Ranma 1/2

Ranma 1/2
2-in-1 Edition
Vol. 13

STORY AND ART BY
RUMIKO TAKAHASHI

RANMA 1/2 Vol. 25, 26
by Rumiko TAKAHASHI
© 1988 Rumiko TAKAHASHI
All rights reserved.
Original Japanese edition published by SHOGAKUKAN.
English translation rights in the United States of America,
Canada, the United Kingdom, Ireland, Australia and New
Zealand arranged with SHOGAKUKAN.

Translation/Kaori Inoue
English Adaptation/Gerard Jones, Matt Thorn
Touch-up Art & Lettering/Erika Terriquez
Design/Yukiko Whitley
Editors/(First Edition) Julie Davis; (Second Edition) Avery Gotoh;
(2-in-1 Edition) Erica Yee

The stories, characters and incidents mentioned in
this publication are entirely fictional.

No portion of this book may be reproduced or transmitted in
any form or by any means without written permission from the
copyright holders.

Printed in the U.S.A.

Published by VIZ Media, LLC
P.O. Box 77010
San Francisco, CA 94107

10 9 8 7 6 5 4 3 2 1
First printing, March 2016

www.viz.com

www.SHONENSUNDAY.COM

PARENTAL ADVISORY
RANMA 1/2 is rated T+ for Older Teen and is
recommended for ages 16 and up. This volume
contains sexual situations and humor.
ratings.viz.com

Ranma 1/2

25・26

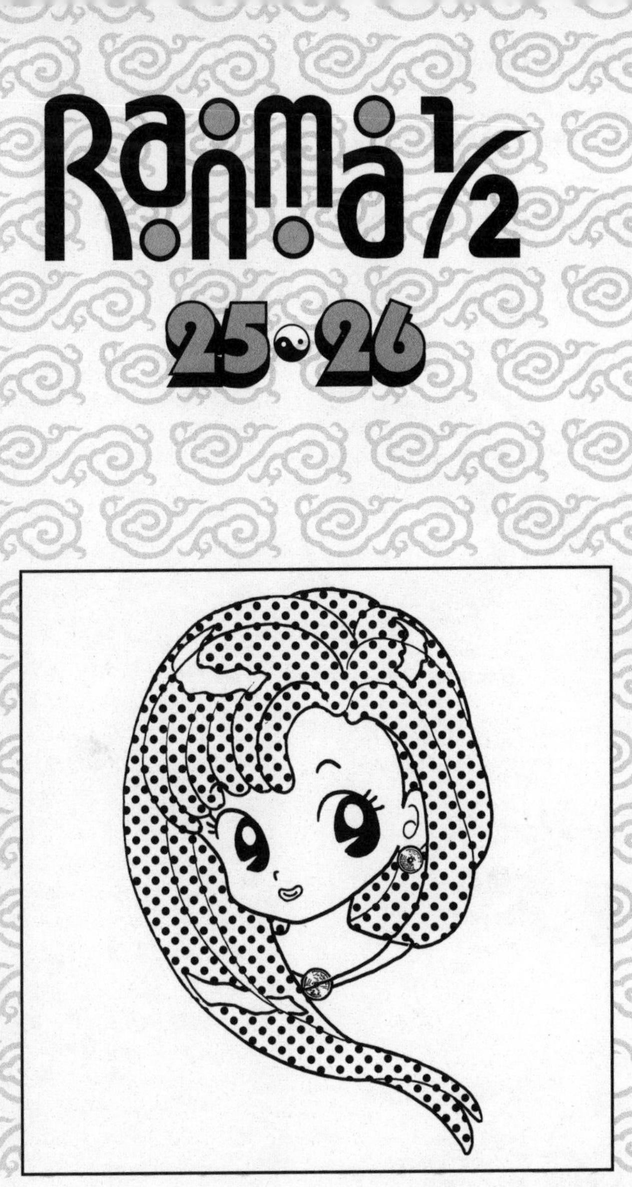

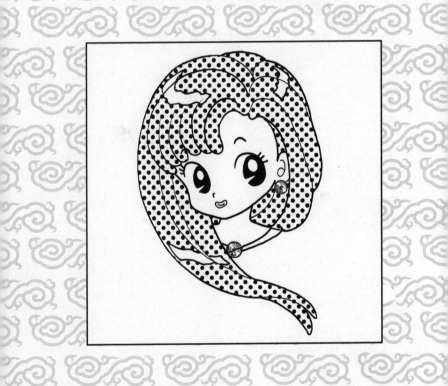

CAST OF CHARACTERS

THE SAOTOMES

Ranma Saotome
Martial artist with an ego that won't let him quit. Changes into a girl when splashed with cold water.

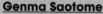

Genma Saotome
Ranma's irresponsible father, recently returned from training his son in China. Changes into a panda.

THE MASTERS

Happosai
Martial arts master who trained both Genma and Soun.

Cologne
Shampoo's great-grandmother, a martial artist and devious matchmaker.

STORY SO FAR

The Tendos are an average, run-of-the-mill Japanese family—at least on the surface. Soun Tendo is the owner and proprietor of the Tendo Dojo, where "Anything-Goes Martial Arts" is practiced. Like the name says, anything goes and usually does.

When Soun's old friend Genma Saotome comes to visit, Soun's three lovely young daughters—Akane, Nabiki and Kasumi—are told that it's time for one of them to become the fiancée of Genma's teenage son, Ranma, as per an agreement made between the two fathers years ago. Youngest daughter Akane—who says she hates boys—is quickly nominated for bridal duty by her sisters.

Unfortunately, Ranma and his father have suffered a strange accident. While training in China, both plunged into one of many cursed springs at the legendary martial arts training ground of Jusenkyo. These springs transform the unlucky dunkee into whoever—or whatever—drowned there hundreds of years ago.

From now on, a splash of cold water turns Ranma's father into a giant panda, and Ranma becomes a beautiful, busty young woman. Hot water reverses the effect...but only until next time.

Ranma and Genma weren't the only ones to take the Jusenkyo plunge—it isn't long before they meet other members of the "cursed." And although their parents are still determined to see Ranma and Akane marry and carry on the dojo, Ranma seems to have a strange talent for accumulating extra fiancées, and Akane has a few suitors of her own. Will the two ever work out their differences and get rid of all these extra people, or will they just call the whole thing off? And will Ranma ever get rid of his curse?

THE TENDOS

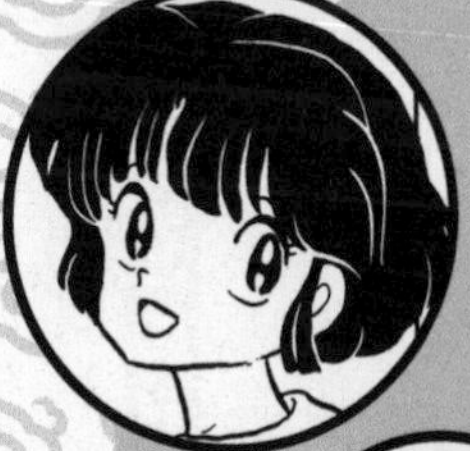

Akane Tendo
A martial artist, a tomboy and Ranma's reluctant fiancée. Has no clue who "P-chan" really is.

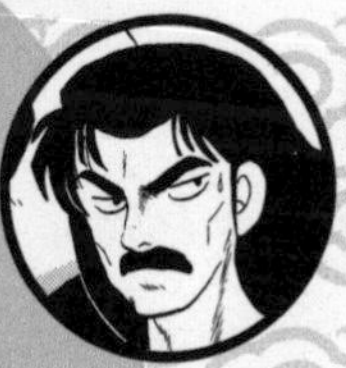

Soun Tendo
Head of the Tendo household and owner of the Tendo Dojo.

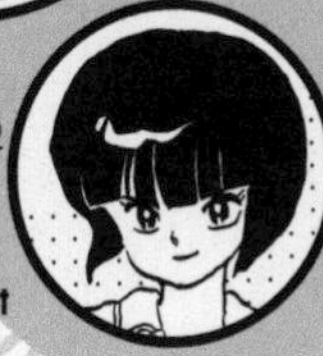

Nabiki Tendo
Always ready to make a buck off others' suffering, coldhearted capitalist Nabiki is the middle Tendo daughter.

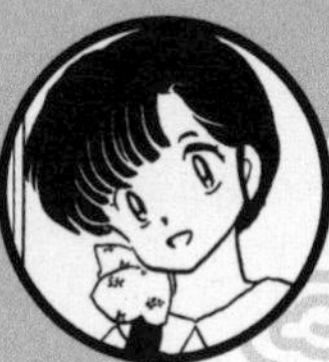

Kasumi Tendo
Sweet-natured eldest daughter and substitute mother figure for the Tendo family.

THE SUITORS

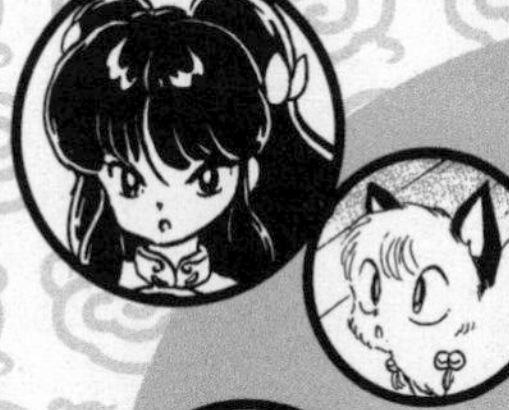

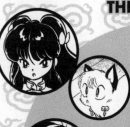

Shampoo
Chinese Amazon warrior who wants to kill girl Ranma and marry boy Ranma. Changes into a cute kitty cat.

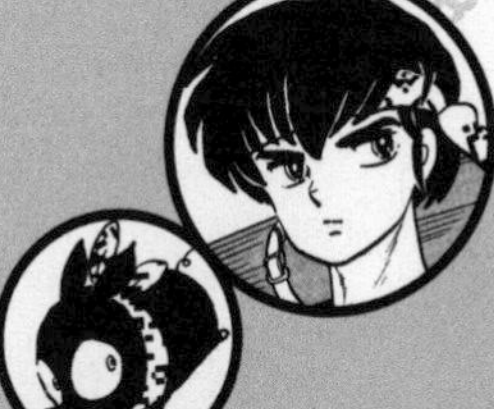

Ryoga Hibiki
A martial artist with a grudge against Ranma, a crush on Akane and no sense of direction. Changes into a piglet Akane calls "P-chan."

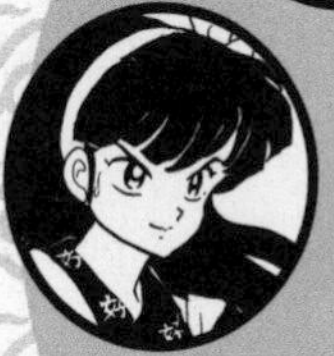

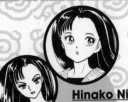

Ukyo Kuonji
Ranma's childhood friend. Has a grudge to settle and a flair for cooking.

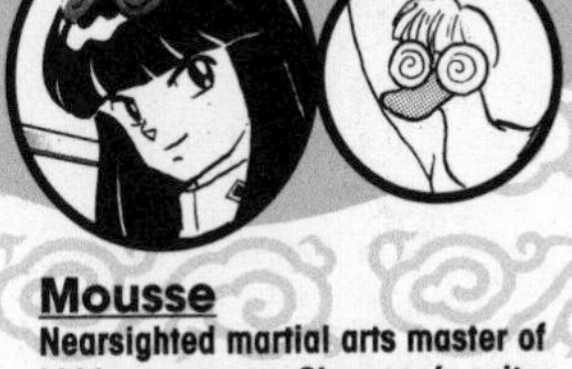

Mousse
Nearsighted martial arts master of hidden weapons. Shampoo's suitor. Changes into a duck.

AND IN THIS CORNER...

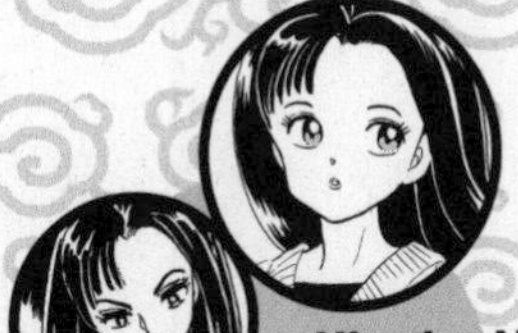

Hinako Ninomiya
A new high school teacher with a reputation for dealing with delinquents.

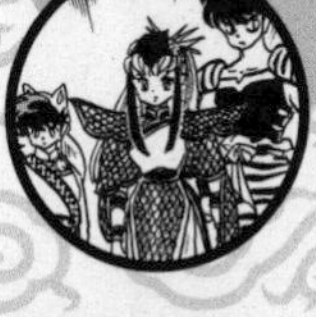

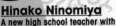

Mint, Herb & Lime
(from left to right)
A trio of Chinese martial artists with special animal powers.

Contents

PART 1
A MAN AGAIN!

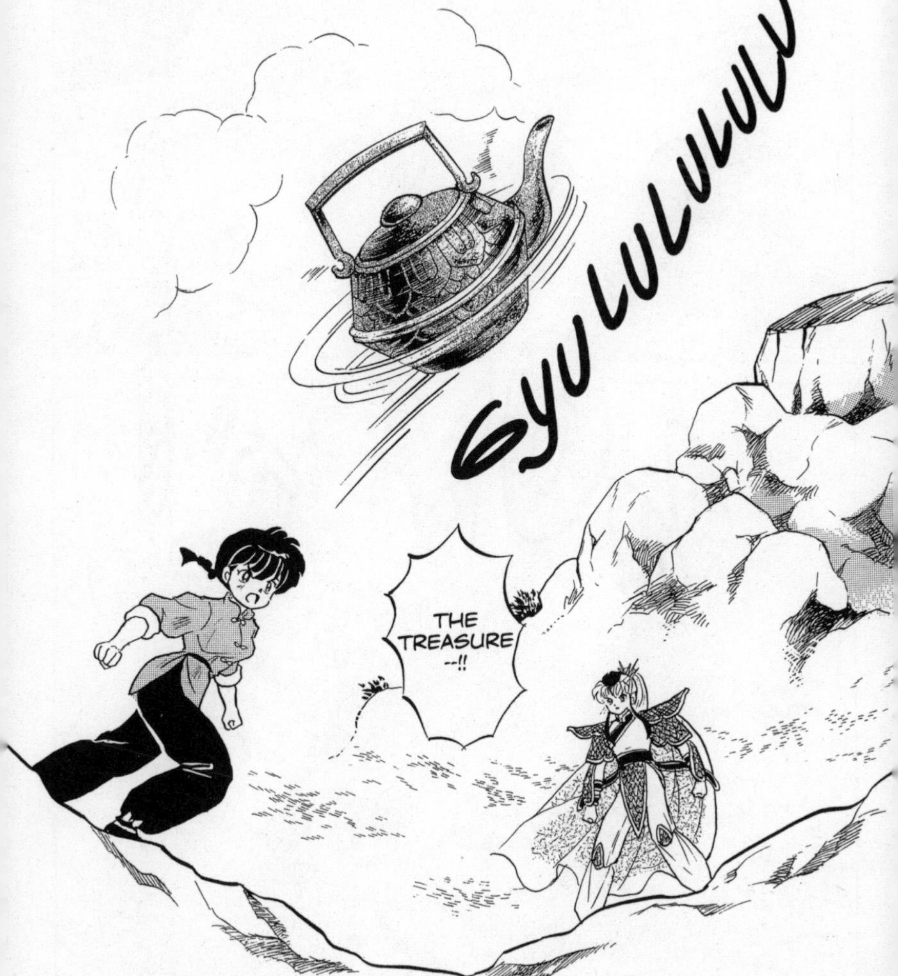
GYU LULULULU
THE TREASURE --!!

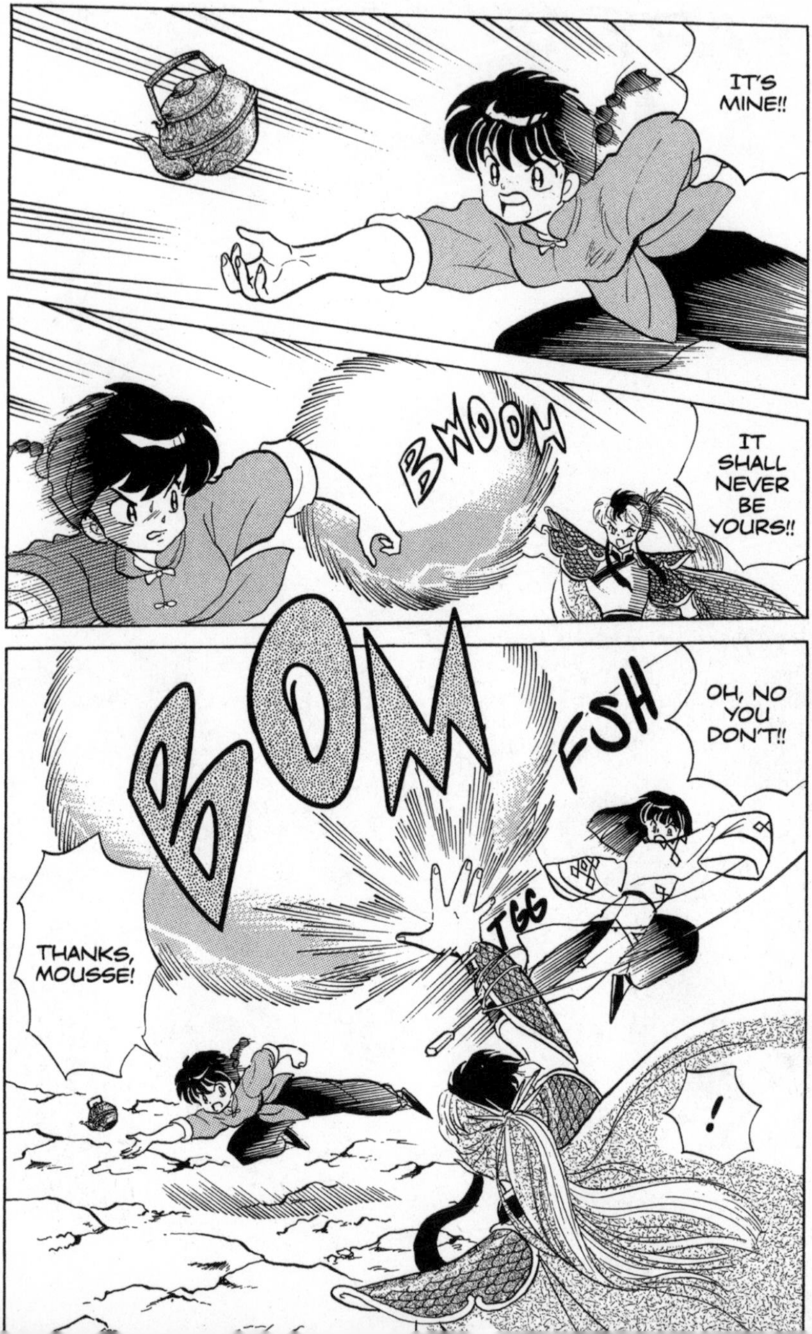
IT'S MINE!!
BWOOH
IT SHALL NEVER BE YOURS!!
OH, NO YOU DON'T!!
FSH
BOM
TGG
THANKS, MOUSSE!
!

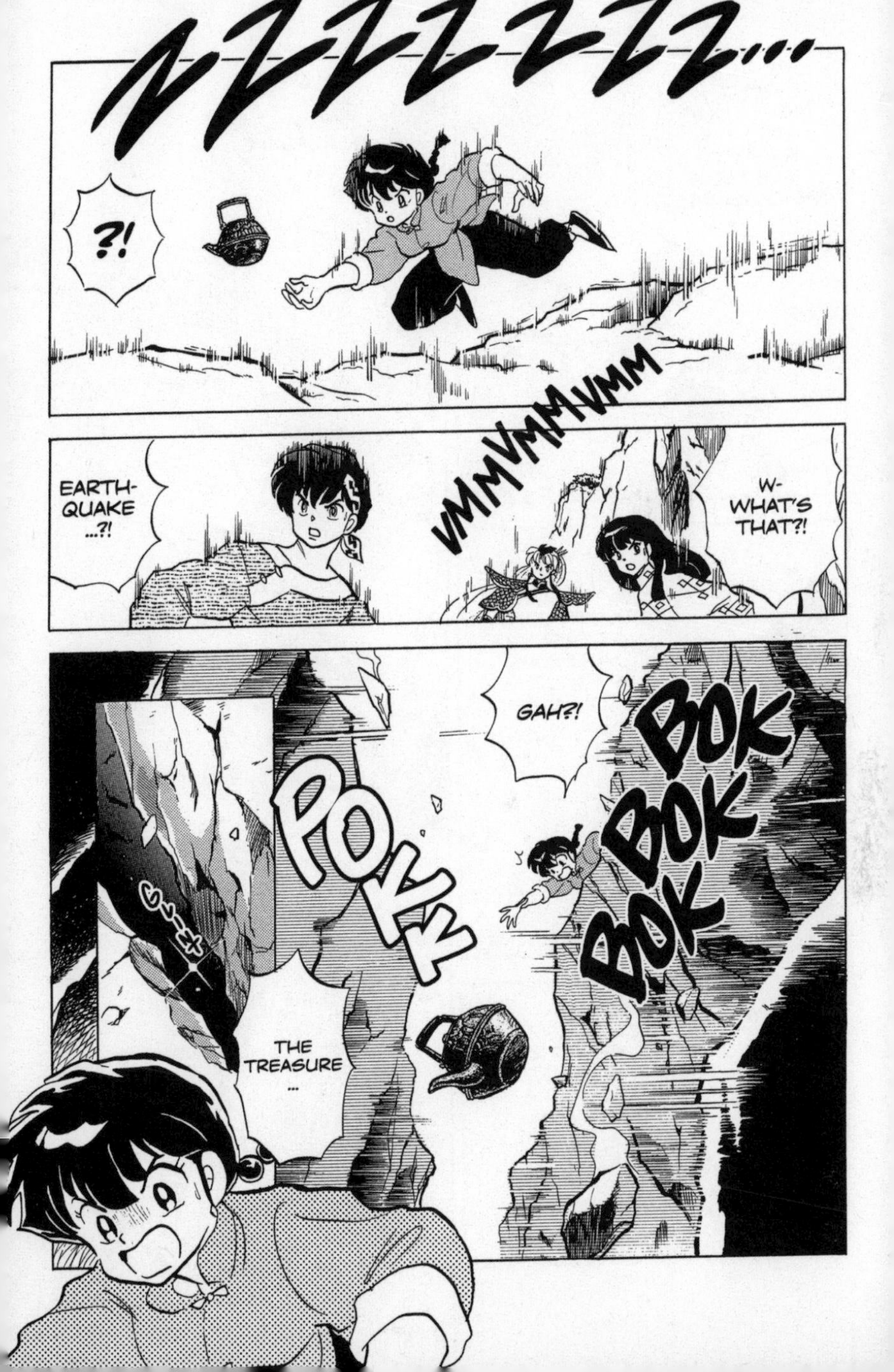
NZZZZZZZ...
?!
VMMVMMVMM
W-WHAT'S THAT?!
EARTH-QUAKE ...?!
BOK BOK BOK
GAH?!
POKK
THE TREASURE ...

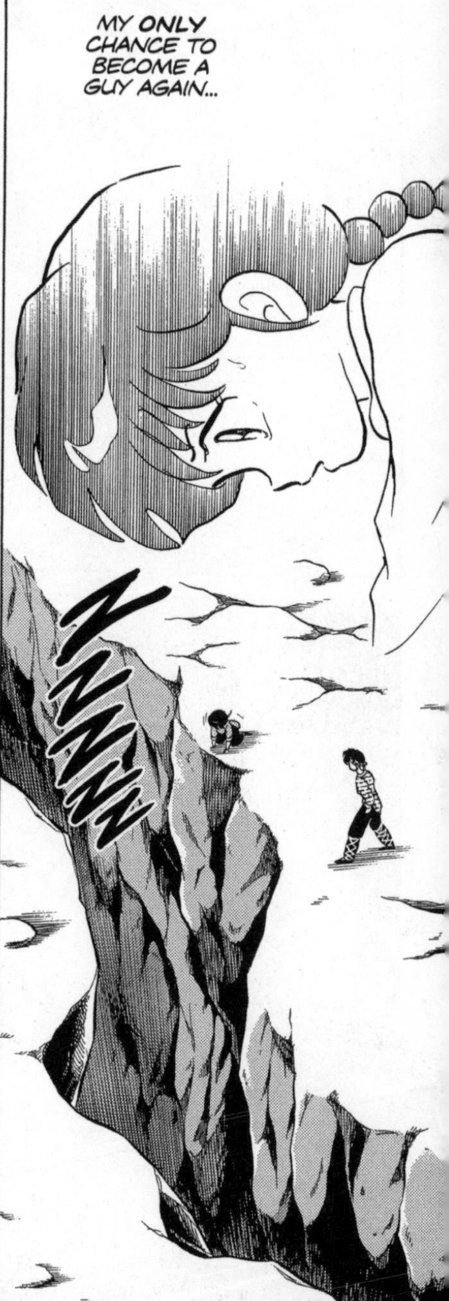
MY ONLY CHANCE TO BECOME A GUY AGAIN...
NNNNN

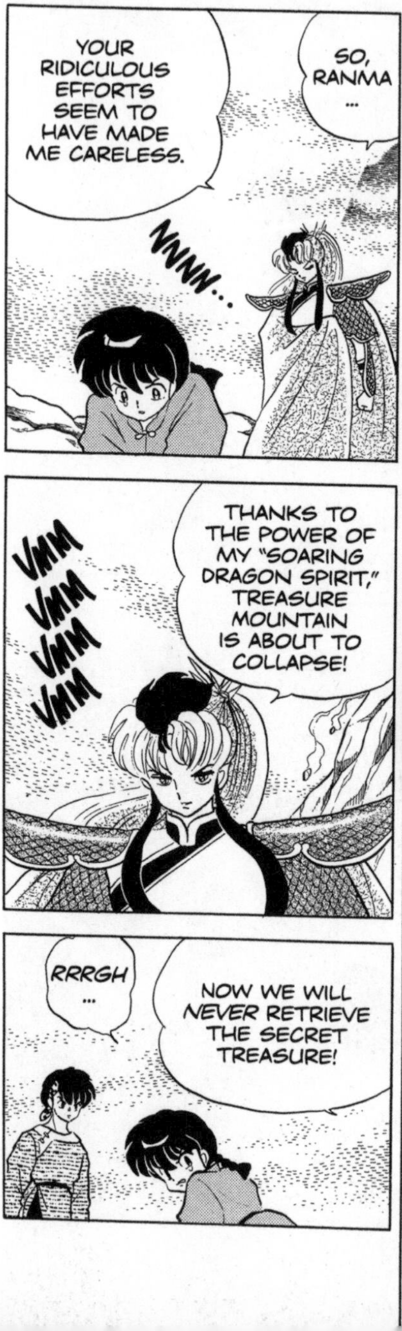
SO, RANMA ...
YOUR RIDICULOUS EFFORTS SEEM TO HAVE MADE ME CARELESS.
NNNN...
THANKS TO THE POWER OF MY "SOARING DRAGON SPIRIT," TREASURE MOUNTAIN IS ABOUT TO COLLAPSE!
VMM VMM VMM VMM
NOW WE WILL NEVER RETRIEVE THE SECRET TREASURE!
RRRGH ...

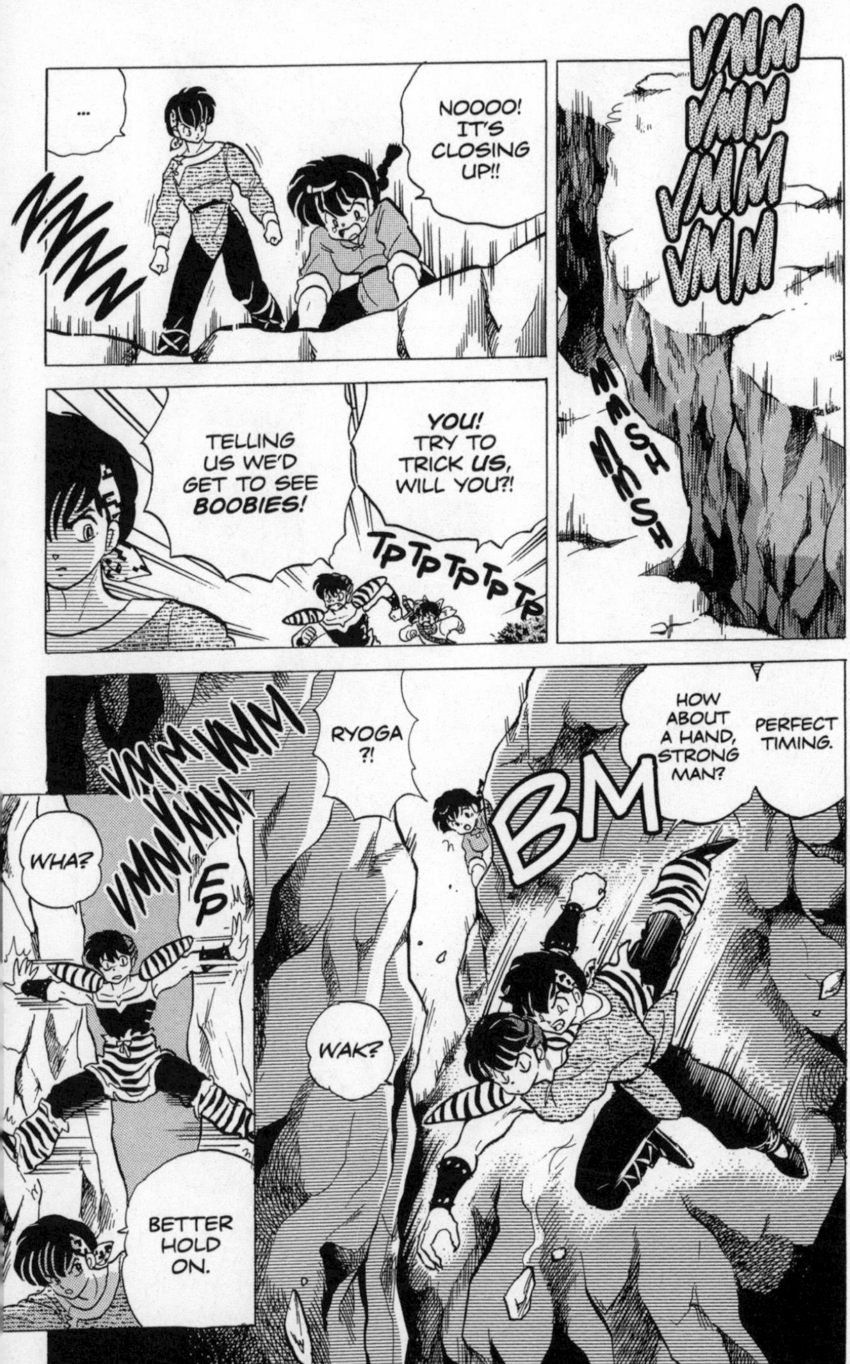
VMM
VMM
VMM
VMM
MESH
MESH
NOOOO! IT'S CLOSING UP!!
...
NNNN
YOU! TRY TO TRICK US, WILL YOU?!
TELLING US WE'D GET TO SEE BOOBIES!
TP TP TP TP TP
PERFECT TIMING.
HOW ABOUT A HAND, STRONG MAN?
BM
RYOGA ?!
VMM VMM VMM VMM VMM
WAK?
WHA?
FP
BETTER HOLD ON.

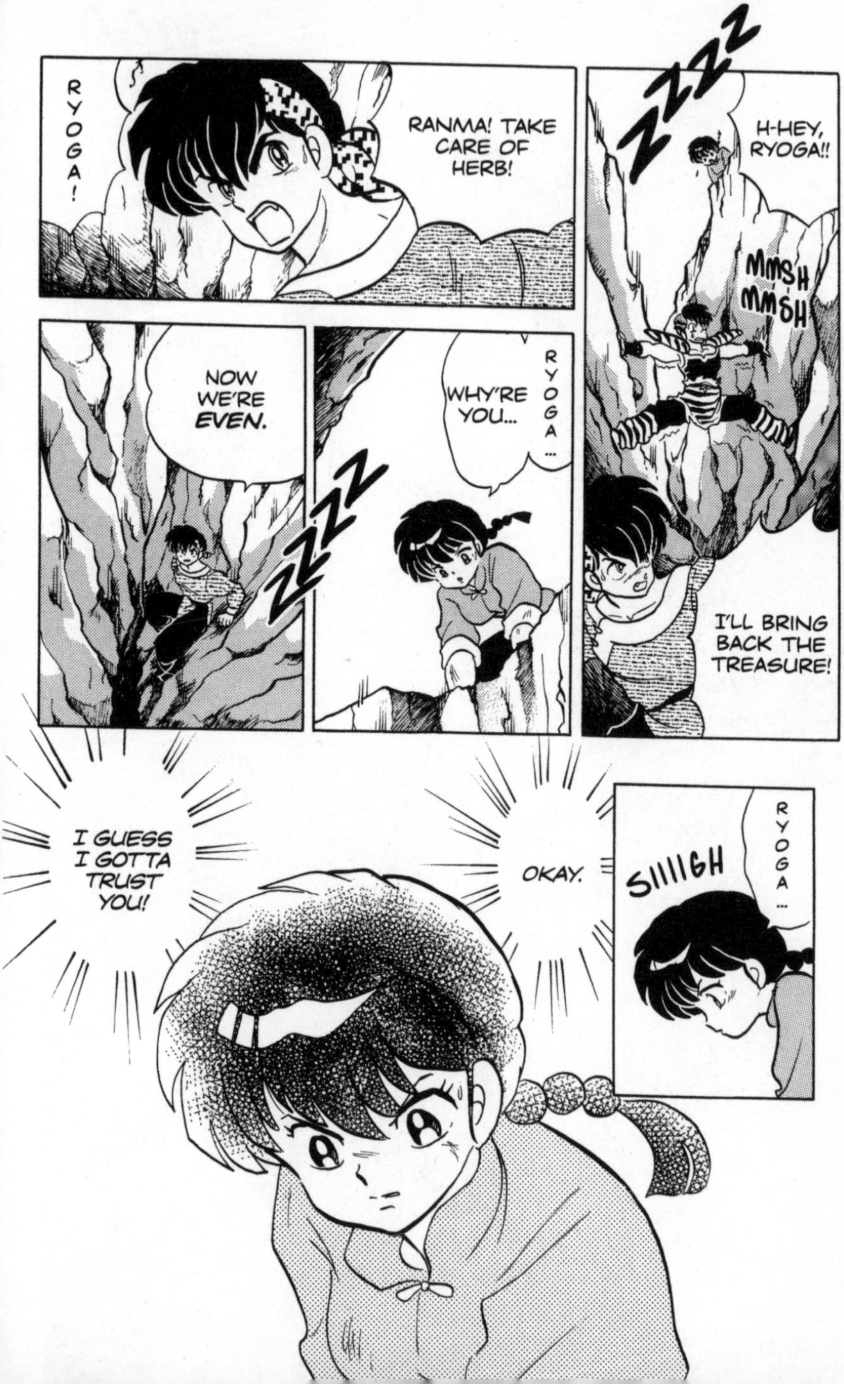
H-HEY, RYOGA!!
ZZZZ
MMSH MMSH
I'LL BRING BACK THE TREASURE!
RANMA! TAKE CARE OF HERB!
RYOGA!
RYOGA...
WHY'RE YOU...
ZZZZ
NOW WE'RE EVEN.
RYOGA...
SIIIIGH
OKAY.
I GUESS I GOTTA TRUST YOU!

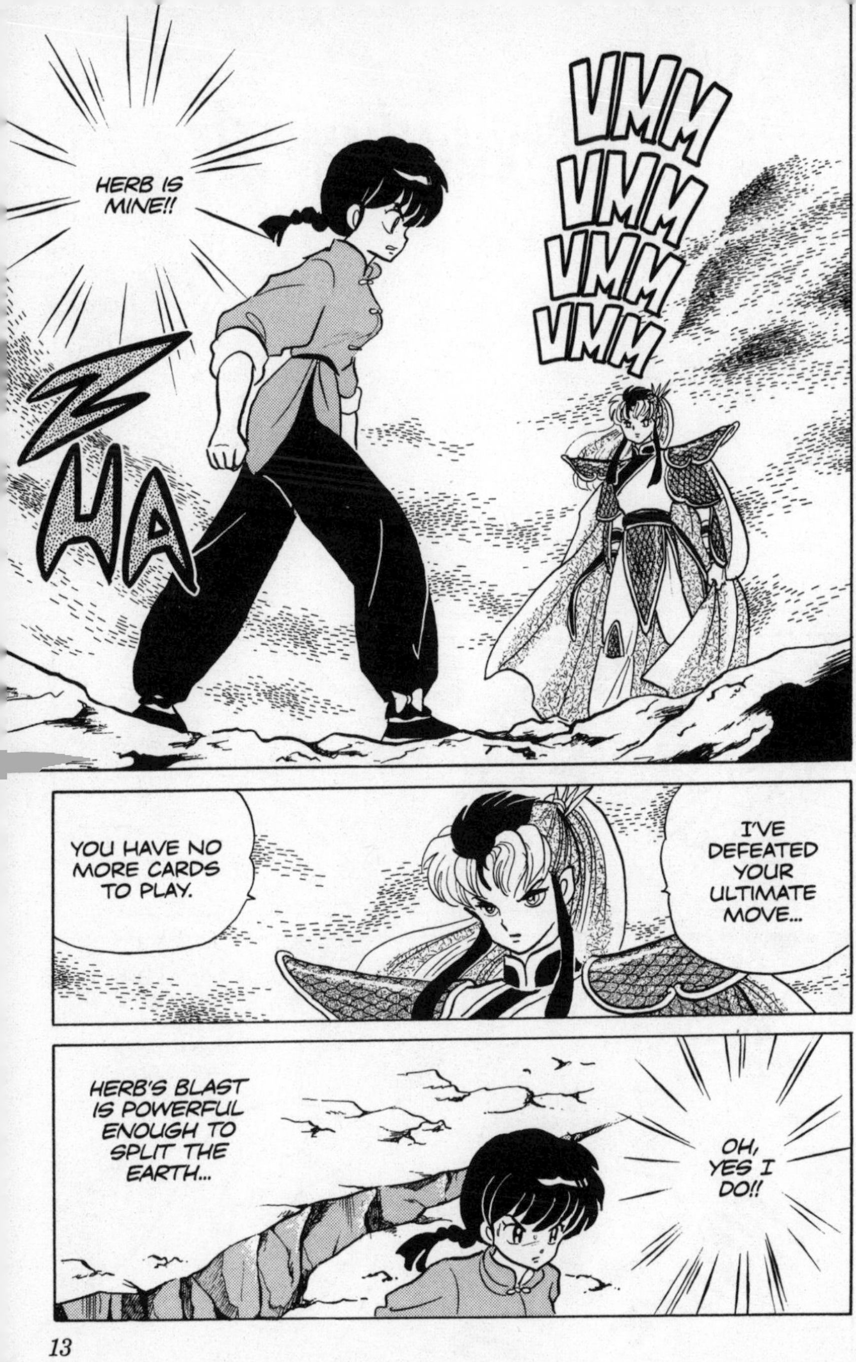
UMM UMM UMM UMM
HERB IS MINE!!
ZHA
I'VE DEFEATED YOUR ULTIMATE MOVE...
YOU HAVE NO MORE CARDS TO PLAY.
OH, YES I DO!!
HERB'S BLAST IS POWERFUL ENOUGH TO SPLIT THE EARTH...

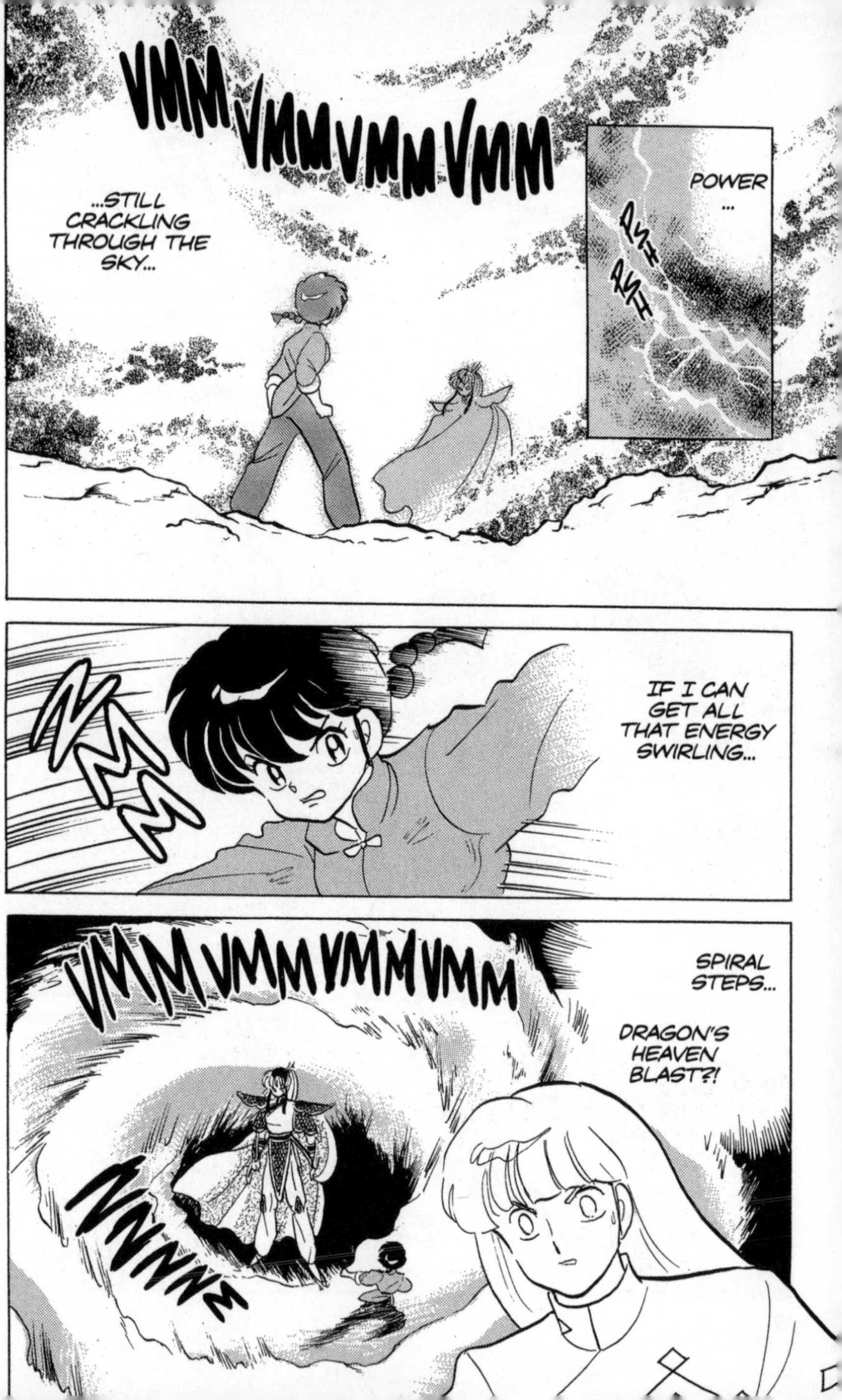
POWER...
VMM VMM VMM VMM
...STILL CRACKLING THROUGH THE SKY...
IF I CAN GET ALL THAT ENERGY SWIRLING...
VMM VMM VMM VMM
SPIRAL STEPS...
DRAGON'S HEAVEN BLAST?!

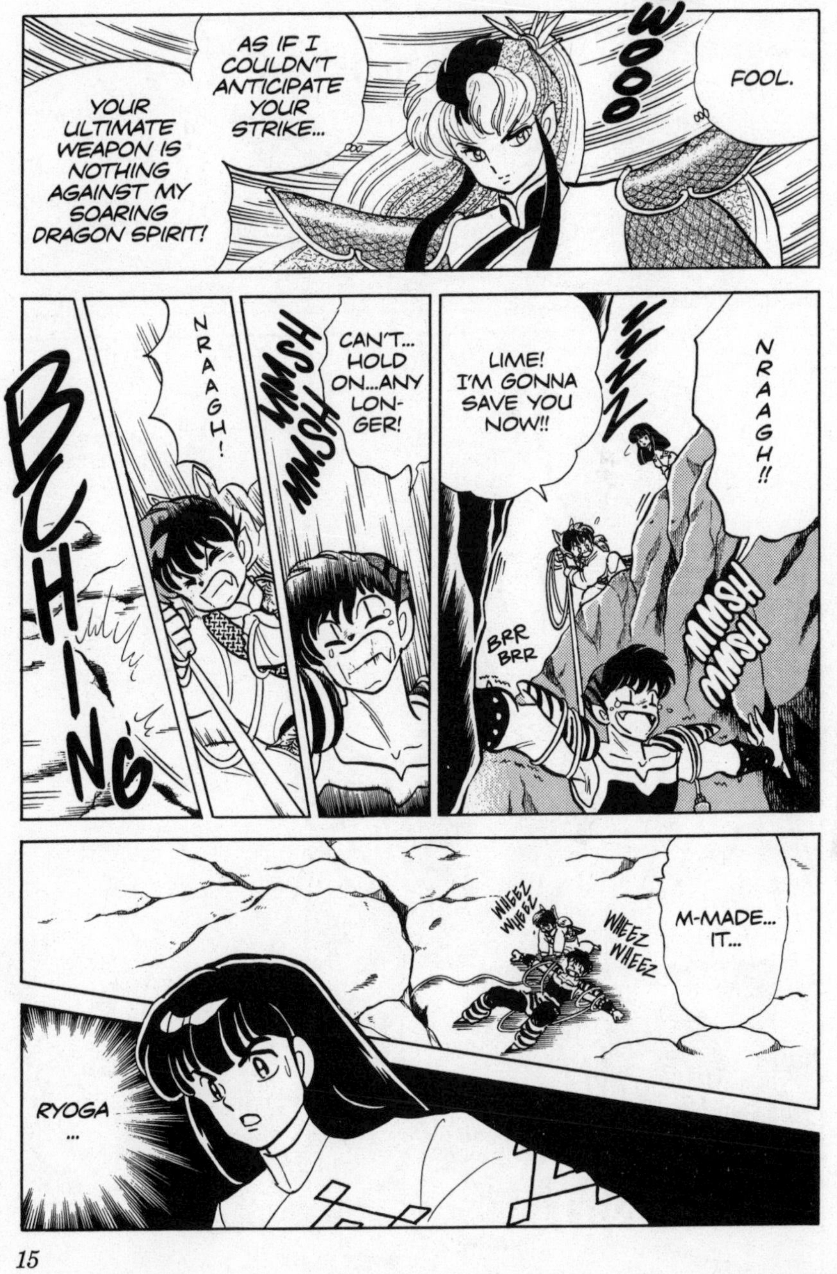
GWOOOO
FOOL.
AS IF I COULDN'T ANTICIPATE YOUR STRIKE...
YOUR ULTIMATE WEAPON IS NOTHING AGAINST MY SOARING DRAGON SPIRIT!
NRAAGH!!
WNNN
LIME! I'M GONNA SAVE YOU NOW!!
MMSH MMSH
BRR BRR
CAN'T... HOLD ON...ANY LON-GER!
MMSH MMSH
NRAAGH!
BUCHING
M-MADE... IT...
WHEEZ WHEEZ
WHEEZ WHEEZ
RYOGA ...

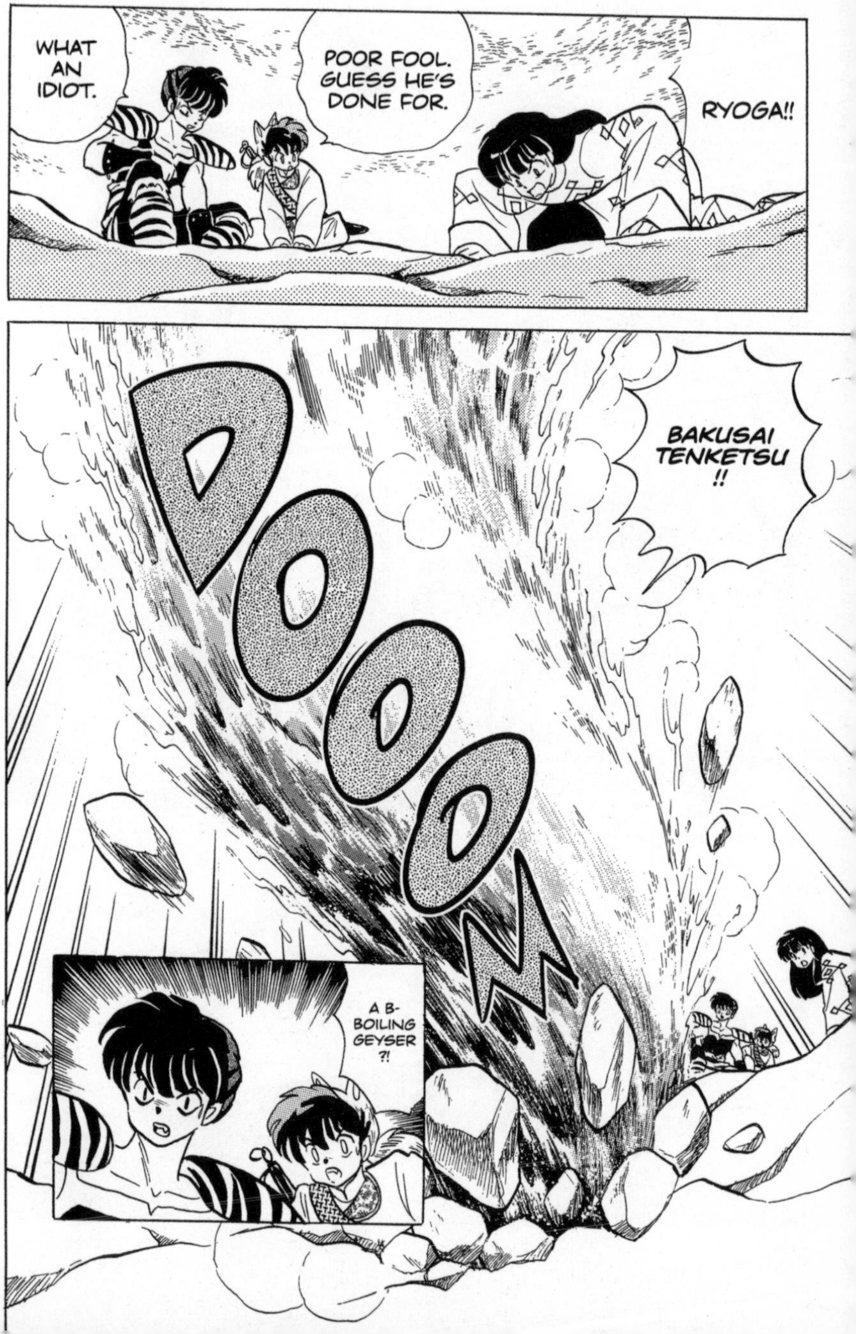
RYOGA!!
POOR FOOL. GUESS HE'S DONE FOR.
WHAT AN IDIOT.
BAKUSAI TENKETSU !!
DOOOOM
A B-BOILING GEYSER ?!

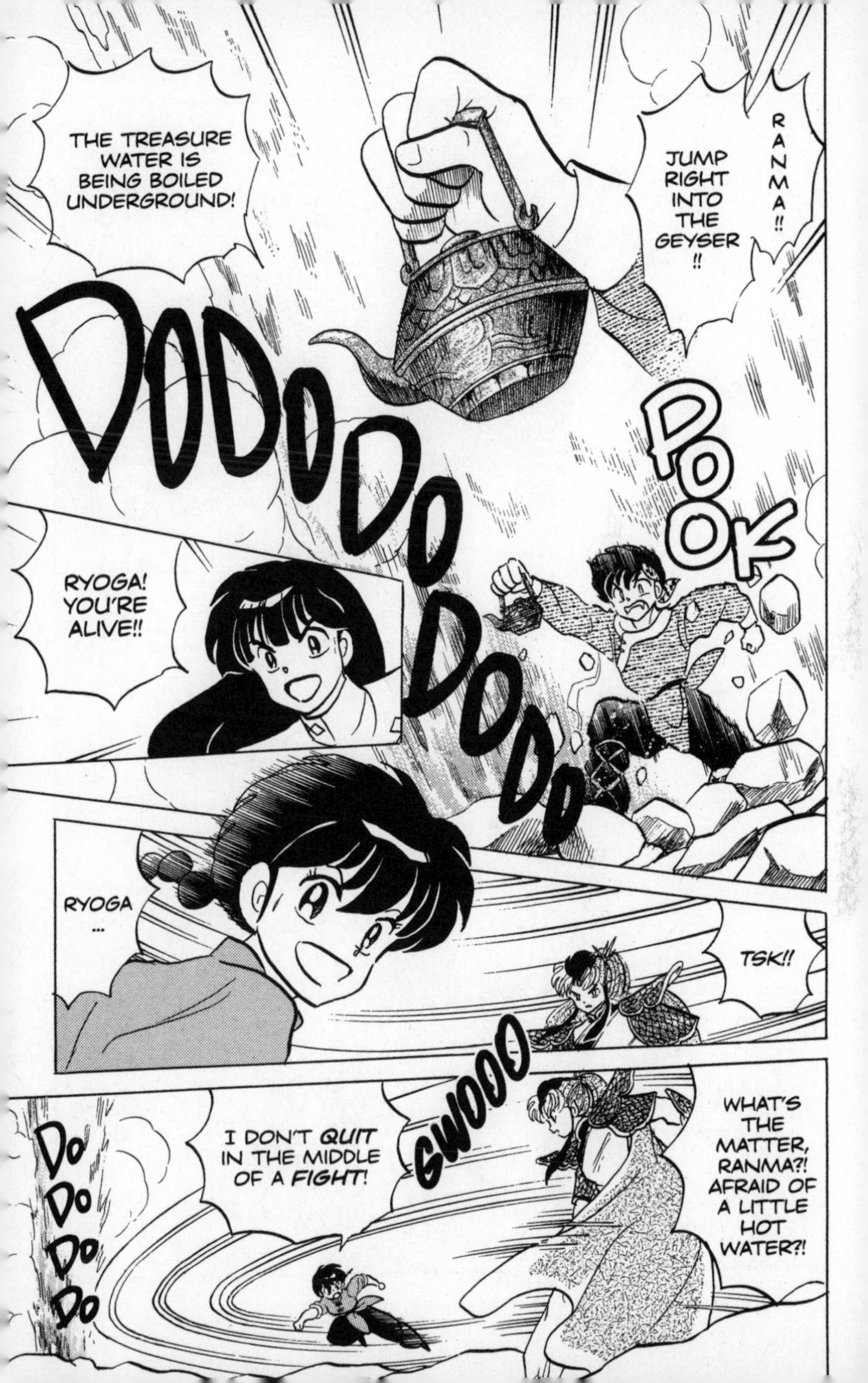
RANMA!!
JUMP RIGHT INTO THE GEYSER!!
THE TREASURE WATER IS BEING BOILED UNDERGROUND!
DODODODODODO
POOK
RYOGA! YOU'RE ALIVE!!
TSK!!
RYOGA ...
WHAT'S THE MATTER, RANMA?! AFRAID OF A LITTLE HOT WATER?!
GWOOO
I DON'T *QUIT* IN THE MIDDLE OF A *FIGHT*!
Do Do Do Do

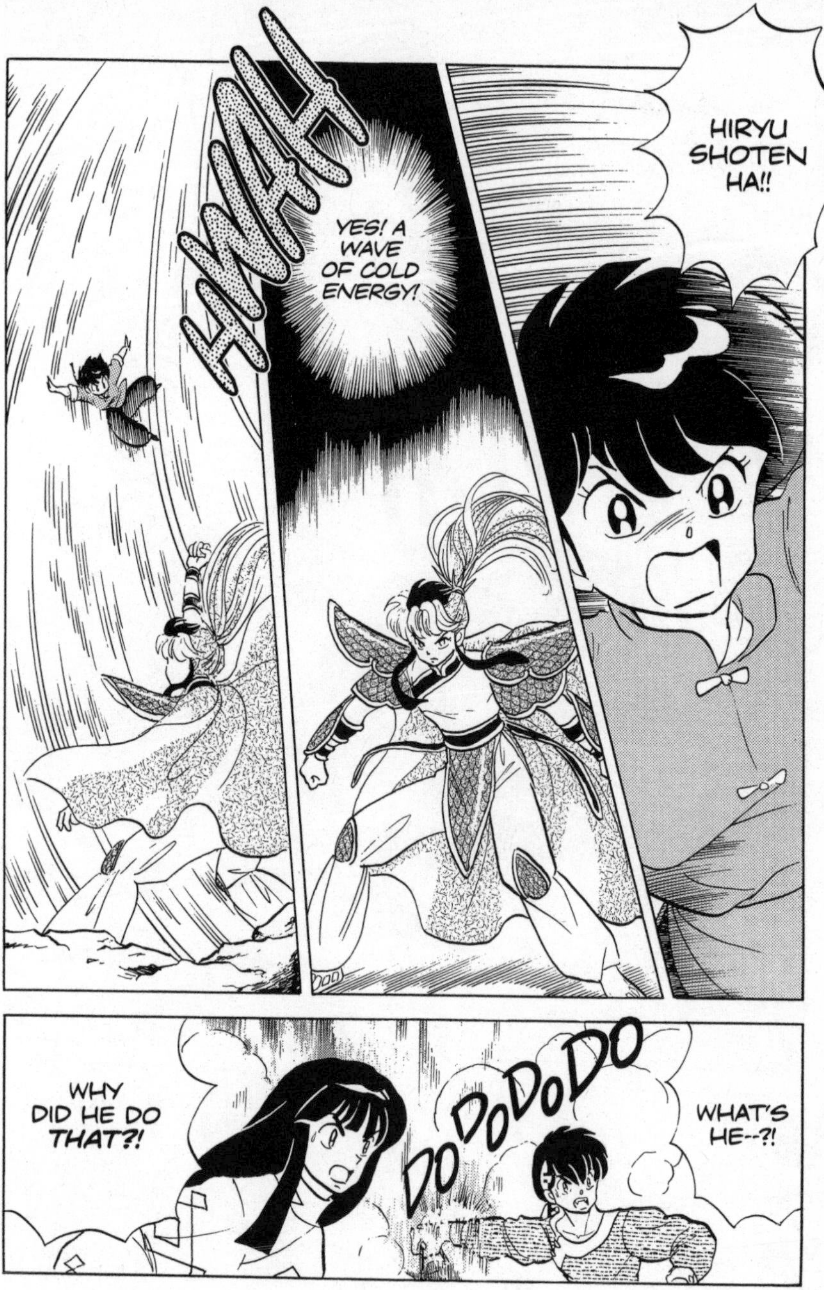
HIRYU SHOTEN HA!!
HWAH
YES! A WAVE OF COLD ENERGY!
WHAT'S HE--?!
DODODODODO
WHY DID HE DO THAT?!

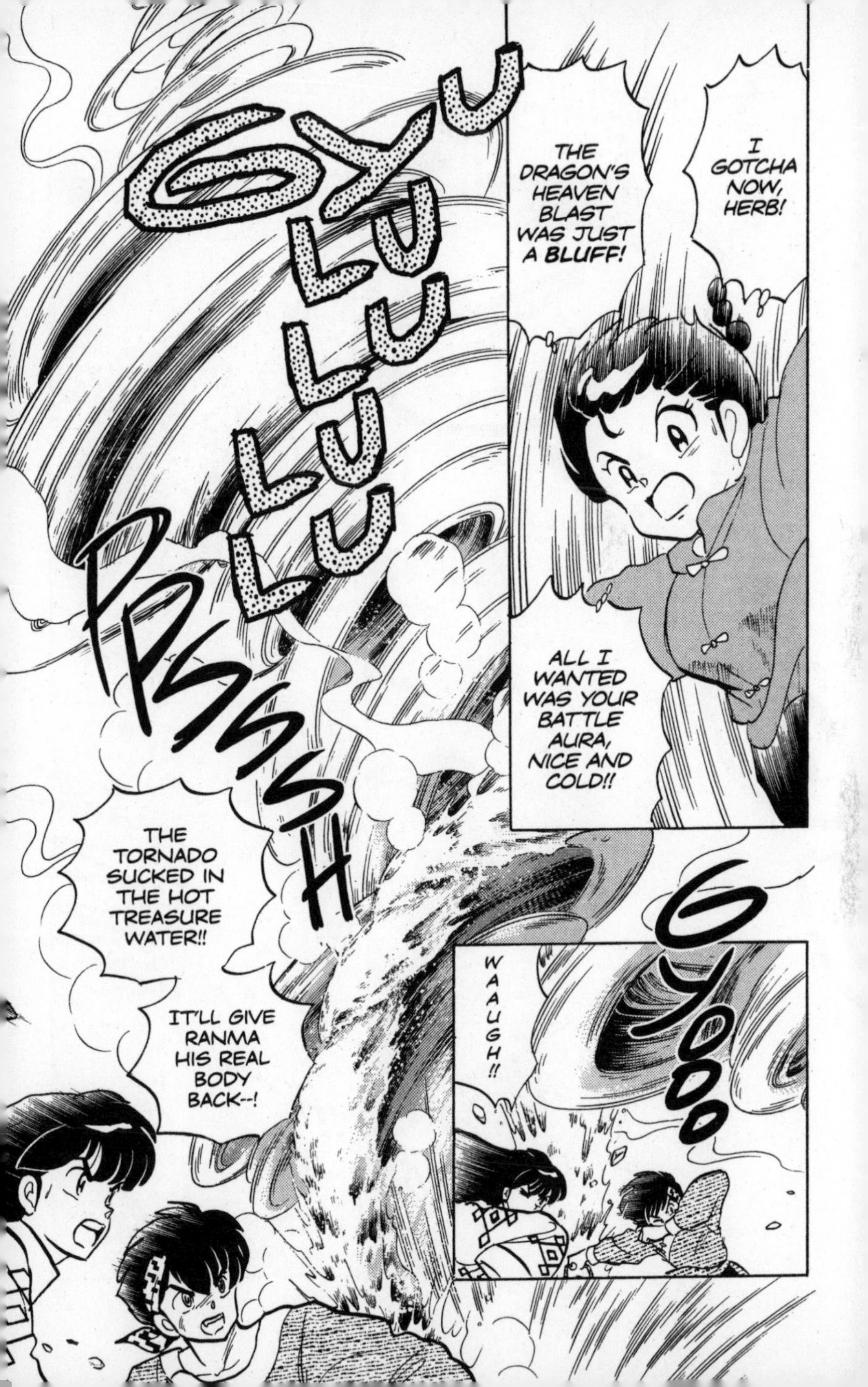
I GOTCHA NOW, HERB!
THE DRAGON'S HEAVEN BLAST WAS JUST A BLUFF!
ALL I WANTED WAS YOUR BATTLE AURA, NICE AND COLD!!
GYOOOO
WAAUGH!!
PSSSH
THE TORNADO SUCKED IN THE HOT TREASURE WATER!!
IT'LL GIVE RANMA HIS REAL BODY BACK--!

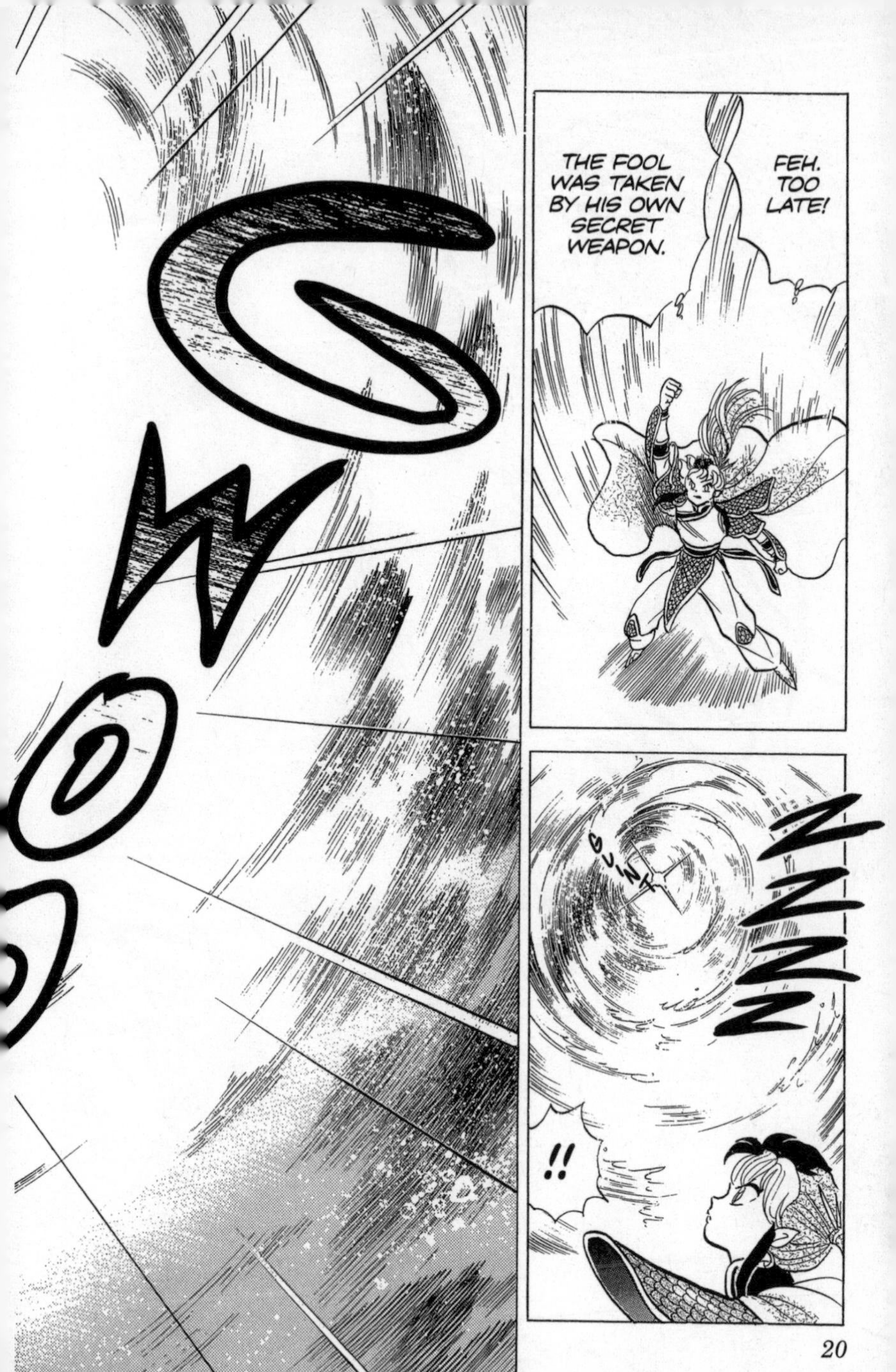
FEH. TOO LATE!
THE FOOL WAS TAKEN BY HIS OWN SECRET WEAPON.
NNNNN
GUINK
!!
GWOO

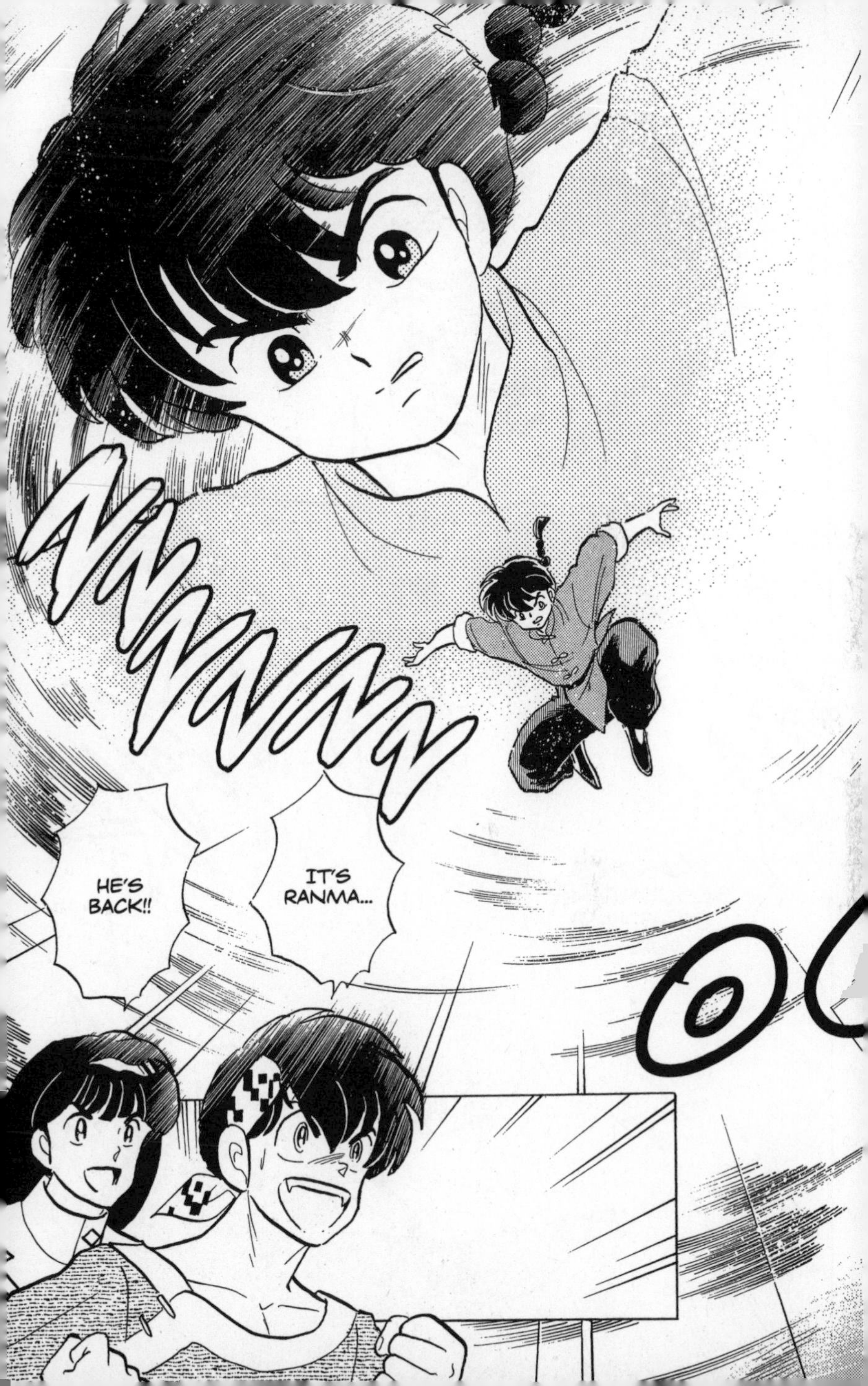
IT'S RANMA...
HE'S BACK!!

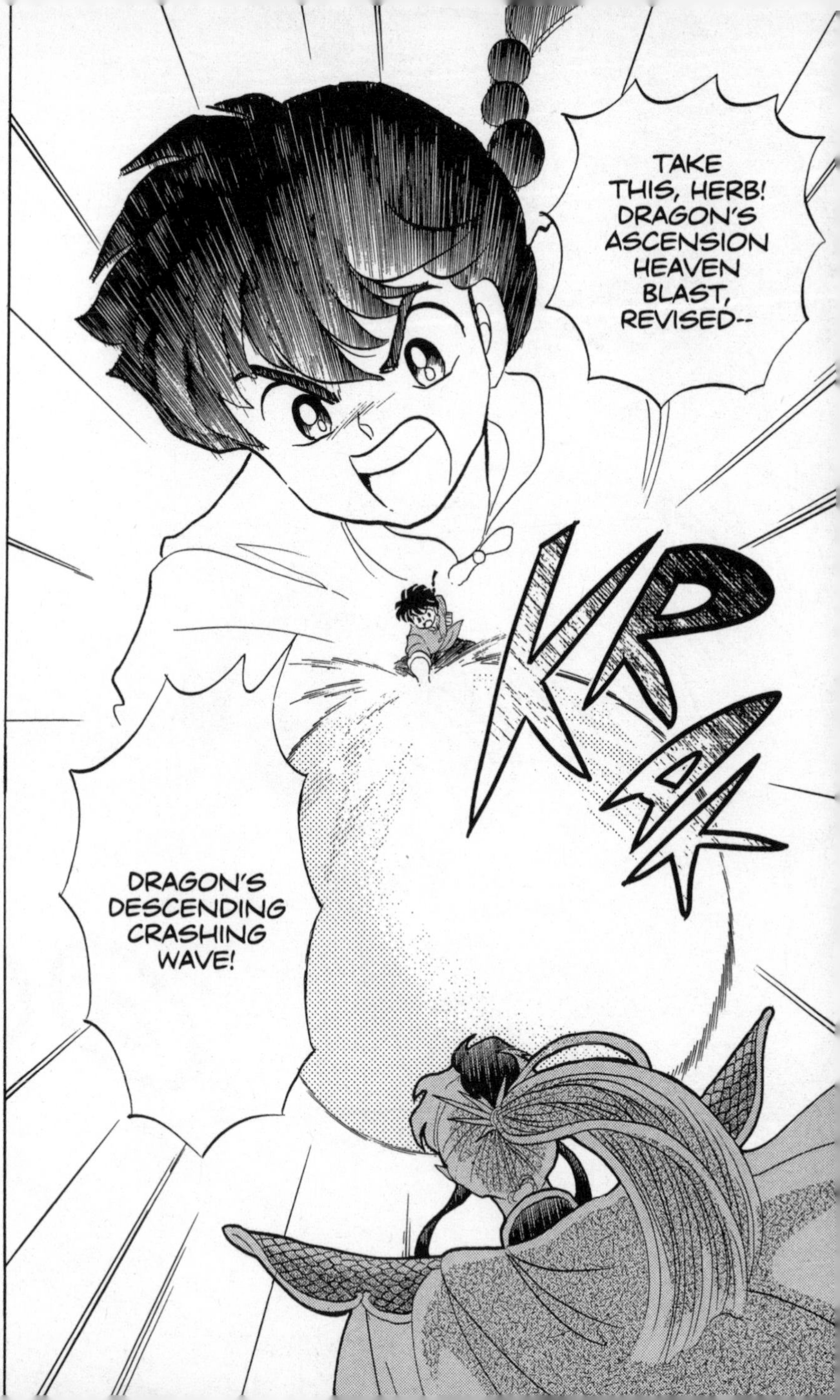
TAKE THIS, HERB! DRAGON'S ASCENSION HEAVEN BLAST, REVISED--
KRAK
DRAGON'S DESCENDING CRASHING WAVE!

PART 2

WELCOME HOME, RANMA!

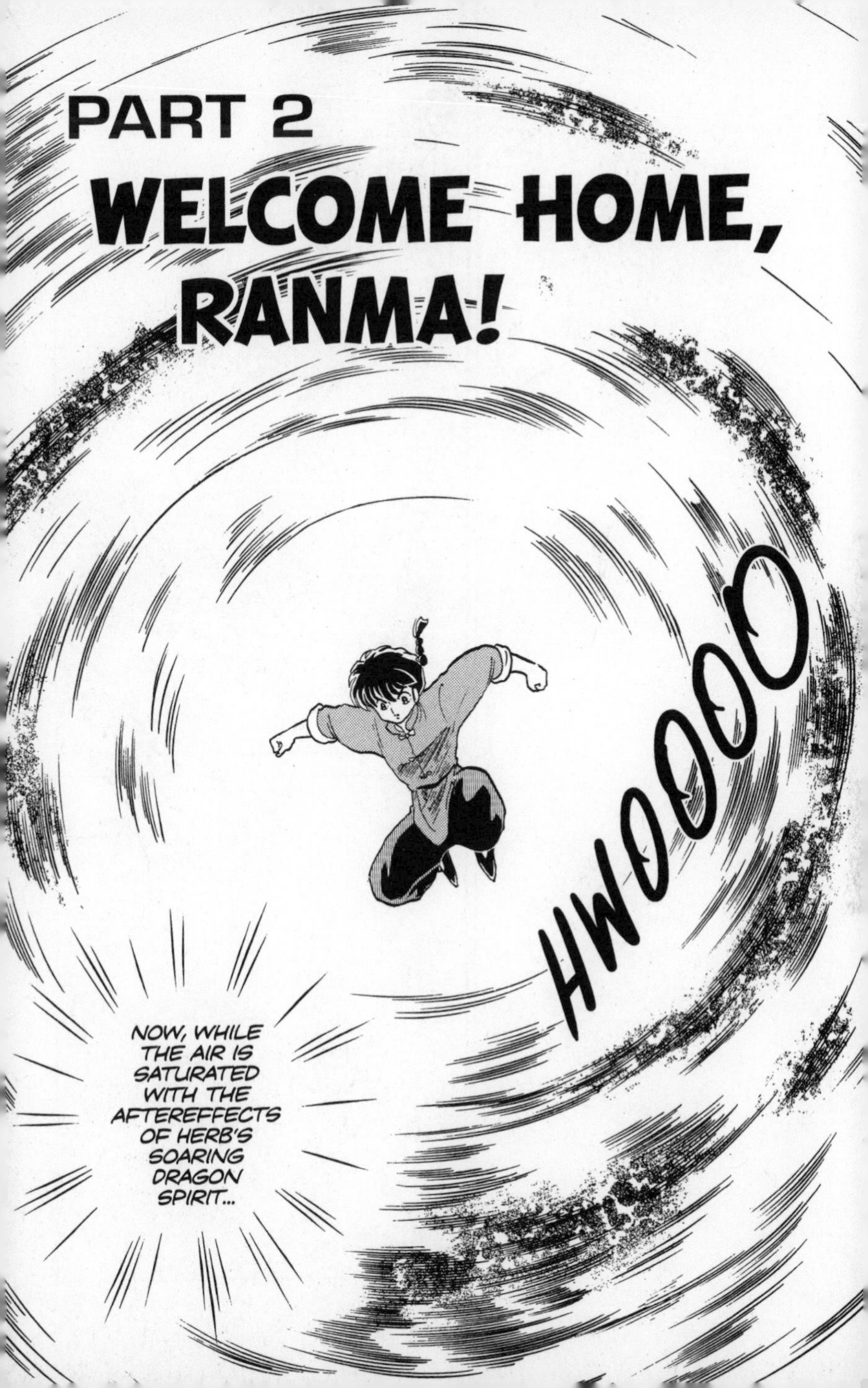
HWOOOO
NOW, WHILE THE AIR IS SATURATED WITH THE AFTEREFFECTS OF HERB'S SOARING DRAGON SPIRIT...

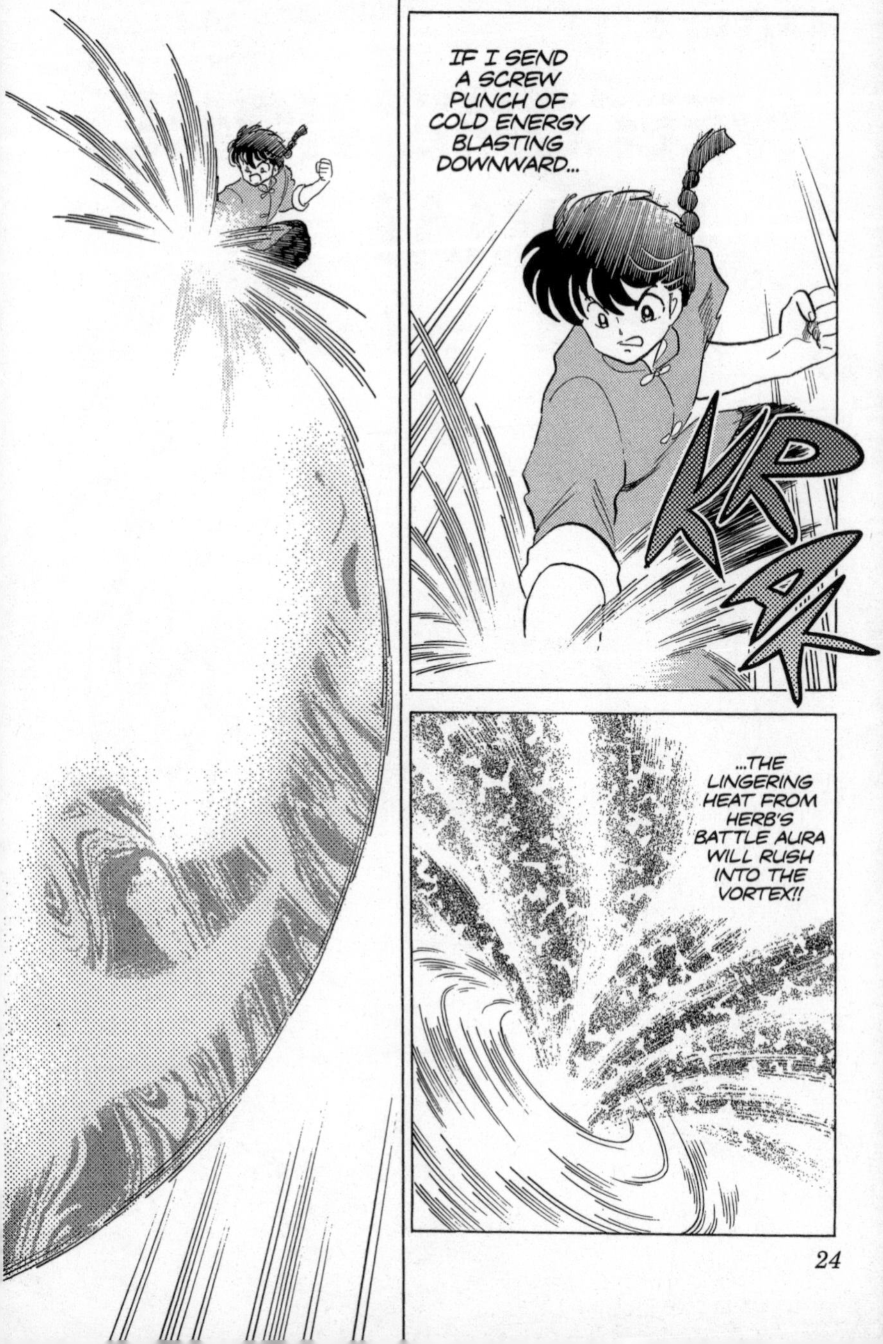
IF I SEND A SCREW PUNCH OF COLD ENERGY BLASTING DOWNWARD...
KRAK
...THE LINGERING HEAT FROM HERB'S BATTLE AURA WILL RUSH INTO THE VORTEX!!

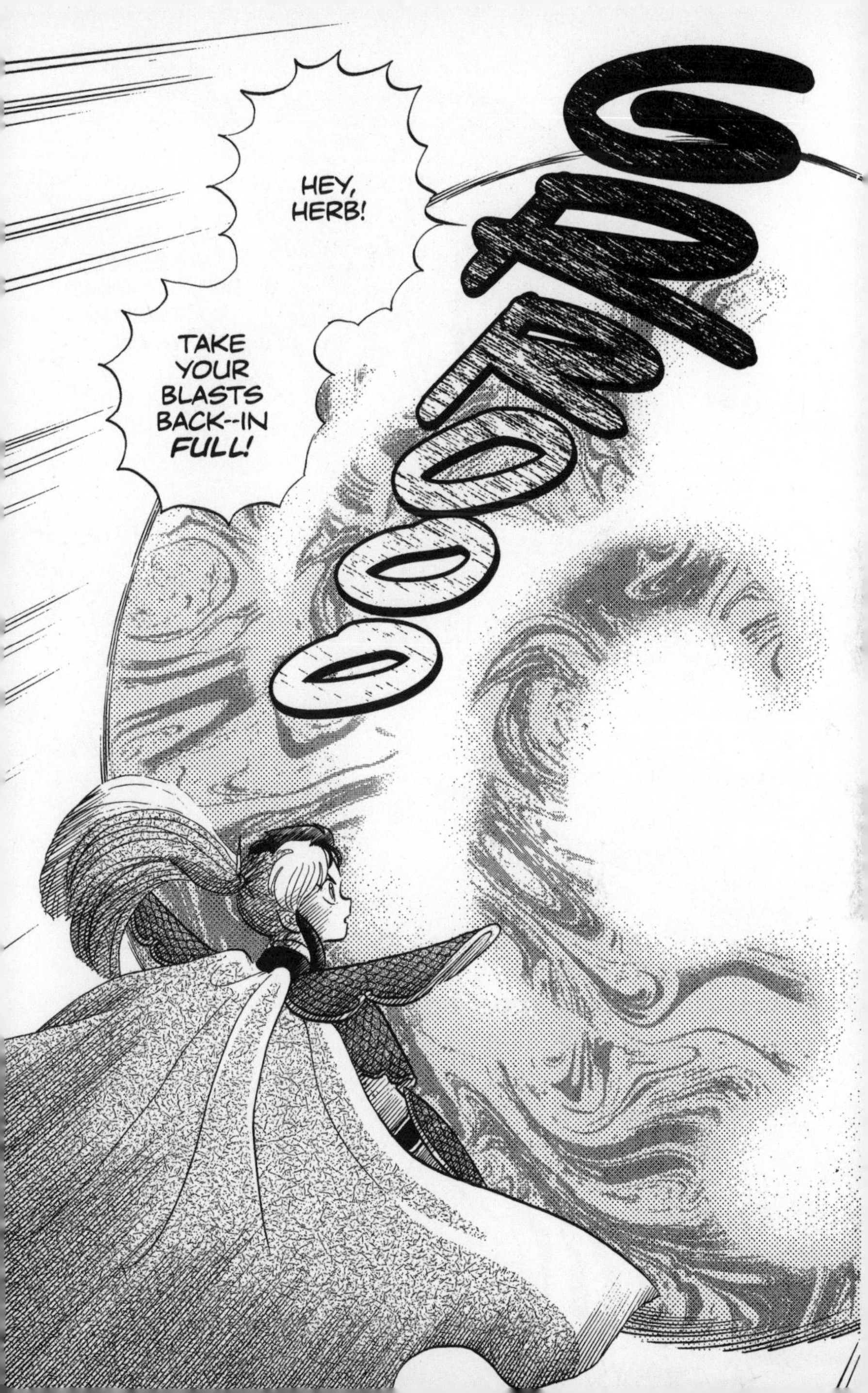
HEY, HERB!
TAKE YOUR BLASTS BACK--IN FULL!

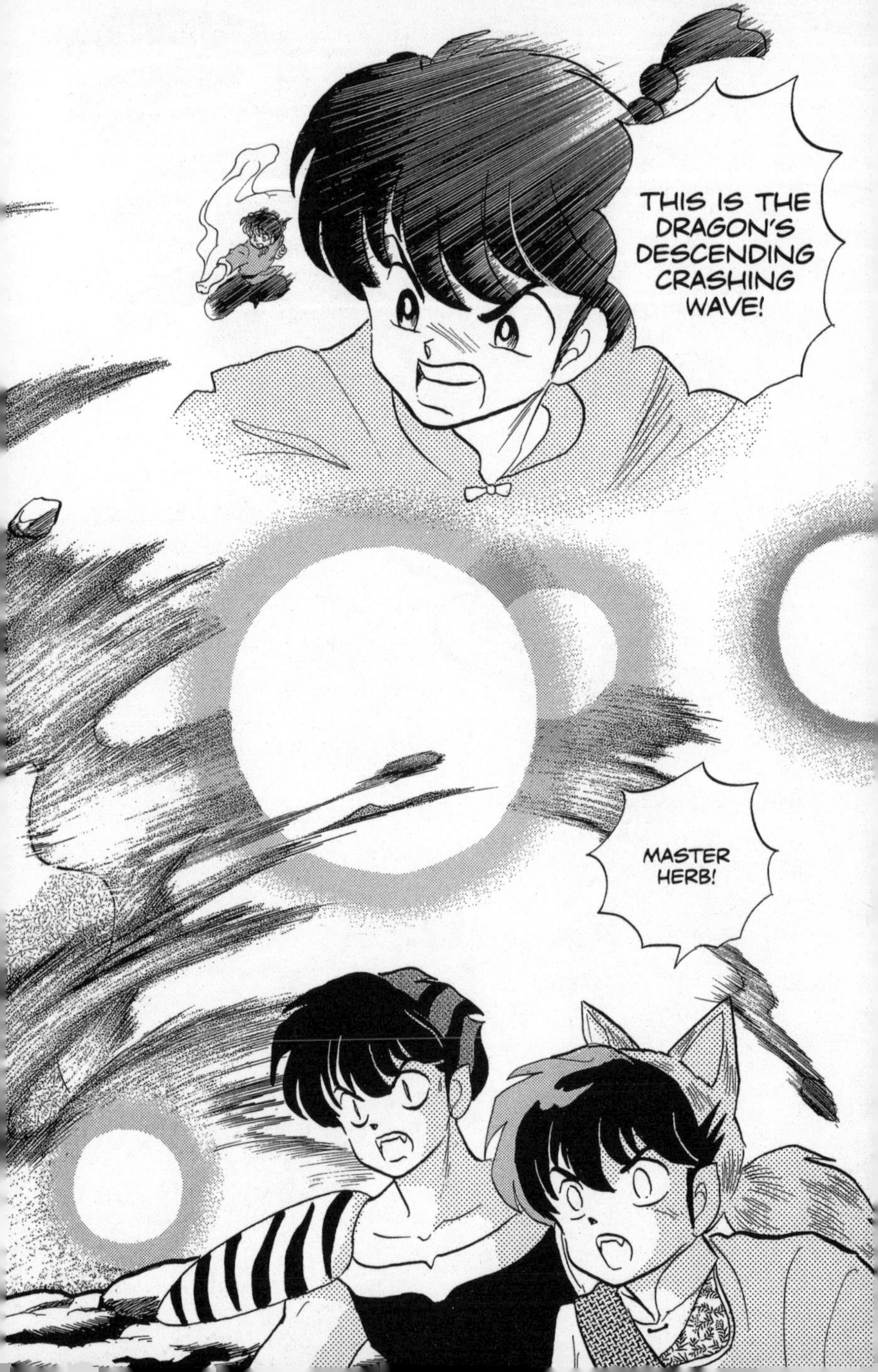
THIS IS THE DRAGON'S DESCENDING CRASHING WAVE!
MASTER HERB!

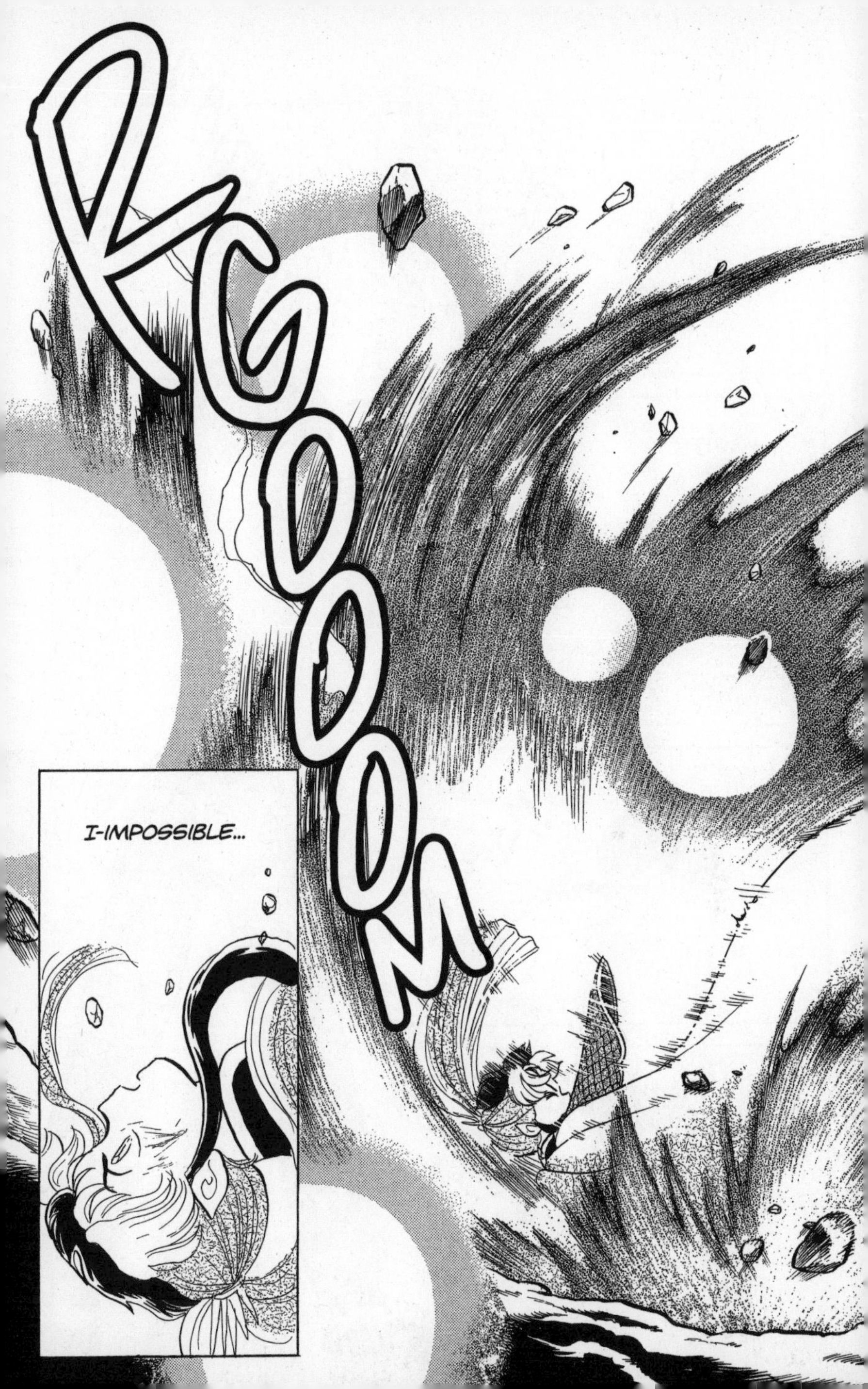

KGOOOOM
I-IMPOSSIBLE...

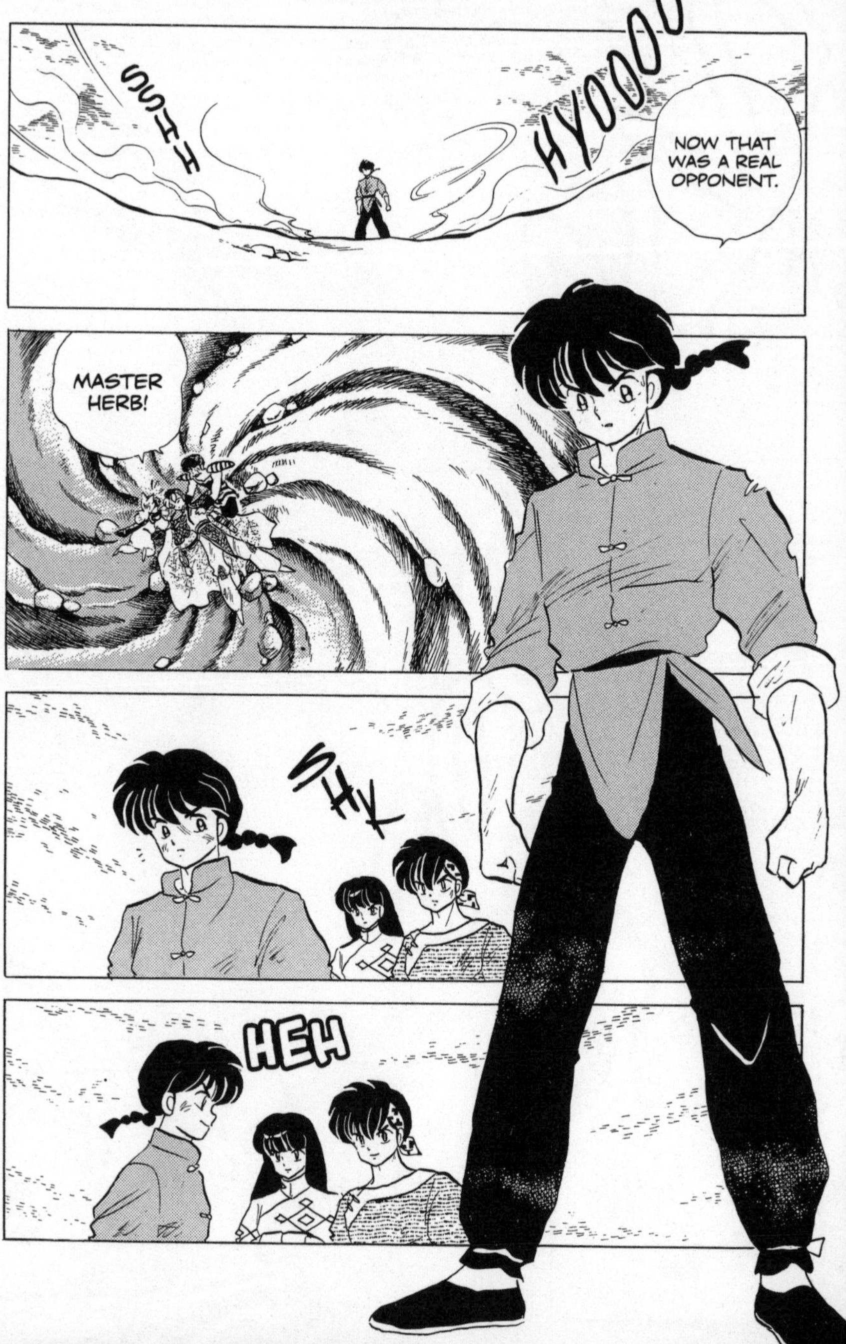
NOW THAT WAS A REAL OPPONENT.
HYOOOO
SSHH
MASTER HERB!
SHK
HEH

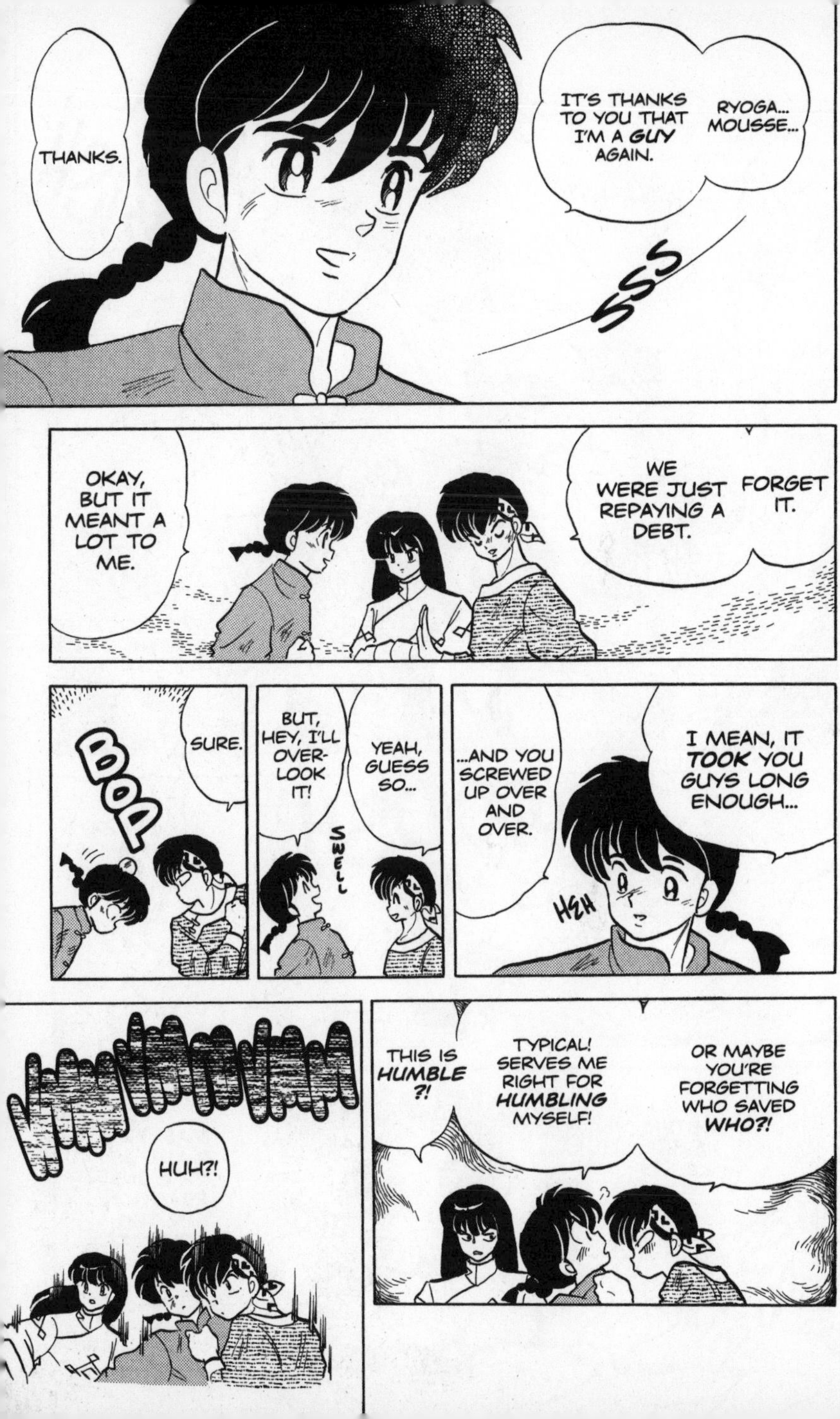
RYOGA... MOUSSE...
IT'S THANKS TO YOU THAT I'M A GUY AGAIN.
SSS
THANKS.
FORGET IT.
WE WERE JUST REPAYING A DEBT.
OKAY, BUT IT MEANT A LOT TO ME.
I MEAN, IT TOOK YOU GUYS LONG ENOUGH...
...AND YOU SCREWED UP OVER AND OVER.
HEH
YEAH, GUESS SO...
BUT, HEY, I'LL OVER-LOOK IT!
SWELL
SURE.
BOP
OR MAYBE YOU'RE FORGETTING WHO SAVED WHO?!
TYPICAL! SERVES ME RIGHT FOR HUMBLING MYSELF!
THIS IS HUMBLE?!
HUH?!

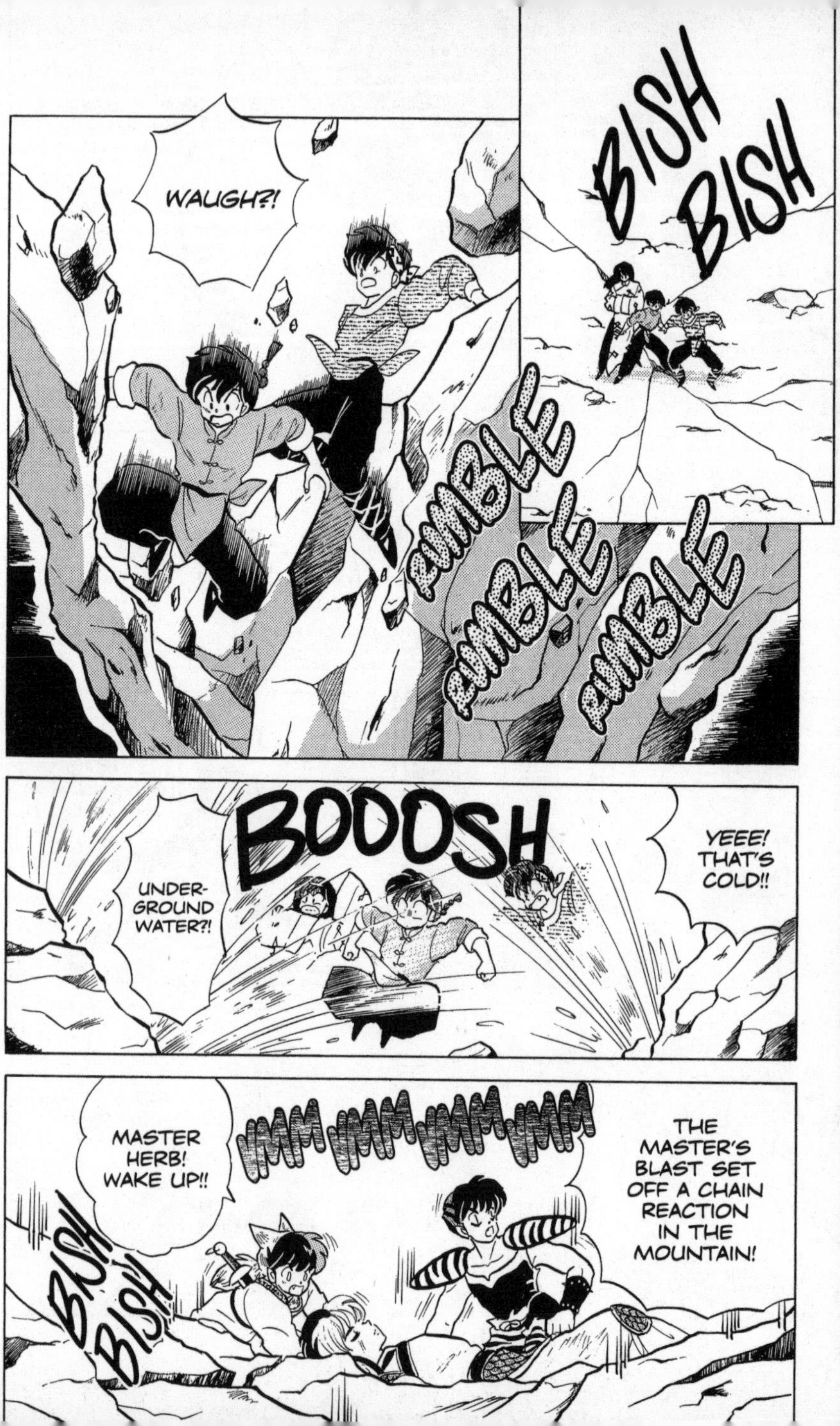
BISH
BISH
WAUGH?!
RUMBLE
RUMBLE
RUMBLE
YEEE! THAT'S COLD!!
BOOOSH
UNDER-GROUND WATER?!
THE MASTER'S BLAST SET OFF A CHAIN REACTION IN THE MOUNTAIN!
VMM VMM VMM VMM
MASTER HERB! WAKE UP!!
BISH
BISH

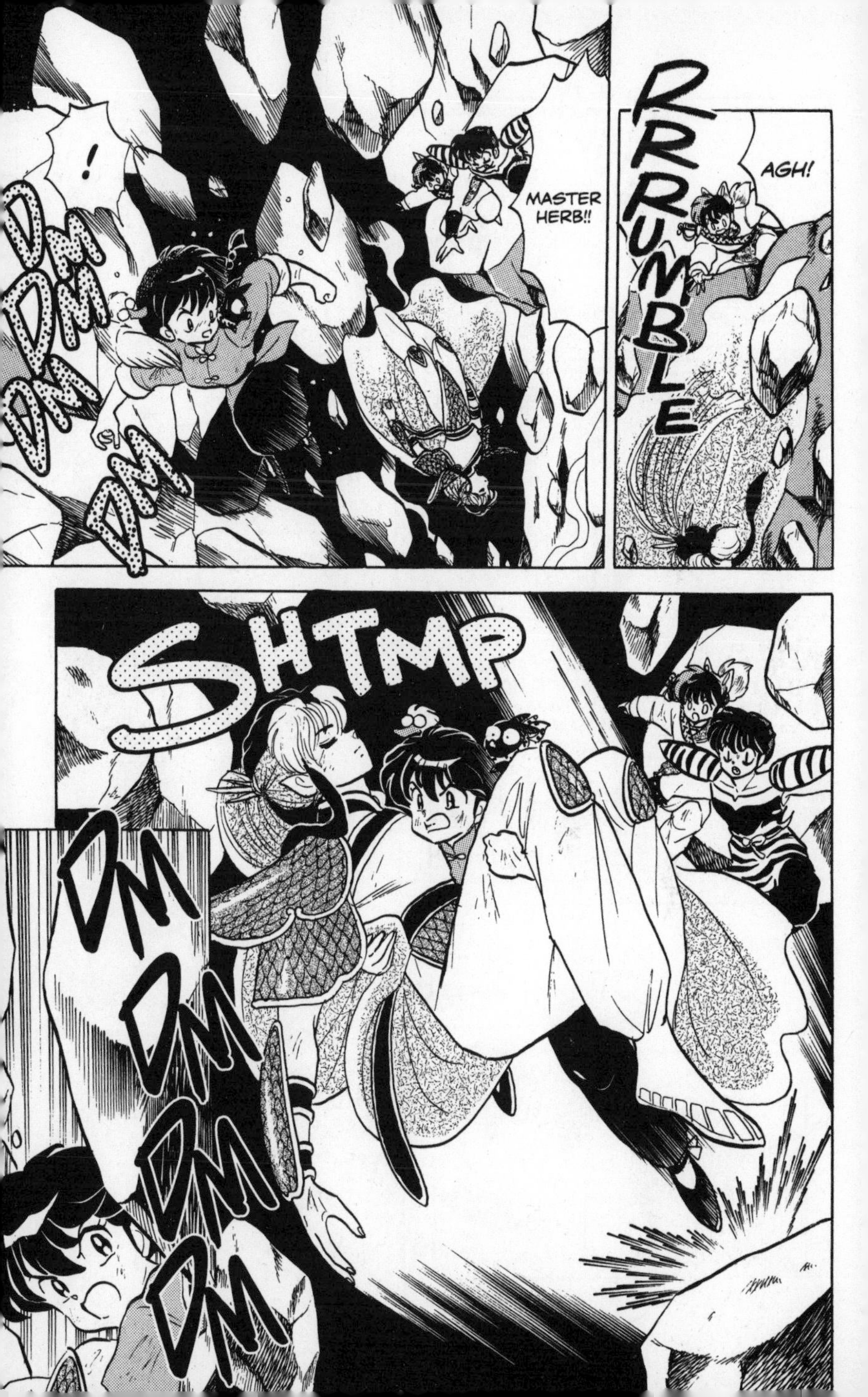
RRRUMBLE
AGH!
MASTER HERB!!
!
DM DM DM
DM
SHTMP
DM DM DM DM DM

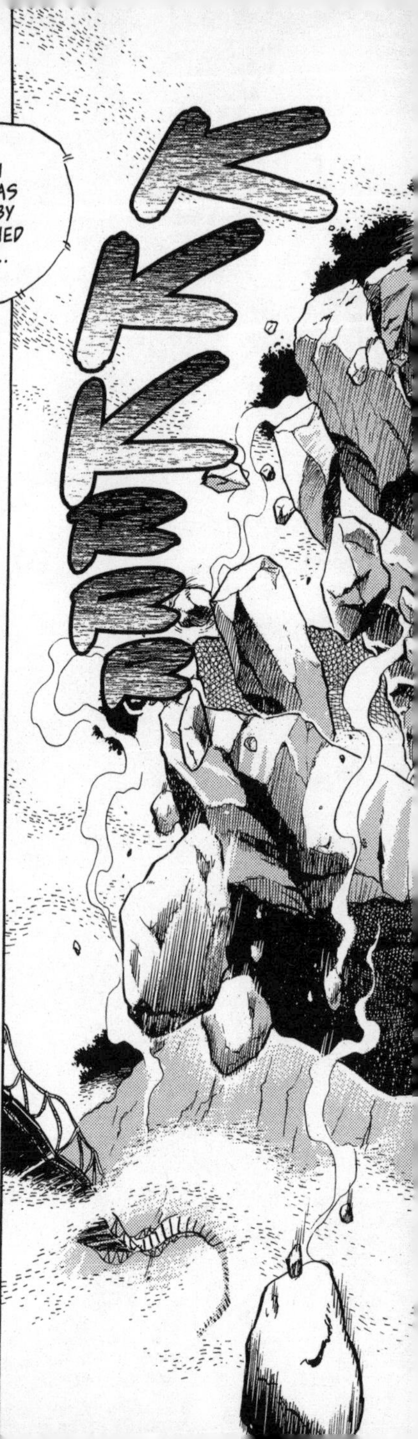

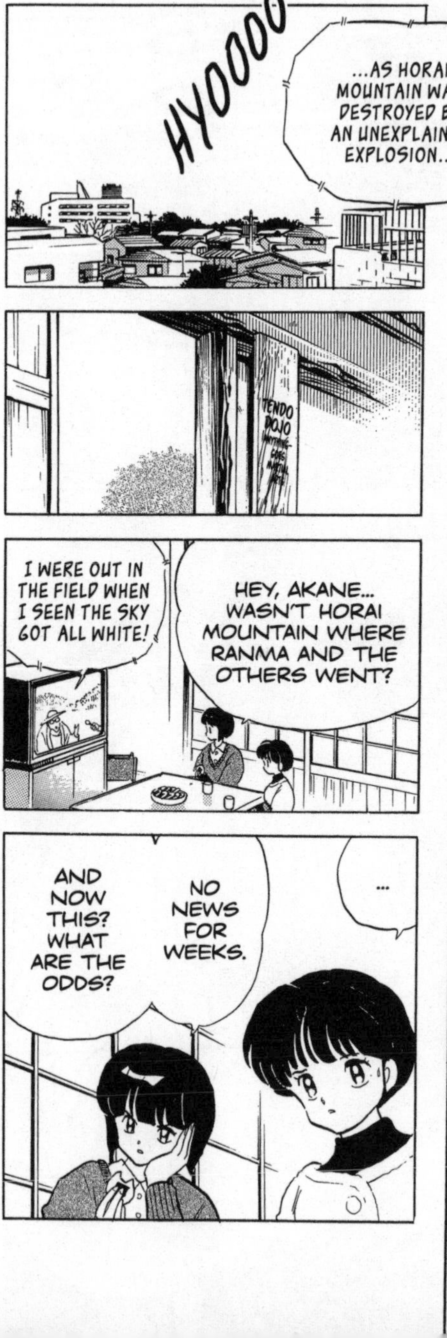
HYOOOO
...AS HORAI MOUNTAIN WAS DESTROYED BY AN UNEXPLAINED EXPLOSION...
TENDO DOJO
HEY, AKANE... WASN'T HORAI MOUNTAIN WHERE RANMA AND THE OTHERS WENT?
I WERE OUT IN THE FIELD WHEN I SEEN THE SKY GOT ALL WHITE!
...
NO NEWS FOR WEEKS.
AND NOW THIS? WHAT ARE THE ODDS?

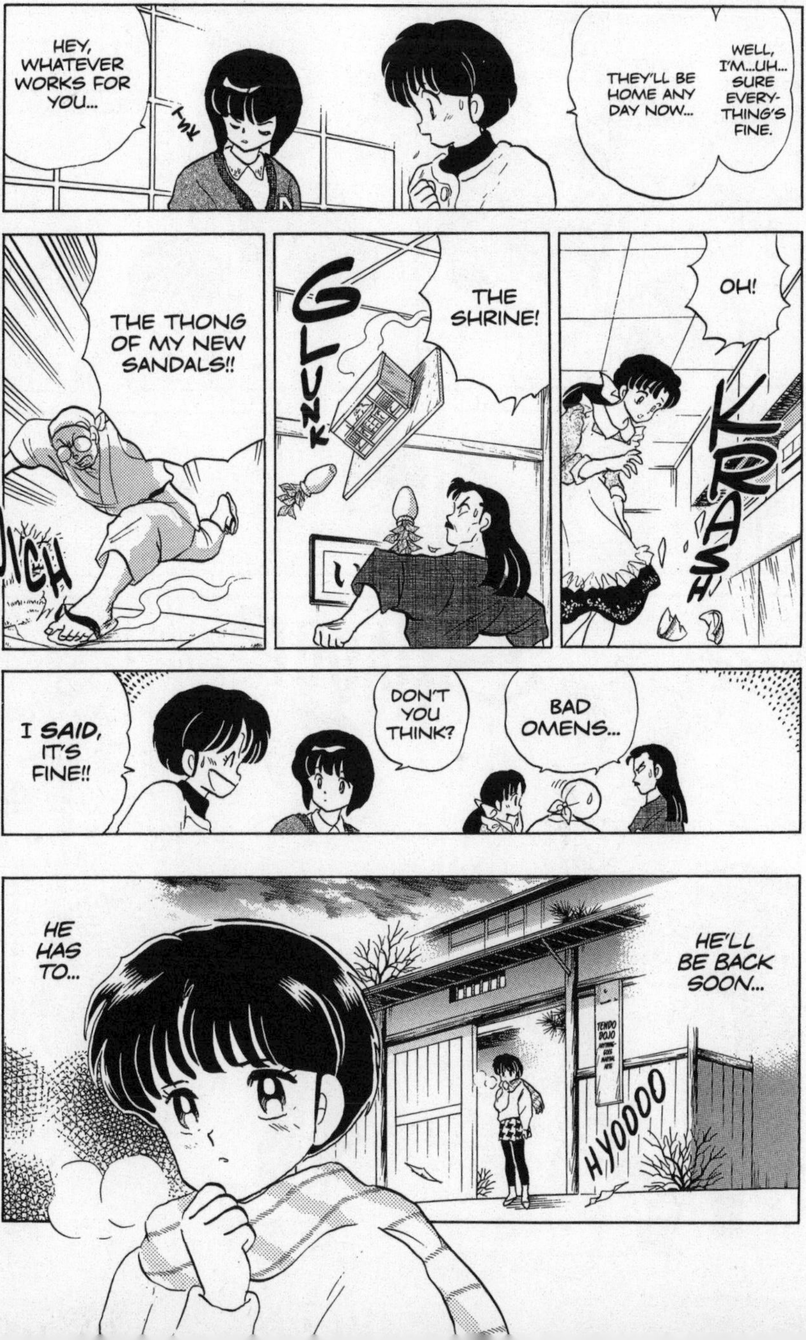
WELL, I'M...UH... SURE EVERY-THING'S FINE.
THEY'LL BE HOME ANY DAY NOW...
HEY, WHATEVER WORKS FOR YOU...
TSK
OH!
KRASH
THE SHRINE!
GLUNK
THE THONG OF MY NEW SANDALS!!
PWICH
BAD OMENS...
DON'T YOU THINK?
I SAID, IT'S FINE!!
HE'LL BE BACK SOON...
TENDO DOJO
HYOOOO
HE HAS TO...

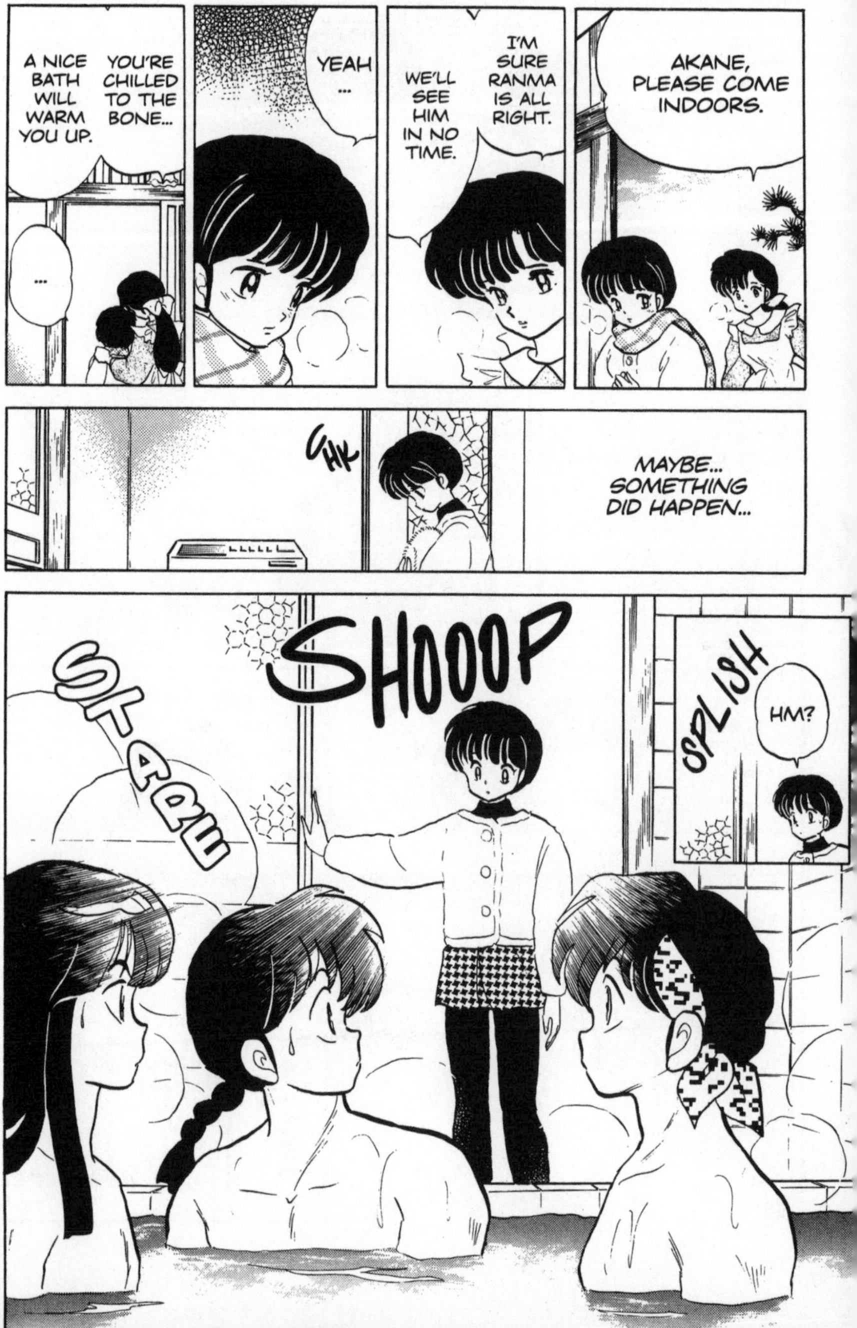
AKANE, PLEASE COME INDOORS.
I'M SURE RANMA IS ALL RIGHT.
WE'LL SEE HIM IN NO TIME.
YEAH ...
YOU'RE CHILLED TO THE BONE...
A NICE BATH WILL WARM YOU UP.
...
MAYBE... SOMETHING DID HAPPEN...
CHK
SPLISH
HM?
SHOOOP
STARE

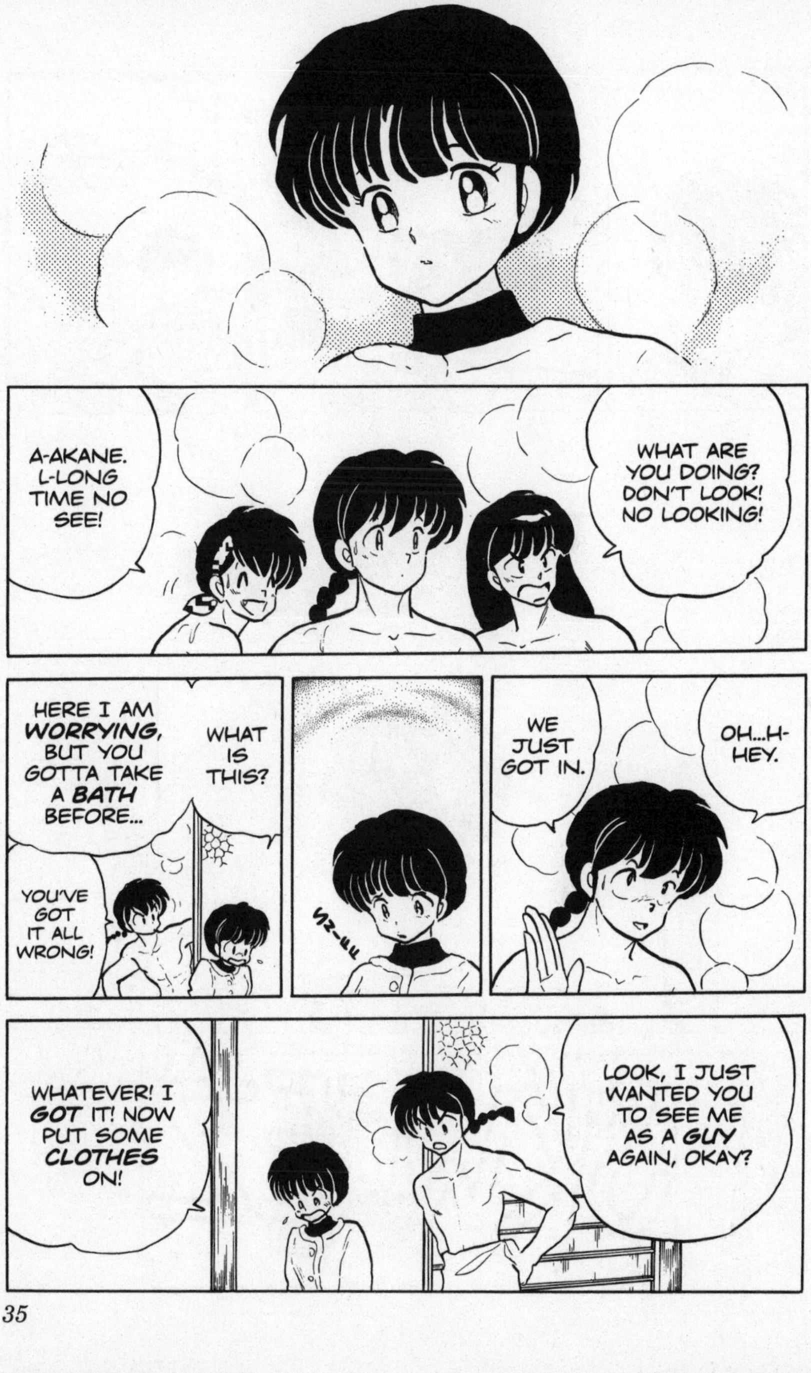
WHAT ARE YOU DOING? DON'T LOOK! NO LOOKING!
A-AKANE. L-LONG TIME NO SEE!
OH...H-HEY.
WE JUST GOT IN.
WHAT IS THIS?
HERE I AM **WORRYING**, BUT YOU GOTTA TAKE A **BATH** BEFORE...
YOU'VE GOT IT ALL WRONG!
LOOK, I JUST WANTED YOU TO SEE ME AS A **GUY** AGAIN, OKAY?
WHATEVER! I **GOT** IT! NOW PUT SOME **CLOTHES** ON!

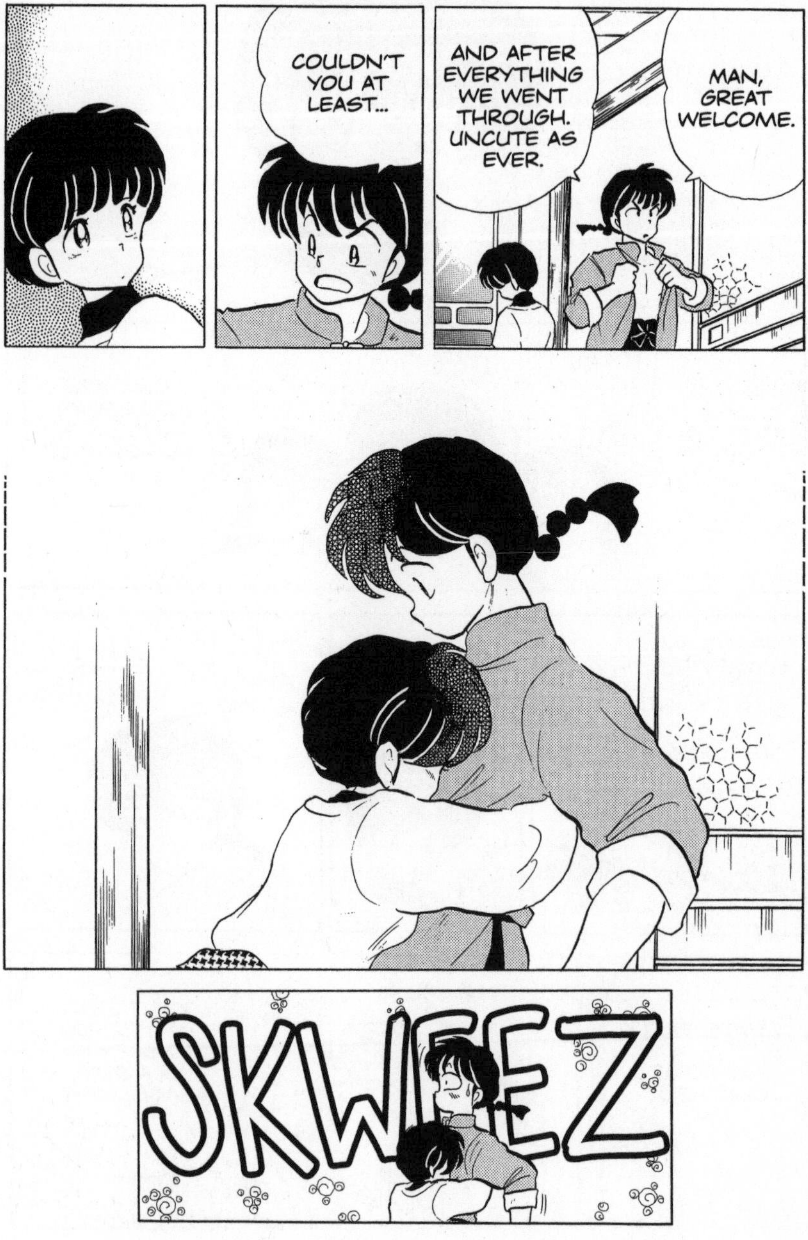
MAN, GREAT WELCOME.
AND AFTER EVERYTHING WE WENT THROUGH. UNCUTE AS EVER.
COULDN'T YOU AT LEAST...
SKWEEZ

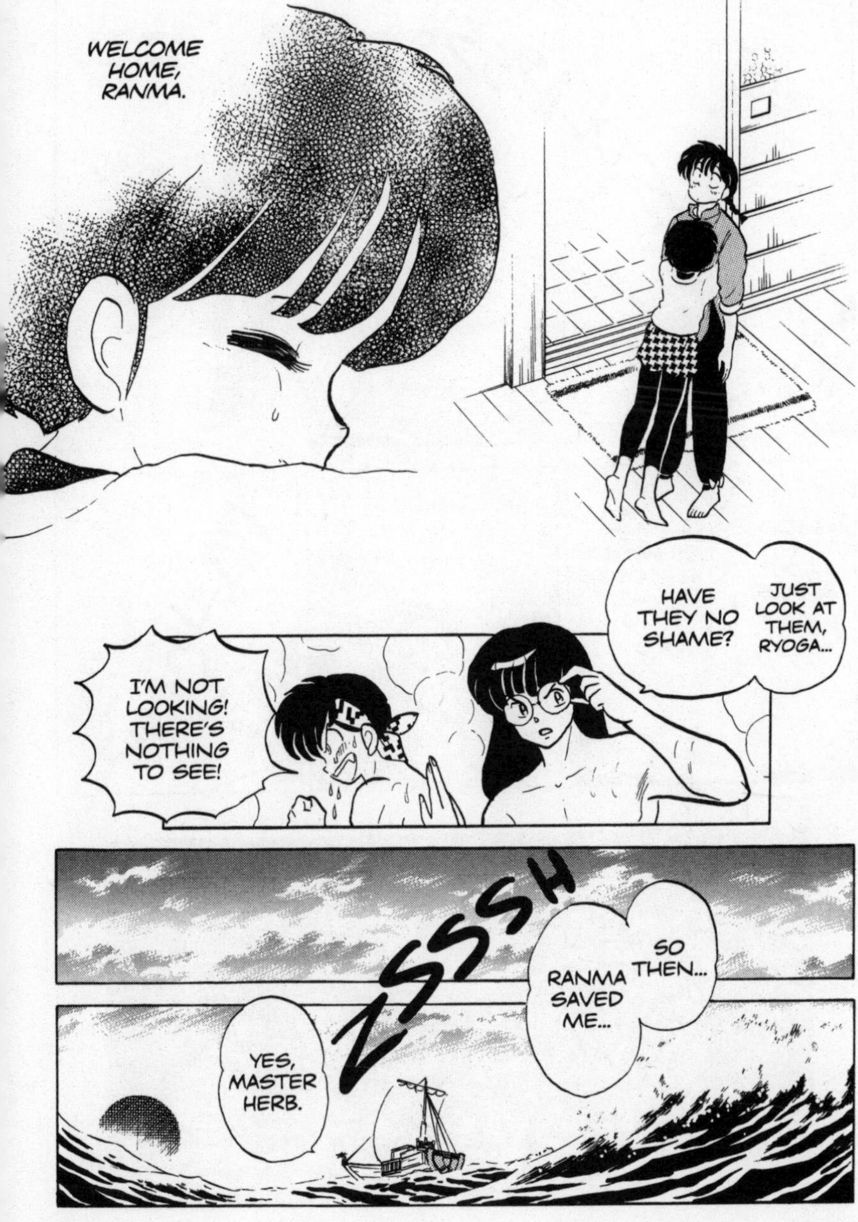
WELCOME HOME, RANMA.
JUST LOOK AT THEM, RYOGA...
HAVE THEY NO SHAME?
I'M NOT LOOKING! THERE'S NOTHING TO SEE!
ZSSSH
SO THEN...
RANMA SAVED ME...
YES, MASTER HERB.

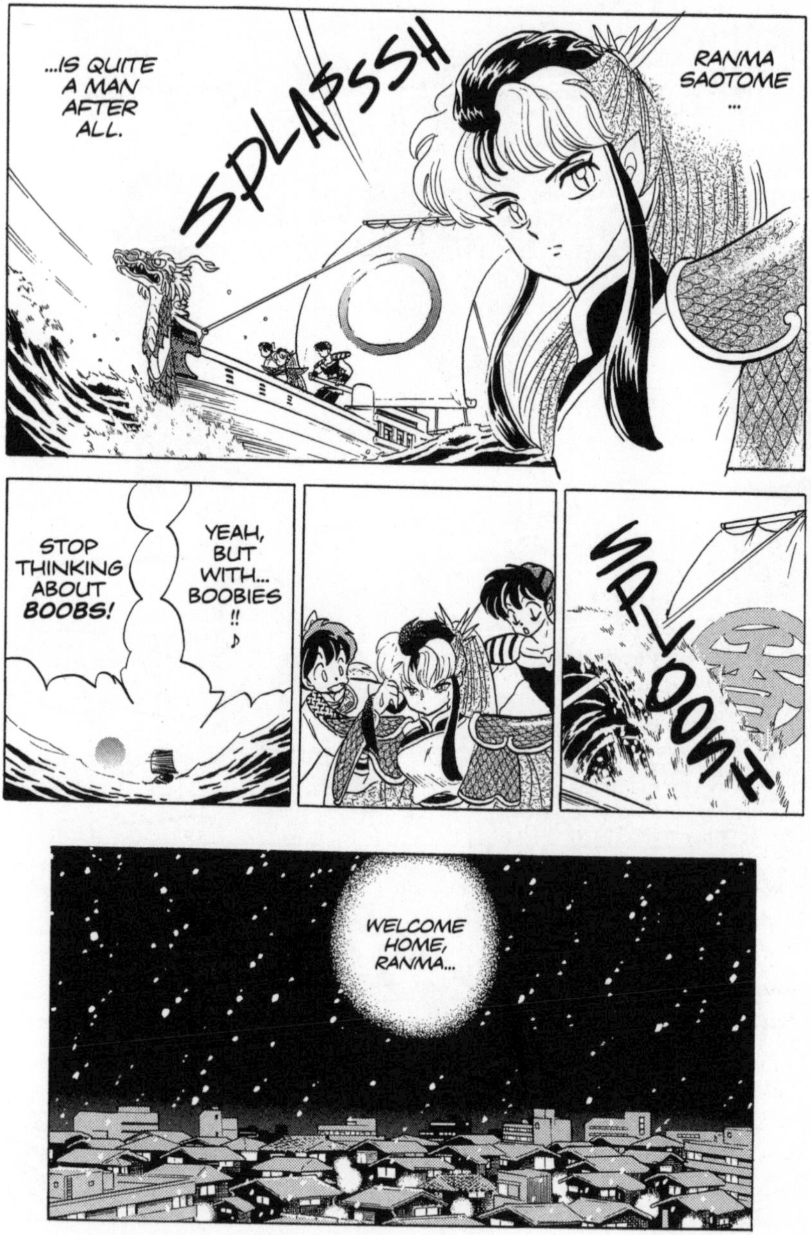

RANMA SAOTOME ...
SPLASSSH
...IS QUITE A MAN AFTER ALL.
SPLOOSH
YEAH, BUT WITH... BOOBIES!! ♪
STOP THINKING ABOUT **BOOBS!**
WELCOME HOME, RANMA...

PART 3
THE ULTIMATE TEACHER!

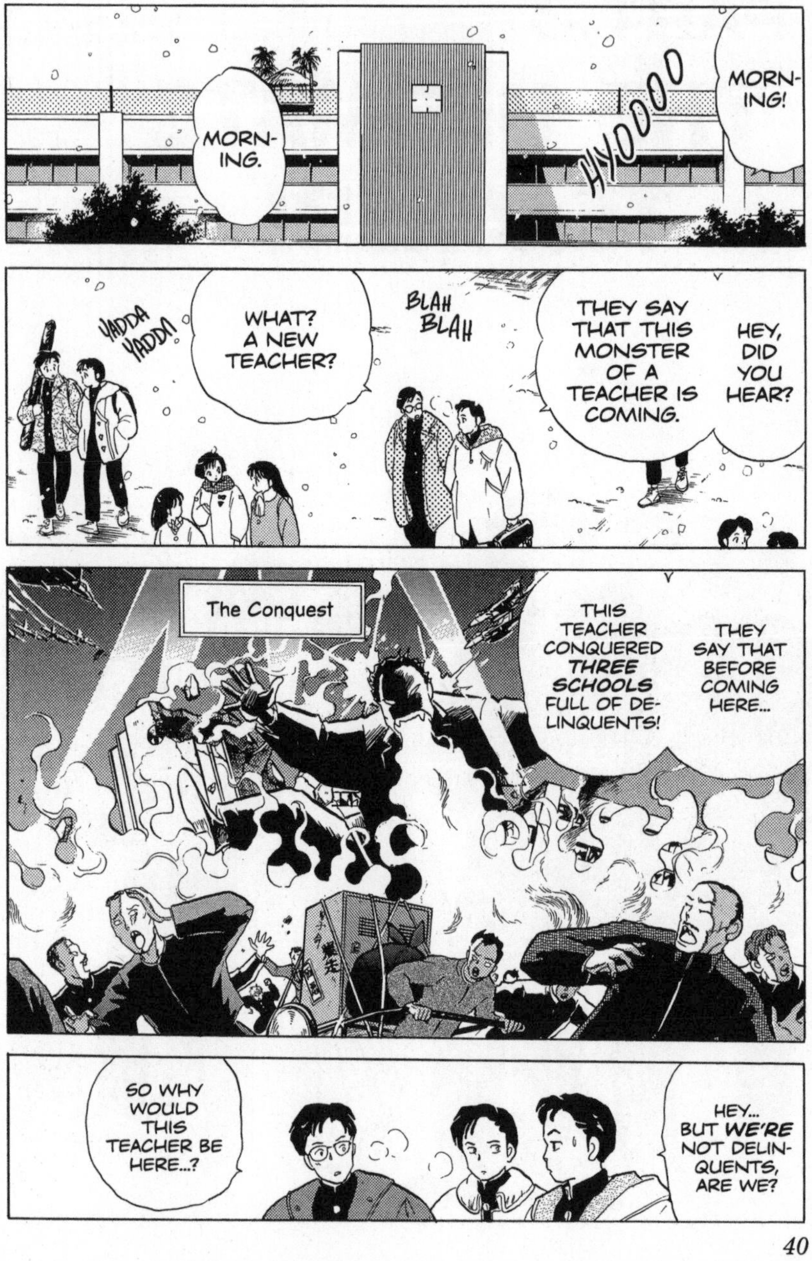
MORN-ING!
HYODOOO
MORN-ING.
HEY, DID YOU HEAR?
THEY SAY THAT THIS MONSTER OF A TEACHER IS COMING.
BLAH BLAH
WHAT? A NEW TEACHER?
YADDA YADDA
THEY SAY THAT BEFORE COMING HERE...
THIS TEACHER CONQUERED **THREE SCHOOLS** FULL OF DE-LINQUENTS!
The Conquest
HEY... BUT **WE'RE** NOT DELIN-QUENTS, ARE WE?
SO WHY WOULD THIS TEACHER BE HERE...?

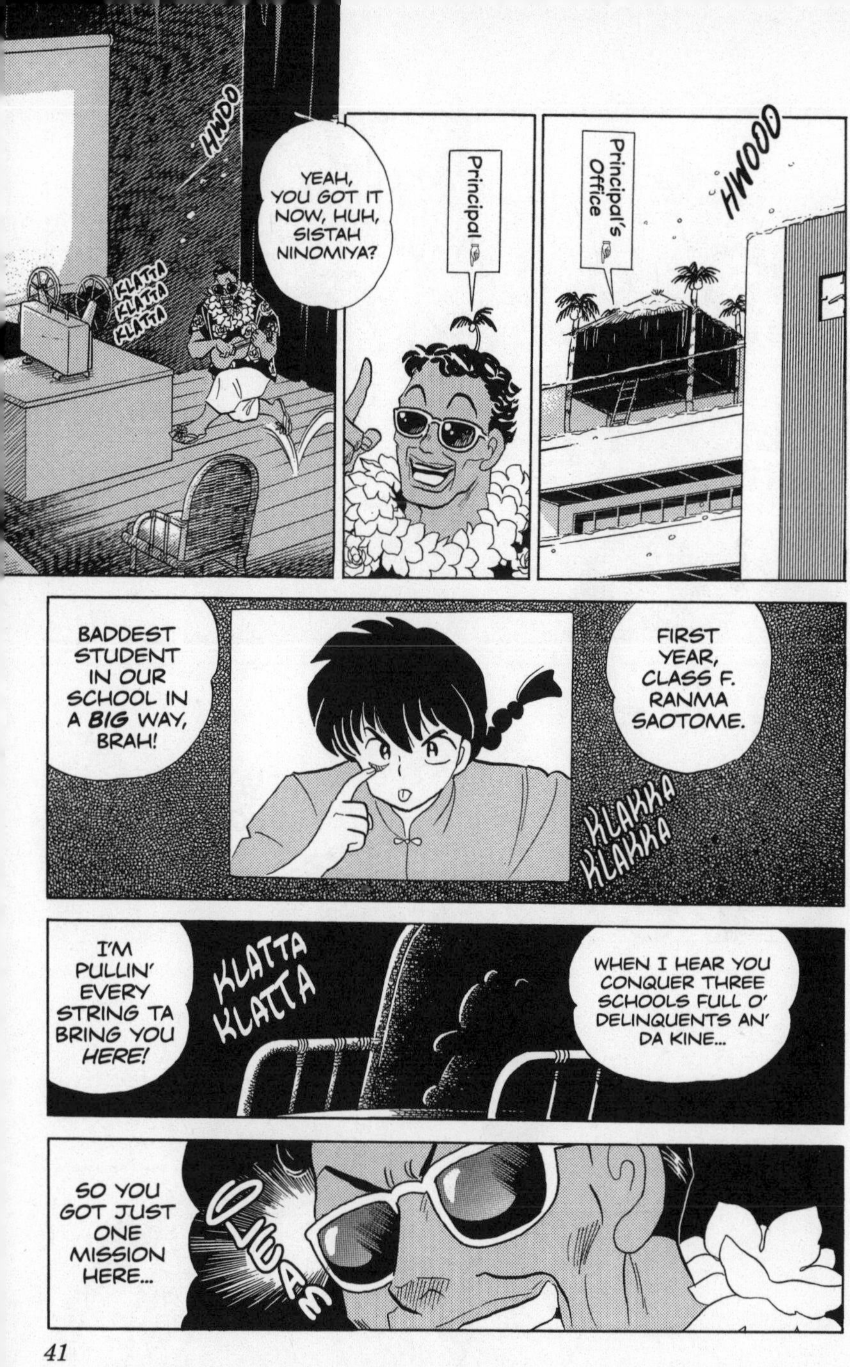
HWOOD
Principal's Office
Principal
YEAH, YOU GOT IT NOW, HUH, SISTAH NINOMIYA?
HWDO
KLATTA KLATTA KLATTA
FIRST YEAR, CLASS F. RANMA SAOTOME.
KLAKKA KLAKKA
BADDEST STUDENT IN OUR SCHOOL IN A BIG WAY, BRAH!
WHEN I HEAR YOU CONQUER THREE SCHOOLS FULL O' DELINQUENTS AN' DA KINE...
KLATTA KLATTA
I'M PULLIN' EVERY STRING TA BRING YOU HERE!
SO YOU GOT JUST ONE MISSION HERE...

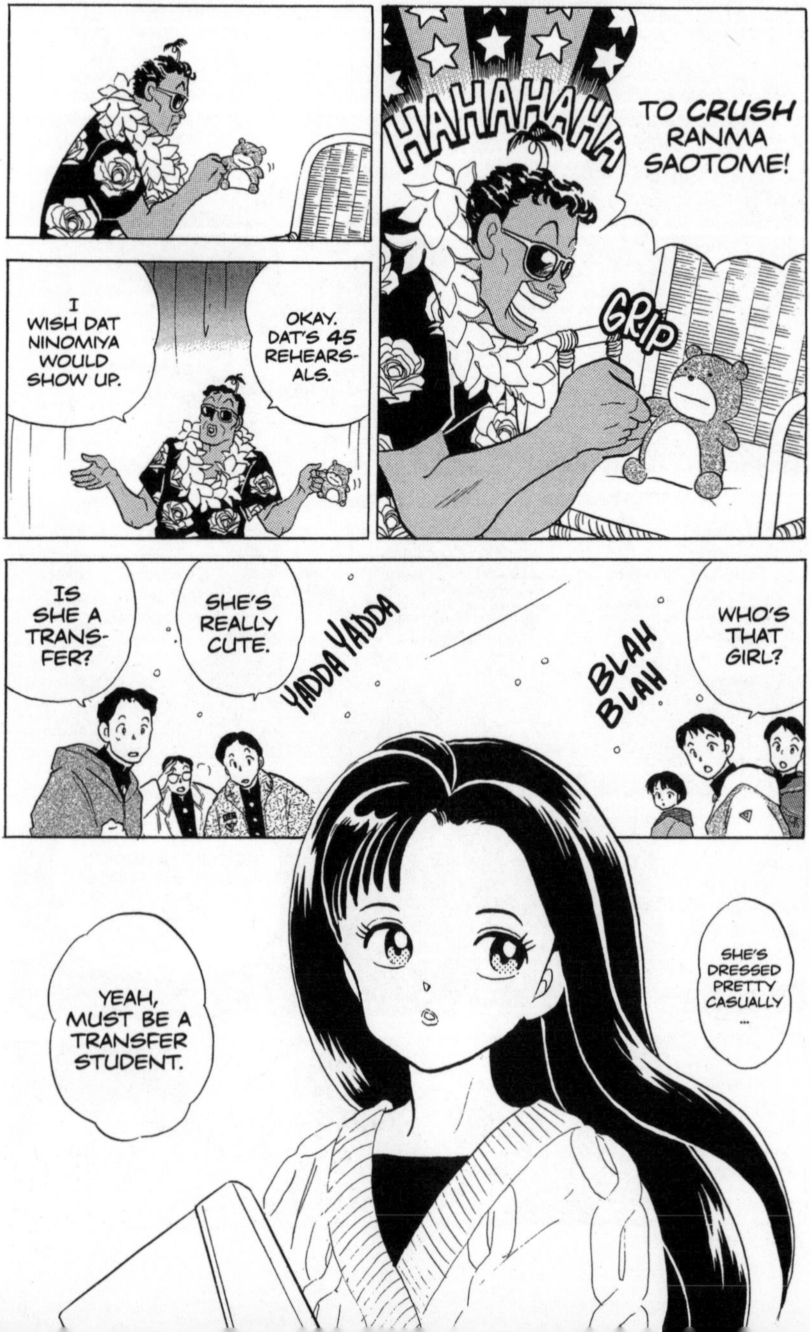
HAHAHAHA
TO CRUSH RANMA SAOTOME!
GRIP
OKAY. DAT'S 45 REHEARSALS.
I WISH DAT NINOMIYA WOULD SHOW UP.
WHO'S THAT GIRL?
BLAH BLAH
YADDA YADDA
SHE'S REALLY CUTE.
IS SHE A TRANSFER?
SHE'S DRESSED PRETTY CASUALLY...
YEAH, MUST BE A TRANSFER STUDENT.

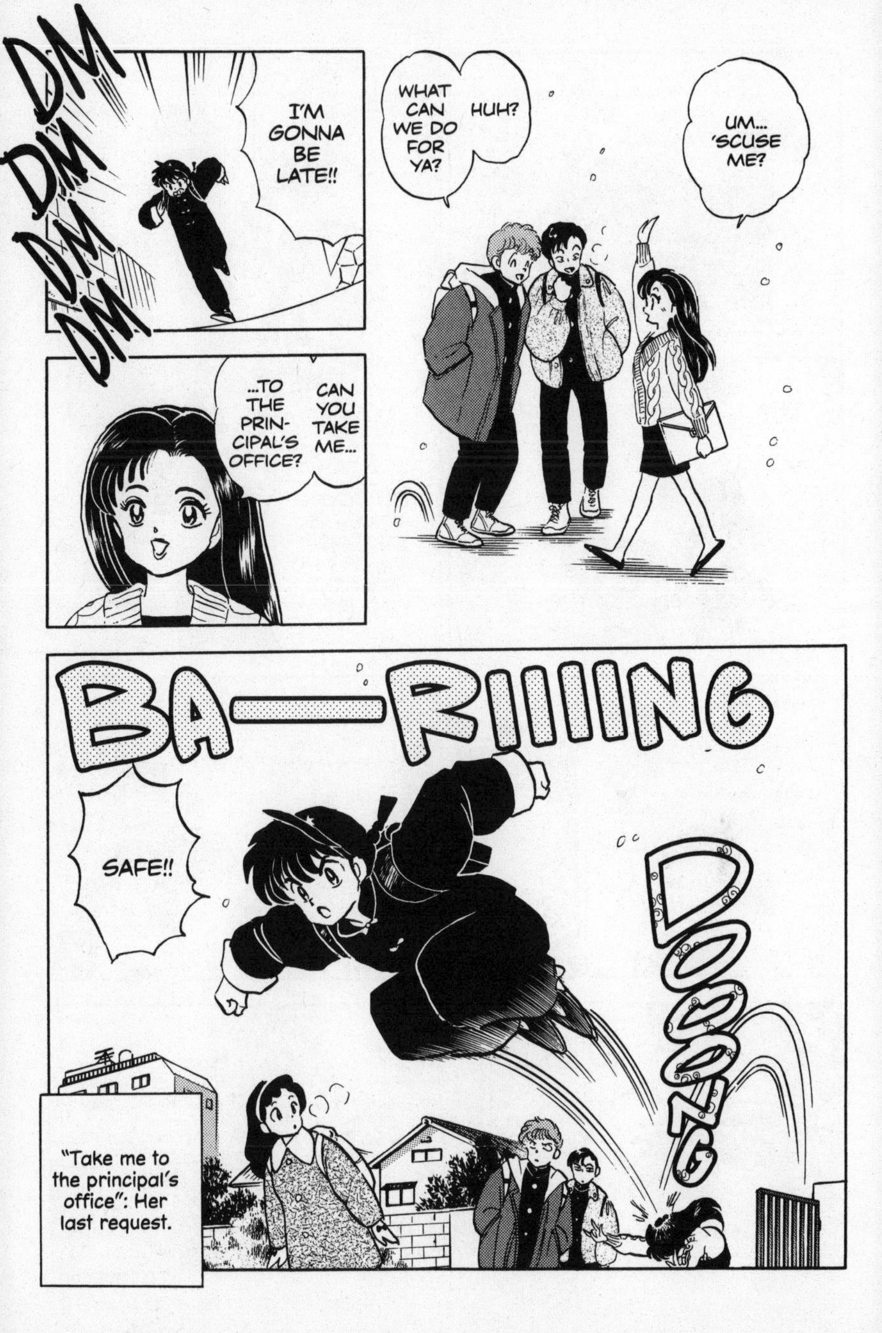
UM... 'SCUSE ME?
HUH?
WHAT CAN WE DO FOR YA?
DM DM DM DM DM
I'M GONNA BE LATE!!
CAN YOU TAKE ME...
...TO THE PRIN-CIPAL'S OFFICE?
BA—RIIIING
SAFE!!
DOOONG
"Take me to the principal's office": Her last request.

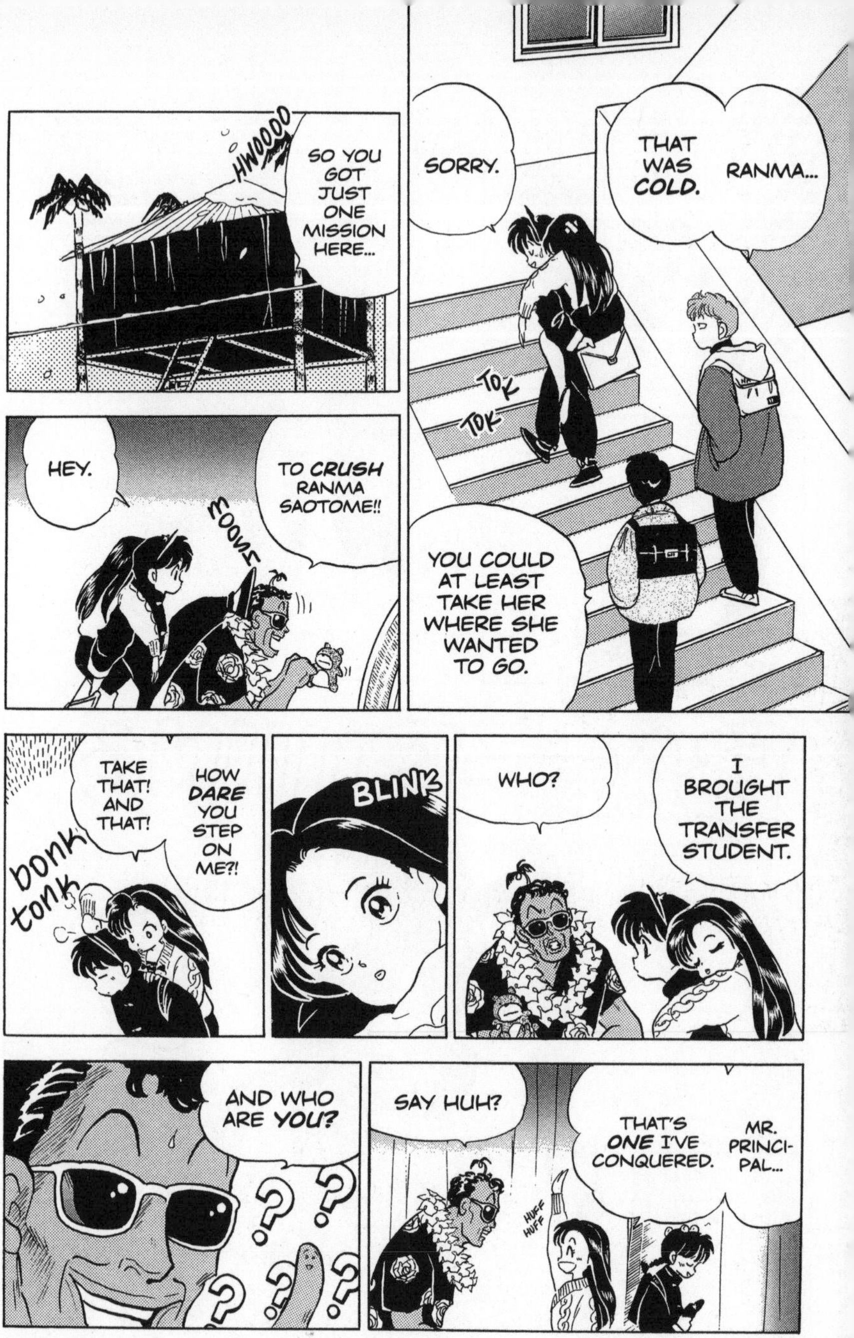
RANMA...
THAT WAS COLD.
SORRY.
TOK TOK
YOU COULD AT LEAST TAKE HER WHERE SHE WANTED TO GO.
HWOOOO
SO YOU GOT JUST ONE MISSION HERE...
TO CRUSH RANMA SAOTOME!!
SWOOSH
HEY.
I BROUGHT THE TRANSFER STUDENT.
WHO?
BLINK
HOW DARE YOU STEP ON ME?!
TAKE THAT! AND THAT!
bonk tonk
MR. PRINCIPAL...
THAT'S ONE I'VE CONQUERED.
HUFF HUFF
SAY HUH?
AND WHO ARE YOU?

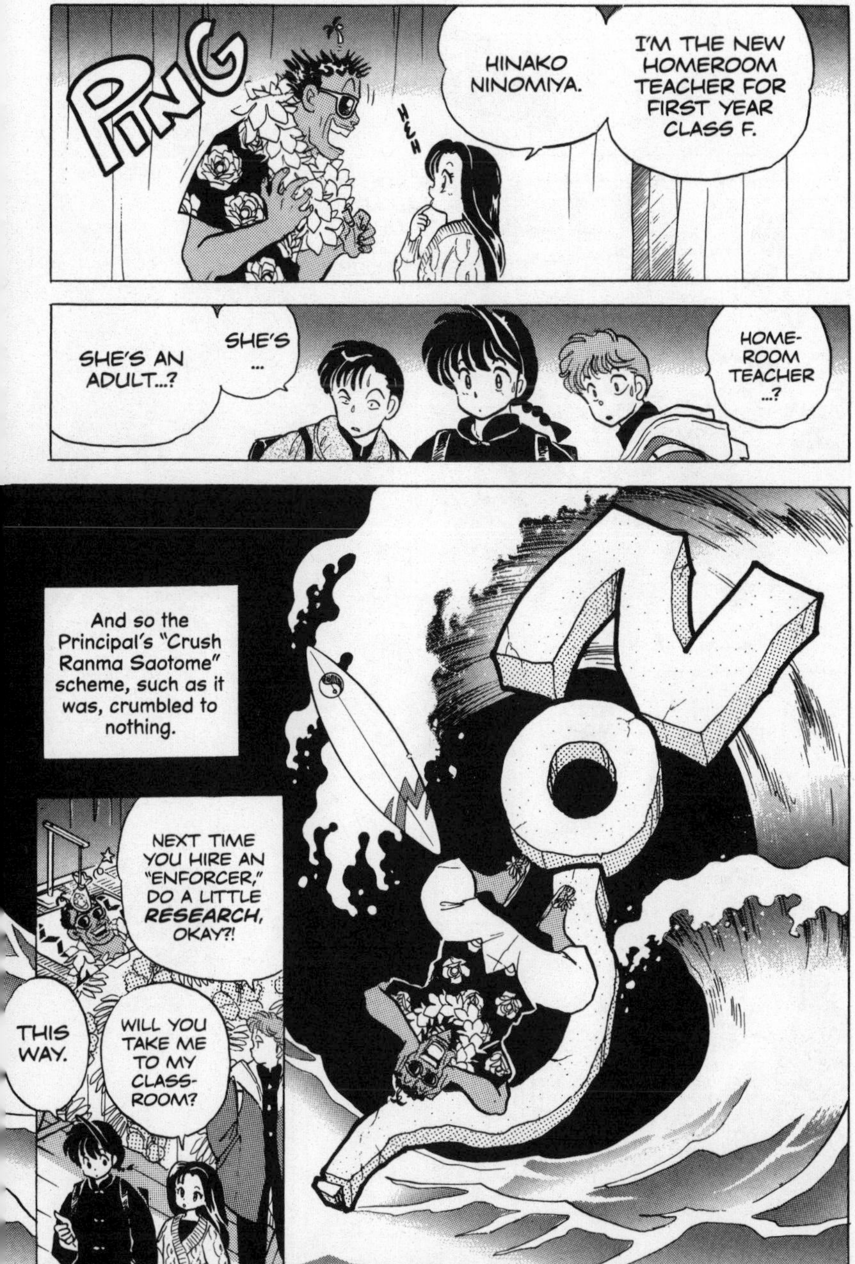
I'M THE NEW HOMEROOM TEACHER FOR FIRST YEAR CLASS F.
HINAKO NINOMIYA.
HEH
PING
HOME-ROOM TEACHER ...?
SHE'S ...
SHE'S AN ADULT...?
And so the Principal's "Crush Ranma Saotome" scheme, such as it was, crumbled to nothing.
NEXT TIME YOU HIRE AN "ENFORCER," DO A LITTLE RESEARCH, OKAY?!
WILL YOU TAKE ME TO MY CLASS-ROOM?
THIS WAY.

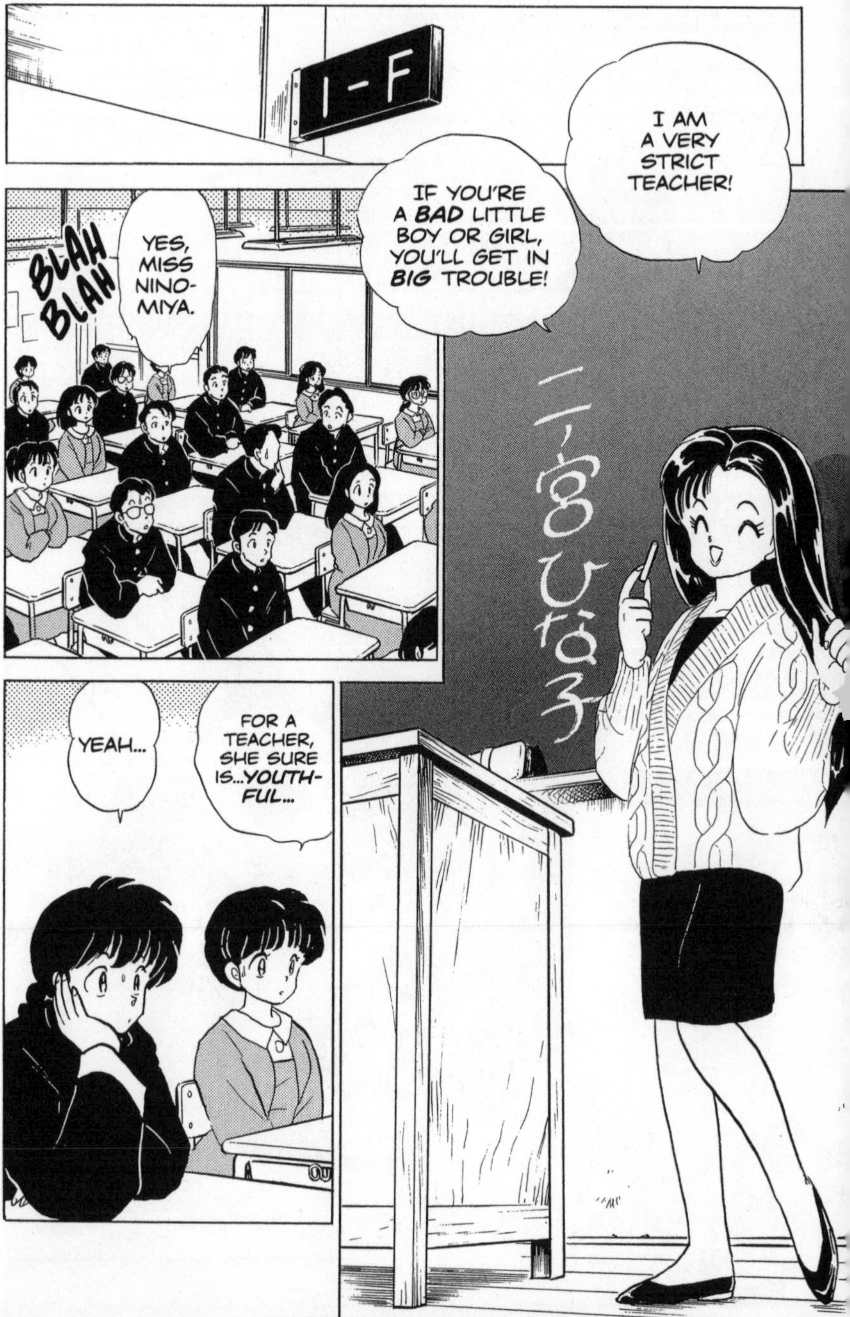
I-F
I AM A VERY STRICT TEACHER!
IF YOU'RE A **BAD** LITTLE BOY OR GIRL, YOU'LL GET IN **BIG** TROUBLE!
二ノ宮ひな子
YES, MISS NINO-MIYA.
BLAH BLAH
FOR A TEACHER, SHE SURE IS...***YOUTH-FUL...***
YEAH...

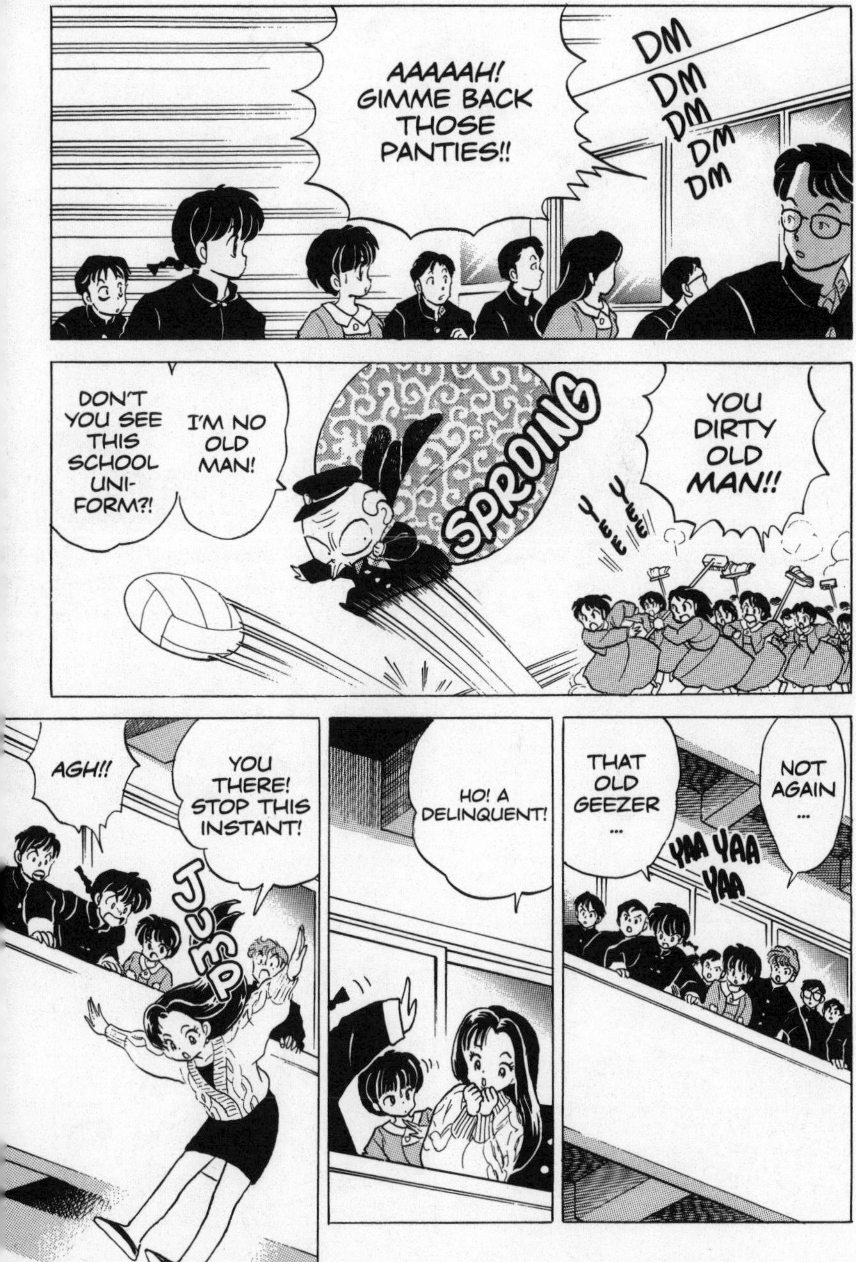
DM DM DM DM DM
AAAAAH! GIMME BACK THOSE PANTIES!!
YOU DIRTY OLD MAN!!
YEE YEE
SPROING
I'M NO OLD MAN!
DON'T YOU SEE THIS SCHOOL UNI-FORM?!
NOT AGAIN ...
THAT OLD GEEZER ...
YAA YAA YAA YAA
HO! A DELINQUENT!
YOU THERE! STOP THIS INSTANT!
AGH!!
JUMP

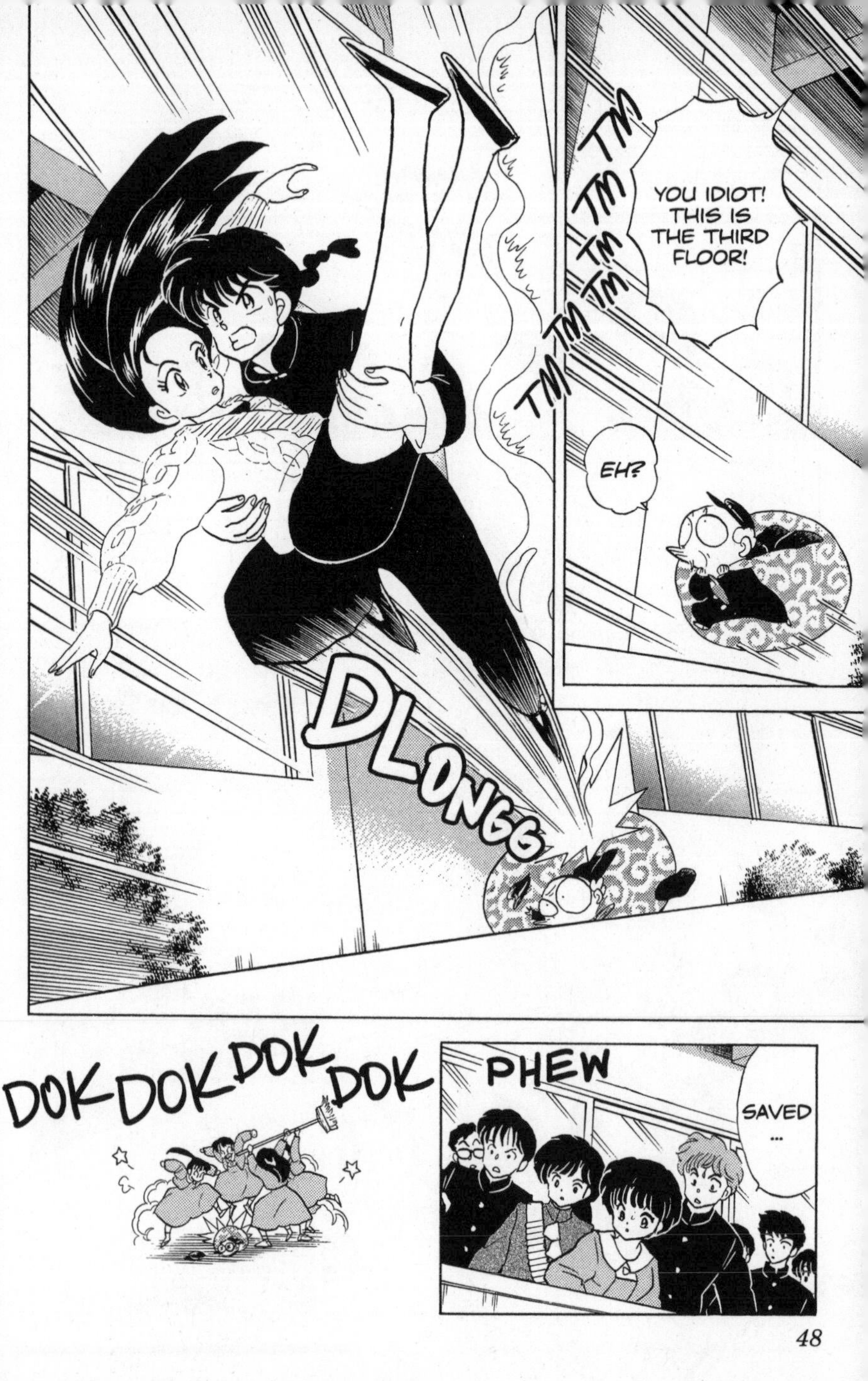
YOU IDIOT! THIS IS THE THIRD FLOOR!
TM TM TM TM TM TM TM
EH?
DLONGG
PHEW
SAVED ...
DOK DOK DOK DOK

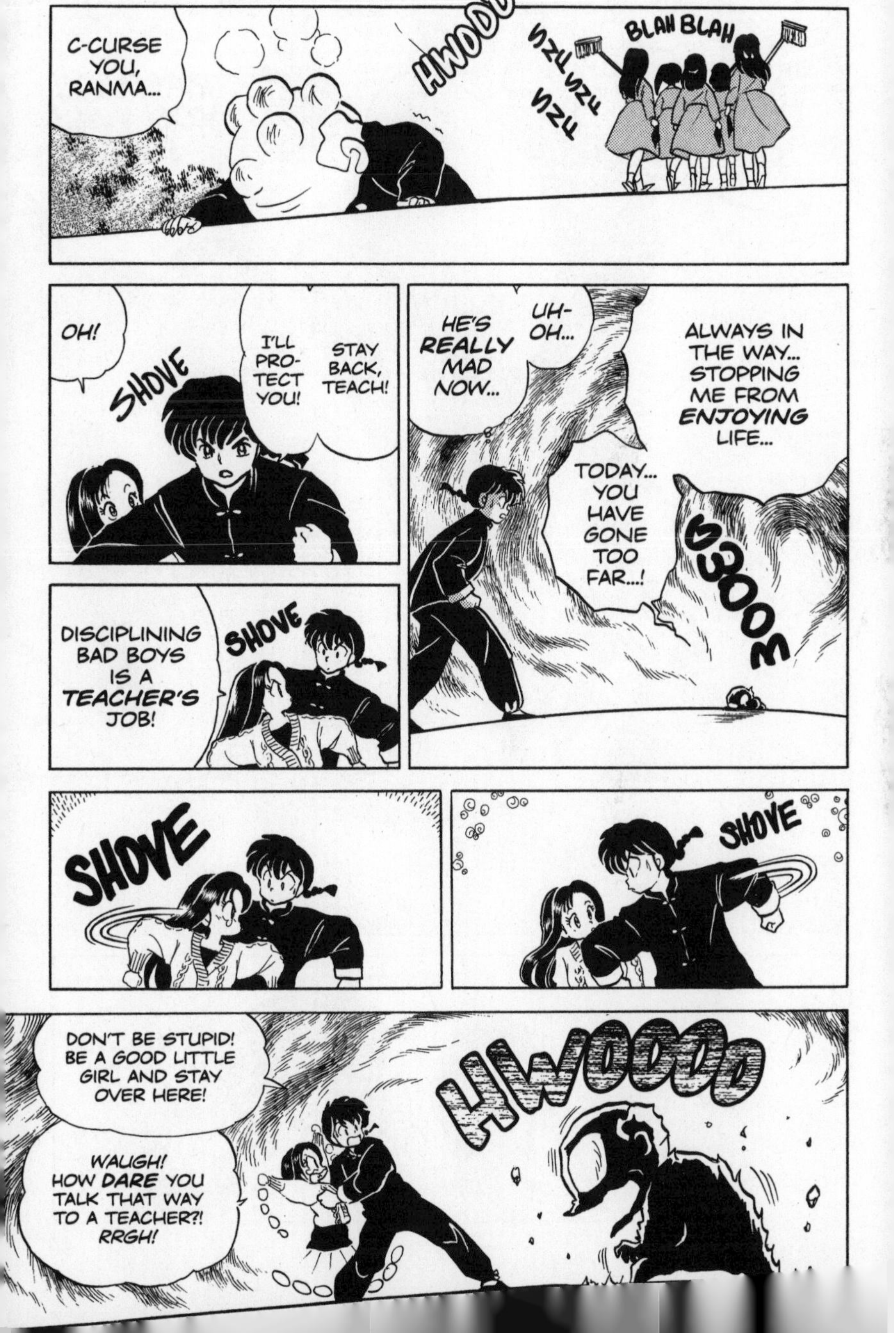
BLAH BLAH
HWOOD
C-CURSE YOU, RANMA...
ALWAYS IN THE WAY... STOPPING ME FROM ENJOYING LIFE...
UH-OH...
HE'S REALLY MAD NOW...
TODAY... YOU HAVE GONE TOO FAR...!
STAY BACK, TEACH!
I'LL PROTECT YOU!
SHOVE
OH!
SHOVE
DISCIPLINING BAD BOYS IS A TEACHER'S JOB!
SHOVE
SHOVE
HWOOOD
DON'T BE STUPID! BE A GOOD LITTLE GIRL AND STAY OVER HERE!
WAUGH! HOW DARE YOU TALK THAT WAY TO A TEACHER?! RRGH!

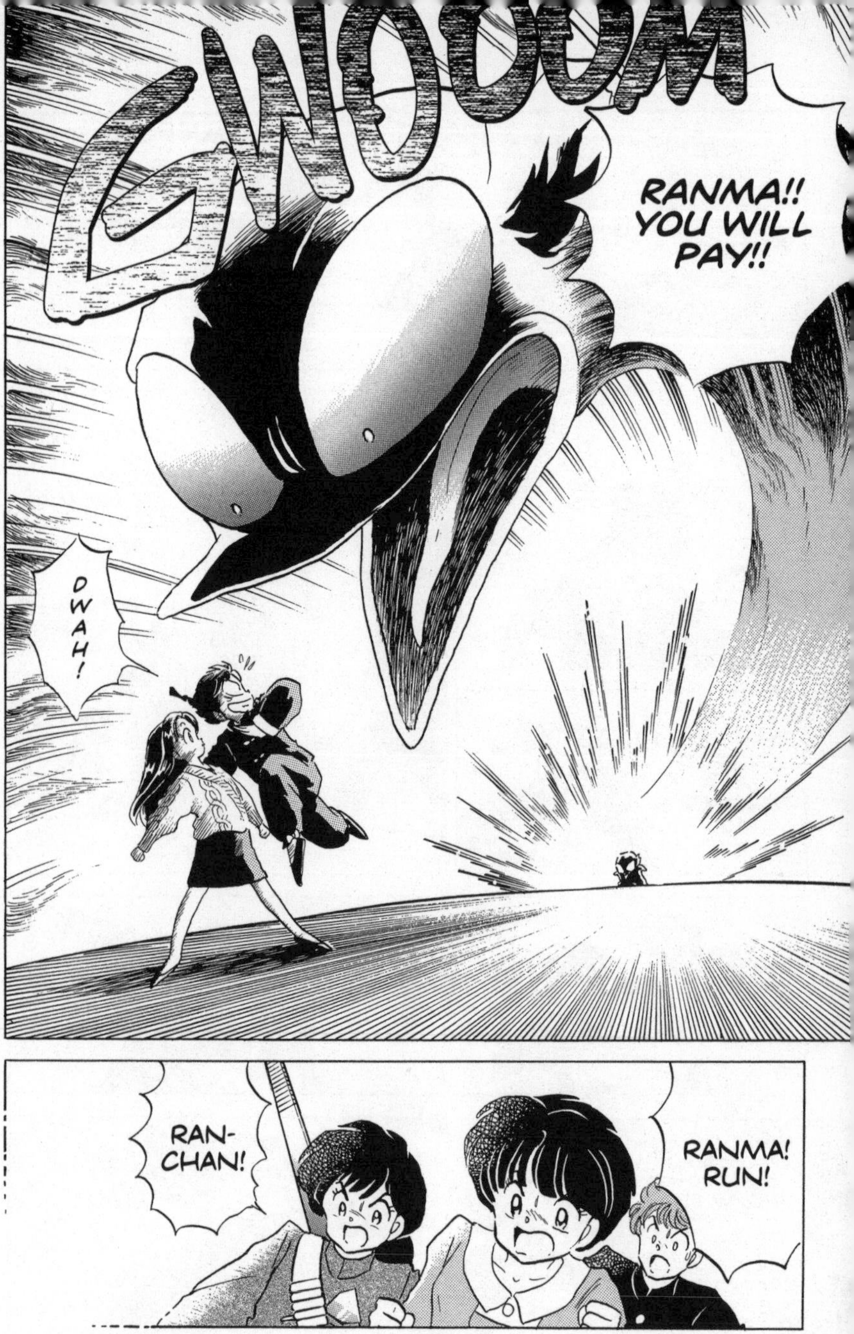

GWOOOM
RANMA!! YOU WILL PAY!!
DWAH!
RANMA! RUN!
RAN-CHAN!

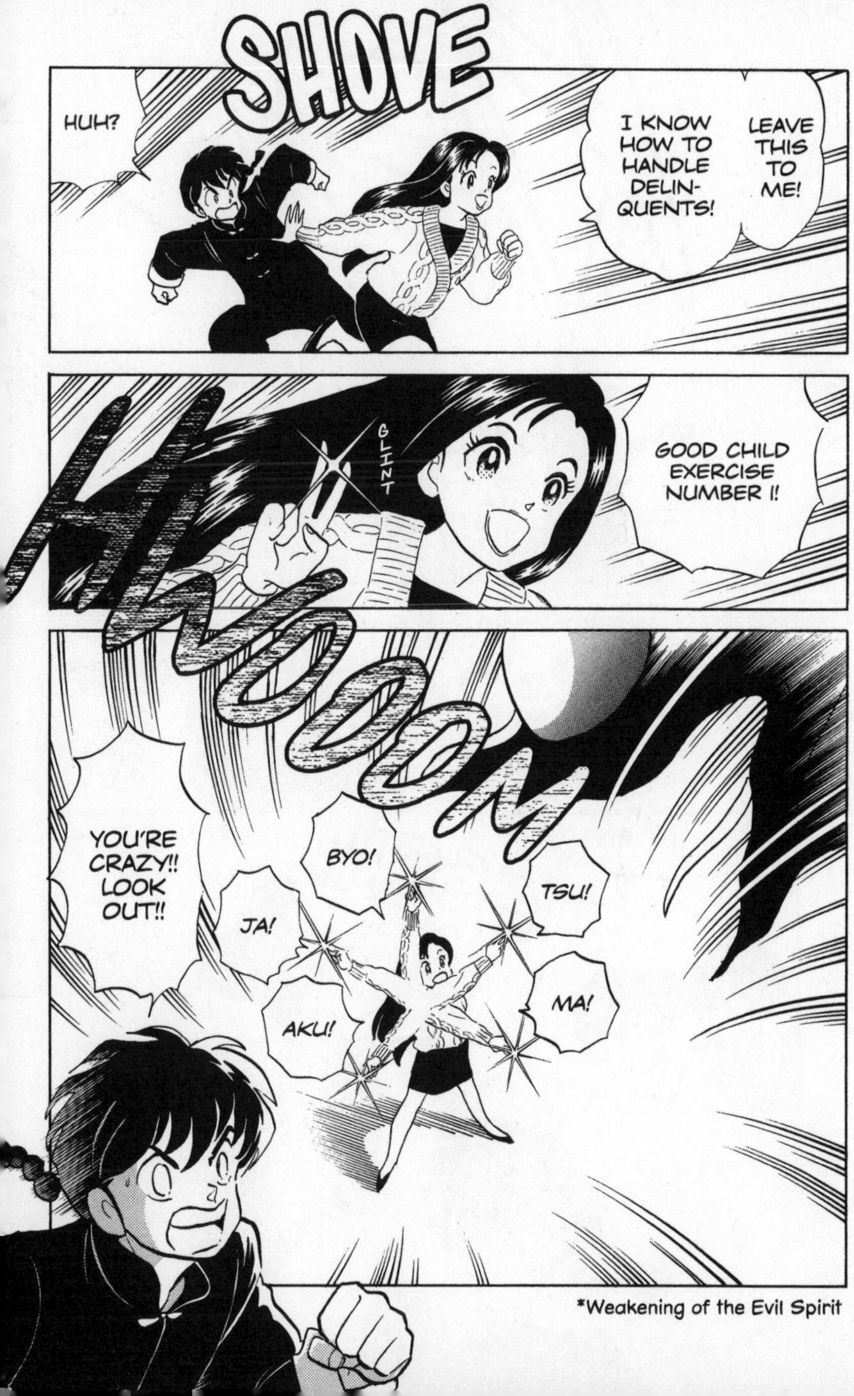
SHOVE
LEAVE THIS TO ME!
I KNOW HOW TO HANDLE DELIN-QUENTS!
HUH?
GLINT
GOOD CHILD EXERCISE NUMBER 1!
HWOOOM
TSU!
BYO!
YOU'RE CRAZY!! LOOK OUT!!
MA!
JA!
AKU!

*Weakening of the Evil Spirit

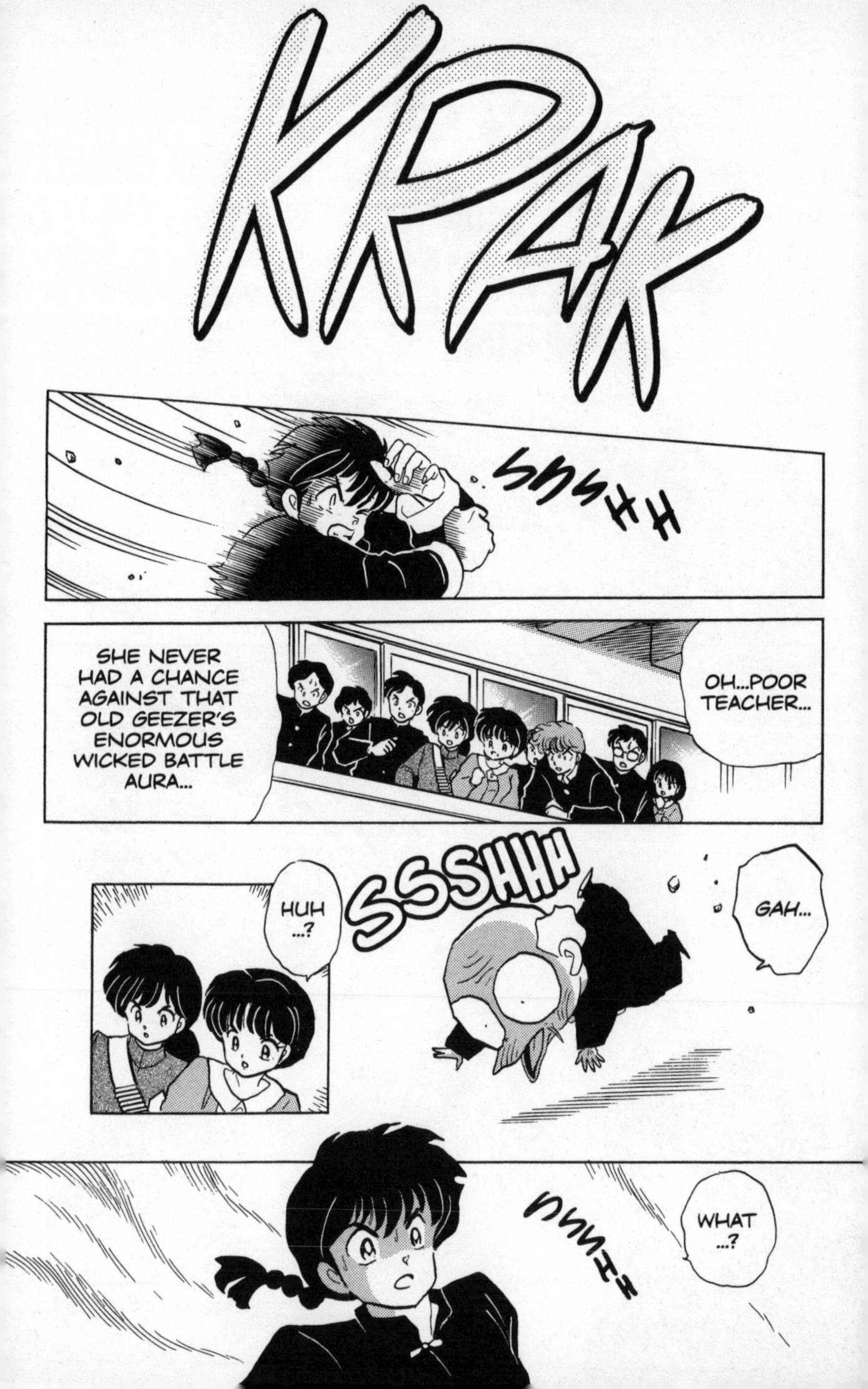
KRAK
SSSHH
OH...POOR TEACHER...
SHE NEVER HAD A CHANCE AGAINST THAT OLD GEEZER'S ENORMOUS WICKED BATTLE AURA...
GAH...
SSSHHH
HUH ...?
WHAT ...?
SSSHH

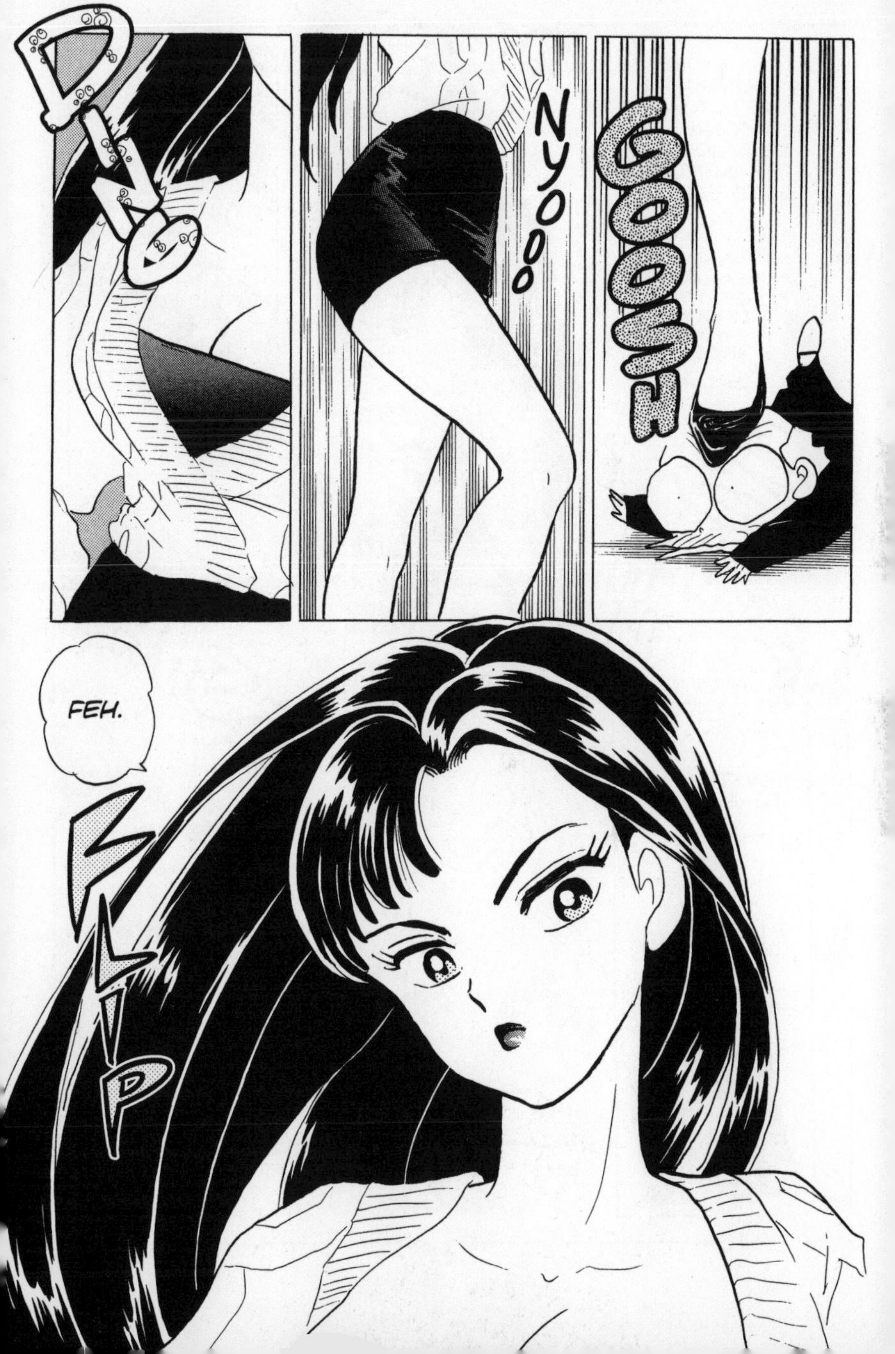
GOOOSH
NYOOOO
DING
FEH.
FLIP

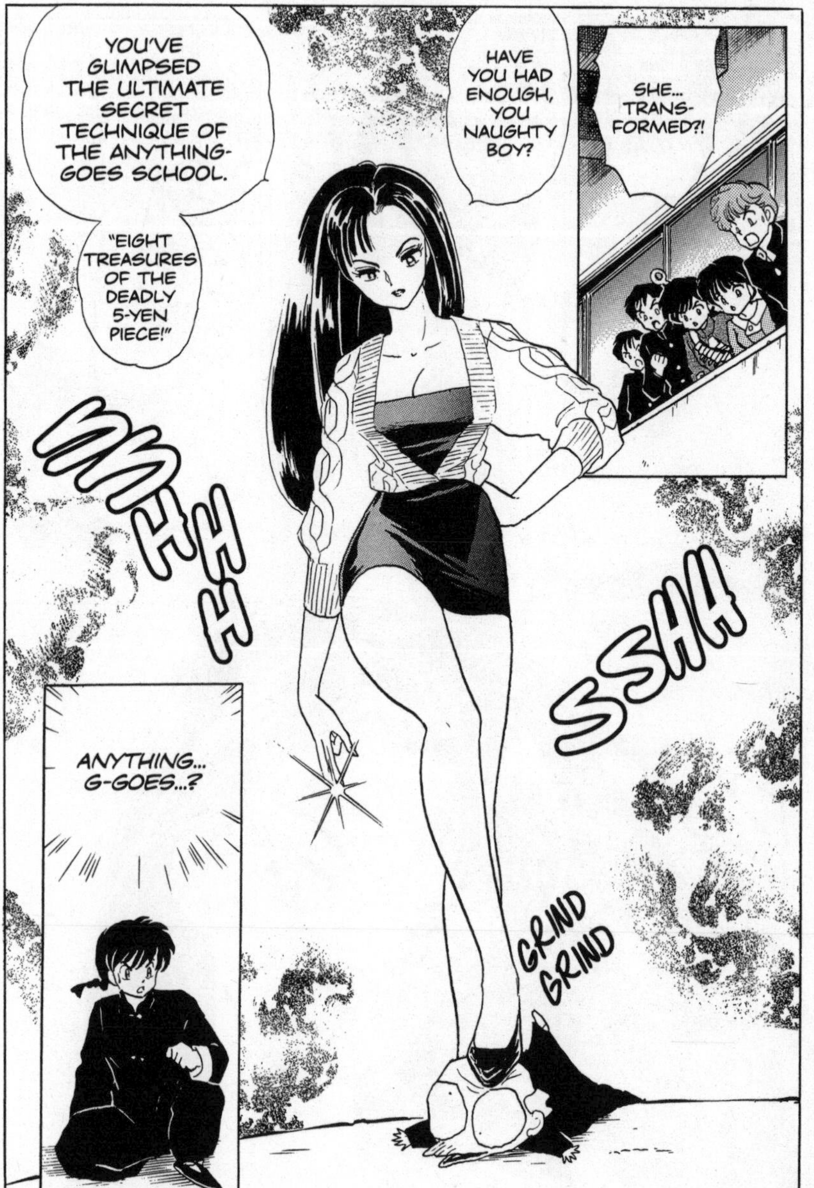
SHE... TRANS-FORMED?!
HAVE YOU HAD ENOUGH, YOU NAUGHTY BOY?
YOU'VE GLIMPSED THE ULTIMATE SECRET TECHNIQUE OF THE ANYTHING-GOES SCHOOL.
"EIGHT TREASURES OF THE DEADLY 5-YEN PIECE!"
SSHH
WHHH
GRIND GRIND
ANYTHING... G-GOES...?

PART 4
THE EIGHT MYSTERIOUS TREASURES

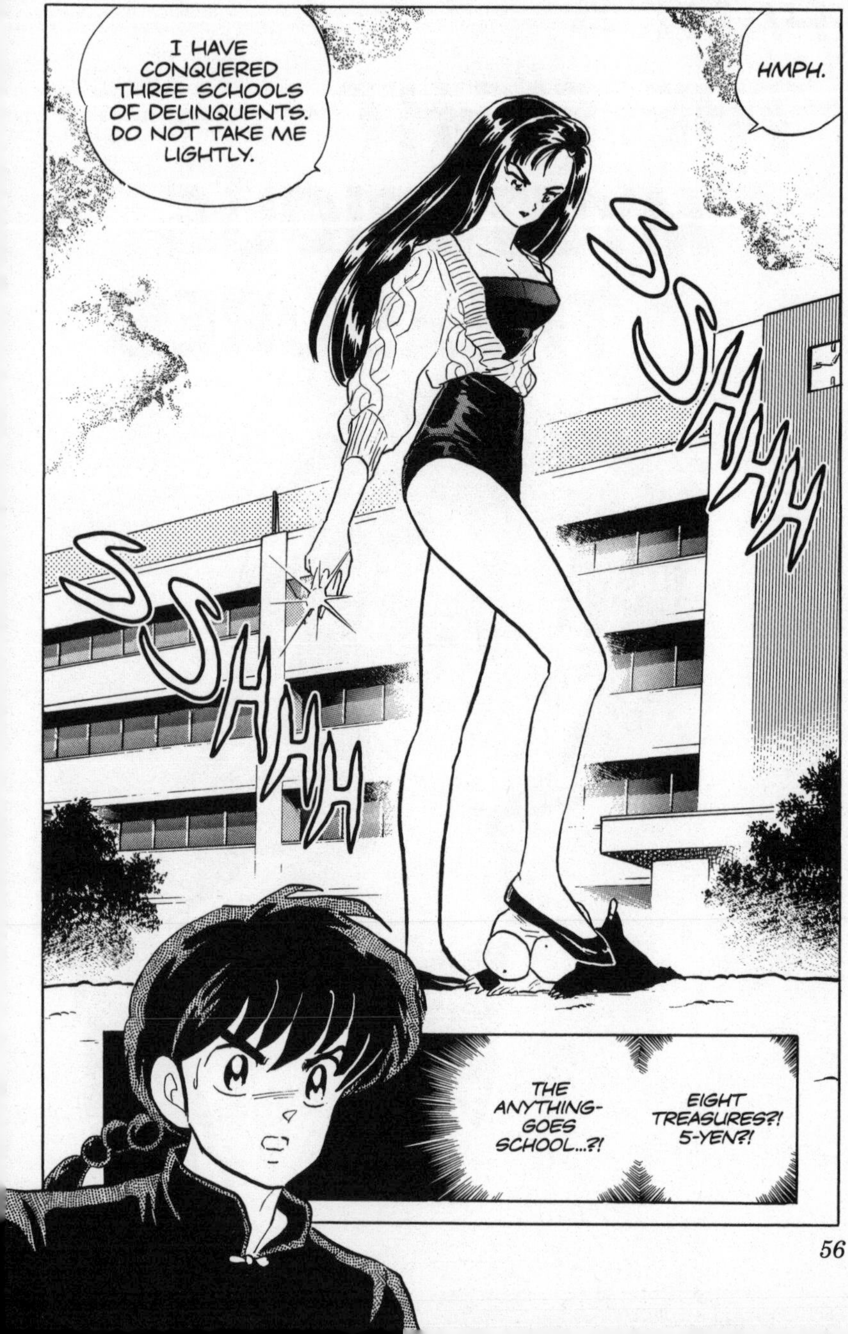
HMPH.
I HAVE CONQUERED THREE SCHOOLS OF DELINQUENTS. DO NOT TAKE ME LIGHTLY.
SSHHH
SSHHHH
EIGHT TREASURES?! 5-YEN?!
THE ANYTHING-GOES SCHOOL...?!

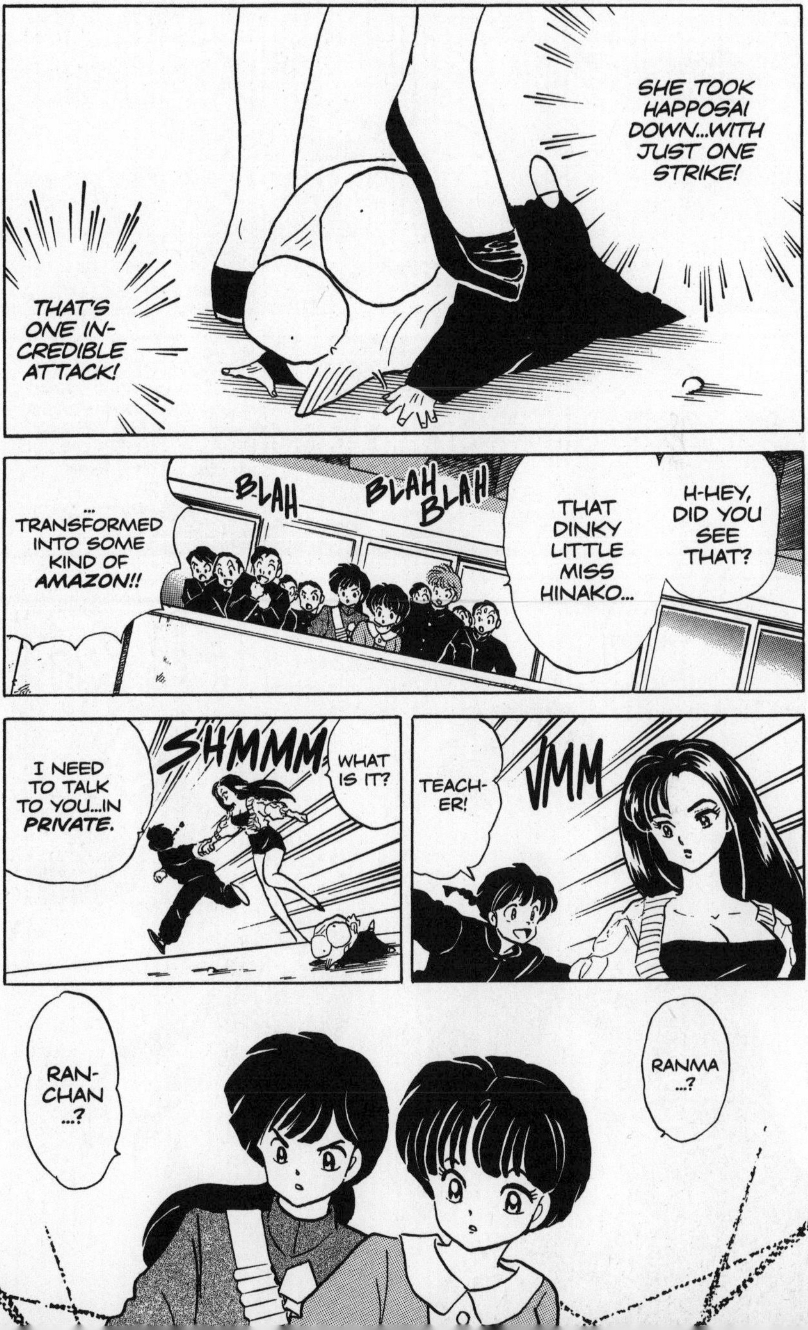
SHE TOOK HAPPOSAI DOWN...WITH JUST ONE STRIKE!
THAT'S ONE IN-CREDIBLE ATTACK!
H-HEY, DID YOU SEE THAT?
THAT DINKY LITTLE MISS HINAKO...
BLAH BLAH BLAH
BLAH
...TRANSFORMED INTO SOME KIND OF AMAZON!!
VMM
TEACH-ER!
WHAT IS IT?
SHMMM
I NEED TO TALK TO YOU...IN PRIVATE.
RANMA ...?
RAN-CHAN ...?

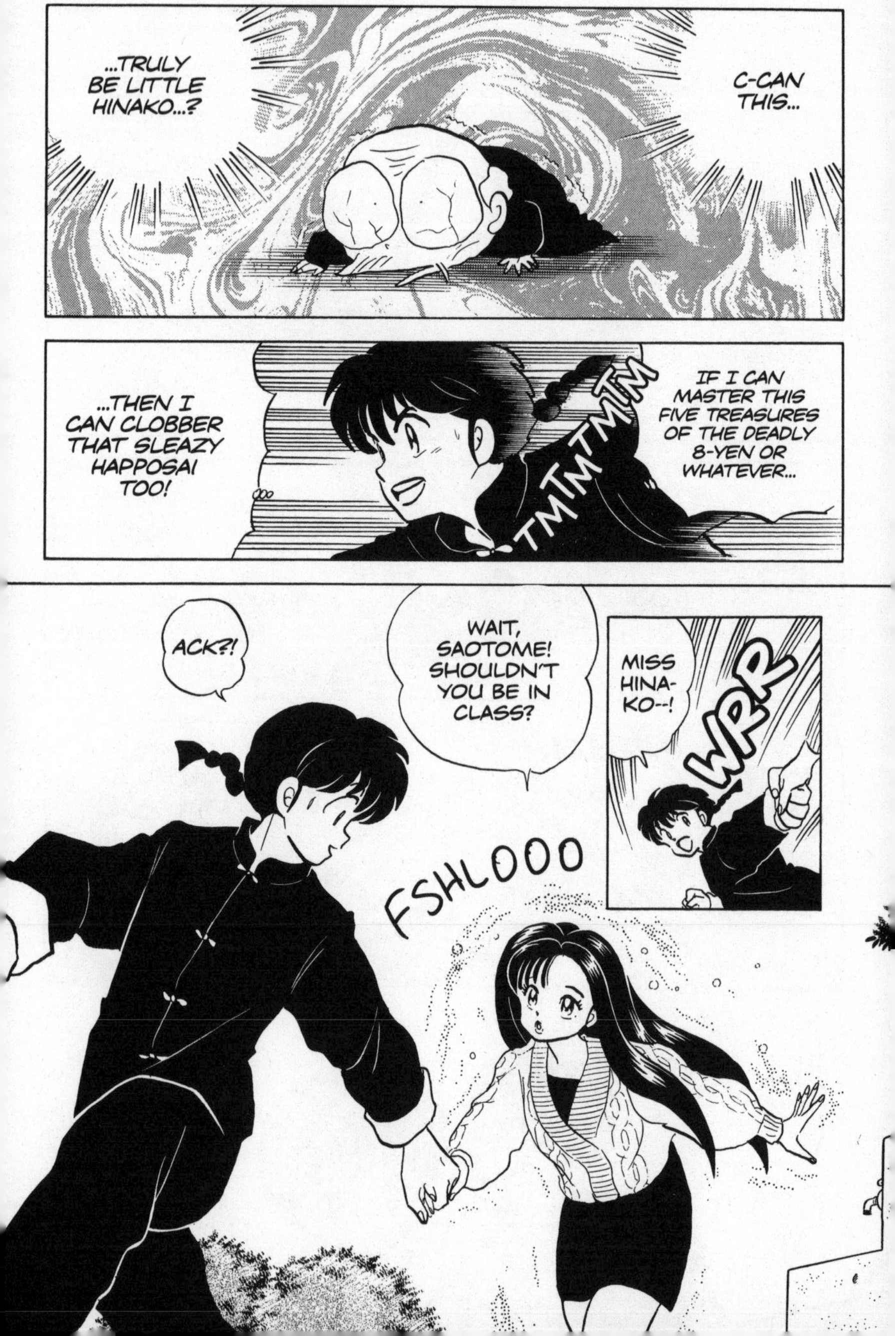
C-CAN THIS...
...TRULY BE LITTLE HINAKO...?
IF I CAN MASTER THIS FIVE TREASURES OF THE DEADLY 8-YEN OR WHATEVER...
TMTMTMTM
...THEN I CAN CLOBBER THAT SLEAZY HAPPOSAI TOO!
MISS HINA-KO--!
WRR
WAIT, SAOTOME! SHOULDN'T YOU BE IN CLASS?
ACK?!
FSHLOOO

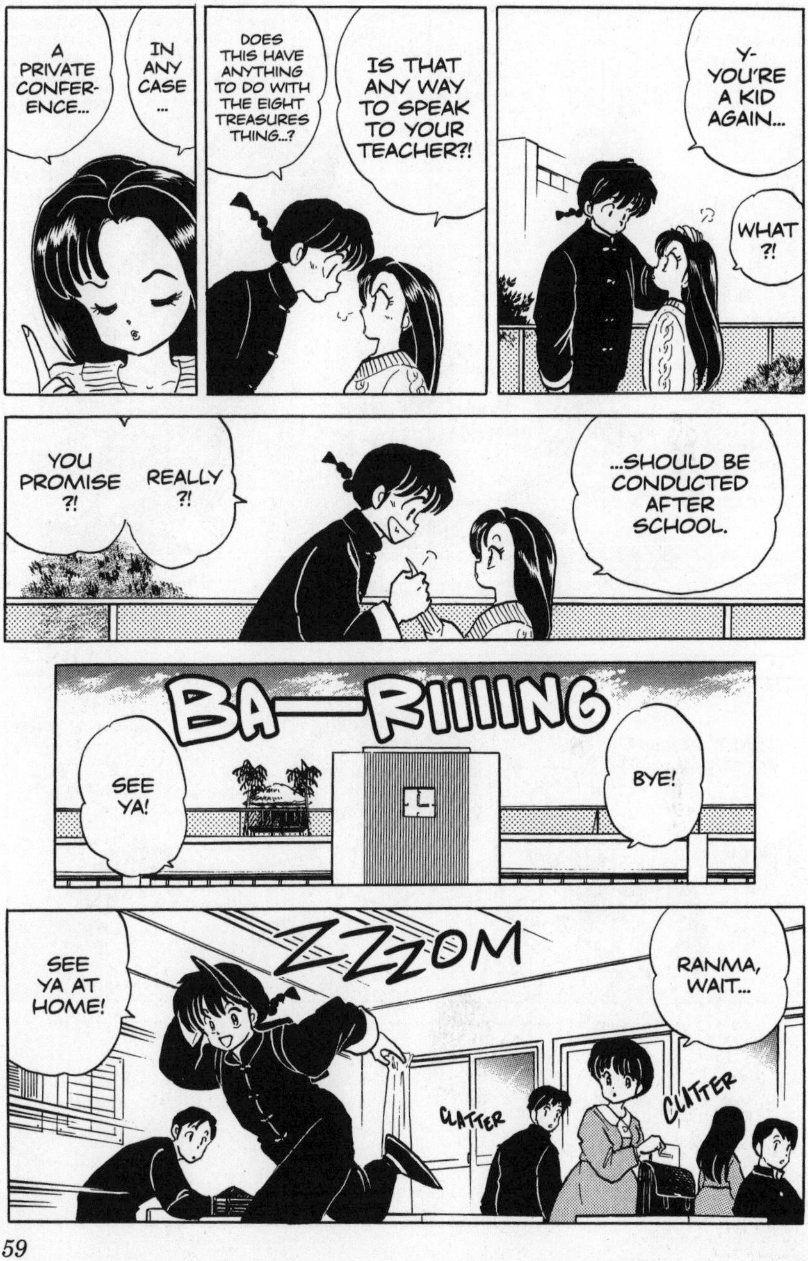

Y- YOU'RE A KID AGAIN...
WHAT ?!
IS THAT ANY WAY TO SPEAK TO YOUR TEACHER?!
DOES THIS HAVE ANYTHING TO DO WITH THE EIGHT TREASURES THING..?
IN ANY CASE ...
A PRIVATE CONFERENCE...
...SHOULD BE CONDUCTED AFTER SCHOOL.
REALLY ?!
YOU PROMISE ?!
BA—RIIIING
BYE!
SEE YA!
RANMA, WAIT...
CLATTER
ZZZOM
CLATTER
SEE YA AT HOME!

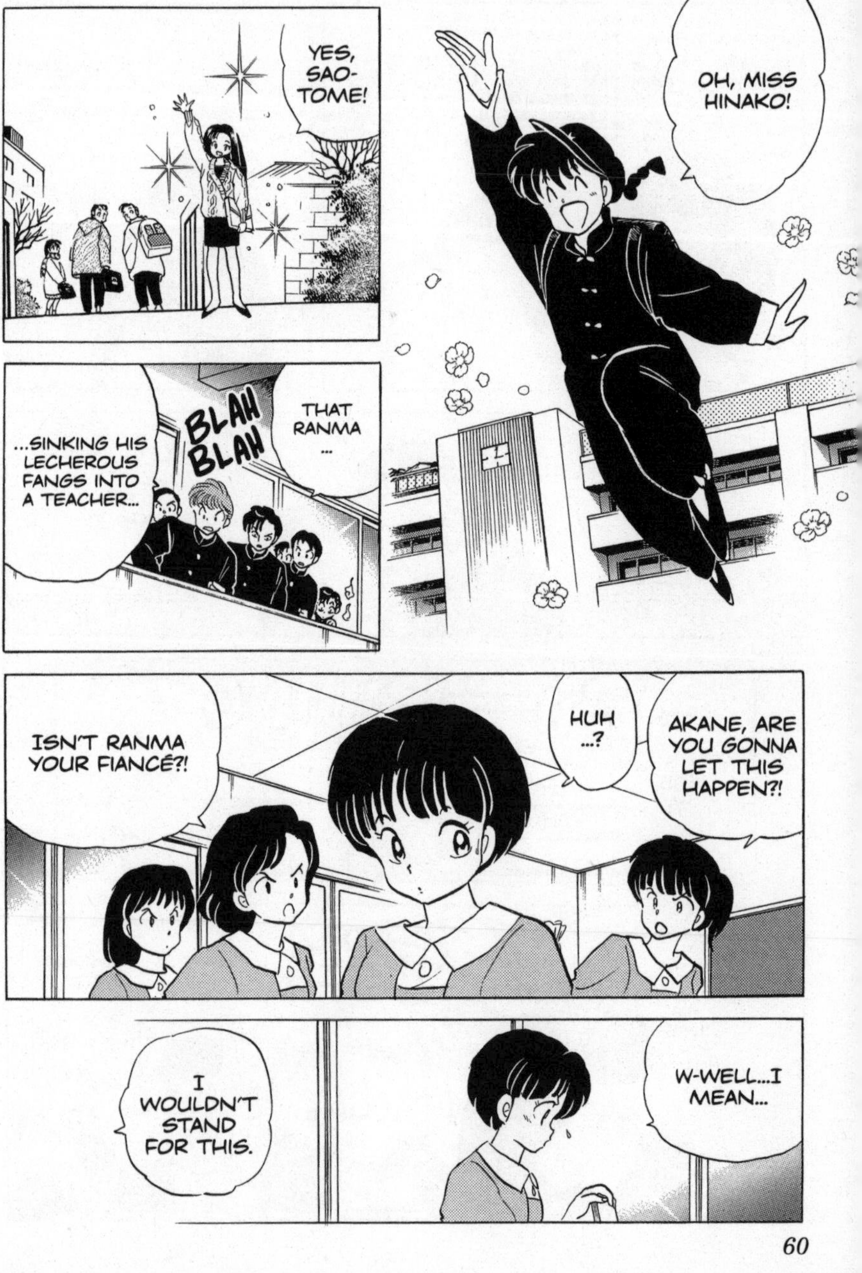
OH, MISS HINAKO!
YES, SAO-TOME!
THAT RANMA ...
BLAH BLAH
...SINKING HIS LECHEROUS FANGS INTO A TEACHER...
AKANE, ARE YOU GONNA LET THIS HAPPEN?!
HUH ...?
ISN'T RANMA YOUR FIANCÉ?!
W-WELL...I MEAN...
I WOULDN'T STAND FOR THIS.

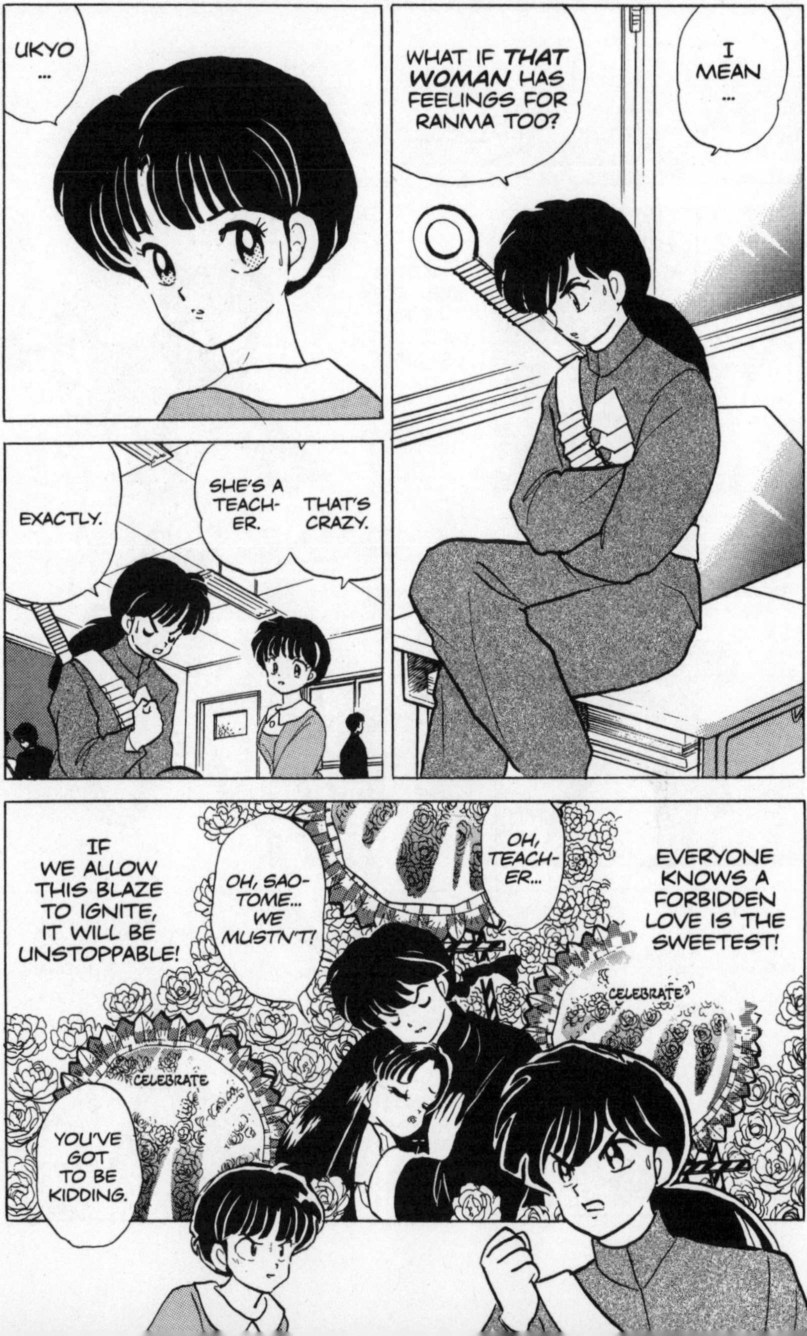
I MEAN ...
WHAT IF *THAT WOMAN* HAS FEELINGS FOR RANMA TOO?
UKYO ...
SHE'S A TEACHER. THAT'S CRAZY.
EXACTLY.
EVERYONE KNOWS A FORBIDDEN LOVE IS THE SWEETEST!
OH, TEACHER...
OH, SAOTOME... WE MUSTN'T!
IF WE ALLOW THIS BLAZE TO IGNITE, IT WILL BE UNSTOPPABLE!
CELEBRATE
CELEBRATE
YOU'VE GOT TO BE KIDDING.

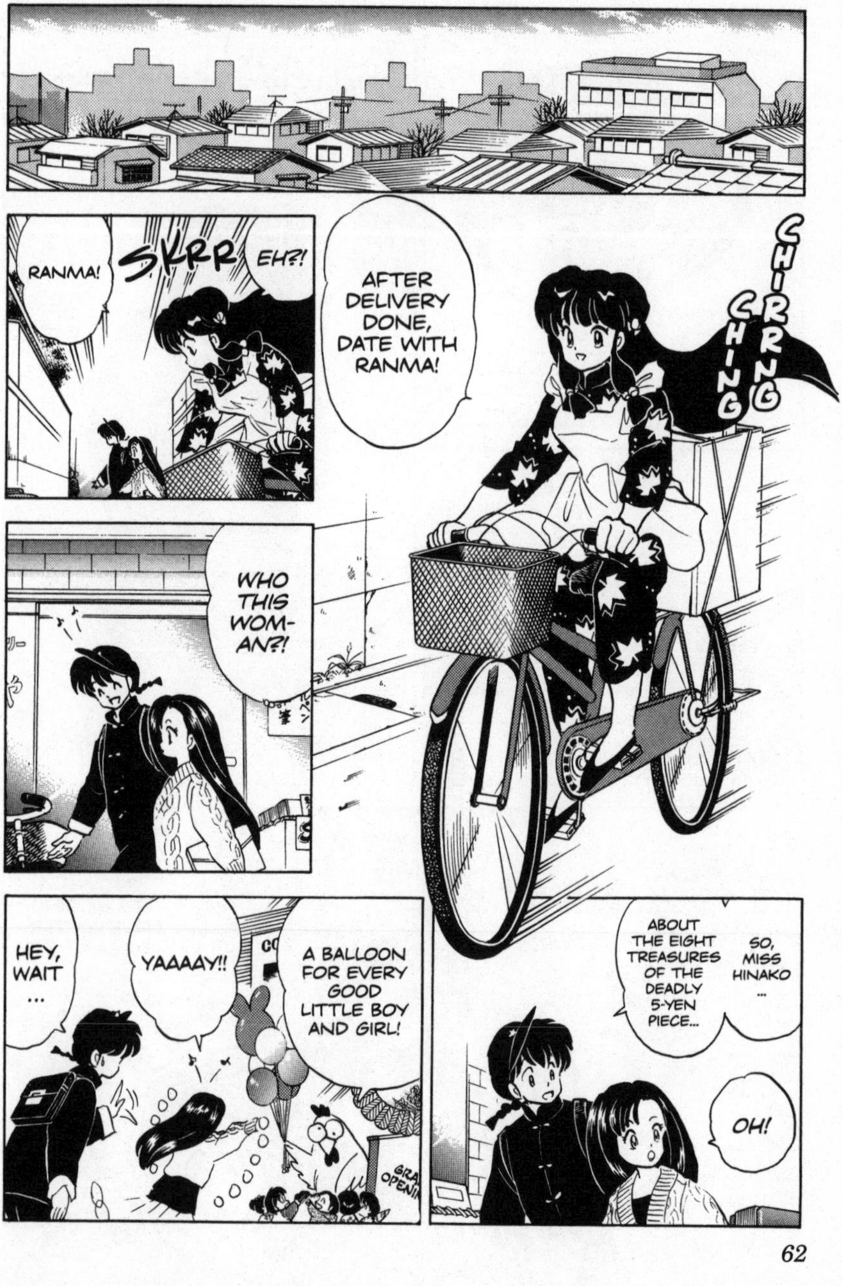
CHIRRRING
CHING
AFTER DELIVERY DONE, DATE WITH RANMA!
EH?!
SKRR
RANMA!
WHO THIS WOM-AN?!
SO, MISS HINAKO ...
ABOUT THE EIGHT TREASURES OF THE DEADLY 5-YEN PIECE...
OH!
A BALLOON FOR EVERY GOOD LITTLE BOY AND GIRL!
YAAAAY!!
HEY, WAIT ...

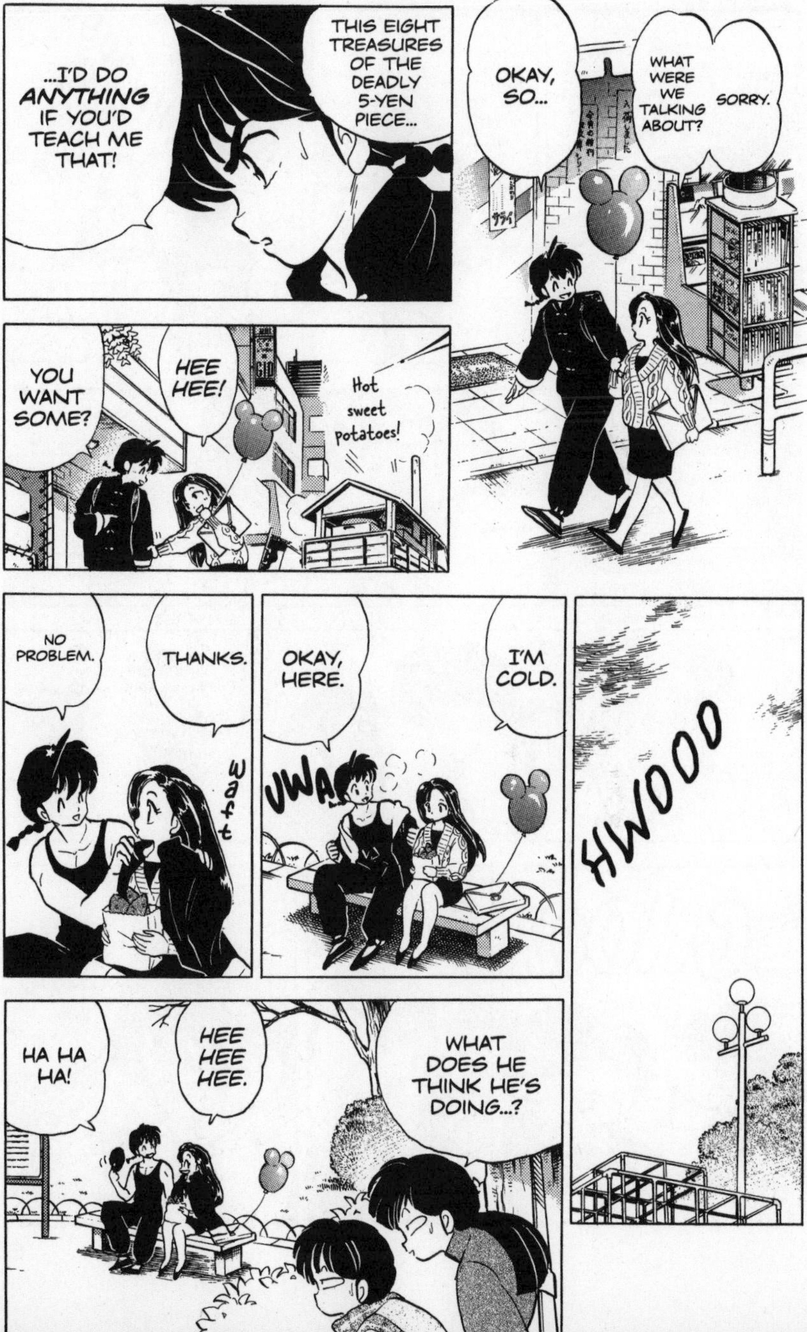
SORRY.
WHAT WERE WE TALKING ABOUT?
OKAY, SO...
THIS EIGHT TREASURES OF THE DEADLY 5-YEN PIECE...
...I'D DO ANYTHING IF YOU'D TEACH ME THAT!
Hot sweet potatoes!
HEE HEE!
YOU WANT SOME?
HWOOD
I'M COLD.
OKAY, HERE.
UWA
THANKS.
NO PROBLEM.
waft
WHAT DOES HE THINK HE'S DOING...?
HEE HEE HEE.
HA HA HA!

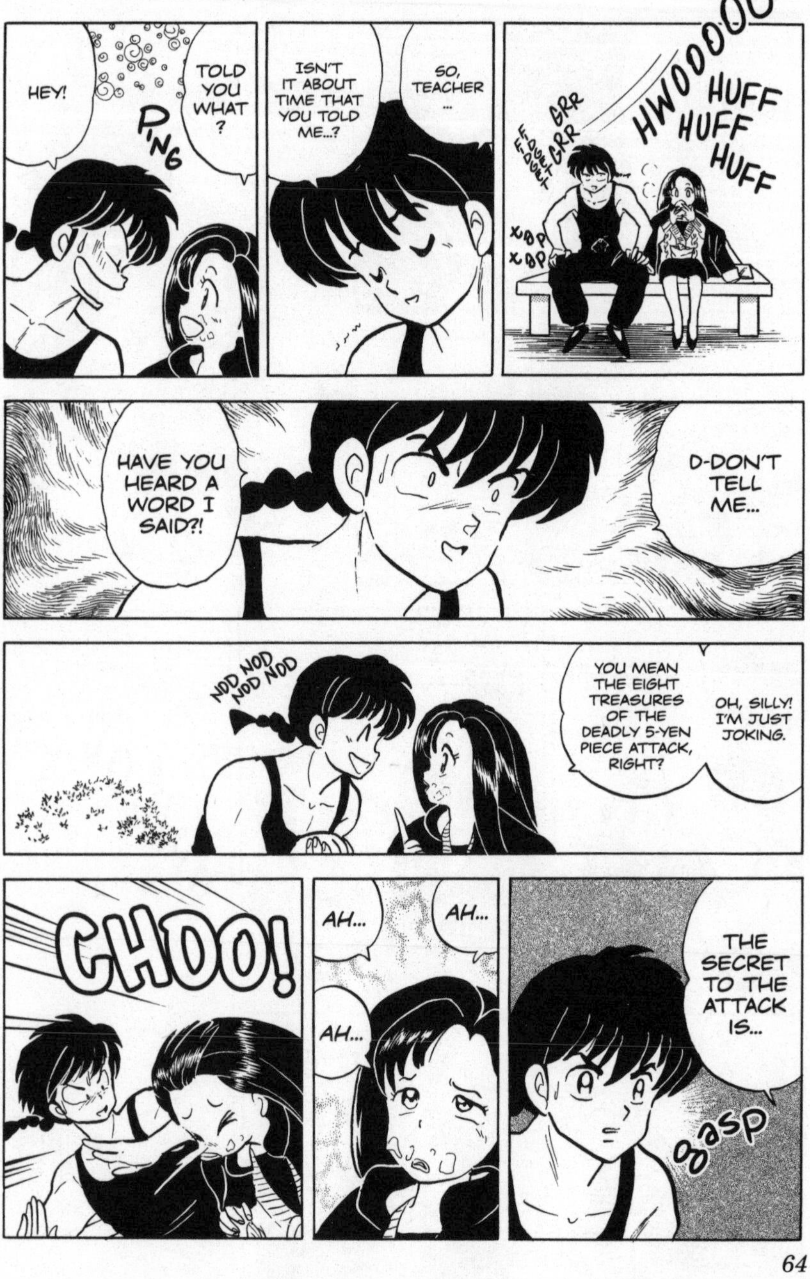
HWOOOOO
HUFF
HUFF
HUFF
GRR
GRR
SO, TEACHER ...
ISN'T IT ABOUT TIME THAT YOU TOLD ME...?
TOLD YOU WHAT ?
PING
HEY!
D-DON'T TELL ME...
HAVE YOU HEARD A WORD I SAID?!
OH, SILLY! I'M JUST JOKING.
YOU MEAN THE EIGHT TREASURES OF THE DEADLY 5-YEN PIECE ATTACK, RIGHT?
NOD NOD
NOD NOD
THE SECRET TO THE ATTACK IS...
gasp
AH...
AH...
AH...
CHOO!

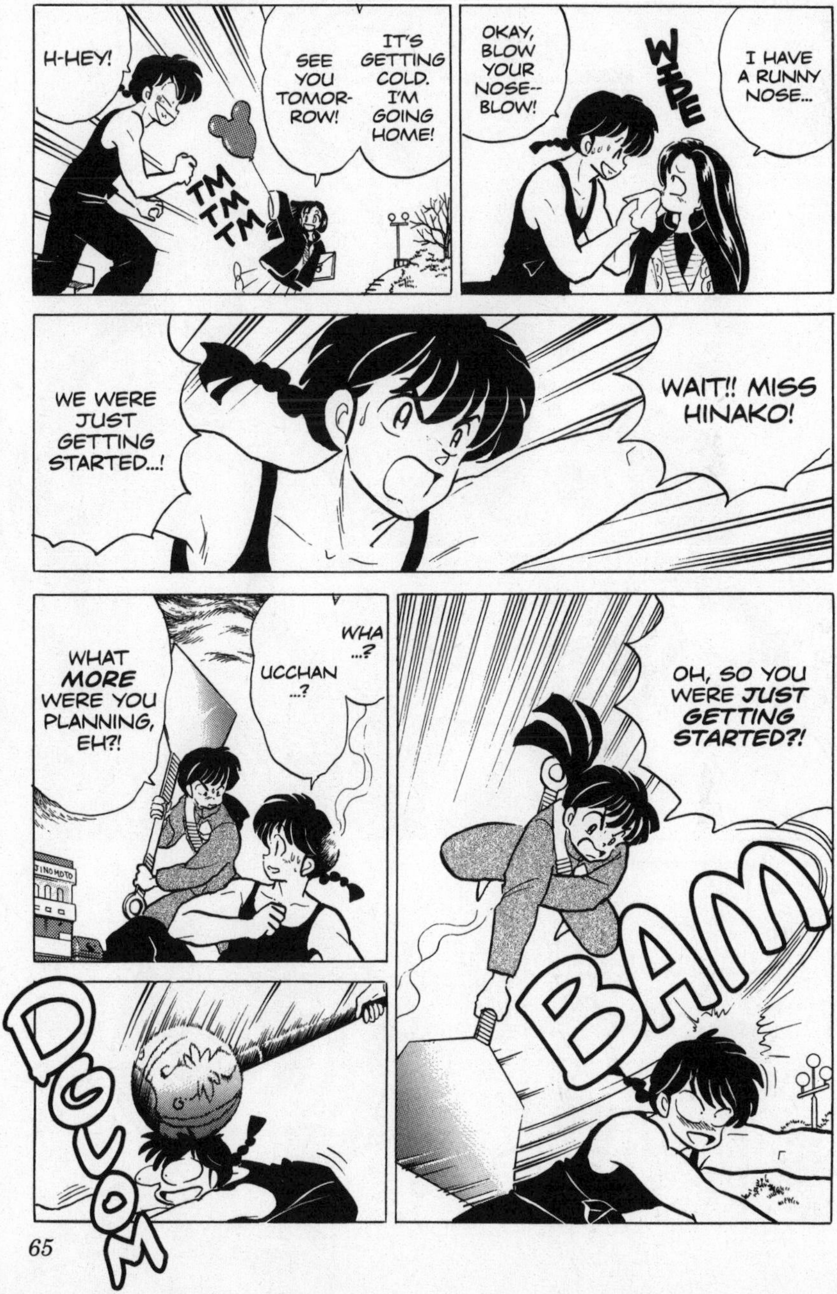
I HAVE A RUNNY NOSE...
WIPE
OKAY, BLOW YOUR NOSE-- BLOW!
IT'S GETTING COLD. I'M GOING HOME!
SEE YOU TOMORROW!
TM TM TM
H-HEY!
WAIT!! MISS HINAKO!
WE WERE JUST GETTING STARTED...!
OH, SO YOU WERE JUST GETTING STARTED?!
BAM
WHA ...?
UCCHAN ...?
WHAT MORE WERE YOU PLANNING, EH?!

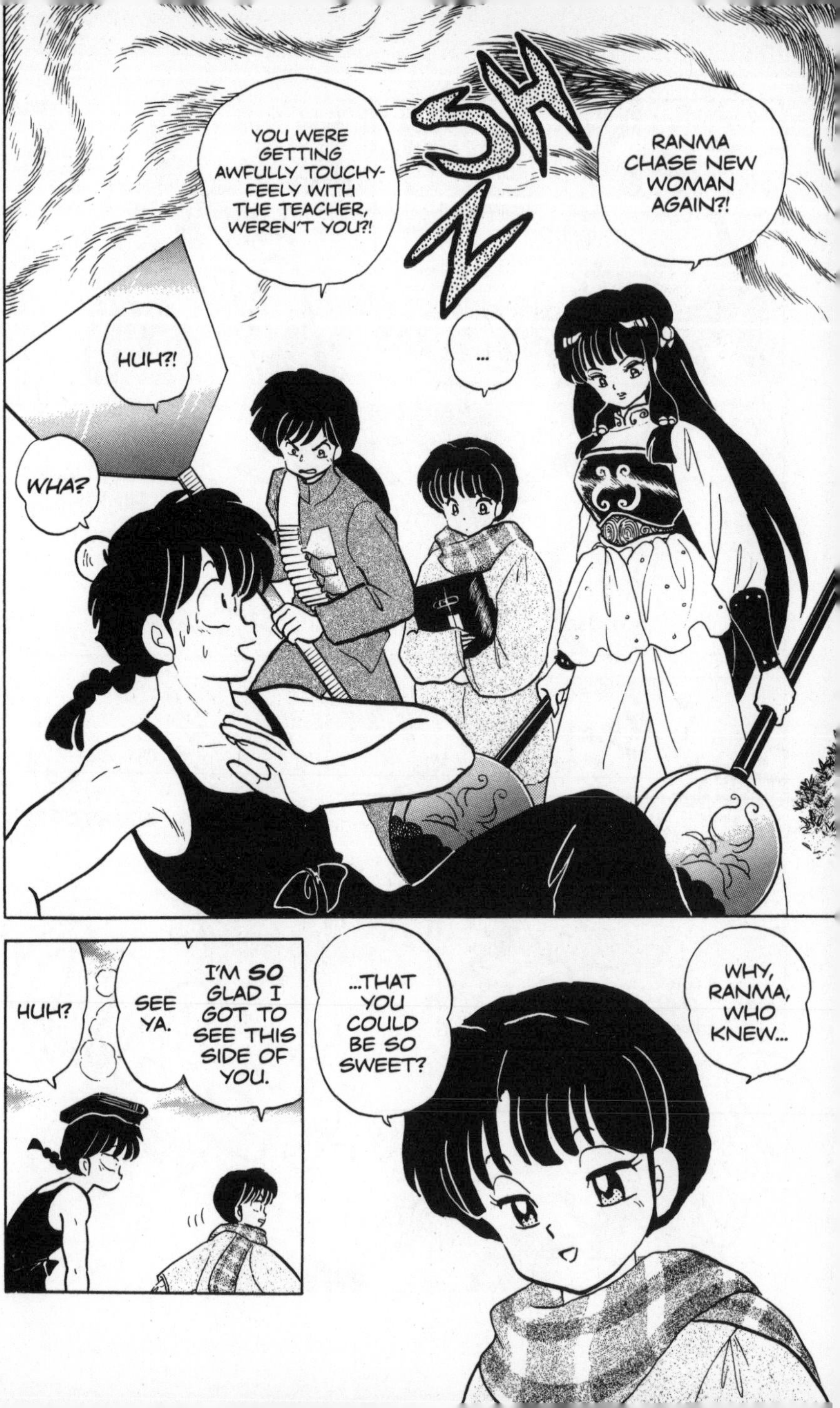
RANMA CHASE NEW WOMAN AGAIN?!
YOU WERE GETTING AWFULLY TOUCHY-FEELY WITH THE TEACHER, WEREN'T YOU?!
...
HUH?!
WHA?
WHY, RANMA, WHO KNEW...
...THAT YOU COULD BE SO SWEET?
I'M **SO** GLAD I GOT TO SEE THIS SIDE OF YOU.
SEE YA.
HUH?

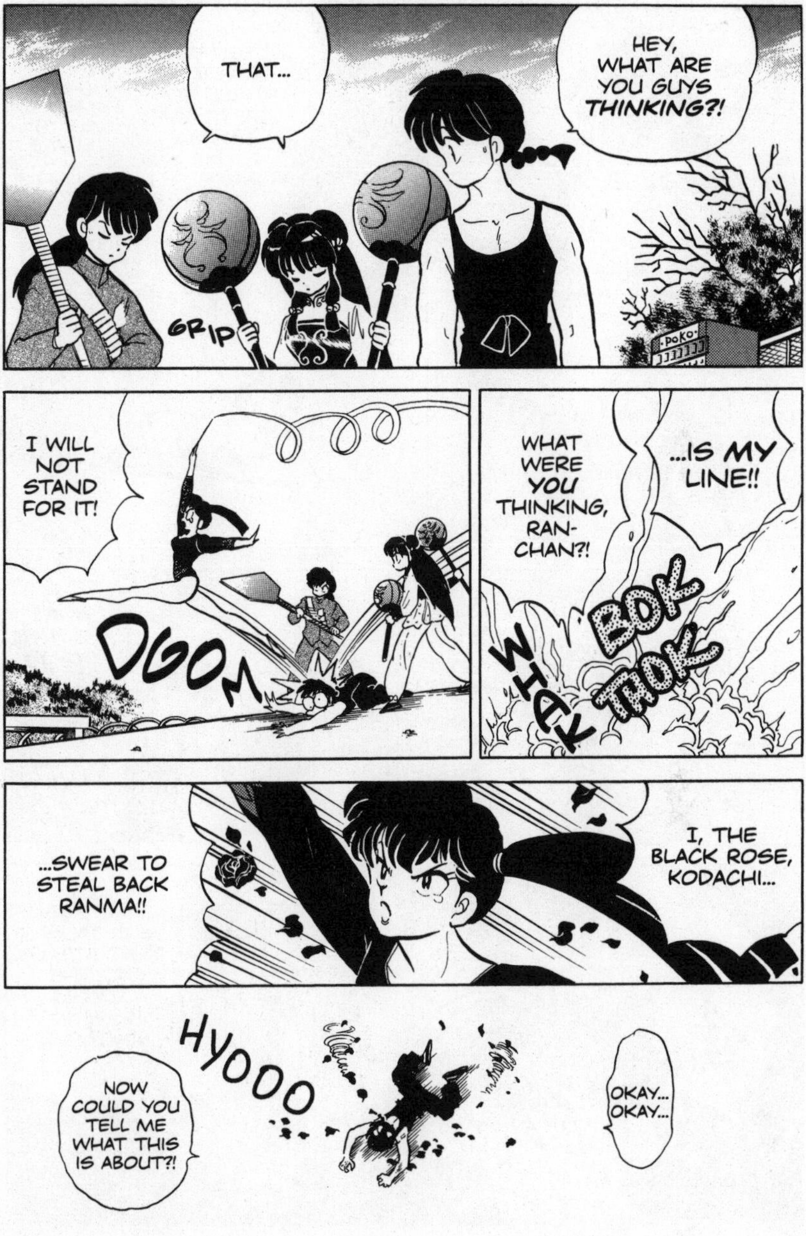
HEY, WHAT ARE YOU GUYS THINKING?!
THAT...
GRIP
...IS MY LINE!!
WHAT WERE YOU THINKING, RAN-CHAN?!
BOK
TROK
WHAK
I WILL NOT STAND FOR IT!
DGOM
I, THE BLACK ROSE, KODACHI...
...SWEAR TO STEAL BACK RANMA!!
OKAY... OKAY...
HYOOO
NOW COULD YOU TELL ME WHAT THIS IS ABOUT?!

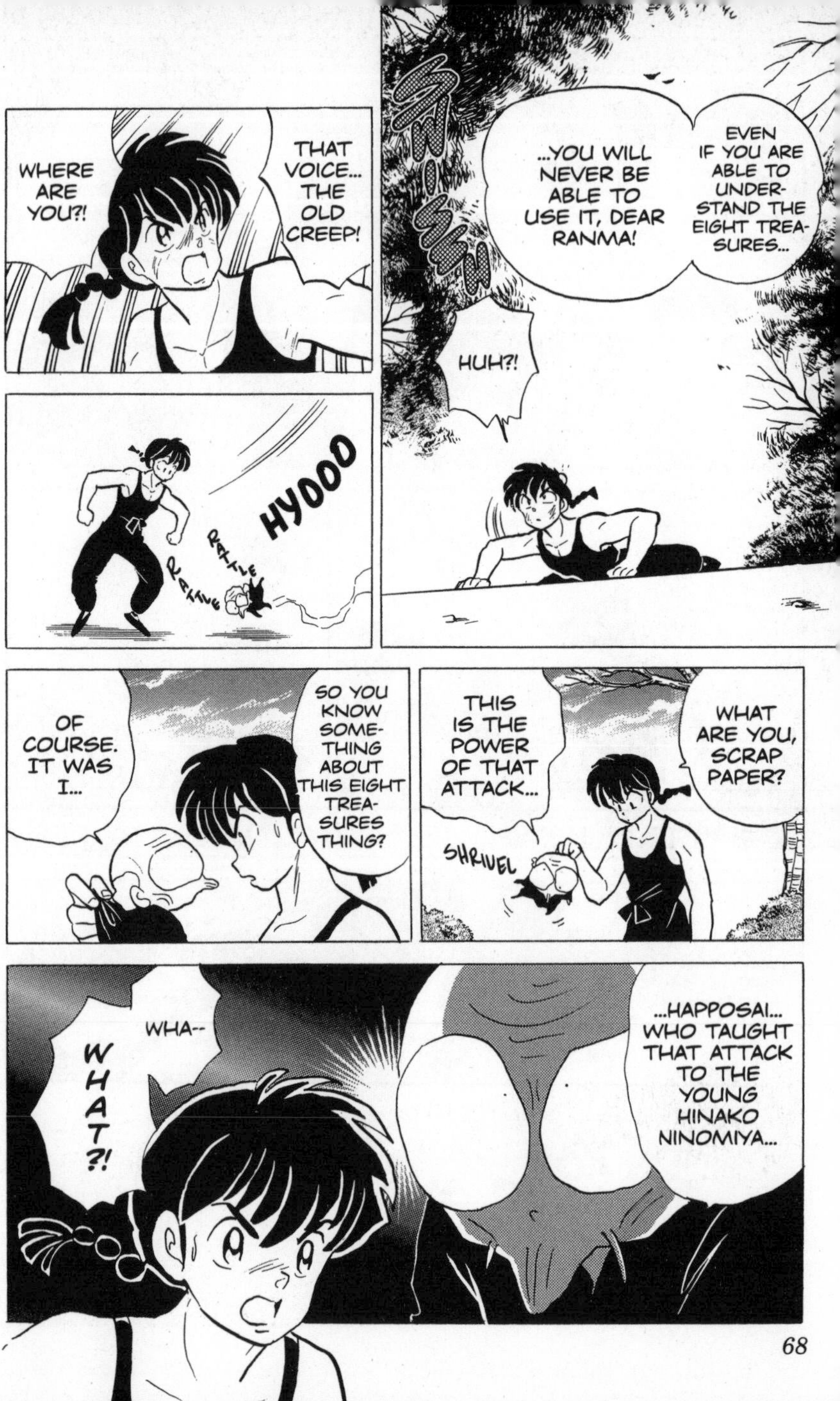
EVEN IF YOU ARE ABLE TO UNDER-STAND THE EIGHT TREA-SURES...
...YOU WILL NEVER BE ABLE TO USE IT, DEAR RANMA!
HUH?!
THAT VOICE... THE OLD CREEP!
WHERE ARE YOU?!
HYOOD
RATTLE
RATTLE
WHAT ARE YOU, SCRAP PAPER?
THIS IS THE POWER OF THAT ATTACK...
SHRIVEL
SO YOU KNOW SOME-THING ABOUT THIS EIGHT TREA-SURES THING?
OF COURSE. IT WAS I...
...HAPPOSAI... WHO TAUGHT THAT ATTACK TO THE YOUNG HINAKO NINOMIYA...
WHA--
WHAT?!

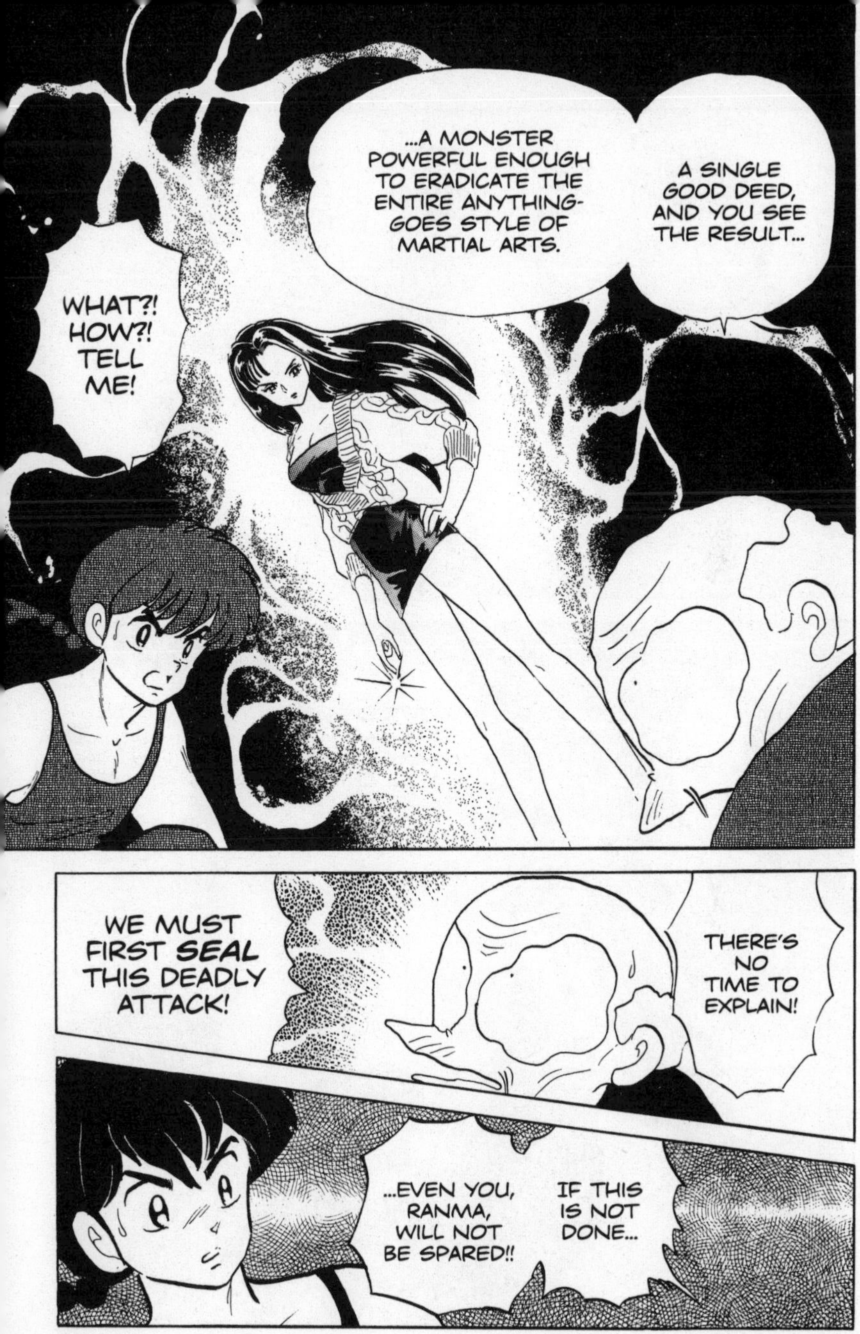
A SINGLE GOOD DEED, AND YOU SEE THE RESULT...
...A MONSTER POWERFUL ENOUGH TO ERADICATE THE ENTIRE ANYTHING-GOES STYLE OF MARTIAL ARTS.
WHAT?! HOW?! TELL ME!
THERE'S NO TIME TO EXPLAIN!
WE MUST FIRST **SEAL** THIS DEADLY ATTACK!
IF THIS IS NOT DONE...
...EVEN YOU, RANMA, WILL NOT BE SPARED!!

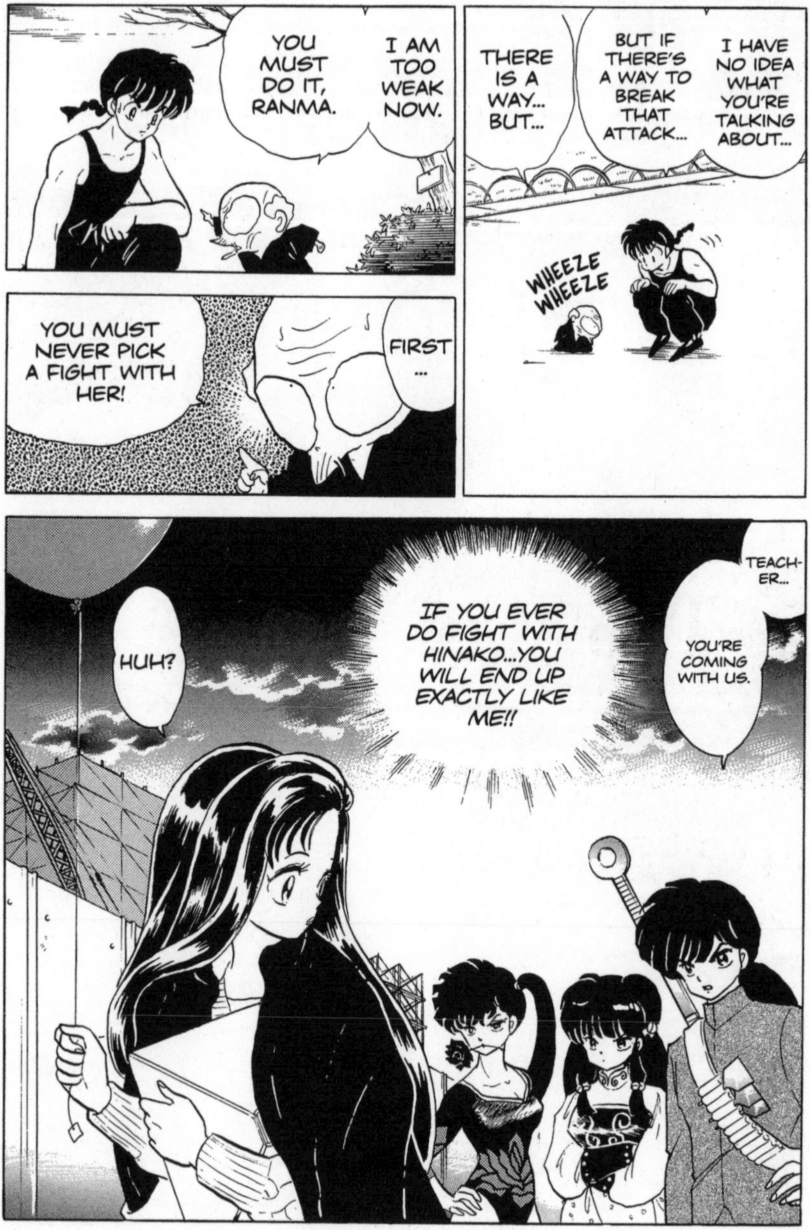
I HAVE NO IDEA WHAT YOU'RE TALKING ABOUT...
BUT IF THERE'S A WAY TO BREAK THAT ATTACK...
THERE IS A WAY... BUT...
WHEEZE WHEEZE
I AM TOO WEAK NOW.
YOU MUST DO IT, RANMA.
FIRST ...
YOU MUST NEVER PICK A FIGHT WITH HER!
TEACH-ER...
YOU'RE COMING WITH US.
IF YOU EVER DO FIGHT WITH HINAKO...YOU WILL END UP EXACTLY LIKE ME!!
HUH?

PART 5
THE WORLD'S MOST POWERFUL WOMAN

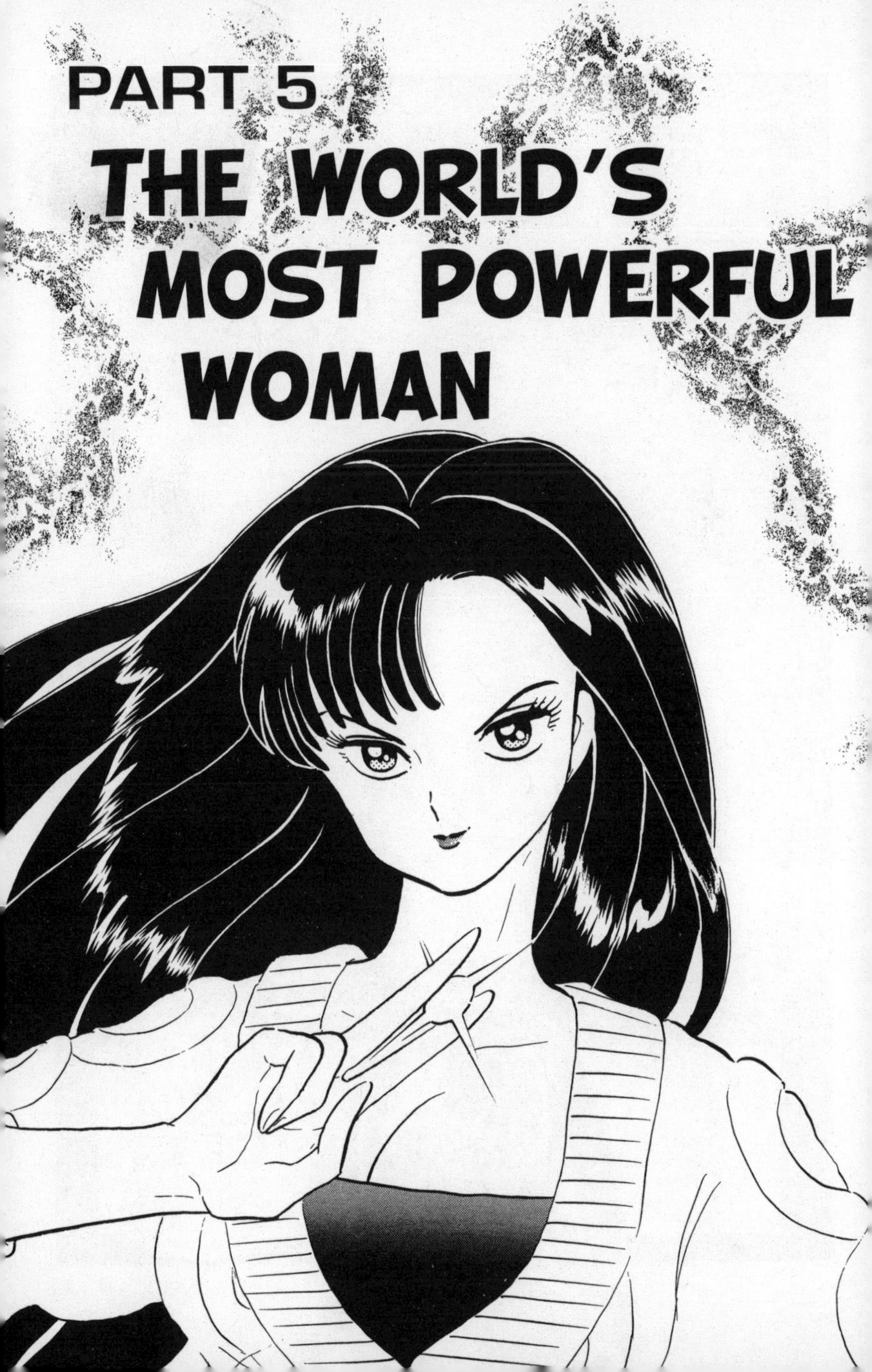

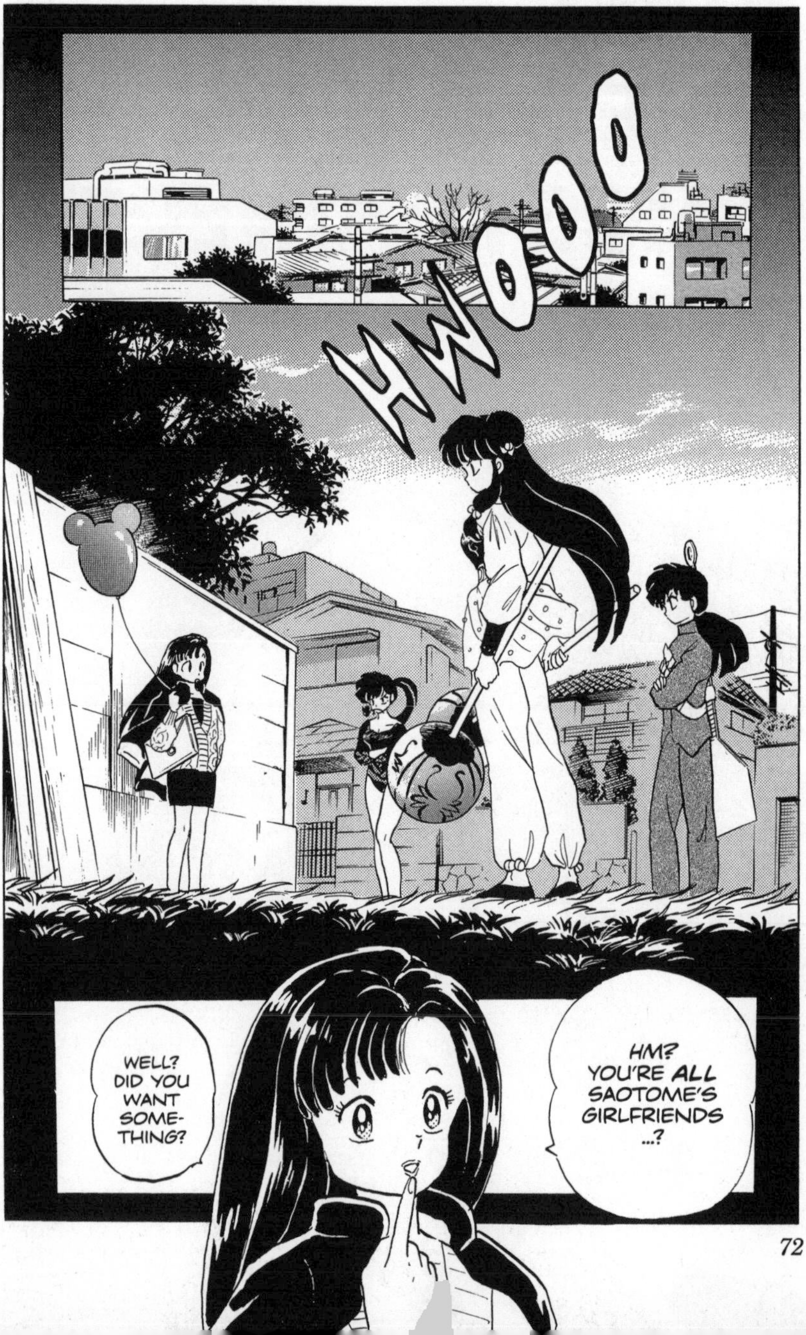
HWOOO
HM? YOU'RE **ALL** SAOTOME'S GIRLFRIENDS ...?
WELL? DID YOU WANT SOME-THING?

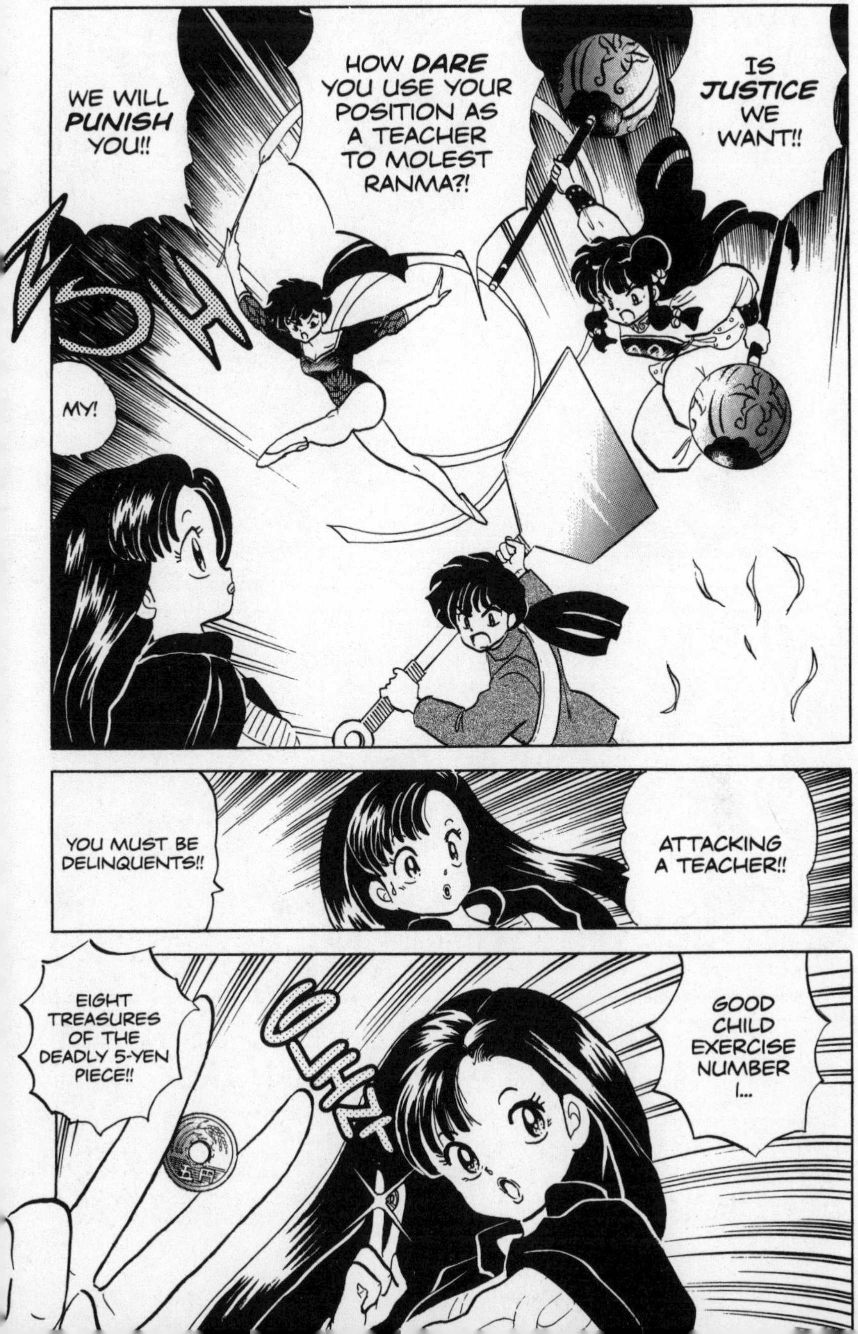
IS JUSTICE WE WANT!!
HOW DARE YOU USE YOUR POSITION AS A TEACHER TO MOLEST RANMA?!
WE WILL PUNISH YOU!!
MY!
ATTACKING A TEACHER!!
YOU MUST BE DELINQUENTS!!
GOOD CHILD EXERCISE NUMBER 1...
EIGHT TREASURES OF THE DEADLY 5-YEN PIECE!!

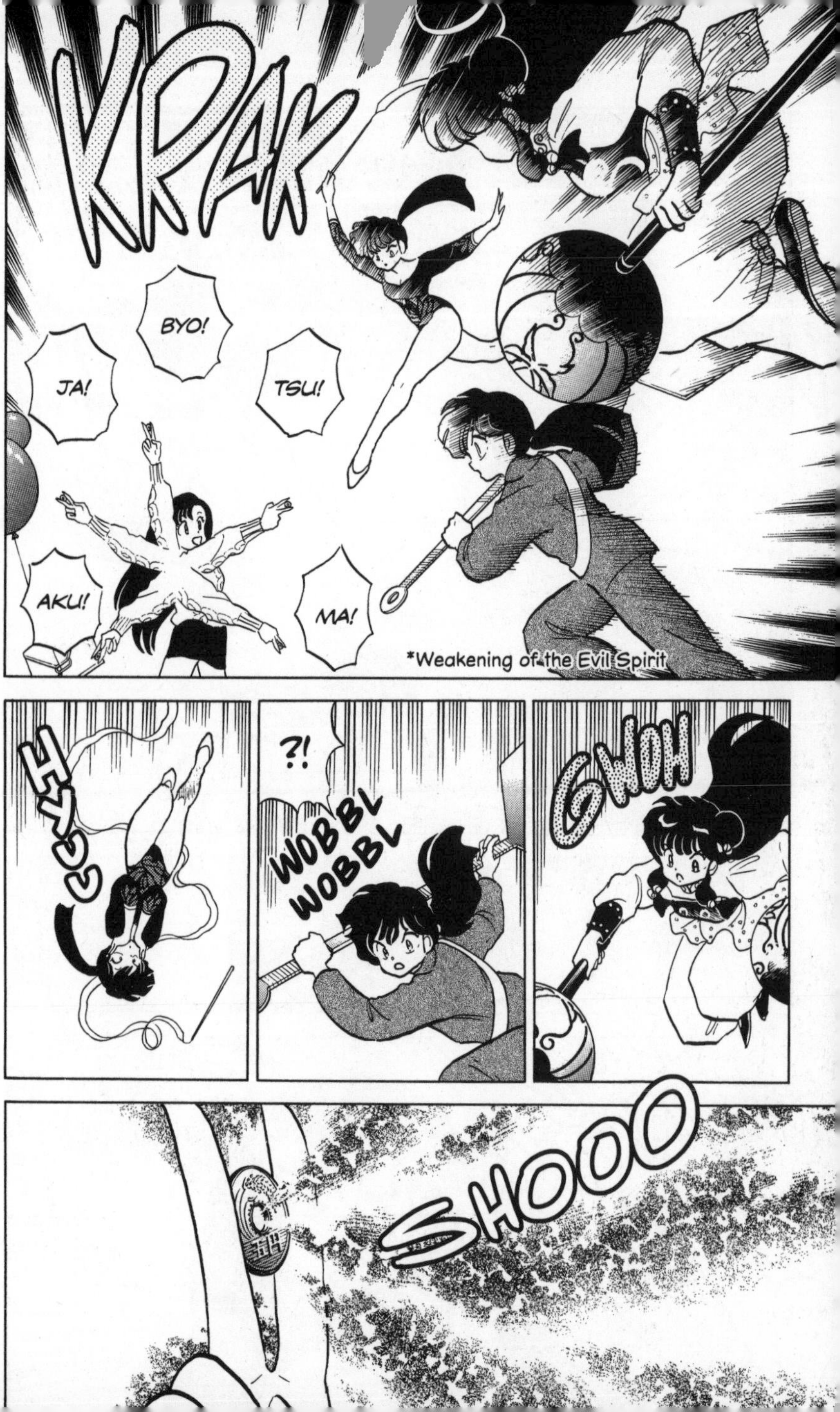
KRAK
TSU!
BYO!
JA!
MA!
AKU!
*Weakening of the Evil Spirit
GWOH
?!
WOBBL WOBBL
SHOOO

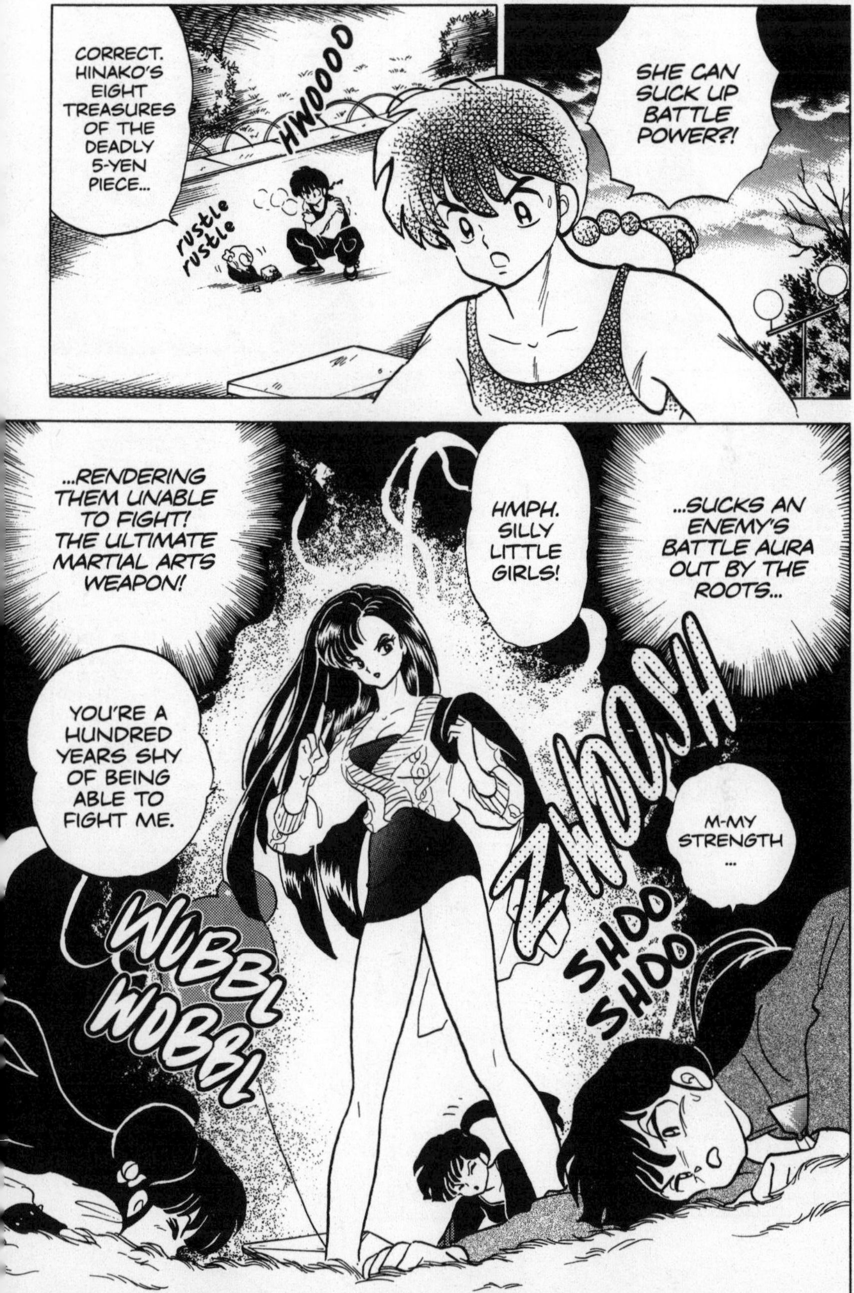
SHE CAN SUCK UP BATTLE POWER?!
CORRECT. HINAKO'S EIGHT TREASURES OF THE DEADLY 5-YEN PIECE...
HWOOOO
rustle rustle
...SUCKS AN ENEMY'S BATTLE AURA OUT BY THE ROOTS...
HMPH. SILLY LITTLE GIRLS!
...RENDERING THEM UNABLE TO FIGHT! THE ULTIMATE MARTIAL ARTS WEAPON!
ZWOOSH
M-MY STRENGTH ...
SHDOO SHDOO
YOU'RE A HUNDRED YEARS SHY OF BEING ABLE TO FIGHT ME.
WIBBL WOBBL

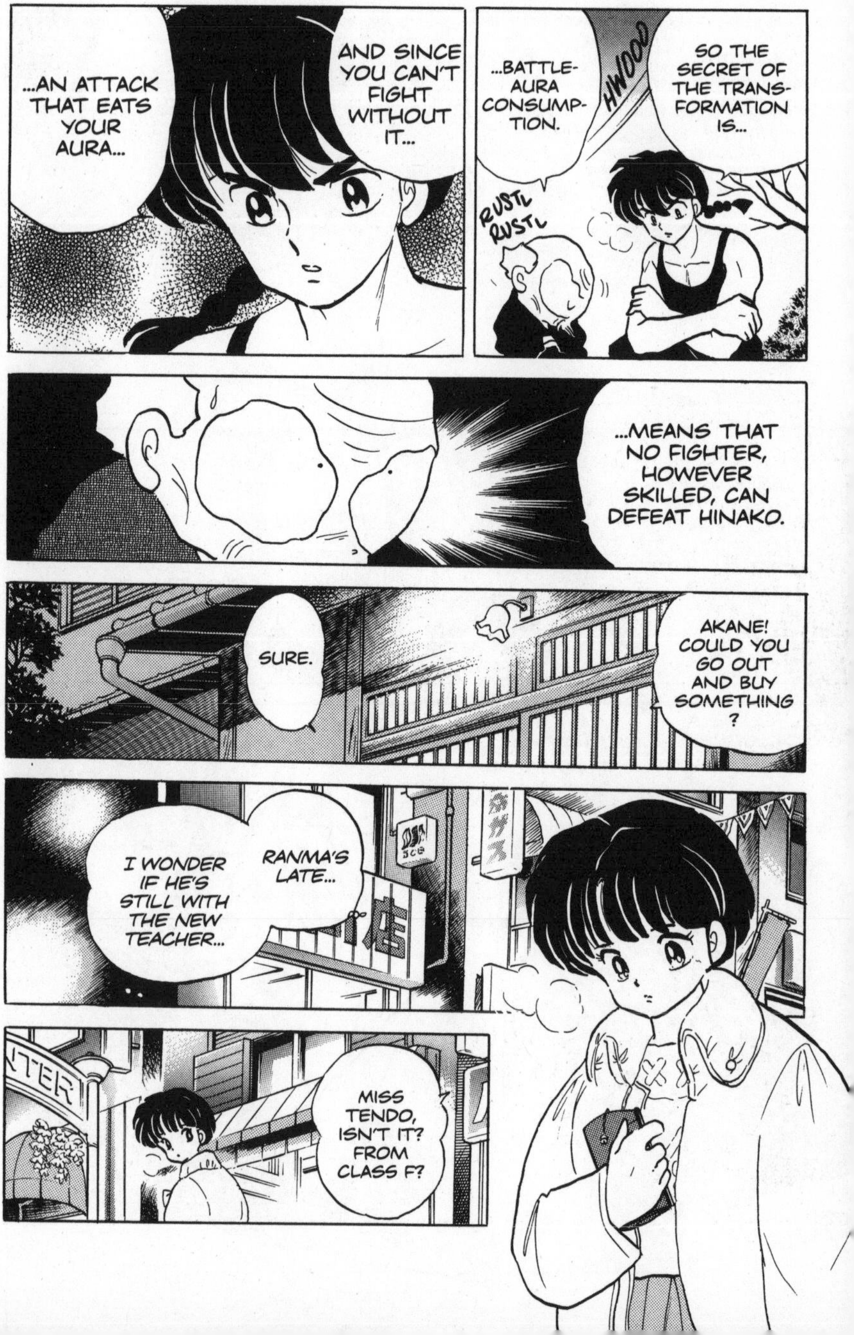
SO THE SECRET OF THE TRANS-FORMATION IS...
HWOOO
...BATTLE-AURA CONSUMP-TION.
RUSTL RUSTL
AND SINCE YOU CAN'T FIGHT WITHOUT IT...
...AN ATTACK THAT EATS YOUR AURA...
...MEANS THAT NO FIGHTER, HOWEVER SKILLED, CAN DEFEAT HINAKO.
AKANE! COULD YOU GO OUT AND BUY SOMETHING ?
SURE.
RANMA'S LATE...
I WONDER IF HE'S STILL WITH THE NEW TEACHER...
MISS TENDO, ISN'T IT? FROM CLASS F?

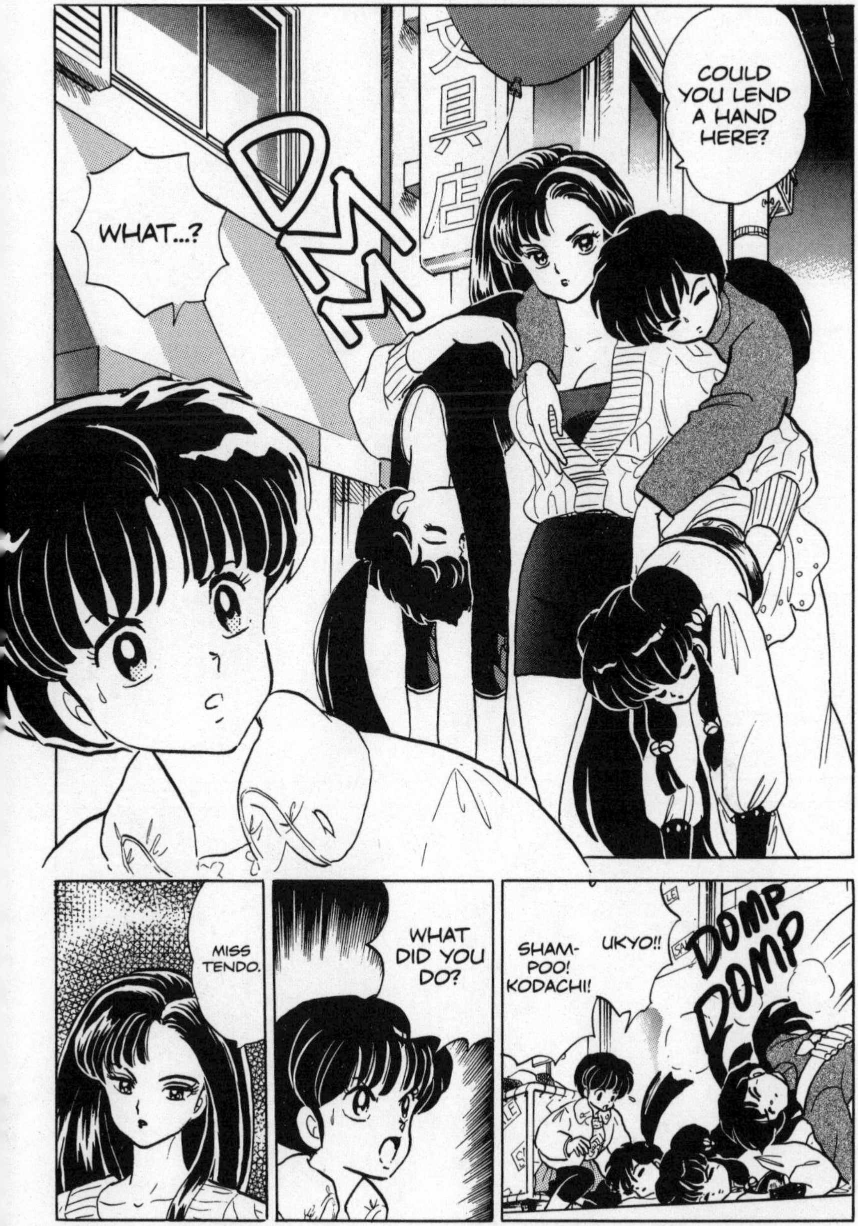
COULD YOU LEND A HAND HERE?
DMM
WHAT...?
DOMP DOMP
SHAM-POO! KODACHI! UKYO!!
WHAT DID YOU DO?
MISS TENDO.

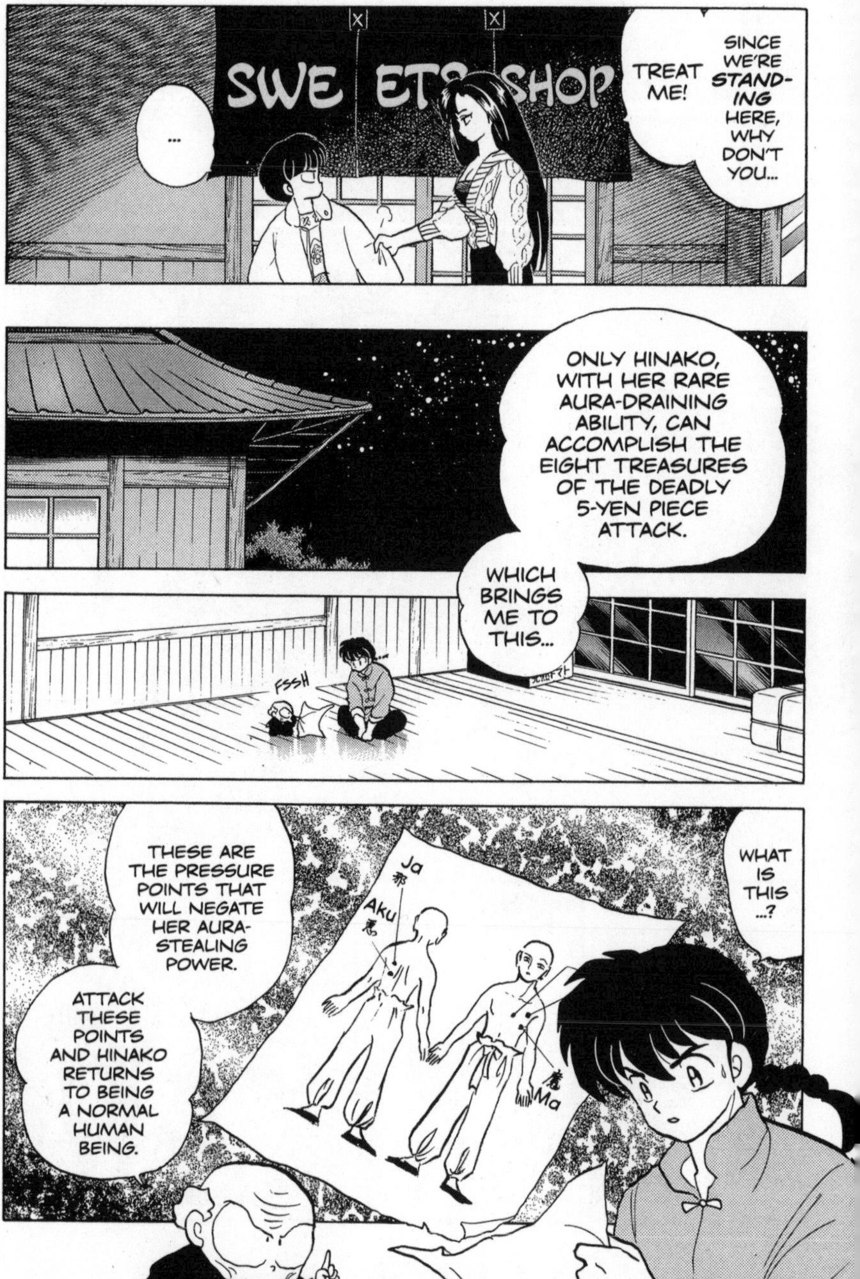
SINCE WE'RE STANDING HERE, WHY DON'T YOU...
TREAT ME!
SWE ETS SHOP
...
ONLY HINAKO, WITH HER RARE AURA-DRAINING ABILITY, CAN ACCOMPLISH THE EIGHT TREASURES OF THE DEADLY 5-YEN PIECE ATTACK.
WHICH BRINGS ME TO THIS...
FSSH
WHAT IS THIS ...?
THESE ARE THE PRESSURE POINTS THAT WILL NEGATE HER AURA-STEALING POWER.
Ja 邪
Aku 悪
魔 Ma
ATTACK THESE POINTS AND HINAKO RETURNS TO BEING A NORMAL HUMAN BEING.

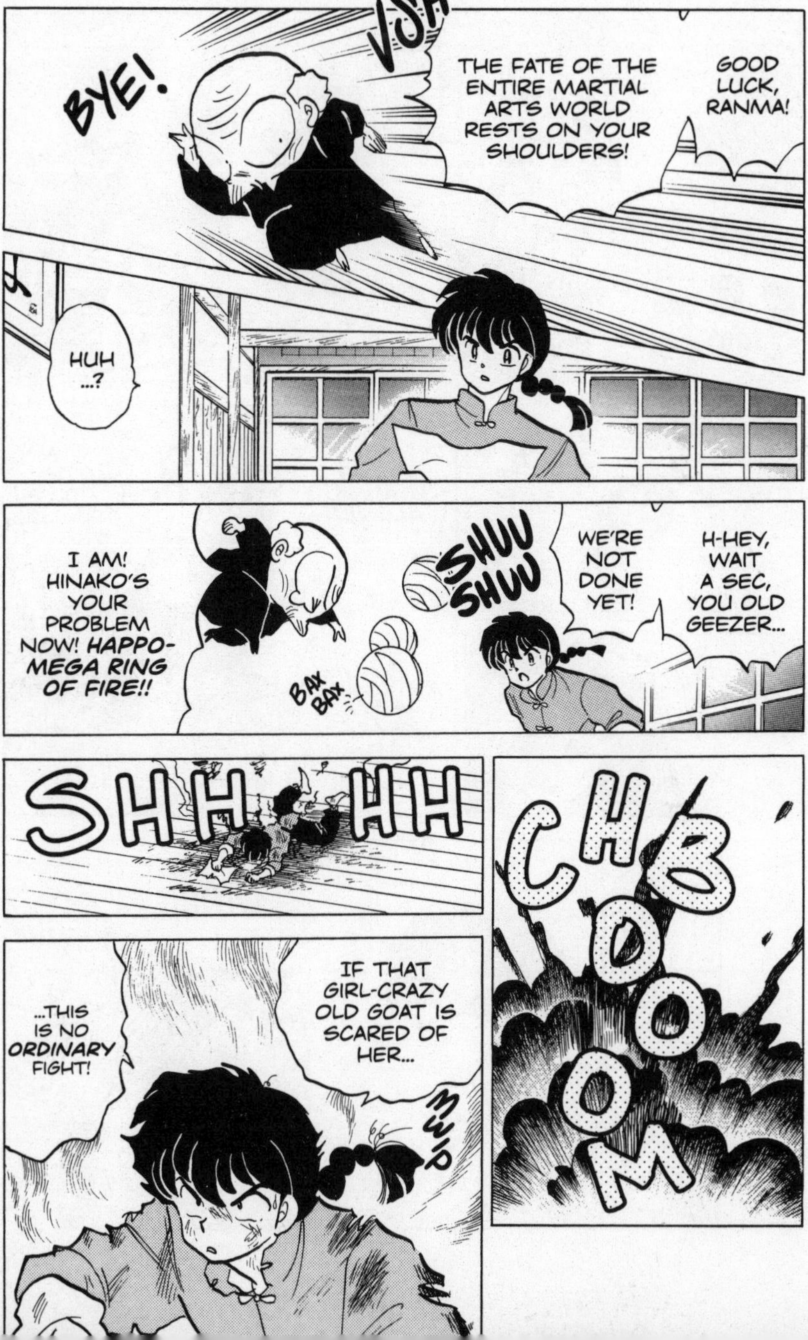

GOOD LUCK, RANMA!
THE FATE OF THE ENTIRE MARTIAL ARTS WORLD RESTS ON YOUR SHOULDERS!
VSH
BYE!
HUH ...?
H-HEY, WAIT A SEC, YOU OLD GEEZER...
WE'RE NOT DONE YET!
SHUU SHUU
BAX BAX
I AM! HINAKO'S YOUR PROBLEM NOW! **HAPPO-MEGA RING OF FIRE!!**
CHBOOOM
SHHHH
IF THAT GIRL-CRAZY OLD GOAT IS SCARED OF HER...
MWIP
...THIS IS NO **ORDINARY** FIGHT!

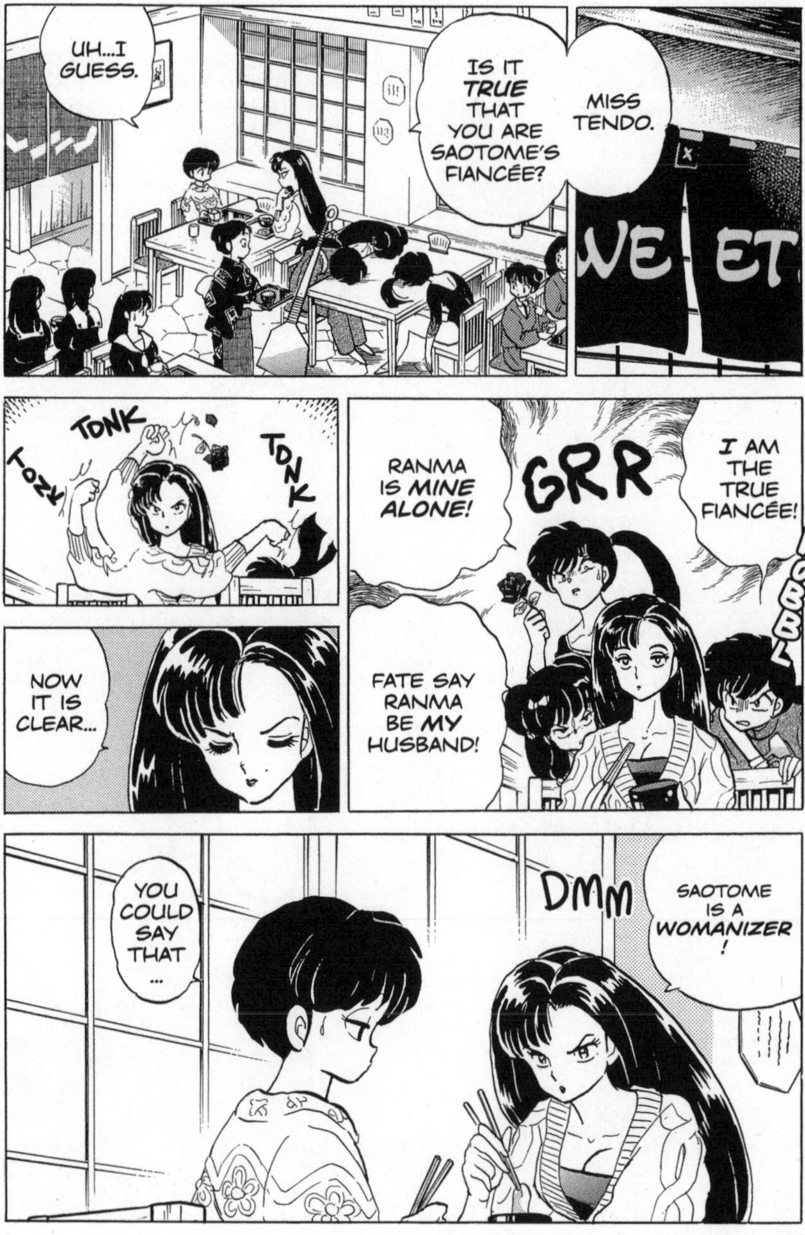
WE ET.
MISS TENDO.
IS IT TRUE THAT YOU ARE SAOTOME'S FIANCÉE?
UH...I GUESS.
I AM THE TRUE FIANCÉE!
WOBBL
GRR
RANMA IS MINE ALONE!
FATE SAY RANMA BE MY HUSBAND!
TONK
TONK
TONK
NOW IT IS CLEAR...
SAOTOME IS A WOMANIZER!
DMM
YOU COULD SAY THAT ...

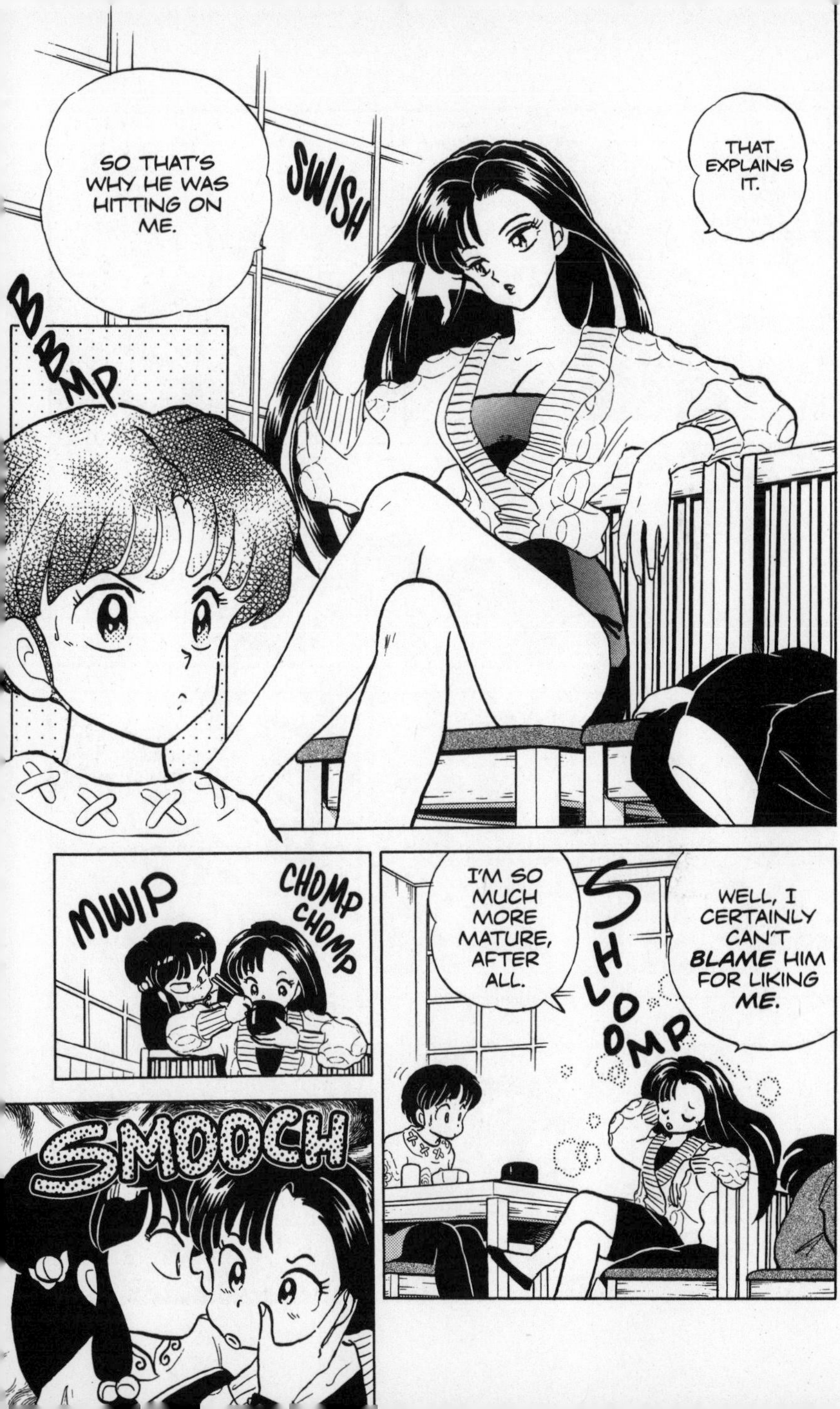
THAT EXPLAINS IT.
SWISH
SO THAT'S WHY HE WAS HITTING ON ME.
WELL, I CERTAINLY CAN'T *BLAME* HIM FOR LIKING *ME.*
SHLOOMP
I'M SO MUCH MORE MATURE, AFTER ALL.
CHOMP CHOMP
MWIP
SMOOCH

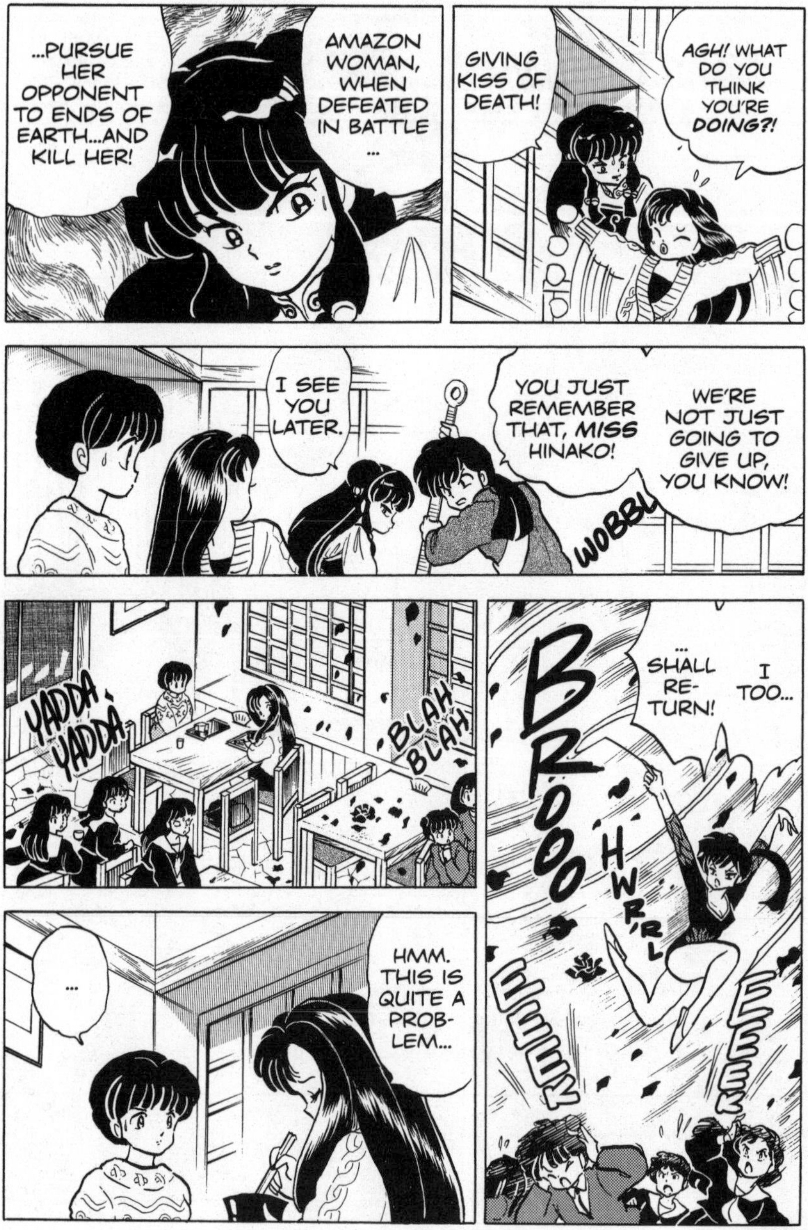
AGH! WHAT DO YOU THINK YOU'RE *DOING?!*
GIVING KISS OF DEATH!
AMAZON WOMAN, WHEN DEFEATED IN BATTLE ...
...PURSUE HER OPPONENT TO ENDS OF EARTH...AND KILL HER!
WE'RE NOT JUST GOING TO GIVE UP, YOU KNOW!
YOU JUST REMEMBER THAT, *MISS* HINAKO!
I SEE YOU LATER.
WOBBL
I TOO...
... SHALL RE-TURN!
BROOOO
HWRRL
EEEEEK
EEEK
BLAH BLAH
YADDA YADDA
HMM. THIS IS QUITE A PROB-LEM...
...

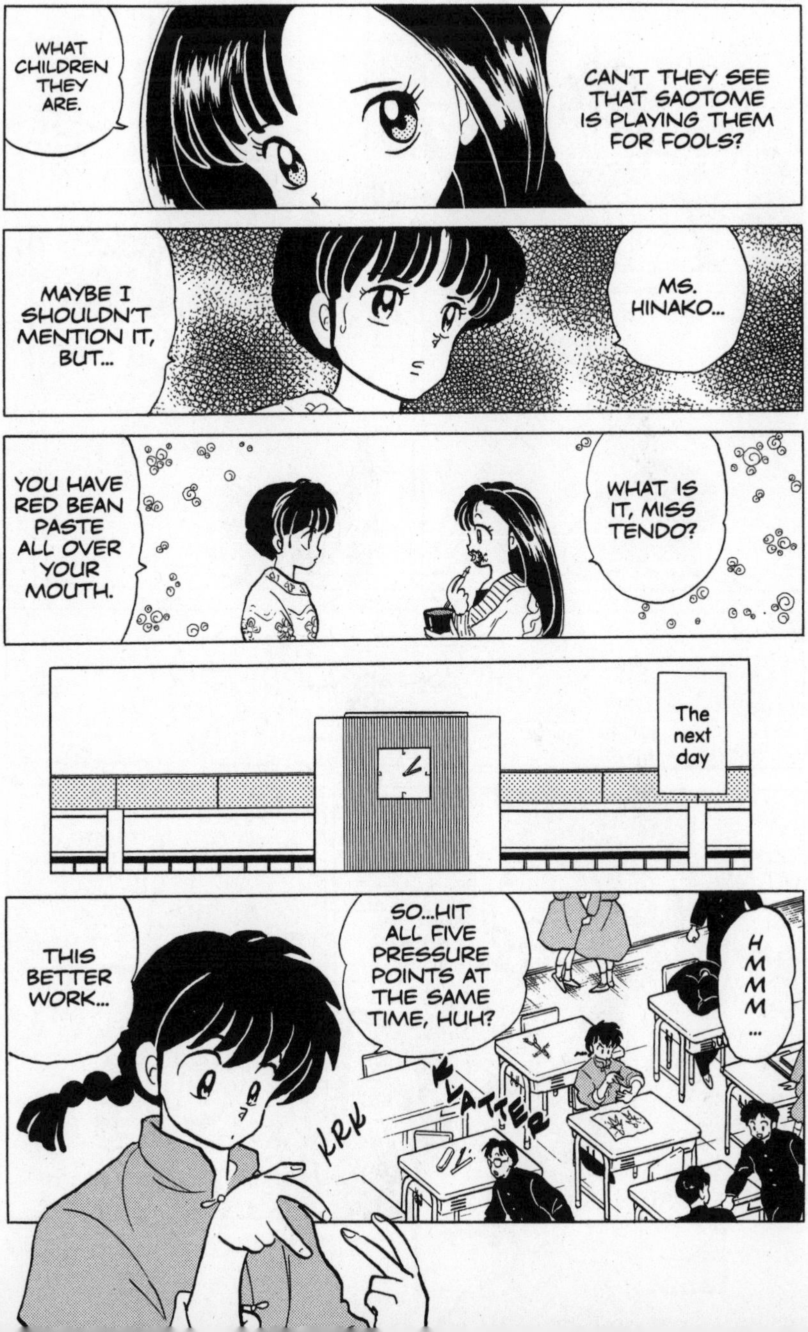
CAN'T THEY SEE THAT SAOTOME IS PLAYING THEM FOR FOOLS?
WHAT CHILDREN THEY ARE.
MS. HINAKO...
MAYBE I SHOULDN'T MENTION IT, BUT...
WHAT IS IT, MISS TENDO?
YOU HAVE RED BEAN PASTE ALL OVER YOUR MOUTH.
The next day
HMMM...
SO...HIT ALL FIVE PRESSURE POINTS AT THE SAME TIME, HUH?
KLATTER
THIS BETTER WORK...
KRK

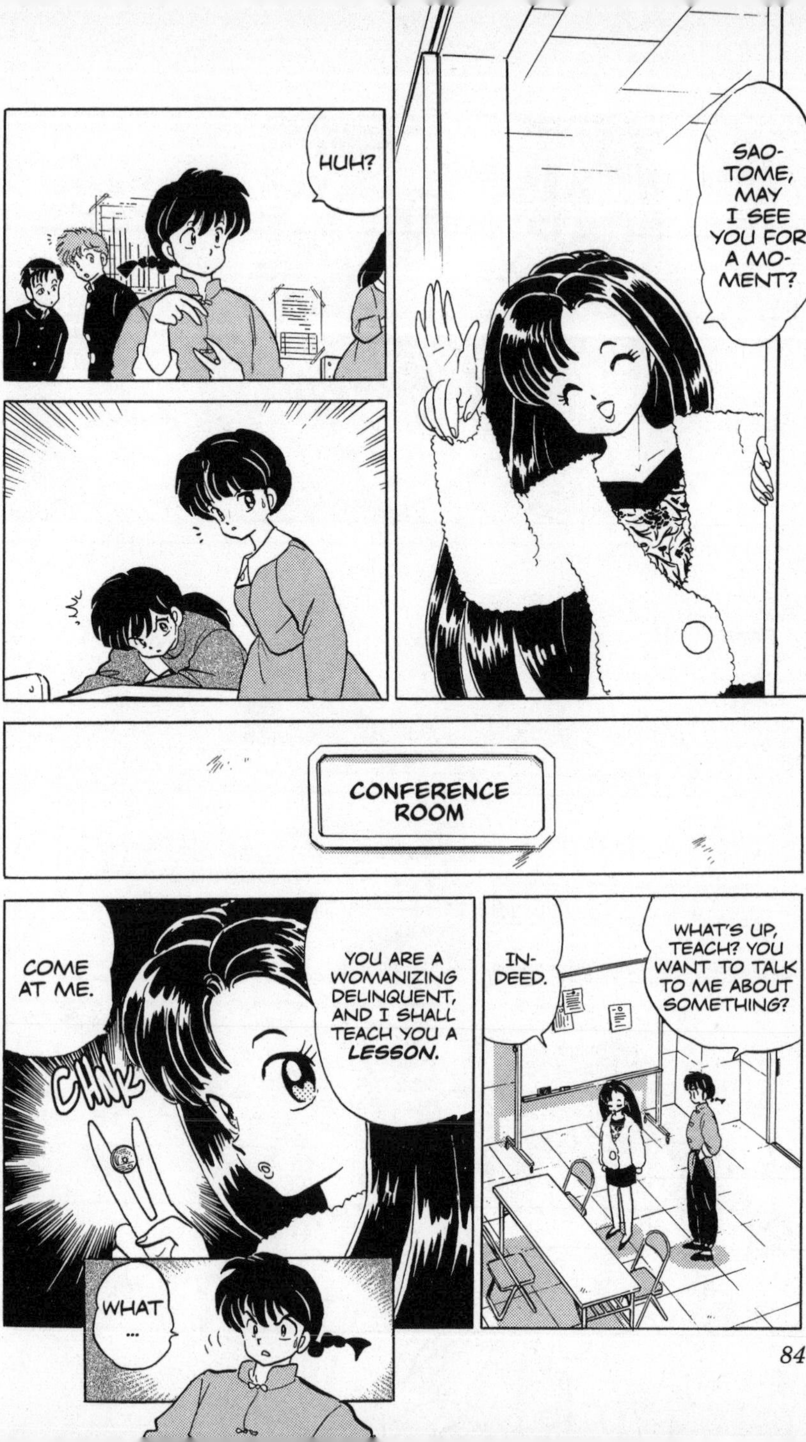
SAO-TOME, MAY I SEE YOU FOR A MO-MENT?
HUH?
CONFERENCE ROOM
WHAT'S UP, TEACH? YOU WANT TO TALK TO ME ABOUT SOMETHING?
IN-DEED.
YOU ARE A WOMANIZING DELINQUENT, AND I SHALL TEACH YOU A *LESSON*.
COME AT ME.
CHNK
WHAT ...

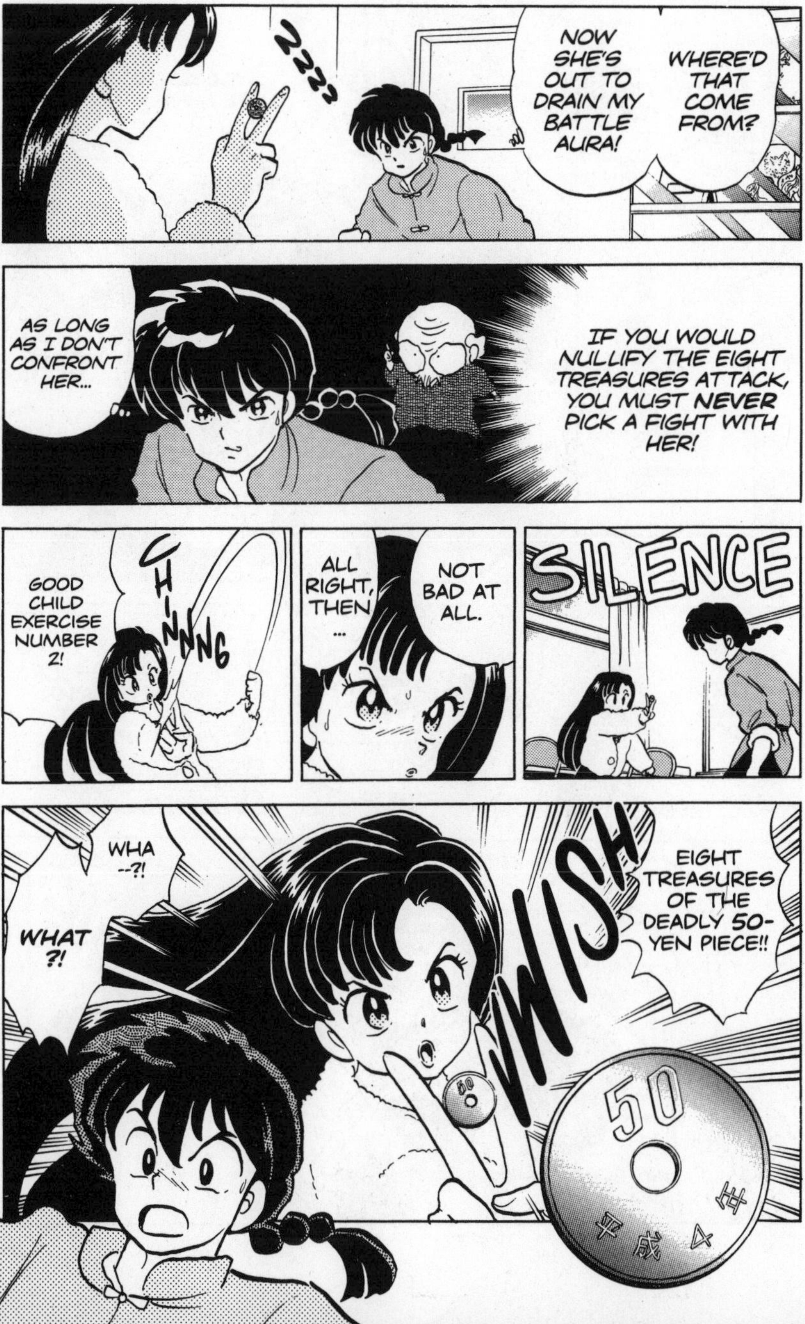
WHERE'D THAT COME FROM?
NOW SHE'S OUT TO DRAIN MY BATTLE AURA!
IF YOU WOULD NULLIFY THE EIGHT TREASURES ATTACK, YOU MUST **NEVER** PICK A FIGHT WITH HER!
AS LONG AS I DON'T CONFRONT HER...
SILENCE
NOT BAD AT ALL.
ALL RIGHT, THEN ...
GOOD CHILD EXERCISE NUMBER 2!
CHINNNG
EIGHT TREASURES OF THE DEADLY 50-YEN PIECE!!
WHISH
WHA --?!
WHAT ?!
50
平成4年

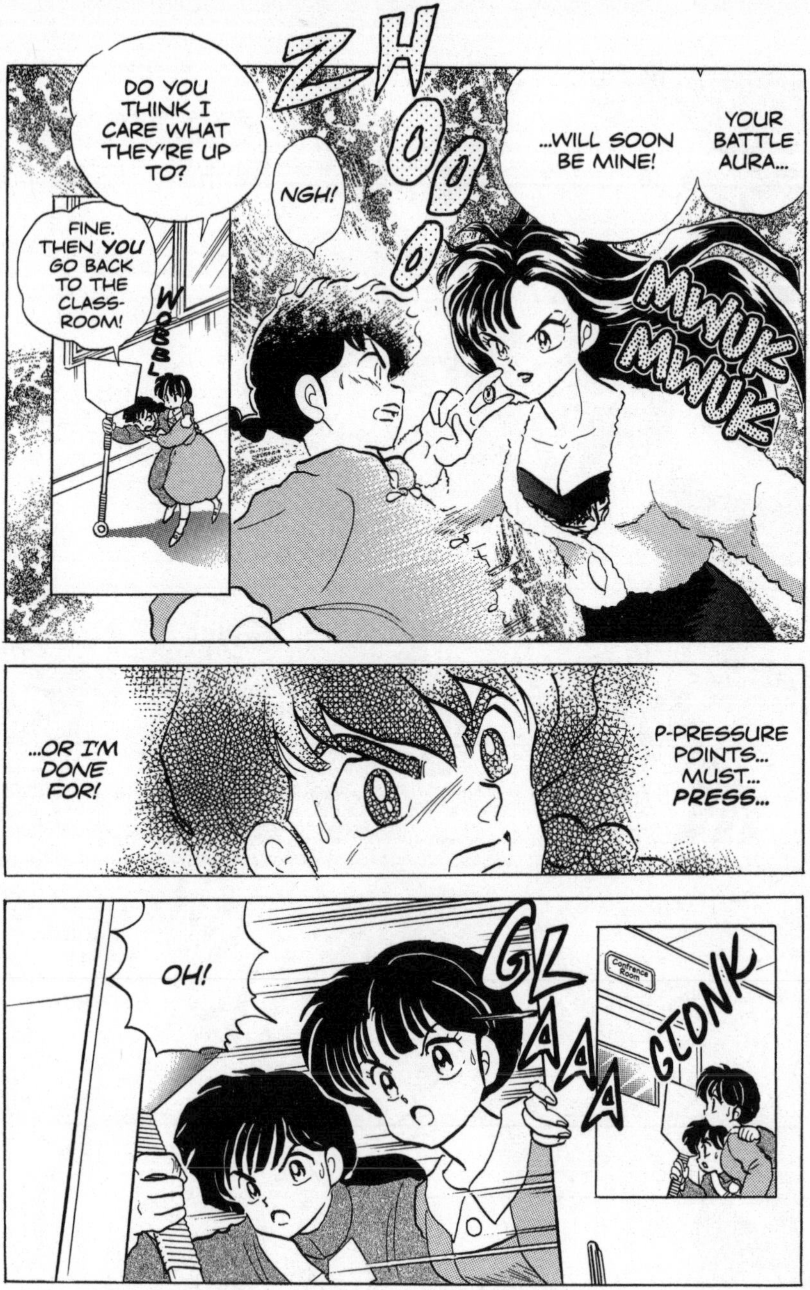
YOUR BATTLE AURA...
...WILL SOON BE MINE!
MWUK MWUK
ZHOOOO
NGH!
DO YOU THINK I CARE WHAT THEY'RE UP TO?
FINE. THEN **YOU** GO BACK TO THE CLASSROOM!
WOBBL
P-PRESSURE POINTS... MUST... **PRESS**...
...OR I'M DONE FOR!
Confrence Room
GLONK
GLAAAA
OH!

PART 6
GO FOR THE PRESSURE POINTS!

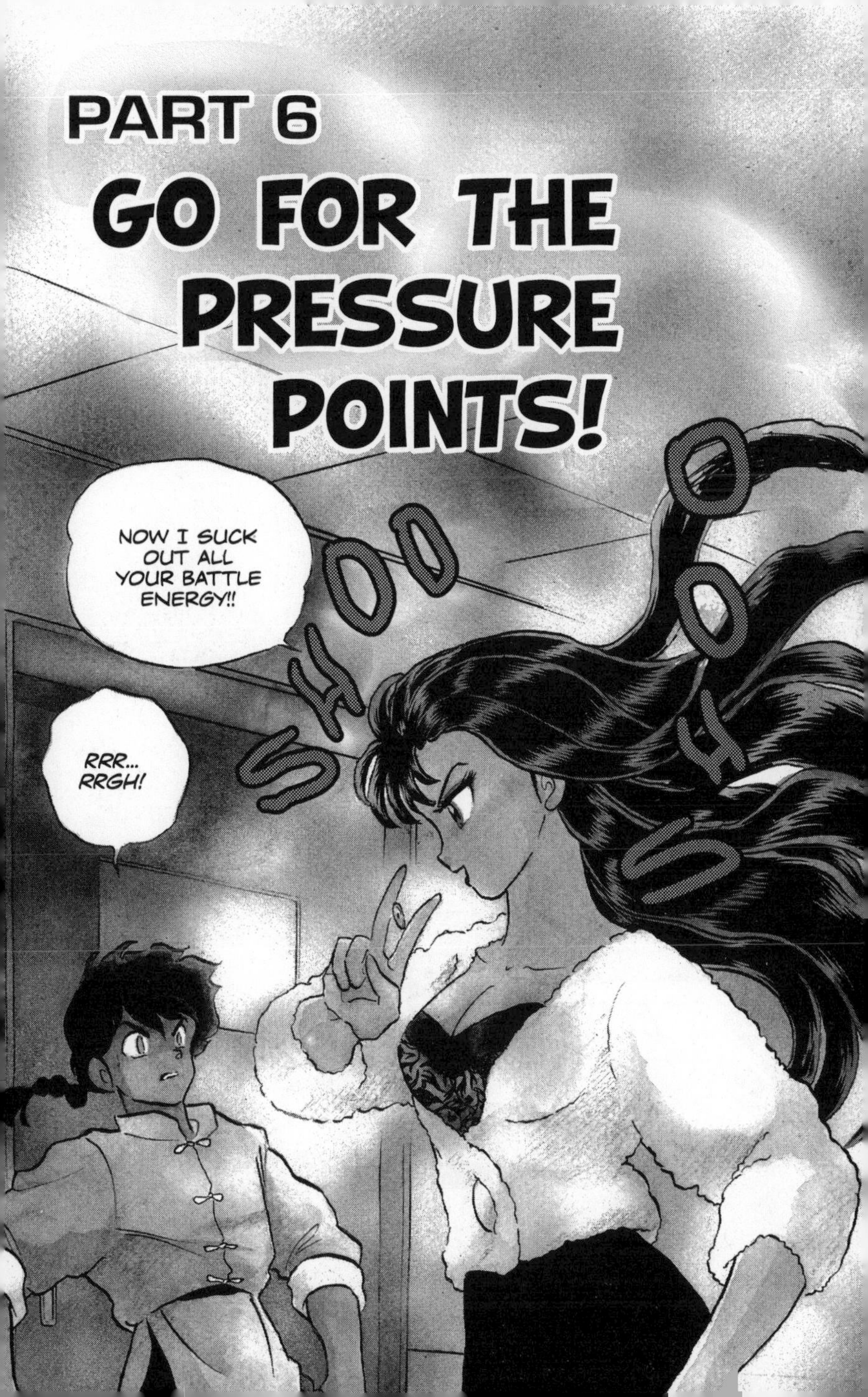
SHOOO
NOW I SUCK OUT ALL YOUR BATTLE ENERGY!!
SHOO
RRR... RRGH!

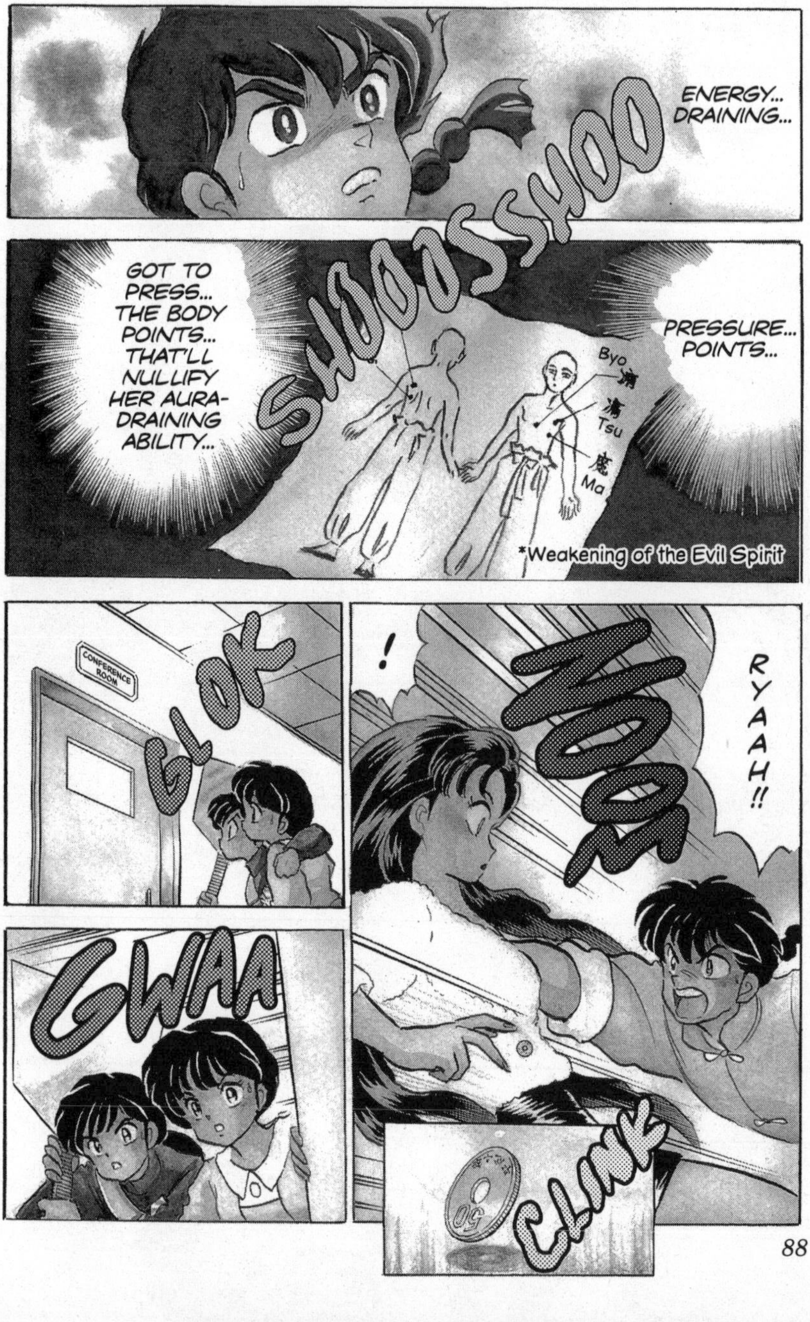
ENERGY... DRAINING...
SHOOSSHOO
PRESSURE... POINTS...
Byo 病
痛 Tsu
魔 Ma
*Weakening of the Evil Spirit
GOT TO PRESS... THE BODY POINTS... THAT'LL NULLIFY HER AURA-DRAINING ABILITY...
RYAAH!!
NOOM
!
CLINK
CLOK
CONFERENCE ROOM
GWAA

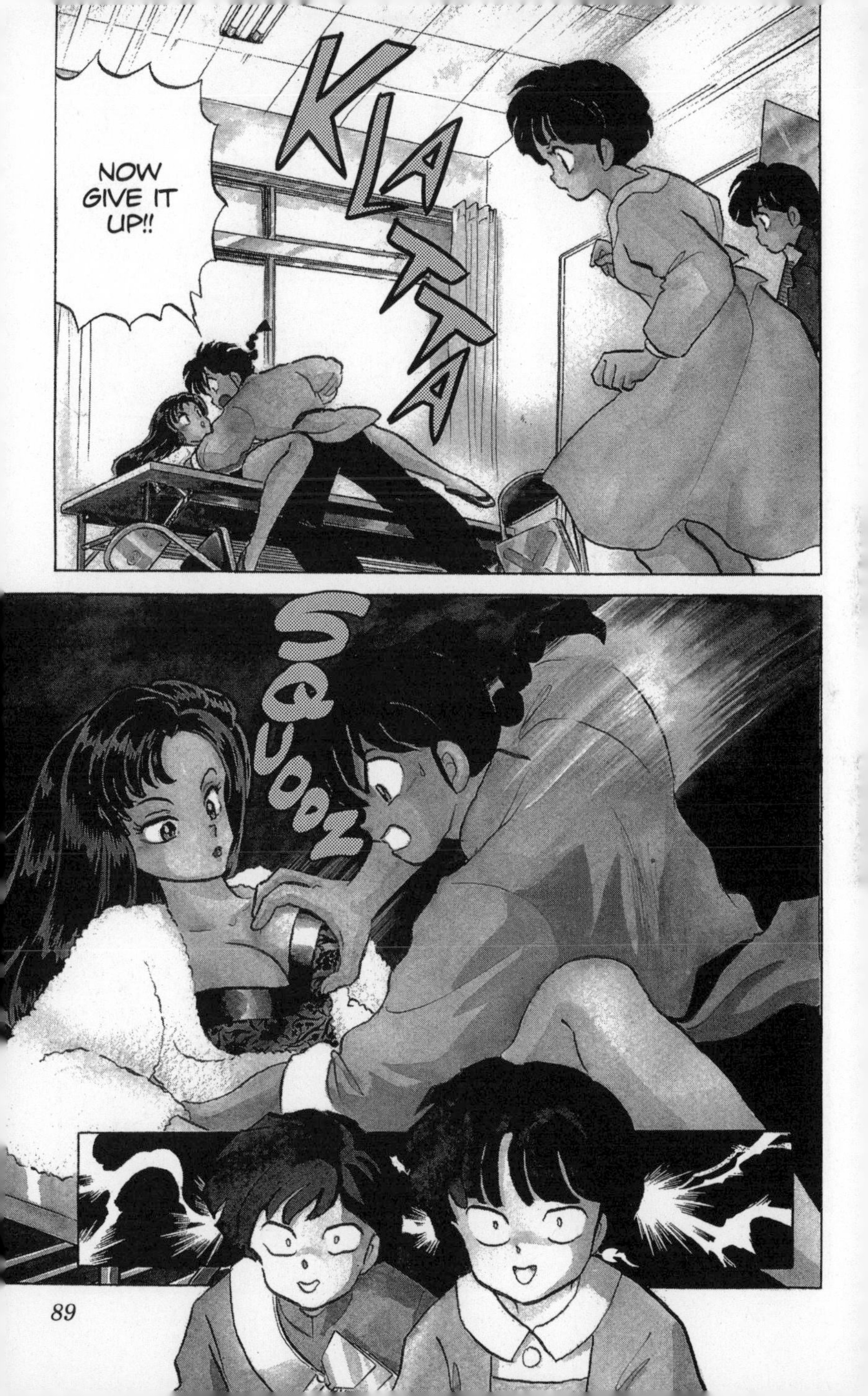
KLATTA
NOW GIVE IT UP!!
SQUOOM

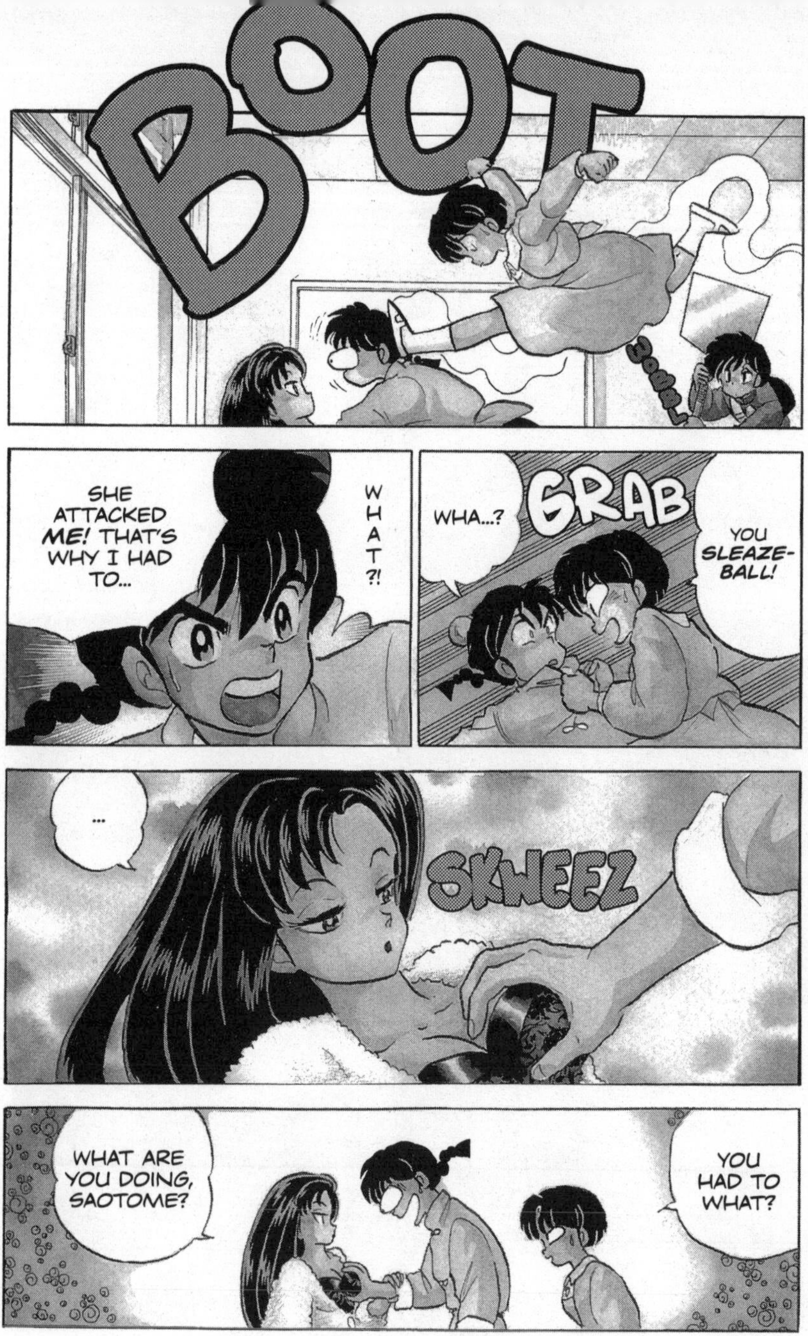
BOOT
GRAB
YOU SLEAZE-BALL!
WHA...?
WHAT?!
SHE ATTACKED ME! THAT'S WHY I HAD TO...
SKWEEZ
...
YOU HAD TO WHAT?
WHAT ARE YOU DOING, SAOTOME?

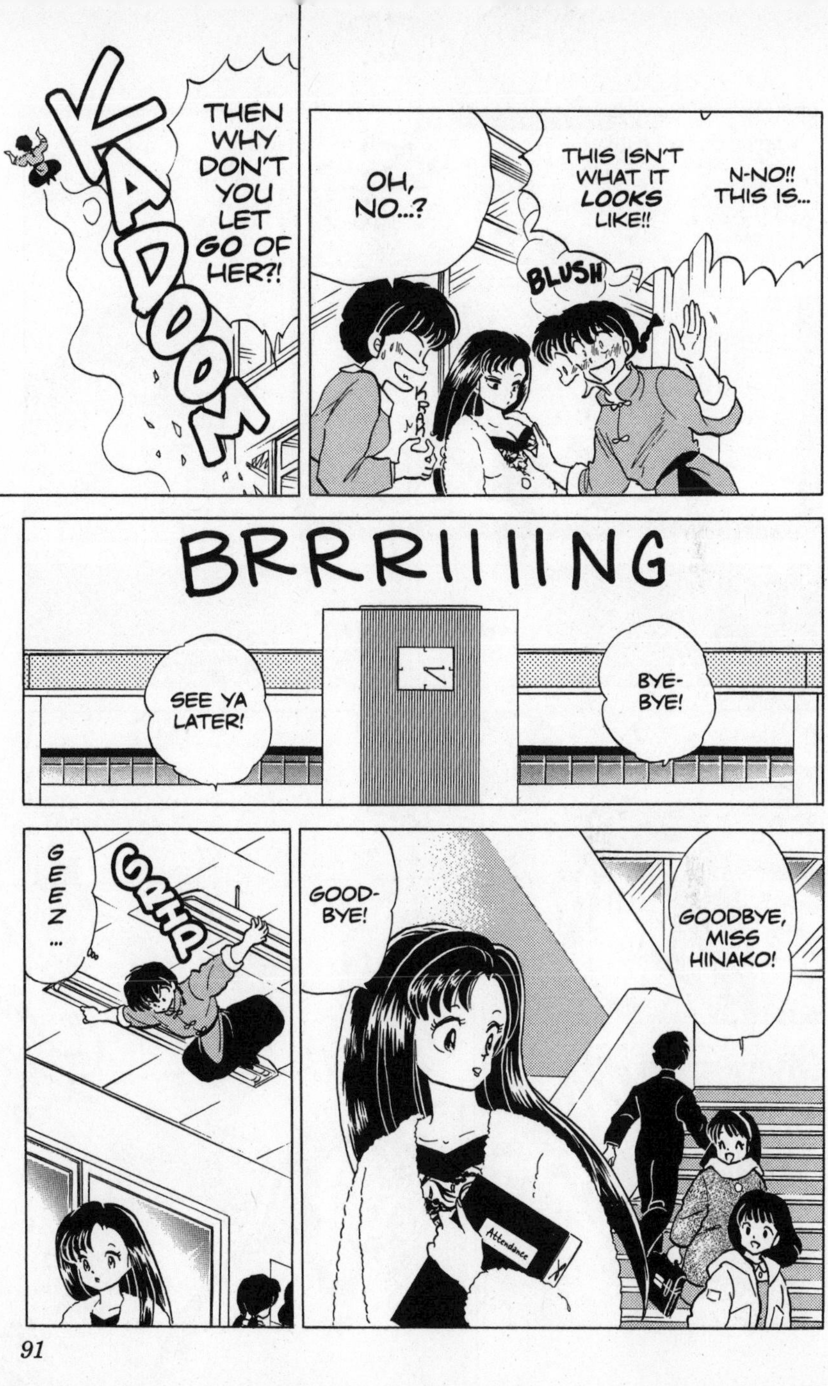
N-NO!! THIS IS...
THIS ISN'T WHAT IT LOOKS LIKE!!
BLUSH
OH, NO...?
KRAK
THEN WHY DON'T YOU LET GO OF HER?!
KADOOM
BRRRIIIING
BYE-BYE!
SEE YA LATER!
GOODBYE, MISS HINAKO!
GOOD-BYE!
Attendance
GRIP
GEEZ...

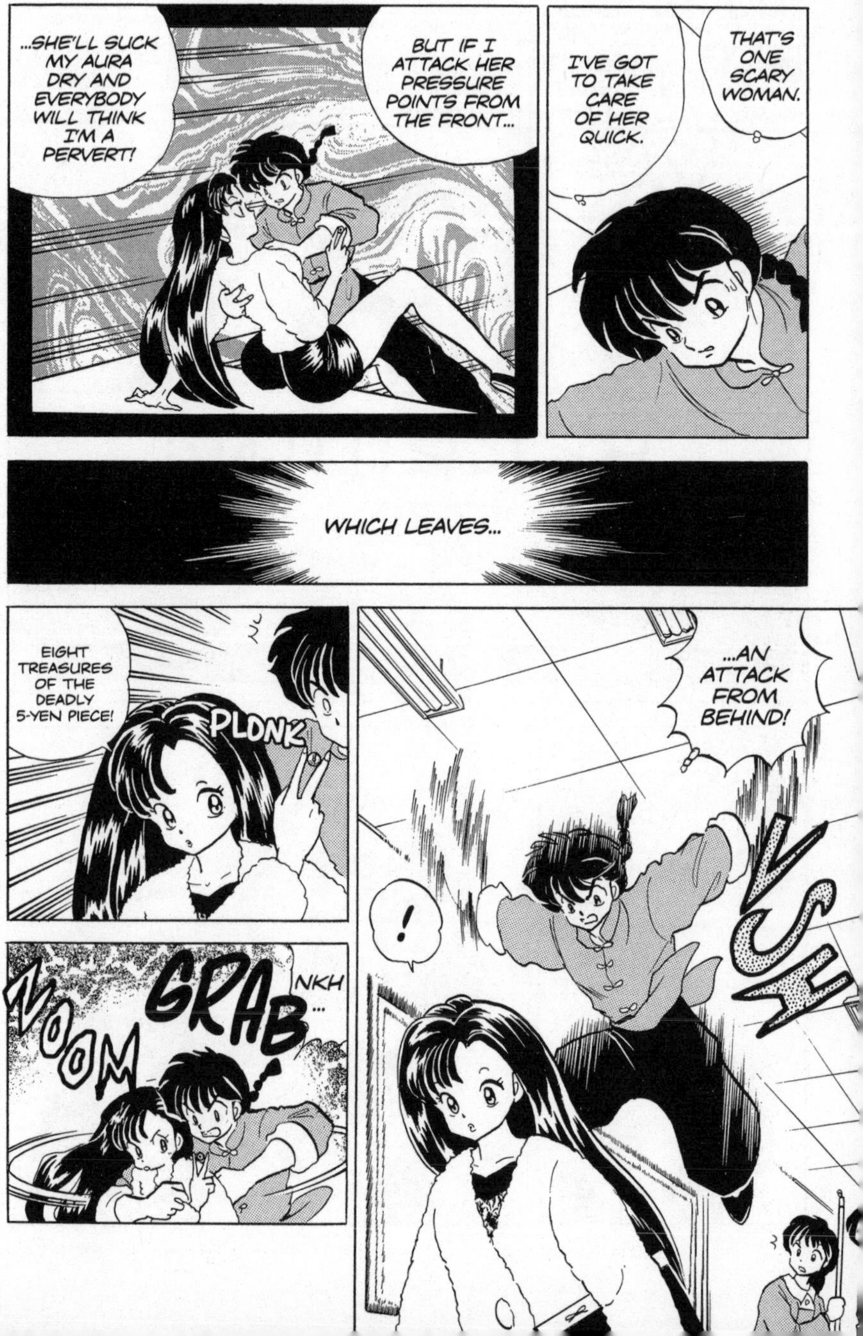
THAT'S ONE SCARY WOMAN.
I'VE GOT TO TAKE CARE OF HER QUICK.
BUT IF I ATTACK HER PRESSURE POINTS FROM THE FRONT...
...SHE'LL SUCK MY AURA DRY AND EVERYBODY WILL THINK I'M A PERVERT!
WHICH LEAVES...
...AN ATTACK FROM BEHIND!
VSH
!
EIGHT TREASURES OF THE DEADLY 5-YEN PIECE!
PLONK
NKH...
GRAB
ZOOM

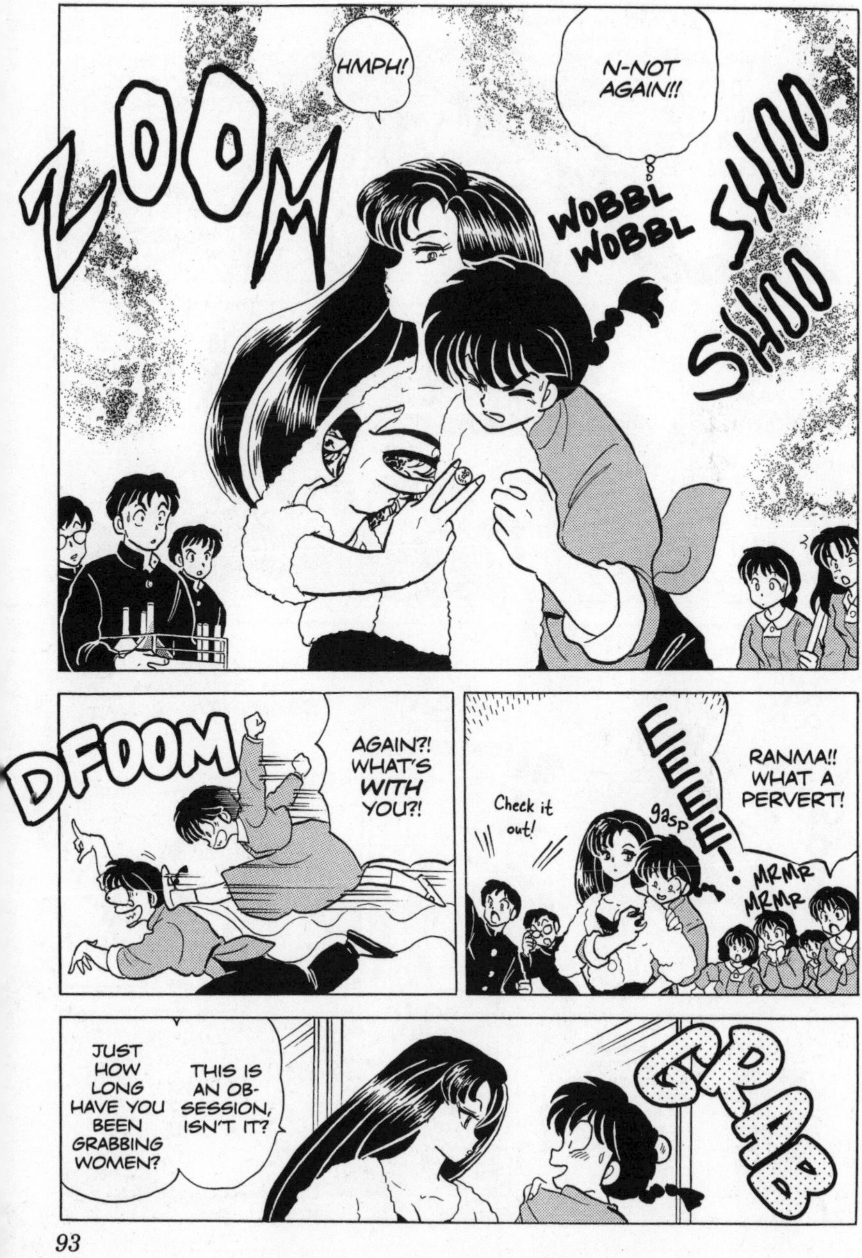
N-NOT AGAIN!!
SHOO SHOO
WOBBL WOBBL
HMPH!
ZOOM
RANMA!! WHAT A PERVERT!
EEEEE!
MRMR MRMR
gasp
Check it out!
AGAIN?! WHAT'S WITH YOU?!
DFOOM
GRAB
THIS IS AN OB-SESSION, ISN'T IT?
JUST HOW LONG HAVE YOU BEEN GRABBING WOMEN?

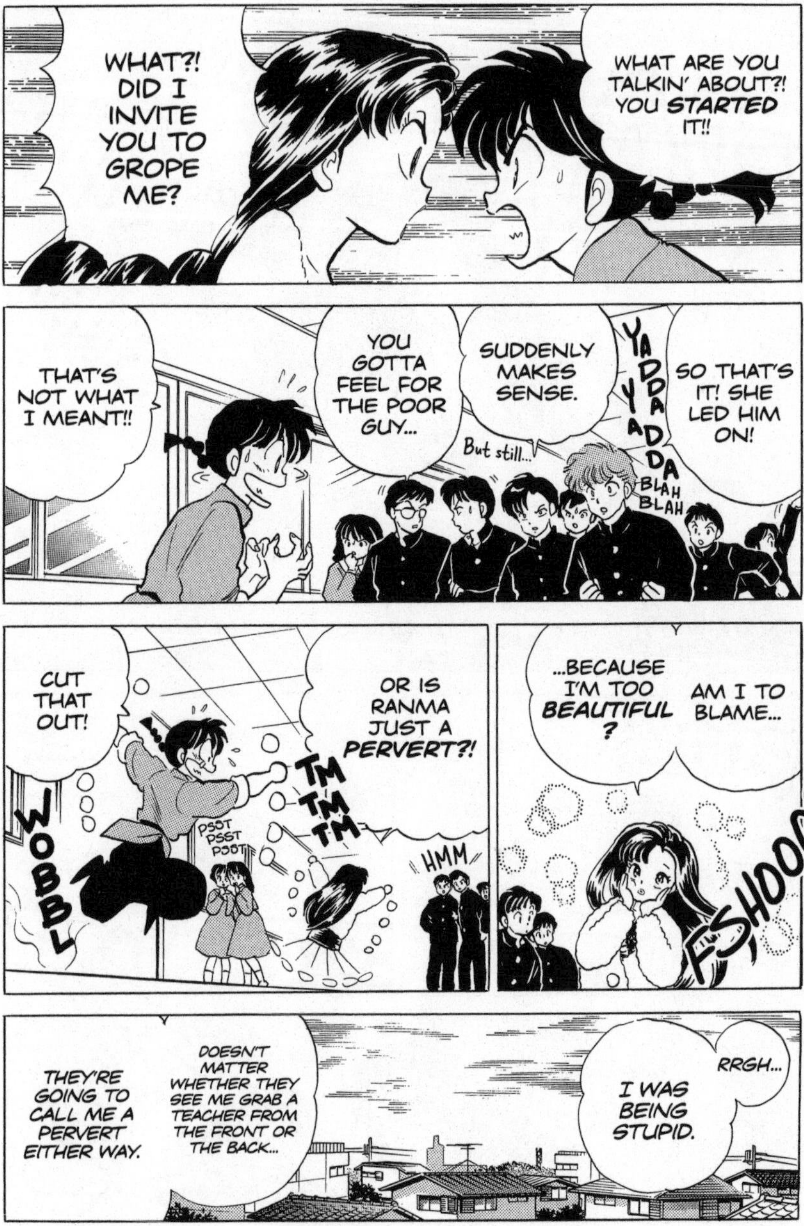
WHAT ARE YOU TALKIN' ABOUT?! YOU STARTED IT!!
WHAT?! DID I INVITE YOU TO GROPE ME?
SO THAT'S IT! SHE LED HIM ON!
YADDA YADDA BLAH BLAH
SUDDENLY MAKES SENSE.
But still...
YOU GOTTA FEEL FOR THE POOR GUY...
THAT'S NOT WHAT I MEANT!!
AM I TO BLAME...
...BECAUSE I'M TOO BEAUTIFUL?
FSHOOOO
OR IS RANMA JUST A PERVERT?!
TM TM TM
HMM
PSST PSST PSST
CUT THAT OUT!
WOBBL
RRGH...
I WAS BEING STUPID.
DOESN'T MATTER WHETHER THEY SEE ME GRAB A TEACHER FROM THE FRONT OR THE BACK...
THEY'RE GOING TO CALL ME A PERVERT EITHER WAY.

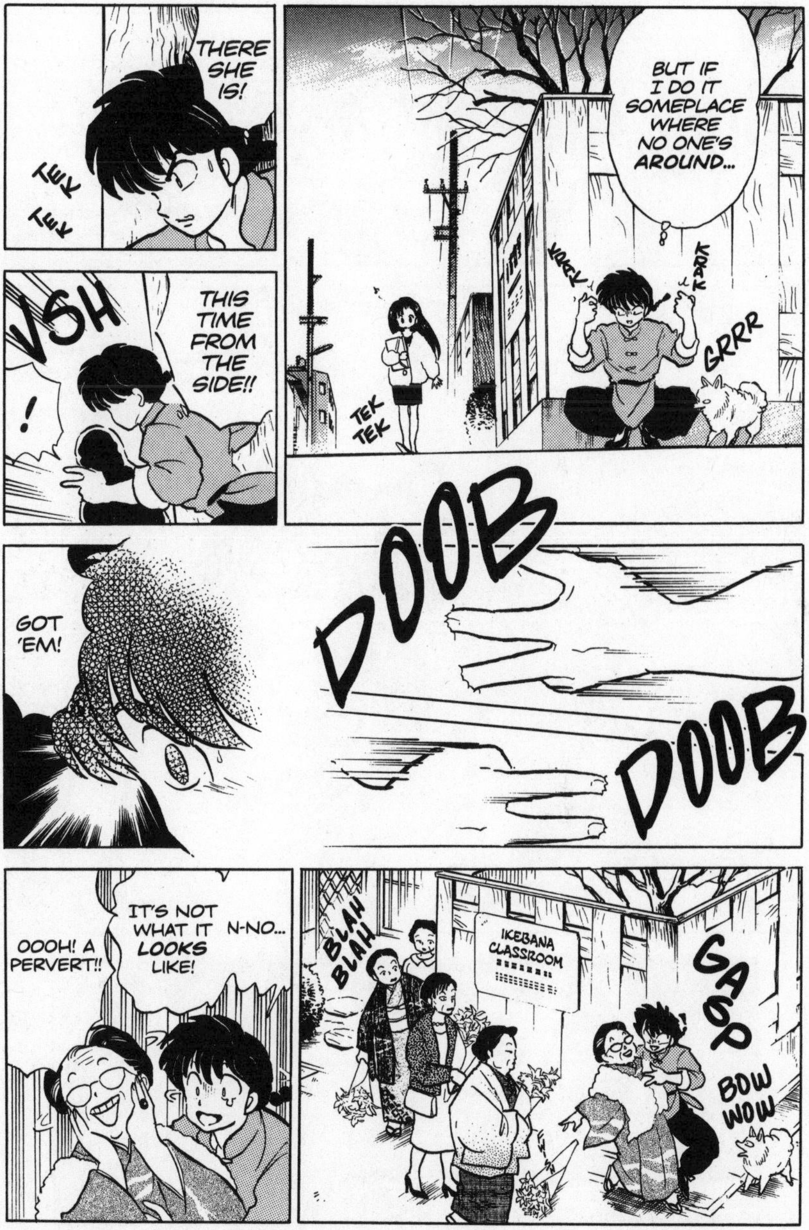
BUT IF I DO IT SOMEPLACE WHERE NO ONE'S AROUND...
KRACK
KRAK
GRRR
TEK TEK
THERE SHE IS!
TEK
TEK
THIS TIME FROM THE SIDE!!
VSH
!
DOOB
DOOB
GOT 'EM!
GASP
BOW WOW
IKEBANA CLASSROOM
BLAH BLAH
N-NO...
IT'S NOT WHAT IT LOOKS LIKE!
OOOH! A PERVERT!!

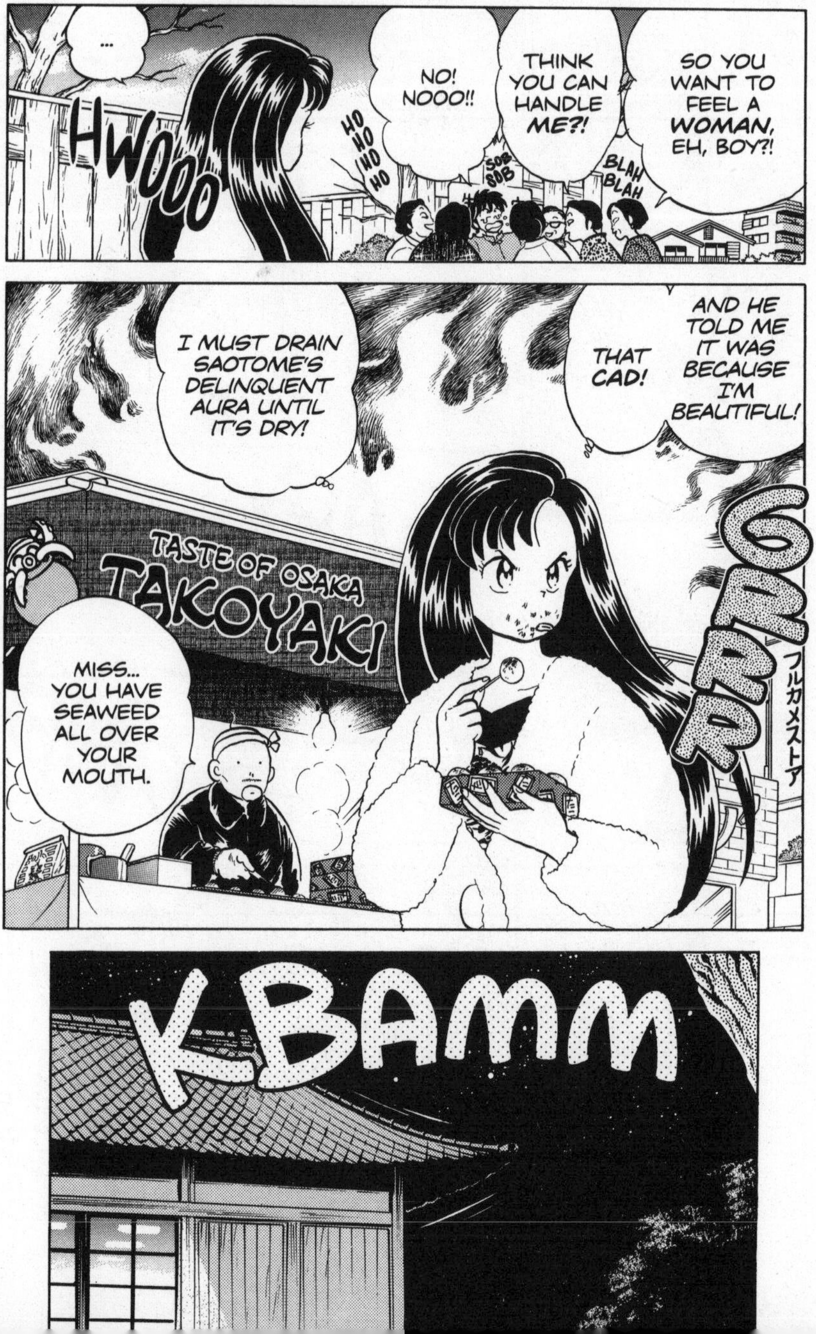
SO YOU WANT TO FEEL A WOMAN, EH, BOY?!
BLAH BLAH
THINK YOU CAN HANDLE ME?!
SOB SOB
NO! NOOO!!
HO HO HO HO
...
HWOOO
AND HE TOLD ME IT WAS BECAUSE I'M BEAUTIFUL!
THAT CAD!
GRRRR
フルカメストア
I MUST DRAIN SAOTOME'S DELINQUENT AURA UNTIL IT'S DRY!
TASTE OF OSAKA TAKOYAKI
MISS... YOU HAVE SEAWEED ALL OVER YOUR MOUTH.
KBAMM

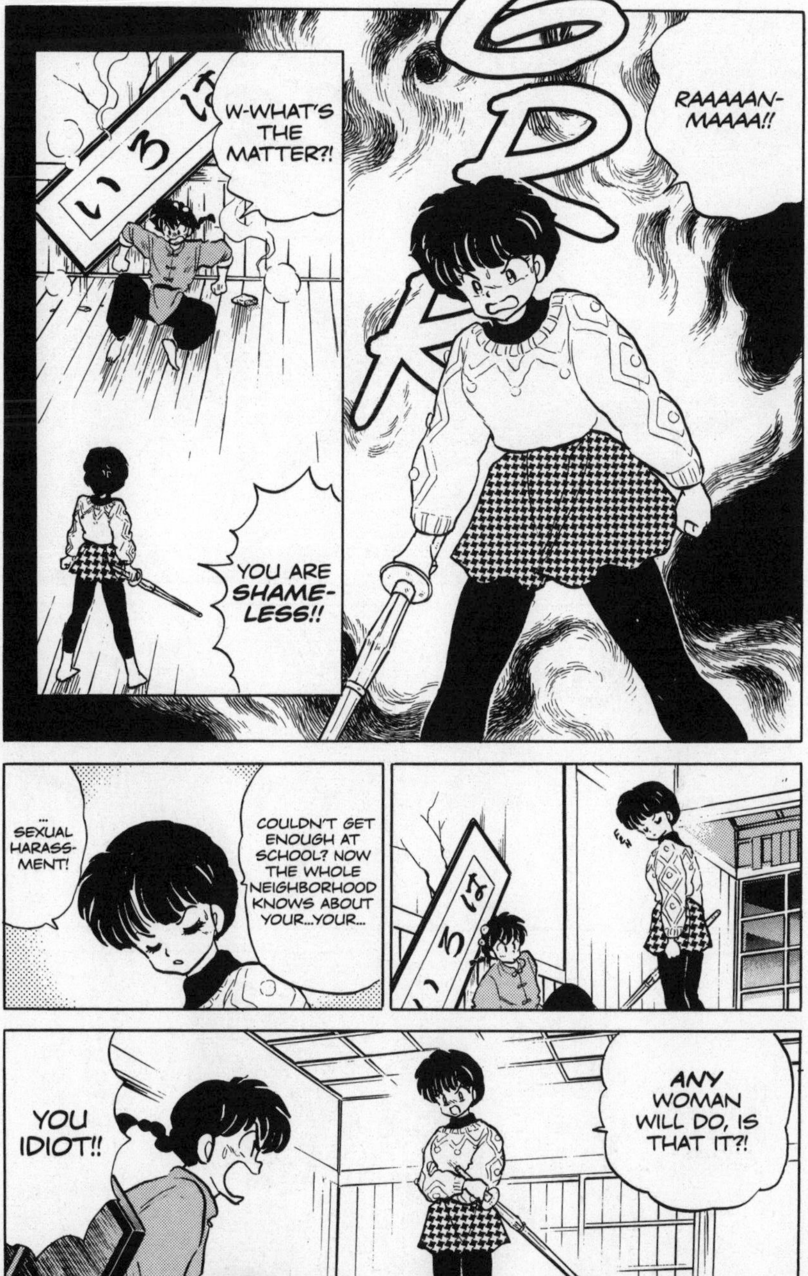
RAAAAAN-MAAAA!!
W-WHAT'S THE MATTER?!
YOU ARE SHAME-LESS!!
COULDN'T GET ENOUGH AT SCHOOL? NOW THE WHOLE NEIGHBORHOOD KNOWS ABOUT YOUR...YOUR...
... SEXUAL HARASS-MENT!
ANY WOMAN WILL DO, IS THAT IT?!
YOU IDIOT!!

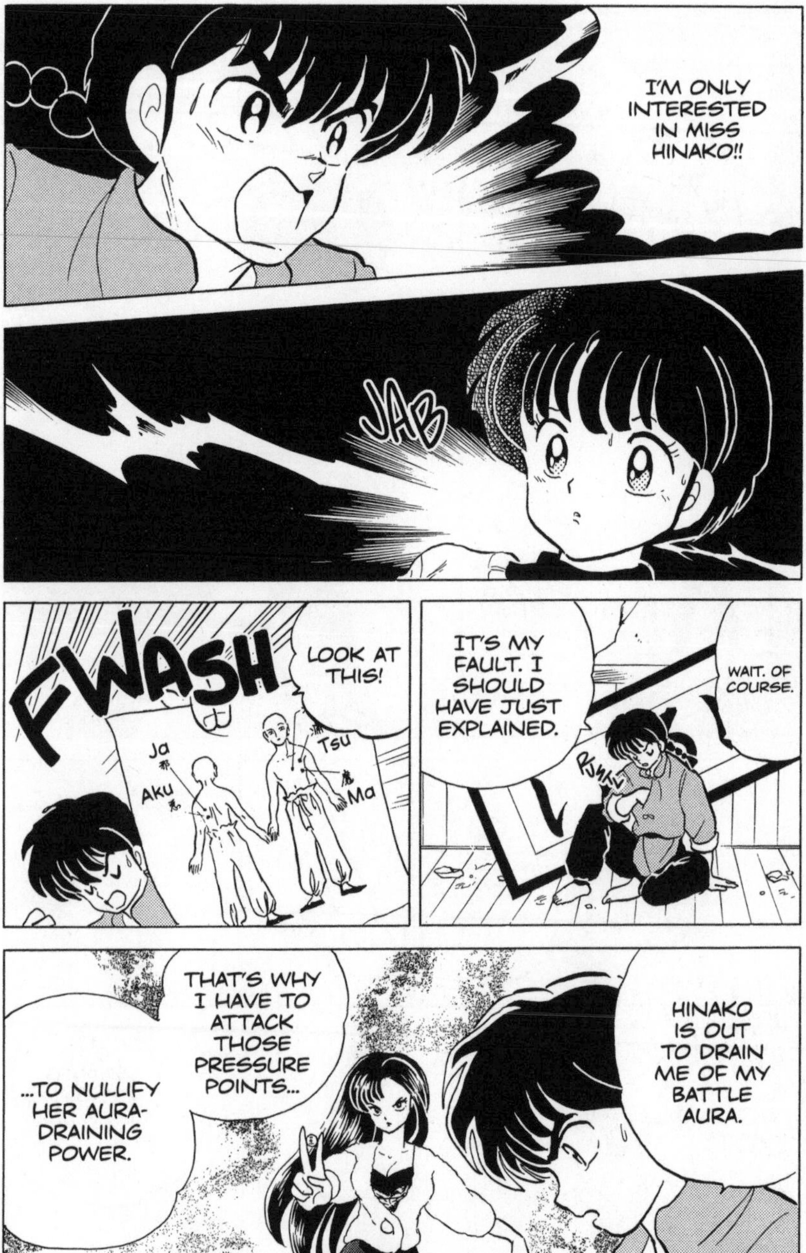
I'M ONLY INTERESTED IN MISS HINAKO!!
JAB
WAIT. OF COURSE.
IT'S MY FAULT. I SHOULD HAVE JUST EXPLAINED.
FWASH
LOOK AT THIS!
Tsu
Ma
Ja
Aku
HINAKO IS OUT TO DRAIN ME OF MY BATTLE AURA.
THAT'S WHY I HAVE TO ATTACK THOSE PRESSURE POINTS...
...TO NULLIFY HER AURA-DRAINING POWER.

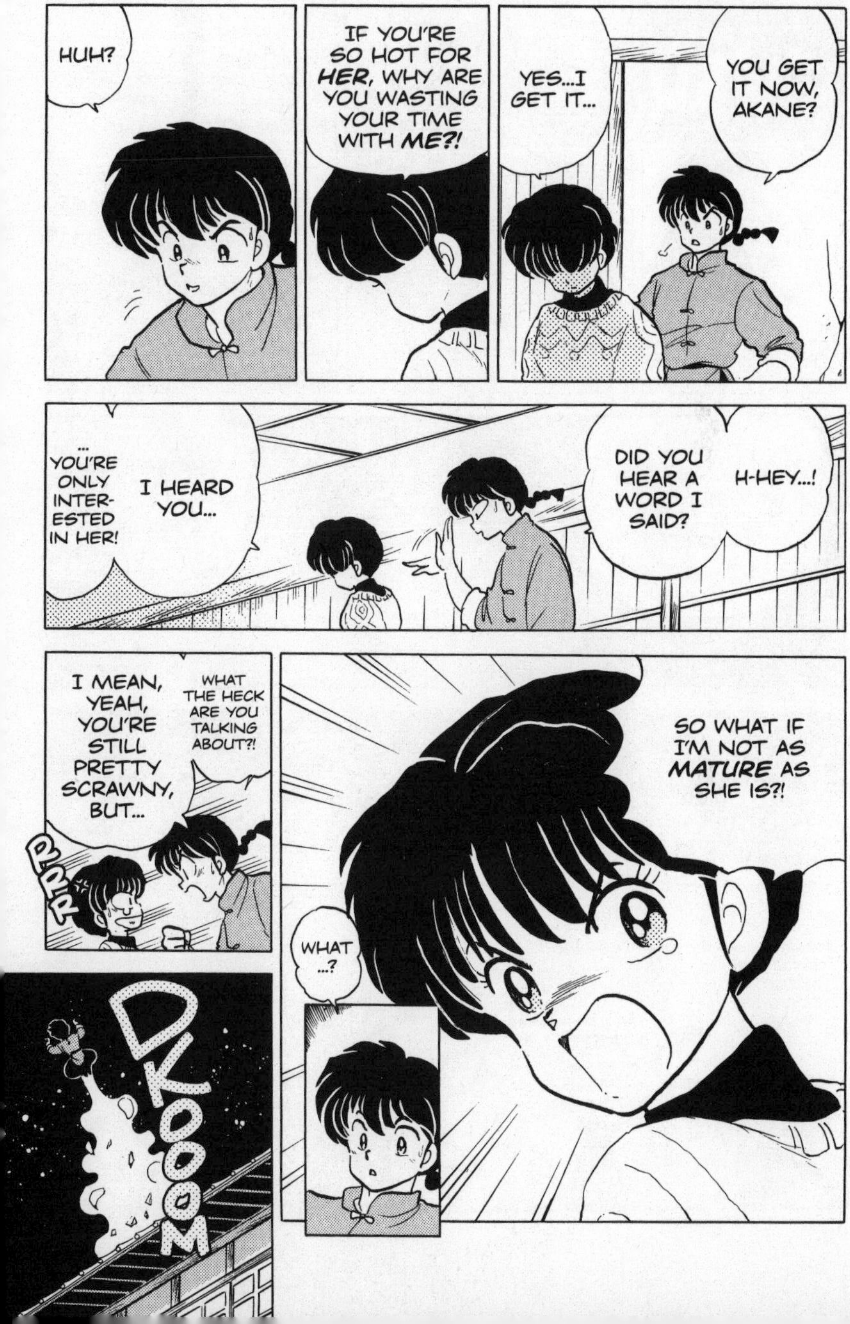
YOU GET IT NOW, AKANE?
YES...I GET IT...
IF YOU'RE SO HOT FOR **HER**, WHY ARE YOU WASTING YOUR TIME WITH **ME?!**
HUH?
H-HEY...!
DID YOU HEAR A WORD I SAID?
I HEARD YOU...
...YOU'RE ONLY INTER-ESTED IN HER!
SO WHAT IF I'M NOT AS **MATURE** AS SHE IS?!
WHAT...?
I MEAN, YEAH, YOU'RE STILL PRETTY SCRAWNY, BUT...
WHAT THE HECK ARE YOU TALKING ABOUT?!
RRR
DKOOOM

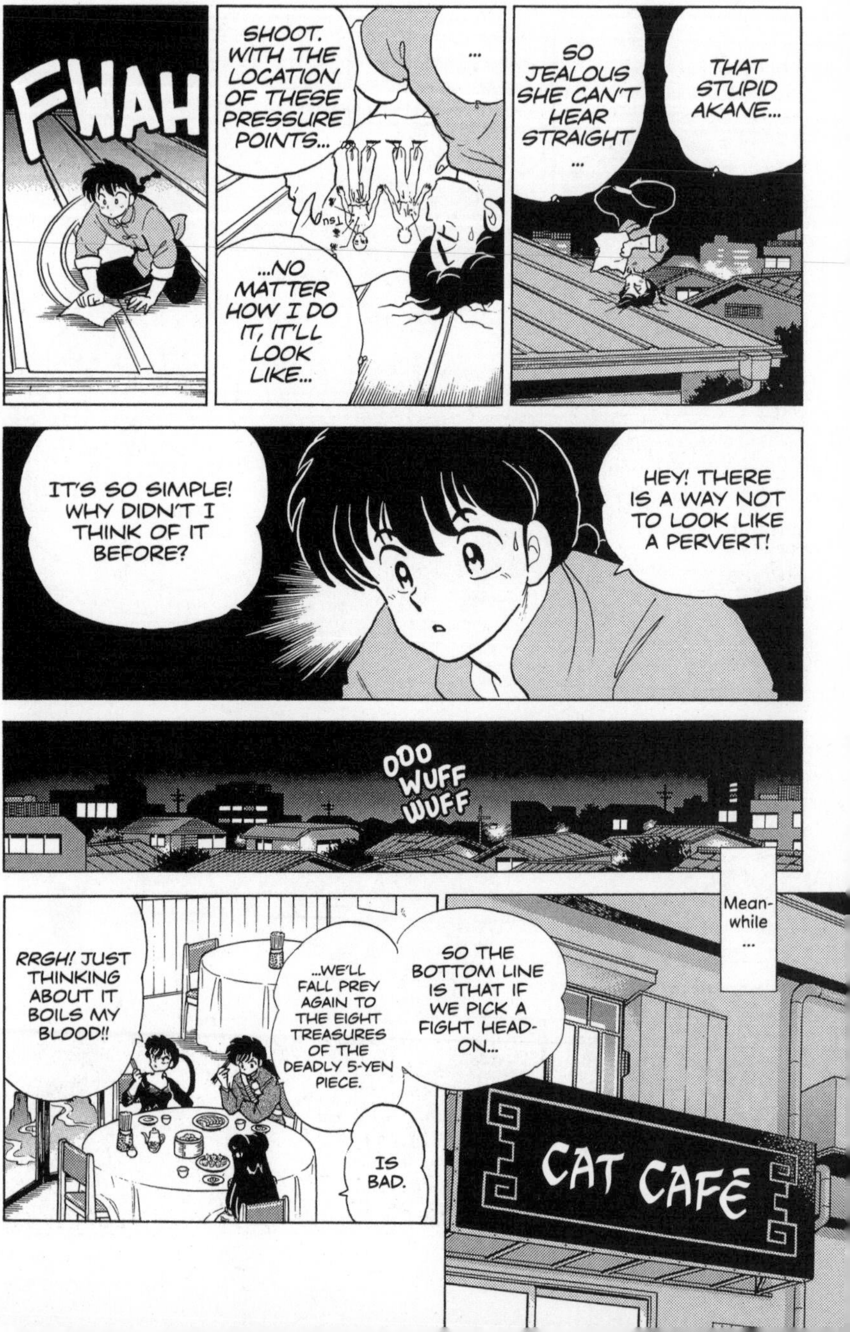
THAT STUPID AKANE...
SO JEALOUS SHE CAN'T HEAR STRAIGHT ...
...
SHOOT. WITH THE LOCATION OF THESE PRESSURE POINTS...
...NO MATTER HOW I DO IT, IT'LL LOOK LIKE...
FWAH
HEY! THERE IS A WAY NOT TO LOOK LIKE A PERVERT!
IT'S SO SIMPLE! WHY DIDN'T I THINK OF IT BEFORE?
OOO WUFF WUFF
Meanwhile ...
CAT CAFÉ
SO THE BOTTOM LINE IS THAT IF WE PICK A FIGHT HEAD-ON...
...WE'LL FALL PREY AGAIN TO THE EIGHT TREASURES OF THE DEADLY 5-YEN PIECE.
IS BAD.
RRGH! JUST THINKING ABOUT IT BOILS MY BLOOD!!

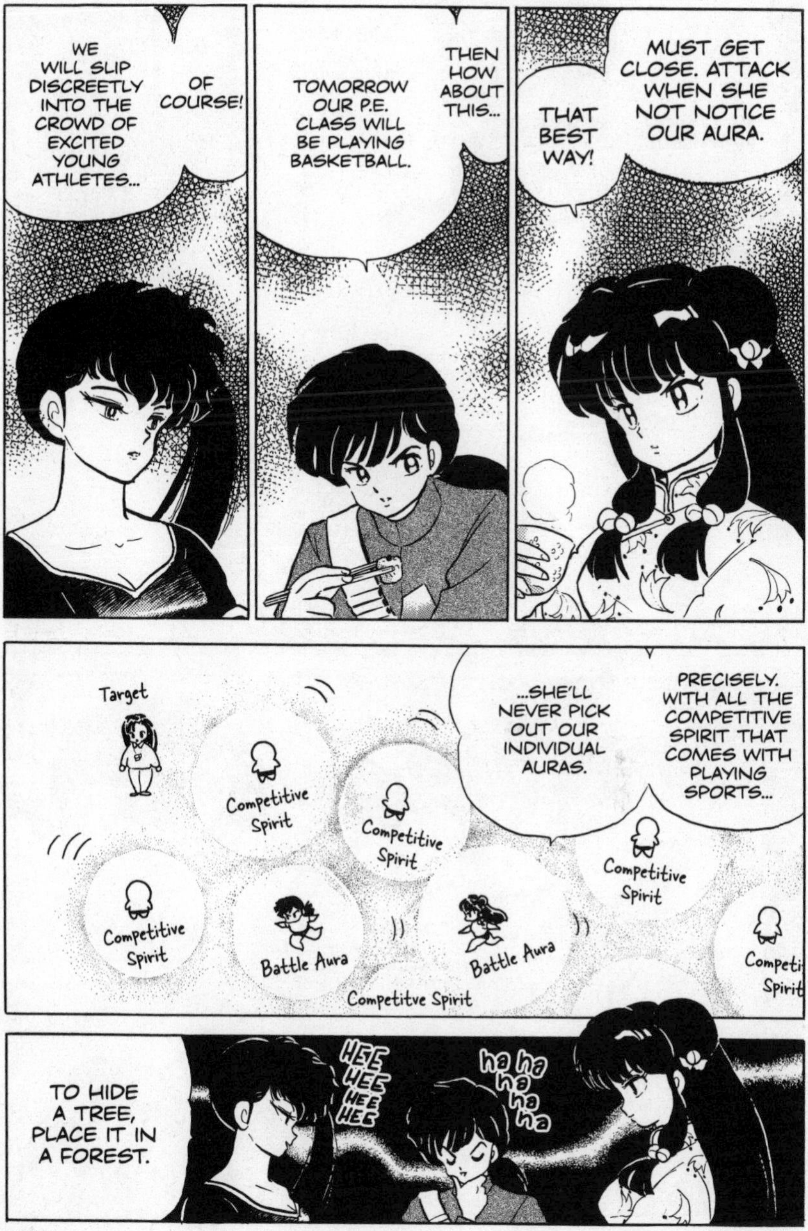
MUST GET CLOSE. ATTACK WHEN SHE NOT NOTICE OUR AURA.
THAT BEST WAY!
THEN HOW ABOUT THIS...
TOMORROW OUR P.E. CLASS WILL BE PLAYING BASKETBALL.
WE WILL SLIP DISCREETLY INTO THE CROWD OF EXCITED YOUNG ATHLETES...
OF COURSE!
PRECISELY. WITH ALL THE COMPETITIVE SPIRIT THAT COMES WITH PLAYING SPORTS...
...SHE'LL NEVER PICK OUT OUR INDIVIDUAL AURAS.
Competitive Spirit
Competitive Spirit
Competitive Spirit
Target
Competitive Spirit
Battle Aura
Battle Aura
Competitive Spirit
Competitve Spirit
ha ha ha ha ha
HEE HEE HEE HEE
TO HIDE A TREE, PLACE IT IN A FOREST.

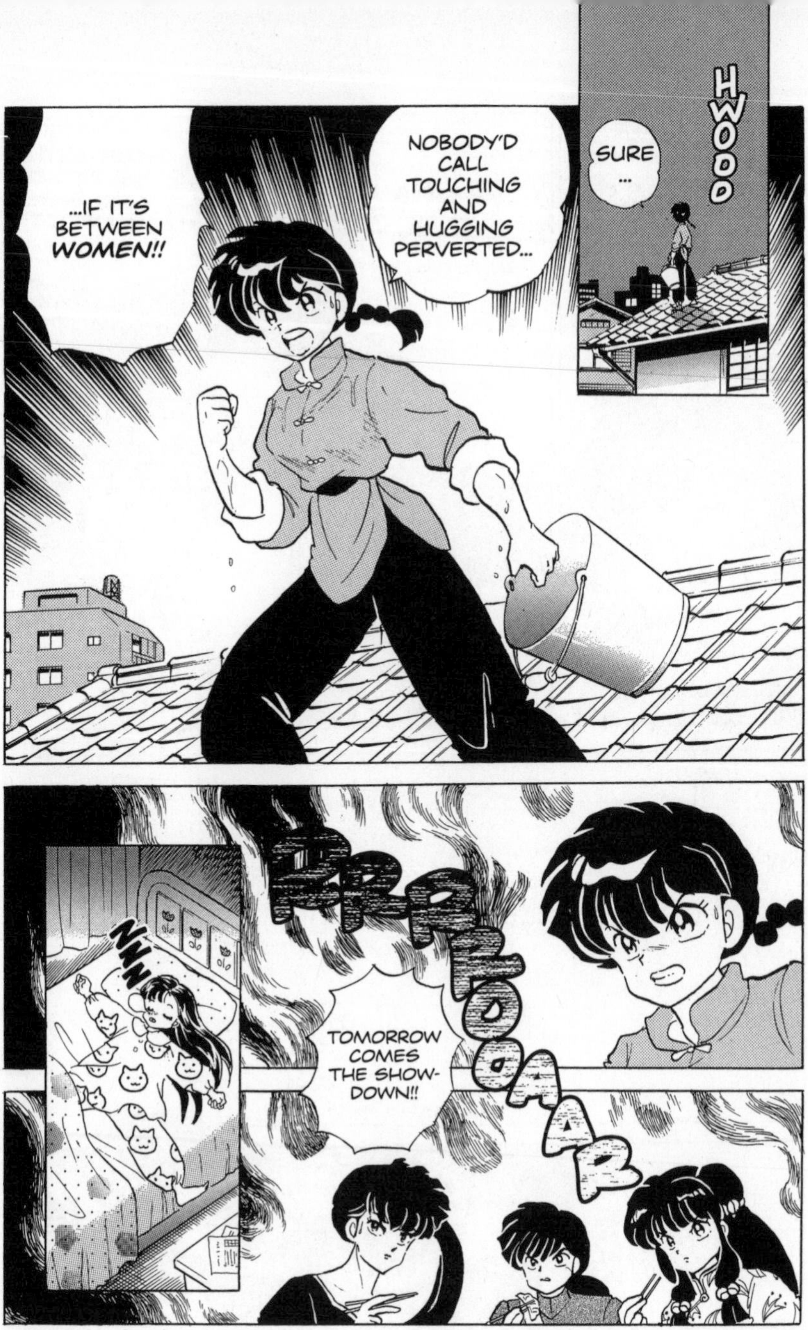
HWOOD
SURE ...
NOBODY'D CALL TOUCHING AND HUGGING PERVERTED...
...IF IT'S BETWEEN WOMEN!!
PRRRZOOAAP
TOMORROW COMES THE SHOW-DOWN!!
NNN

PART 7
THE FORMATION FROM HELL

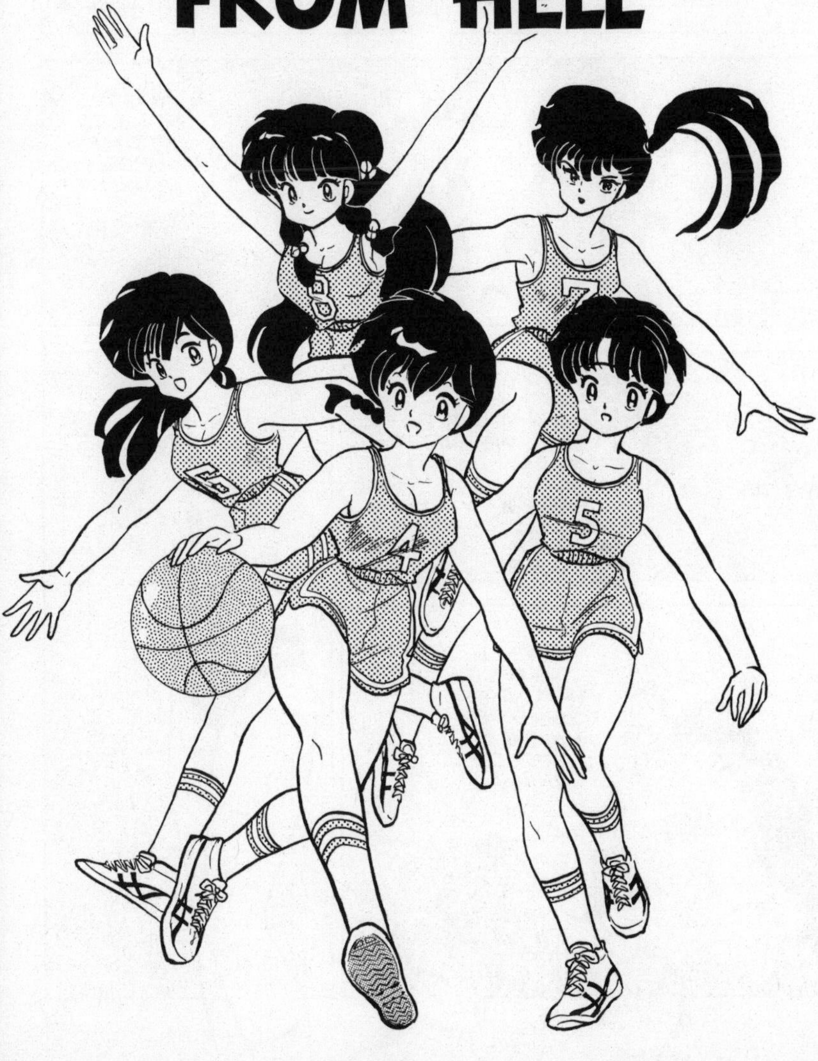

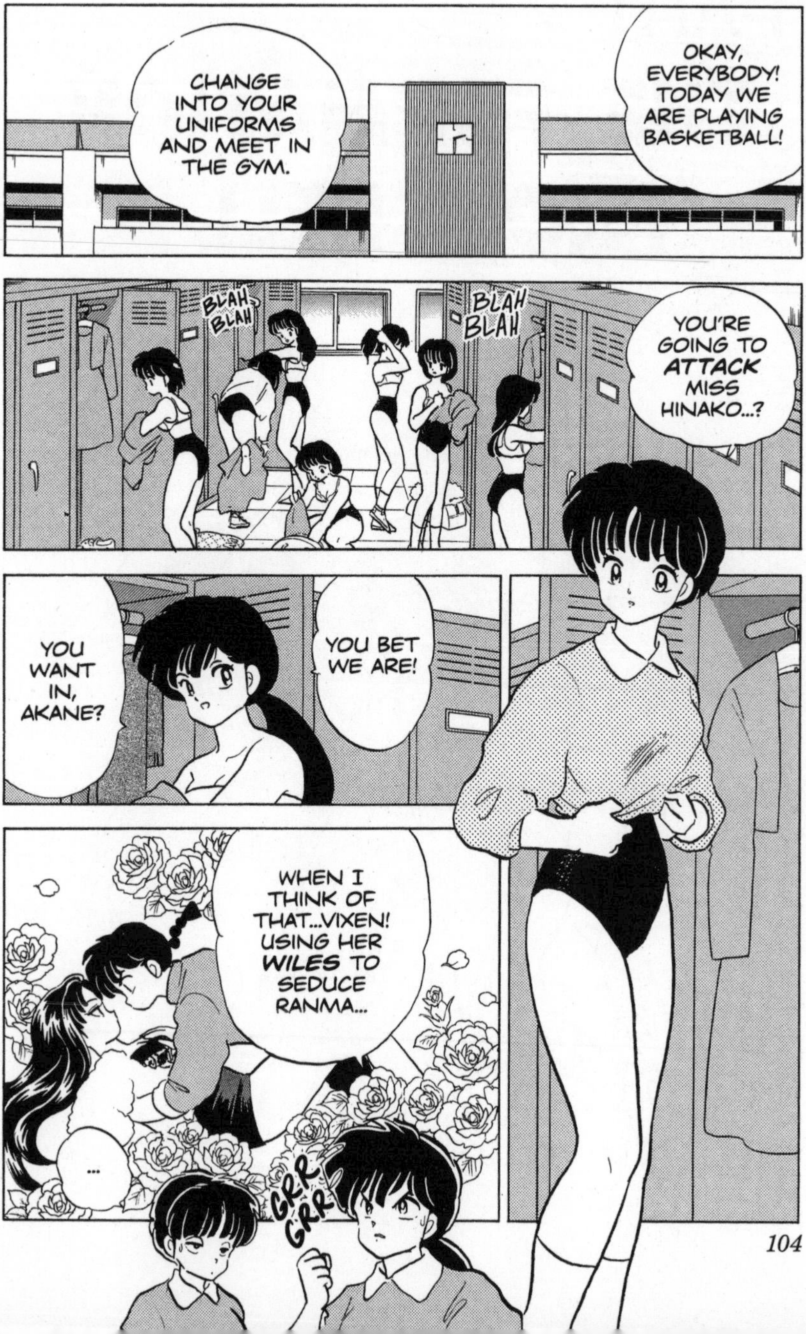

OKAY, EVERYBODY! TODAY WE ARE PLAYING BASKETBALL!
CHANGE INTO YOUR UNIFORMS AND MEET IN THE GYM.
YOU'RE GOING TO ATTACK MISS HINAKO...?
BLAH BLAH
BLAH BLAH
YOU BET WE ARE!
YOU WANT IN, AKANE?
WHEN I THINK OF THAT...VIXEN! USING HER WILES TO SEDUCE RANMA...
...
GRR GRR

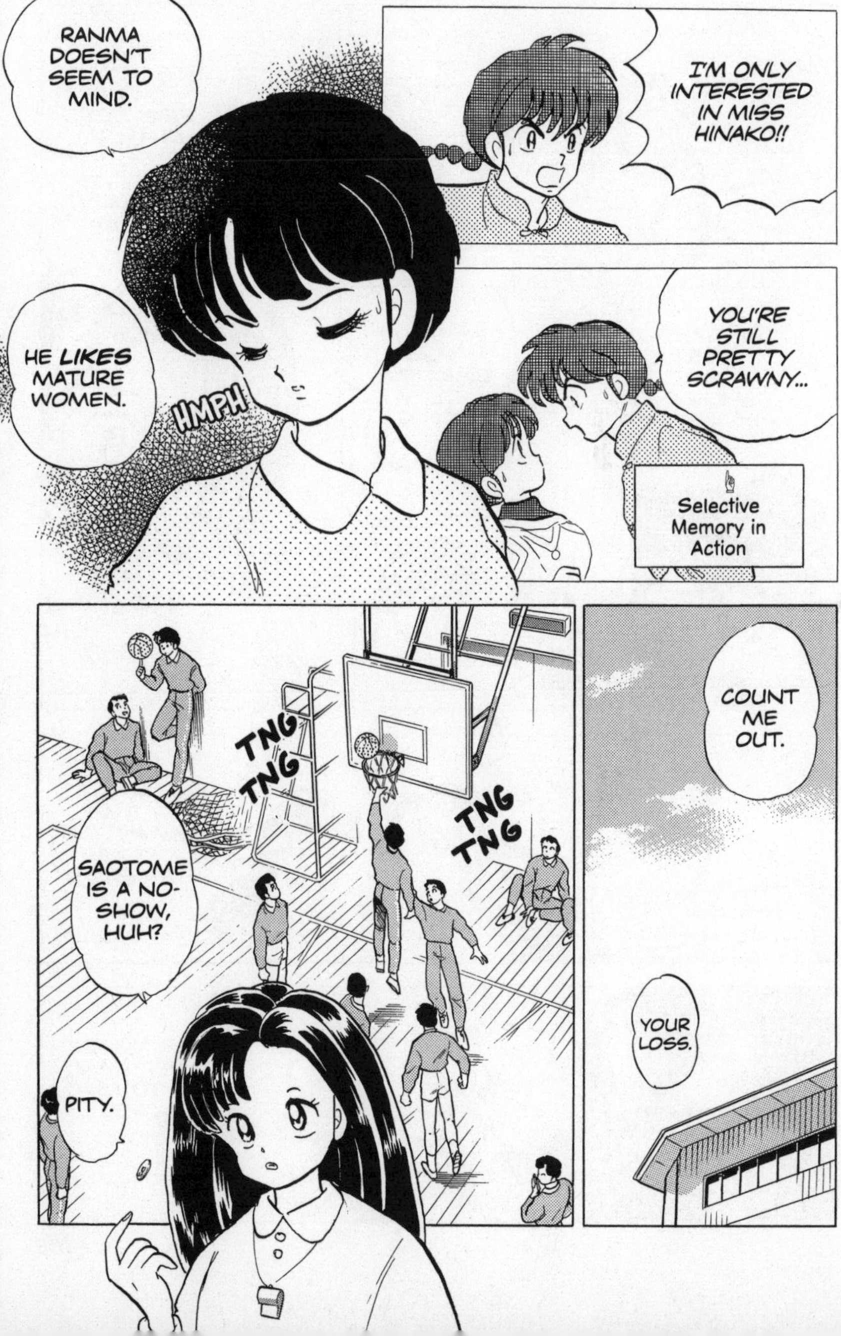
I'M ONLY INTERESTED IN MISS HINAKO!!
RANMA DOESN'T SEEM TO MIND.
YOU'RE STILL PRETTY SCRAWNY...
Selective Memory in Action
HE *LIKES* MATURE WOMEN.
HMPH
COUNT ME OUT.
YOUR LOSS.
TNG TNG
TNG TNG
SAOTOME IS A NO-SHOW, HUH?
PITY.

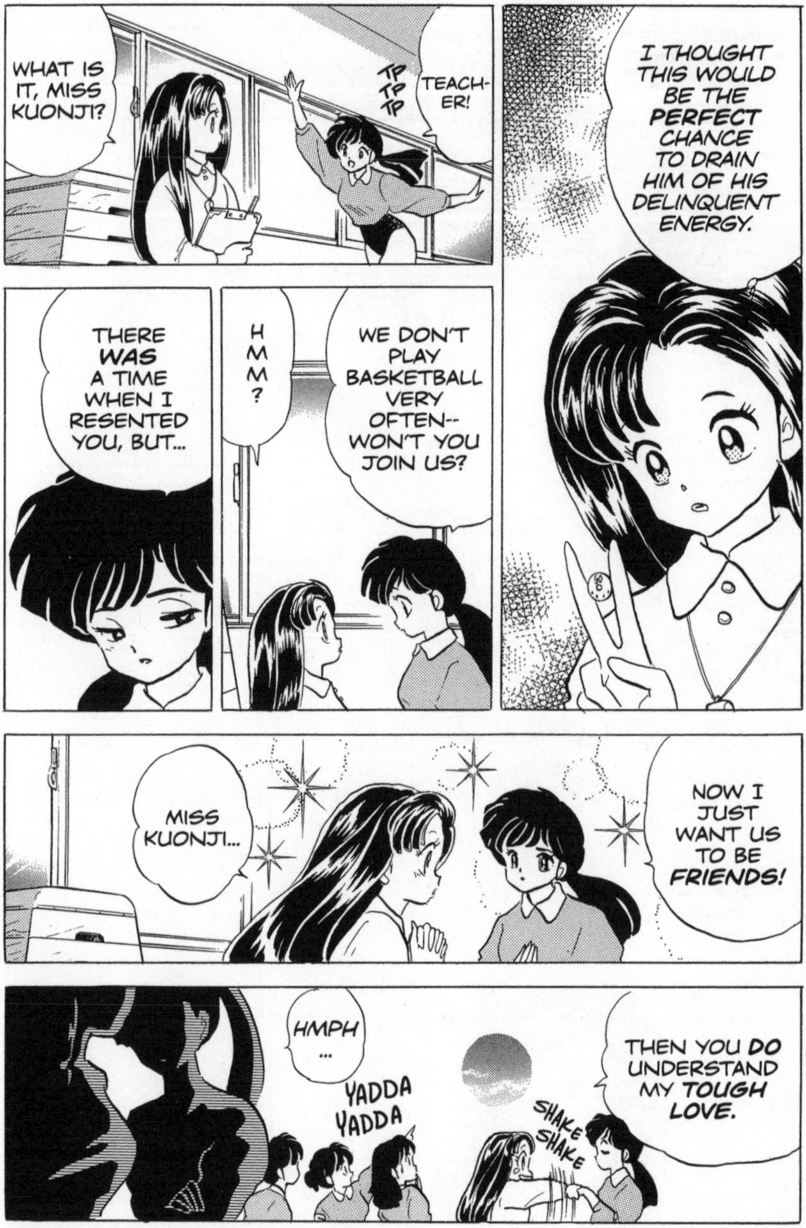
I THOUGHT THIS WOULD BE THE **PERFECT** CHANCE TO DRAIN HIM OF HIS DELINQUENT ENERGY.
TEACHER!
TP TP TP
WHAT IS IT, MISS KUONJI?
WE DON'T PLAY BASKETBALL VERY OFTEN-- WON'T YOU JOIN US?
HMM?
THERE **WAS** A TIME WHEN I RESENTED YOU, BUT...
NOW I JUST WANT US TO BE **FRIENDS!**
MISS KUONJI...
THEN YOU **DO** UNDERSTAND MY **TOUGH LOVE.**
SHAKE SHAKE
YADDA YADDA
HMPH...

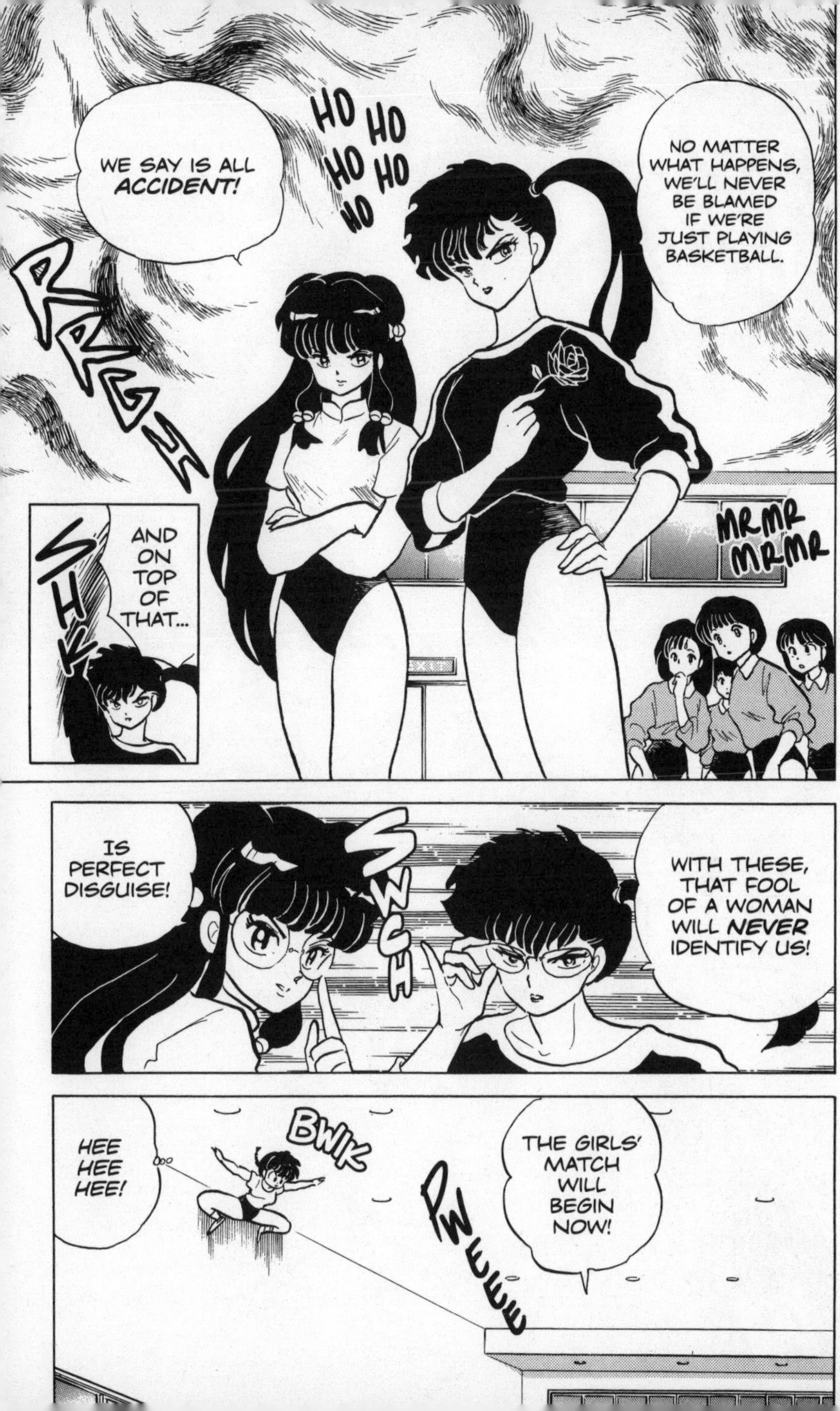
NO MATTER WHAT HAPPENS, WE'LL NEVER BE BLAMED IF WE'RE JUST PLAYING BASKETBALL.
HO HO HO HO HO
WE SAY IS ALL *ACCIDENT!*
RAGGH
MRMR MRMR
AND ON TOP OF THAT...
SHK
WITH THESE, THAT FOOL OF A WOMAN WILL *NEVER* IDENTIFY US!
SWCH
IS PERFECT DISGUISE!
THE GIRLS' MATCH WILL BEGIN NOW!
PWEEEE
BWIK
HEE HEE HEE!

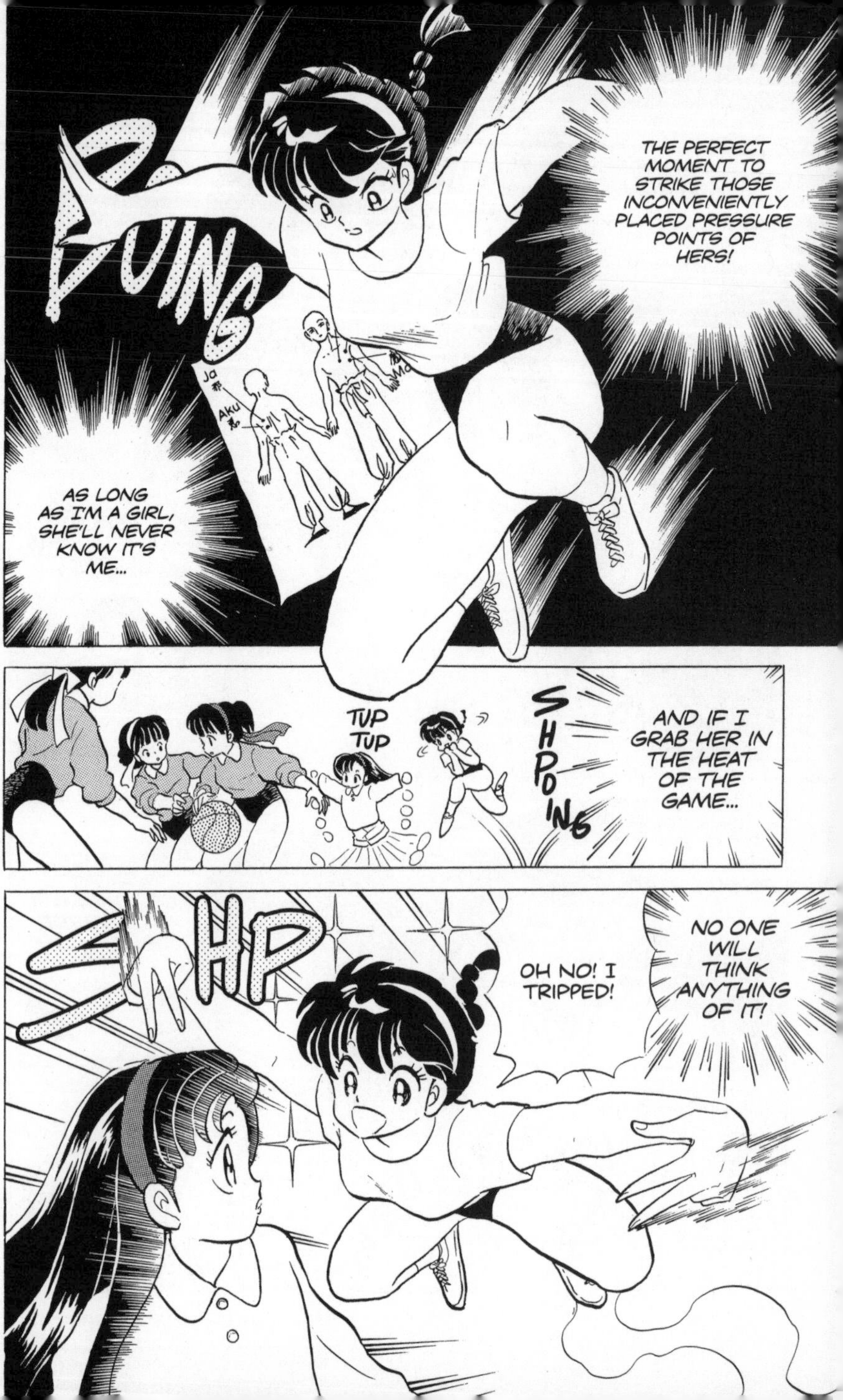
THE PERFECT MOMENT TO STRIKE THOSE INCONVENIENTLY PLACED PRESSURE POINTS OF HERS!
Ma
Ja
Aku
AS LONG AS I'M A GIRL, SHE'LL NEVER KNOW IT'S ME...
AND IF I GRAB HER IN THE HEAT OF THE GAME...
SHPOING
TUP TUP
NO ONE WILL THINK ANYTHING OF IT!
OH NO! I TRIPPED!
SHP

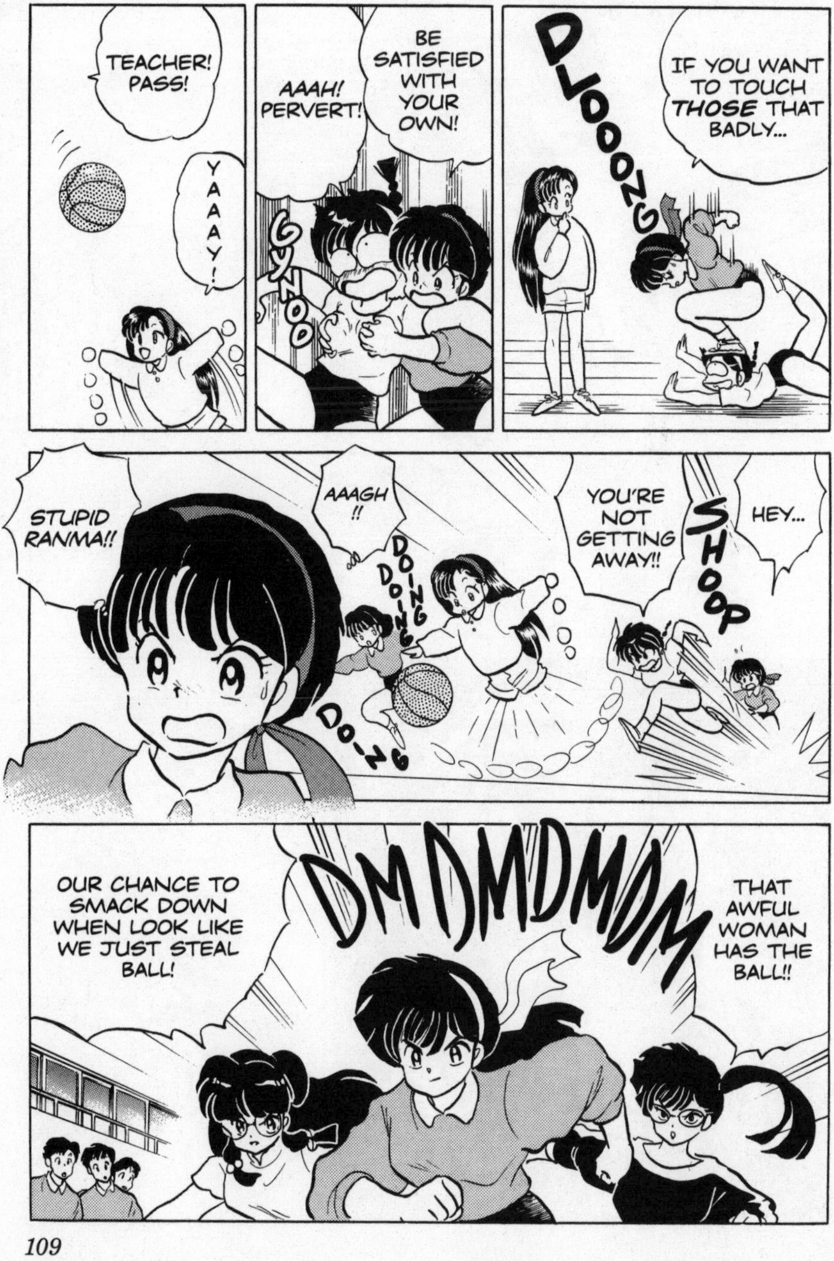
IF YOU WANT TO TOUCH *THOSE* THAT BADLY...
DLOOOONG
BE SATISFIED WITH YOUR OWN!
AAAH! PERVERT!
GYNOO
TEACHER! PASS!
YAAAAY!
HEY...
SHOOP
YOU'RE NOT GETTING AWAY!!
DOING DOING
AAAGH!!
DO-ING
STUPID RANMA!!
THAT AWFUL WOMAN HAS THE BALL!!
DMDMDMDM
OUR CHANCE TO SMACK DOWN WHEN LOOK LIKE WE JUST STEAL BALL!

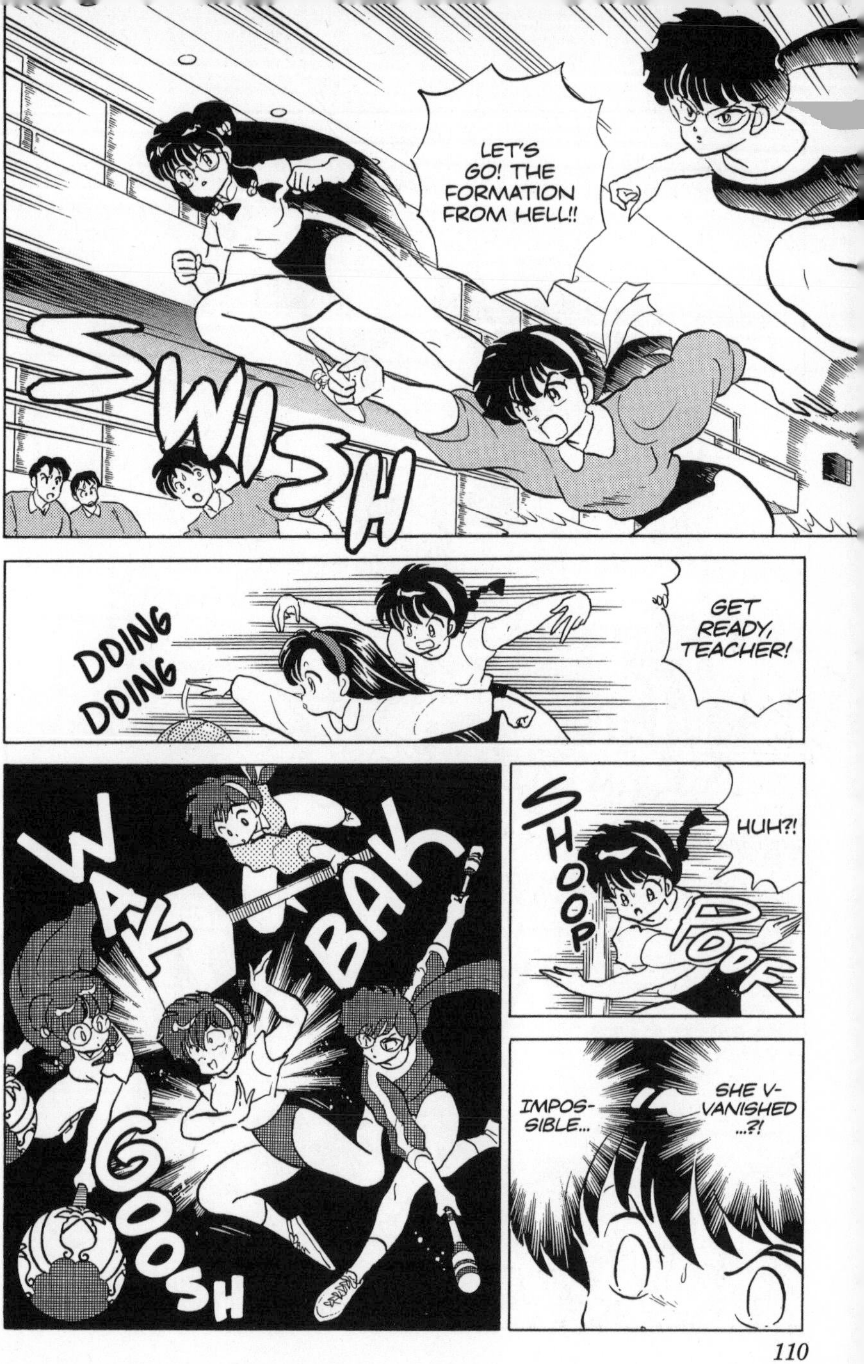
LET'S GO! THE FORMATION FROM HELL!!
SWISH
GET READY, TEACHER!
DDOING DDOING
HUH?!
POOF
SHOOP
SHE V-VANISHED ...?!
IMPOSSIBLE...
BAK
WAK
GOOSH

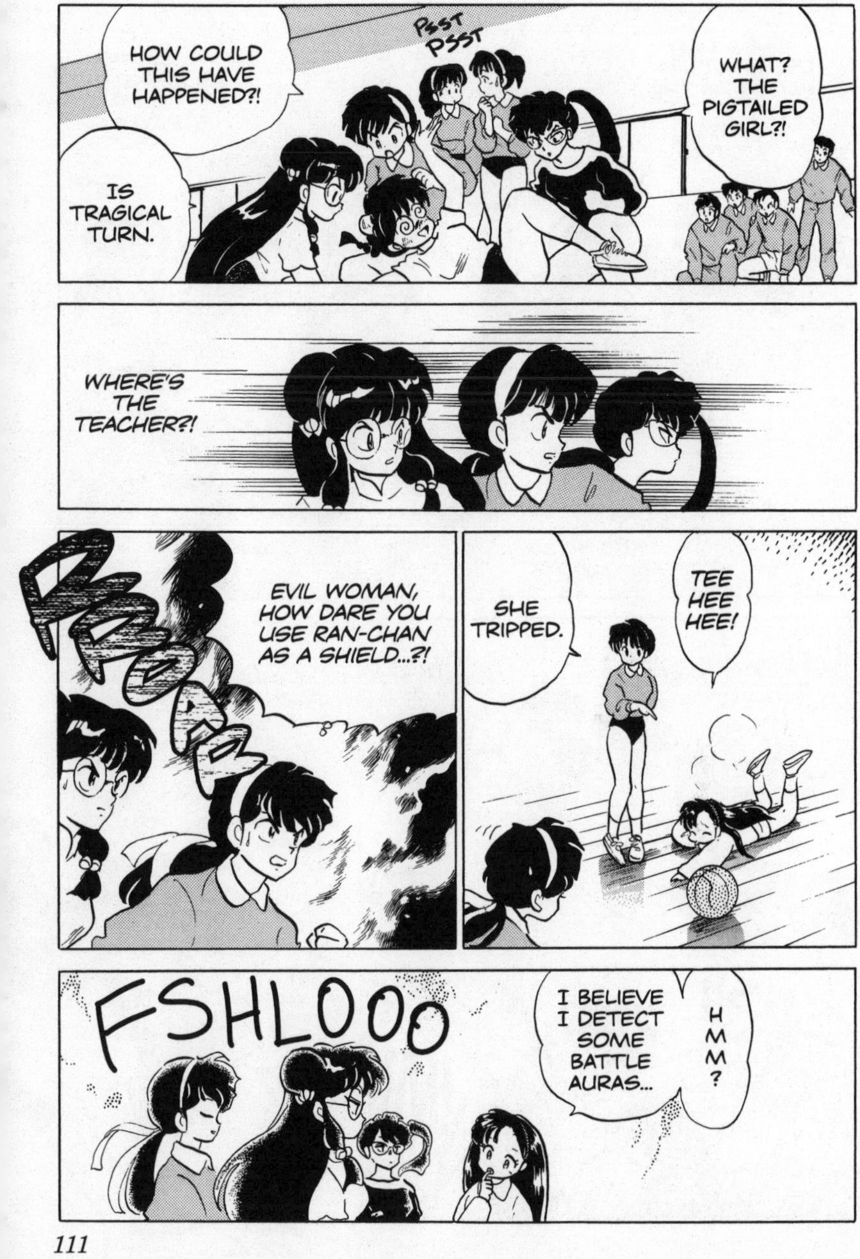
WHAT? THE PIGTAILED GIRL?!
PSST PSST
HOW COULD THIS HAVE HAPPENED?!
IS TRAGICAL TURN.
WHERE'S THE TEACHER?!
TEE HEE HEE!
SHE TRIPPED.
EVIL WOMAN, HOW DARE YOU USE RAN-CHAN AS A SHIELD...?!
HMM?
I BELIEVE I DETECT SOME BATTLE AURAS...
FSHLOOO

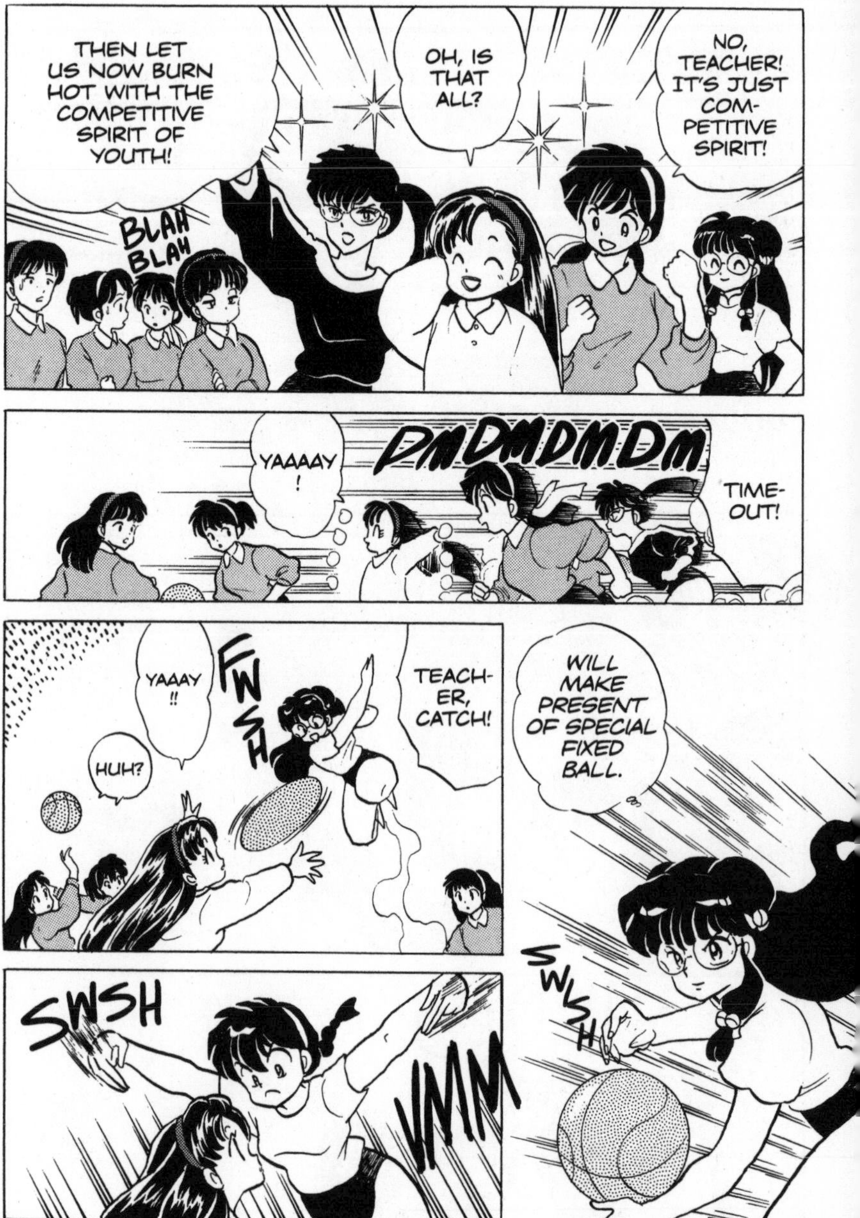
NO, TEACHER! IT'S JUST COM-PETITIVE SPIRIT!
OH, IS THAT ALL?
THEN LET US NOW BURN HOT WITH THE COMPETITIVE SPIRIT OF YOUTH!
BLAH BLAH
TIME-OUT!
DMDMDMDMDM
YAAAAY!
WILL MAKE PRESENT OF SPECIAL FIXED BALL.
SWSH
TEACH-ER, CATCH!
FWSH
YAAAY!!
HUH?
VMM
SWSH

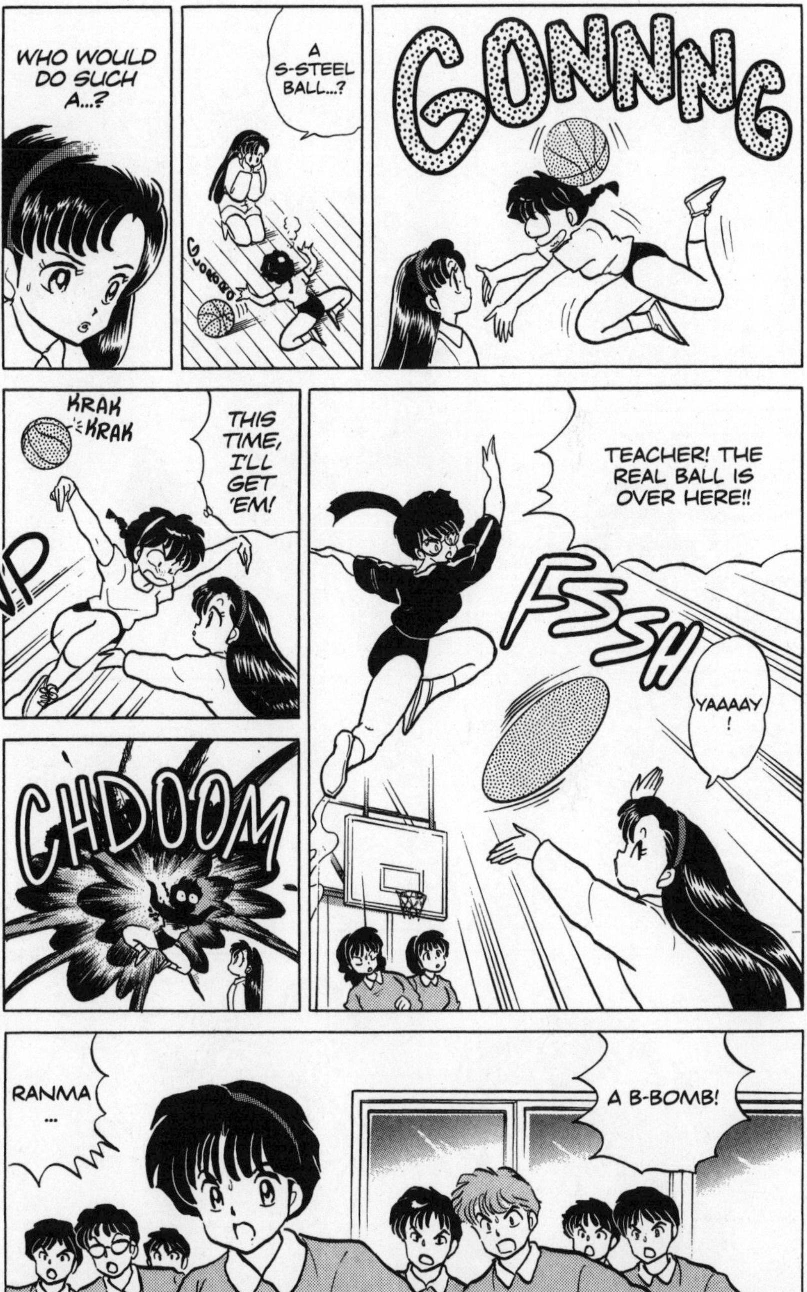
GONNNG
A S-STEEL BALL...?
WHO WOULD DO SUCH A...?
TEACHER! THE REAL BALL IS OVER HERE!!
FSSH
YAAAAY!
KRAK KRAK
THIS TIME, I'LL GET 'EM!
VP
CHDOOM
A B-BOMB!
RANMA ...

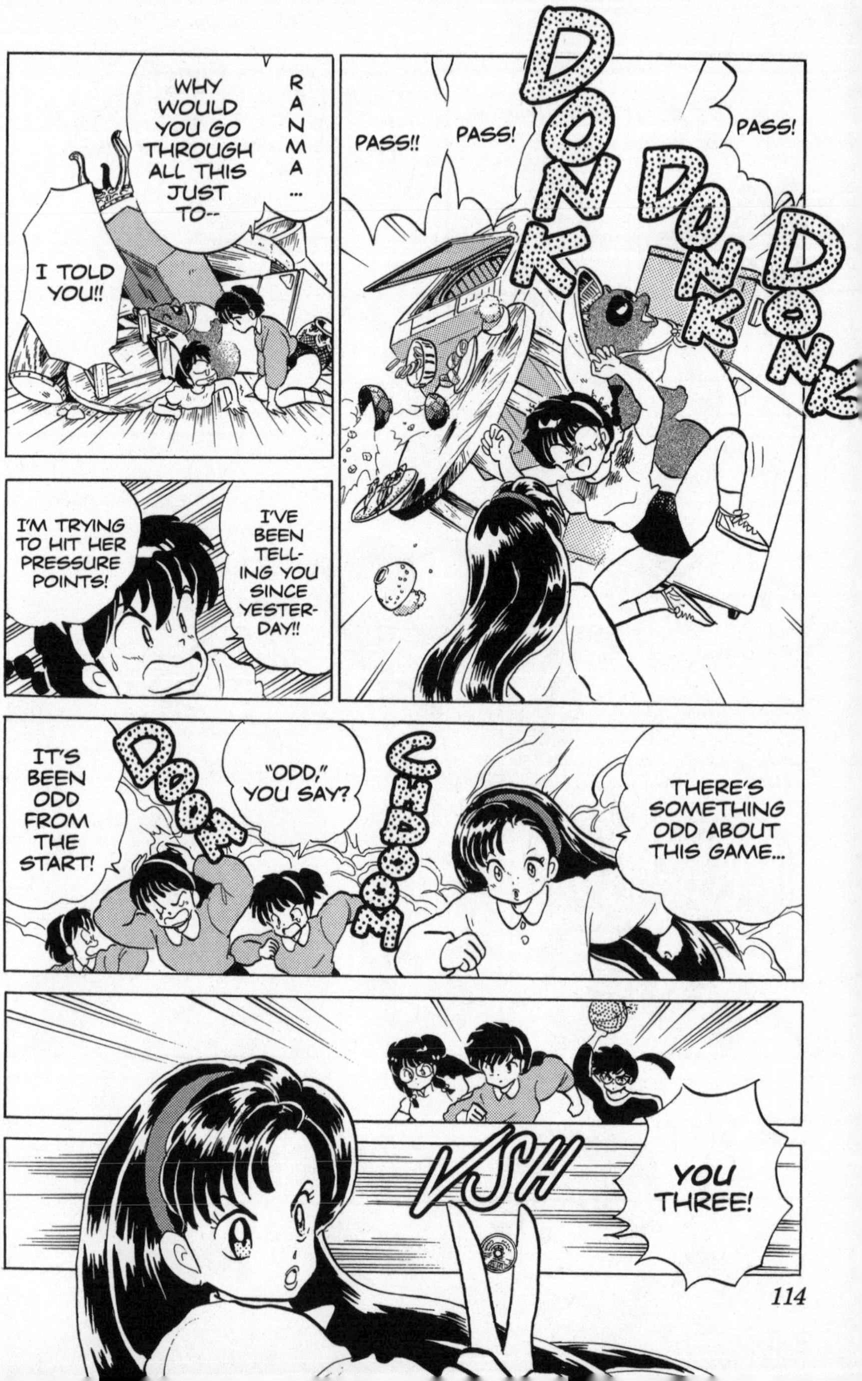
PASS!
DONK
DONK
DONK
PASS!
PASS!!
RANMA...
WHY WOULD YOU GO THROUGH ALL THIS JUST TO--
I TOLD YOU!!
I'VE BEEN TELL-ING YOU SINCE YESTER-DAY!!
I'M TRYING TO HIT HER PRESSURE POINTS!
THERE'S SOMETHING ODD ABOUT THIS GAME...
CHDOOM
"ODD," YOU SAY?
DOOM
IT'S BEEN ODD FROM THE START!
YOU THREE!
VSH

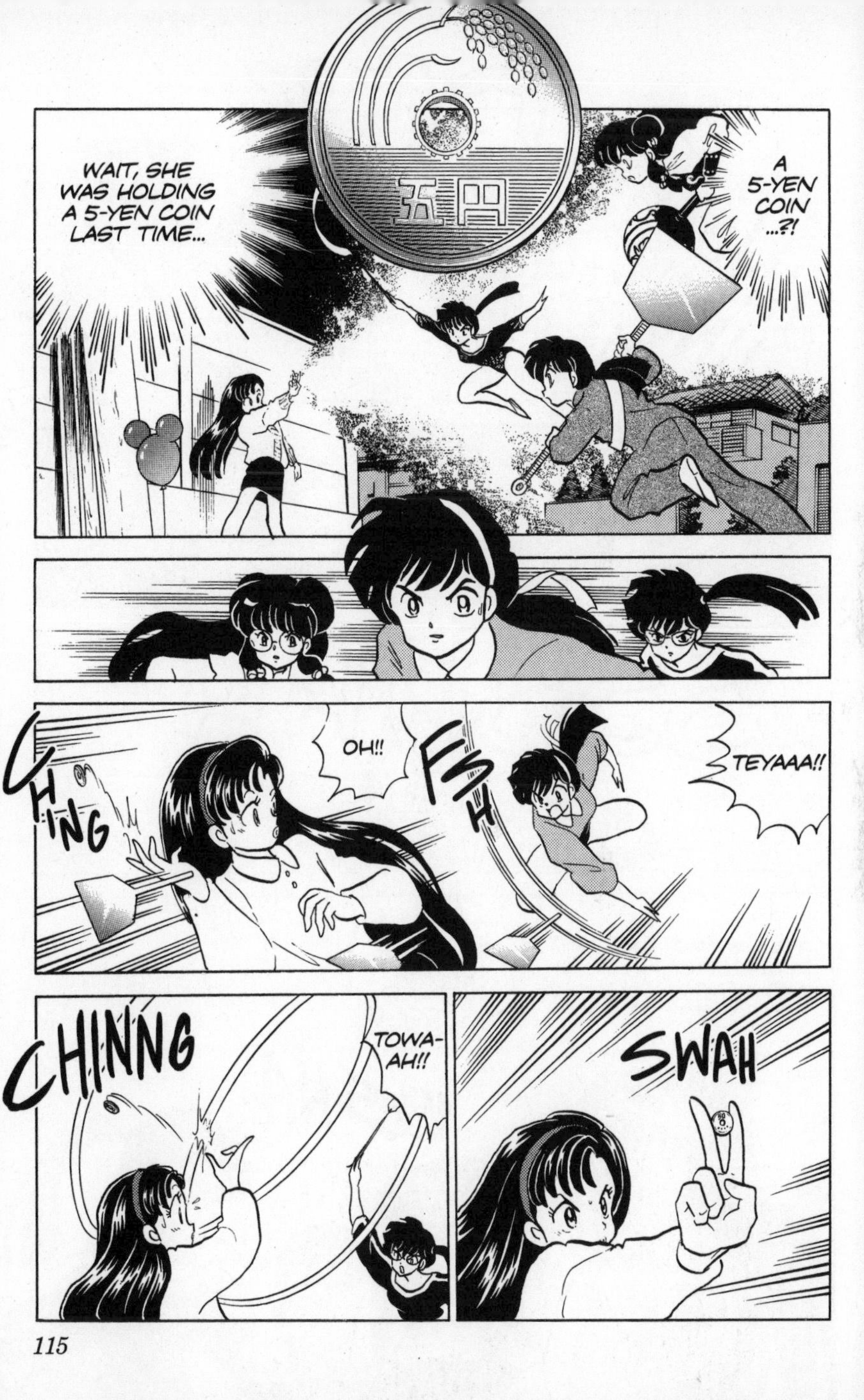
A 5-YEN COIN ...?!
WAIT, SHE WAS HOLDING A 5-YEN COIN LAST TIME...
TEYAAA!!
FSH
OH!!
CHING
SWAH
TOWA-AH!!
CHINNG

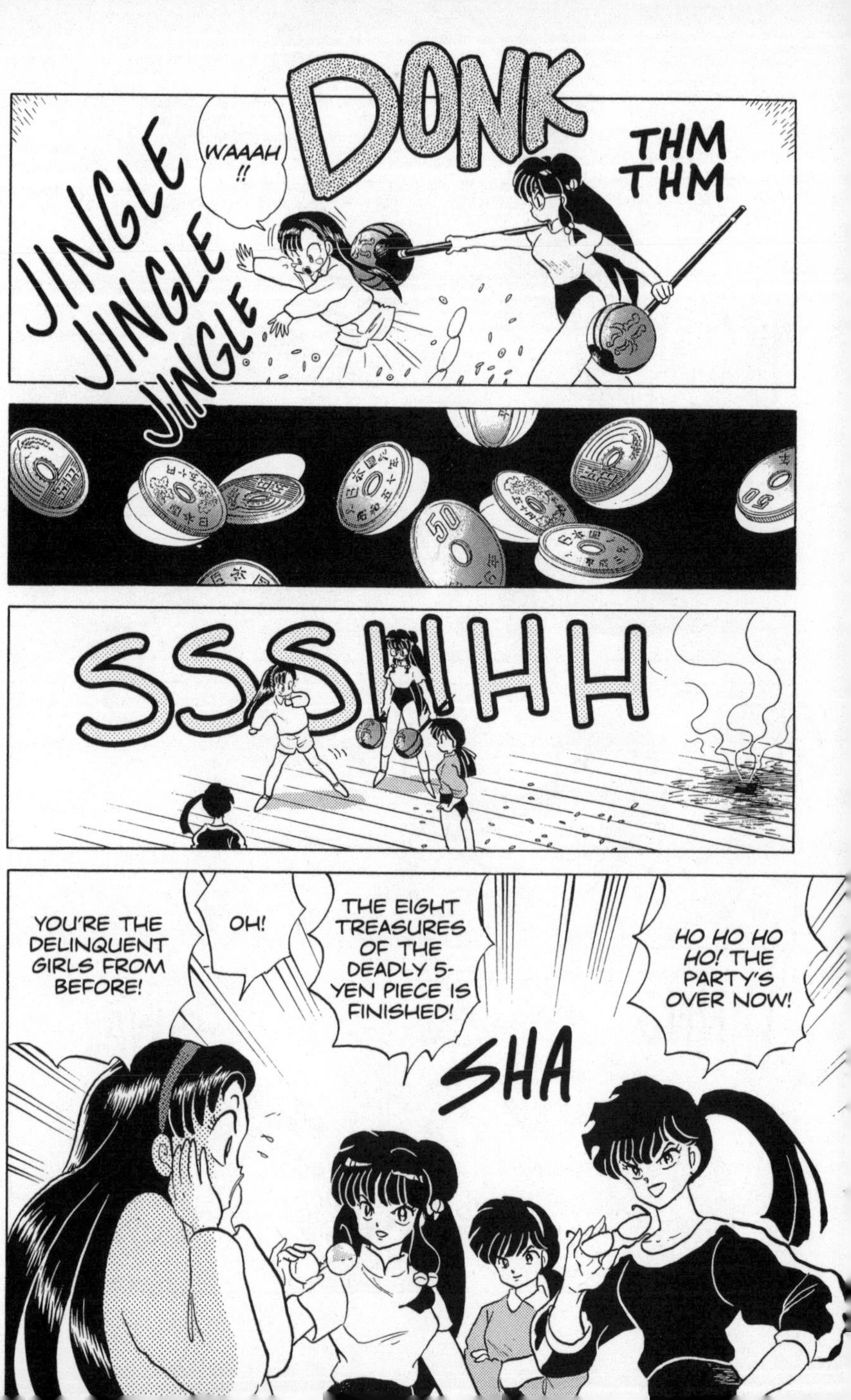
DONK
THM THM
WAAAH !!
JINGLE JINGLE JINGLE
SSSHHH
HO HO HO HO! THE PARTY'S OVER NOW!
SHA
THE EIGHT TREASURES OF THE DEADLY 5-YEN PIECE IS FINISHED!
OH!
YOU'RE THE DELINQUENT GIRLS FROM BEFORE!

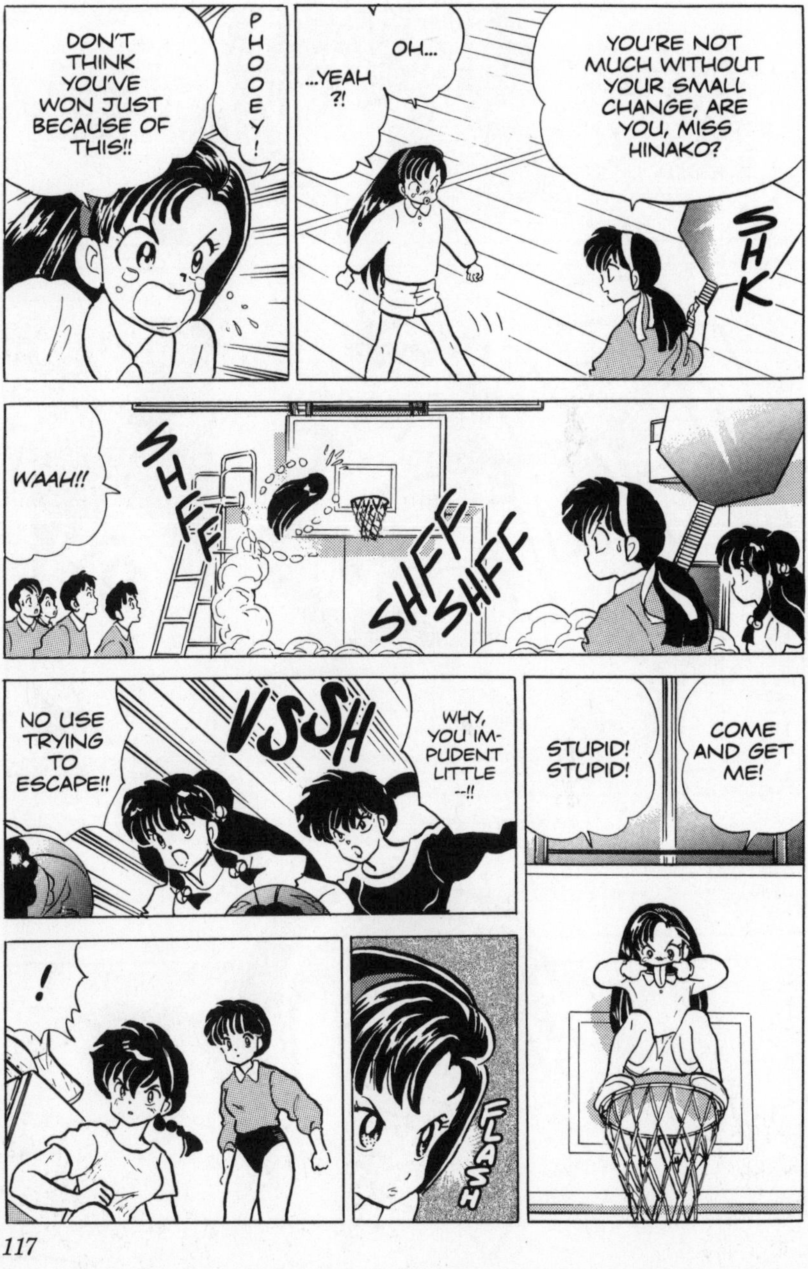
YOU'RE NOT MUCH WITHOUT YOUR SMALL CHANGE, ARE YOU, MISS HINAKO?
OH...
...YEAH ?!
SHK
PHOOEY!
DON'T THINK YOU'VE WON JUST BECAUSE OF THIS!!
SHFF
WAAH!!
SHFF SHFF
COME AND GET ME!
STUPID! STUPID!
WHY, YOU IMPUDENT LITTLE --!!
VSSH
NO USE TRYING TO ESCAPE!!
FLASH
!

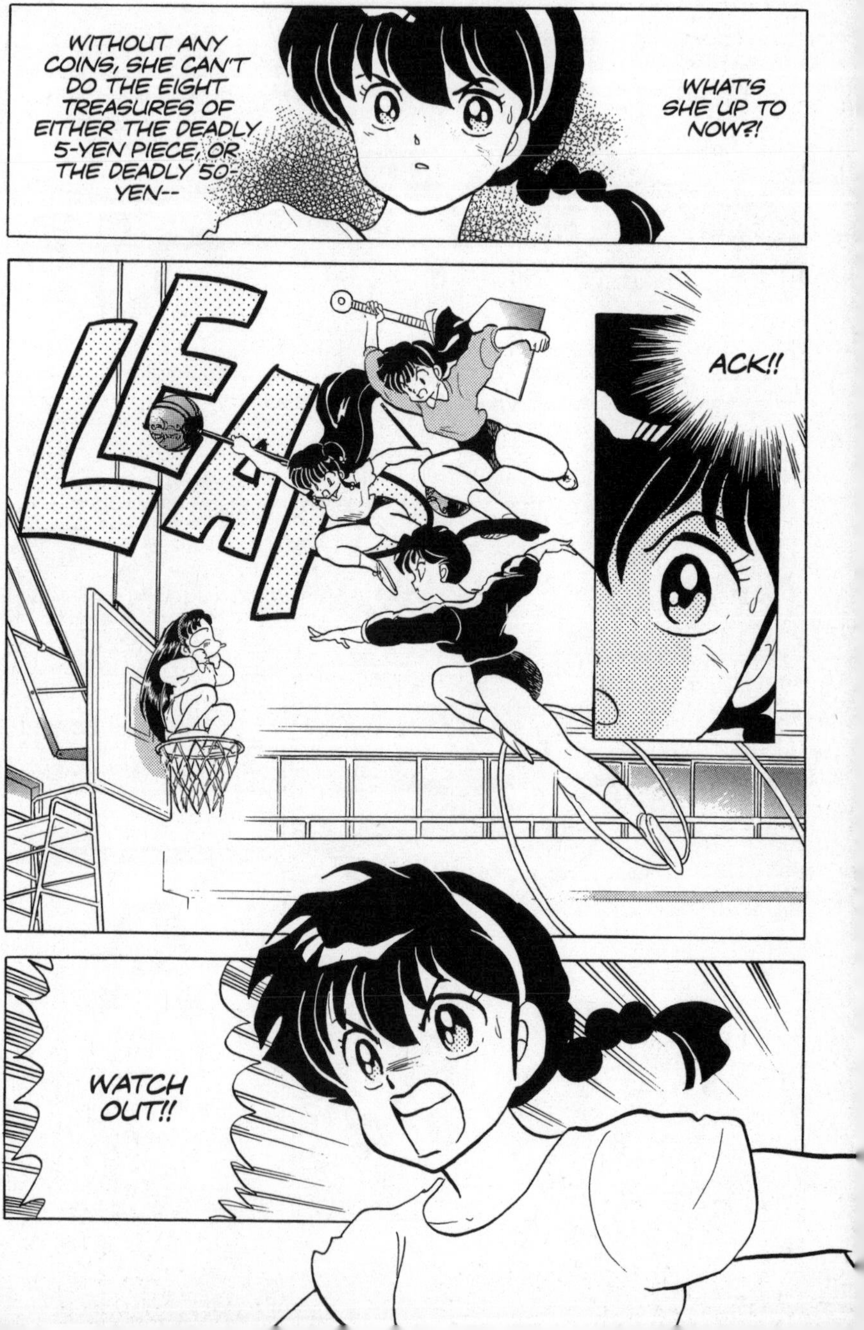
WHAT'S SHE UP TO NOW?!
WITHOUT ANY COINS, SHE CAN'T DO THE EIGHT TREASURES OF EITHER THE DEADLY 5-YEN PIECE, OR THE DEADLY 50-YEN--
ACK!!
LEAP
WATCH OUT!!

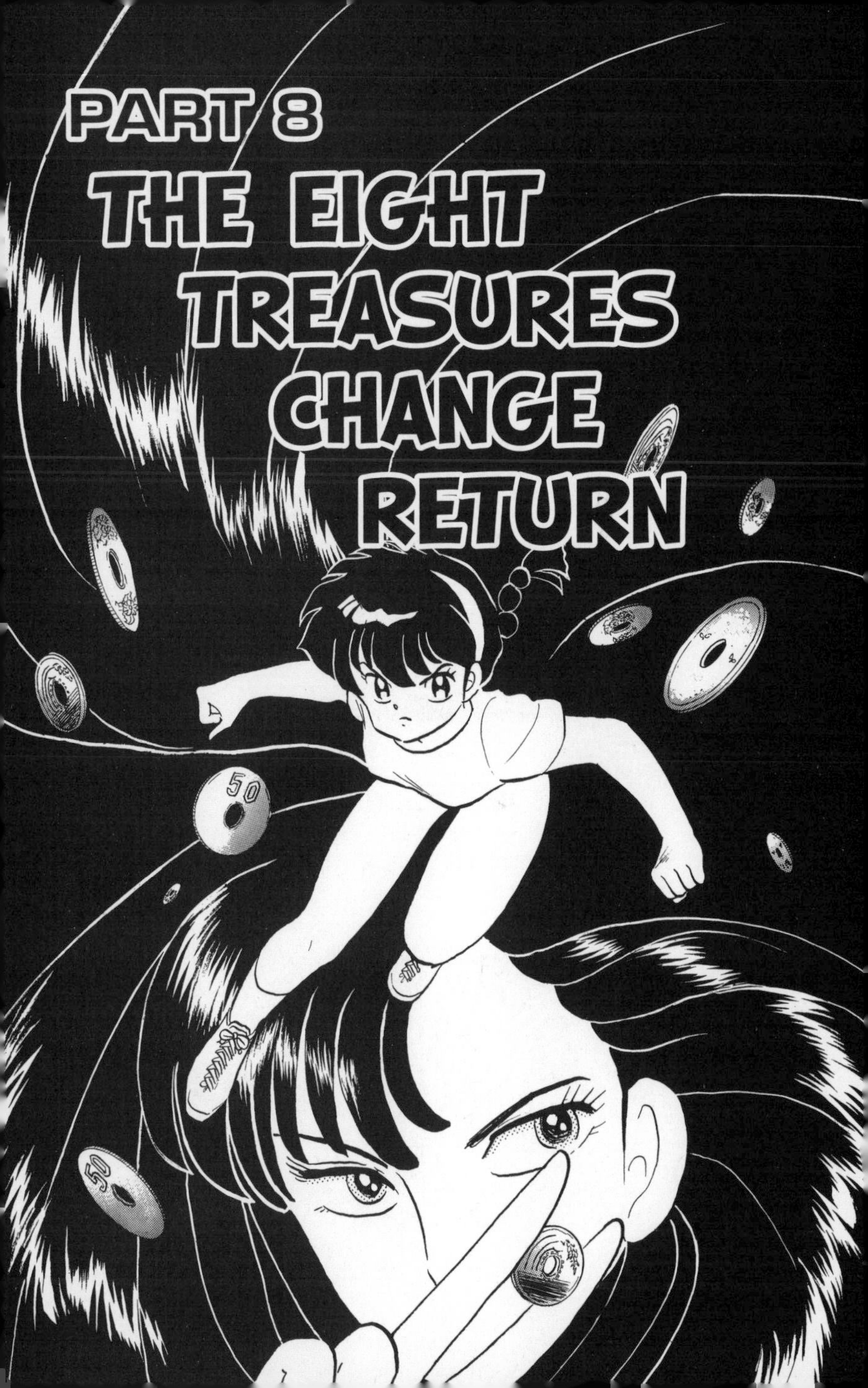
PART 8
THE EIGHT TREASURES CHANGE RETURN
50
50

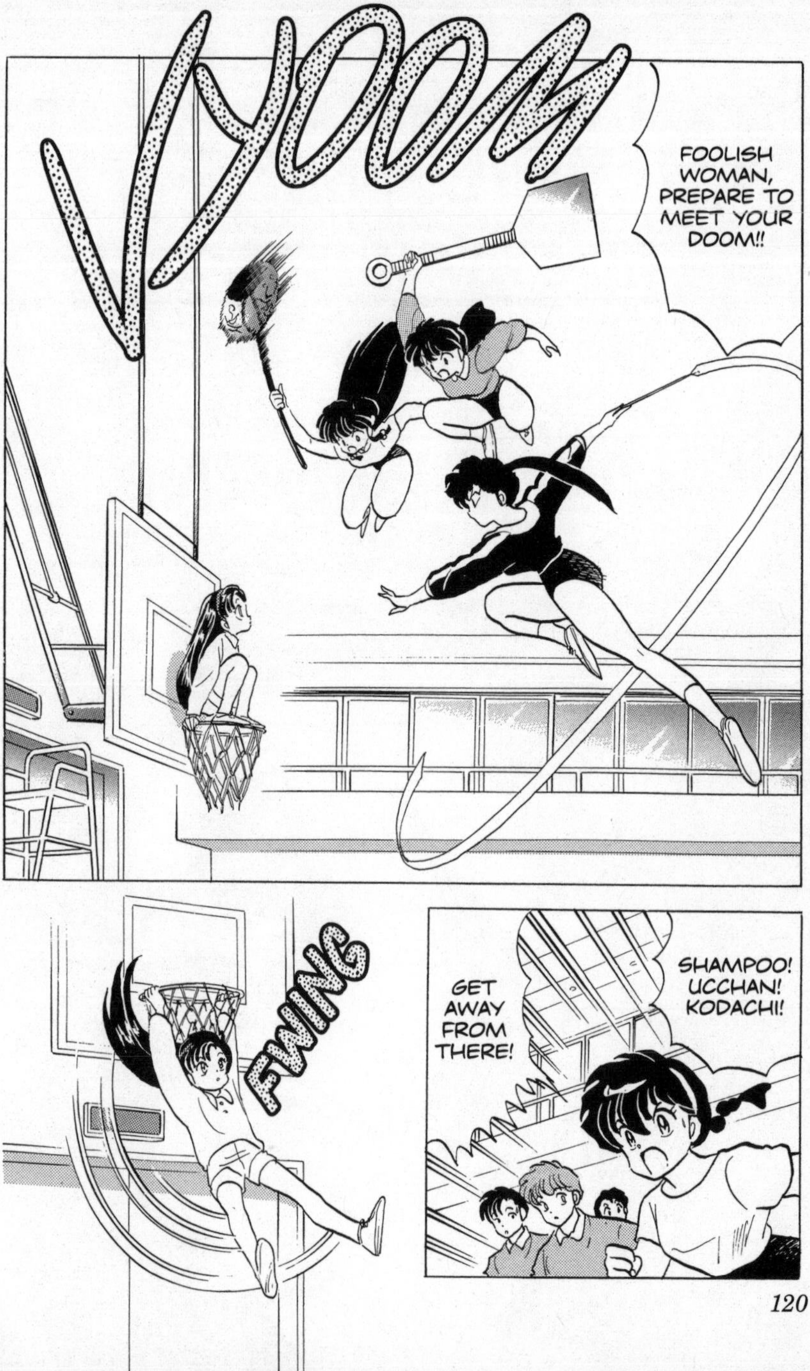
VROOM
FOOLISH WOMAN, PREPARE TO MEET YOUR DOOM!!
SHAMPOO! UCCHAN! KODACHI!
GET AWAY FROM THERE!
FWING

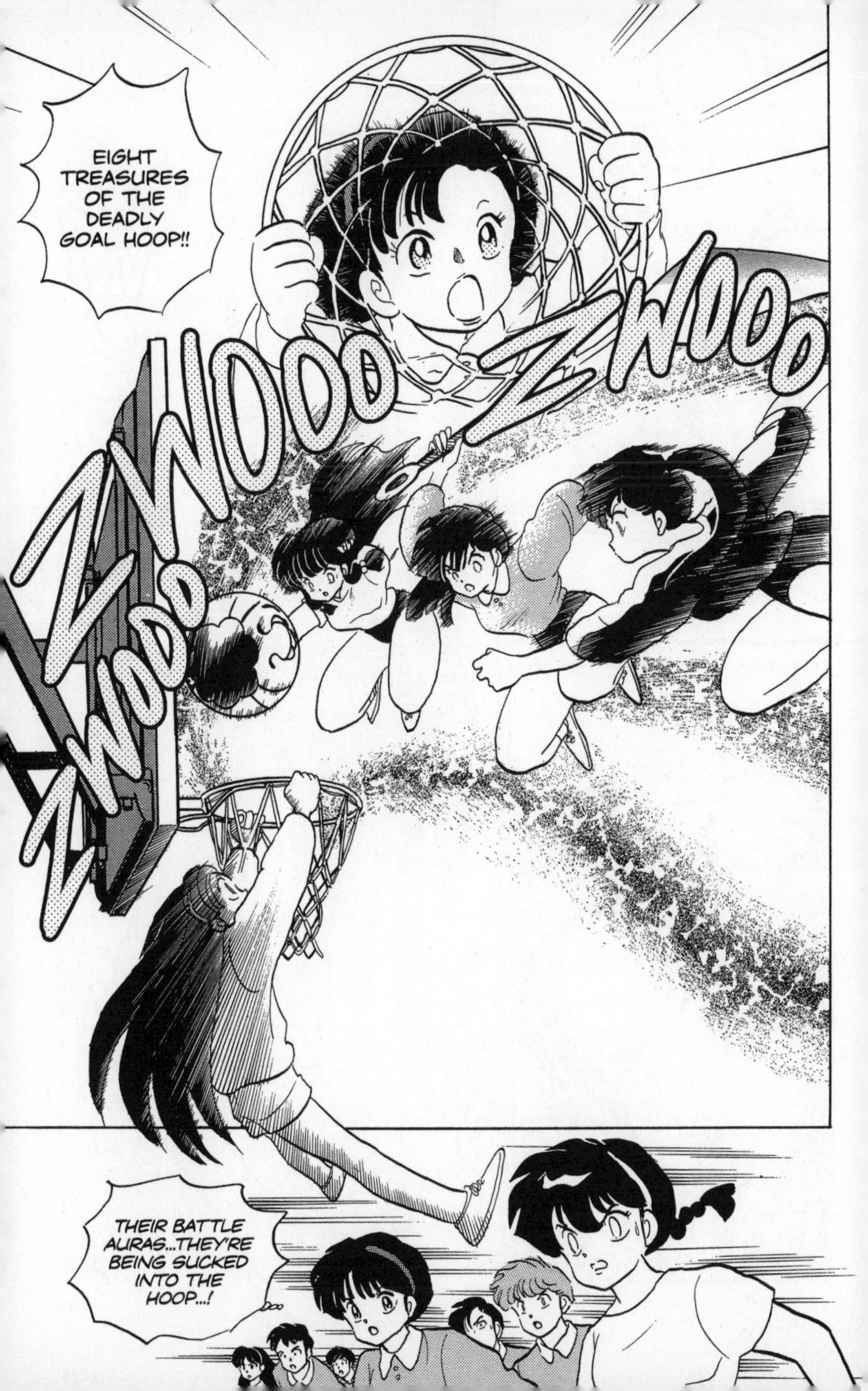
EIGHT TREASURES OF THE DEADLY GOAL HOOP!!
ZWOOO ZWOOO
ZWOOO
THEIR BATTLE AURAS...THEY'RE BEING SUCKED INTO THE HOOP...!

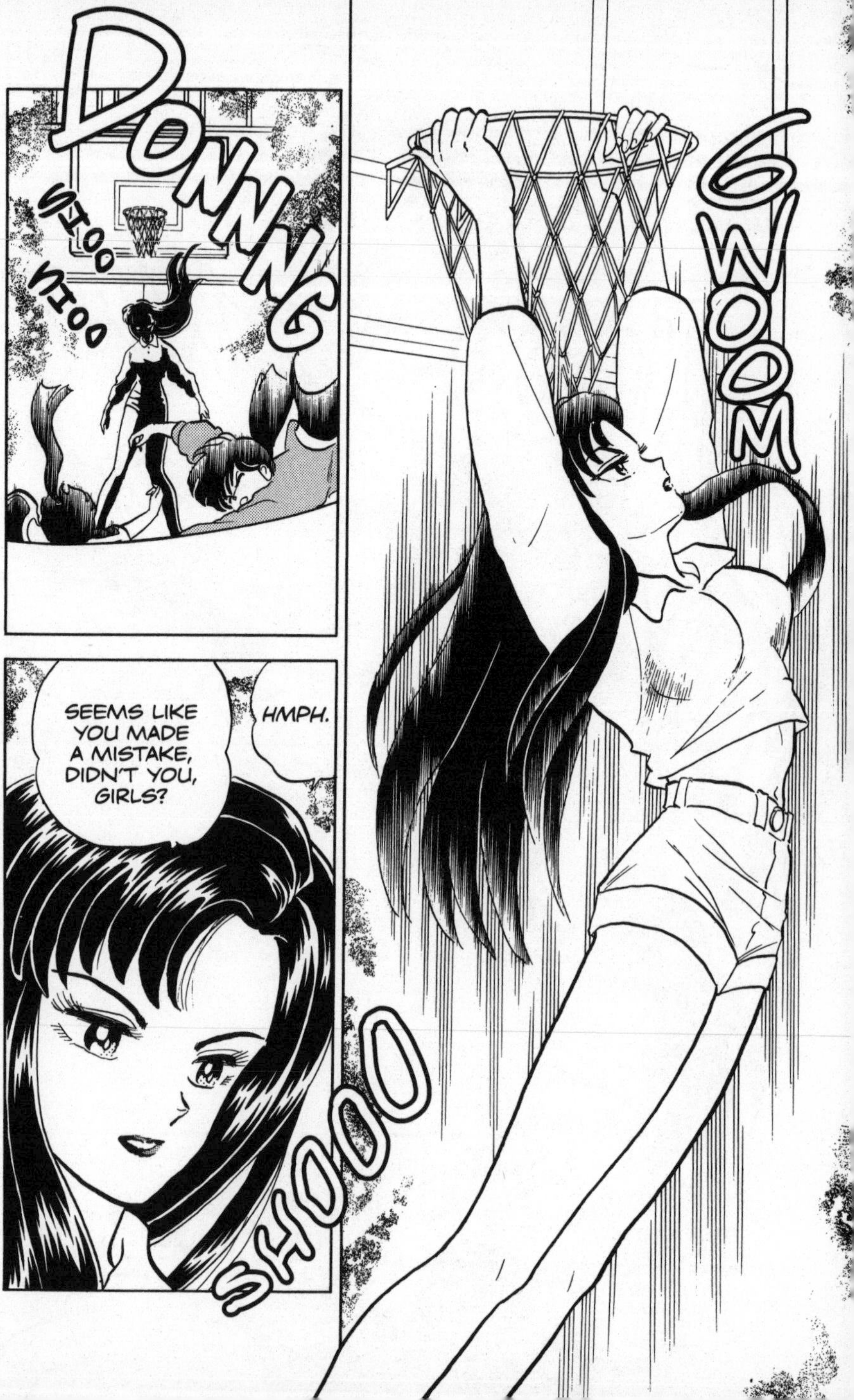
GWOOM
SHOOOO
DONNNG
SHOO SHOO
HMPH.
SEEMS LIKE YOU MADE A MISTAKE, DIDN'T YOU, GIRLS?

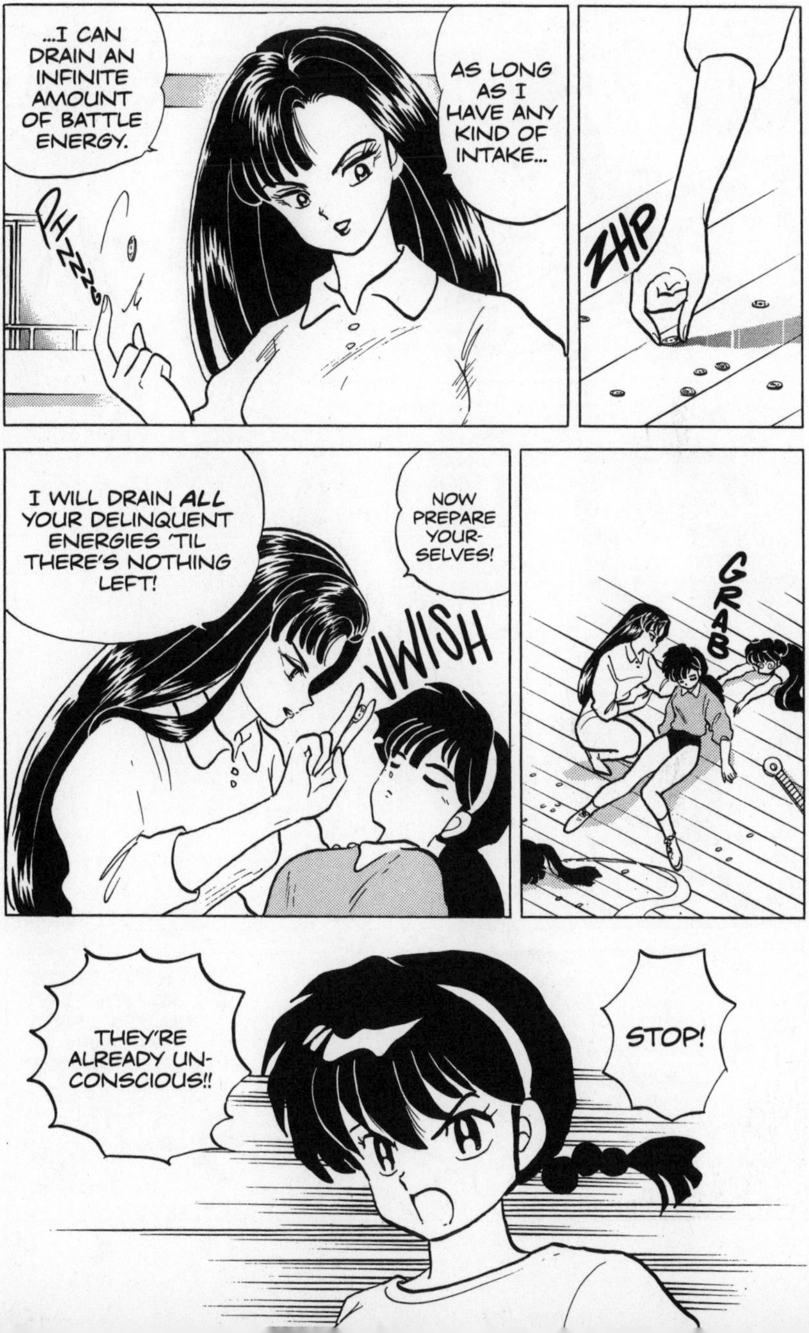
ZHP
AS LONG AS I HAVE ANY KIND OF INTAKE...
...I CAN DRAIN AN INFINITE AMOUNT OF BATTLE ENERGY.
PHZZZZ
GRAB
NOW PREPARE YOUR-SELVES!
I WILL DRAIN ALL YOUR DELINQUENT ENERGIES 'TIL THERE'S NOTHING LEFT!
VWISH
STOP!
THEY'RE ALREADY UN-CONSCIOUS!!

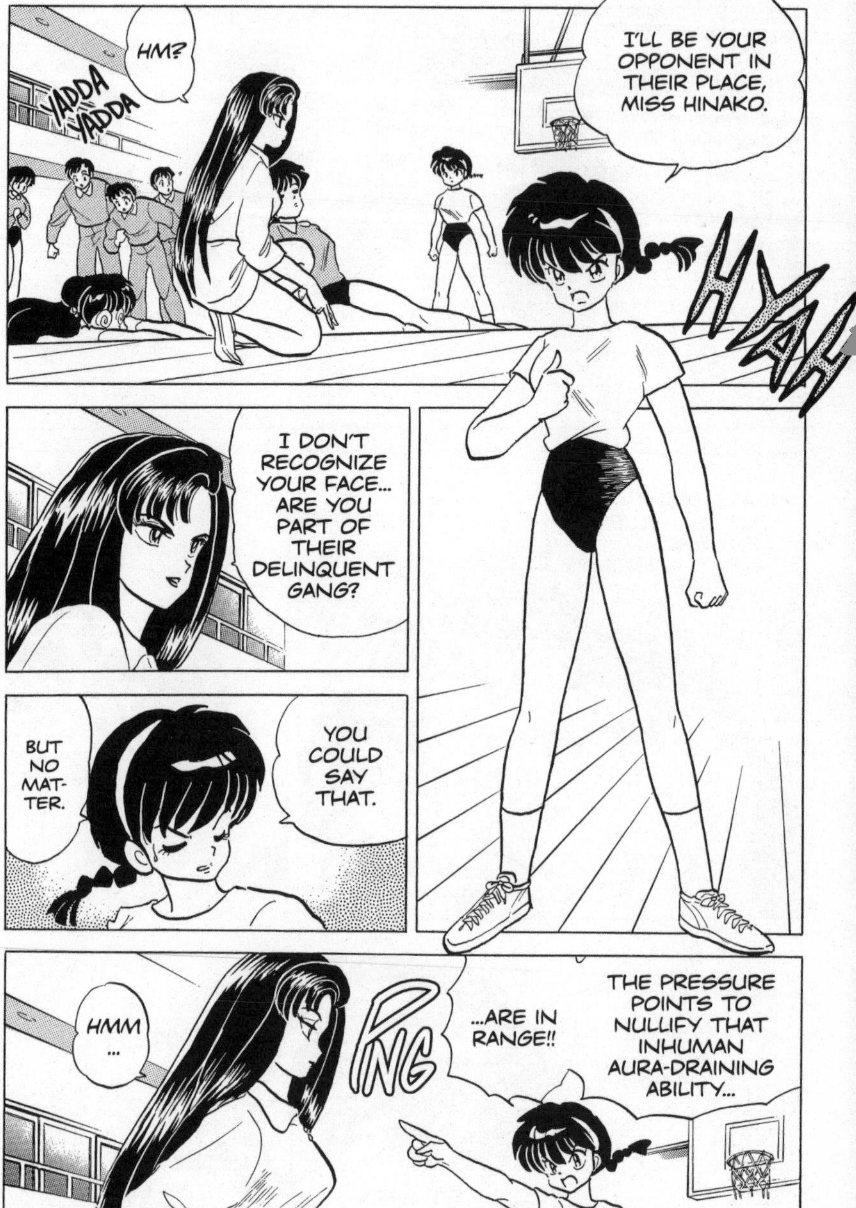
I'LL BE YOUR OPPONENT IN THEIR PLACE, MISS HINAKO.
HYAH
HM?
YADDA YADDA
I DON'T RECOGNIZE YOUR FACE... ARE YOU PART OF THEIR DELINQUENT GANG?
YOU COULD SAY THAT.
BUT NO MAT-TER.
THE PRESSURE POINTS TO NULLIFY THAT INHUMAN AURA-DRAINING ABILITY...
...ARE IN RANGE!!
PING
HMM ...

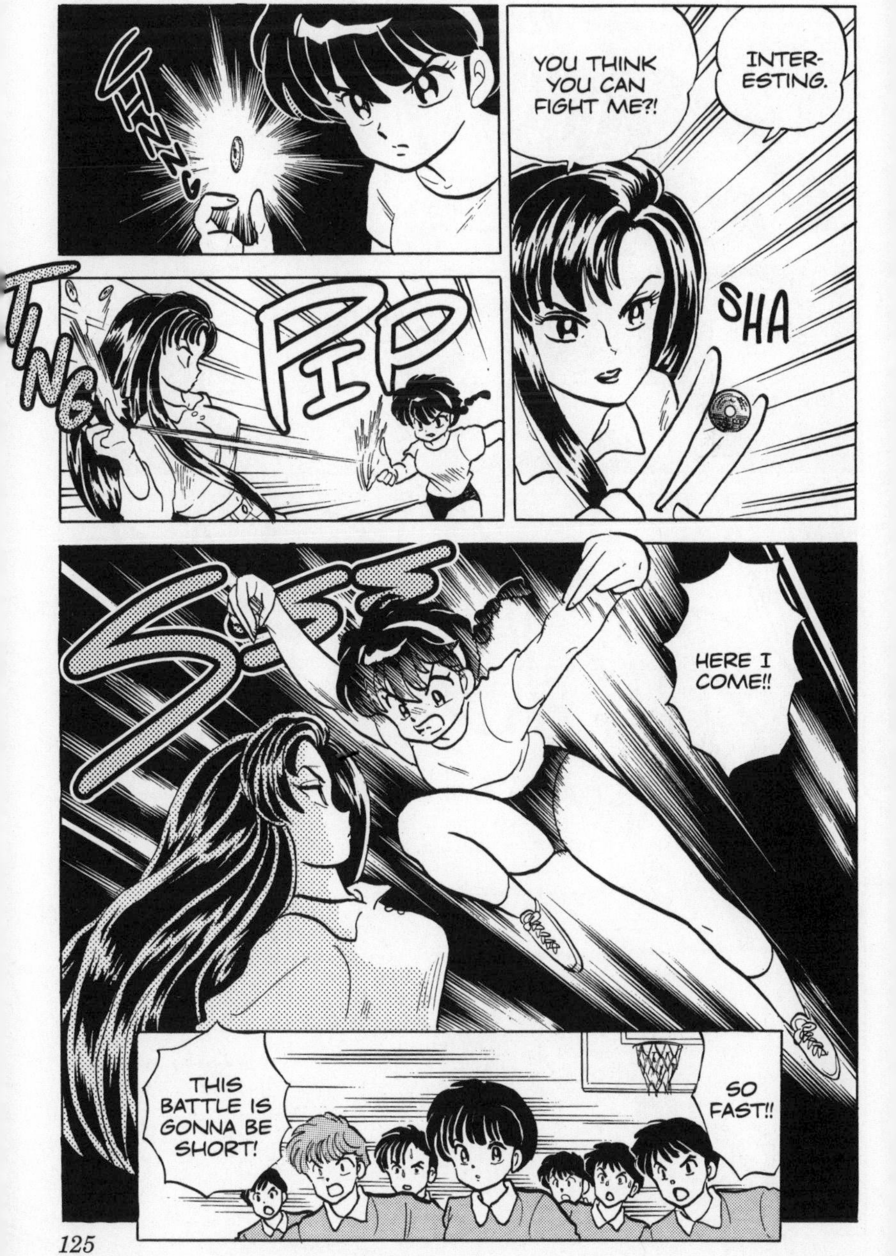
INTER-ESTING.
YOU THINK YOU CAN FIGHT ME?!
SHA
TING
PIP
HERE I COME!!
SO FAST!!
THIS BATTLE IS GONNA BE SHORT!

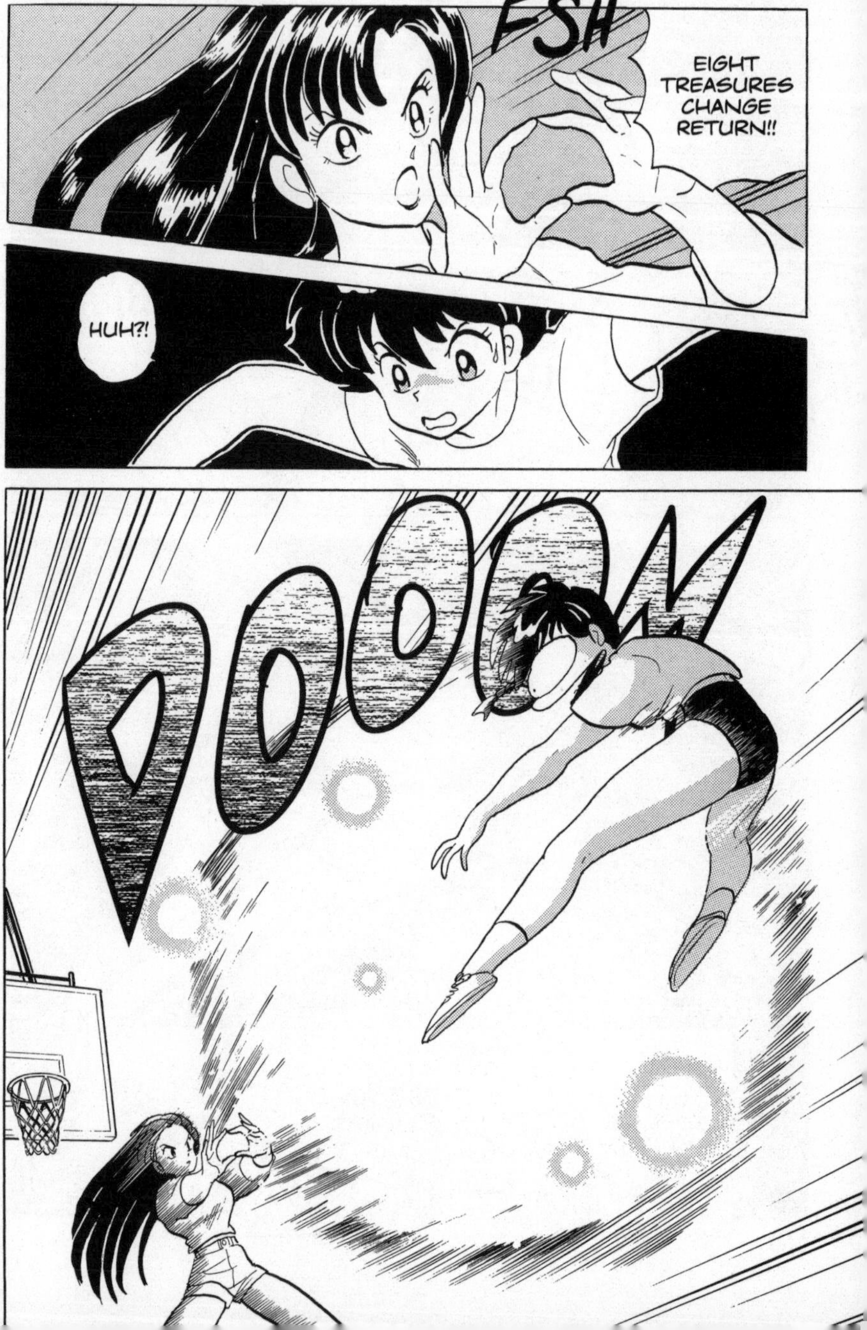
FSH
EIGHT TREASURES CHANGE RETURN!!
HUH?!
DOOOOM

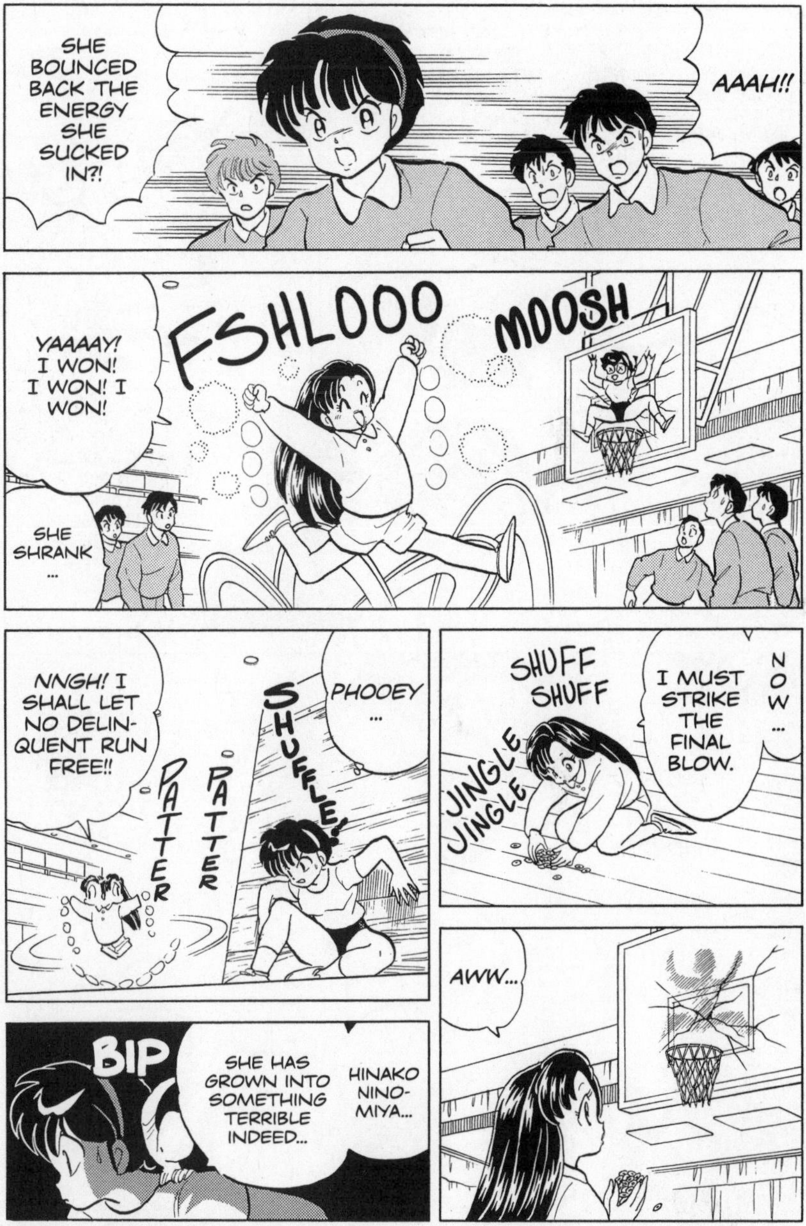
AAAH!!
SHE BOUNCED BACK THE ENERGY SHE SUCKED IN?!
MOOSH
FSHLOOO
YAAAAY! I WON! I WON! I WON!
SHE SHRANK ...
NOW ...
I MUST STRIKE THE FINAL BLOW.
SHUFF SHUFF
JINGLE JINGLE
PHOOEY ...
SHUFFLE!
NNGH! I SHALL LET NO DELIN-QUENT RUN FREE!!
PATTER PATTER
AWW...
HINAKO NINO-MIYA...
SHE HAS GROWN INTO SOMETHING TERRIBLE INDEED...
BIP

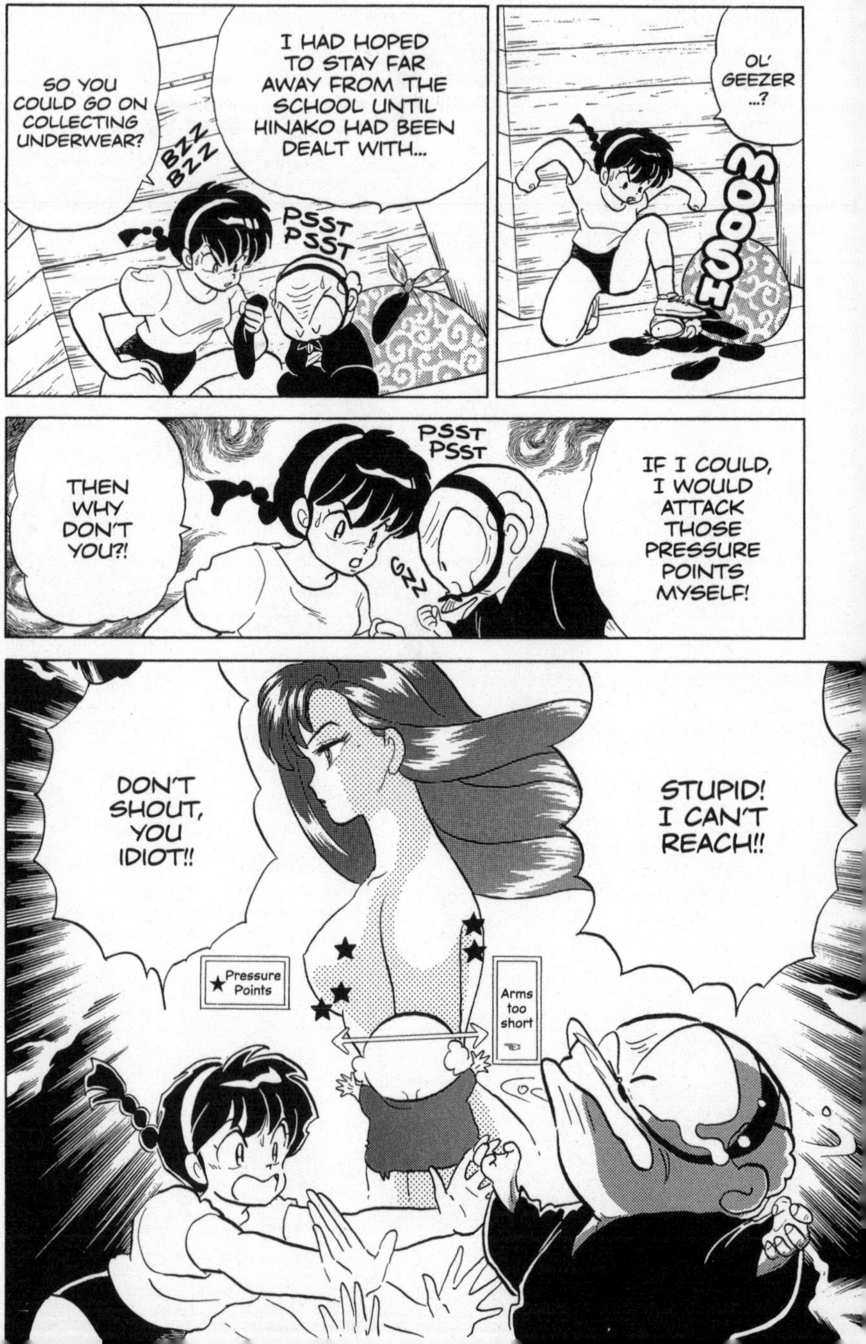
OL' GEEZER ...?
MOOSH
I HAD HOPED TO STAY FAR AWAY FROM THE SCHOOL UNTIL HINAKO HAD BEEN DEALT WITH...
SO YOU COULD GO ON COLLECTING UNDERWEAR?
BZZ BZZ
PSST PSST
IF I COULD, I WOULD ATTACK THOSE PRESSURE POINTS MYSELF!
PSST PSST
THEN WHY DON'T YOU?!
GZZ
STUPID! I CAN'T REACH!!
DON'T SHOUT, YOU IDIOT!!
Arms too short
★ Pressure Points

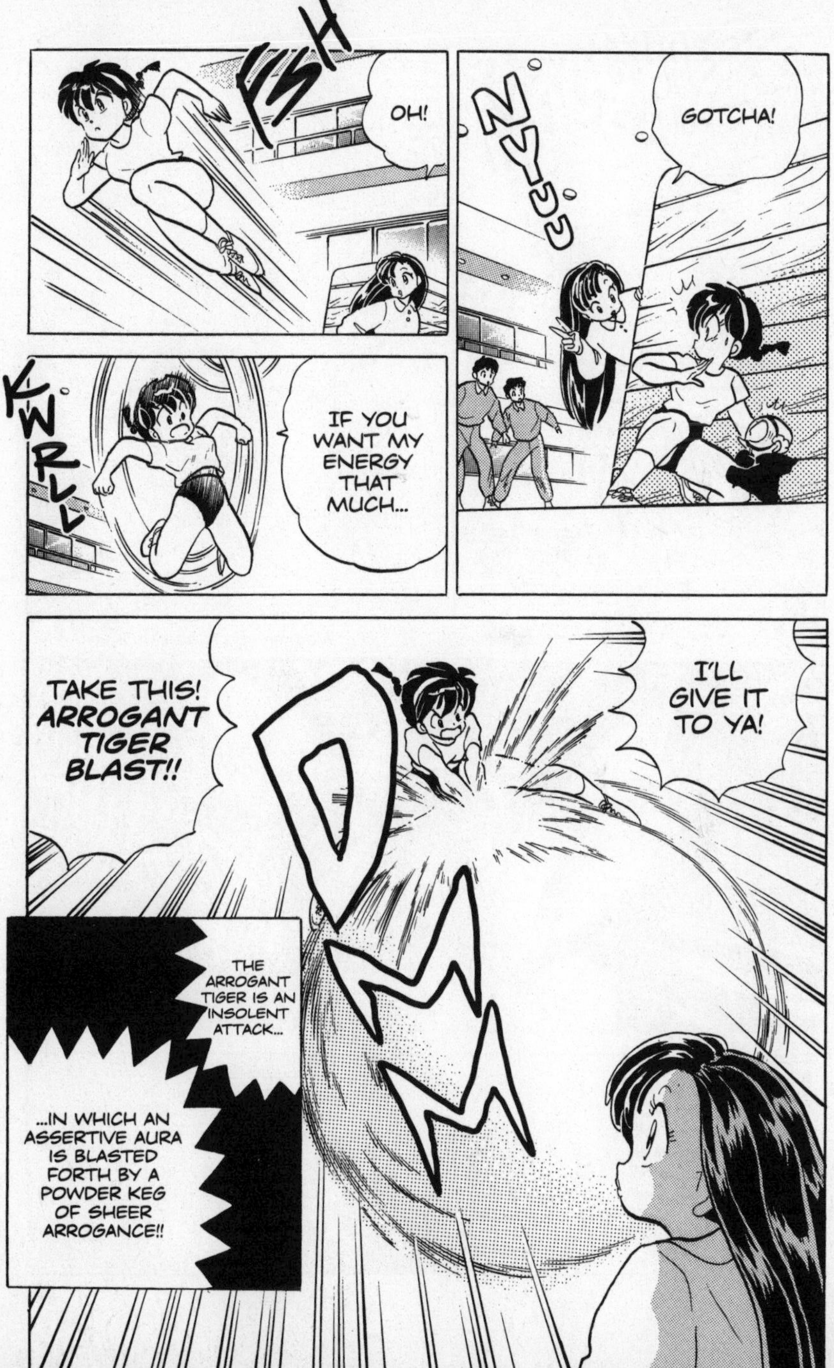
NYUUU
GOTCHA!
FSH
OH!
KWRLLL
IF YOU WANT MY ENERGY THAT MUCH...
I'LL GIVE IT TO YA!
TAKE THIS! ***ARROGANT TIGER BLAST!!***
DOM
THE ARROGANT TIGER IS AN INSOLENT ATTACK...
...IN WHICH AN ASSERTIVE AURA IS BLASTED FORTH BY A POWDER KEG OF SHEER ARROGANCE!!

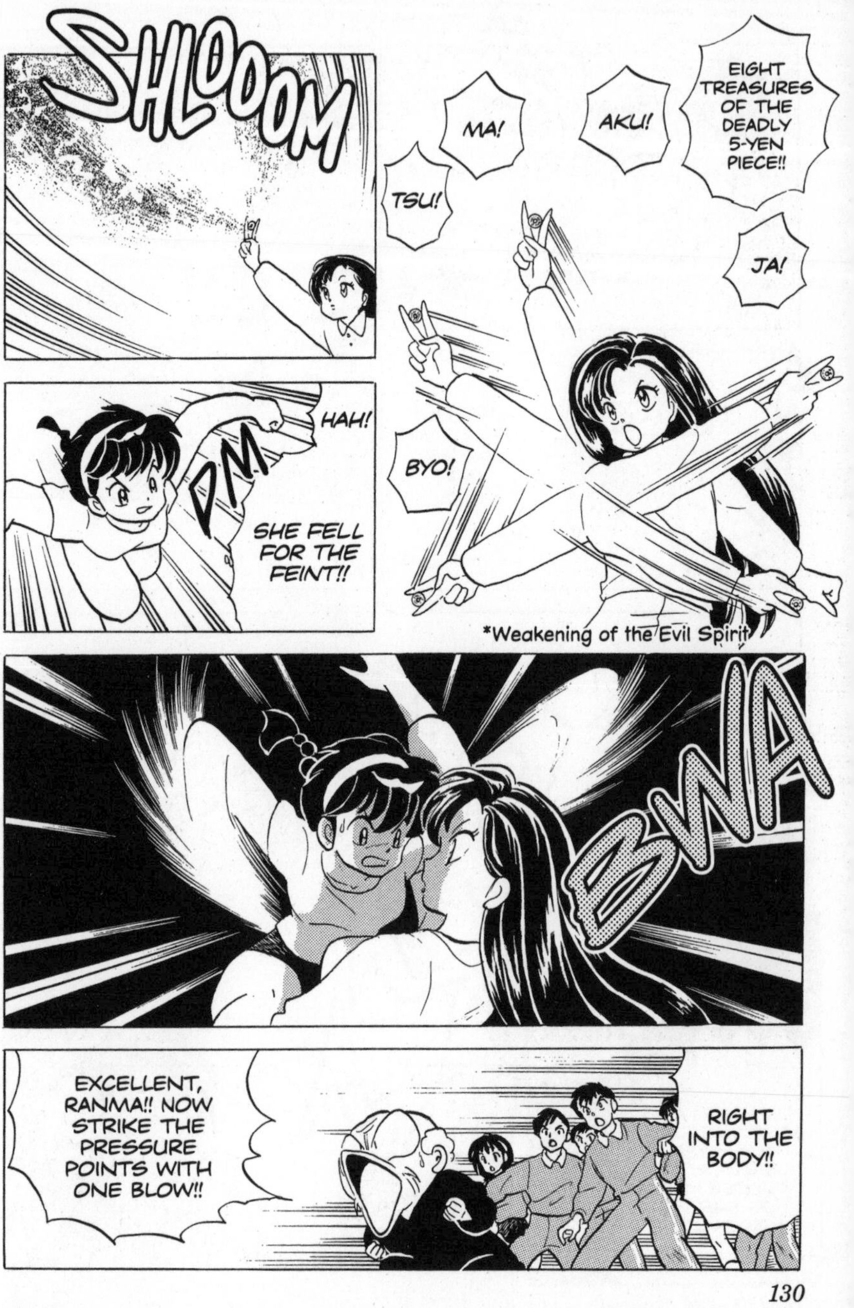
EIGHT TREASURES OF THE DEADLY 5-YEN PIECE!!
JA!
AKU!
MA!
TSU!
BYO!
*Weakening of the Evil Spirit
SHLOOOM
HAH!
DM
SHE FELL FOR THE FEINT!!
BWA
RIGHT INTO THE BODY!!
EXCELLENT, RANMA!! NOW STRIKE THE PRESSURE POINTS WITH ONE BLOW!!

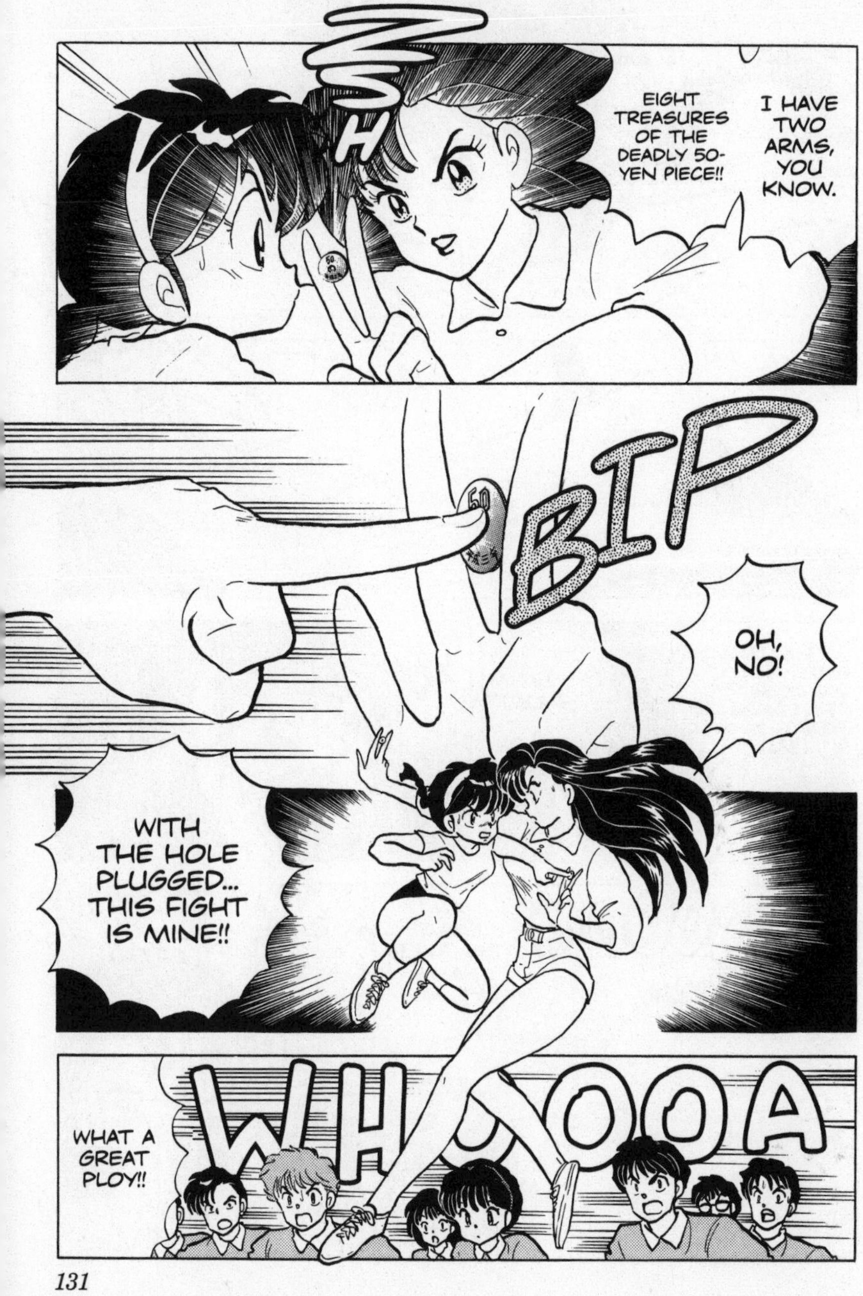
I HAVE TWO ARMS, YOU KNOW.
EIGHT TREASURES OF THE DEADLY 50-YEN PIECE!!
BIP
OH, NO!
WITH THE HOLE PLUGGED... THIS FIGHT IS MINE!!
WHAT A GREAT PLOY!!

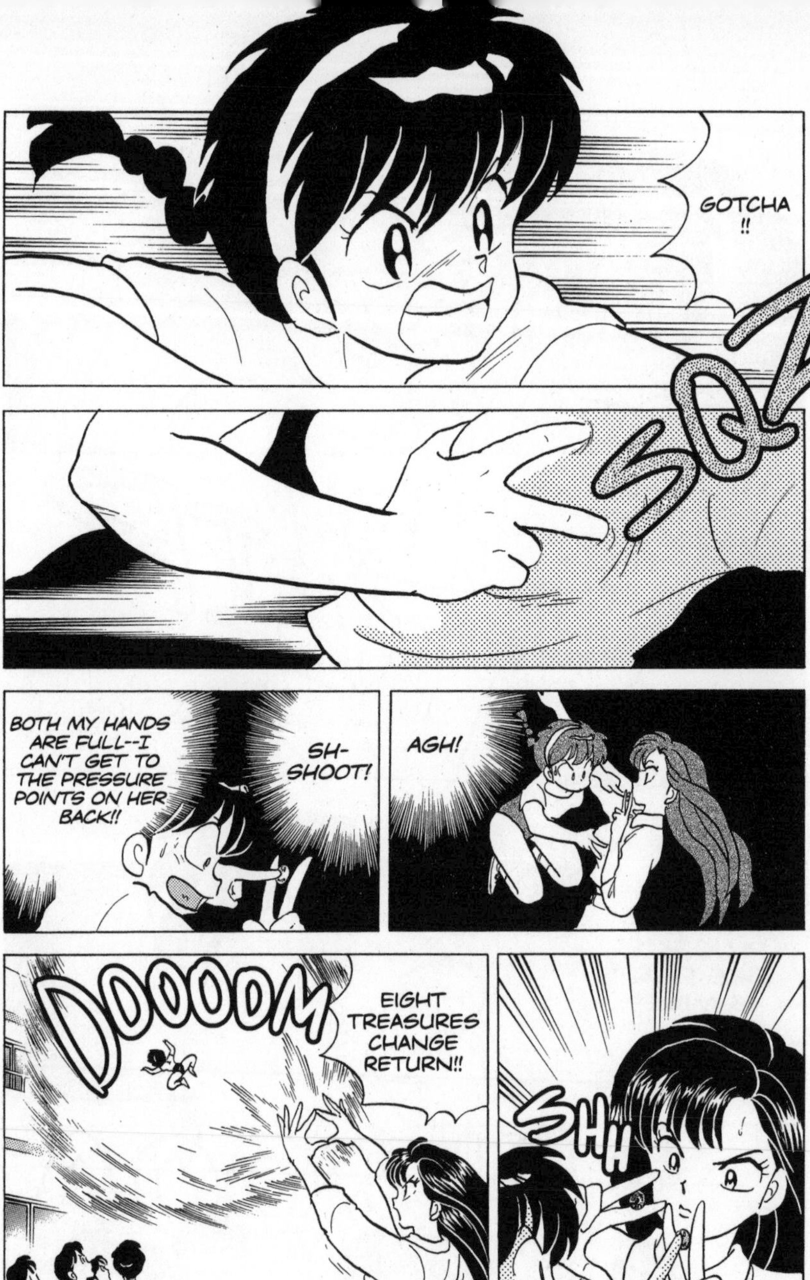
GOTCHA
!!
SQZ
AGH!
SH-
SHOOT!
BOTH MY HANDS
ARE FULL--I
CAN'T GET TO
THE PRESSURE
POINTS ON HER
BACK!!
SHH
EIGHT
TREASURES
CHANGE
RETURN!!
DOOOOM

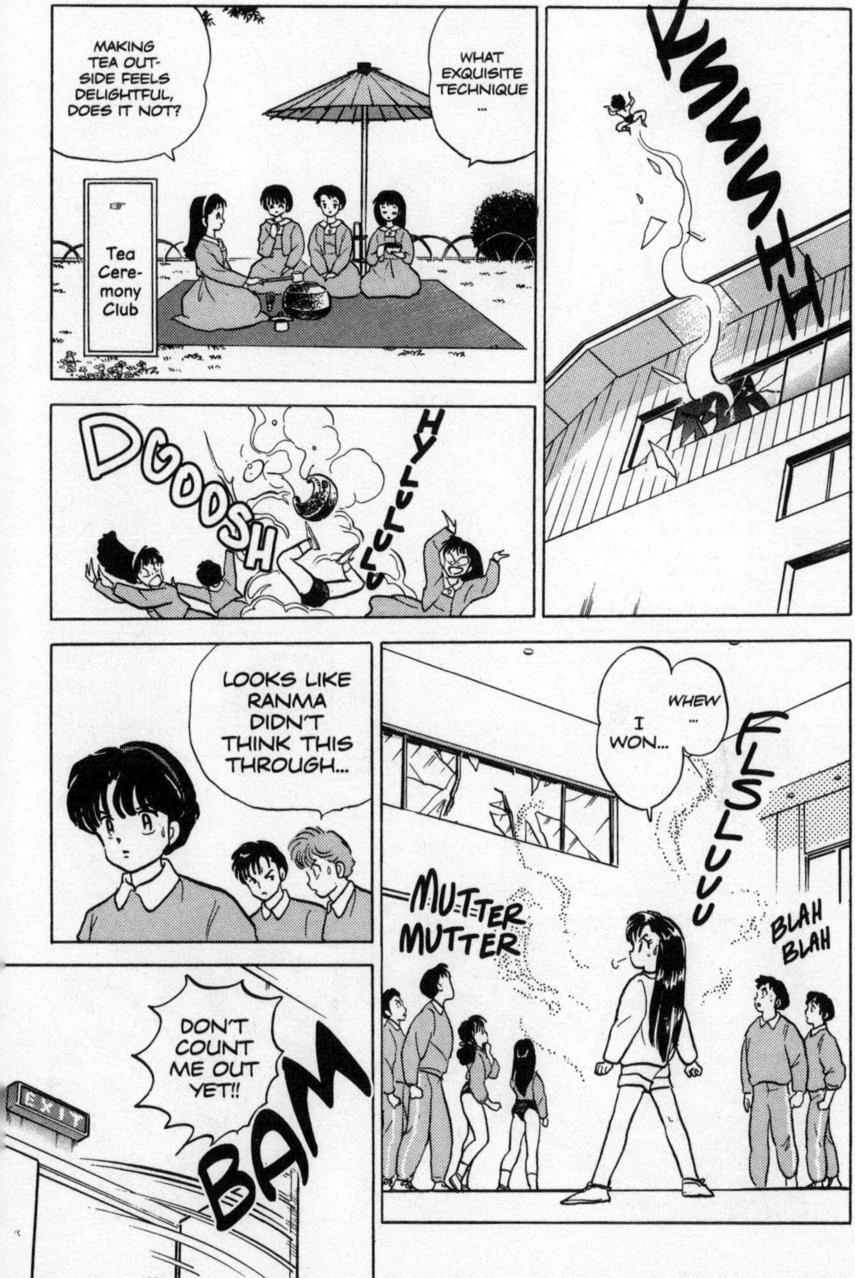
KWSSSHHH
MAKING TEA OUT-SIDE FEELS DELIGHTFUL, DOES IT NOT?
WHAT EXQUISITE TECHNIQUE ...
Tea Ceremony Club
HYULULULU
DGOOSH
WHEW ... I WON...
FLSLUUUU
BLAH BLAH
MUTTER MUTTER
LOOKS LIKE RANMA DIDN'T THINK THIS THROUGH...
DON'T COUNT ME OUT YET!!
BAM
EXIT

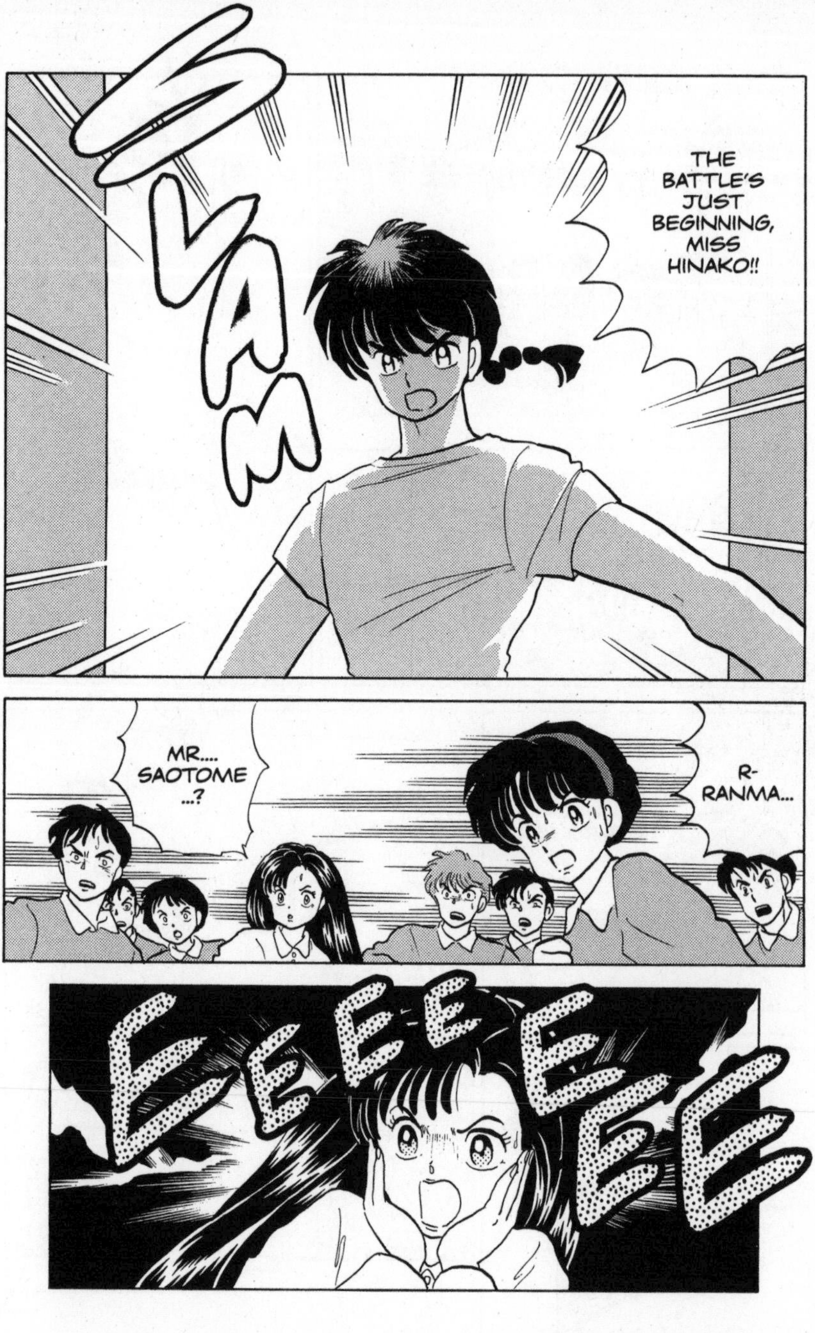

SLAM
THE BATTLE'S JUST BEGINNING, MISS HINAKO!!
R-RANMA...
MR.... SAOTOME ...?
EEEEEEE

PART 9

THE ULTIMATE HEALTH REGIMEN

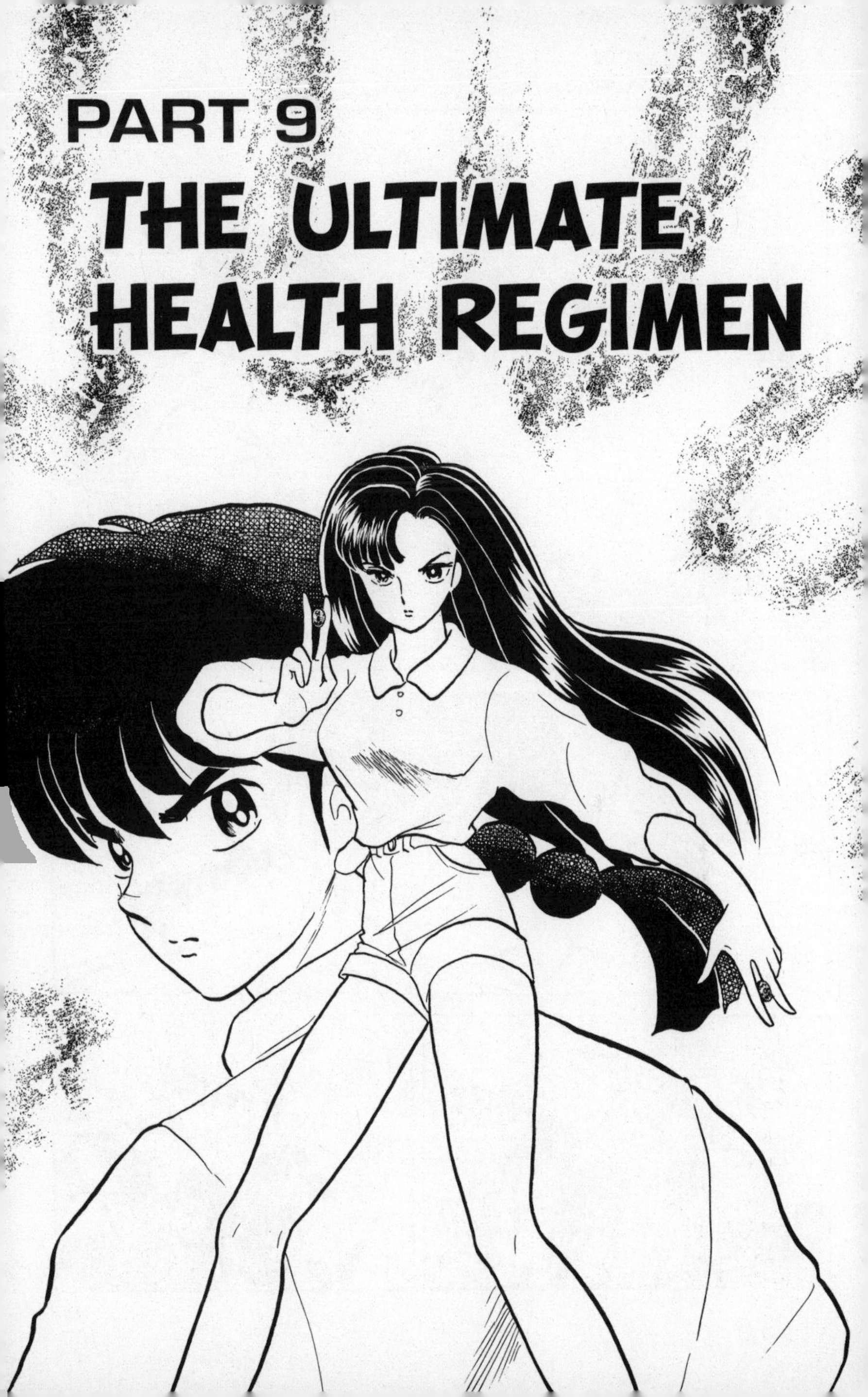

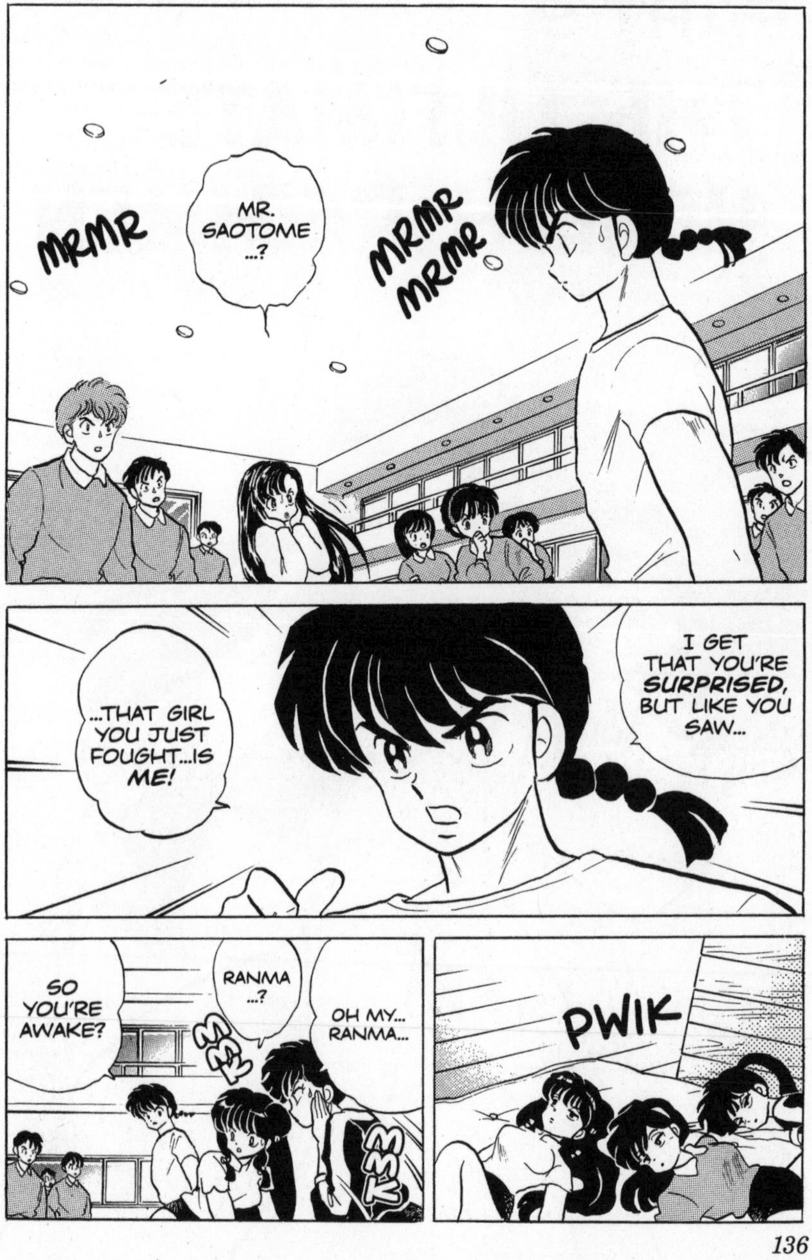

MRMR MRMR
MR. SAOTOME ...?
MRMR
I GET THAT YOU'RE SURPRISED, BUT LIKE YOU SAW...
...THAT GIRL YOU JUST FOUGHT...IS ME!
PWIK
OH MY... RANMA...
RANMA ...?
MMK
MMK
SO YOU'RE AWAKE?

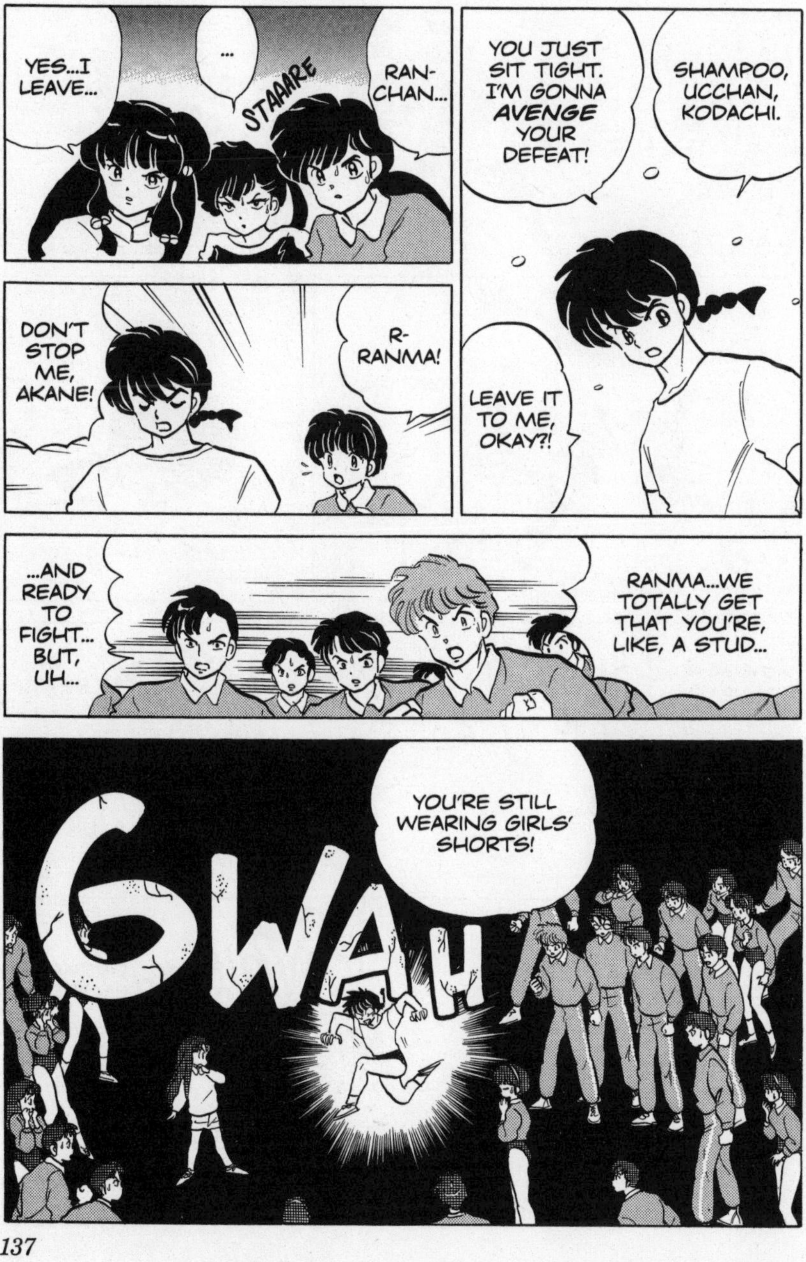
SHAMPOO, UCCHAN, KODACHI.
YOU JUST SIT TIGHT. I'M GONNA **AVENGE** YOUR DEFEAT!
LEAVE IT TO ME, OKAY?!
RAN-CHAN...
STAAARE
...
YES...I LEAVE...
R-RANMA!
DON'T STOP ME, AKANE!
RANMA...WE TOTALLY GET THAT YOU'RE, LIKE, A STUD...
...AND READY TO FIGHT... BUT, UH...
YOU'RE STILL WEARING GIRLS' SHORTS!
GWAH

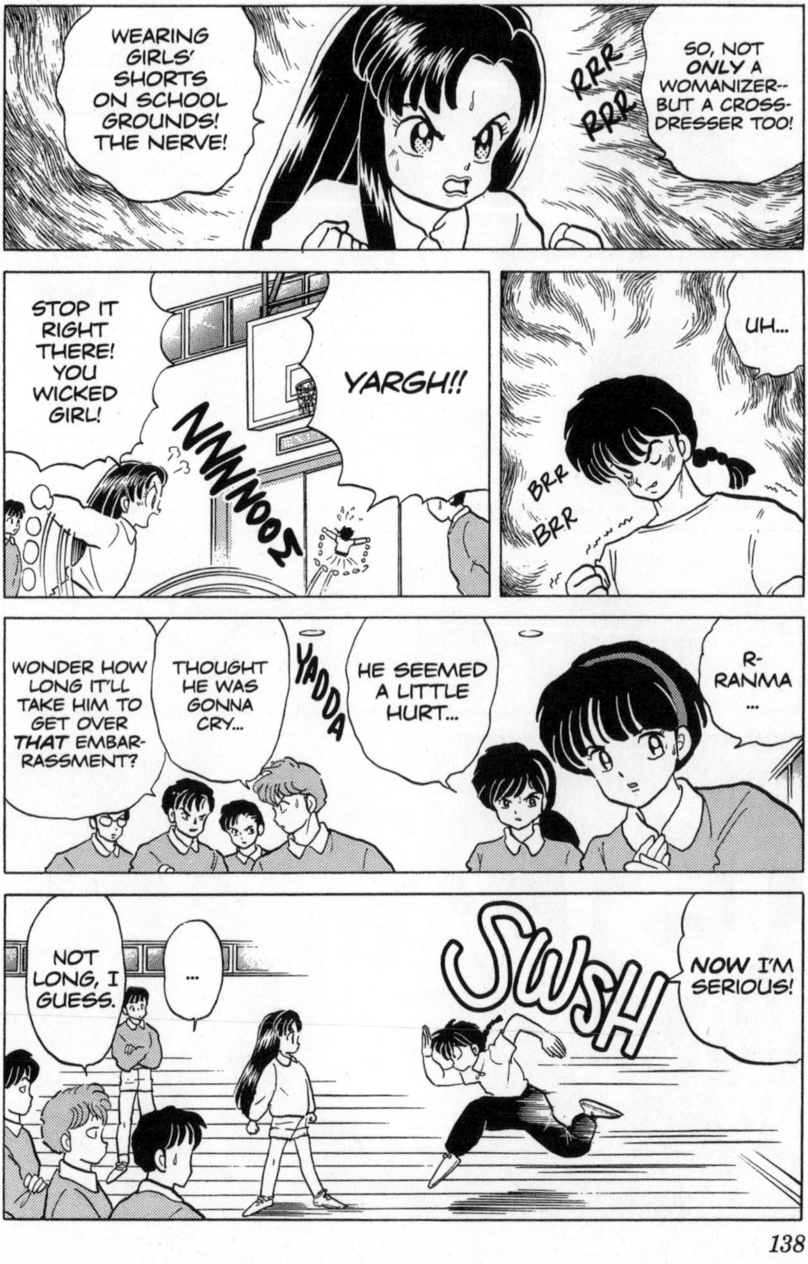
SO, NOT ONLY A WOMANIZER-- BUT A CROSS-DRESSER TOO!
RRR RRR
WEARING GIRLS' SHORTS ON SCHOOL GROUNDS! THE NERVE!
UH...
BRR BRR
STOP IT RIGHT THERE! YOU WICKED GIRL!
YARGH!!
ZOOONNNN
R-RANMA ...
HE SEEMED A LITTLE HURT...
YADDA
THOUGHT HE WAS GONNA CRY...
WONDER HOW LONG IT'LL TAKE HIM TO GET OVER THAT EMBARRASSMENT?
NOW I'M SERIOUS!
SWSH
...
NOT LONG, I GUESS.

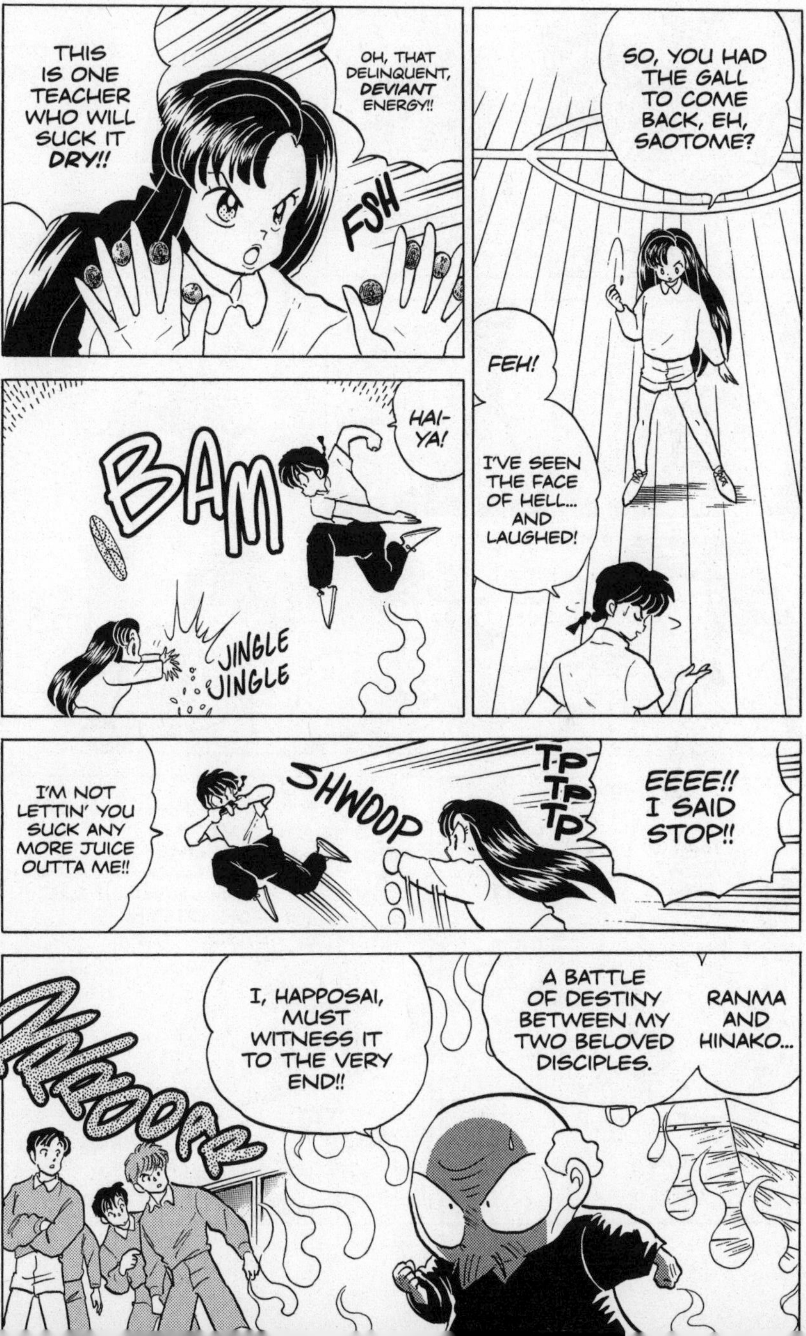
SO, YOU HAD THE GALL TO COME BACK, EH, SAOTOME?
FEH!
I'VE SEEN THE FACE OF HELL... AND LAUGHED!
OH, THAT DELINQUENT, DEVIANT ENERGY!!
FSH
THIS IS ONE TEACHER WHO WILL SUCK IT DRY!!
HAI-YA!
BAM
JINGLE JINGLE
EEEE!! I SAID STOP!!
T-P TP TP
SHWOOP
I'M NOT LETTIN' YOU SUCK ANY MORE JUICE OUTTA ME!!
RANMA AND HINAKO...
A BATTLE OF DESTINY BETWEEN MY TWO BELOVED DISCIPLES.
I, HAPPOSAI, MUST WITNESS IT TO THE VERY END!!

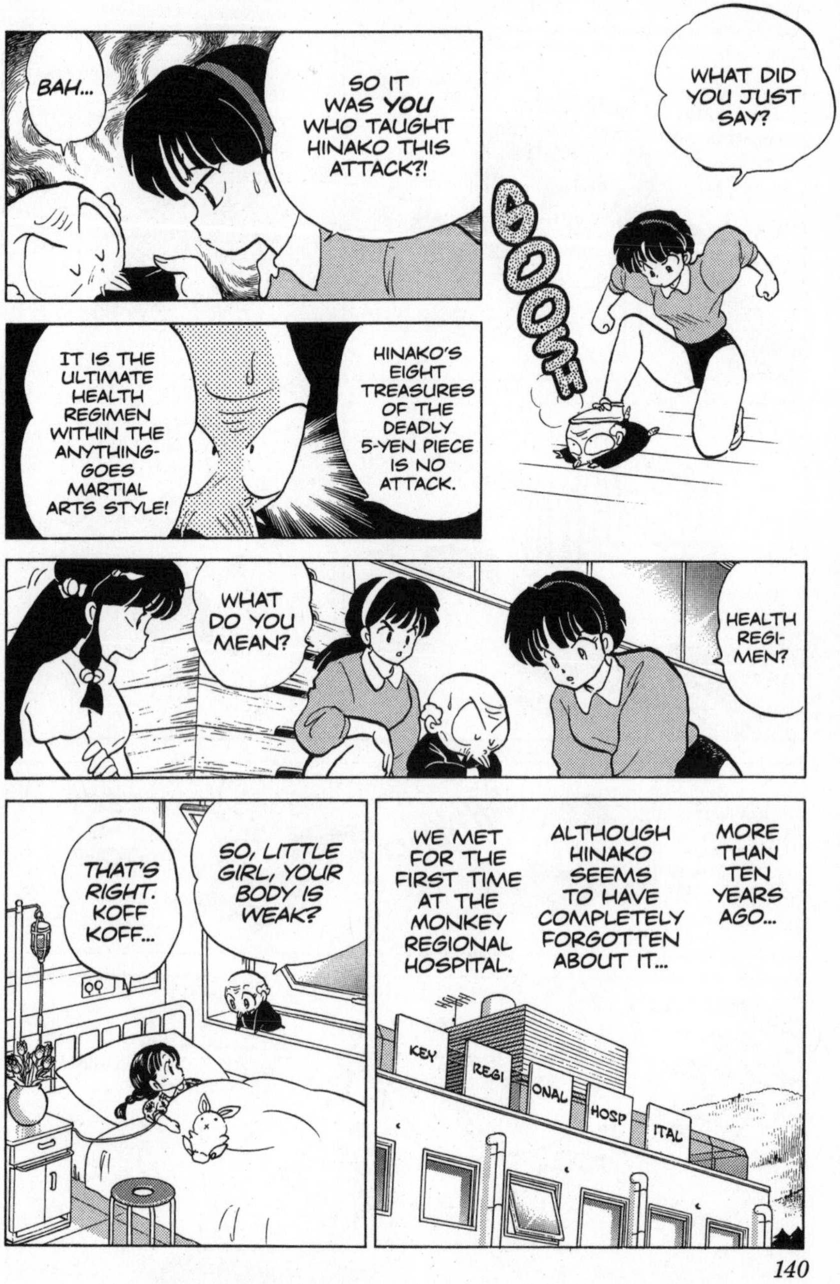
WHAT DID YOU JUST SAY?
BOOSH
SO IT WAS YOU WHO TAUGHT HINAKO THIS ATTACK?!
BAH...
HINAKO'S EIGHT TREASURES OF THE DEADLY 5-YEN PIECE IS NO ATTACK.
IT IS THE ULTIMATE HEALTH REGIMEN WITHIN THE ANYTHING-GOES MARTIAL ARTS STYLE!
HEALTH REGI-MEN?
WHAT DO YOU MEAN?
MORE THAN TEN YEARS AGO...
ALTHOUGH HINAKO SEEMS TO HAVE COMPLETELY FORGOTTEN ABOUT IT...
WE MET FOR THE FIRST TIME AT THE MONKEY REGIONAL HOSPITAL.
KEY
REGI
ONAL
HOSP
ITAL
SO, LITTLE GIRL, YOUR BODY IS WEAK?
THAT'S RIGHT. KOFF KOFF...

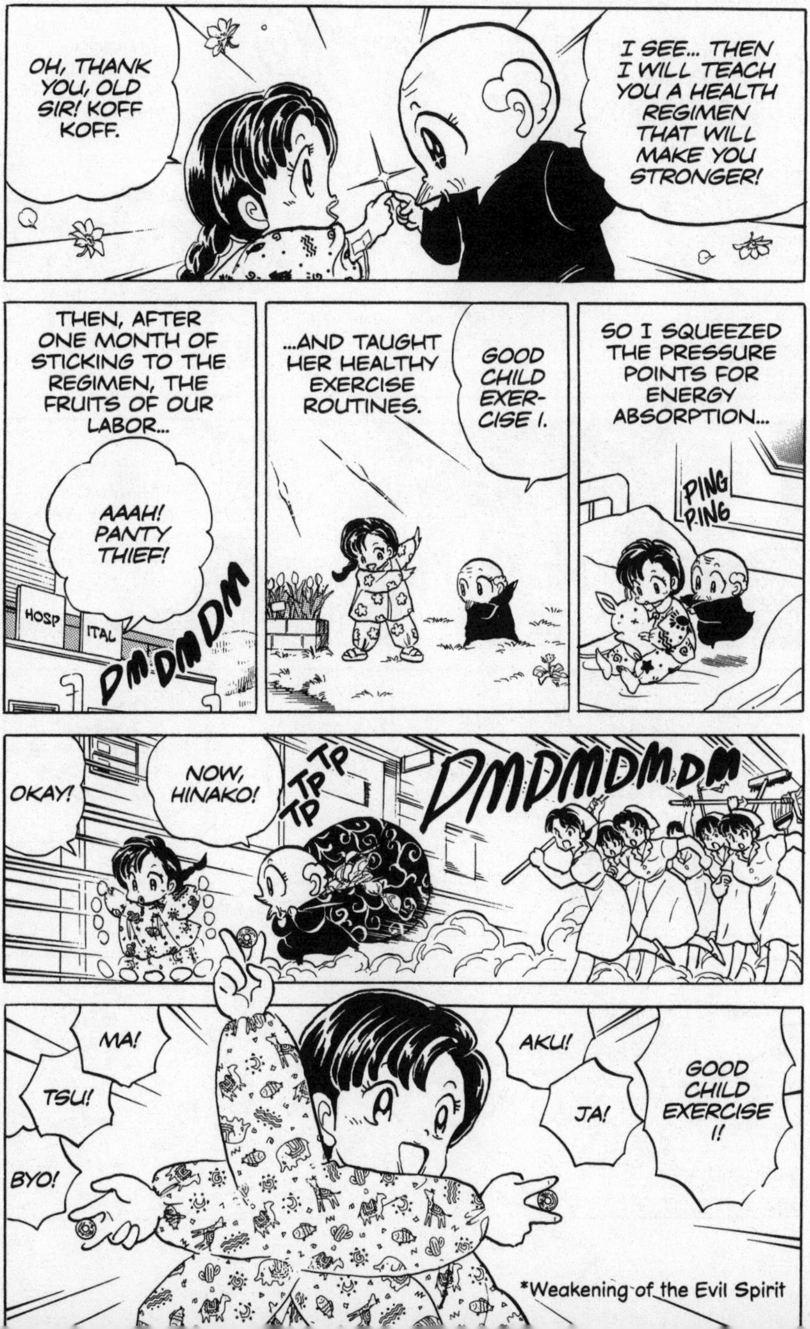
I SEE... THEN I WILL TEACH YOU A HEALTH REGIMEN THAT WILL MAKE YOU STRONGER!
OH, THANK YOU, OLD SIR! KOFF KOFF.
SO I SQUEEZED THE PRESSURE POINTS FOR ENERGY ABSORPTION...
PING PING
...AND TAUGHT HER HEALTHY EXERCISE ROUTINES.
GOOD CHILD EXER-CISE 1.
THEN, AFTER ONE MONTH OF STICKING TO THE REGIMEN, THE FRUITS OF OUR LABOR...
AAAH! PANTY THIEF!
HOSP
ITAL
DMDMDM
DMDMDMDMDM
TP TP TP
NOW, HINAKO!
OKAY!
AKU!
GOOD CHILD EXERCISE 1!
JA!
MA!
TSU!
BYO!
*Weakening of the Evil Spirit

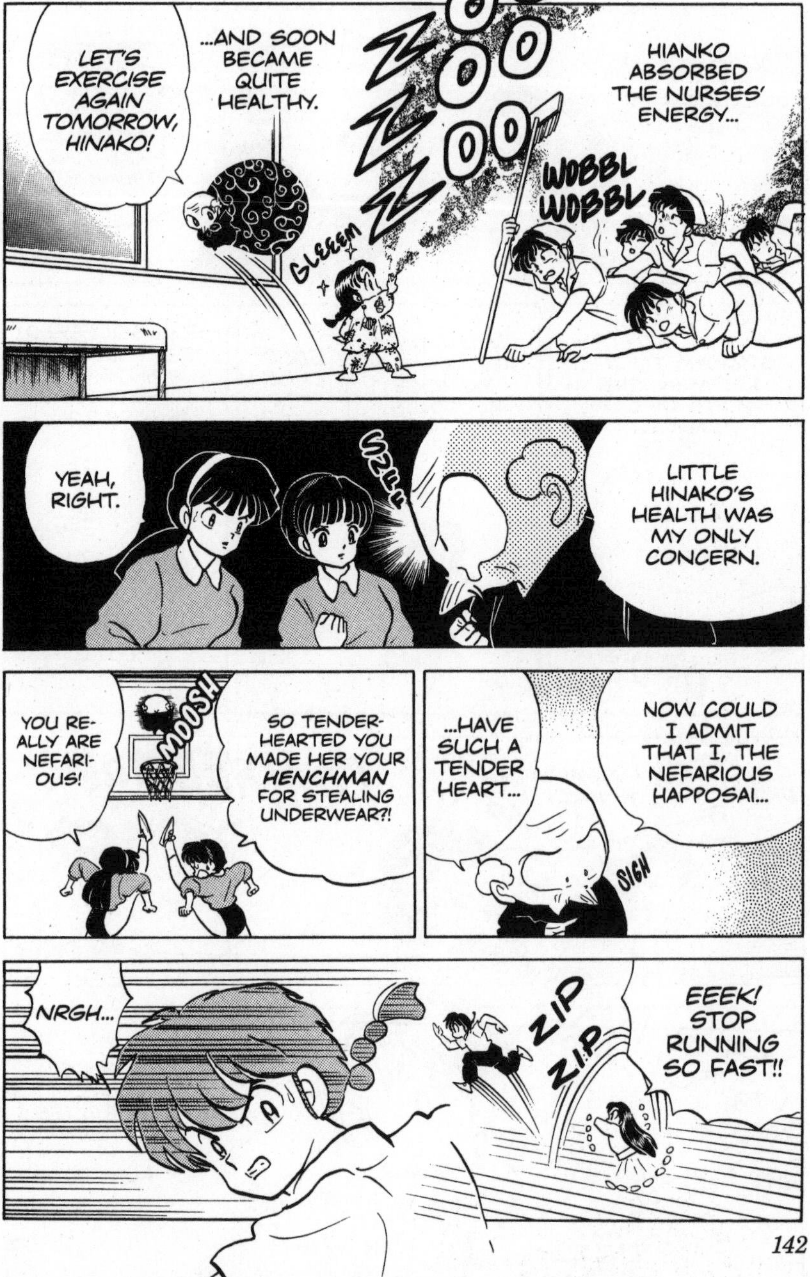
HIANKO ABSORBED THE NURSES' ENERGY...
WOBBL WOBBL
...AND SOON BECAME QUITE HEALTHY.
GLEEEM
LET'S EXERCISE AGAIN TOMORROW, HINAKO!
LITTLE HINAKO'S HEALTH WAS MY ONLY CONCERN.
YEAH, RIGHT.
NOW COULD I ADMIT THAT I, THE NEFARIOUS HAPPOSAI...
...HAVE SUCH A TENDER HEART...
SIGH
SO TENDER-HEARTED YOU MADE HER YOUR **HENCHMAN** FOR STEALING UNDERWEAR?!
MOOSH
YOU RE-ALLY ARE NEFARI-OUS!
EEEK! STOP RUNNING SO FAST!!
ZIP ZIP
NRGH...

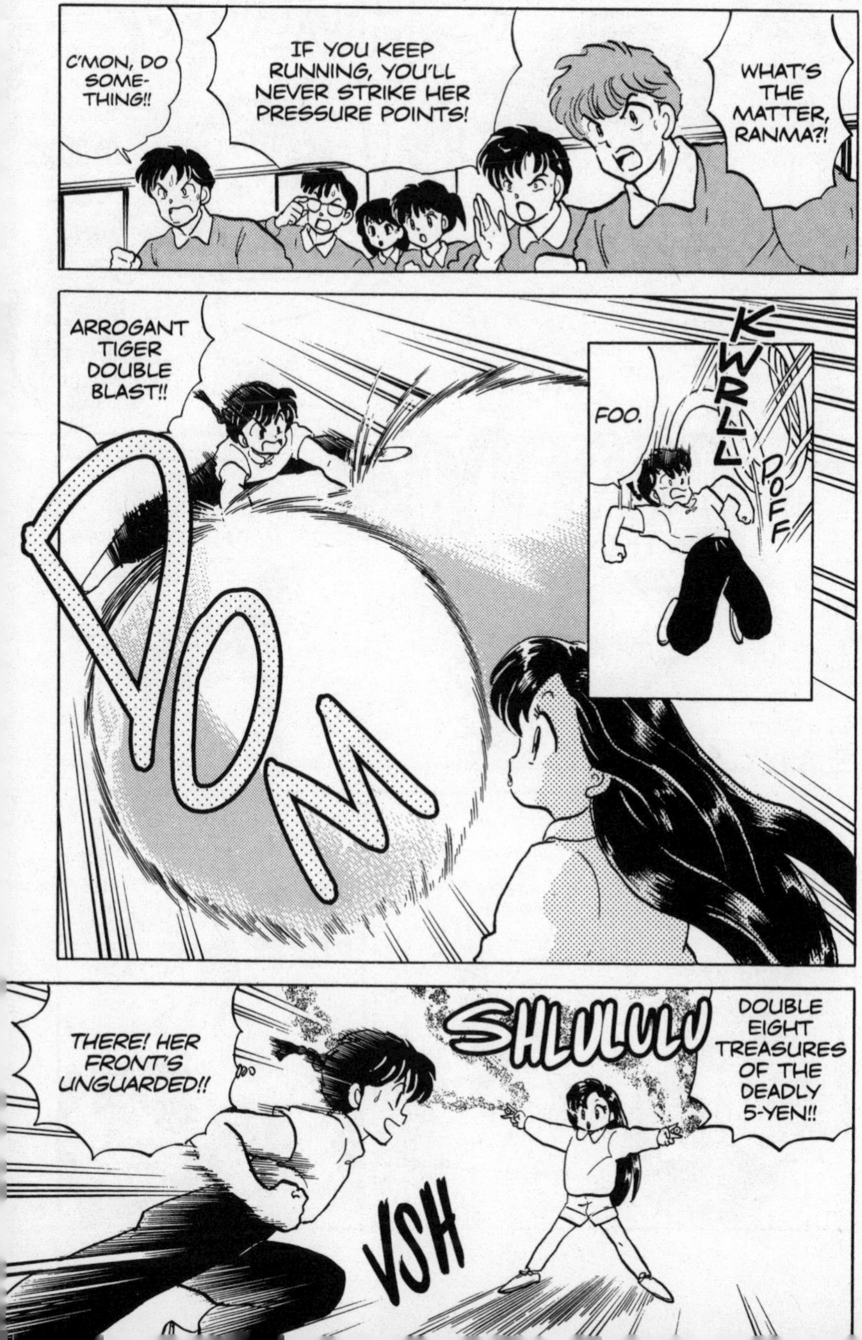
WHAT'S THE MATTER, RANMA?!
IF YOU KEEP RUNNING, YOU'LL NEVER STRIKE HER PRESSURE POINTS!
C'MON, DO SOME-THING!!
KWRLL
FOO.
POFF
ARROGANT TIGER DOUBLE BLAST!!
DOOM
DOUBLE EIGHT TREASURES OF THE DEADLY 5-YEN!!
SHLULULU
THERE! HER FRONT'S UNGUARDED!!
VSH

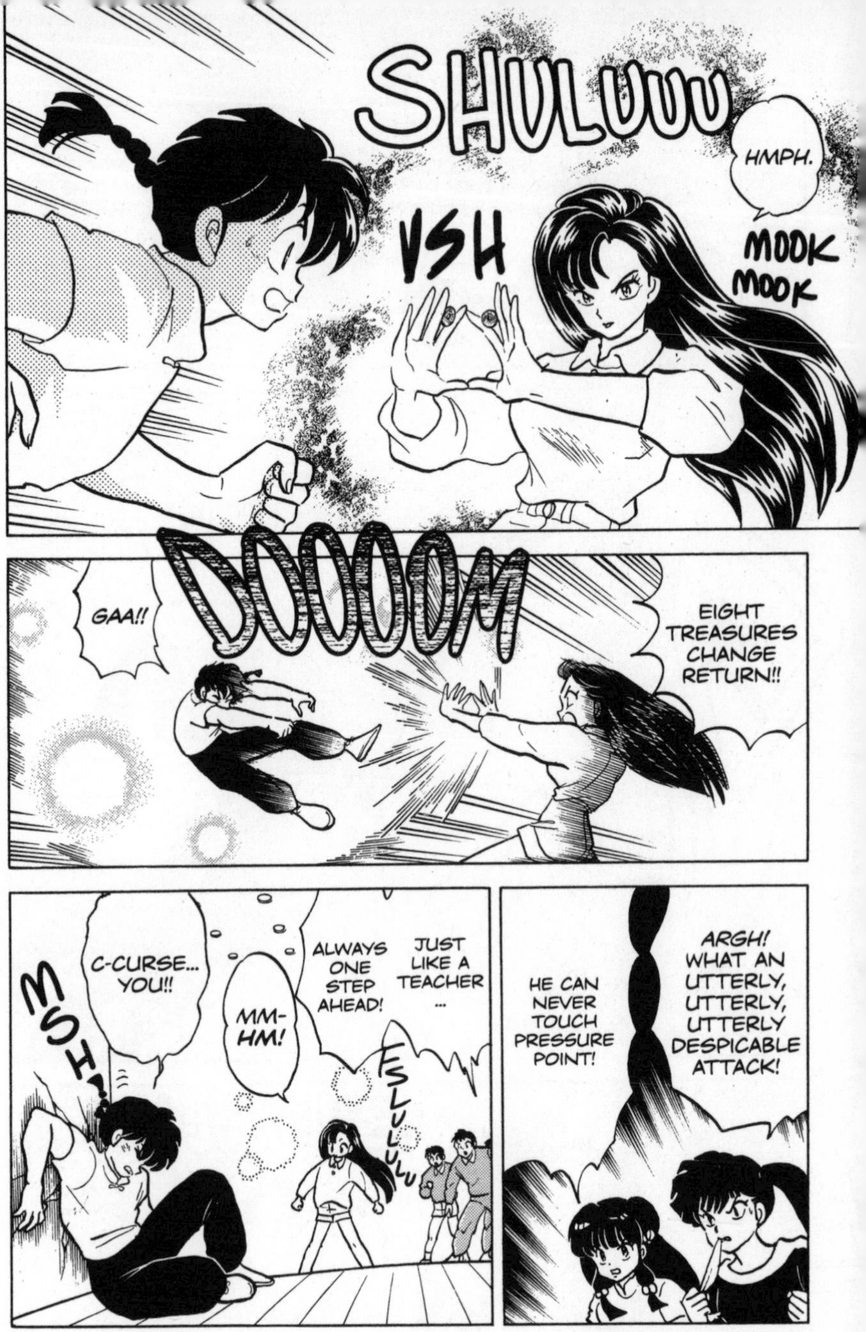
SHULUUU
HMPH.
MOOK MOOK
VSH
DOOOOM
EIGHT TREASURES CHANGE RETURN!!
GAA!!
ARGH! WHAT AN UTTERLY, UTTERLY, UTTERLY DESPICABLE ATTACK!
HE CAN NEVER TOUCH PRESSURE POINT!
JUST LIKE A TEACHER ...
ALWAYS ONE STEP AHEAD!
MM-HM!
C-CURSE... YOU!!
SLULULU
MSH

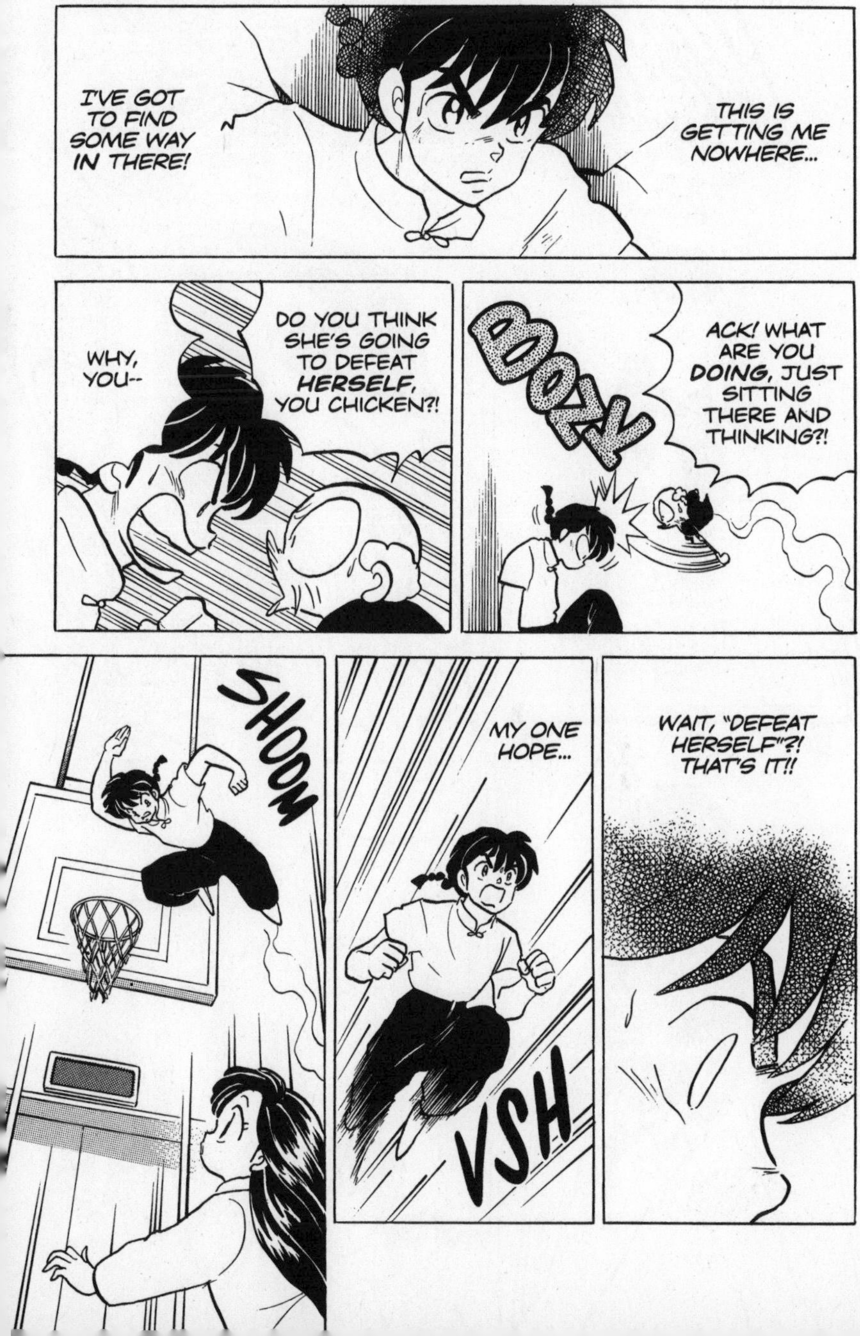
THIS IS GETTING ME NOWHERE...
I'VE GOT TO FIND SOME WAY IN THERE!
BOZK
ACK! WHAT ARE YOU DOING, JUST SITTING THERE AND THINKING?!
DO YOU THINK SHE'S GOING TO DEFEAT HERSELF, YOU CHICKEN?!
WHY, YOU--
WAIT, "DEFEAT HERSELF"?! THAT'S IT!!
MY ONE HOPE...
VSH
SHOOM

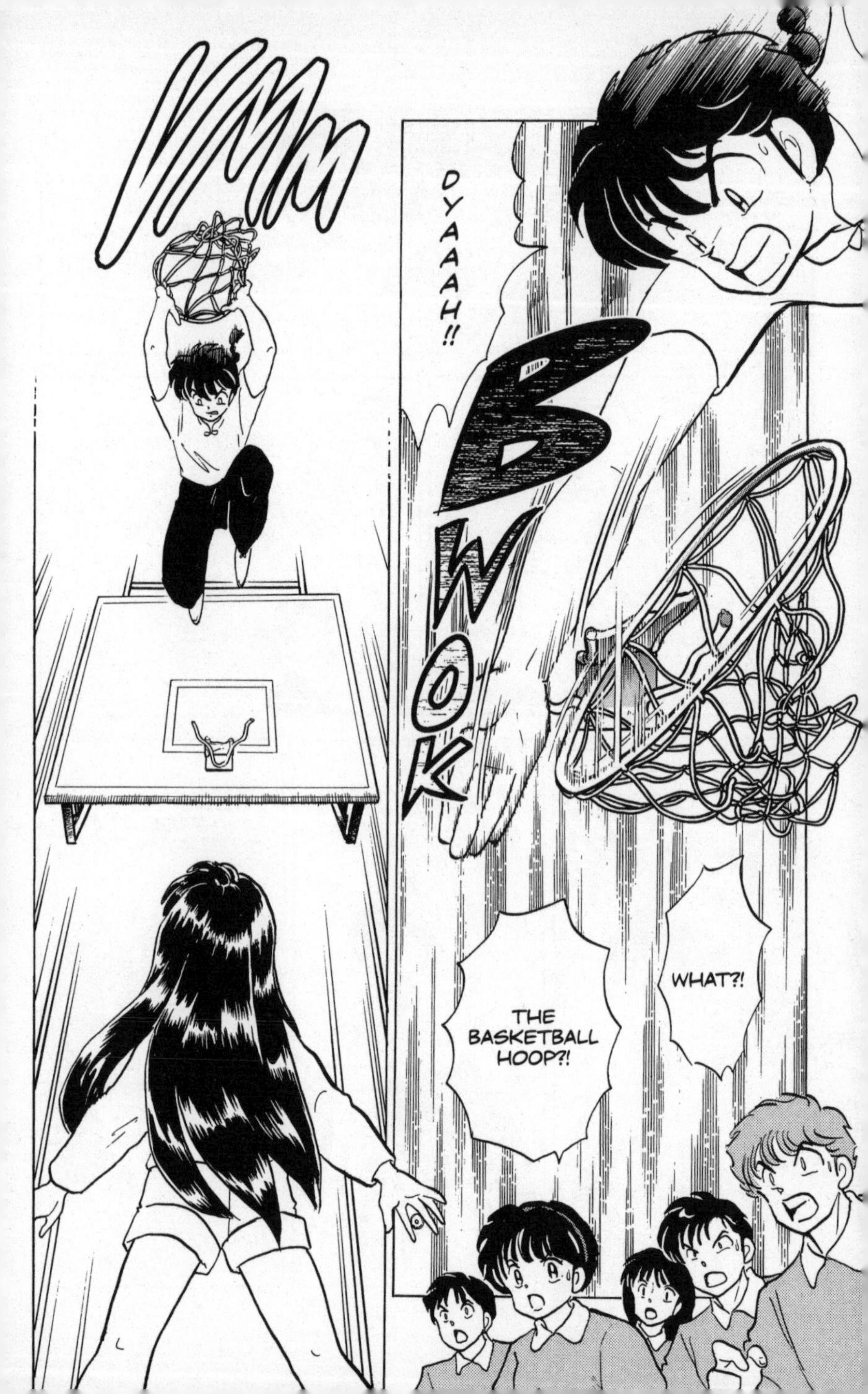
OYAAAAH!!
BWOK
WHAT?!
THE BASKETBALL HOOP?!
VMM

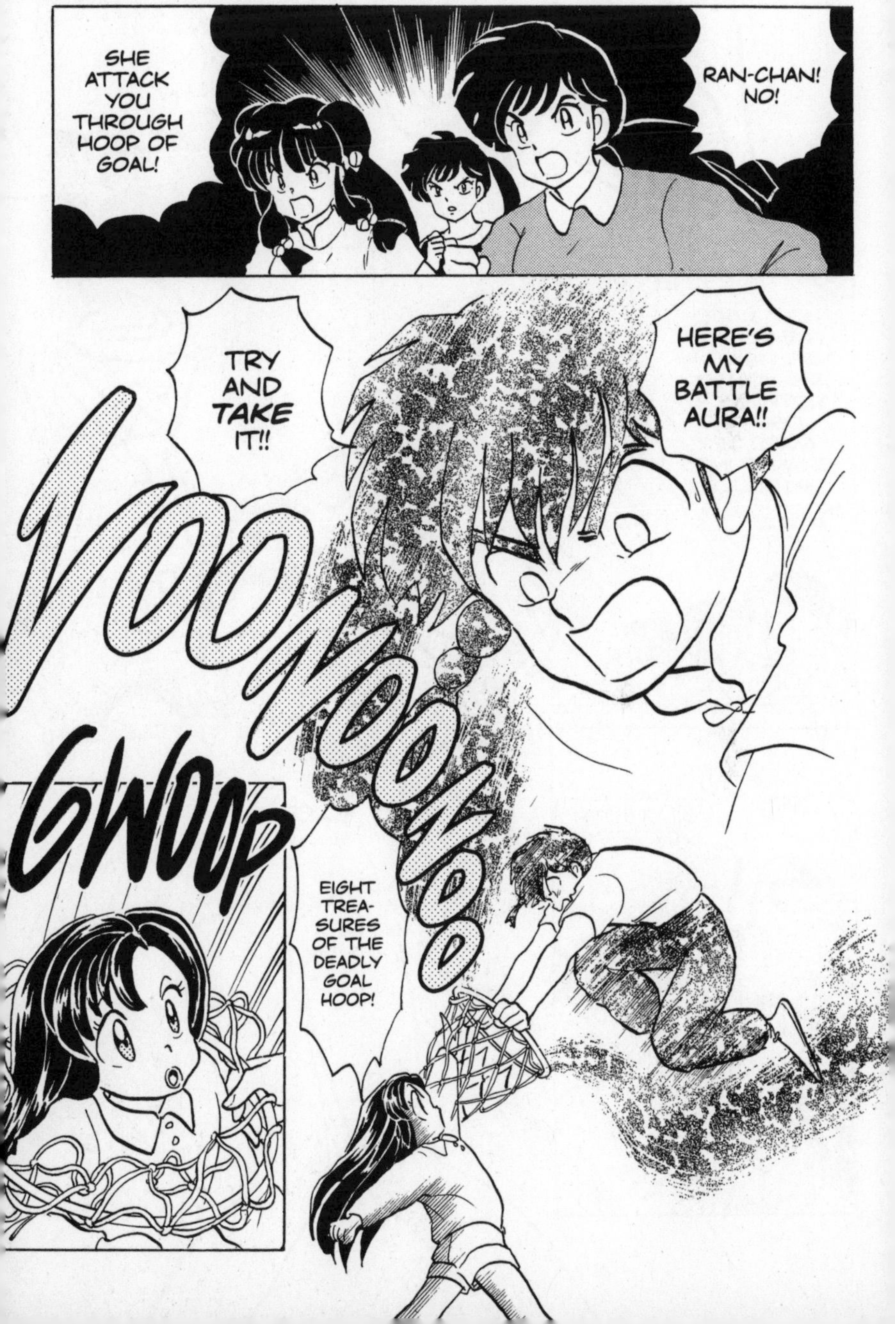
RAN-CHAN! NO!
SHE ATTACK YOU THROUGH HOOP OF GOAL!
HERE'S MY BATTLE AURA!!
TRY AND TAKE IT!!
VOOOOOOOOO
GWOOP
EIGHT TREA-SURES OF THE DEADLY GOAL HOOP!

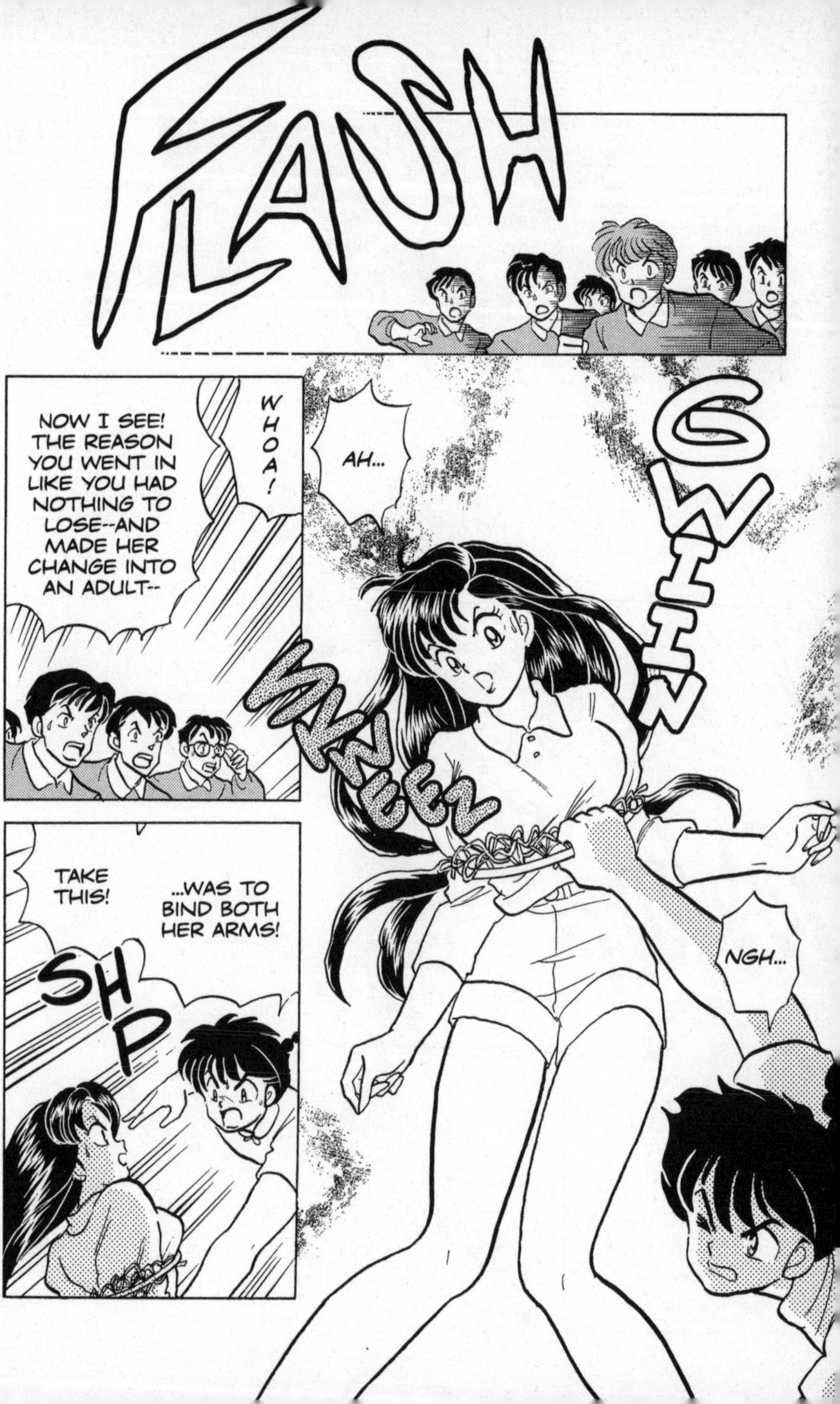
FLASH
AH...
GWIIIN
WWEEN
NGH...
WHOA!
NOW I SEE! THE REASON YOU WENT IN LIKE YOU HAD NOTHING TO LOSE--AND MADE HER CHANGE INTO AN ADULT--
...WAS TO BIND BOTH HER ARMS!
TAKE THIS!
SHP

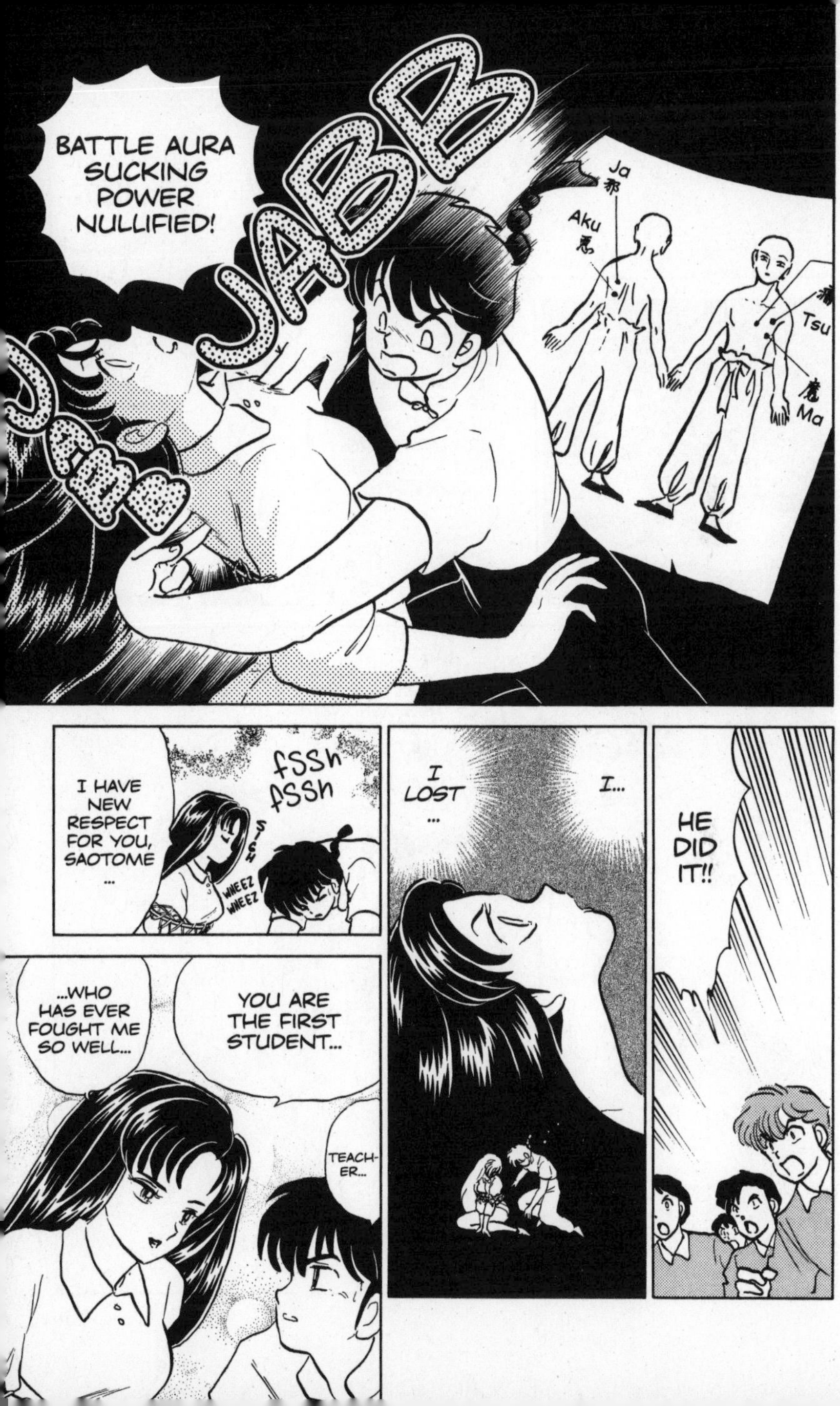
BATTLE AURA SUCKING POWER NULLIFIED!
JABB
JABB
Ja 邪
Aku 悪
Tsu
魔 Ma
HE DID IT!!
I...
I LOST ...
fssh fssh
I HAVE NEW RESPECT FOR YOU, SAOTOME ...
SIGH
WHEEZ WHEEZ
YOU ARE THE FIRST STUDENT...
...WHO HAS EVER FOUGHT ME SO WELL...
TEACHER...

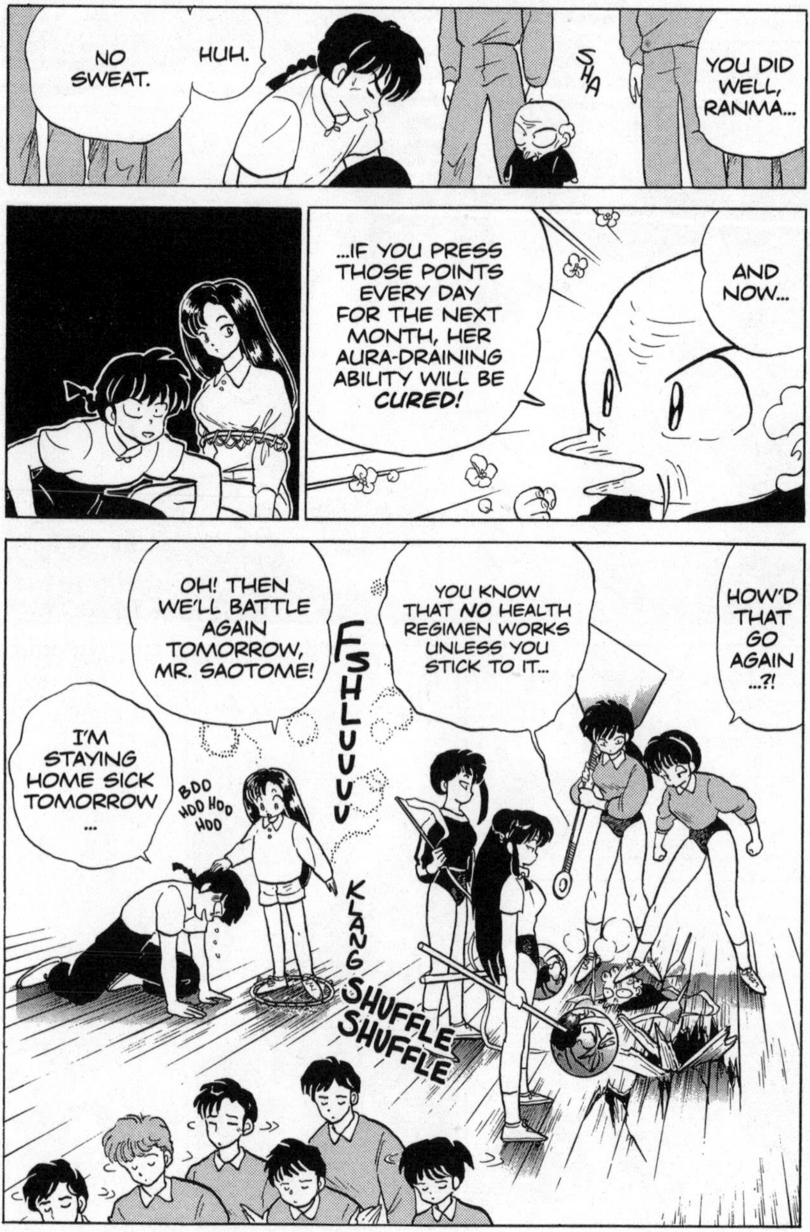
YOU DID WELL, RANMA...
SHA
HUH.
NO SWEAT.
AND NOW...
...IF YOU PRESS THOSE POINTS EVERY DAY FOR THE NEXT MONTH, HER AURA-DRAINING ABILITY WILL BE CURED!
HOW'D THAT GO AGAIN ...?!
YOU KNOW THAT NO HEALTH REGIMEN WORKS UNLESS YOU STICK TO IT...
FSHLUUUUU
OH! THEN WE'LL BATTLE AGAIN TOMORROW, MR. SAOTOME!
I'M STAYING HOME SICK TOMORROW ...
BDO HOO HOO HOO
KLANG
SHUFFLE SHUFFLE

PART 10
AKANE'S JOURNEY

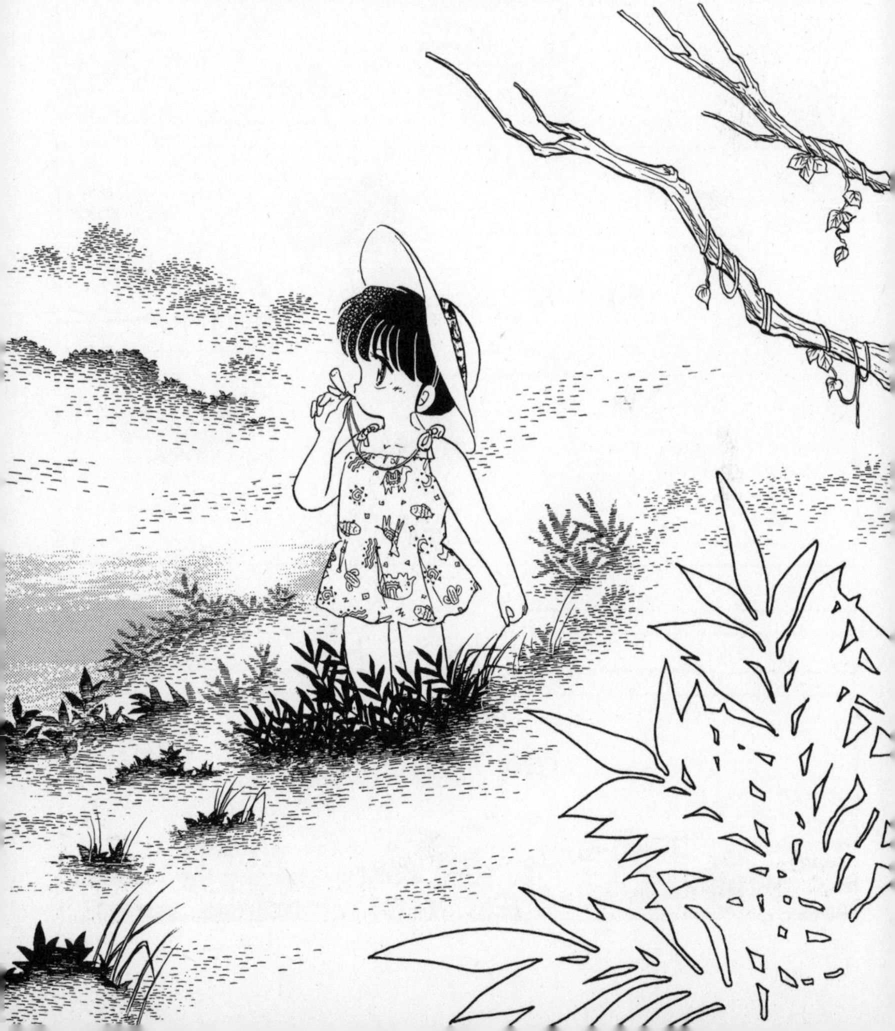

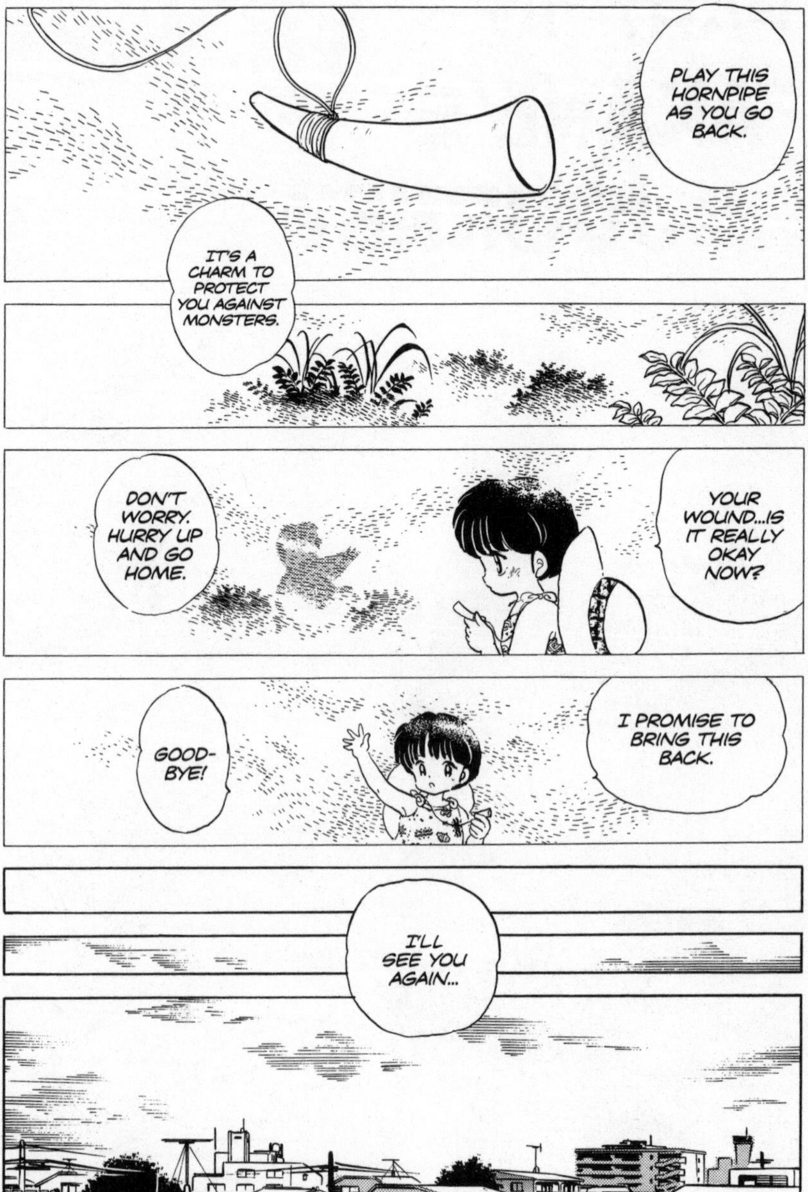
PLAY THIS HORNPIPE AS YOU GO BACK.
IT'S A CHARM TO PROTECT YOU AGAINST MONSTERS.
YOUR WOUND...IS IT REALLY OKAY NOW?
DON'T WORRY. HURRY UP AND GO HOME.
I PROMISE TO BRING THIS BACK.
GOOD-BYE!
I'LL SEE YOU AGAIN...

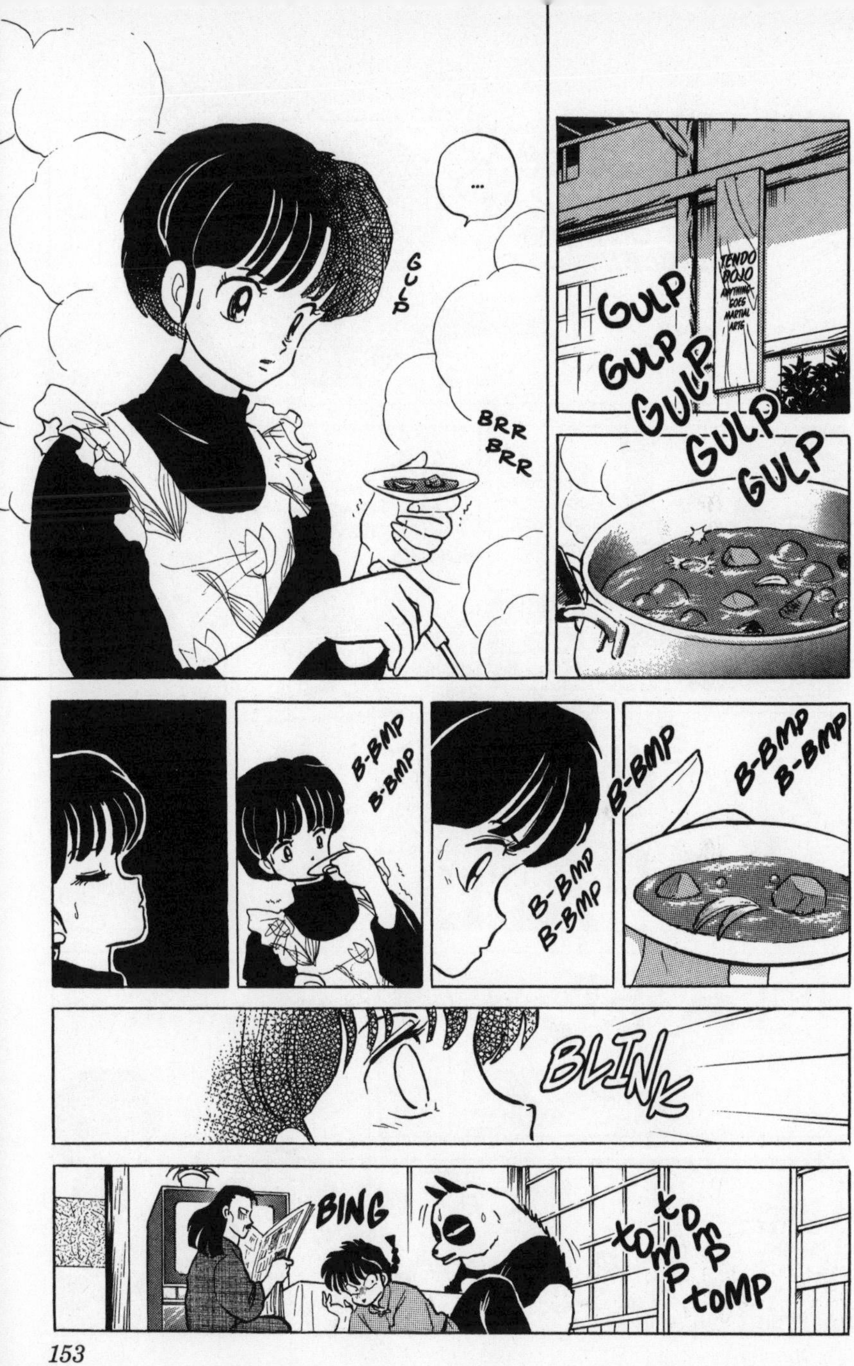
TENDO DOJO ANYTHING-GOES MARTIAL ARTS
GULP
GULP
GULP
GULP
GULP
...
GULP
BRR
BRR
B-BMP
B-BMP
B-BMP
B-BMP
B-BMP
B-BMP
B-BMP
B-BMP
BLINK
tomp tomp
tomp tomp
BING

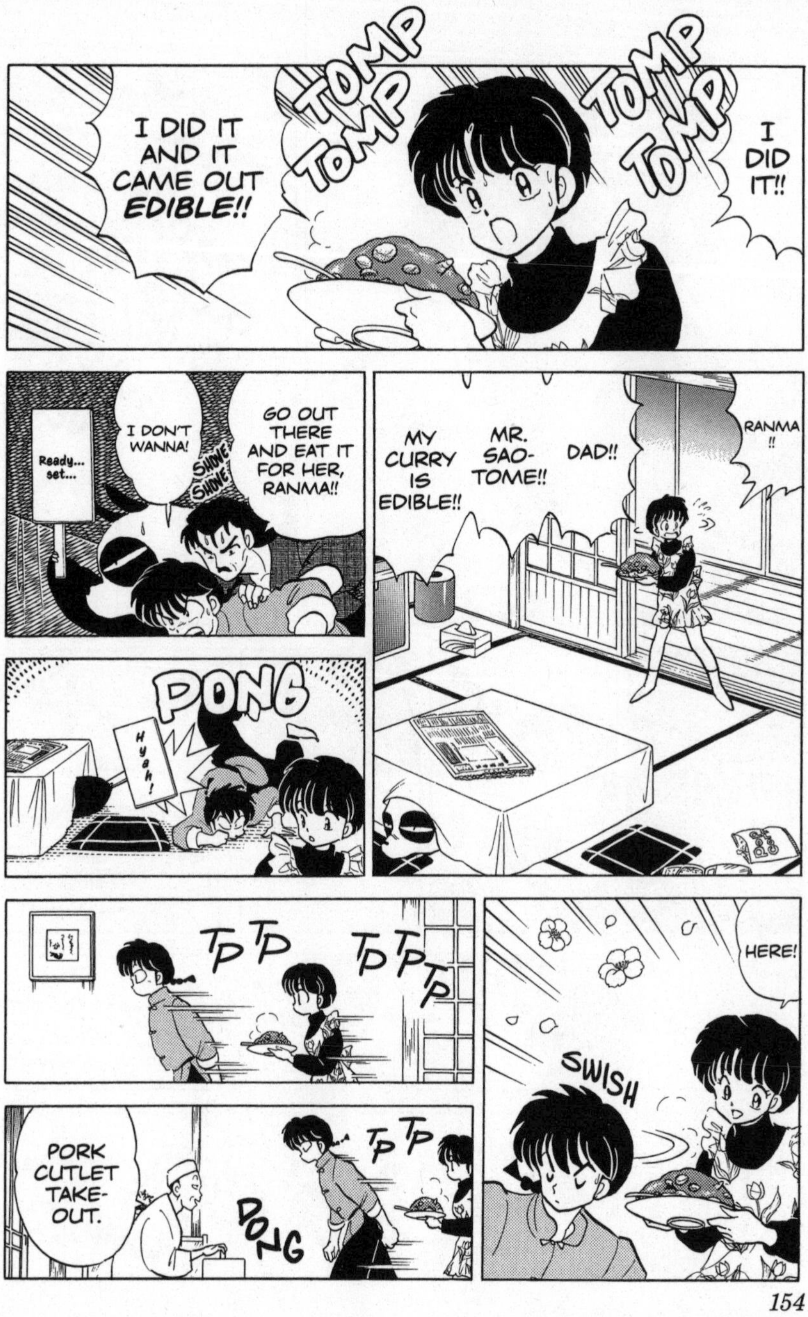
I DID IT!!
TOMP TOMP
TOMP TOMP
I DID IT AND IT CAME OUT EDIBLE!!
RANMA!!
DAD!!
MR. SAO-TOME!!
MY CURRY IS EDIBLE!!
GO OUT THERE AND EAT IT FOR HER, RANMA!!
SHOVE SHOVE
I DON'T WANNA!
Ready... set...
PONG
Hyah!
HERE!
SWISH
TP TP TP TP
TP TP
TP TP
DONG
PORK CUTLET TAKE-OUT.

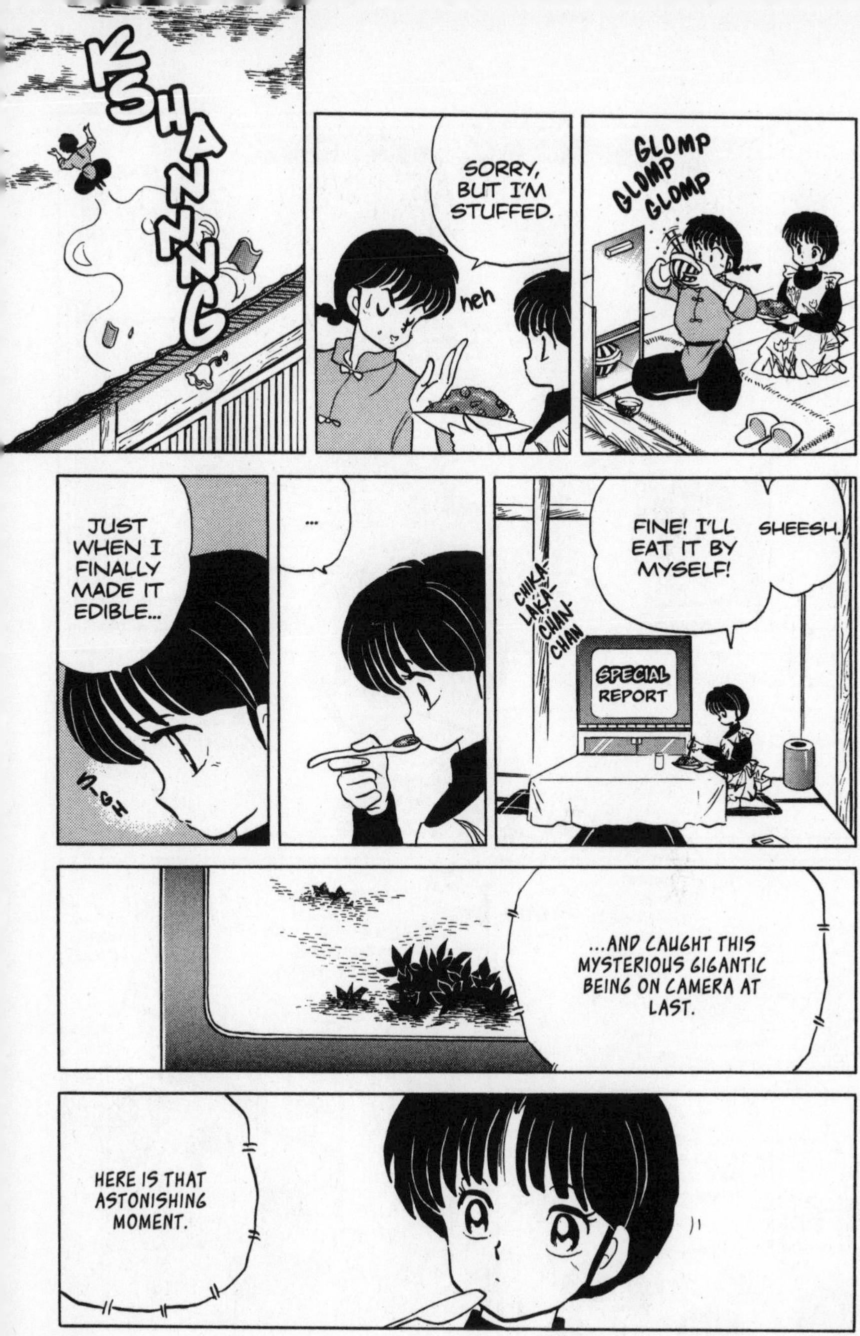
GLOMP
GLOMP
GLOMP
SORRY, BUT I'M STUFFED.
neh
KSHANNNG
SHEESH.
FINE! I'LL EAT IT BY MYSELF!
CHIKA-LAKA-CHAN-CHAN
SPECIAL REPORT
...
JUST WHEN I FINALLY MADE IT EDIBLE...
...AND CAUGHT THIS MYSTERIOUS GIGANTIC BEING ON CAMERA AT LAST.
HERE IS THAT ASTONISHING MOMENT.

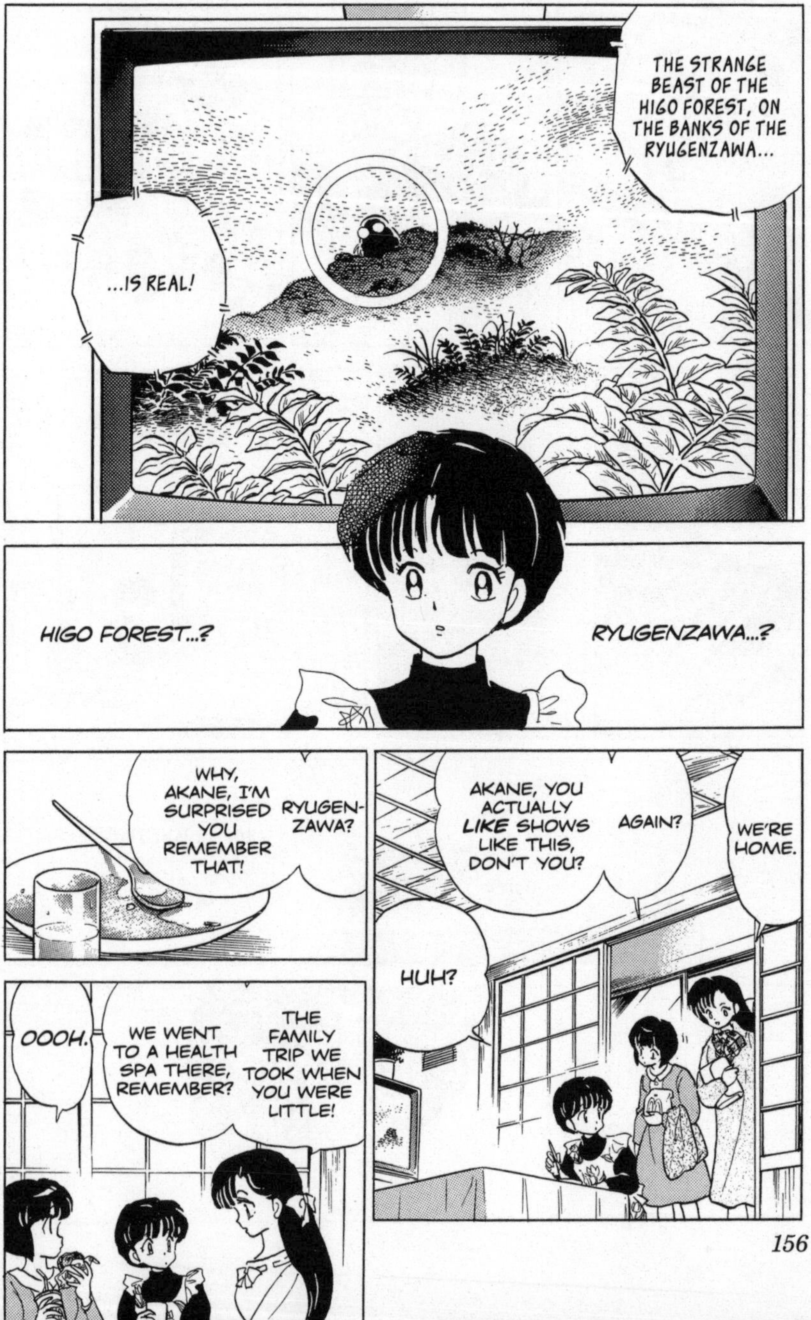
THE STRANGE BEAST OF THE HIGO FOREST, ON THE BANKS OF THE RYUGENZAWA...
...IS REAL!
RYUGENZAWA...?
HIGO FOREST...?
WE'RE HOME.
AGAIN?
AKANE, YOU ACTUALLY *LIKE* SHOWS LIKE THIS, DON'T YOU?
HUH?
RYUGEN-ZAWA?
WHY, AKANE, I'M SURPRISED YOU REMEMBER THAT!
THE FAMILY TRIP WE TOOK WHEN YOU WERE LITTLE!
WE WENT TO A HEALTH SPA THERE, REMEMBER?
OOOH.

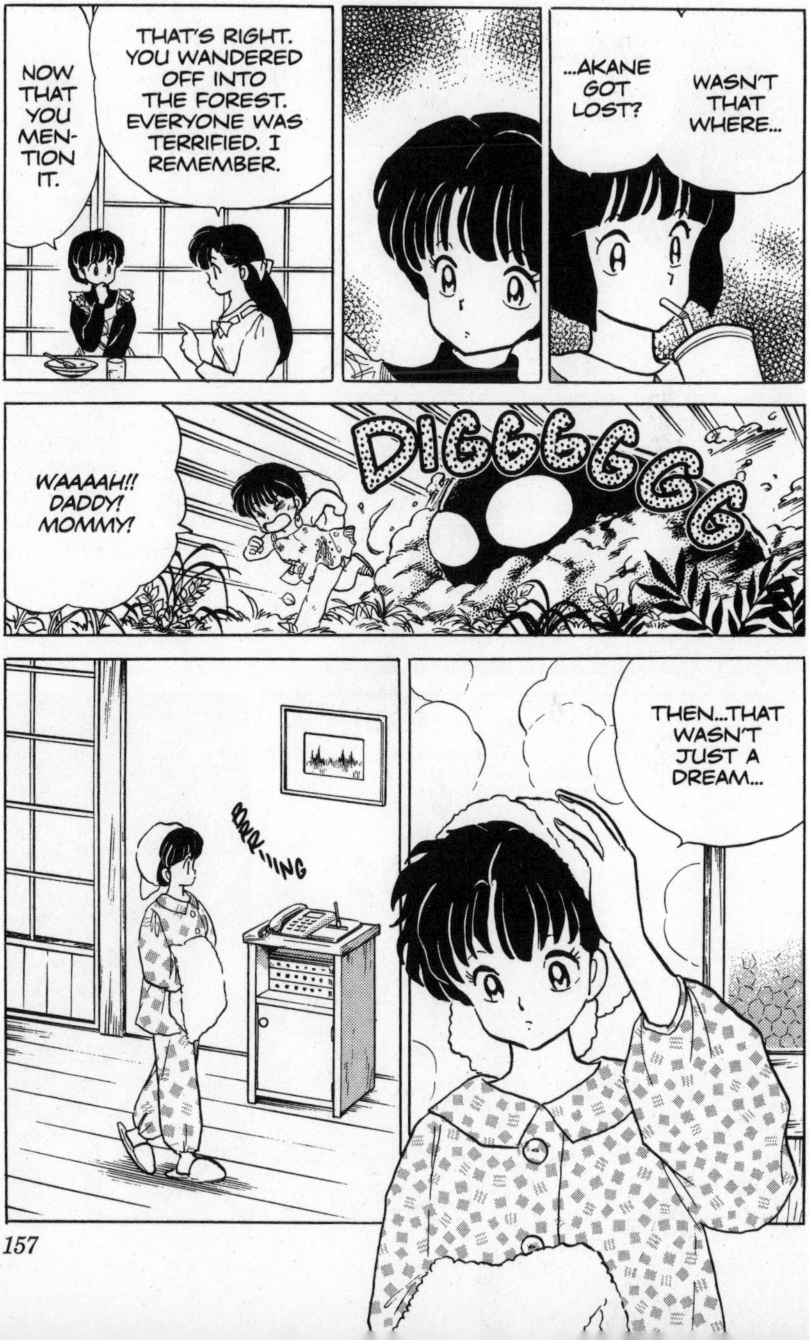
WASN'T THAT WHERE...
...AKANE GOT LOST?
THAT'S RIGHT. YOU WANDERED OFF INTO THE FOREST. EVERYONE WAS TERRIFIED. I REMEMBER.
NOW THAT YOU MEN-TION IT.
DIGGGGGG
WAAAAH!! DADDY! MOMMY!
THEN...THAT WASN'T JUST A DREAM...
BRRR''ING

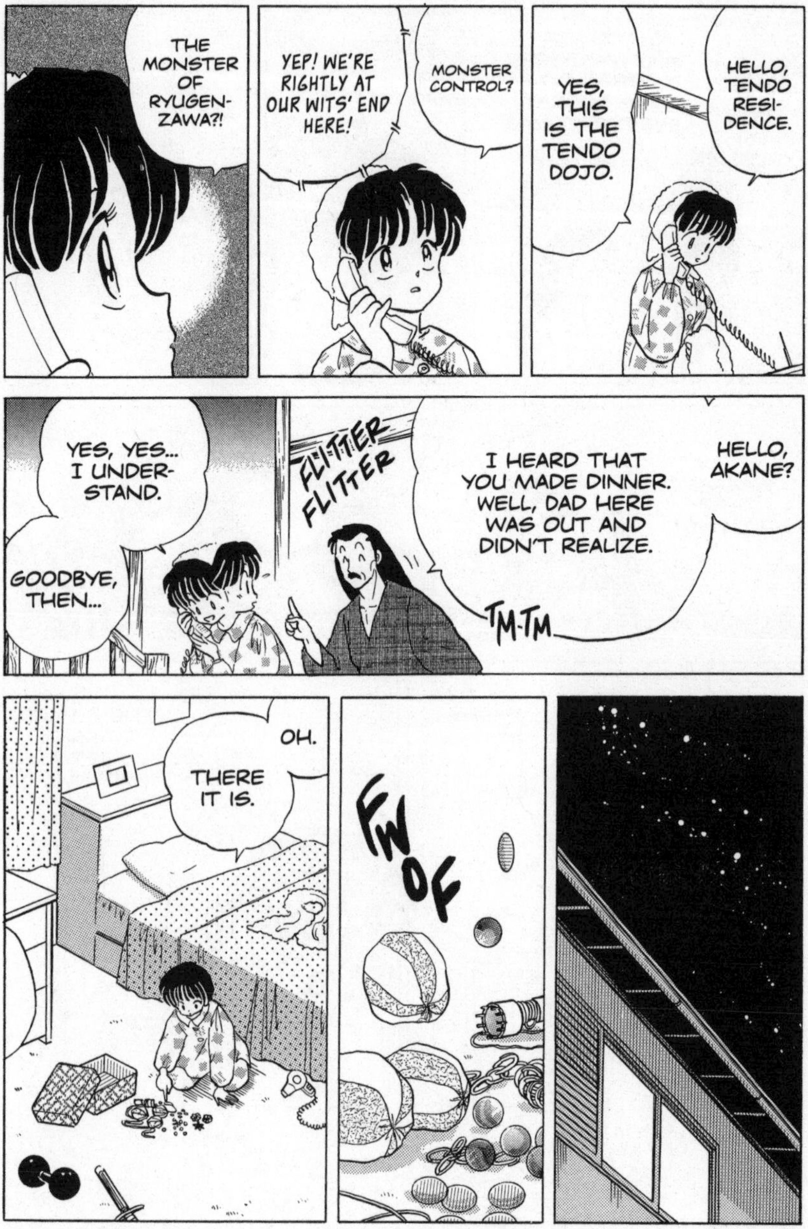
HELLO, TENDO RESI-DENCE.
YES, THIS IS THE TENDO DOJO.
MONSTER CONTROL?
YEP! WE'RE RIGHTLY AT OUR WITS' END HERE!
THE MONSTER OF RYUGEN-ZAWA?!
HELLO, AKANE?
I HEARD THAT YOU MADE DINNER. WELL, DAD HERE WAS OUT AND DIDN'T REALIZE.
TM-TM
FLITTER FLITTER
YES, YES... I UNDER-STAND.
GOODBYE, THEN...
FWOF
OH.
THERE IT IS.

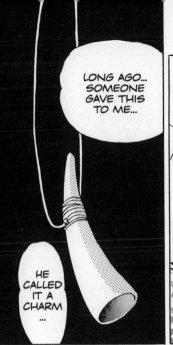

A HORN-PIPE...
LONG AGO... SOMEONE GAVE THIS TO ME...
HE CALLED IT A CHARM ...
CHEEP CHEEP
FATHER, COME QUICK!!
VMM
AKANE LEFT HOME?!
A FAREWELL NOTE?!
I'm off to Ryugenzawa. Don't worry about me.

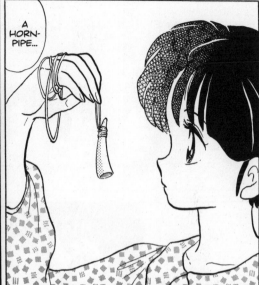

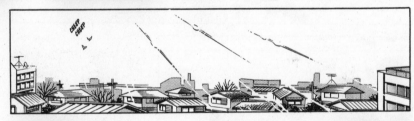

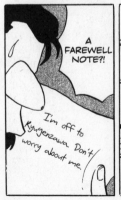

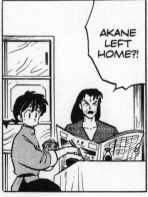

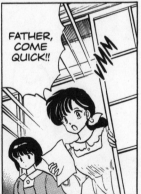

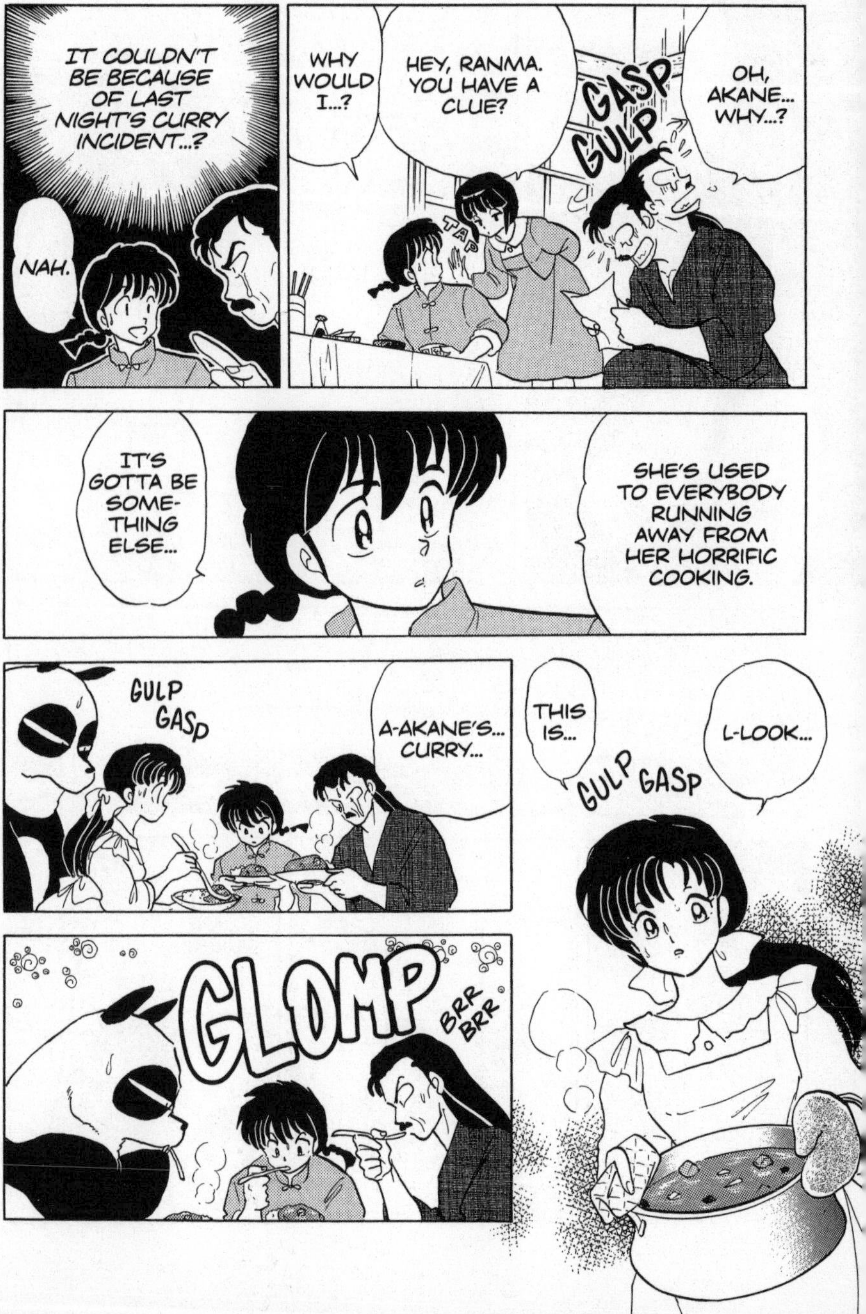
OH, AKANE... WHY...?
GASP GULP
HEY, RANMA. YOU HAVE A CLUE?
WHY WOULD I...?
TAP
IT COULDN'T BE BECAUSE OF LAST NIGHT'S CURRY INCIDENT...?
NAH.
SHE'S USED TO EVERYBODY RUNNING AWAY FROM HER HORRIFIC COOKING.
IT'S GOTTA BE SOME-THING ELSE...
L-LOOK...
THIS IS...
GULP GASP
A-AKANE'S... CURRY...
GULP GASP
GLOMP
BRR BRR

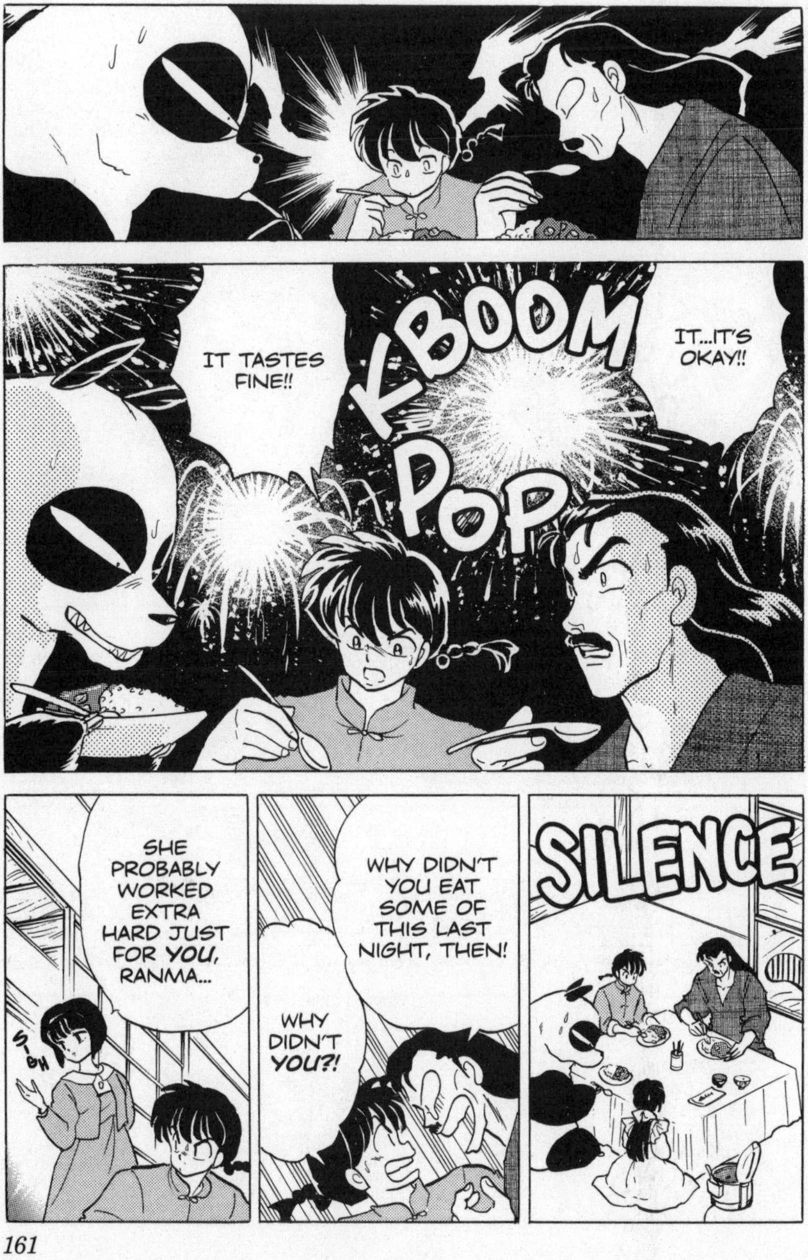
IT...IT'S OKAY!!
KBOOM
IT TASTES FINE!!
POP
SILENCE
WHY DIDN'T YOU EAT SOME OF THIS LAST NIGHT, THEN!
WHY DIDN'T YOU?!
SHE PROBABLY WORKED EXTRA HARD JUST FOR YOU, RANMA...
SIGH

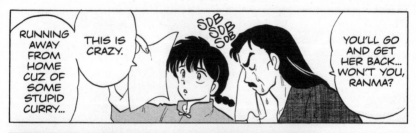

YOU'LL GO AND GET HER BACK... WON'T YOU, RANMA?
SOB SOB SOB
THIS IS CRAZY.
RUNNING AWAY FROM HOME CUZ OF SOME STUPID CURRY...
RAAAAAN-MAAAA!!
DM DM DM DM DM DM
NNNN...
YESSIR.
LEAVING RIGHT NOW.
KTANK KTANK
WELL, MONSTER CONTROL IS THE RESPONSIBILITY OF A MARTIAL ARTIST.
I'LL JUST TELL DAD ABOUT IT WHEN I GET HOME.

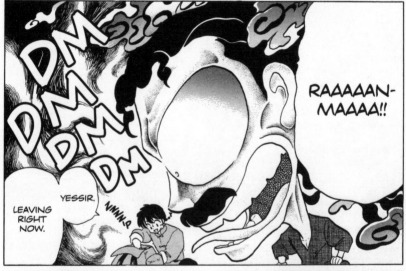

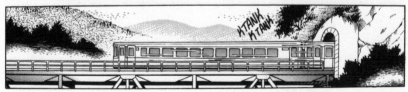

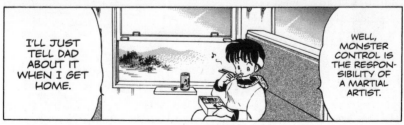

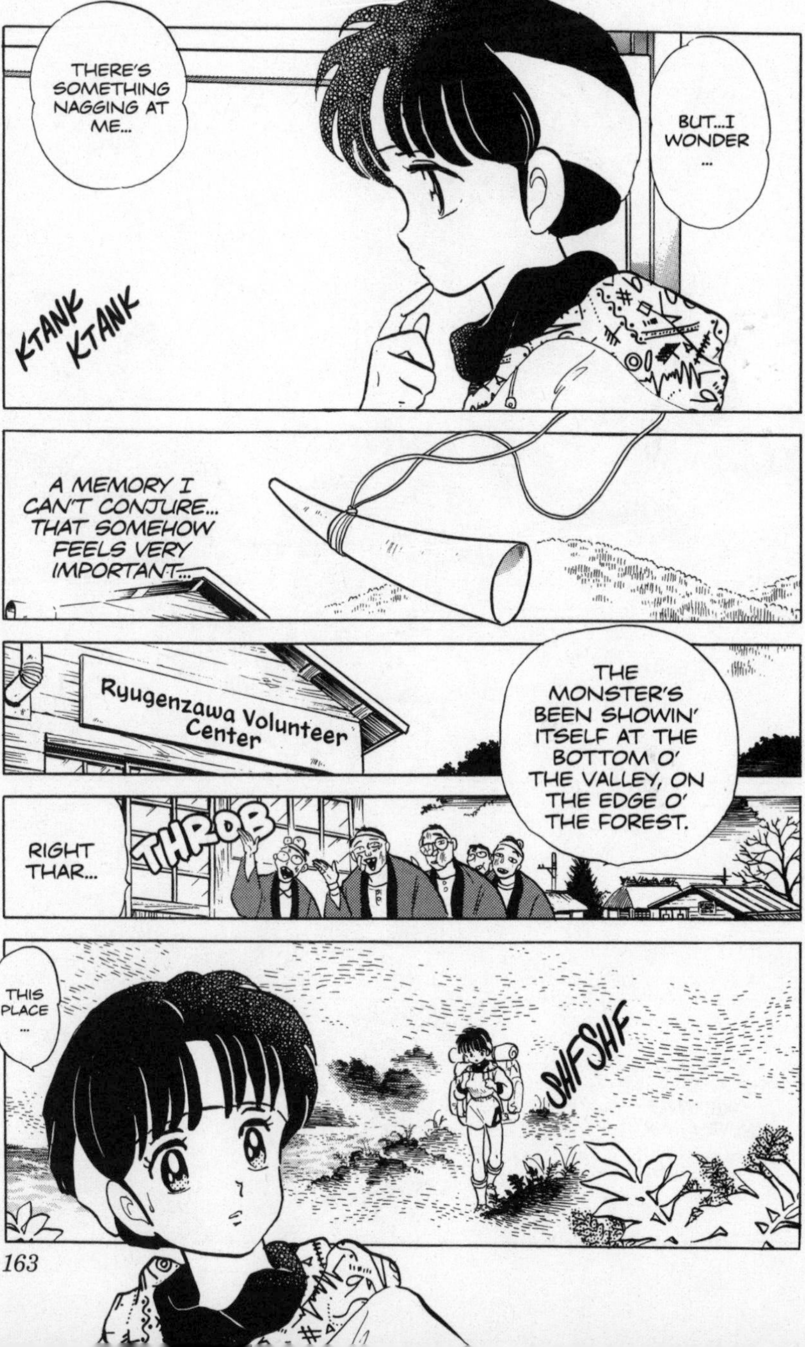
BUT...I WONDER ...
THERE'S SOMETHING NAGGING AT ME...
KTANK KTANK
A MEMORY I CAN'T CONJURE... THAT SOMEHOW FEELS VERY IMPORTANT...
Ryugenzawa Volunteer Center
THE MONSTER'S BEEN SHOWIN' ITSELF AT THE BOTTOM O' THE VALLEY, ON THE EDGE O' THE FOREST.
THROB
RIGHT THAR...
SHFSHF
THIS PLACE ...

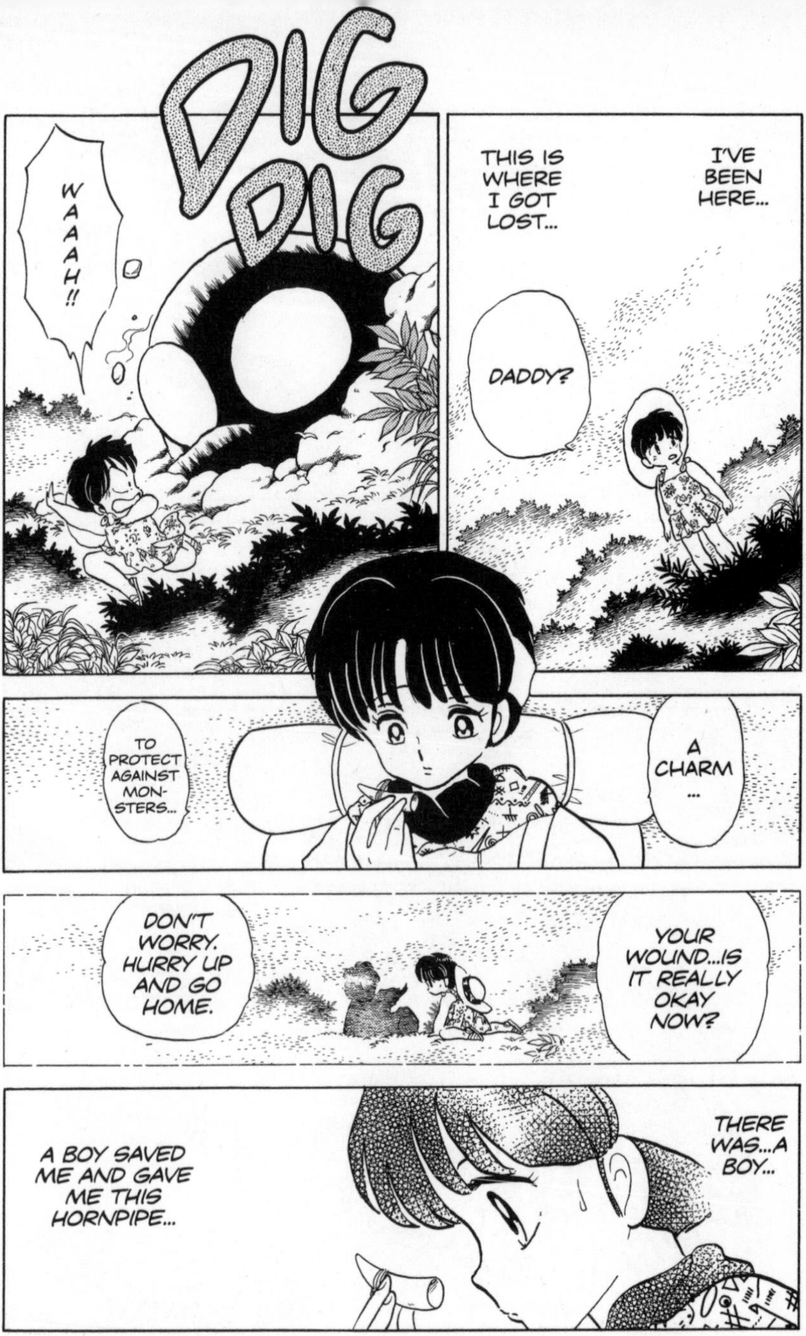
I'VE BEEN HERE...
THIS IS WHERE I GOT LOST...
DADDY?
DIG DIG
WAAAAH!!
A CHARM...
TO PROTECT AGAINST MON-STERS...
YOUR WOUND...IS IT REALLY OKAY NOW?
DON'T WORRY. HURRY UP AND GO HOME.
THERE WAS...A BOY...
A BOY SAVED ME AND GAVE ME THIS HORNPIPE...

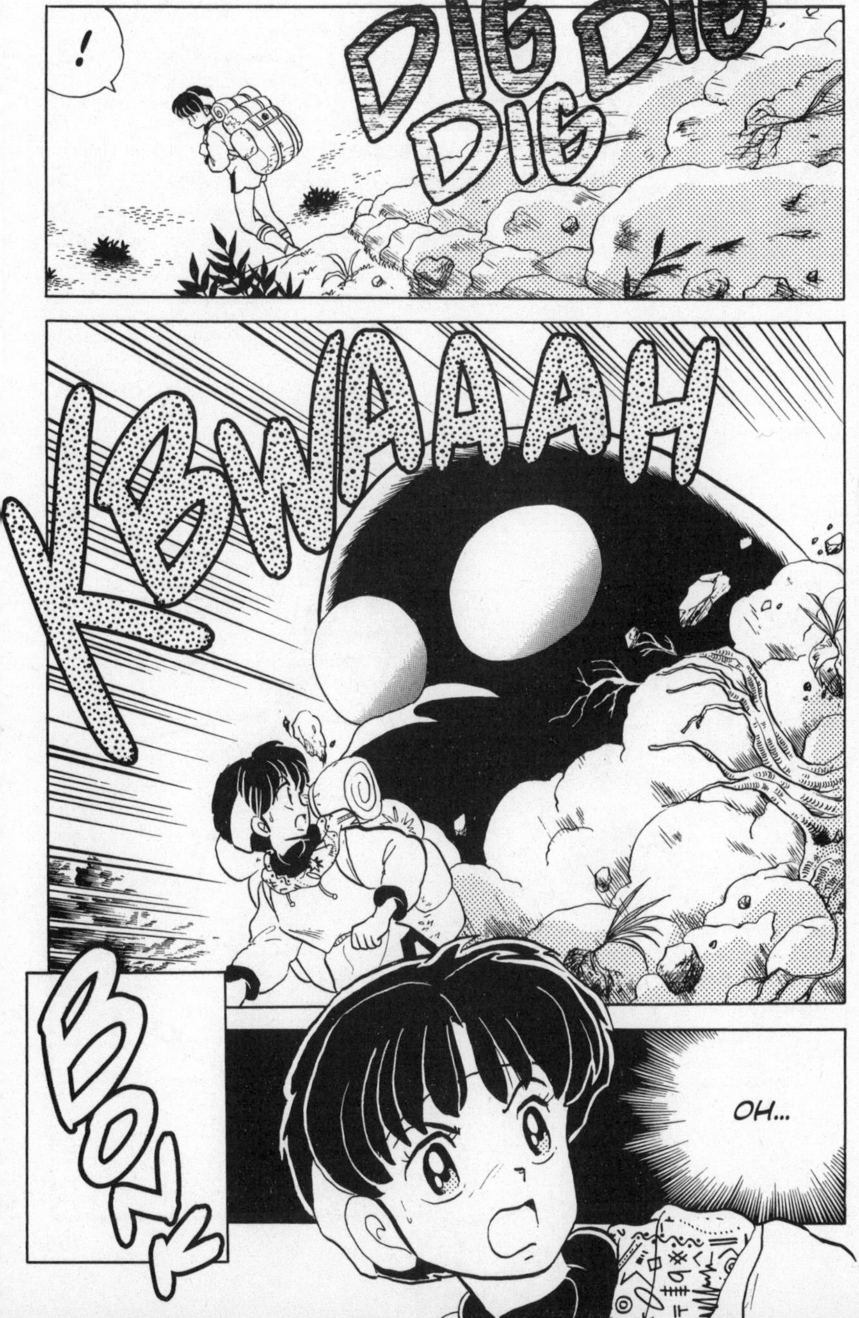
!
DIG DIG DIG
KBWAAAH
OH...
BOLK

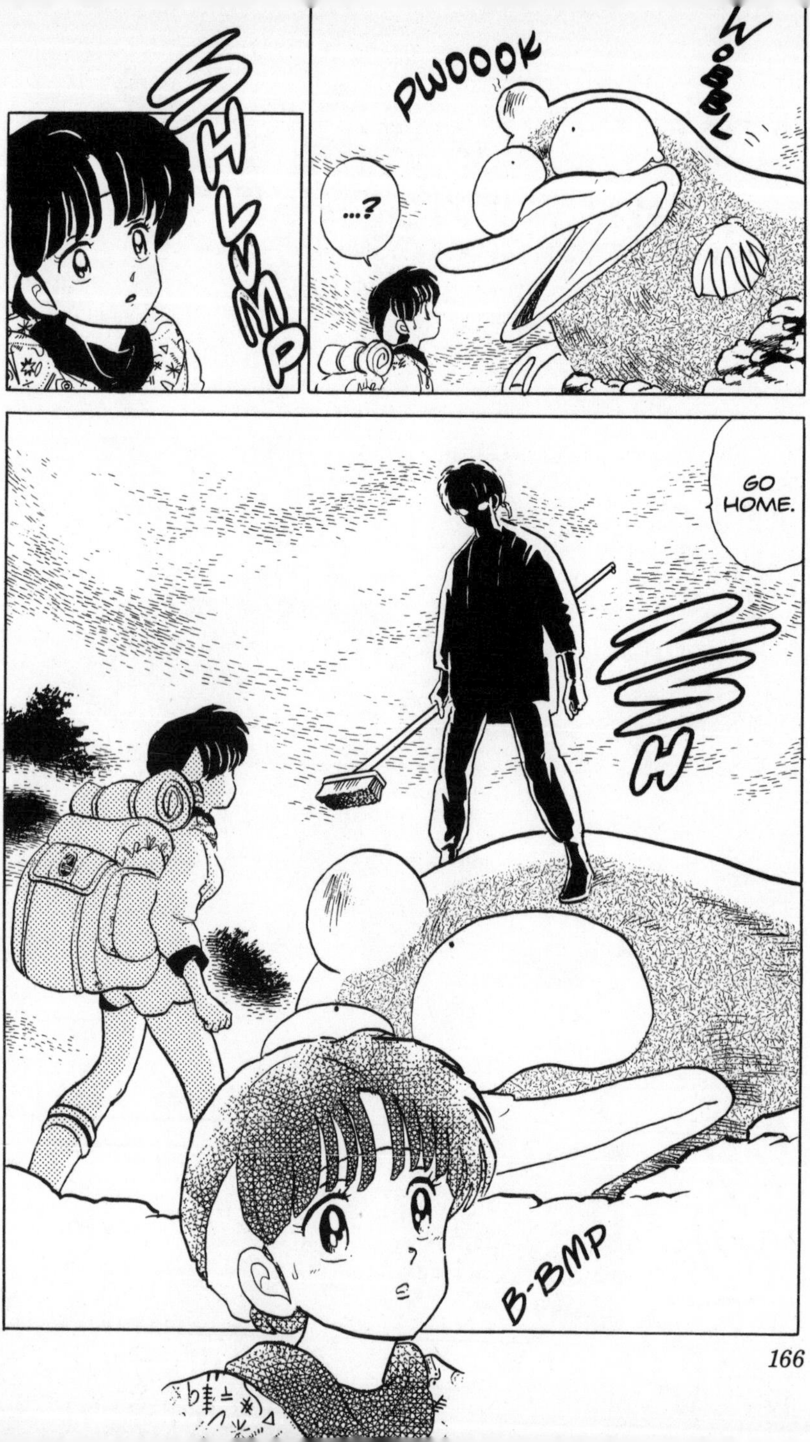
WOBBL
PWOOOK
...?
SHLUMP
GO HOME.
WSSH
B-BMP

PART 11
RECOVERED MEMORIES

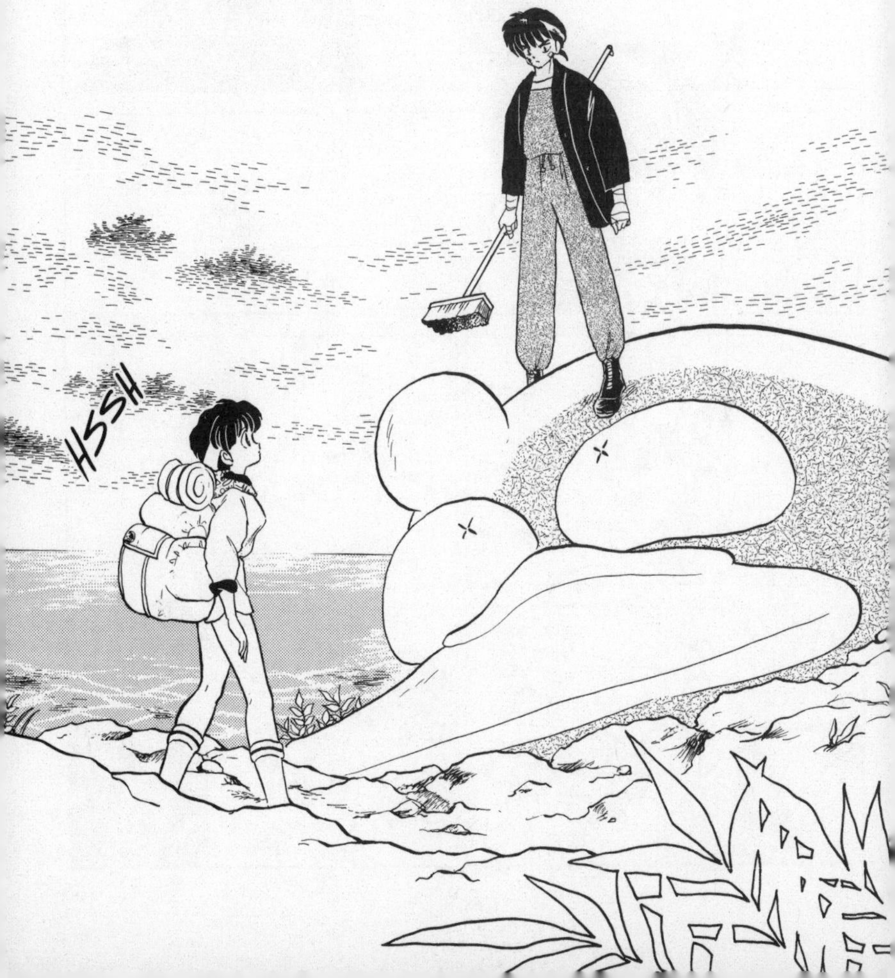
HSSH

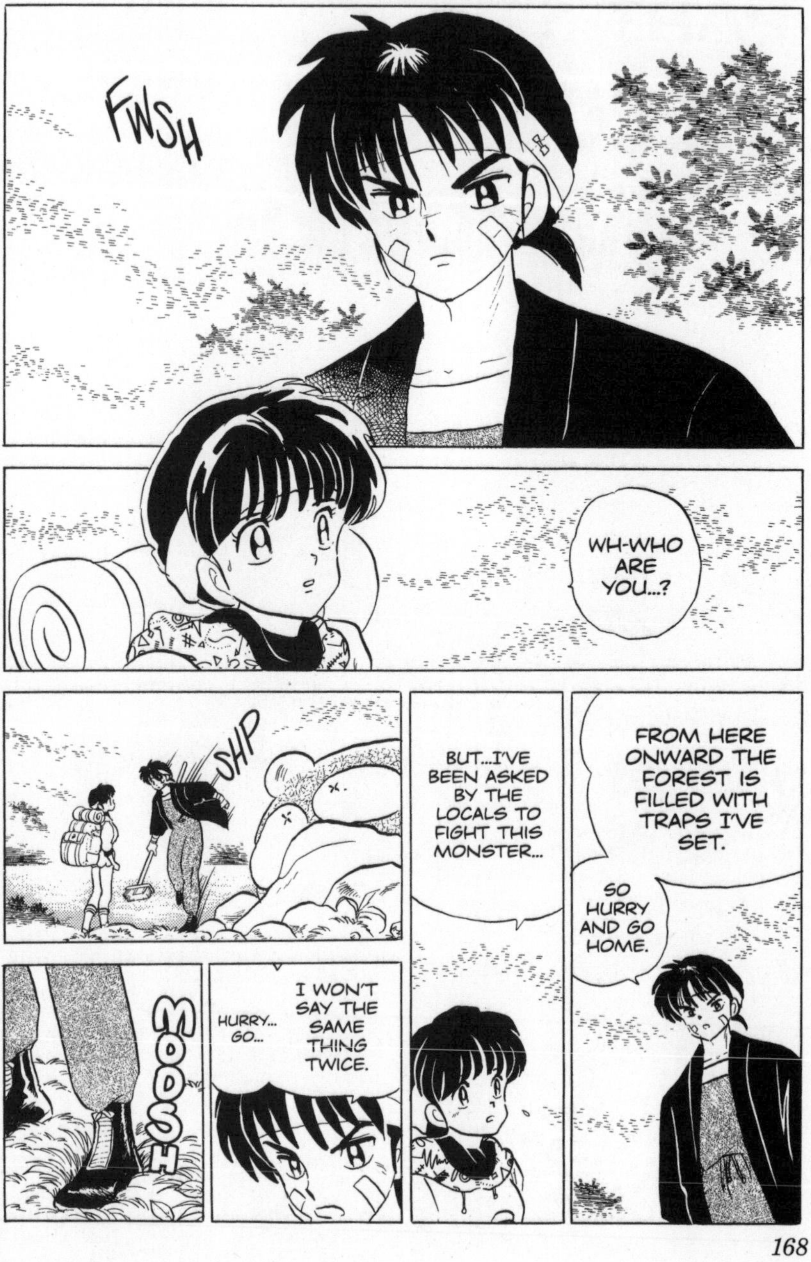
FWSH
WH-WHO ARE YOU...?
FROM HERE ONWARD THE FOREST IS FILLED WITH TRAPS I'VE SET.
SO HURRY AND GO HOME.
BUT...I'VE BEEN ASKED BY THE LOCALS TO FIGHT THIS MONSTER...
SHP
I WON'T SAY THE SAME THING TWICE.
HURRY... GO...
MOOSH

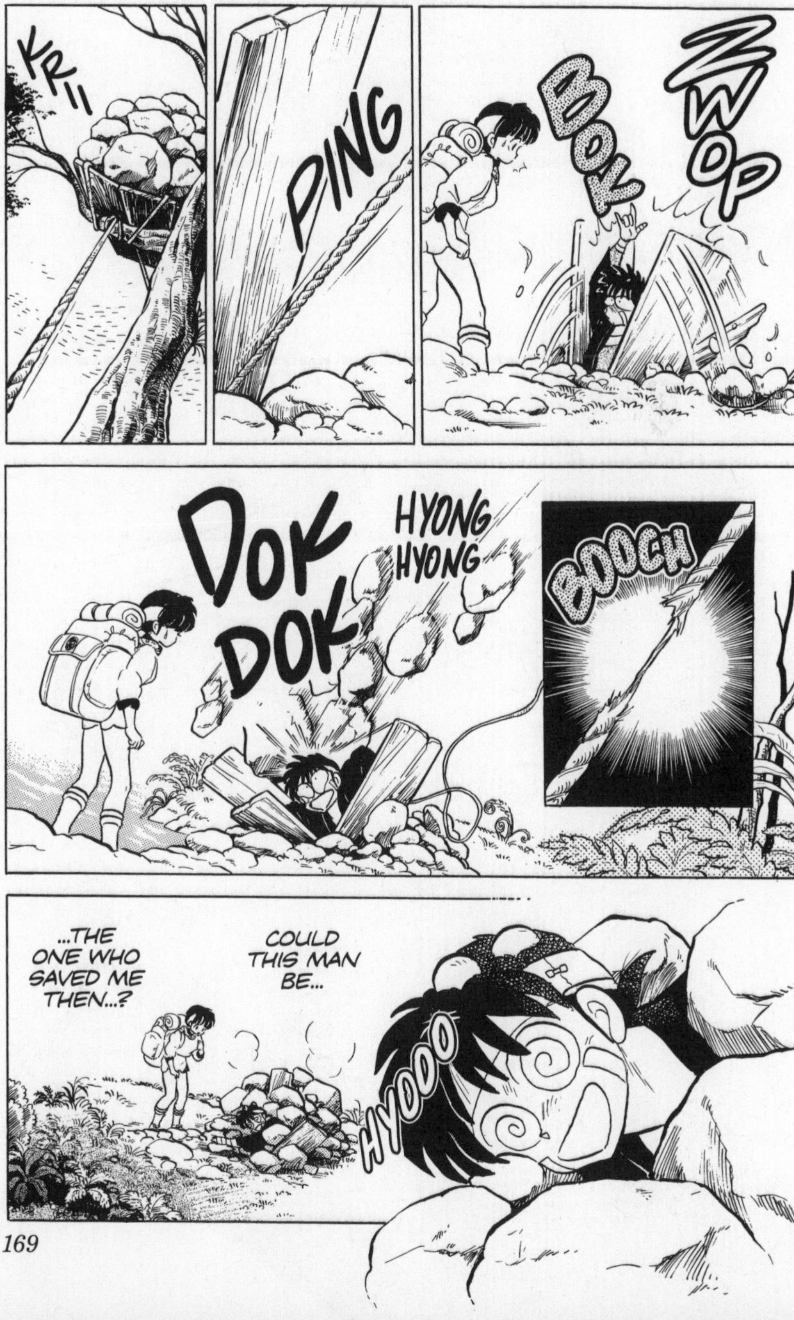
ZWOP
BOW
PING
KRII
BOOCH
HYONG HYONG
DOK DOK
COULD THIS MAN BE...
...THE ONE WHO SAVED ME THEN...?
HYODO

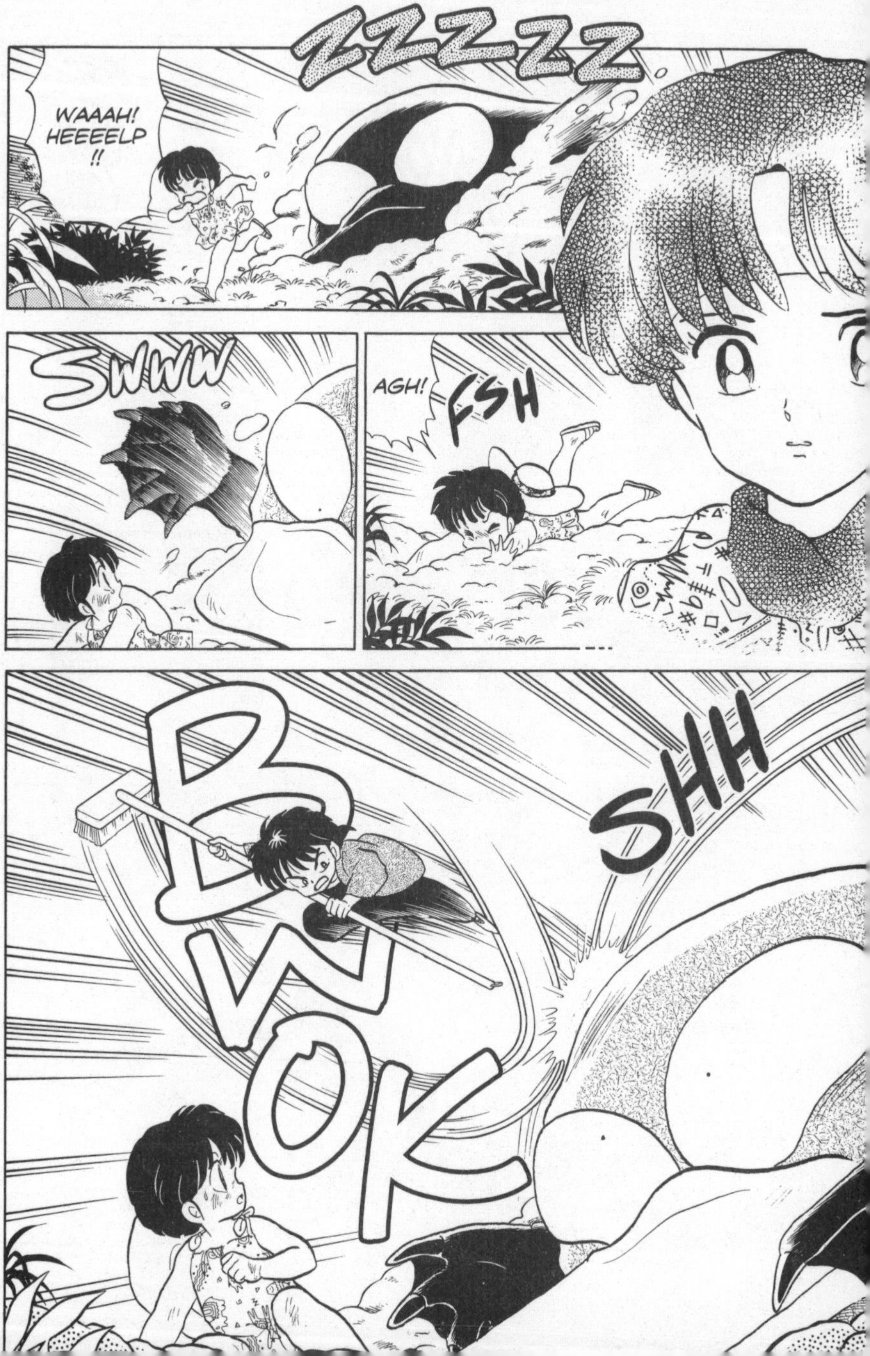
ZZZZZZ
WAAAH! HEEEELP !!
AGH!
FSH
SWWW
SHH
BWOK

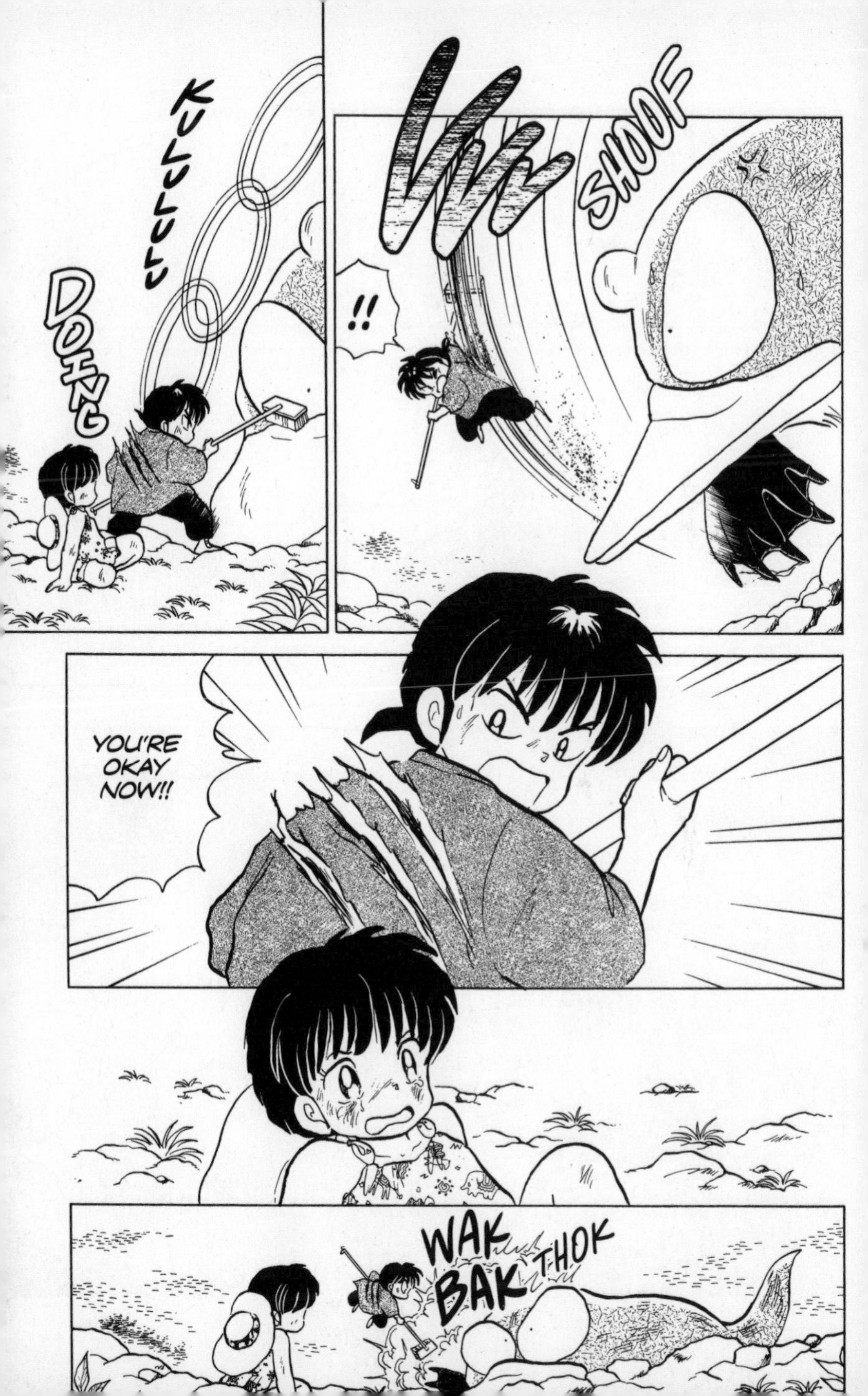
SHOOF
!!
KULULULULU
DOING
YOU'RE OKAY NOW!!
WAK
BAK
THOK

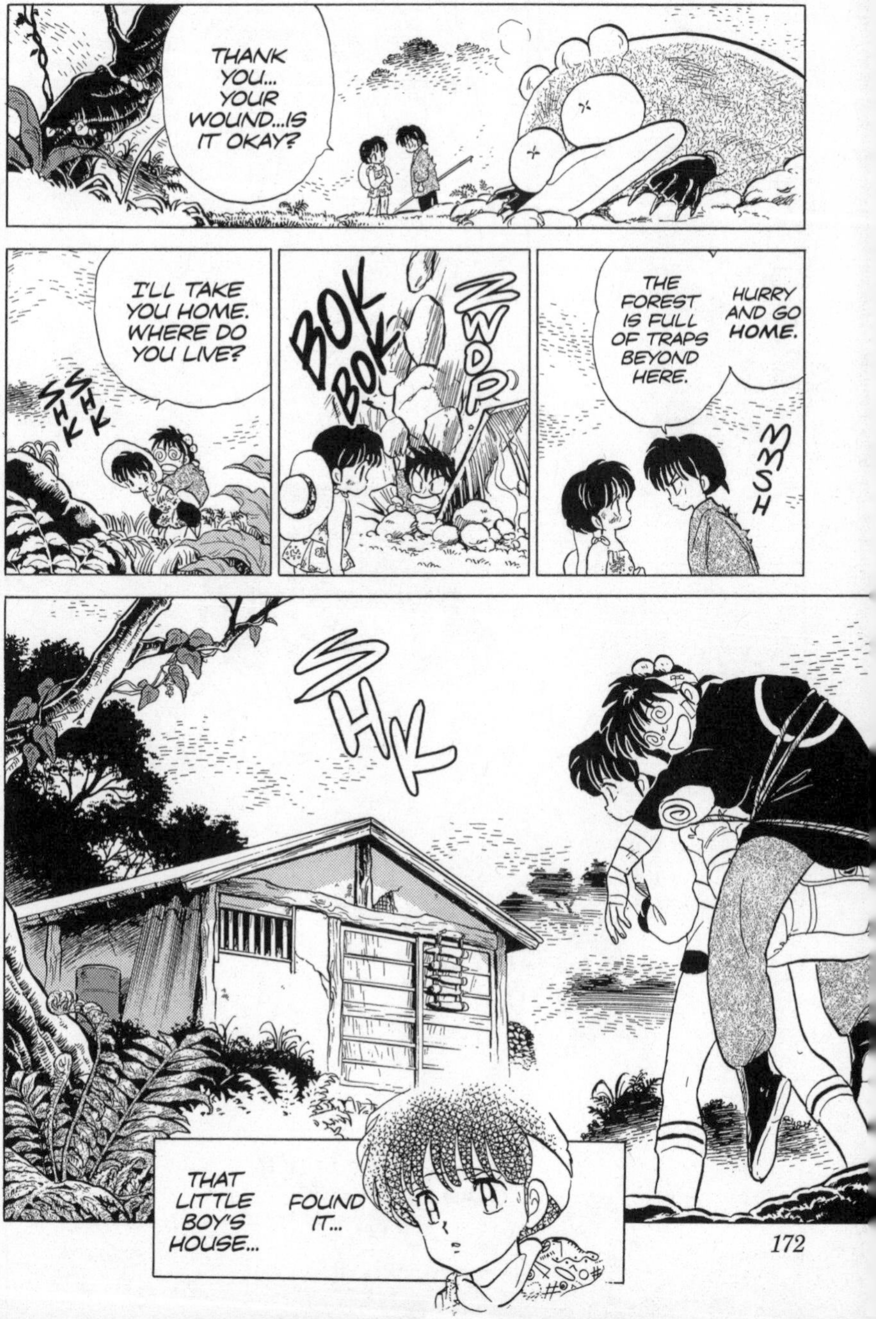
THANK YOU... YOUR WOUND...IS IT OKAY?
HURRY AND GO HOME.
THE FOREST IS FULL OF TRAPS BEYOND HERE.
MMSH
ZWDP
BOK BOK
I'LL TAKE YOU HOME. WHERE DO YOU LIVE?
SHK SHK
SHK
THAT LITTLE BOY'S HOUSE...
FOUND IT...

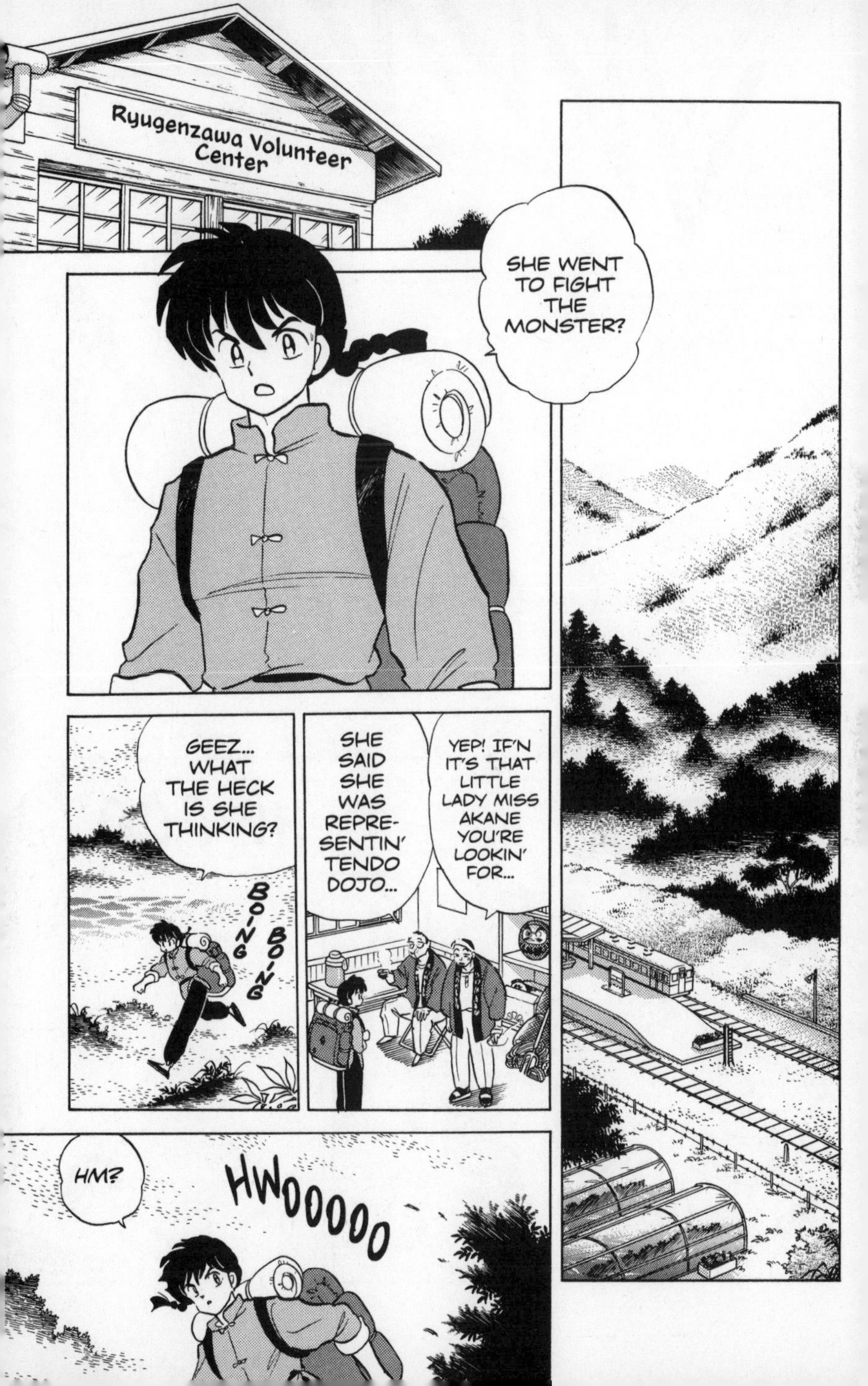
SHE WENT TO FIGHT THE MONSTER?
Ryugenzawa Volunteer Center
YEP! IF'N IT'S THAT LITTLE LADY MISS AKANE YOU'RE LOOKIN' FOR...
SHE SAID SHE WAS REPRE-SENTIN' TENDO DOJO...
GEEZ... WHAT THE HECK IS SHE THINKING?
BOING BOING
HM?
HWOOOOOO

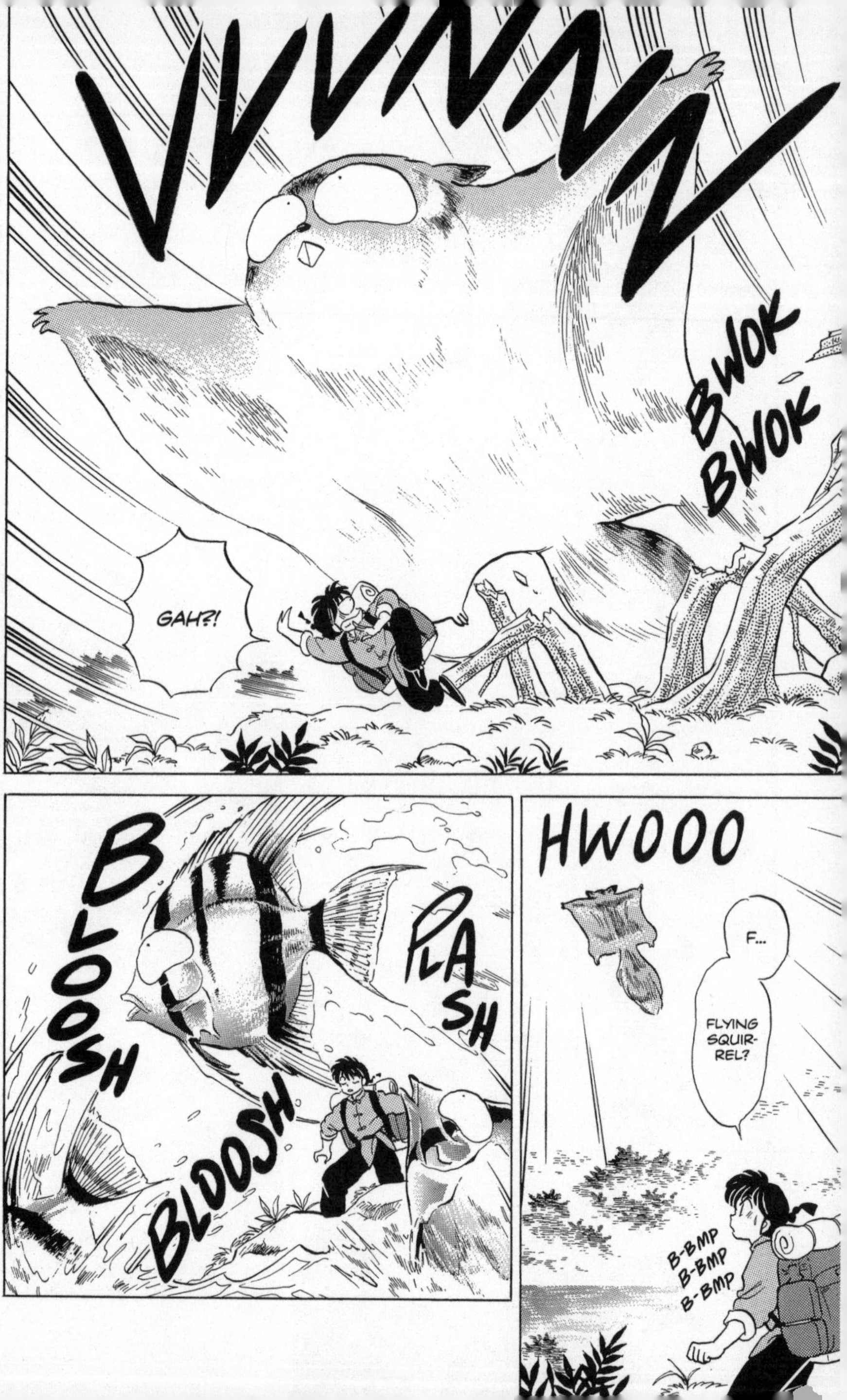
VVVNNN
BWOK BWOK
GAH?!
HWOOO
F...
FLYING SQUIR-REL?
B-BMP B-BMP B-BMP
BLOOSH
PLASH
BLOOSH

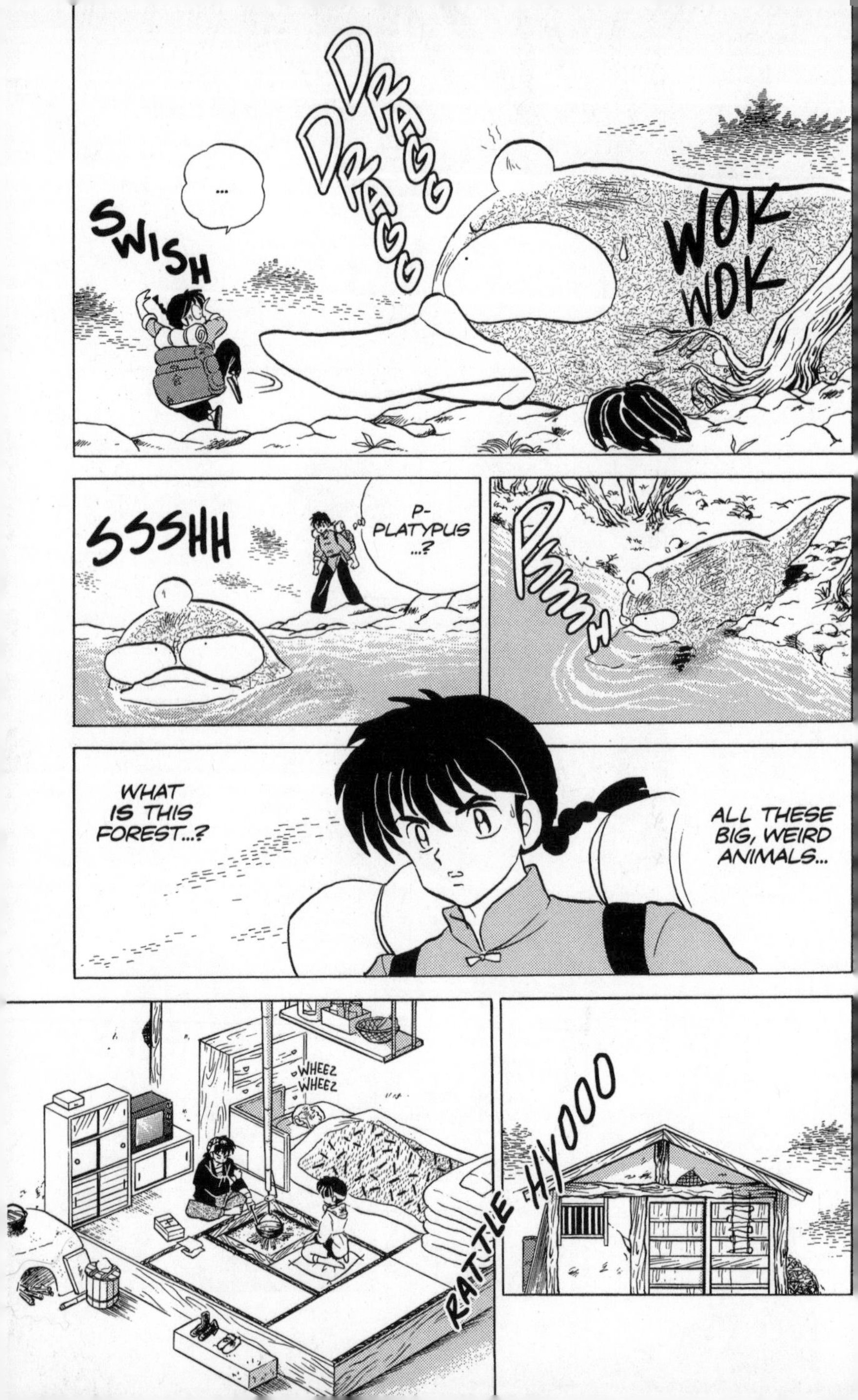
WOK WOK
DRAGU DRAGU
...
SWISH
P-PLATYPUS...?
SSSHH
ALL THESE BIG, WEIRD ANIMALS...
WHAT IS THIS FOREST...?
HYOOO
RATTLE
WHEEZ WHEEZ

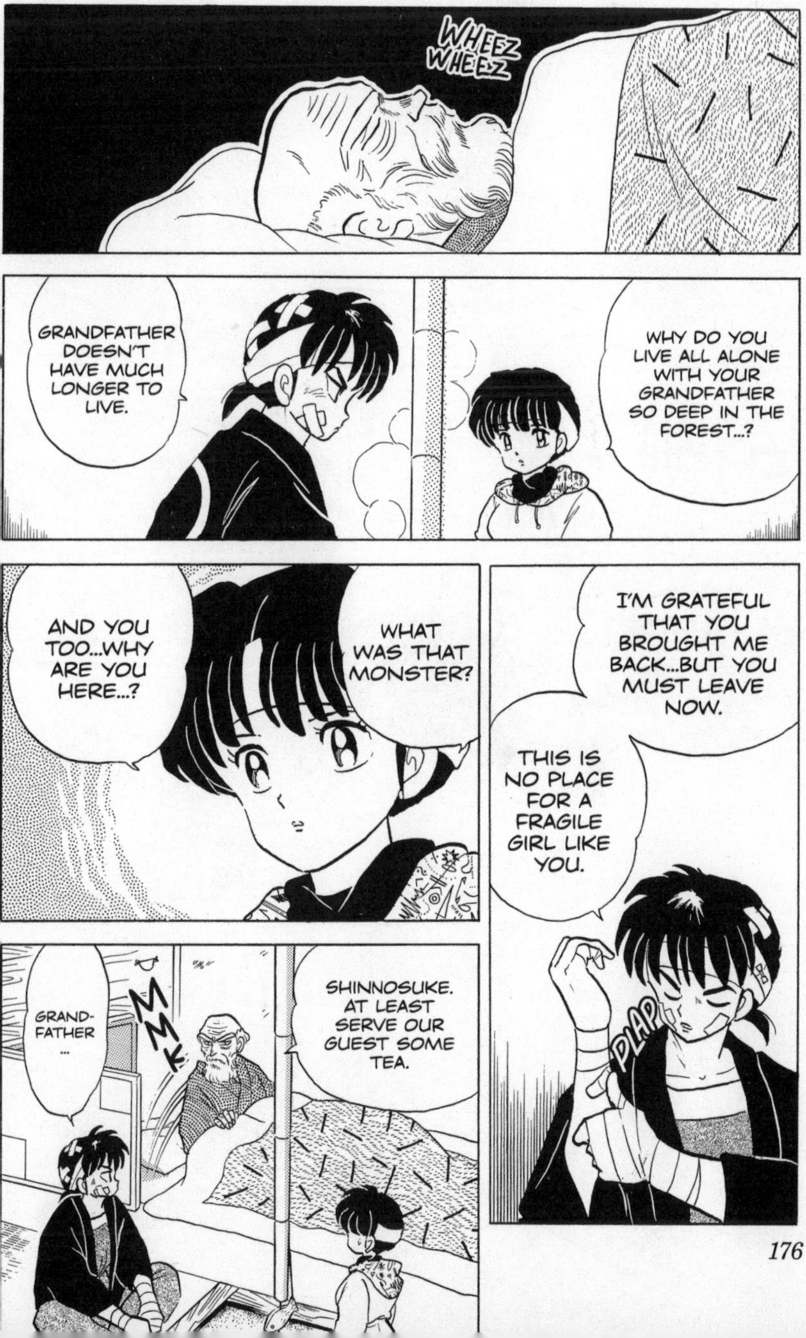
WHEEZ WHEEZ
WHY DO YOU LIVE ALL ALONE WITH YOUR GRANDFATHER SO DEEP IN THE FOREST...?
GRANDFATHER DOESN'T HAVE MUCH LONGER TO LIVE.
I'M GRATEFUL THAT YOU BROUGHT ME BACK...BUT YOU MUST LEAVE NOW.
THIS IS NO PLACE FOR A FRAGILE GIRL LIKE YOU.
PLAP
WHAT WAS THAT MONSTER?
AND YOU TOO...WHY ARE YOU HERE...?
SHINNOSUKE. AT LEAST SERVE OUR GUEST SOME TEA.
MMK
GRAND-FATHER ...

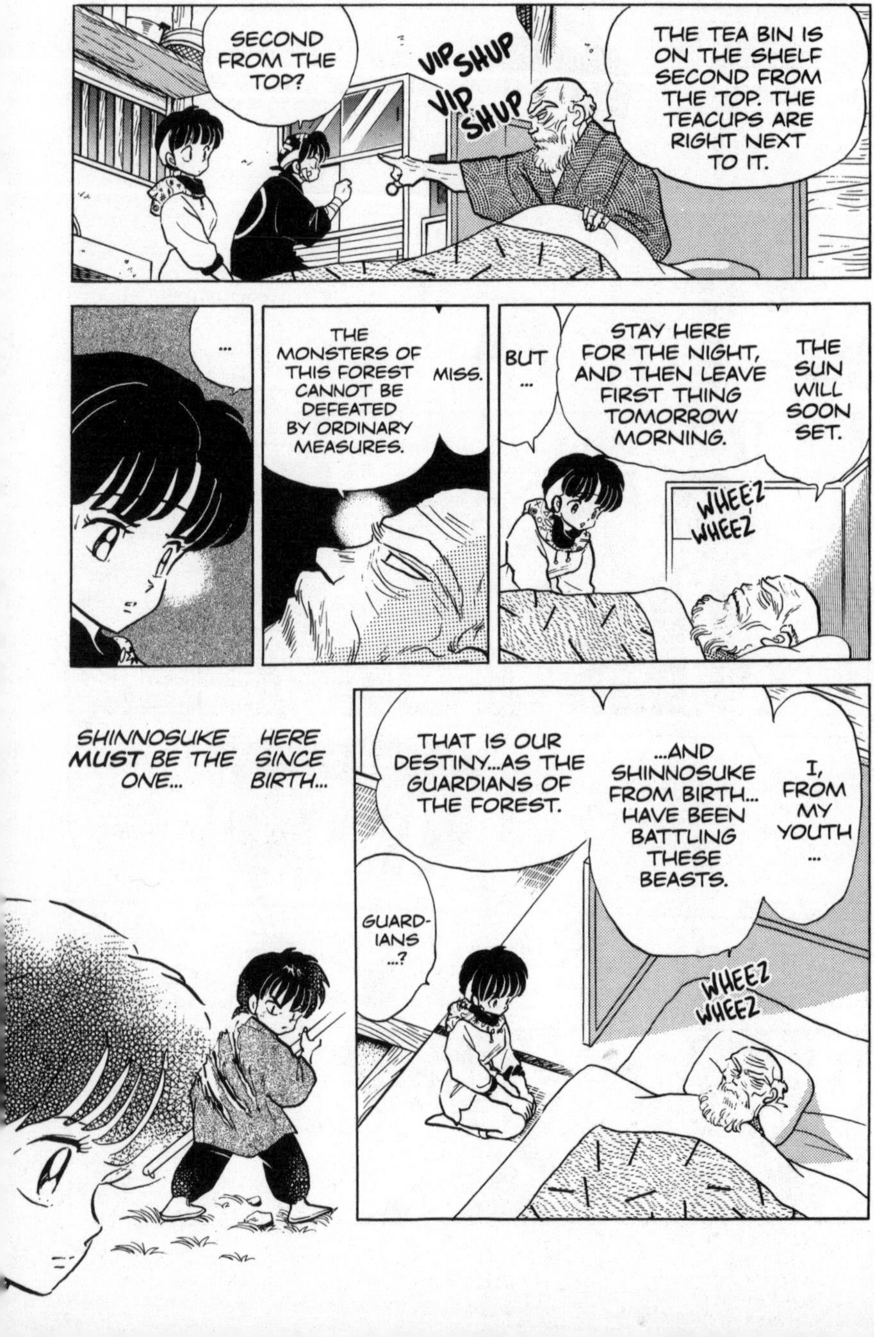
THE TEA BIN IS ON THE SHELF SECOND FROM THE TOP. THE TEACUPS ARE RIGHT NEXT TO IT.
VIP SHUP
VIP SHUP
SECOND FROM THE TOP?
THE SUN WILL SOON SET.
STAY HERE FOR THE NIGHT, AND THEN LEAVE FIRST THING TOMORROW MORNING.
BUT ...
WHEEZ WHEEZ
MISS.
THE MONSTERS OF THIS FOREST CANNOT BE DEFEATED BY ORDINARY MEASURES.
...
I, FROM MY YOUTH ...
...AND SHINNOSUKE FROM BIRTH... HAVE BEEN BATTLING THESE BEASTS.
THAT IS OUR DESTINY...AS THE GUARDIANS OF THE FOREST.
GUARD-IANS ...?
WHEEZ WHEEZ
HERE SINCE BIRTH...
SHINNOSUKE MUST BE THE ONE...

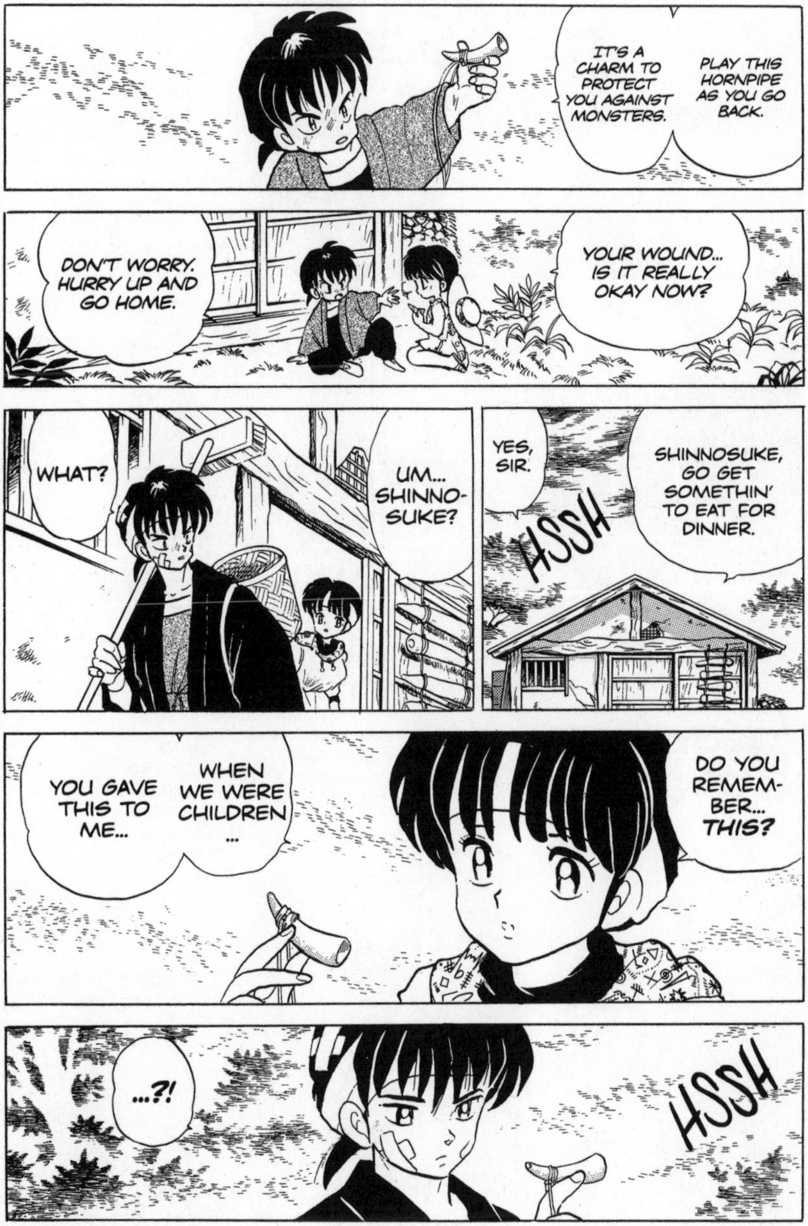
PLAY THIS HORNPIPE AS YOU GO BACK.
IT'S A CHARM TO PROTECT YOU AGAINST MONSTERS.
YOUR WOUND... IS IT REALLY OKAY NOW?
DON'T WORRY. HURRY UP AND GO HOME.
SHINNOSUKE, GO GET SOMETHIN' TO EAT FOR DINNER.
YES, SIR.
HSSH
UM... SHINNOSUKE?
WHAT?
DO YOU REMEMBER... THIS?
WHEN WE WERE CHILDREN...
YOU GAVE THIS TO ME...
HSSH
...?!

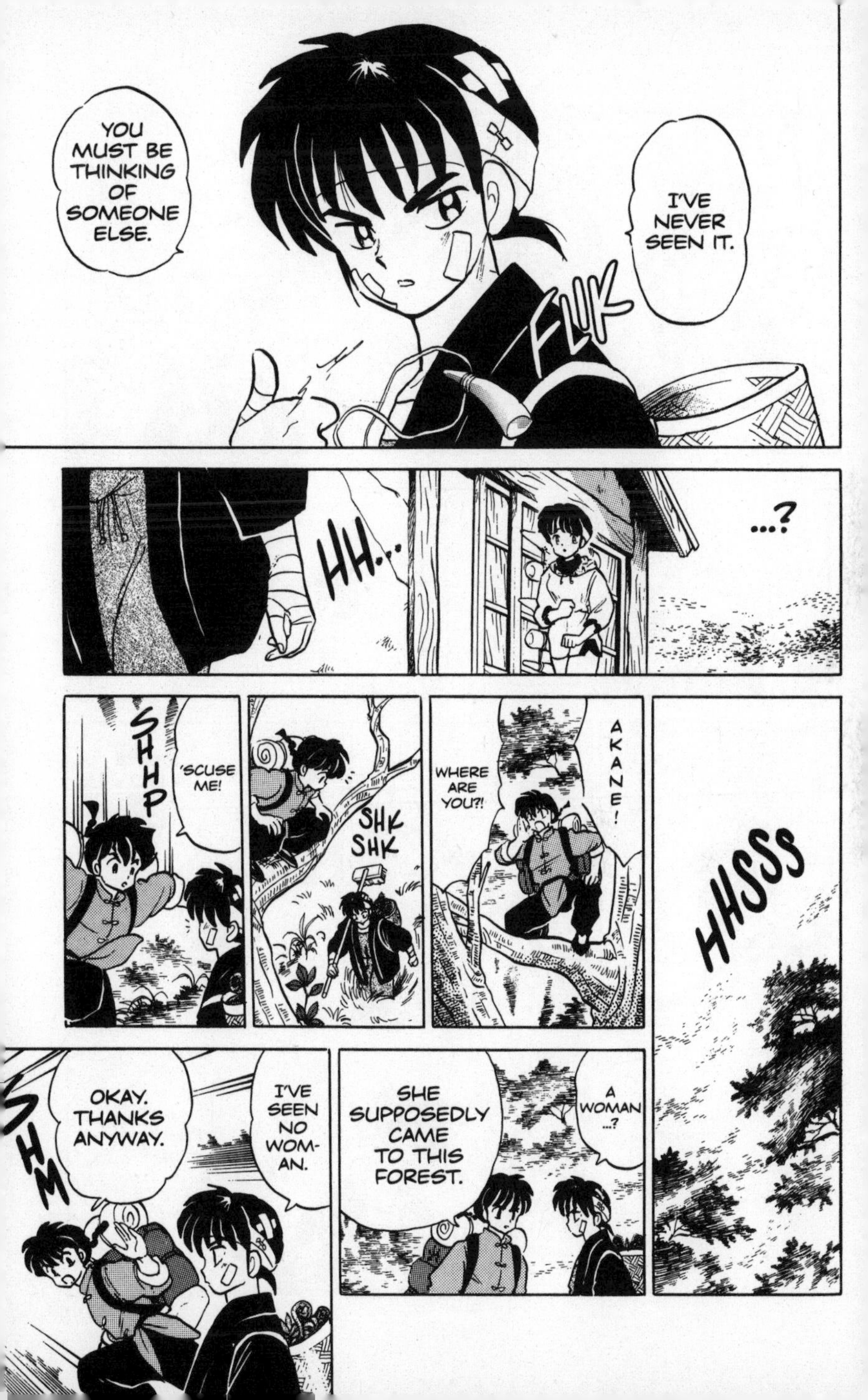
I'VE NEVER SEEN IT.
FLIK
YOU MUST BE THINKING OF SOMEONE ELSE.
...?
HH...
HHSSS
AKANE!
WHERE ARE YOU?!
SHK SHK
SHHP
'SCUSE ME!
A WOMAN ...?
SHE SUPPOSEDLY CAME TO THIS FOREST.
I'VE SEEN NO WOM-AN.
OKAY. THANKS ANYWAY.
SHM

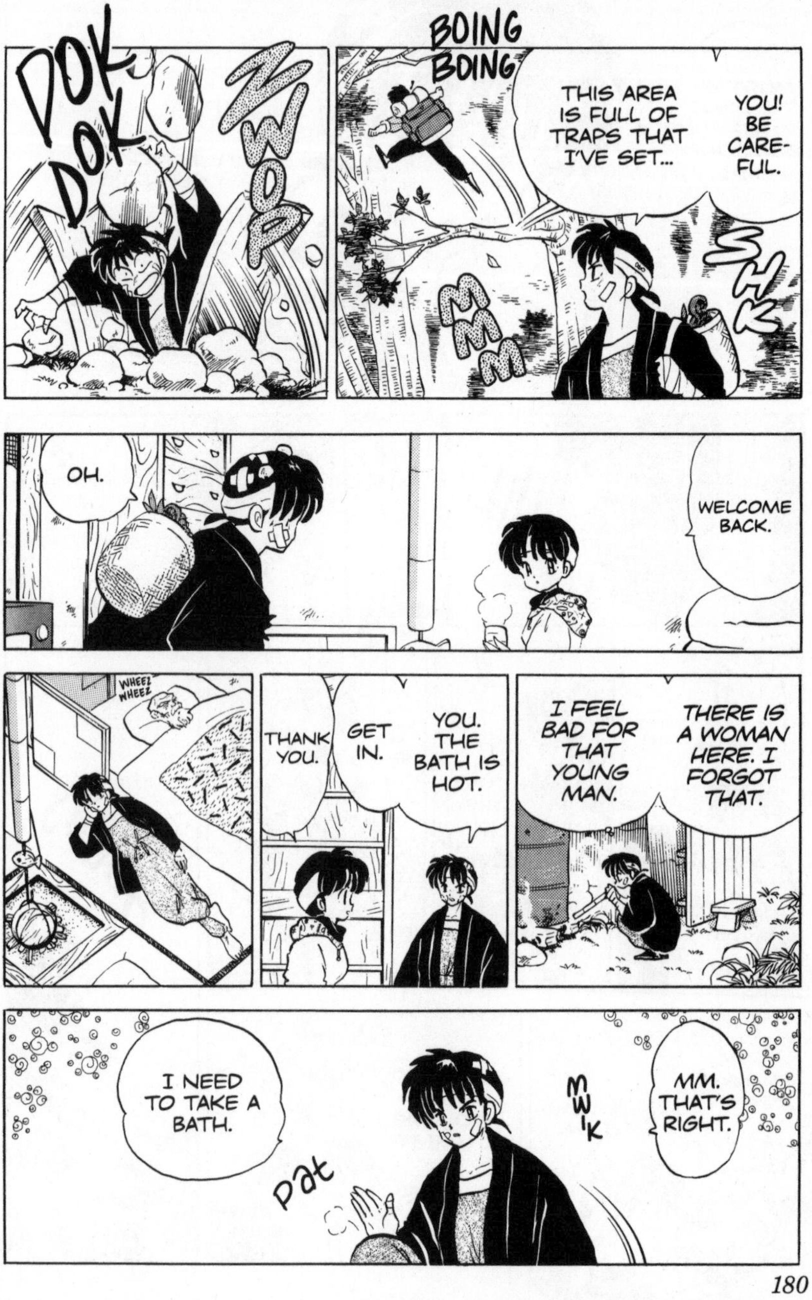
BOING
BOING
YOU! BE CAREFUL.
THIS AREA IS FULL OF TRAPS THAT I'VE SET...
MMM
SHK
DOK DOK
ZWOP
WELCOME BACK.
OH.
THERE IS A WOMAN HERE. I FORGOT THAT.
I FEEL BAD FOR THAT YOUNG MAN.
YOU. THE BATH IS HOT.
GET IN.
THANK YOU.
WHEEZ WHEEZ
MM. THAT'S RIGHT.
MWIK
I NEED TO TAKE A BATH.
pat

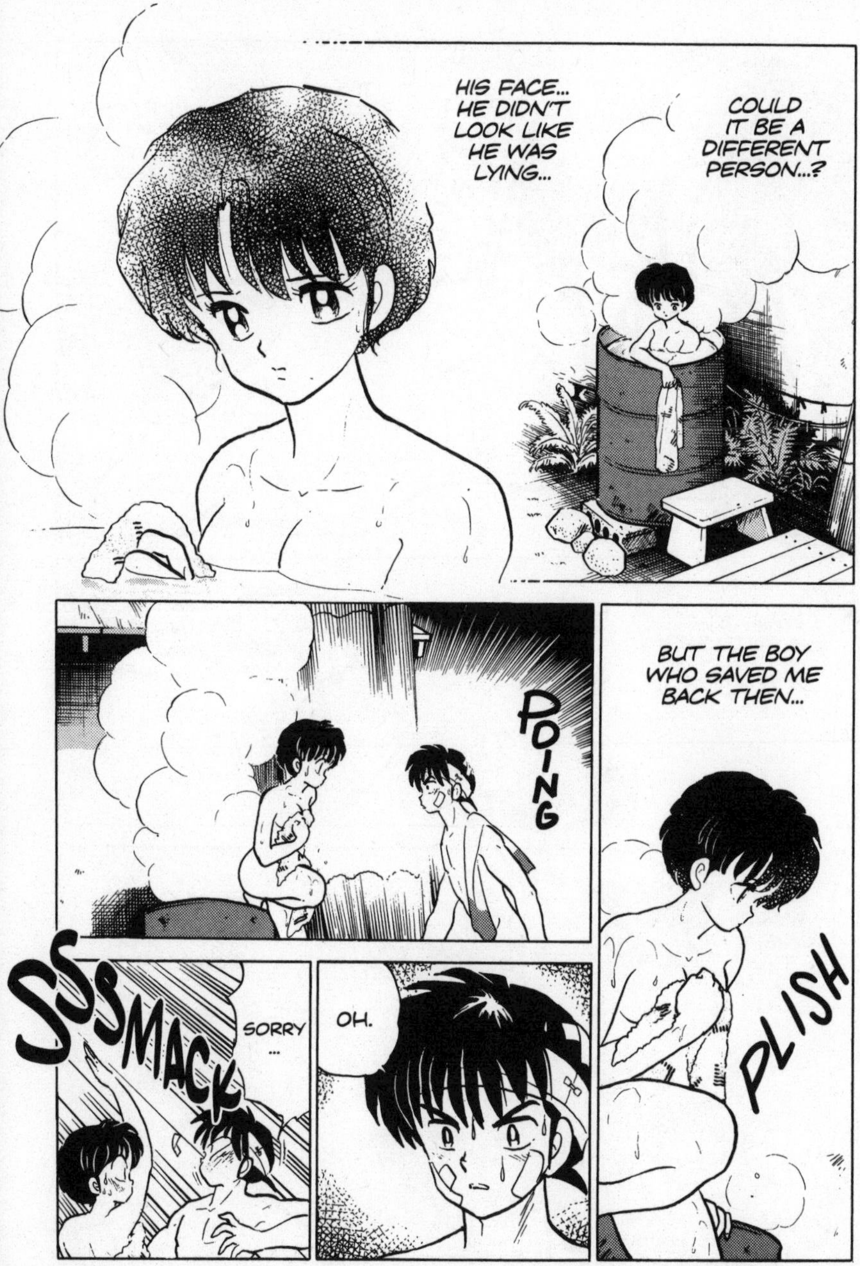
COULD IT BE A DIFFERENT PERSON...?
HIS FACE... HE DIDN'T LOOK LIKE HE WAS LYING...
BUT THE BOY WHO SAVED ME BACK THEN...
PLISH
POING
OH.
SORRY...
SSSMACK

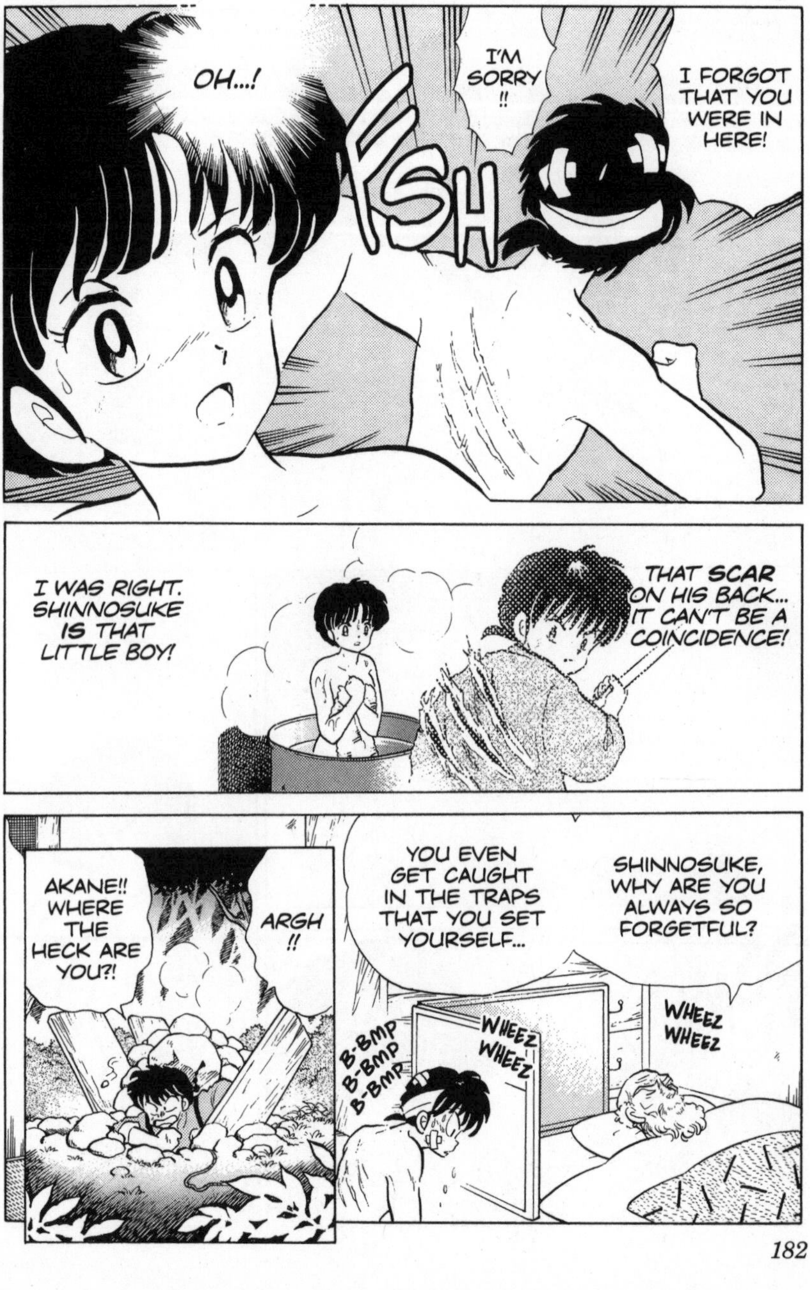
I FORGOT THAT YOU WERE IN HERE!
I'M SORRY !!
FSH
OH...!
THAT SCAR ON HIS BACK... IT CAN'T BE A COINCIDENCE!
I WAS RIGHT. SHINNOSUKE IS THAT LITTLE BOY!
SHINNOSUKE, WHY ARE YOU ALWAYS SO FORGETFUL?
YOU EVEN GET CAUGHT IN THE TRAPS THAT YOU SET YOURSELF...
WHEEZ WHEEZ
WHEEZ WHEEZ
B-BMP B-BMP B-BMP
ARGH !!
AKANE!! WHERE THE HECK ARE YOU?!

PART 12
THE SECRET OF THE FOREST

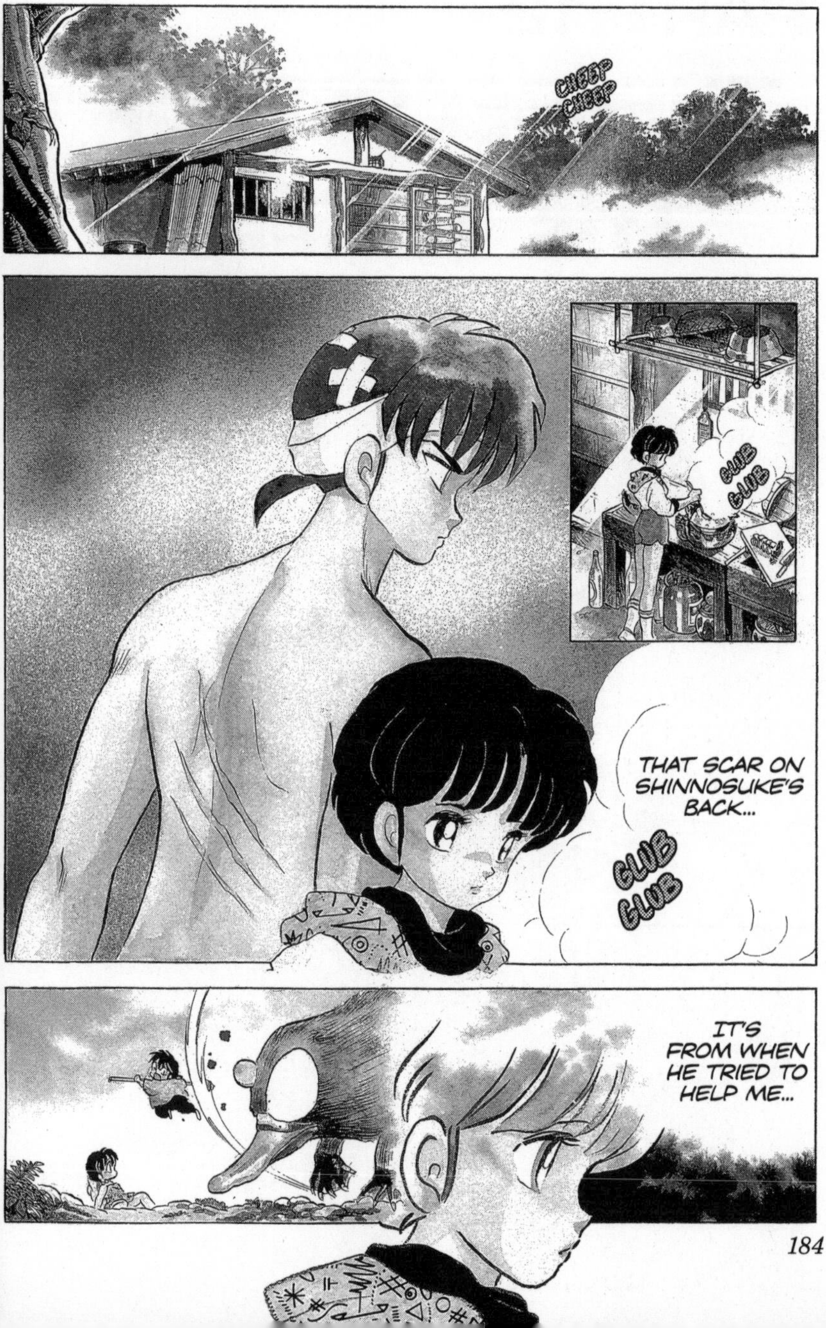
CHEEP CHEEP
GLUB GLUB
THAT SCAR ON SHINNOSUKE'S BACK...
GLUB GLUB
IT'S FROM WHEN HE TRIED TO HELP ME...

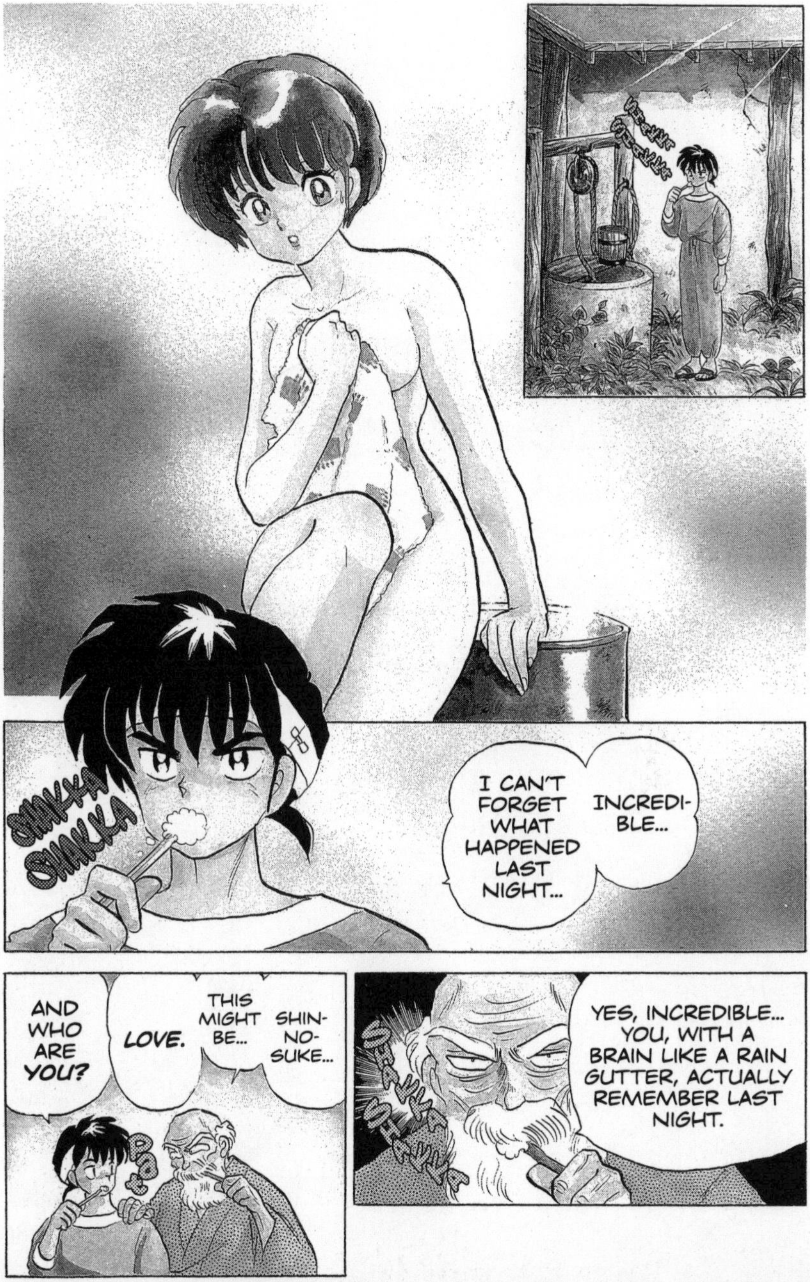
SHAKKA SHAKKA
SHAKKA SHAKKA
INCREDI-BLE...
I CAN'T FORGET WHAT HAPPENED LAST NIGHT...
YES, INCREDIBLE... YOU, WITH A BRAIN LIKE A RAIN GUTTER, ACTUALLY REMEMBER LAST NIGHT.
SHIN-NO-SUKE...
THIS MIGHT BE...
LOVE.
AND WHO ARE **YOU?**

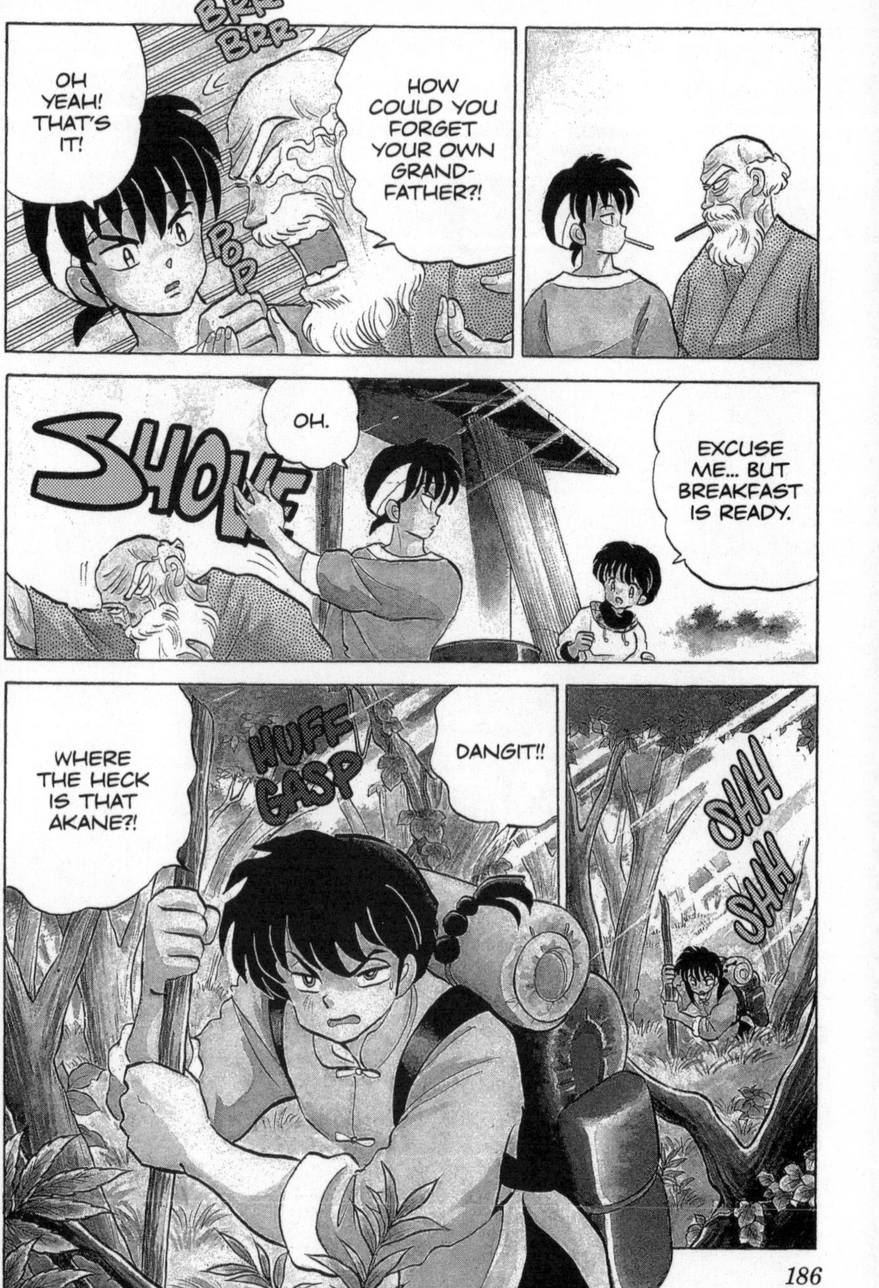
BRR BRR
HOW COULD YOU FORGET YOUR OWN GRAND-FATHER?!
OH YEAH! THAT'S IT!
POP
EXCUSE ME... BUT BREAKFAST IS READY.
OH.
OHH SHH
DANGIT!!
HUFF GASP
WHERE THE HECK IS THAT AKANE?!

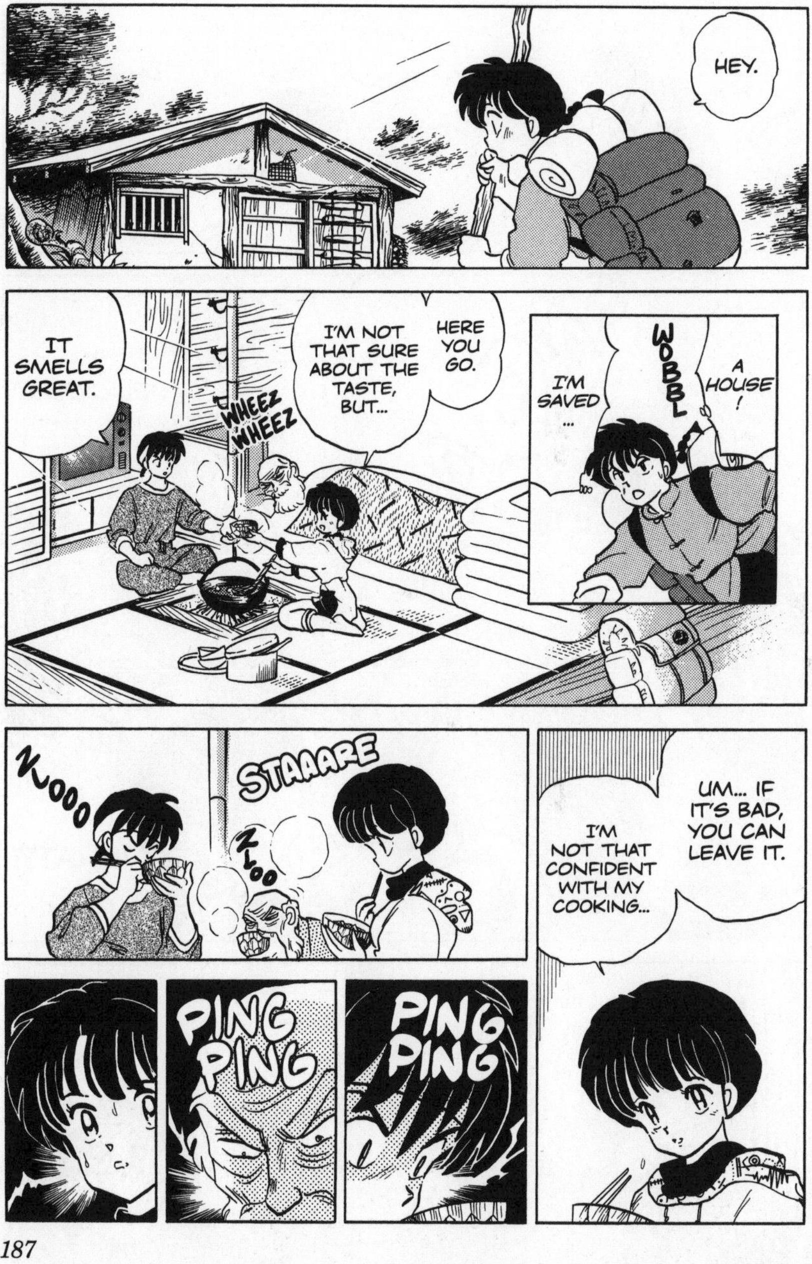
HEY.
A HOUSE!
WOBBL
I'M SAVED...
HERE YOU GO.
I'M NOT THAT SURE ABOUT THE TASTE, BUT...
WHEEZ WHEEZ
IT SMELLS GREAT.
UM... IF IT'S BAD, YOU CAN LEAVE IT.
I'M NOT THAT CONFIDENT WITH MY COOKING...
STAAARE
ZLOO
ZLOOO
PING PING
PING PING

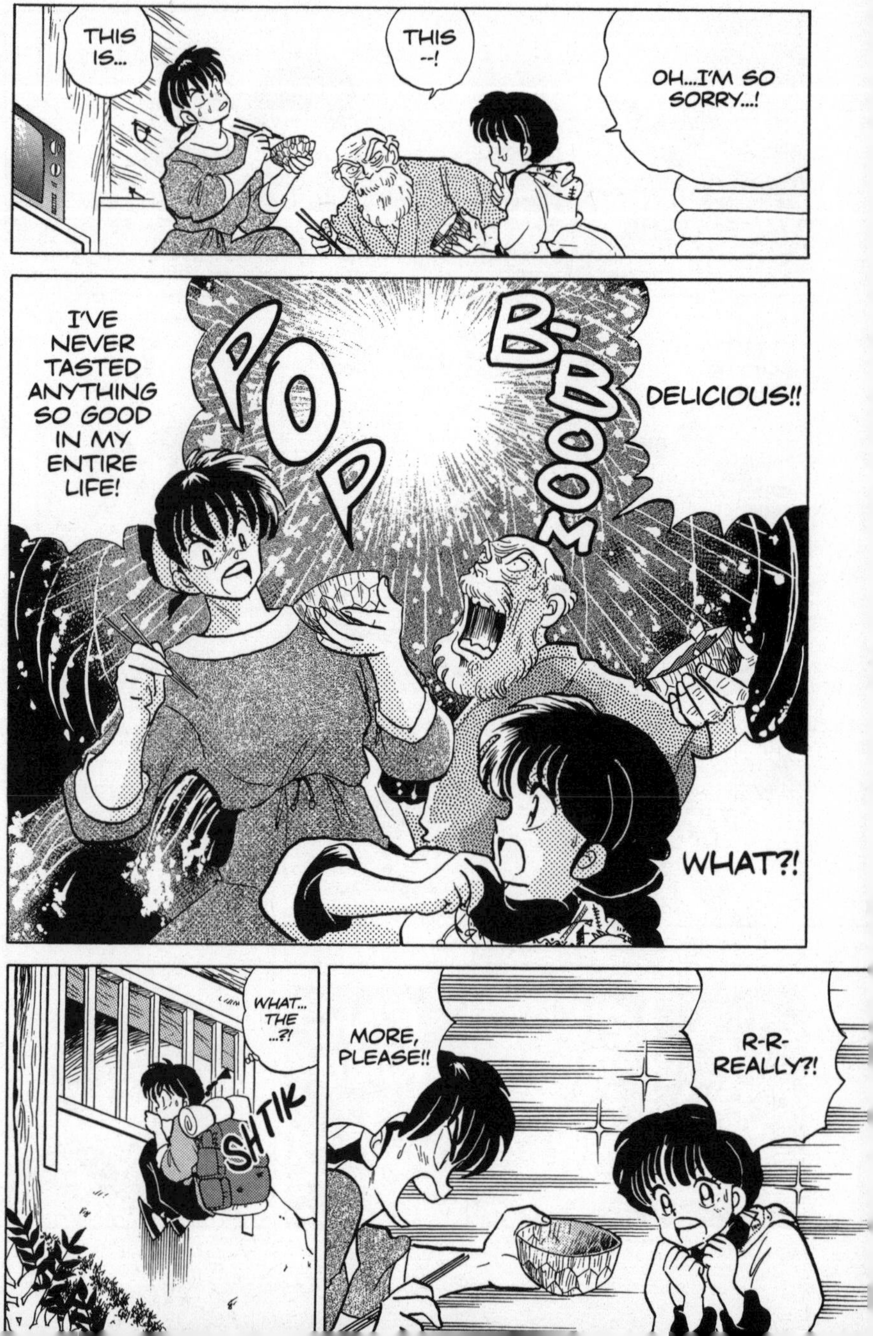
OH...I'M SO SORRY...!
THIS --!
THIS IS...
DELICIOUS!!
B-BOOM
POP
I'VE NEVER TASTED ANYTHING SO GOOD IN MY ENTIRE LIFE!
WHAT?!
R-R-REALLY?!
MORE, PLEASE!!
WHAT... THE ...?!
SHTIK

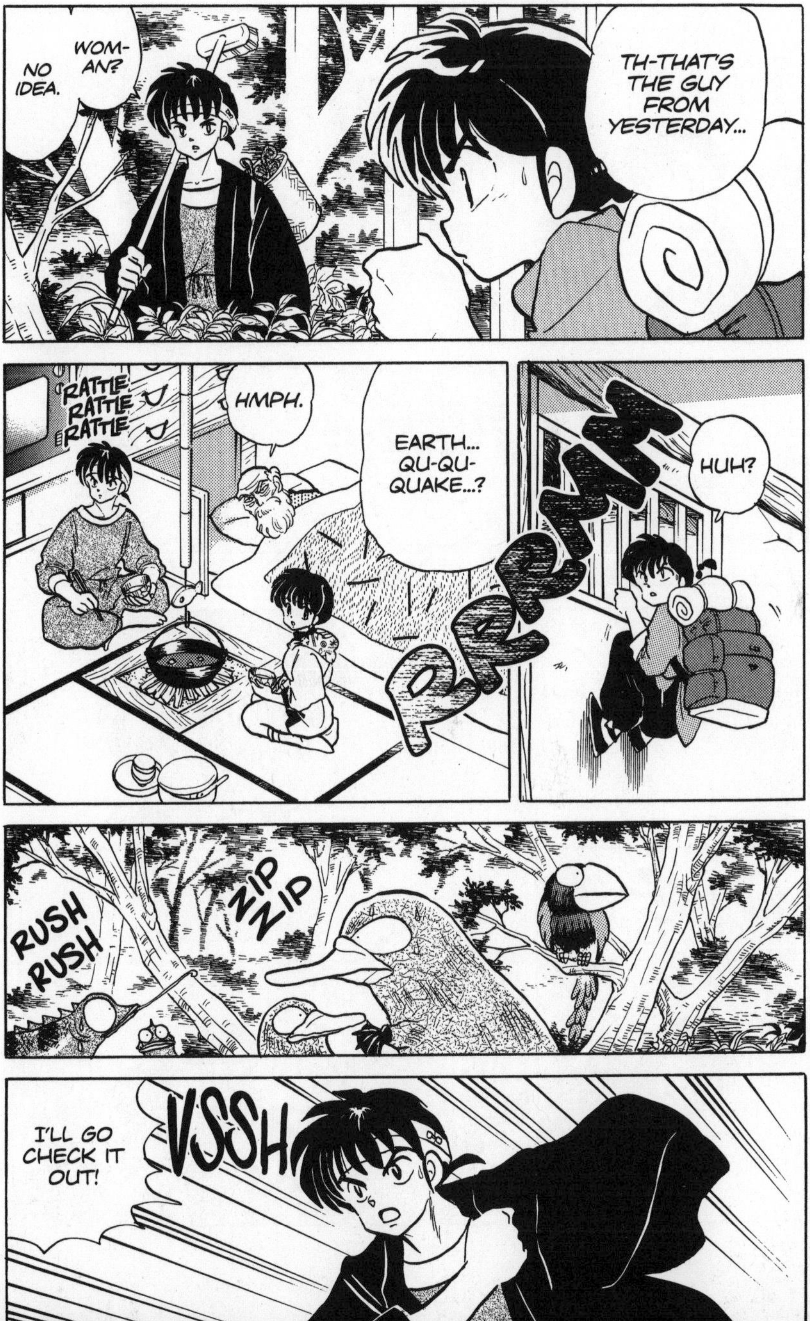
TH-THAT'S THE GUY FROM YESTERDAY...
WOM-AN?
NO IDEA.
HUH?
PRRMM
EARTH... QU-QU-QUAKE...?
HMPH.
RATTLE RATTLE RATTLE
ZIP ZIP
RUSH RUSH
VSSH
I'LL GO CHECK IT OUT!

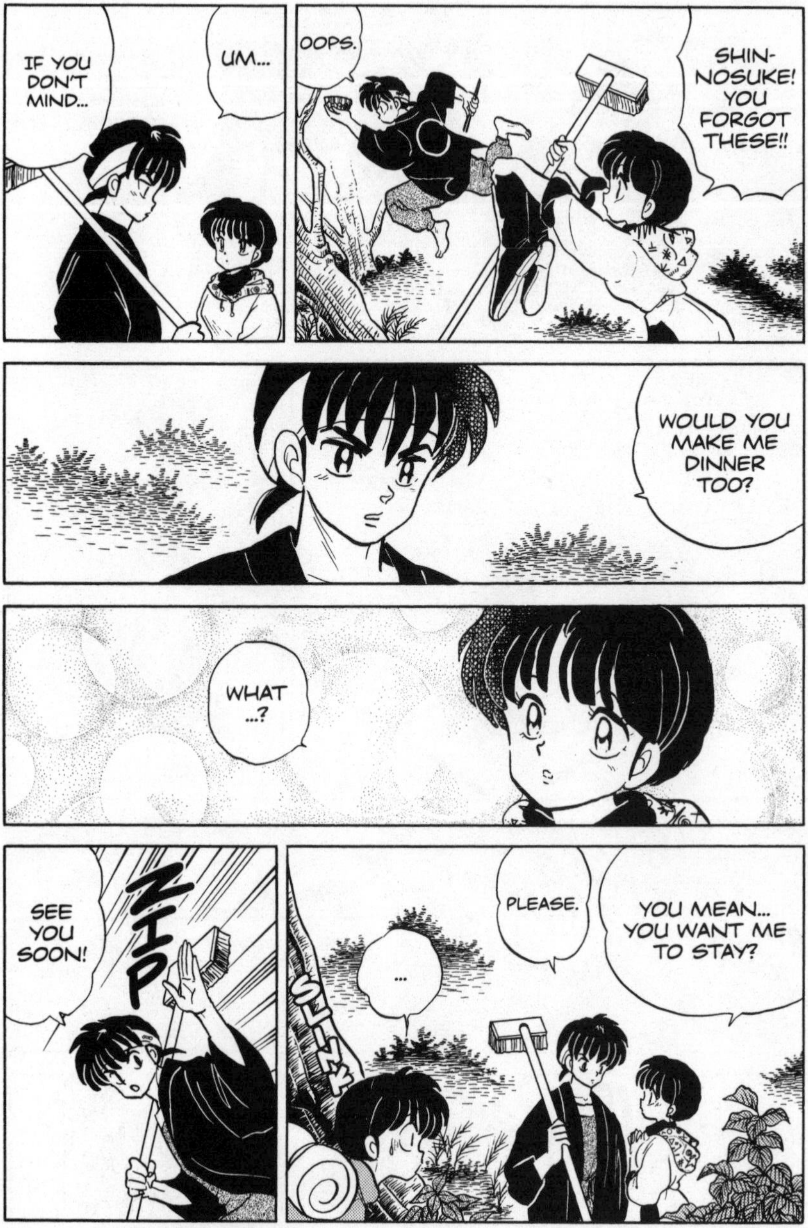
SHIN-NOSUKE! YOU FORGOT THESE!!
OOPS.
UM...
IF YOU DON'T MIND...
WOULD YOU MAKE ME DINNER TOO?
WHAT ...?
YOU MEAN... YOU WANT ME TO STAY?
PLEASE.
...
SLINK
ZIP
SEE YOU SOON!

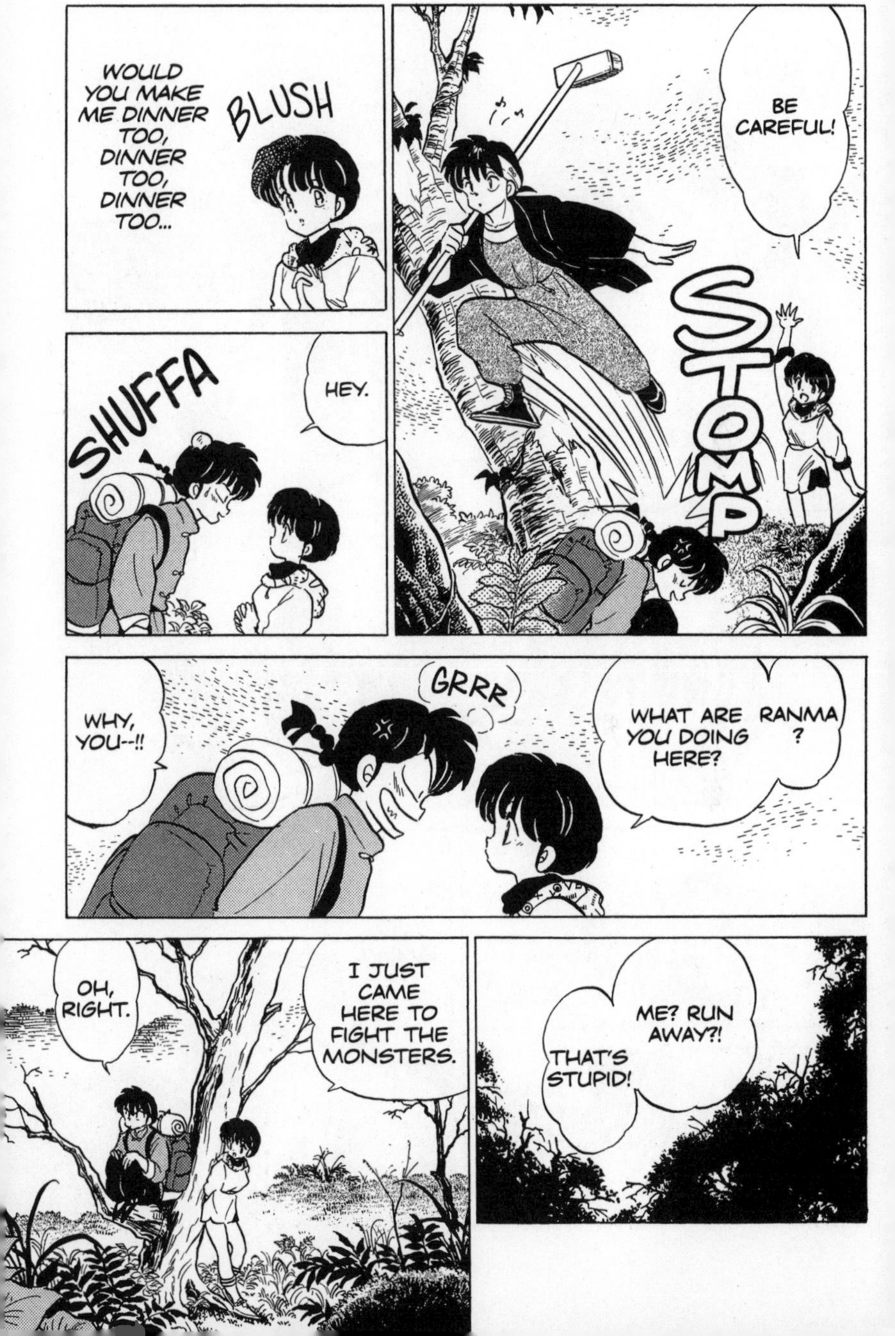
BE CAREFUL!
STOMP
WOULD YOU MAKE ME DINNER TOO, DINNER TOO, DINNER TOO...
BLUSH
HEY.
SHUFFA
RANMA? WHAT ARE YOU DOING HERE?
GRRR
WHY, YOU--!!
ME? RUN AWAY?!
THAT'S STUPID!
I JUST CAME HERE TO FIGHT THE MONSTERS.
OH, RIGHT.

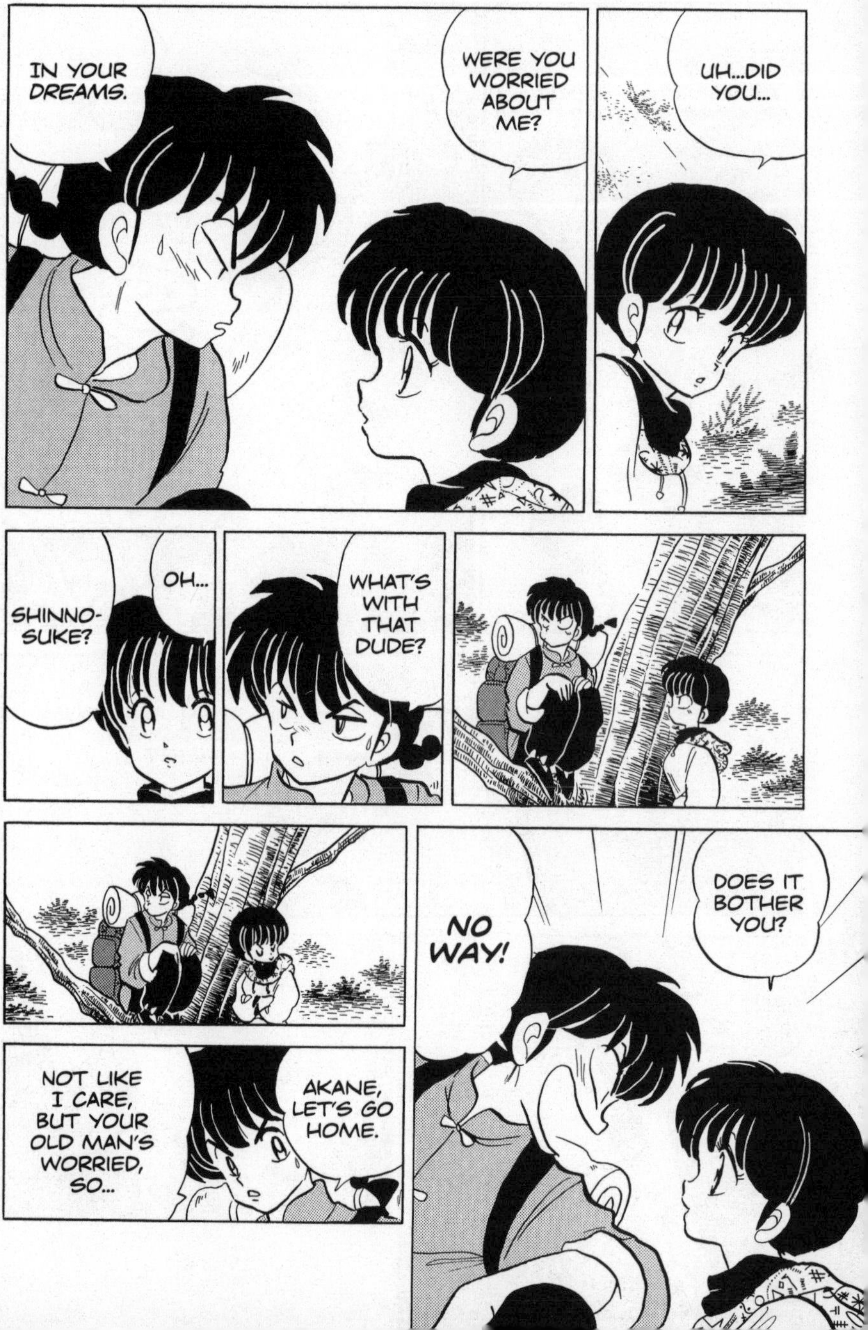
UH...DID YOU...
WERE YOU WORRIED ABOUT ME?
IN YOUR DREAMS.
WHAT'S WITH THAT DUDE?
OH...
SHINNO-SUKE?
DOES IT BOTHER YOU?
NO WAY!
AKANE, LET'S GO HOME.
NOT LIKE I CARE, BUT YOUR OLD MAN'S WORRIED, SO...

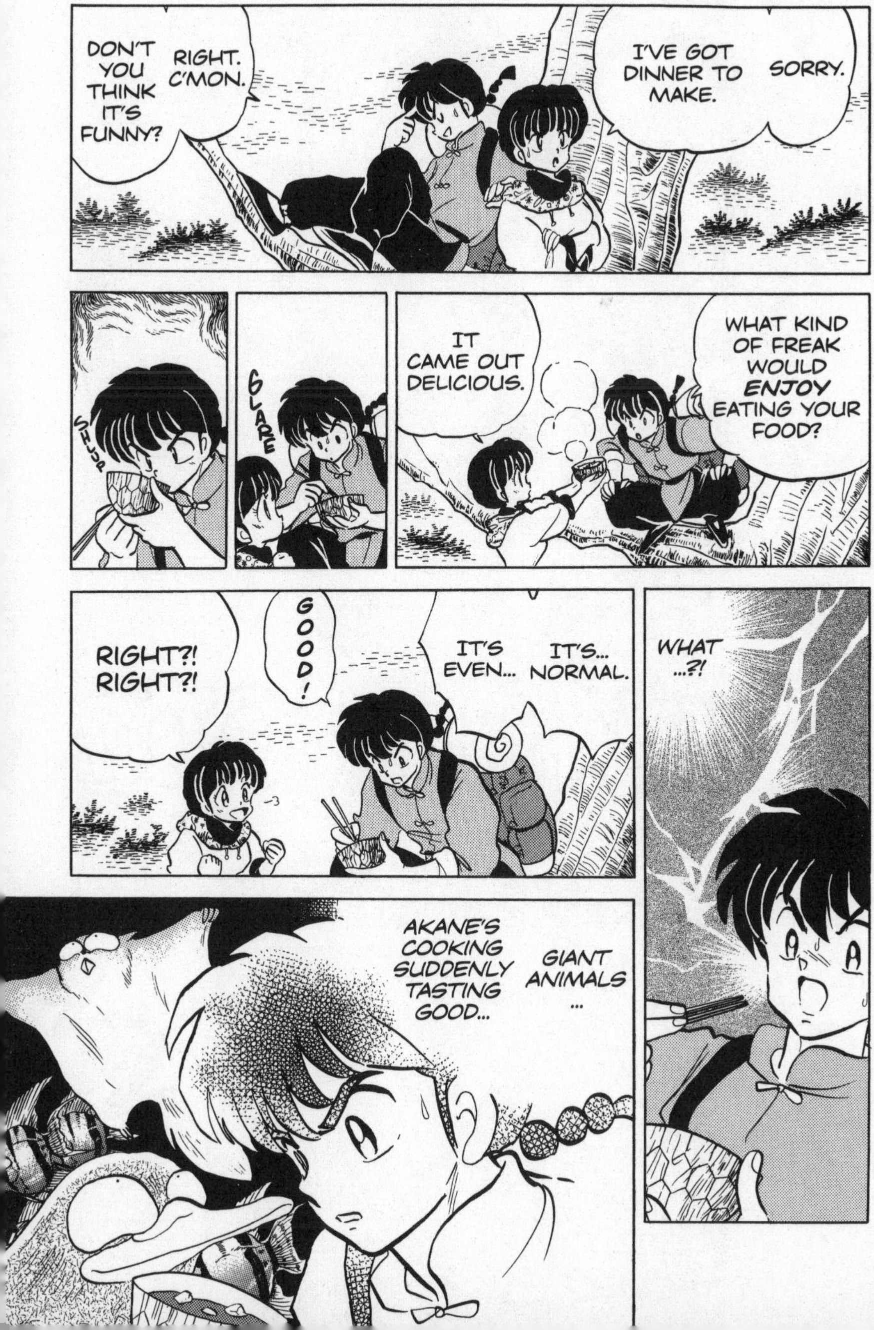
SORRY.
I'VE GOT DINNER TO MAKE.
RIGHT. C'MON.
DON'T YOU THINK IT'S FUNNY?
WHAT KIND OF FREAK WOULD *ENJOY* EATING YOUR FOOD?
IT CAME OUT DELICIOUS.
GLARE
SHLUP
WHAT ...?!
IT'S... NORMAL.
IT'S EVEN...
GOOD!
RIGHT?! RIGHT?!
GIANT ANIMALS ...
AKANE'S COOKING SUDDENLY TASTING GOOD...

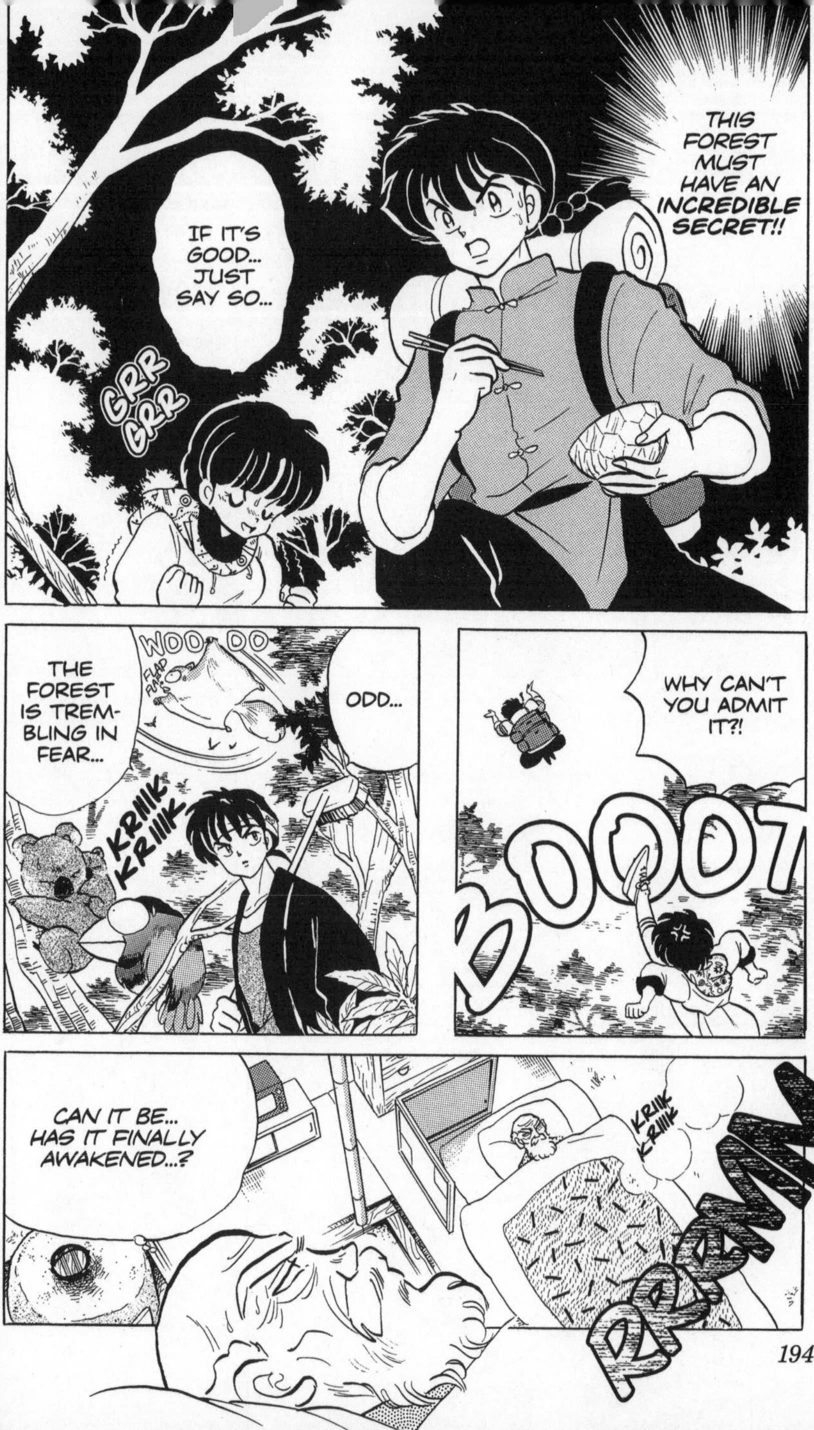
THIS FOREST MUST HAVE AN INCREDIBLE SECRET!!
IF IT'S GOOD... JUST SAY SO...
GRR GRR
WHY CAN'T YOU ADMIT IT?!
BOOOT
WOO DO
FLAP FLAP
ODD...
THE FOREST IS TREMBLING IN FEAR...
KRIIIK KRIIIK
RRRMMM
KRIIK KRIIK
CAN IT BE... HAS IT FINALLY AWAKENED...?

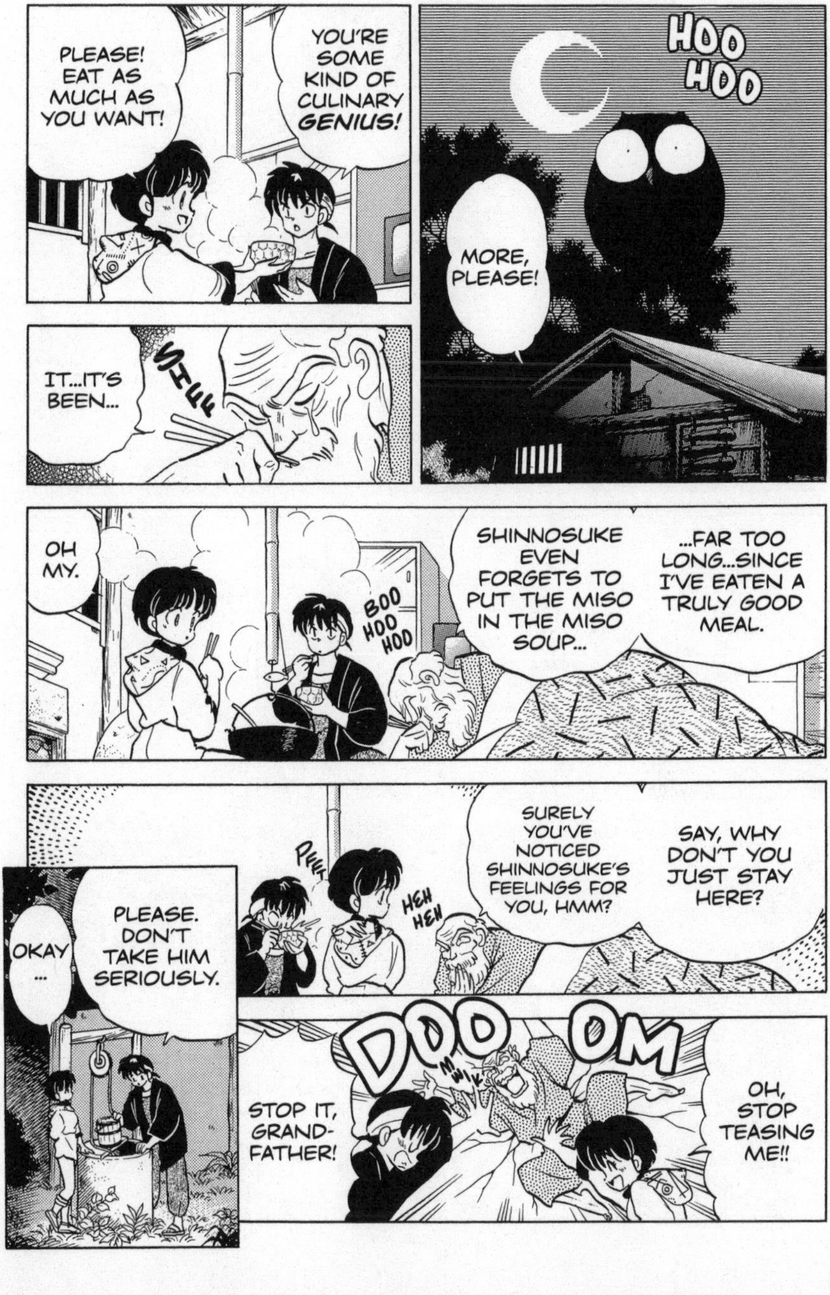
HOO HOO
MORE, PLEASE!
YOU'RE SOME KIND OF CULINARY GENIUS!
PLEASE! EAT AS MUCH AS YOU WANT!
IT...IT'S BEEN...
...FAR TOO LONG...SINCE I'VE EATEN A TRULY GOOD MEAL.
SHINNOSUKE EVEN FORGETS TO PUT THE MISO IN THE MISO SOUP...
BOO HOO HOO
OH MY.
SAY, WHY DON'T YOU JUST STAY HERE?
SURELY YOU'VE NOTICED SHINNOSUKE'S FEELINGS FOR YOU, HMM?
HEH HEH
OH, STOP TEASING ME!!
DOO OM
STOP IT, GRAND-FATHER!
PLEASE. DON'T TAKE HIM SERIOUSLY.
OKAY ...

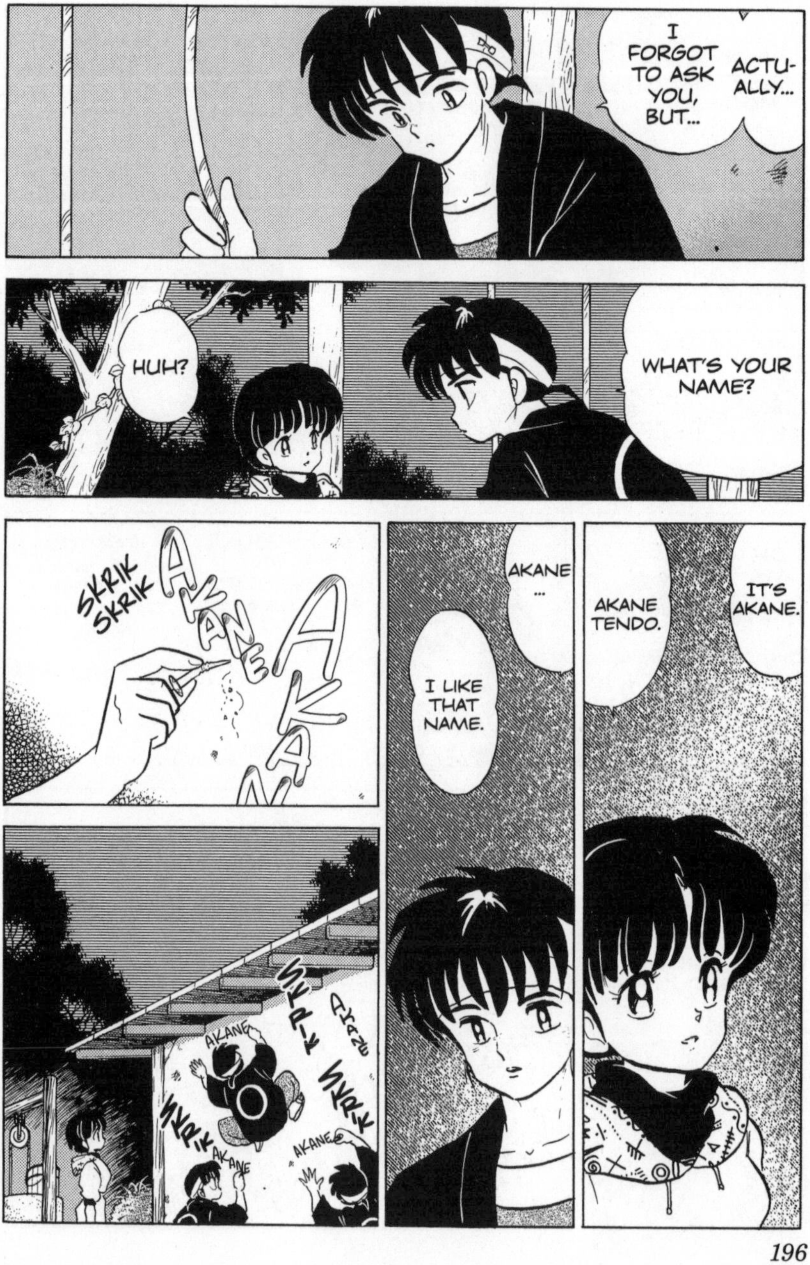
ACTU-ALLY...
I FORGOT TO ASK YOU, BUT...
WHAT'S YOUR NAME?
HUH?
IT'S AKANE.
AKANE TENDO.
AKANE...
I LIKE THAT NAME.
SKRIK SKRIK
AKANE
AKANE
SKRIK
SKRIK
SKRIK
AKANE
AKANE
AKANE
AKANE

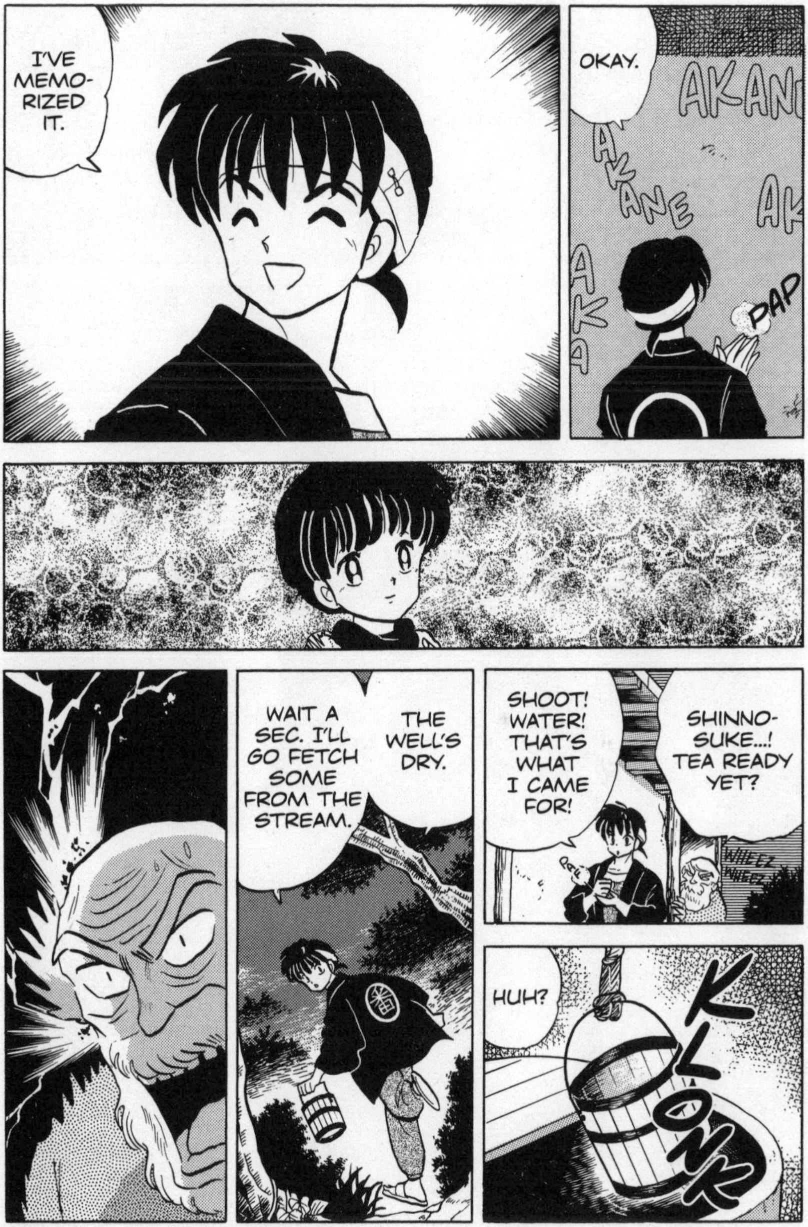
OKAY.
AKAN
AKANE
AK
AKA
PAP
I'VE MEMORIZED IT.
SHINNOSUKE...! TEA READY YET?
SHOOT! WATER! THAT'S WHAT I CAME FOR!
PAP
WHEEZ WHEEZ
HUH?
KLONK
THE WELL'S DRY.
WAIT A SEC. I'LL GO FETCH SOME FROM THE STREAM.

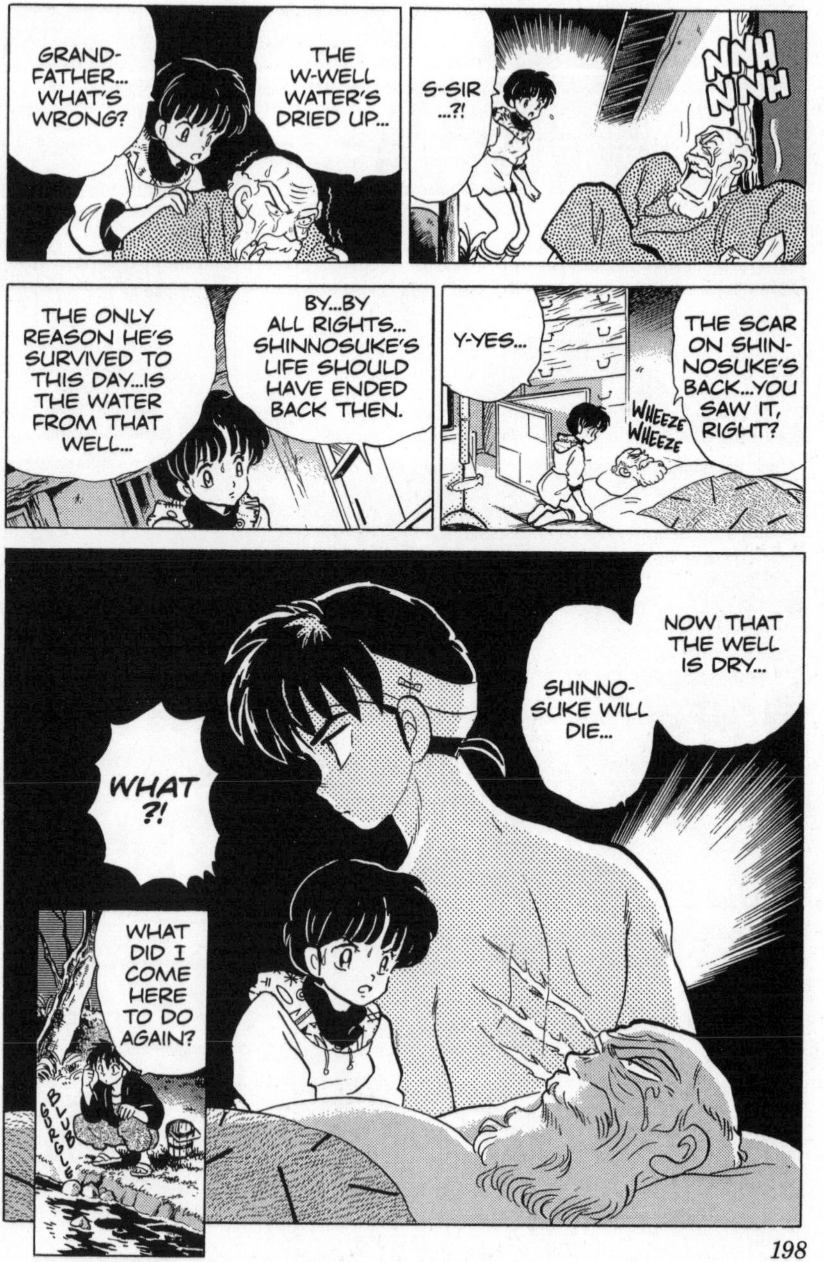
NNH NNH
S-SIR ...?!
THE W-WELL WATER'S DRIED UP...
GRAND-FATHER... WHAT'S WRONG?
THE SCAR ON SHIN-NOSUKE'S BACK...YOU SAW IT, RIGHT?
WHEEZE WHEEZE
Y-YES...
BY...BY ALL RIGHTS... SHINNOSUKE'S LIFE SHOULD HAVE ENDED BACK THEN.
THE ONLY REASON HE'S SURVIVED TO THIS DAY...IS THE WATER FROM THAT WELL...
NOW THAT THE WELL IS DRY...
SHINNO-SUKE WILL DIE...
WHAT ?!
WHAT DID I COME HERE TO DO AGAIN?
GURGLE BLUB

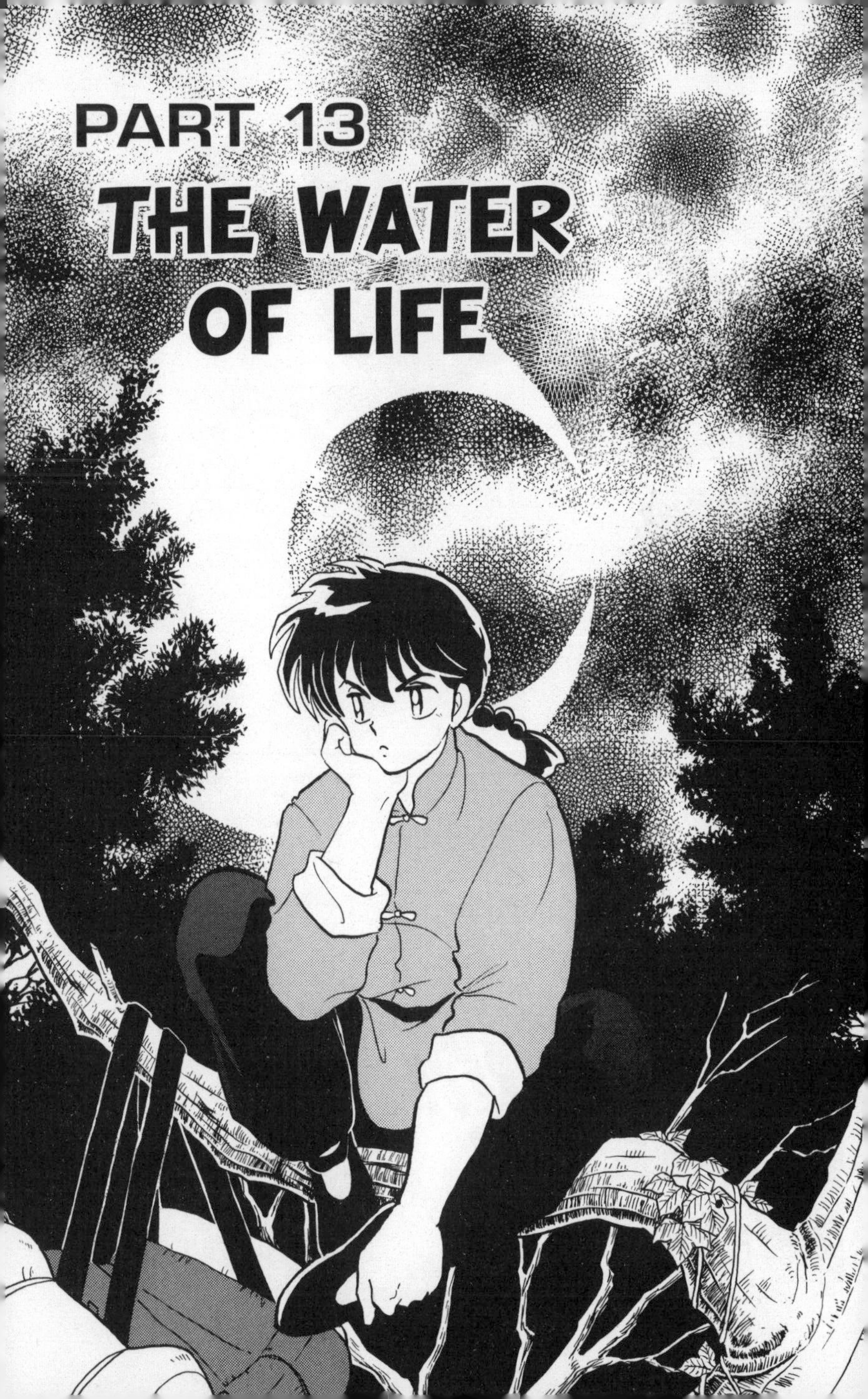
PART 13
THE WATER OF LIFE

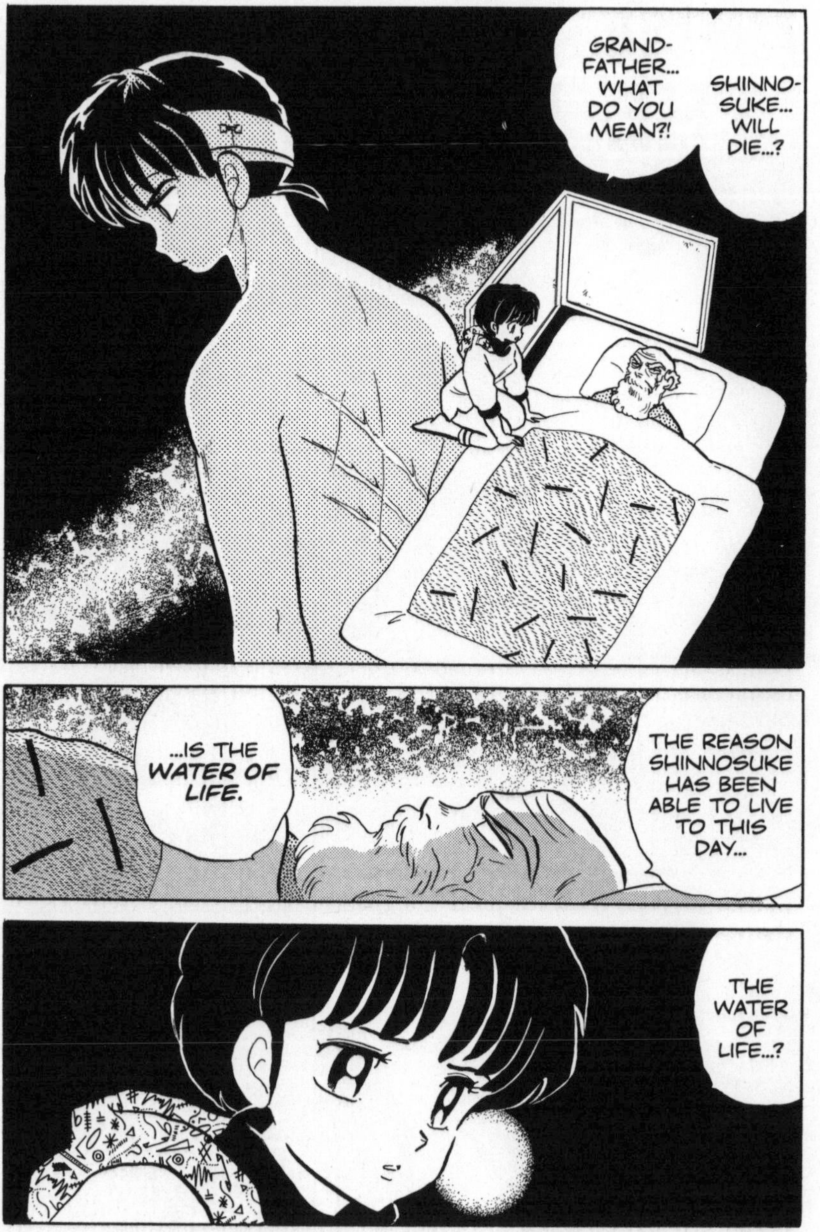
SHINNOSUKE... WILL DIE...?
GRANDFATHER... WHAT DO YOU MEAN?!
THE REASON SHINNOSUKE HAS BEEN ABLE TO LIVE TO THIS DAY...
...IS THE WATER OF LIFE.
THE WATER OF LIFE...?

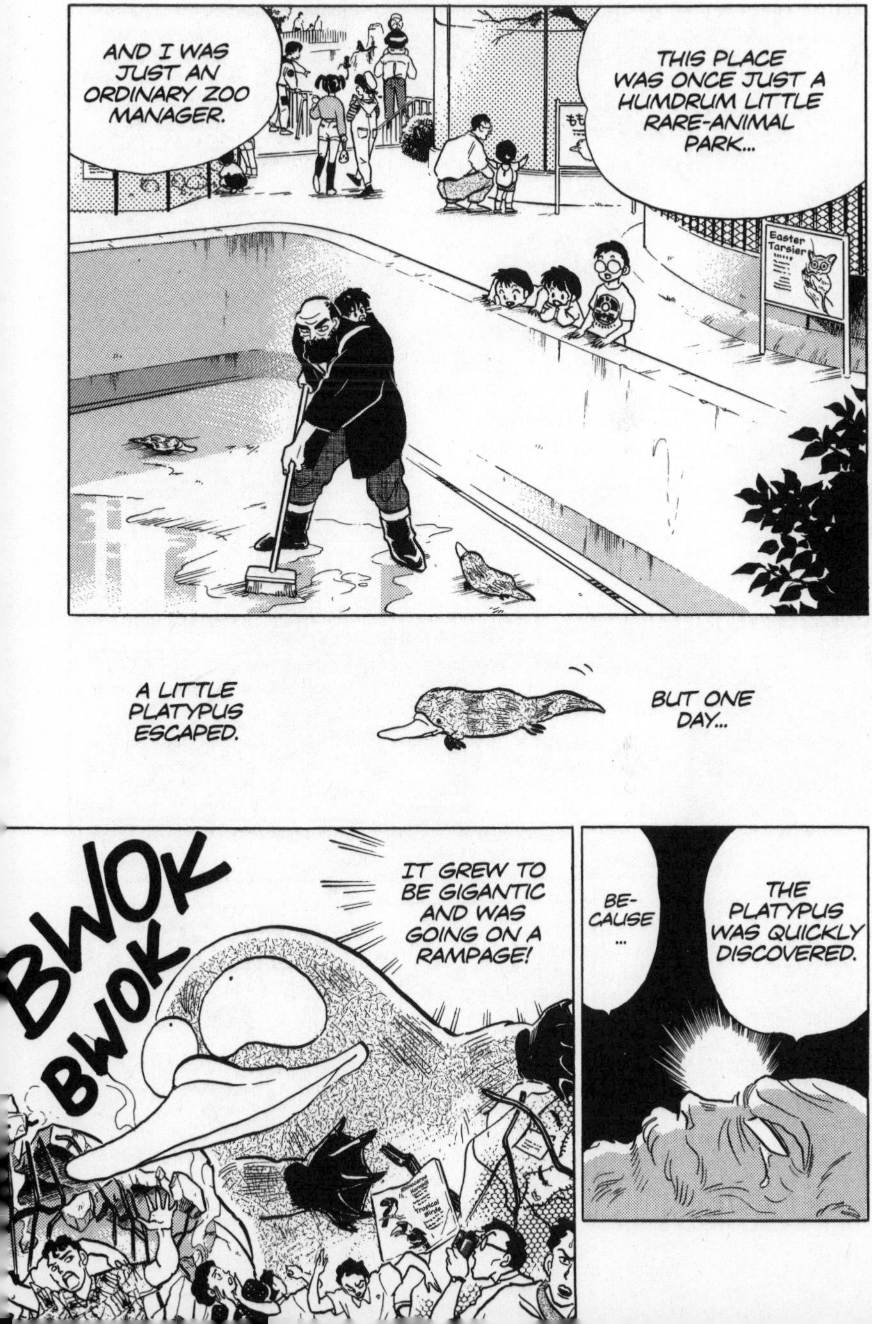
THIS PLACE WAS ONCE JUST A HUMDRUM LITTLE RARE-ANIMAL PARK...
AND I WAS JUST AN ORDINARY ZOO MANAGER.
Easter Tarsier
BUT ONE DAY...
A LITTLE PLATYPUS ESCAPED.
THE PLATYPUS WAS QUICKLY DISCOVERED.
BE-CAUSE ...
IT GREW TO BE GIGANTIC AND WAS GOING ON A RAMPAGE!
BWOK
BWOK
Tropical Birds

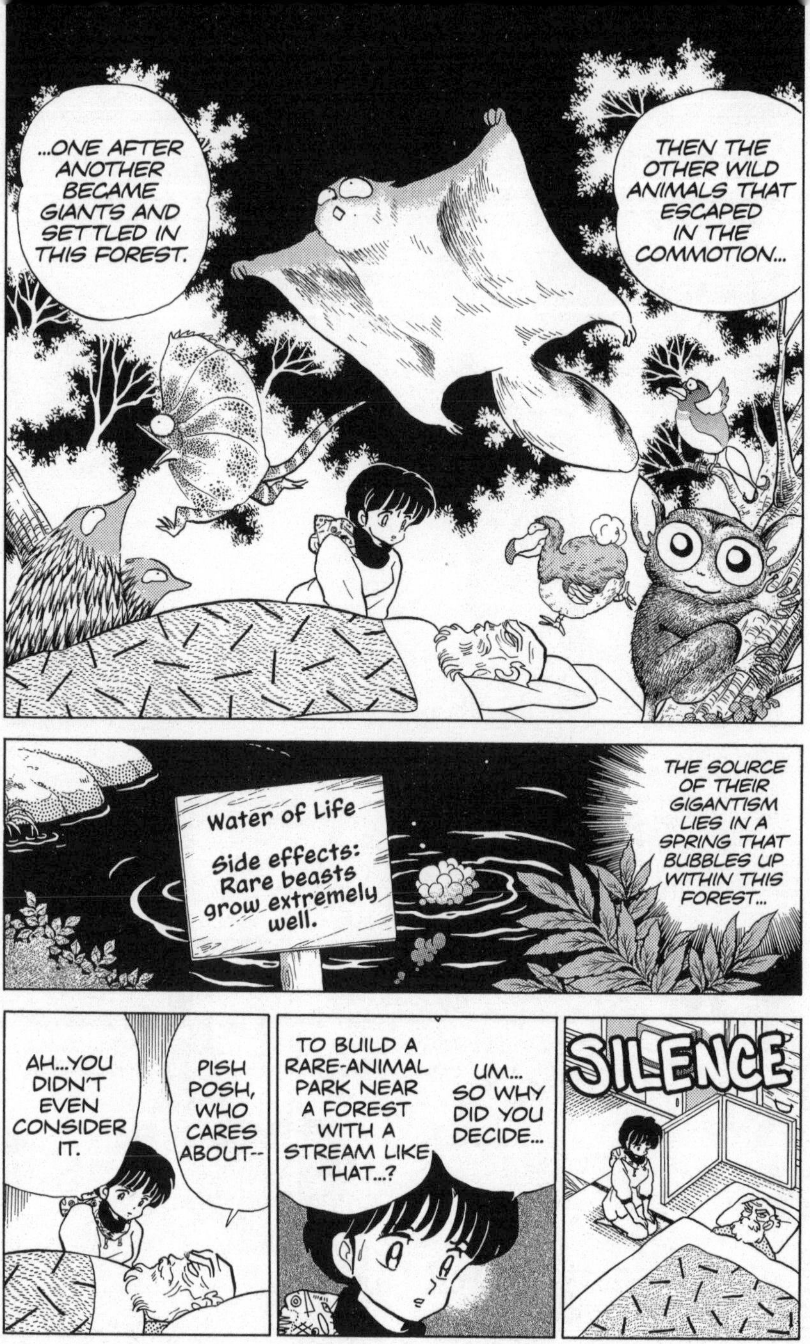
THEN THE OTHER WILD ANIMALS THAT ESCAPED IN THE COMMOTION...
...ONE AFTER ANOTHER BECAME GIANTS AND SETTLED IN THIS FOREST.
THE SOURCE OF THEIR GIGANTISM LIES IN A SPRING THAT BUBBLES UP WITHIN THIS FOREST...
Water of Life
Side effects: Rare beasts grow extremely well.
SILENCE
UM... SO WHY DID YOU DECIDE...
TO BUILD A RARE-ANIMAL PARK NEAR A FOREST WITH A STREAM LIKE THAT...?
PISH POSH, WHO CARES ABOUT--
AH...YOU DIDN'T EVEN CONSIDER IT.

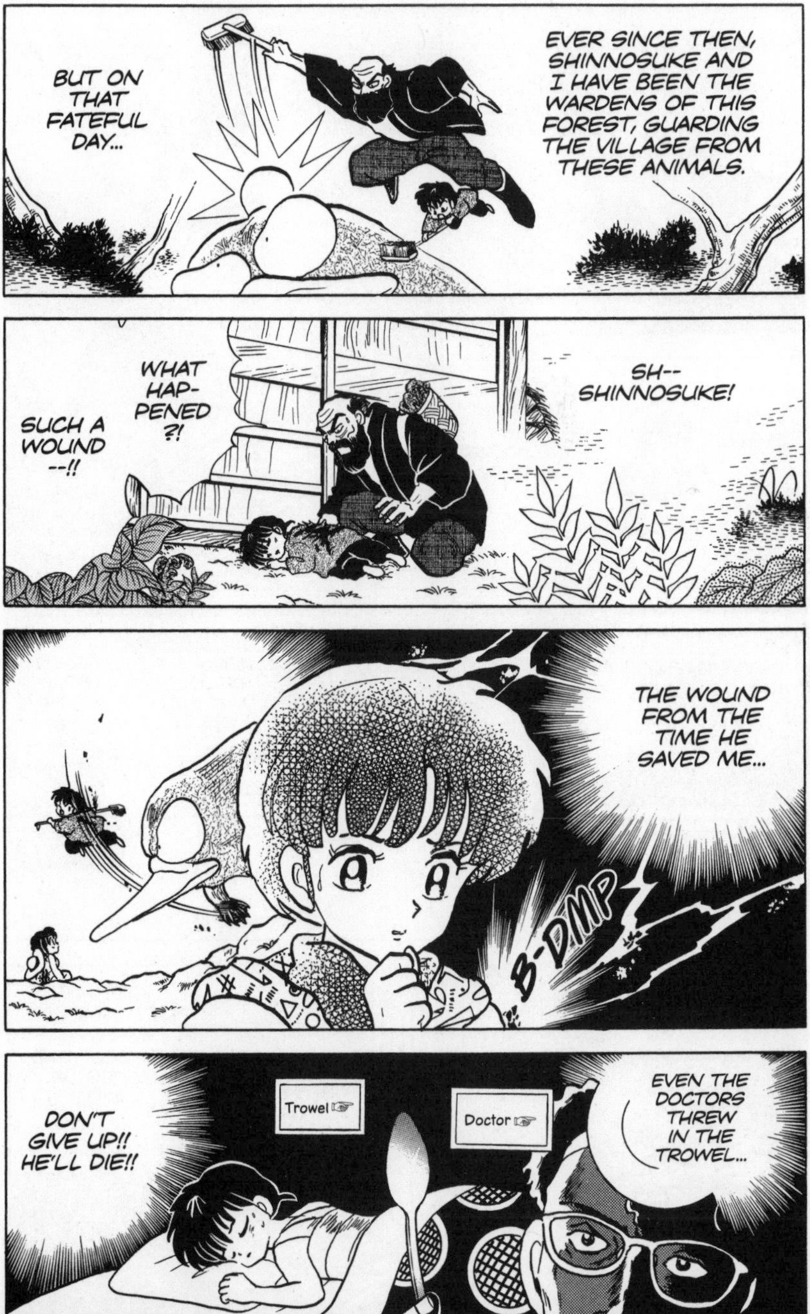
EVER SINCE THEN, SHINNOSUKE AND I HAVE BEEN THE WARDENS OF THIS FOREST, GUARDING THE VILLAGE FROM THESE ANIMALS.
BUT ON THAT FATEFUL DAY...
SH-- SHINNOSUKE!
WHAT HAP-PENED ?!
SUCH A WOUND --!!
THE WOUND FROM THE TIME HE SAVED ME...
B-DMP
EVEN THE DOCTORS THREW IN THE TROWEL...
Doctor ☞
Trowel ☞
DON'T GIVE UP!! HE'LL DIE!!

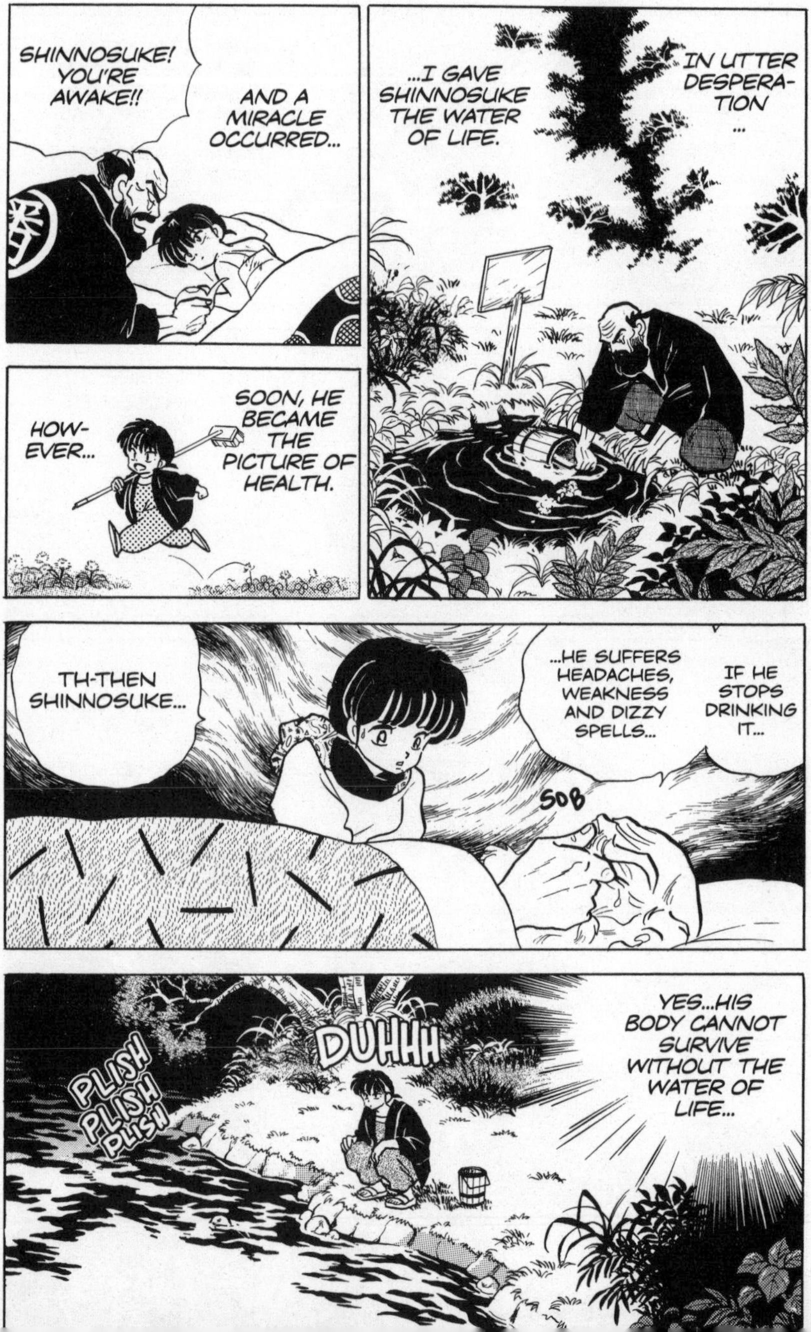

IN UTTER DESPERATION...
...I GAVE SHINNOSUKE THE WATER OF LIFE.
AND A MIRACLE OCCURRED...
SHINNOSUKE! YOU'RE AWAKE!!
SOON, HE BECAME THE PICTURE OF HEALTH.
HOW-EVER...
IF HE STOPS DRINKING IT...
...HE SUFFERS HEADACHES, WEAKNESS AND DIZZY SPELLS...
SOB
TH-THEN SHINNOSUKE...
YES...HIS BODY CANNOT SURVIVE WITHOUT THE WATER OF LIFE...
DUHHH
PLISH PLISH PLISH

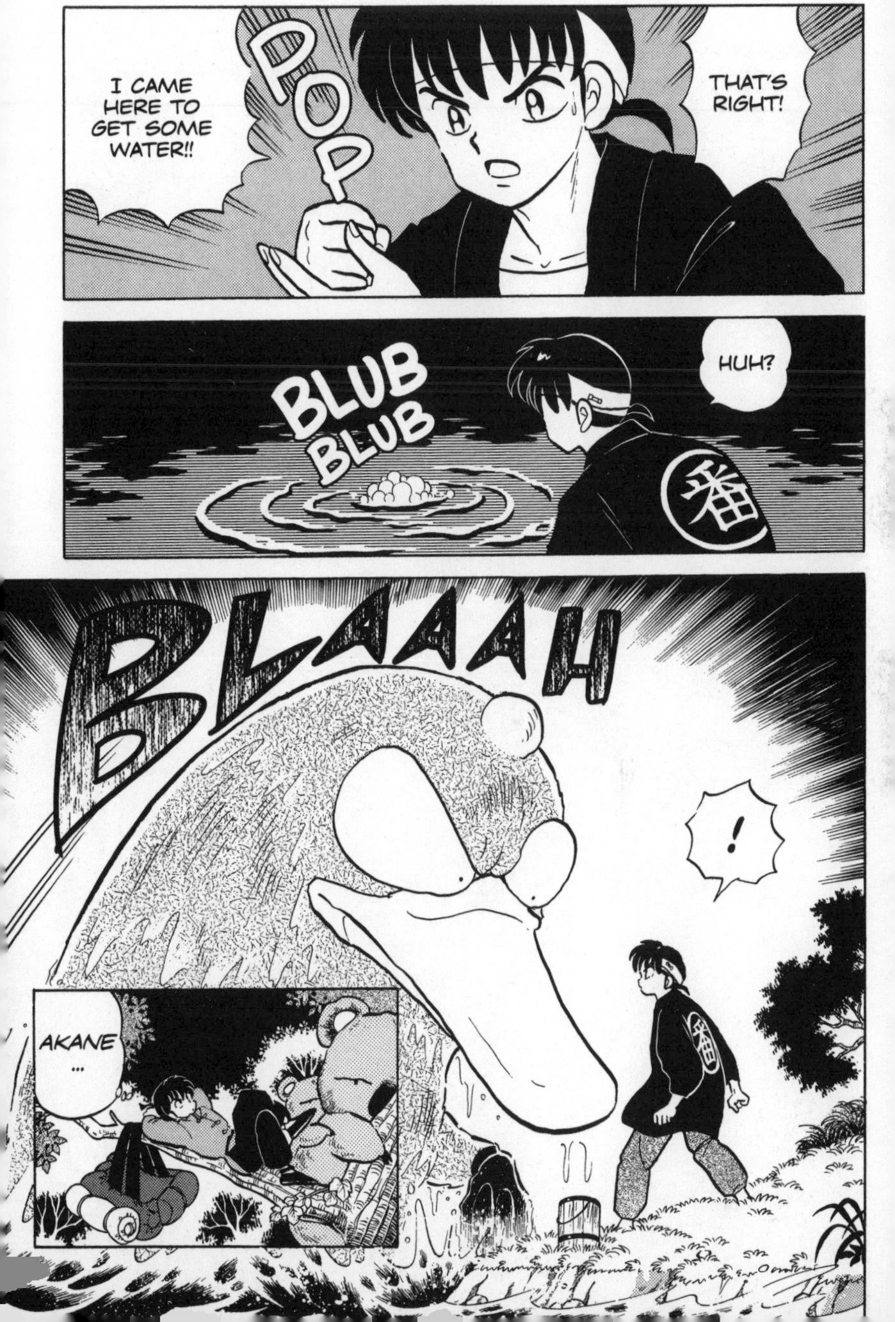
THAT'S RIGHT!
POP
I CAME HERE TO GET SOME WATER!!
HUH?
BLUB BLUB
BLAAAH
!
AKANE ...

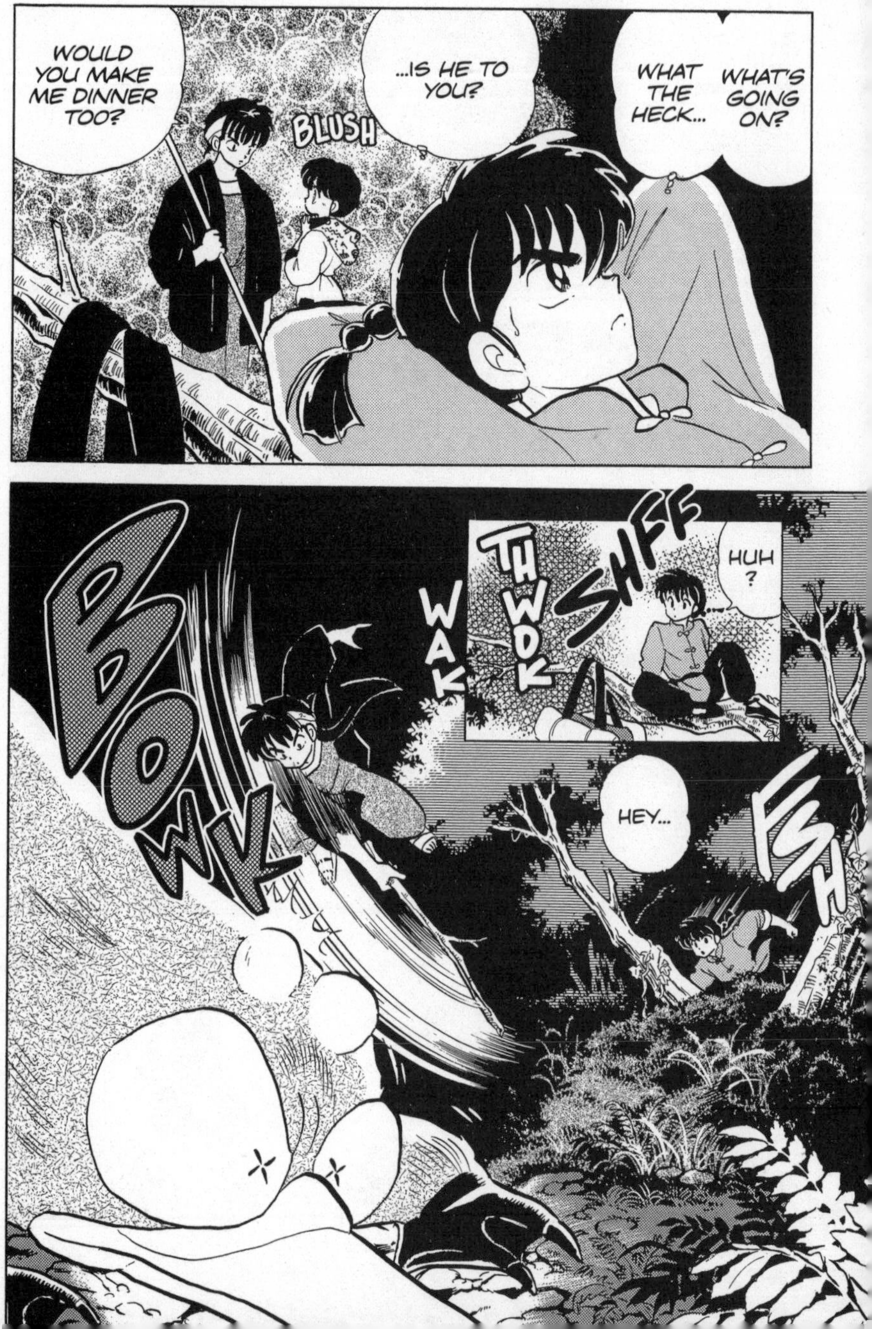
WHAT'S GOING ON?
WHAT THE HECK...
...IS HE TO YOU?
BLUSH
WOULD YOU MAKE ME DINNER TOO?
HUH ?
SHFF
THWDK
WAK
FSH
HEY...
BOWK

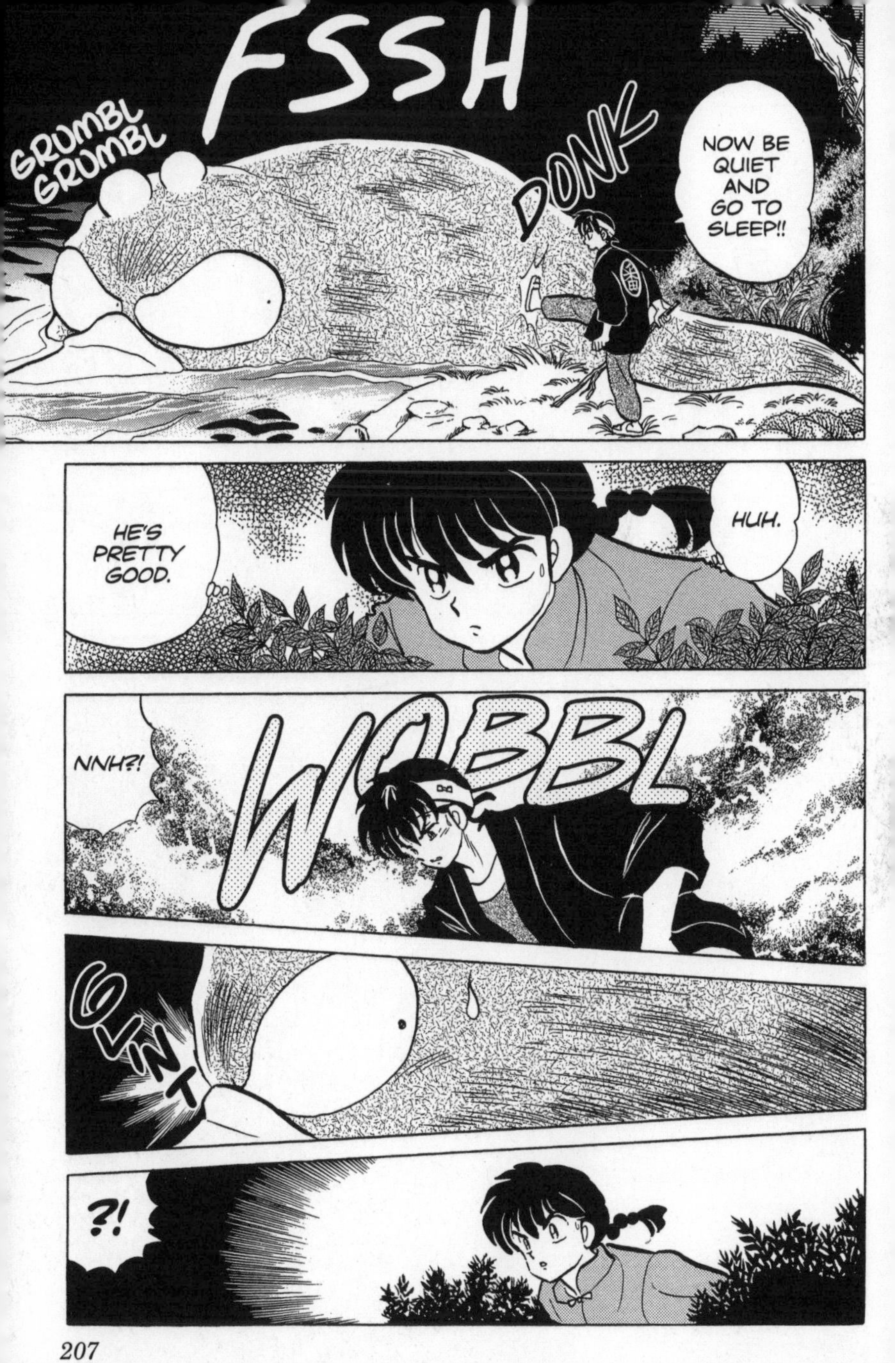
NOW BE QUIET AND GO TO SLEEP!!
DONK
FSSH
GRUMBL GRUMBL
HUH.
HE'S PRETTY GOOD.
WOBBL
NNH?!
GLINT
?!

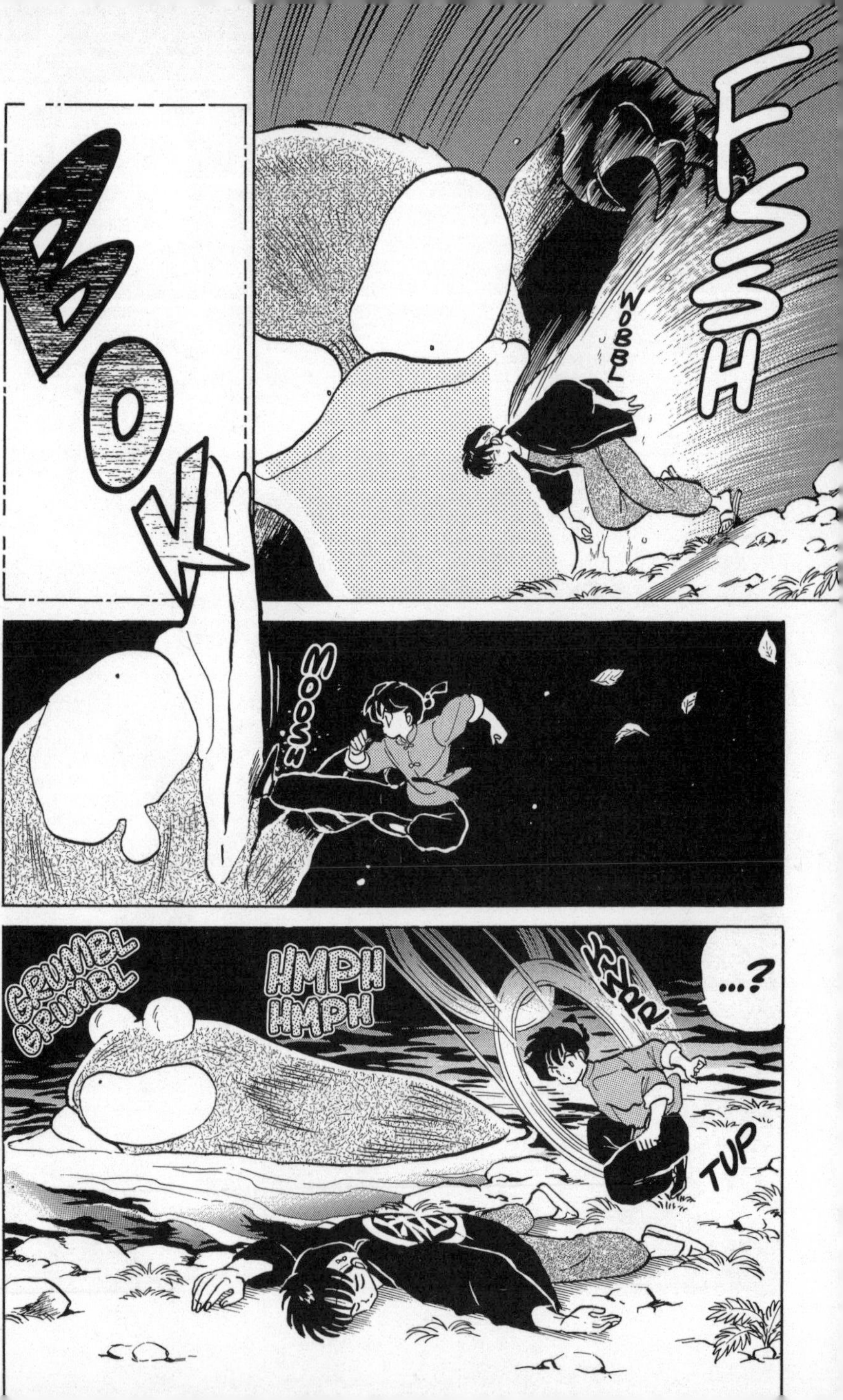

FSSSH
WOBBL
BOK
WOOSH
...?
TUP
HMPH HMPH
GRUMBL GRUMBL

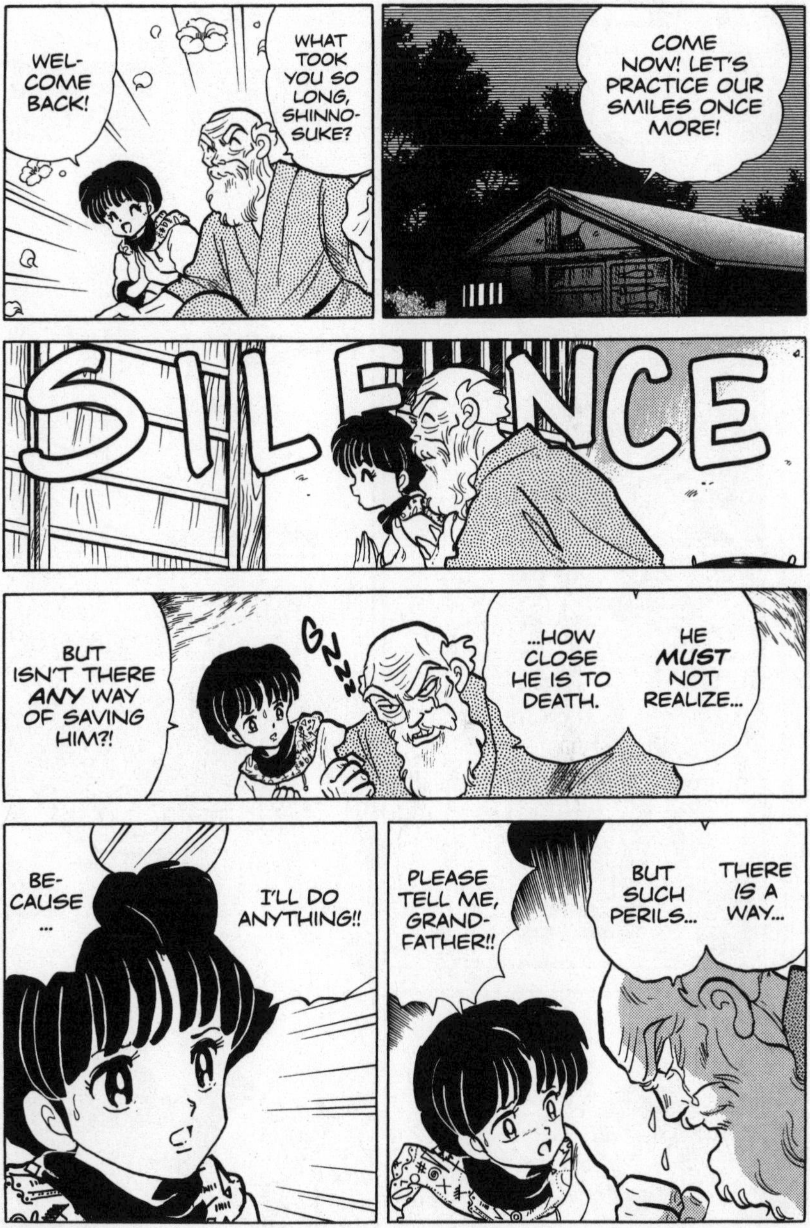
COME NOW! LET'S PRACTICE OUR SMILES ONCE MORE!
WHAT TOOK YOU SO LONG, SHINNO-SUKE?
WEL-COME BACK!
SILENCE
HE MUST NOT REALIZE...
...HOW CLOSE HE IS TO DEATH.
GNNN
BUT ISN'T THERE ANY WAY OF SAVING HIM?!
THERE IS A WAY...
BUT SUCH PERILS...
PLEASE TELL ME, GRAND-FATHER!!
I'LL DO ANYTHING!!
BE-CAUSE ...

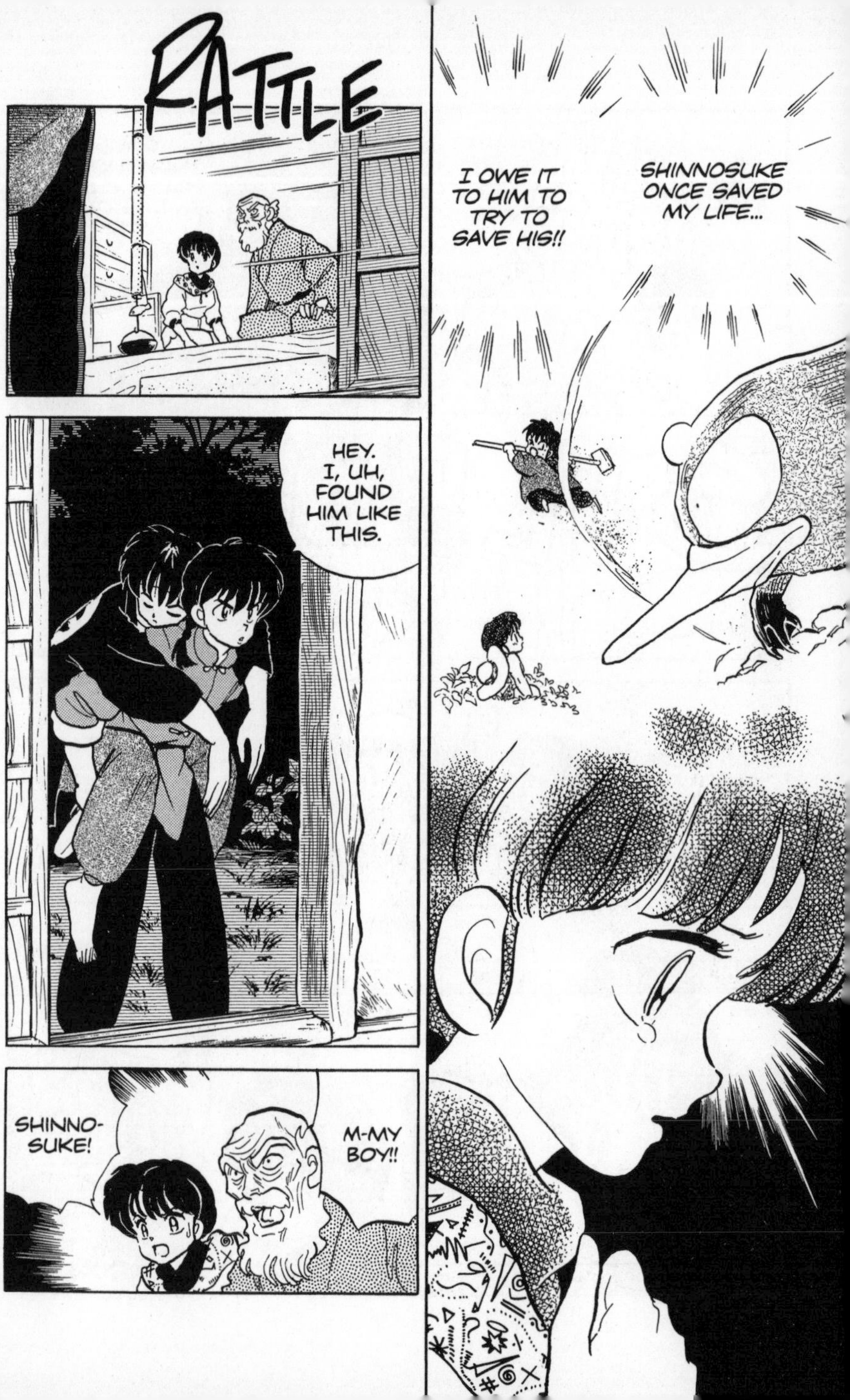
SHINNOSUKE ONCE SAVED MY LIFE...
I OWE IT TO HIM TO TRY TO SAVE HIS!!
RATTLE
HEY. I, UH, FOUND HIM LIKE THIS.
M-MY BOY!!
SHINNO-SUKE!

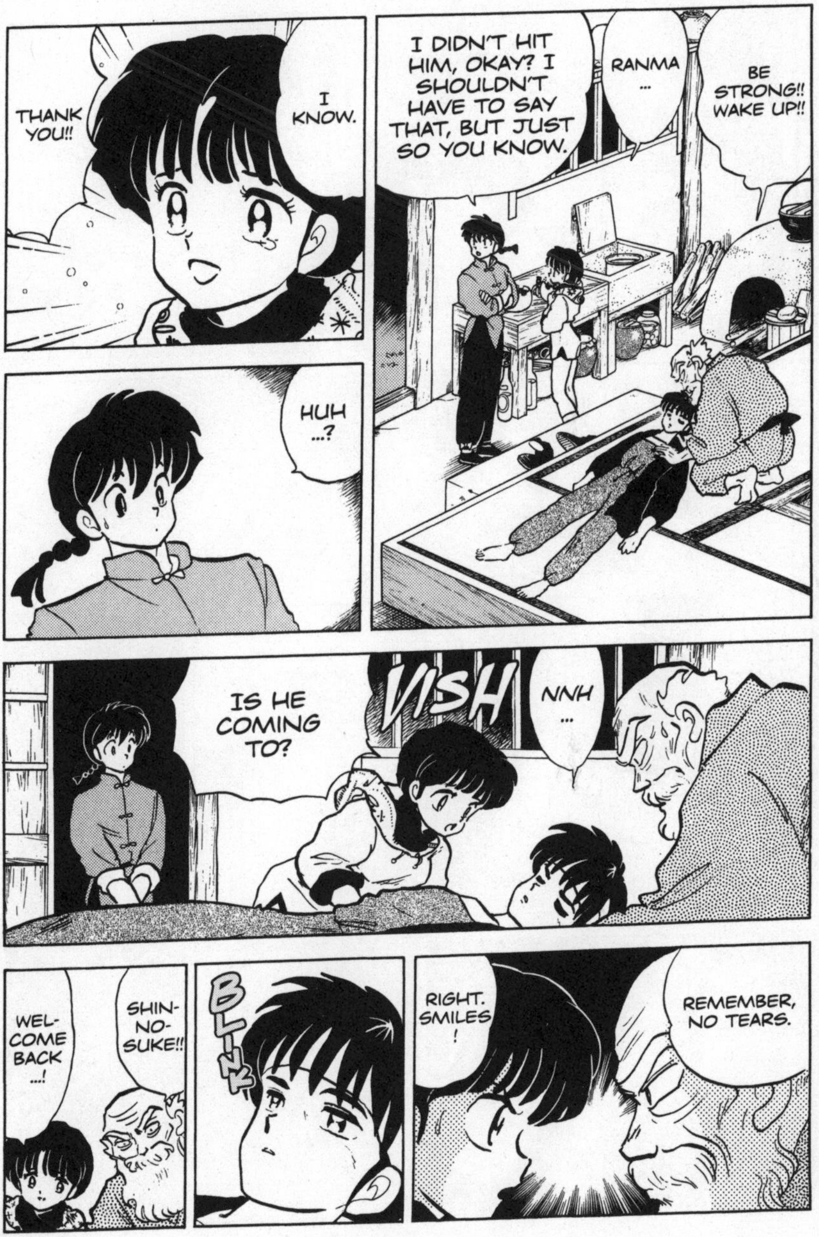
BE STRONG!! WAKE UP!!
RANMA ...
I DIDN'T HIT HIM, OKAY? I SHOULDN'T HAVE TO SAY THAT, BUT JUST SO YOU KNOW.
I KNOW.
THANK YOU!!
HUH ...?
NNH ...
VISH
IS HE COMING TO?
REMEMBER, NO TEARS.
RIGHT. SMILES !
BLINK
SHIN-NO-SUKE!!
WEL-COME BACK ...!

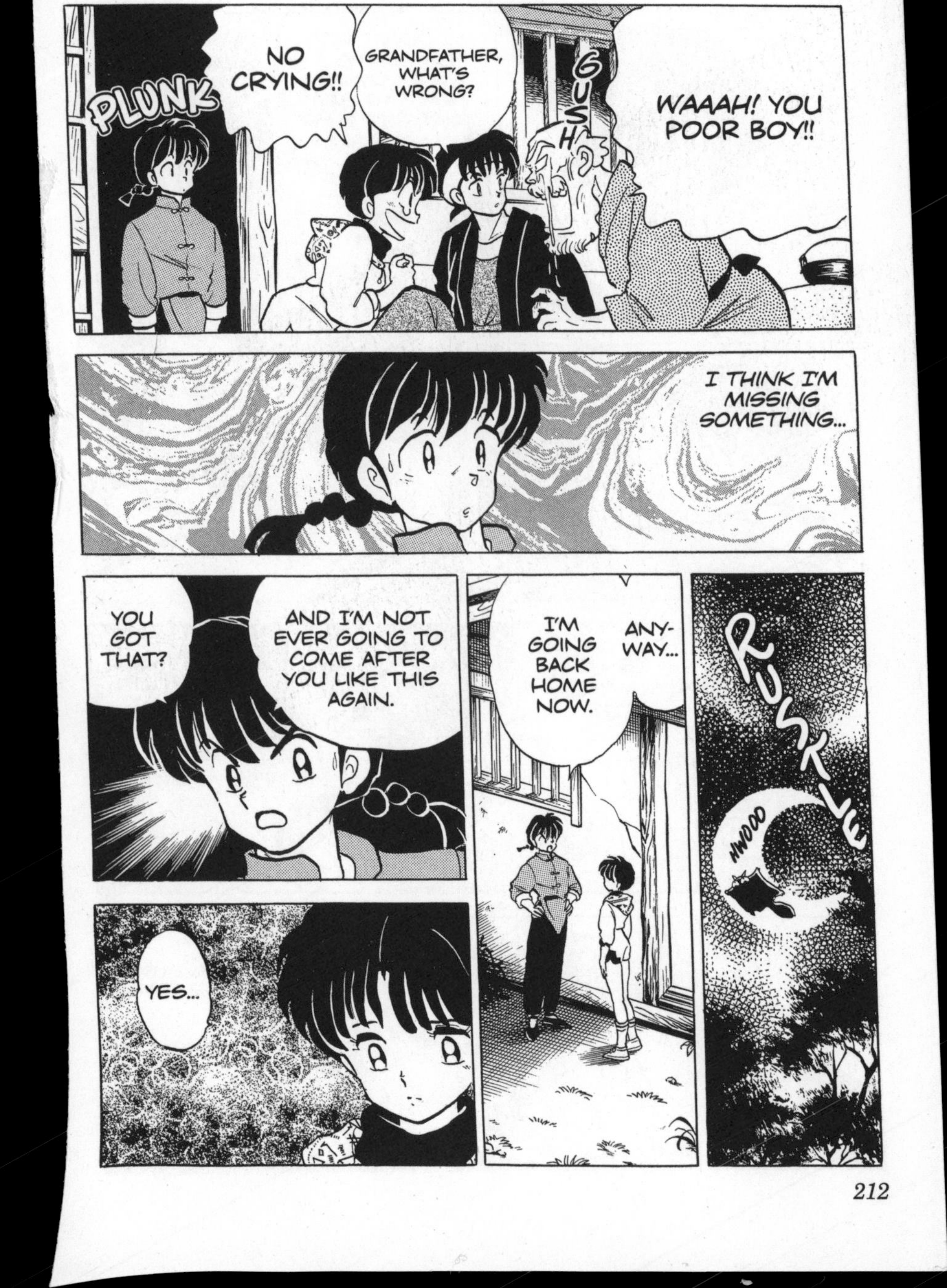
WAAAH! YOU POOR BOY!!
GUSH
GRANDFATHER, WHAT'S WRONG?
NO CRYING!!
PLUNK
I THINK I'M MISSING SOMETHING...
RUSKLE
HWOOO
ANY-WAY...
I'M GOING BACK HOME NOW.
AND I'M NOT EVER GOING TO COME AFTER YOU LIKE THIS AGAIN.
YOU GOT THAT?
YES...

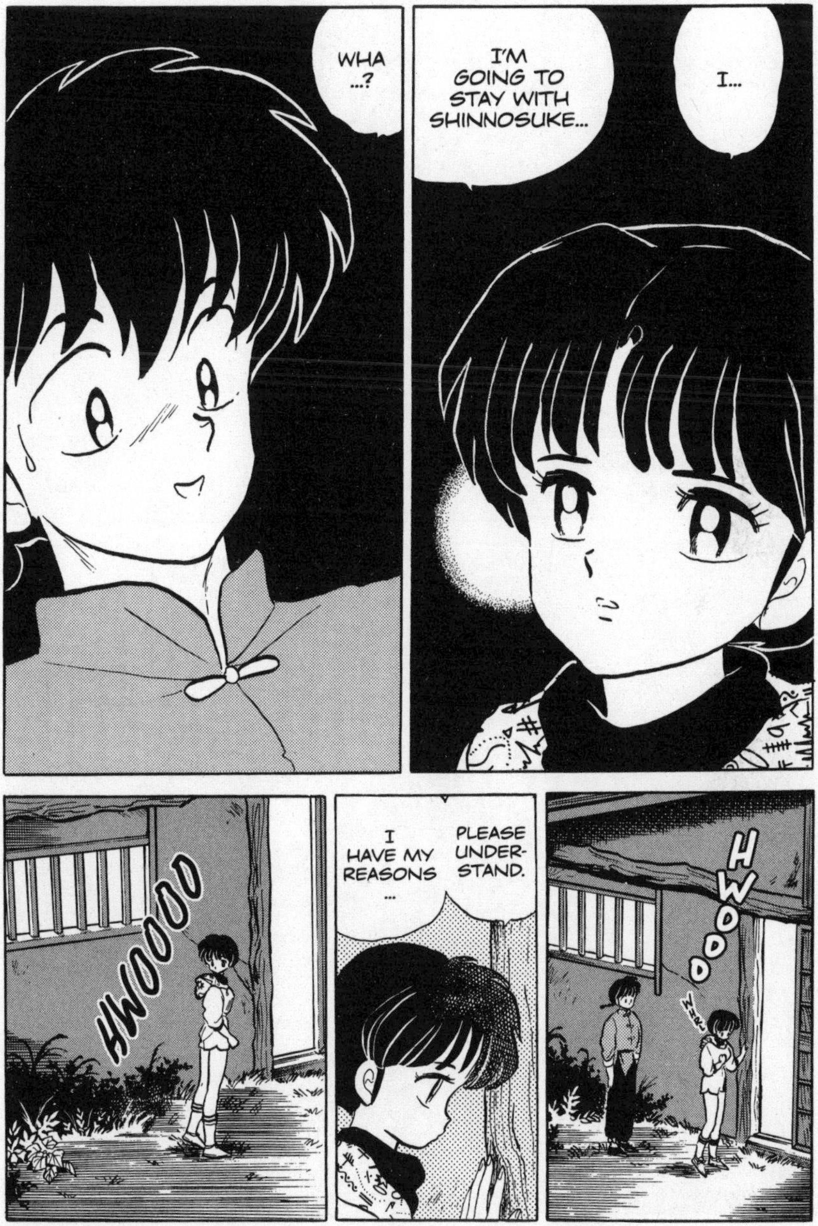
I...
I'M GOING TO STAY WITH SHINNOSUKE...
WHA ...?
HWOODD
WHRL
PLEASE UNDER-STAND.
I HAVE MY REASONS ...
HWOOOO

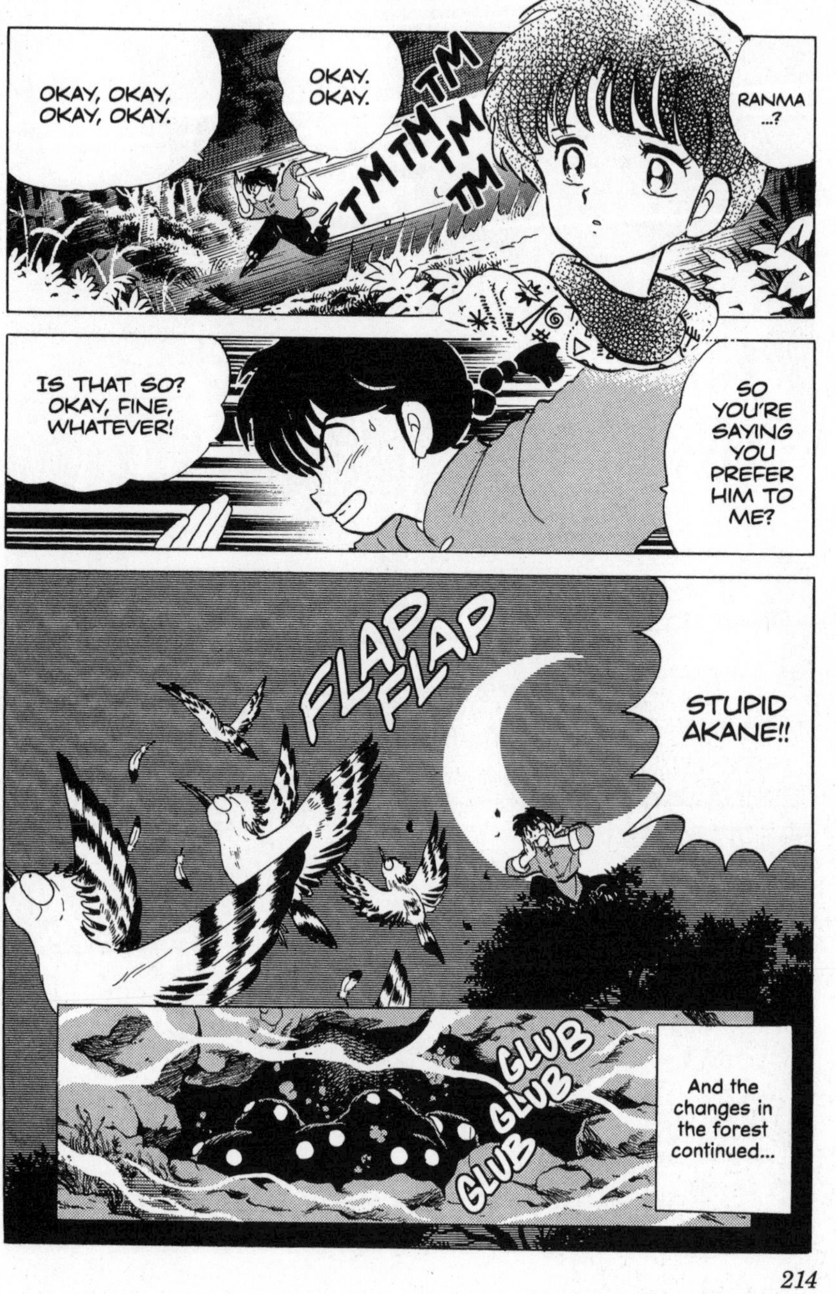
RANMA ...?
TM TM TM TM TM TM TM
OKAY. OKAY.
OKAY, OKAY, OKAY, OKAY.
SO YOU'RE SAYING YOU PREFER HIM TO ME?
IS THAT SO? OKAY, FINE, WHATEVER!
STUPID AKANE!!
FLAP FLAP
And the changes in the forest continued...
GLUB GLUB GLUB

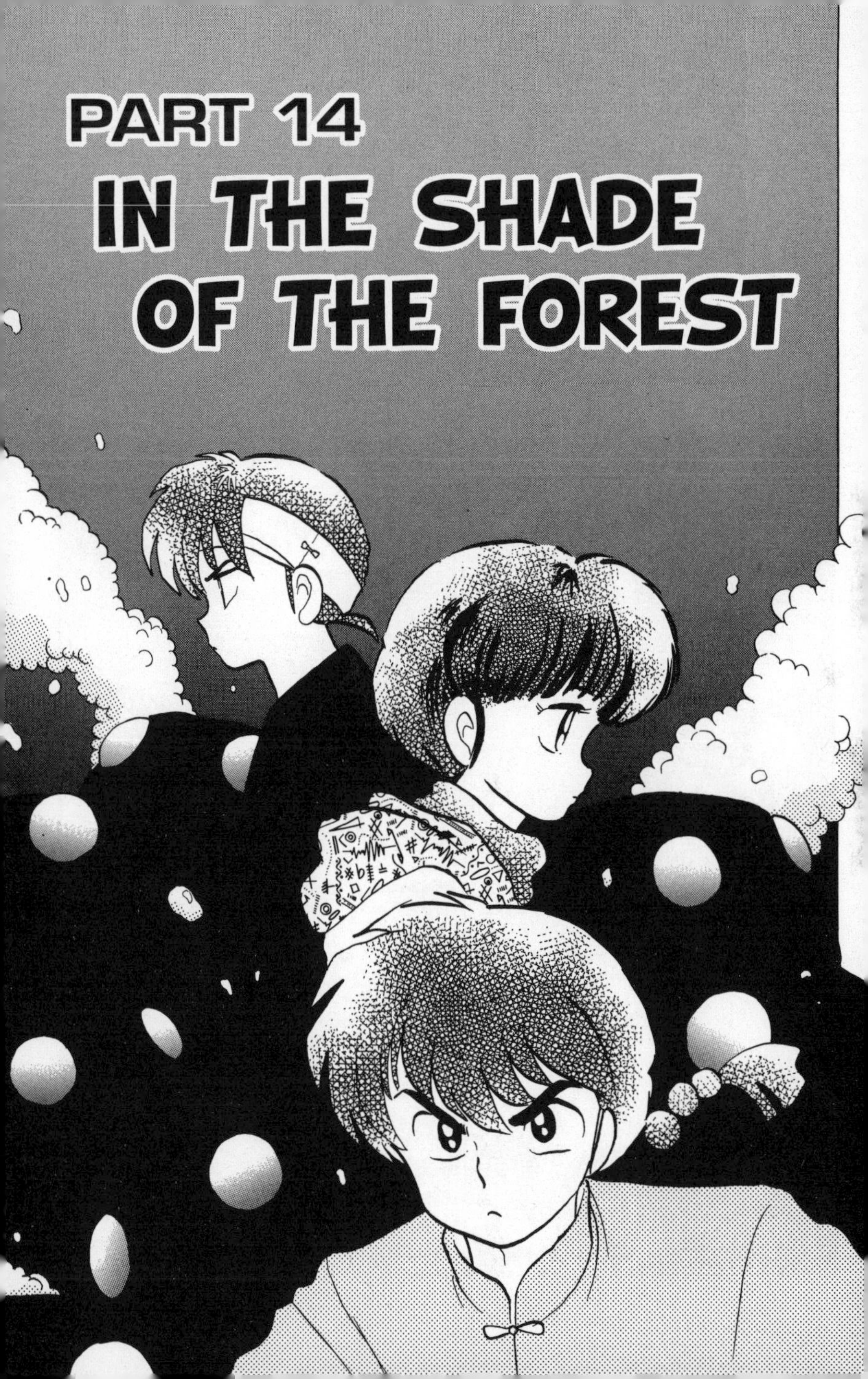
PART 14
IN THE SHADE OF THE FOREST

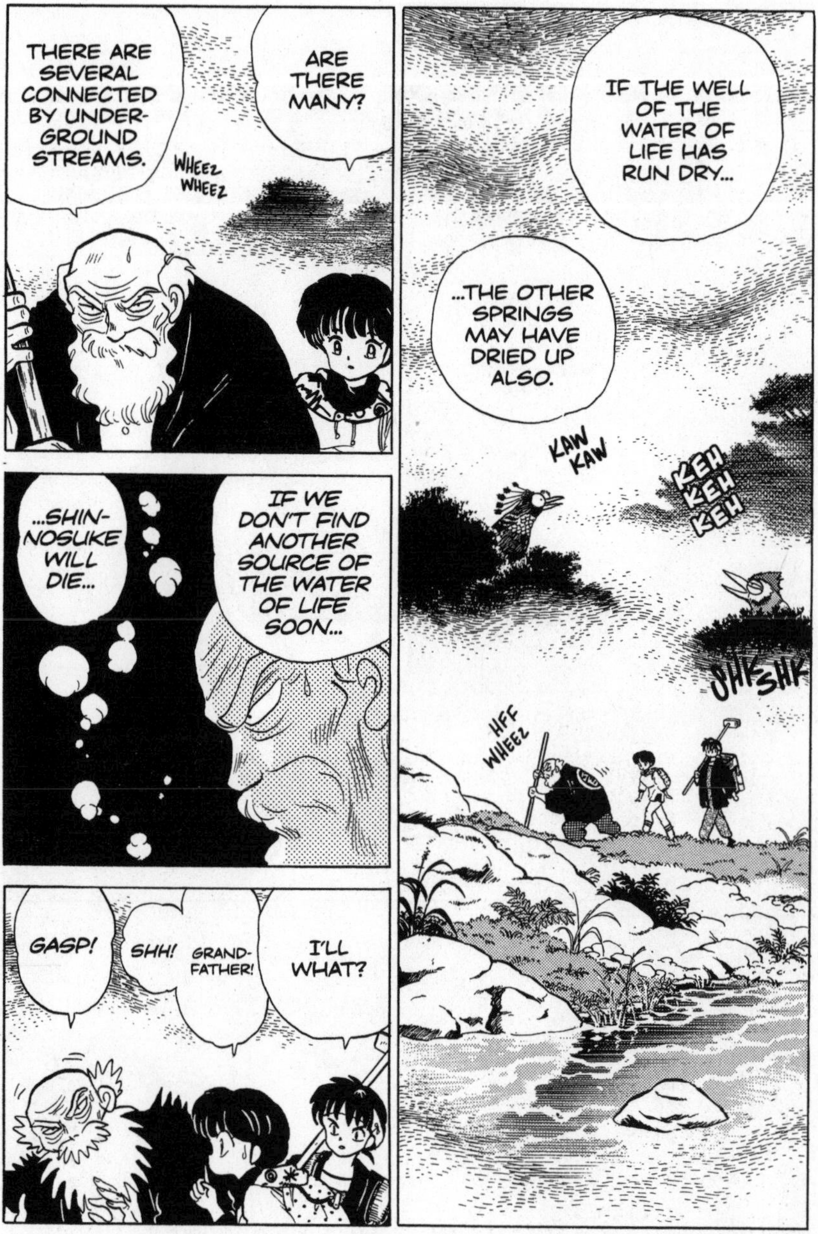
IF THE WELL OF THE WATER OF LIFE HAS RUN DRY...
...THE OTHER SPRINGS MAY HAVE DRIED UP ALSO.
KAW KAW
KEH KEH KEH
SHK SHK
HFF WHEEZ
ARE THERE MANY?
THERE ARE SEVERAL CONNECTED BY UNDERGROUND STREAMS.
WHEEZ WHEEZ
IF WE DON'T FIND ANOTHER SOURCE OF THE WATER OF LIFE SOON...
...SHINNOSUKE WILL DIE...
I'LL WHAT?
GRANDFATHER!
SHH!
GASP!

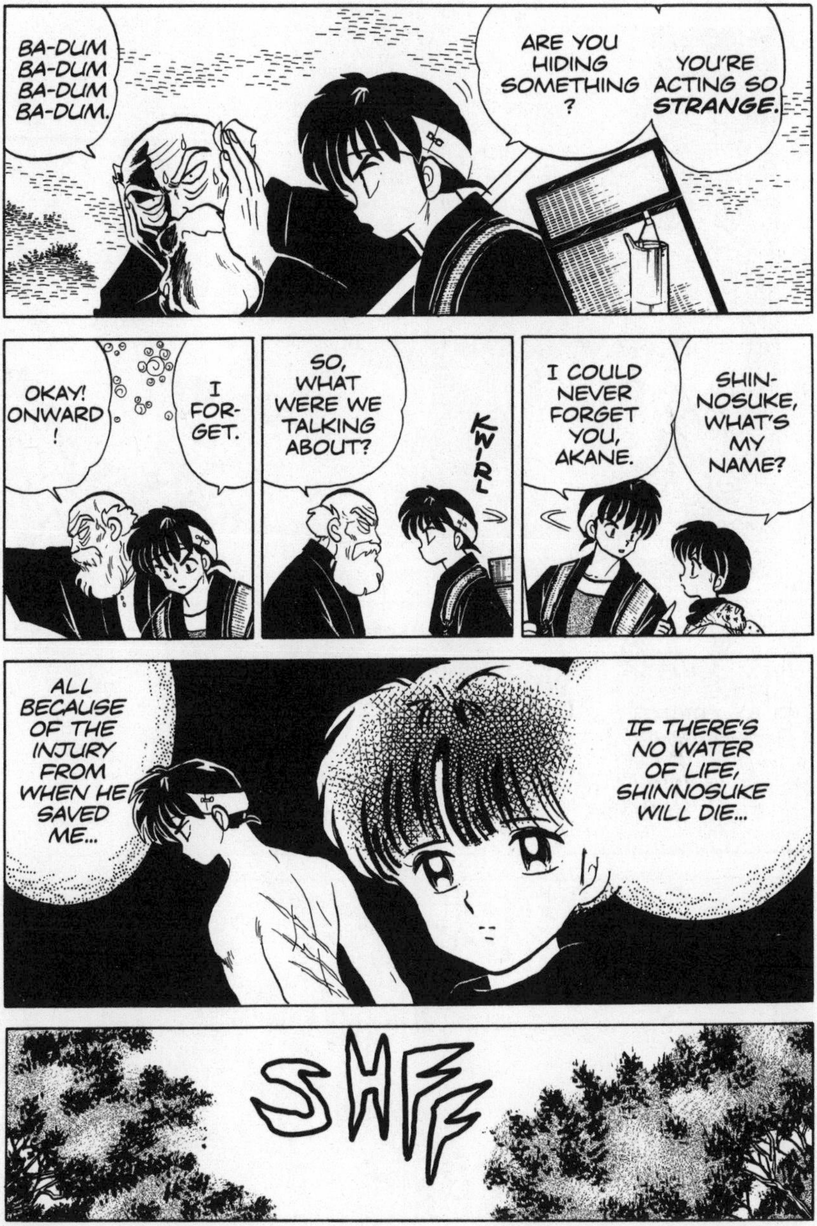
YOU'RE ACTING SO STRANGE.
ARE YOU HIDING SOMETHING ?
BA-DUM BA-DUM BA-DUM BA-DUM.
SHIN-NOSUKE, WHAT'S MY NAME?
I COULD NEVER FORGET YOU, AKANE.
KWIRL
SO, WHAT WERE WE TALKING ABOUT?
I FOR-GET.
OKAY! ONWARD !
IF THERE'S NO WATER OF LIFE, SHINNOSUKE WILL DIE...
ALL BECAUSE OF THE INJURY FROM WHEN HE SAVED ME...
SHFF

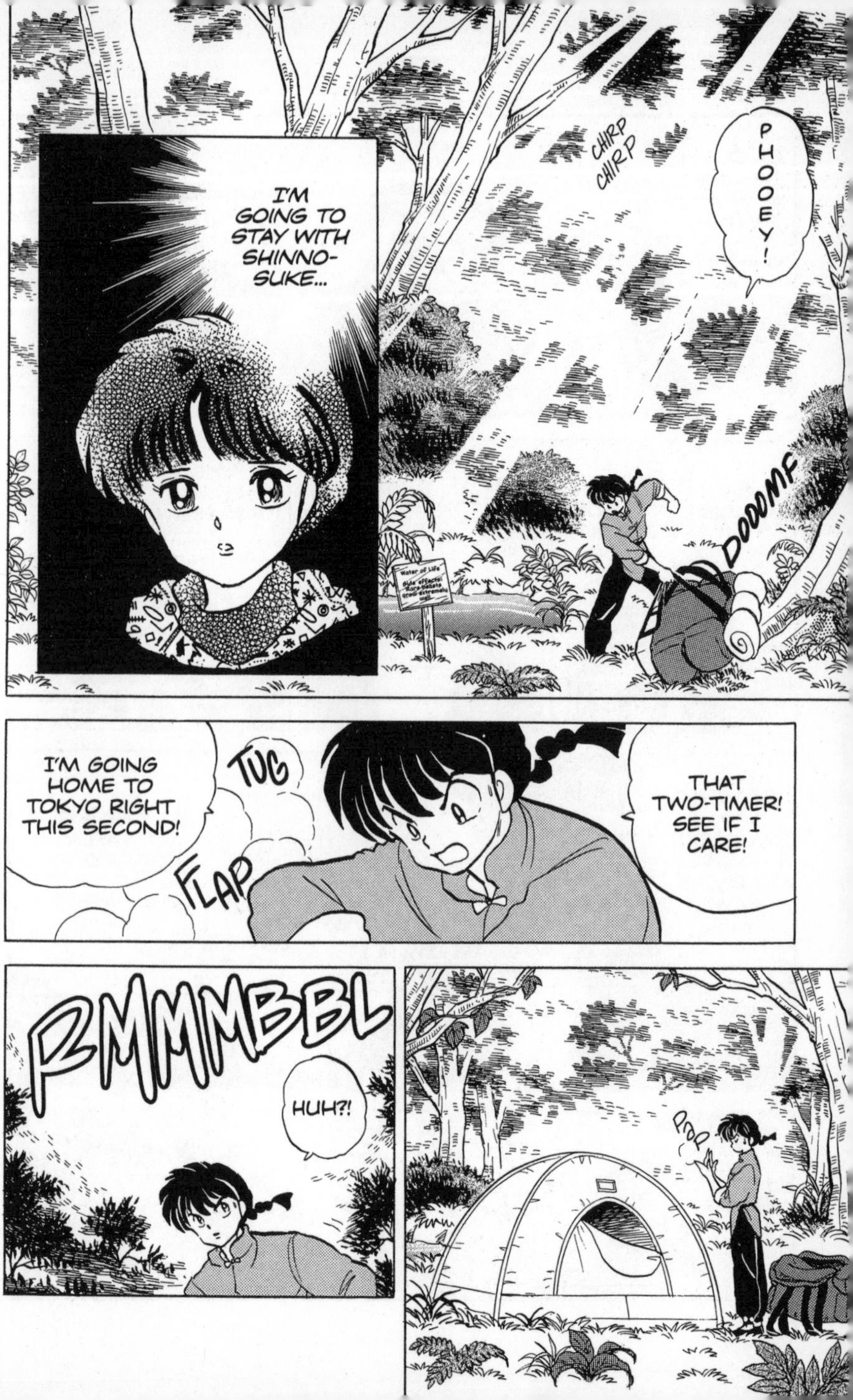
CHIRP CHIRP
PHOOEY!
Water of Life
Side effects: Rare beasts grow extremely well
DOOOMF
I'M GOING TO STAY WITH SHINNO-SUKE...
THAT TWO-TIMER! SEE IF I CARE!
TUG
I'M GOING HOME TO TOKYO RIGHT THIS SECOND!
FLAP
RMMMBBL
HUH?!

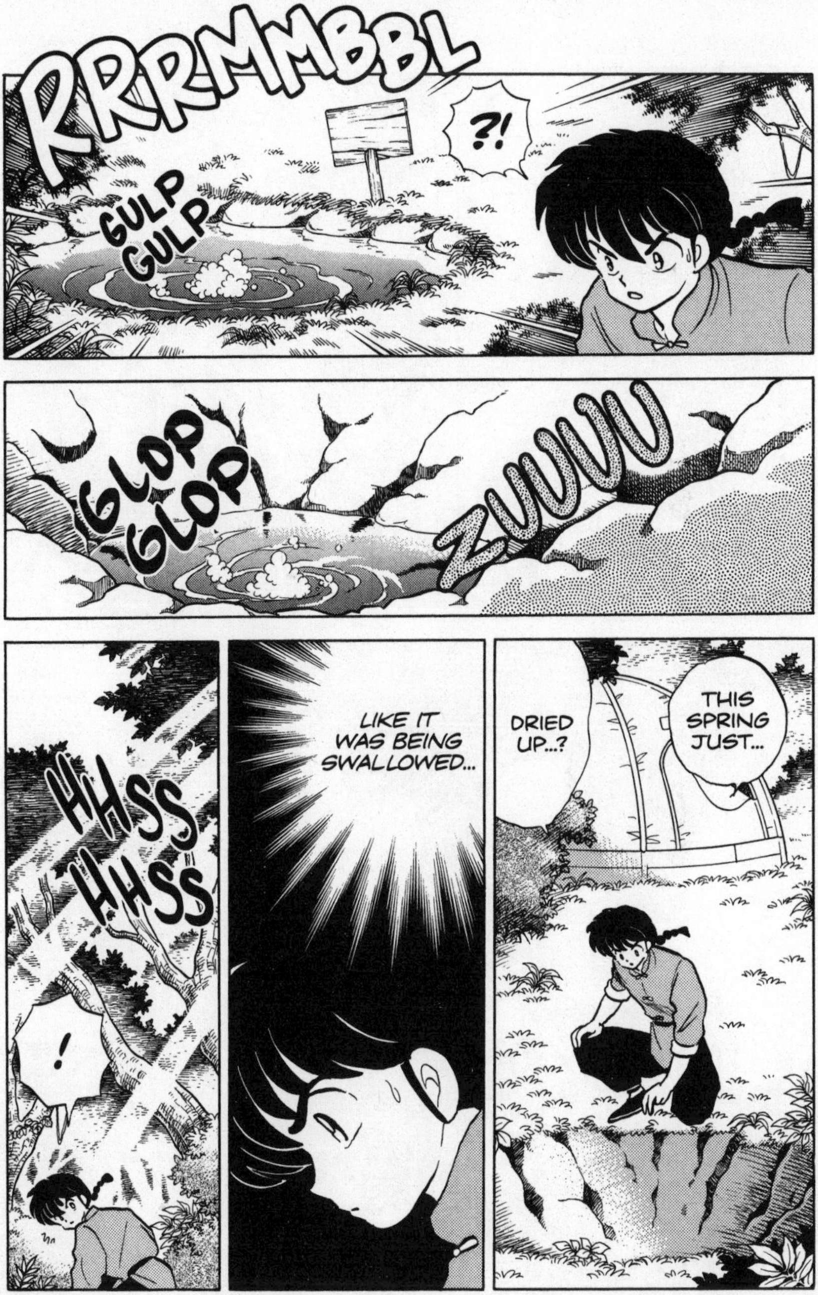
RRRMMBBL
?!
GULP GULP
ZUUUU
GLOP GLOP
THIS SPRING JUST...
DRIED UP...?
LIKE IT WAS BEING SWALLOWED...
HHSS HHSS
!

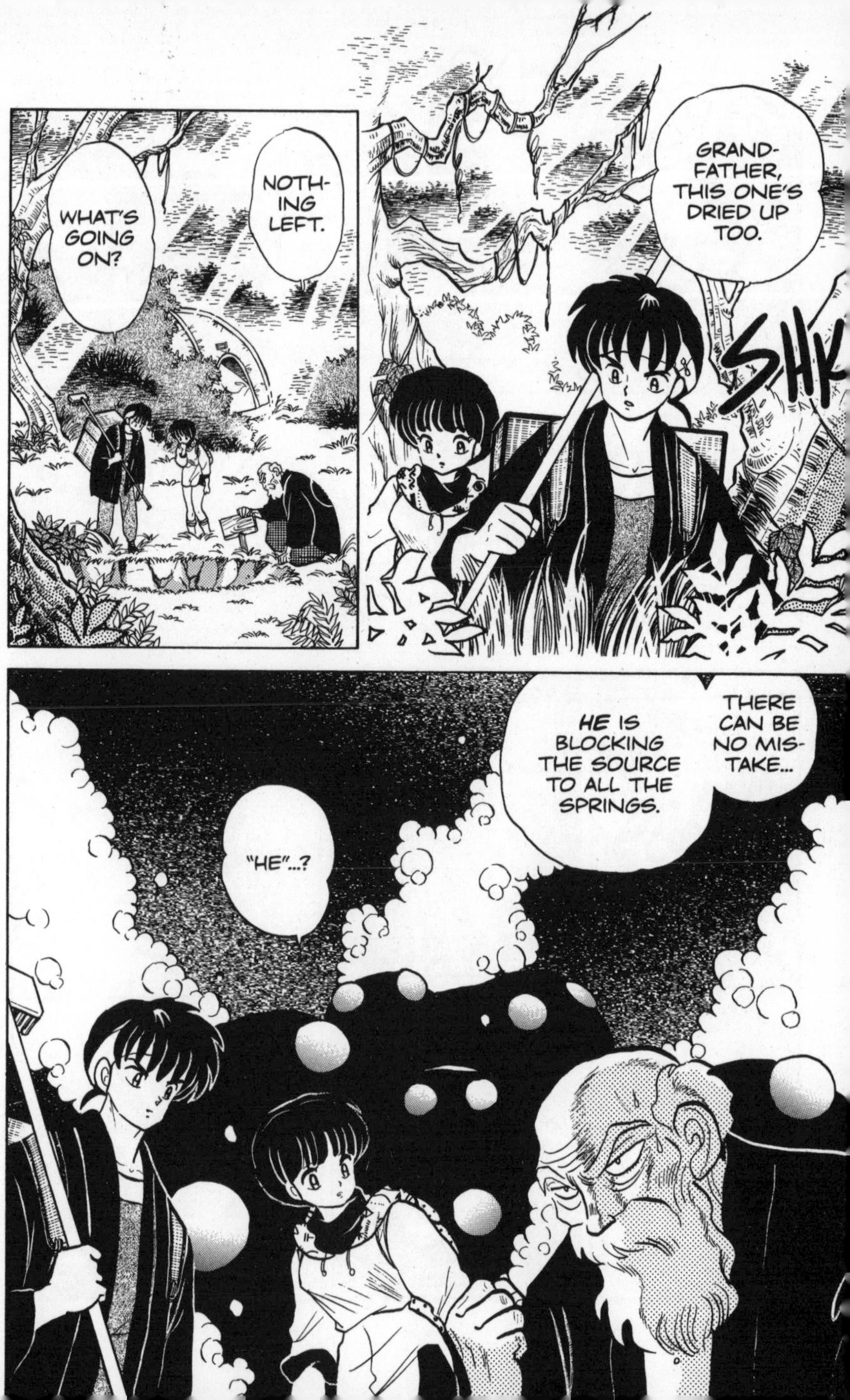
GRAND-FATHER, THIS ONE'S DRIED UP TOO.
SHK
NOTH-ING LEFT.
WHAT'S GOING ON?
THERE CAN BE NO MIS-TAKE...
HE IS BLOCKING THE SOURCE TO ALL THE SPRINGS.
"HE"...?

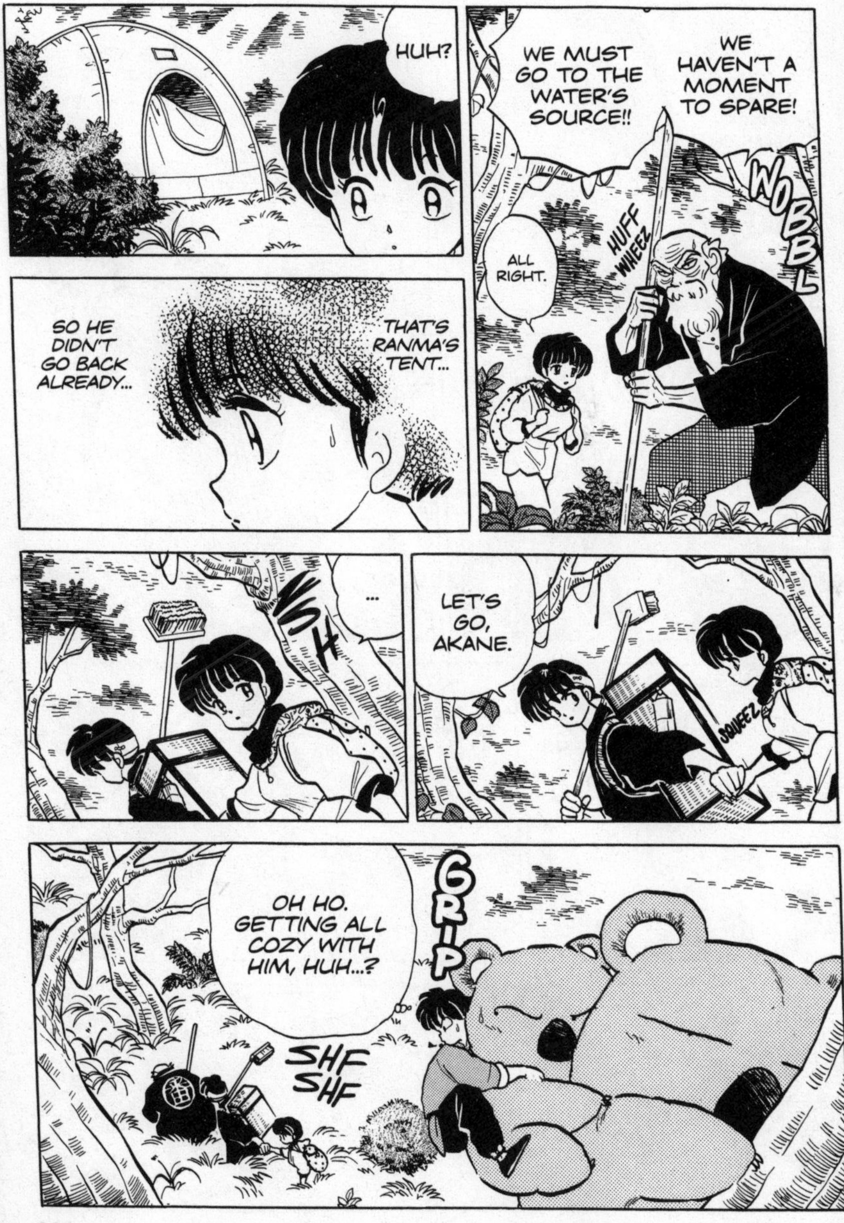
WE HAVEN'T A MOMENT TO SPARE!
WE MUST GO TO THE WATER'S SOURCE!!
WOBBL
HUFF WHEEZ
ALL RIGHT.
HUH?
THAT'S RANMA'S TENT...
SO HE DIDN'T GO BACK ALREADY...
LET'S GO, AKANE.
SQUEEZ
WSH
...
GRIP
OH HO. GETTING ALL COZY WITH HIM, HUH...?
SHF SHF

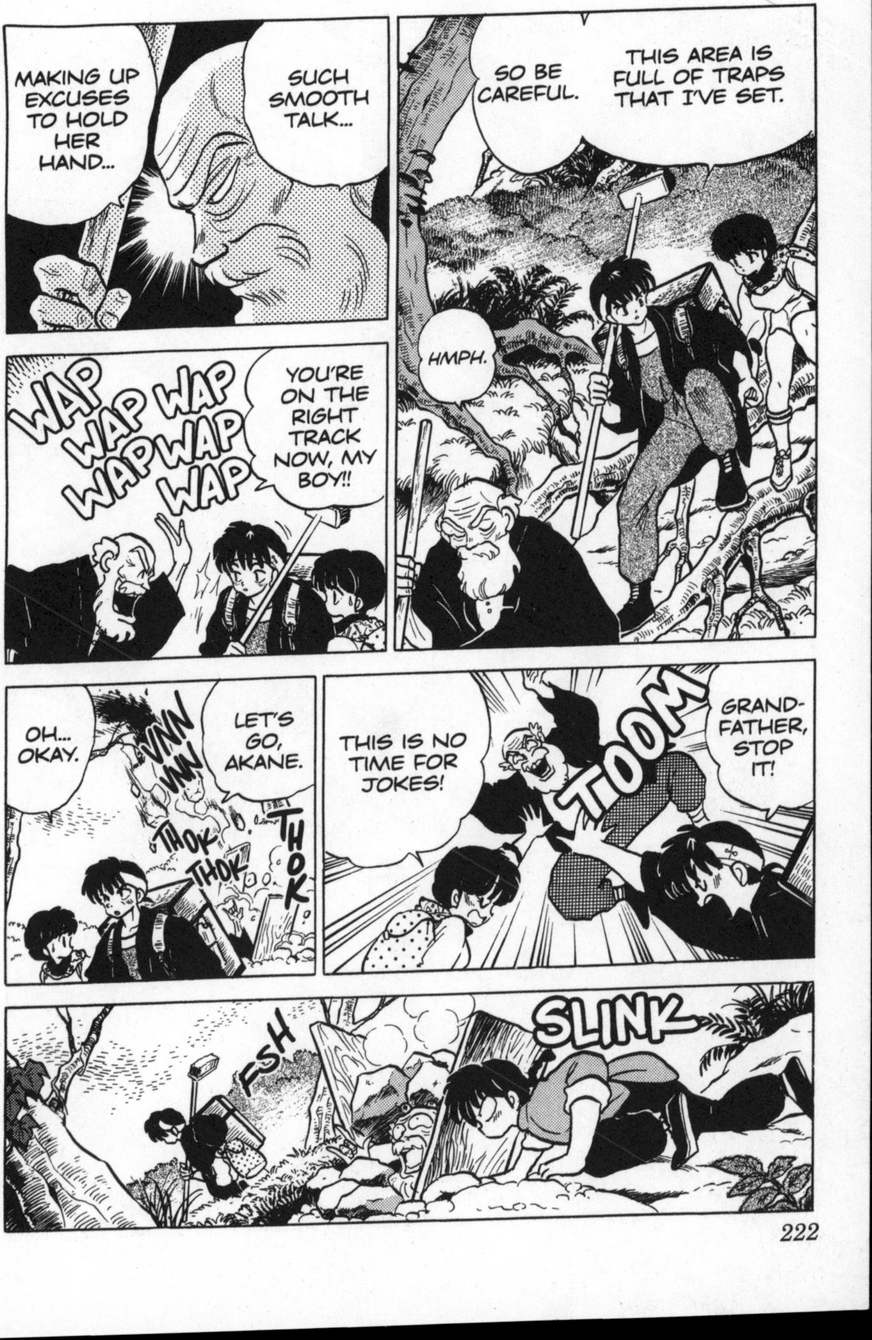
THIS AREA IS FULL OF TRAPS THAT I'VE SET.
SO BE CAREFUL.
HMPH.
SUCH SMOOTH TALK...
MAKING UP EXCUSES TO HOLD HER HAND...
YOU'RE ON THE RIGHT TRACK NOW, MY BOY!!
WAP WAP WAP WAP WAP WAP WAP
GRAND-FATHER, STOP IT!
TOOM
THIS IS NO TIME FOR JOKES!
LET'S GO, AKANE.
VNN VNN
OH... OKAY.
THOK THOK THOK
SLINK
FSH

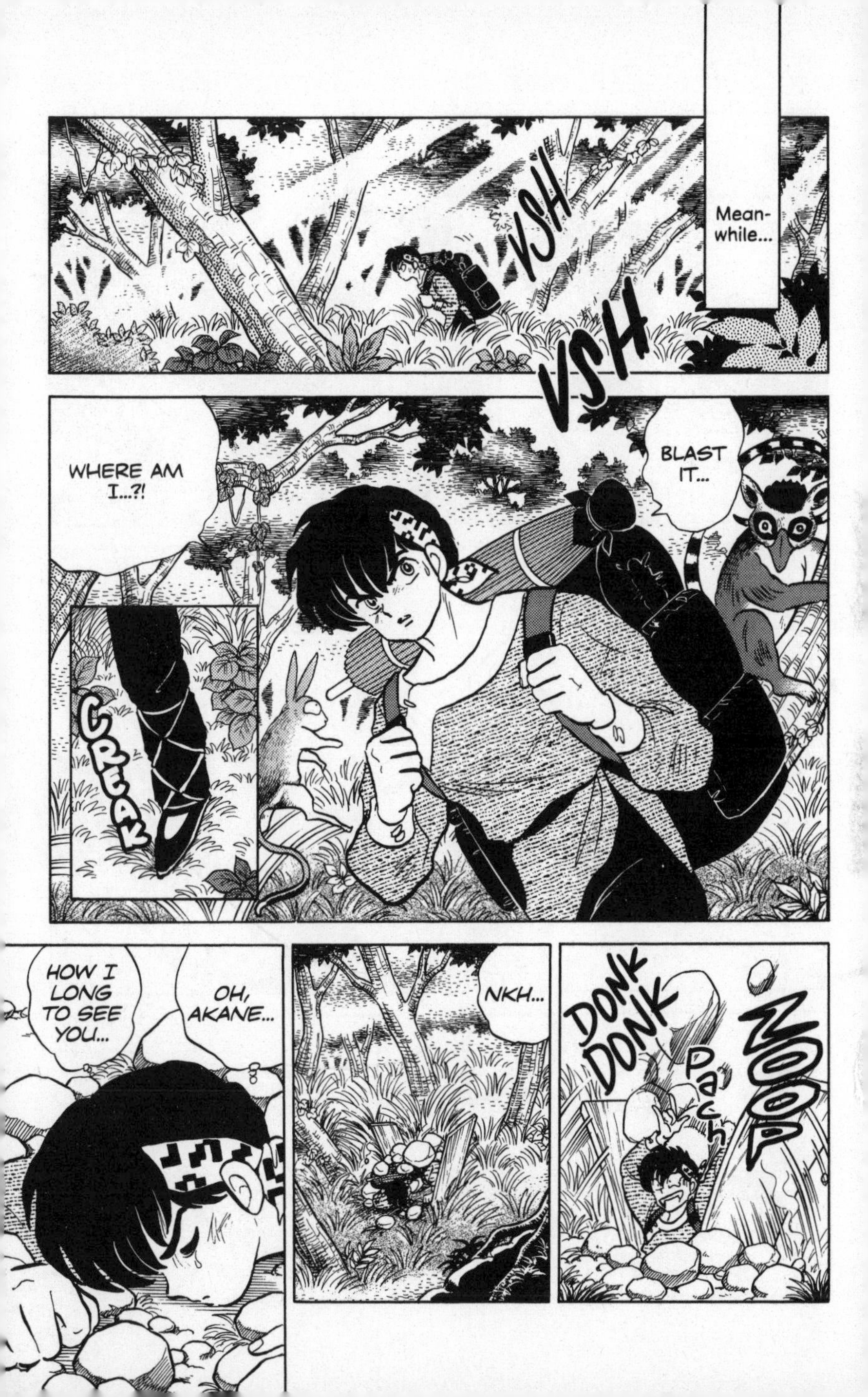
Mean-while...
VSH
VSH
BLAST IT...
WHERE AM I...?!
CREAK
ZOOP
DONK DONK
Pach
NKH...
OH, AKANE...
HOW I LONG TO SEE YOU...

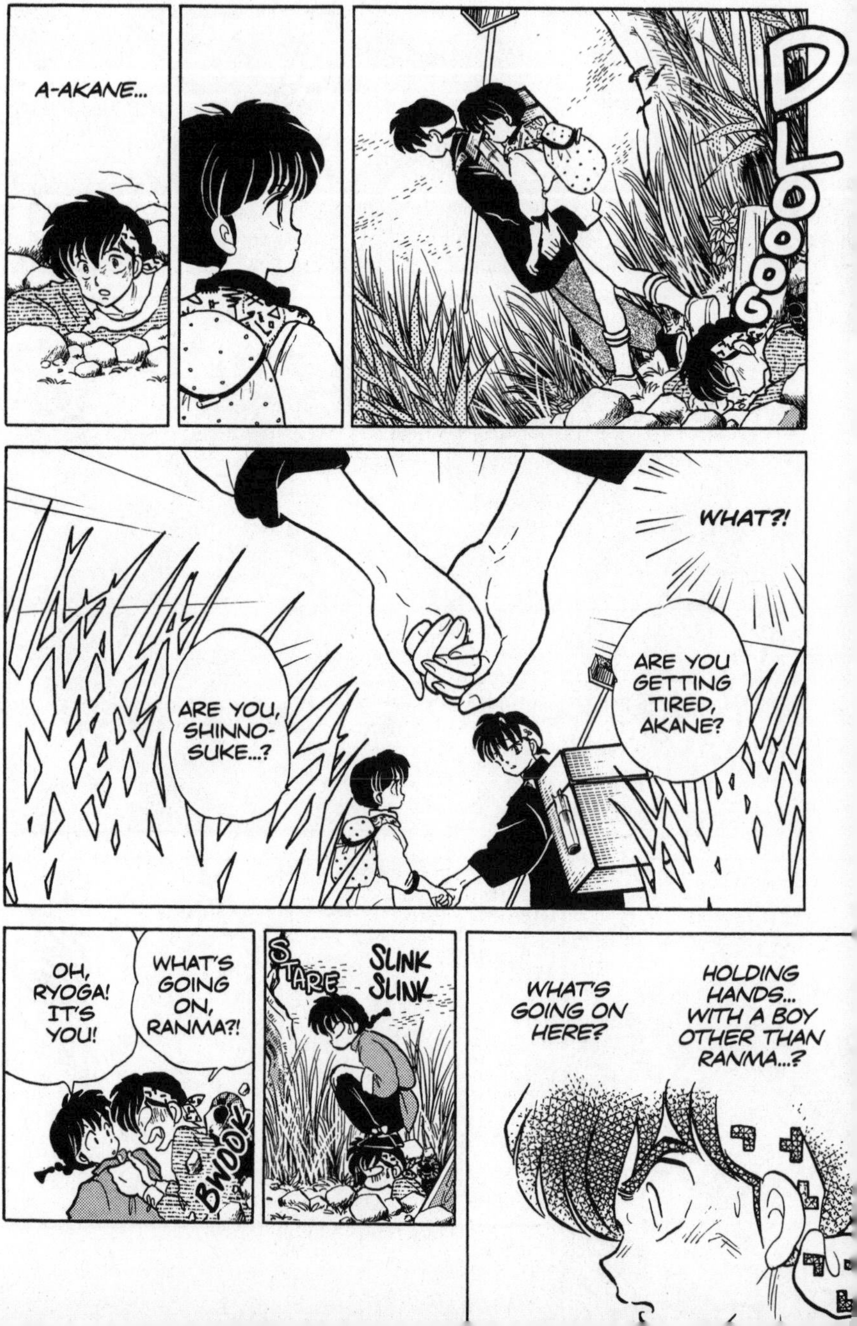
DLOOOG
A-AKANE...
WHAT?!
ARE YOU GETTING TIRED, AKANE?
ARE YOU, SHINNO-SUKE...?
HOLDING HANDS... WITH A BOY OTHER THAN RANMA...?
WHAT'S GOING ON HERE?
SLINK SLINK
STARE
WHAT'S GOING ON, RANMA?!
OH, RYOGA! IT'S YOU!
BWOOK

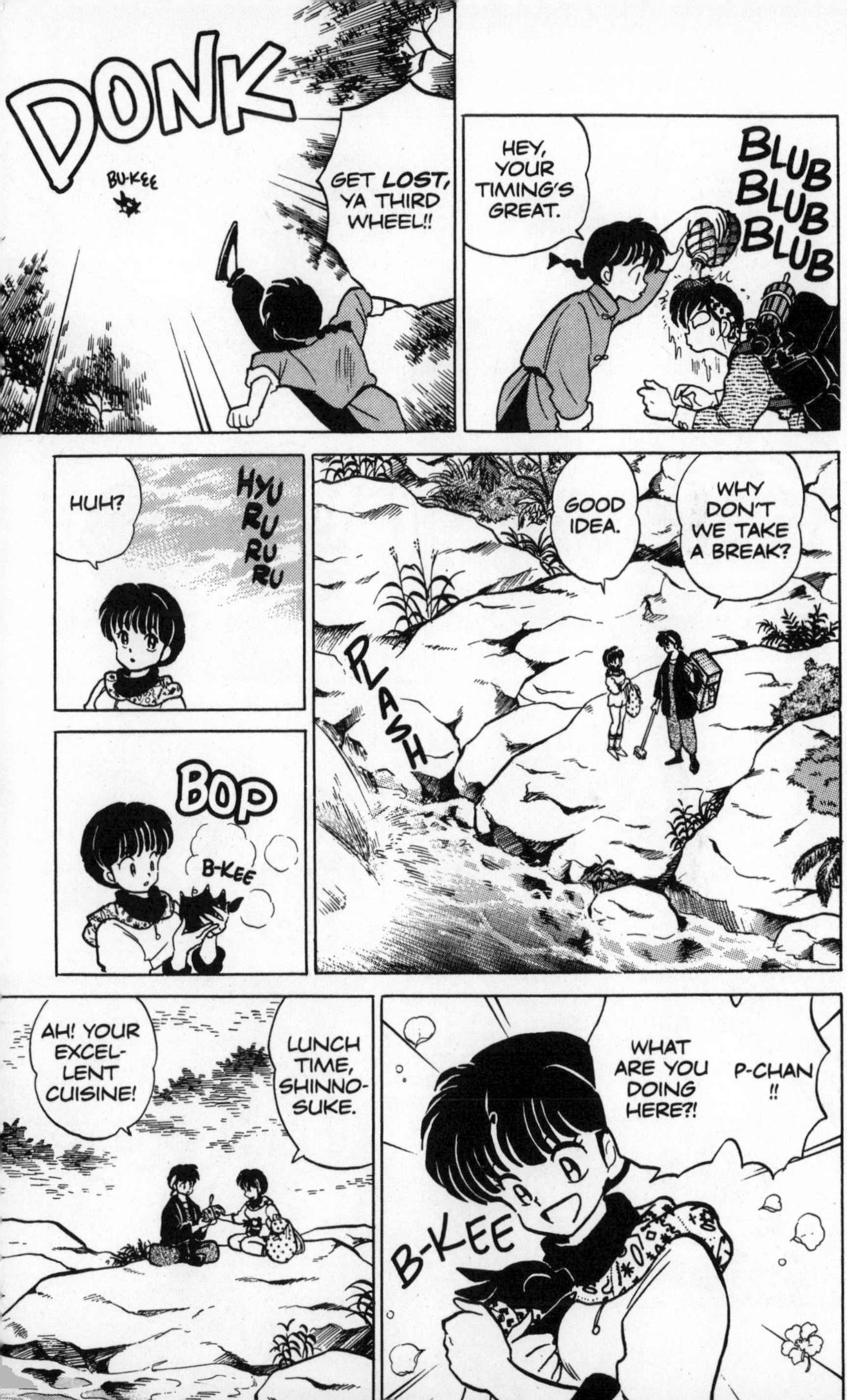
BLUB BLUB BLUB
HEY, YOUR TIMING'S GREAT.
DONK
GET LOST, YA THIRD WHEEL!!
BU-KEE
WHY DON'T WE TAKE A BREAK?
GOOD IDEA.
PLASH
HYU RU RU RU
HUH?
BOP
B-KEE
P-CHAN!!
WHAT ARE YOU DOING HERE?!
B-KEE
LUNCH TIME, SHINNO-SUKE.
AH! YOUR EXCEL-LENT CUISINE!

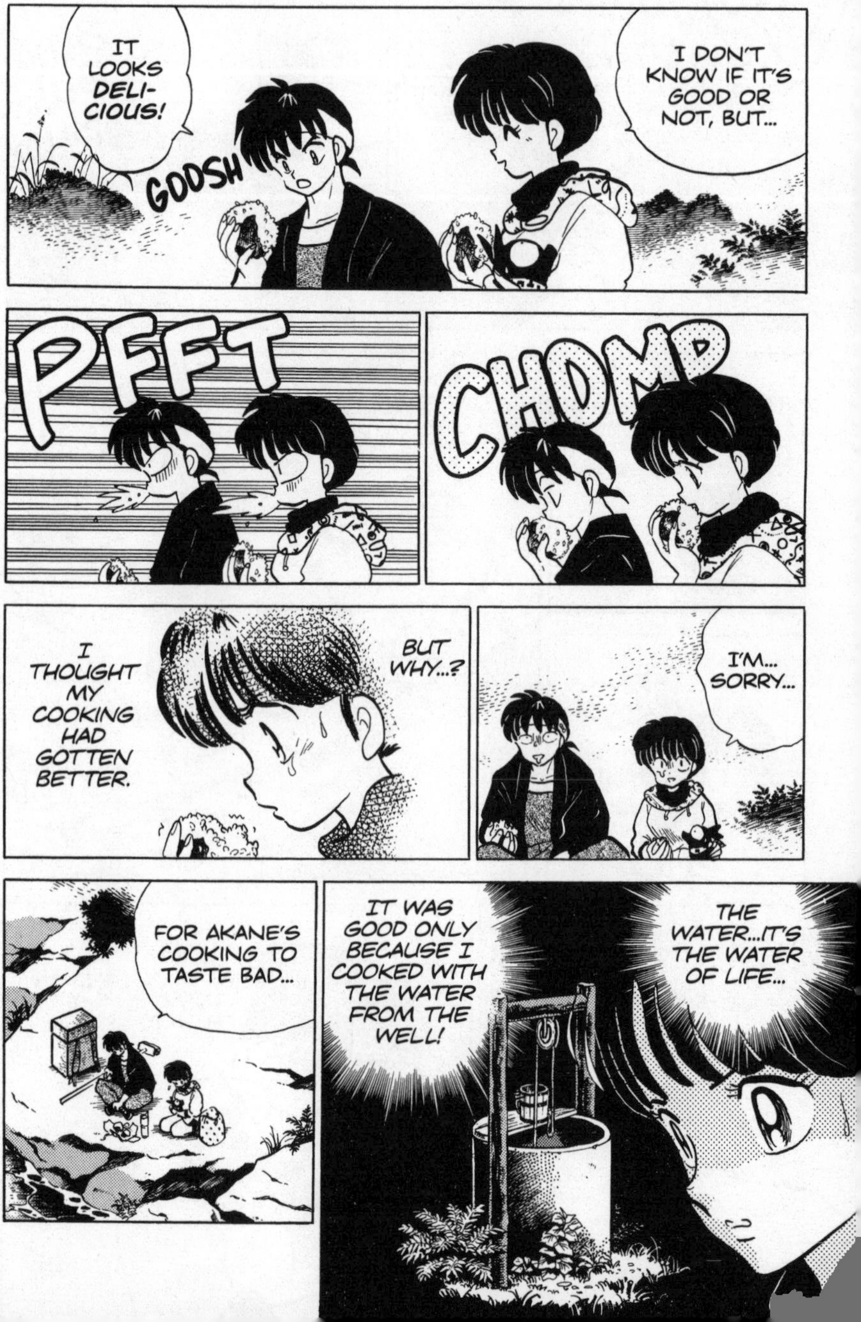
I DON'T KNOW IF IT'S GOOD OR NOT, BUT...
IT LOOKS DELI-CIOUS!
GODSH
CHOMP
PFFT
I'M... SORRY...
BUT WHY..?
I THOUGHT MY COOKING HAD GOTTEN BETTER.
THE WATER...IT'S THE WATER OF LIFE...
IT WAS GOOD ONLY BECAUSE I COOKED WITH THE WATER FROM THE WELL!
FOR AKANE'S COOKING TO TASTE BAD...

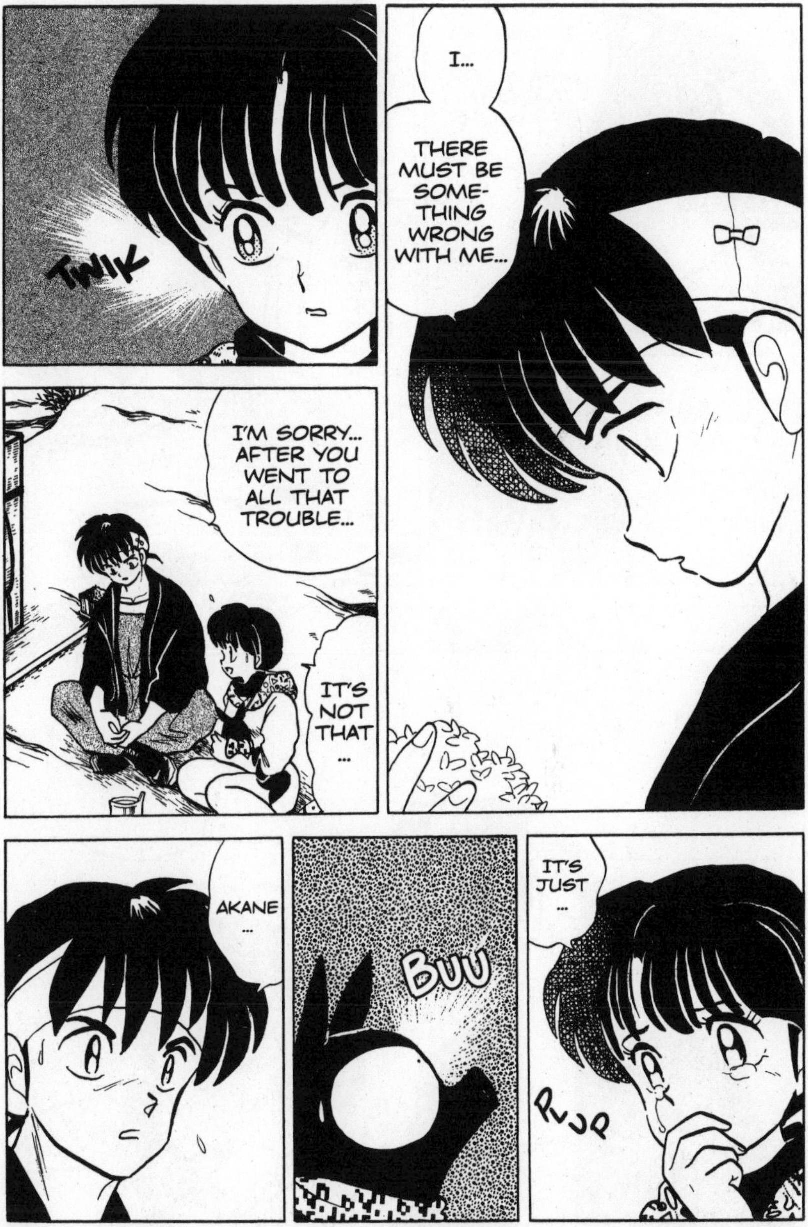
I...
THERE MUST BE SOME-THING WRONG WITH ME...
TWIK
I'M SORRY... AFTER YOU WENT TO ALL THAT TROUBLE...
IT'S NOT THAT ...
IT'S JUST ...
BUU
AKANE ...

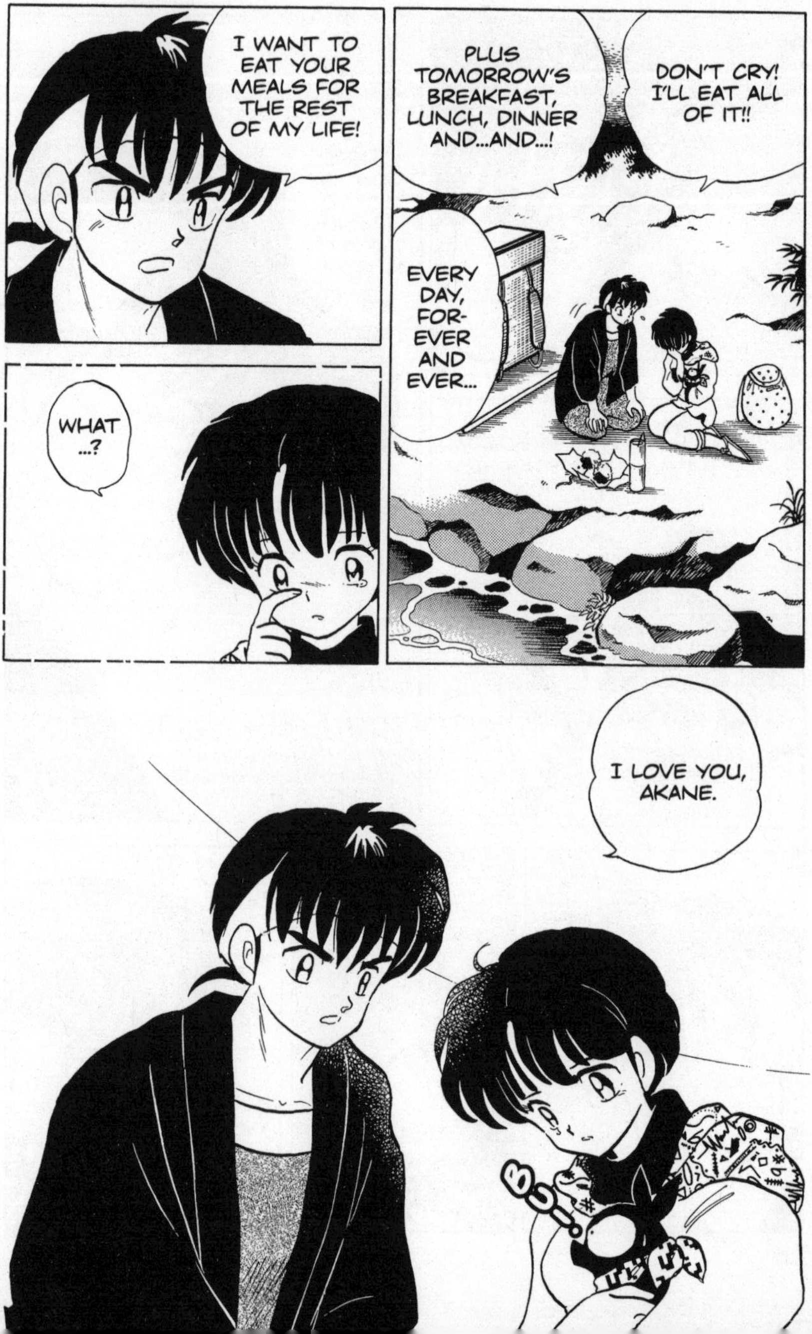
DON'T CRY! I'LL EAT ALL OF IT!!
PLUS TOMORROW'S BREAKFAST, LUNCH, DINNER AND...AND...!
EVERY DAY, FOR-EVER AND EVER...
I WANT TO EAT YOUR MEALS FOR THE REST OF MY LIFE!
WHAT ...?
I LOVE YOU, AKANE.

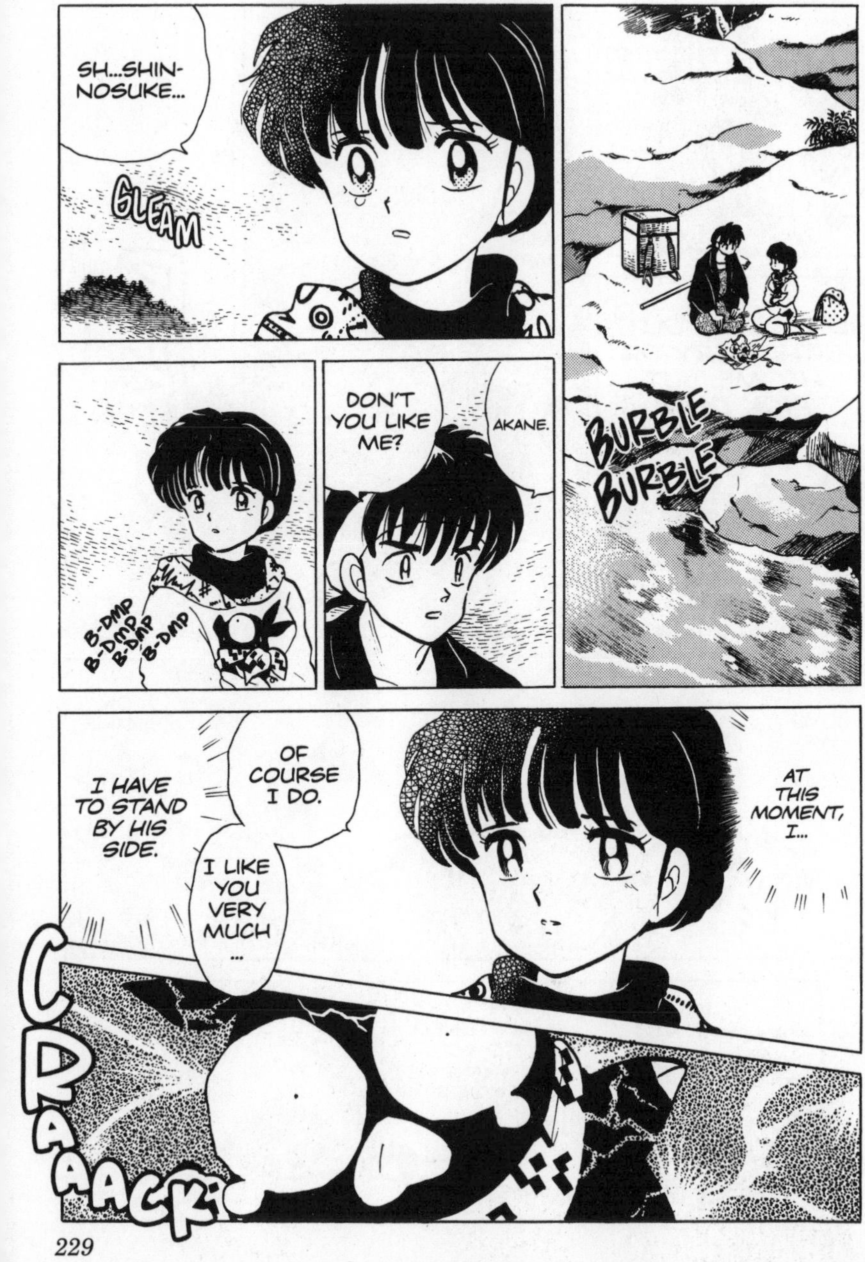
BURBLE
BURBLE
SH...SHIN-NOSUKE...
GLEAM
AKANE.
DON'T YOU LIKE ME?
B-DMP B-DMP B-DMP B-DMP
AT THIS MOMENT, I...
OF COURSE I DO.
I LIKE YOU VERY MUCH...
I HAVE TO STAND BY HIS SIDE.
CRAAACK

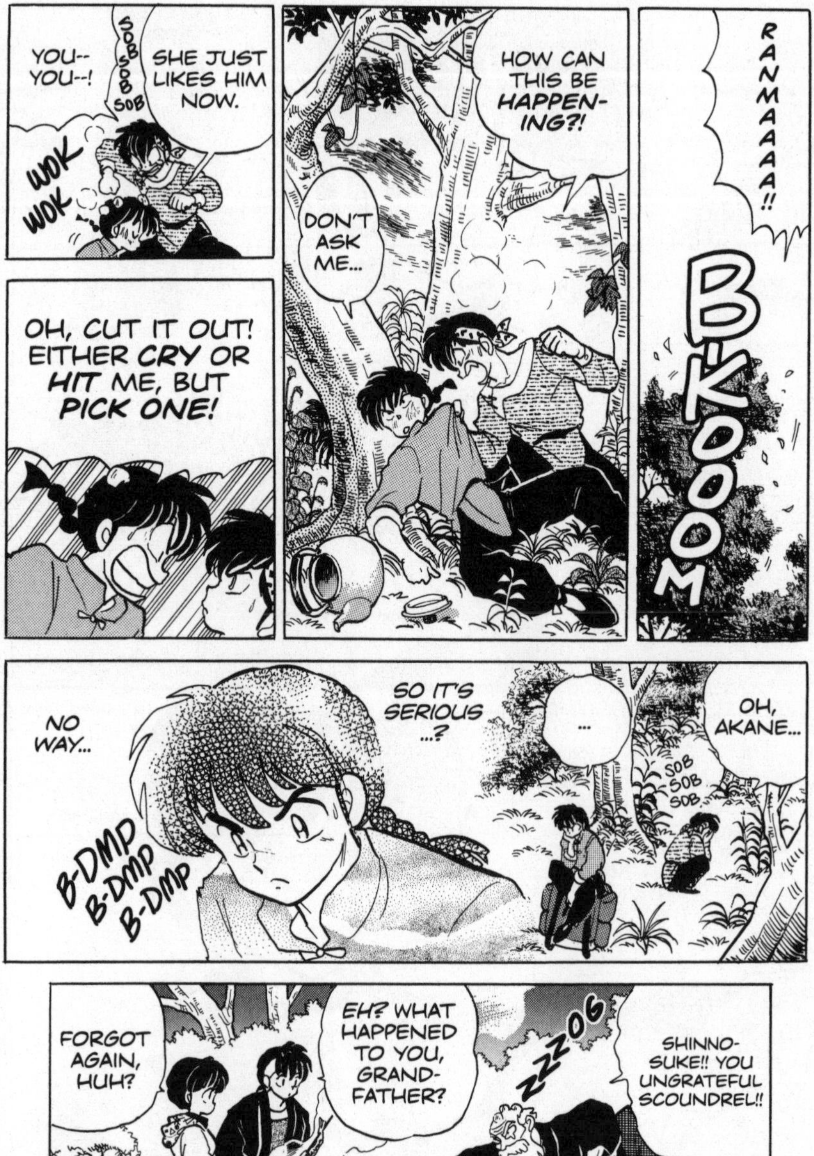
RANMAAAAA!!
B-KOOOOM
HOW CAN THIS BE HAPPENING?!
DON'T ASK ME...
SHE JUST LIKES HIM NOW.
SOB SOB SOB SOB
YOU-- YOU--!
WOK WOK
OH, CUT IT OUT! EITHER CRY OR HIT ME, BUT PICK ONE!
OH, AKANE...
SOB SOB SOB
...
SO IT'S SERIOUS ...?
NO WAY...
B-DMP B-DMP B-DMP
SHINNOSUKE!! YOU UNGRATEFUL SCOUNDREL!!
ZZZOG
EH? WHAT HAPPENED TO YOU, GRANDFATHER?
FORGOT AGAIN, HUH?

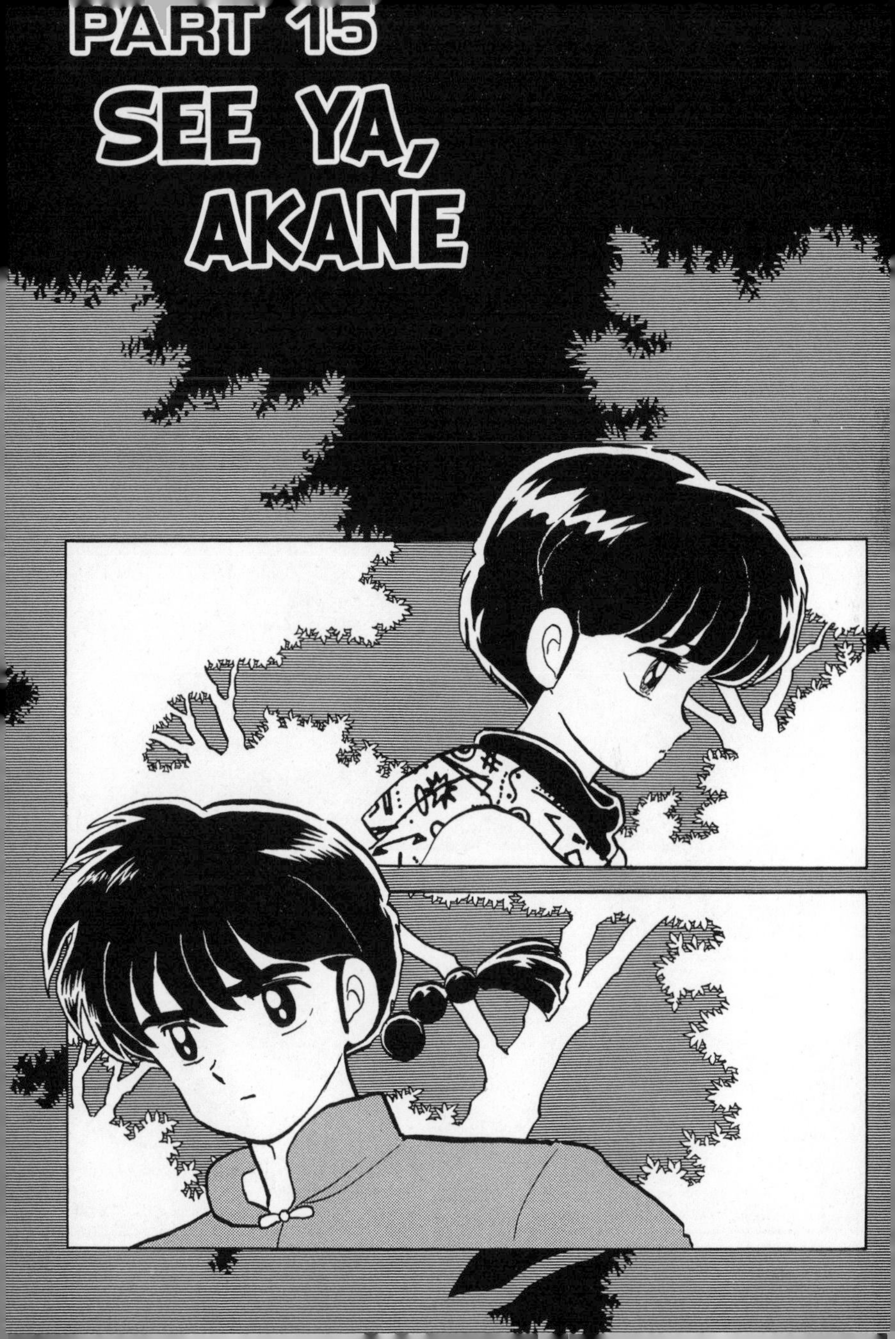
PART 15
SEE YA, AKANE

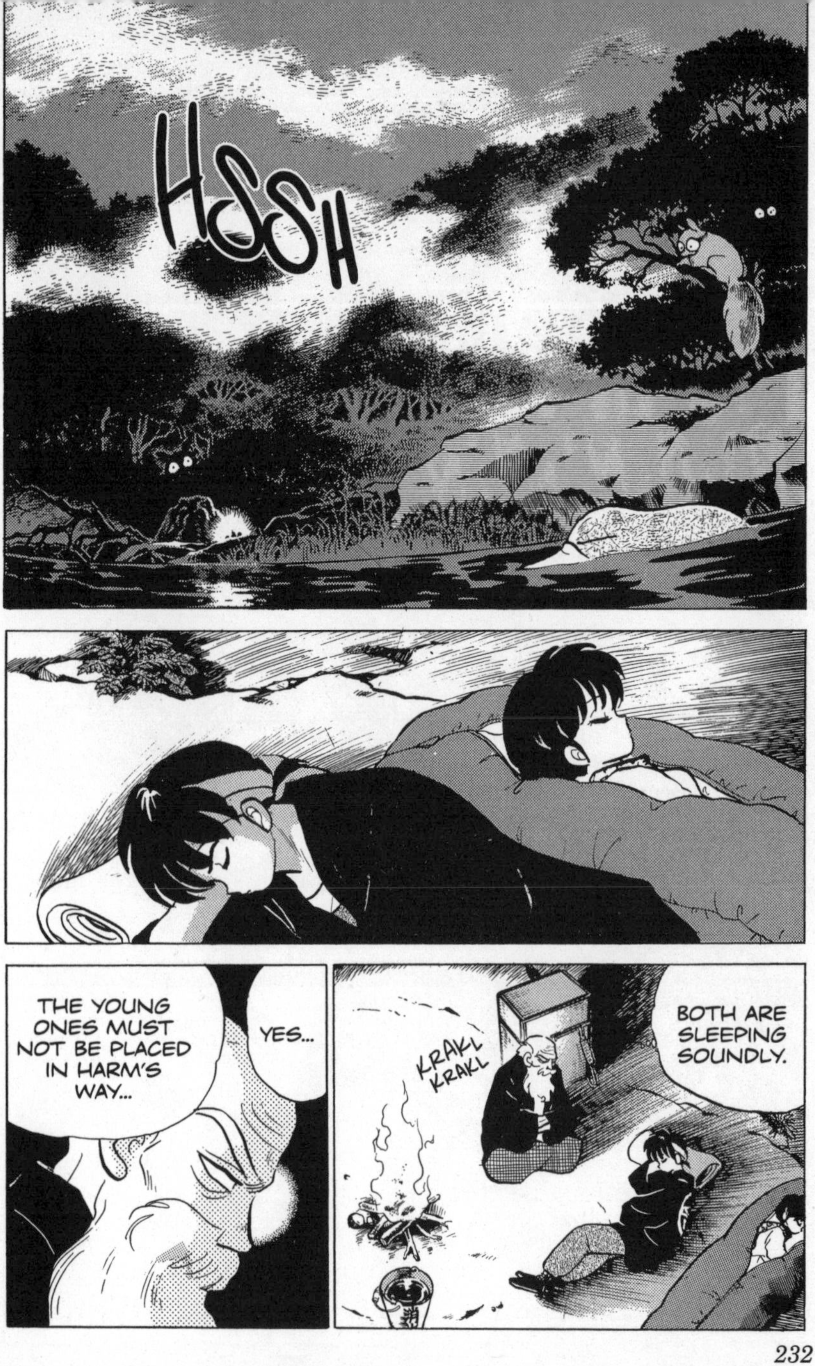
HSSH
BOTH ARE SLEEPING SOUNDLY.
KRAKL KRAKL
YES...
THE YOUNG ONES MUST NOT BE PLACED IN HARM'S WAY...

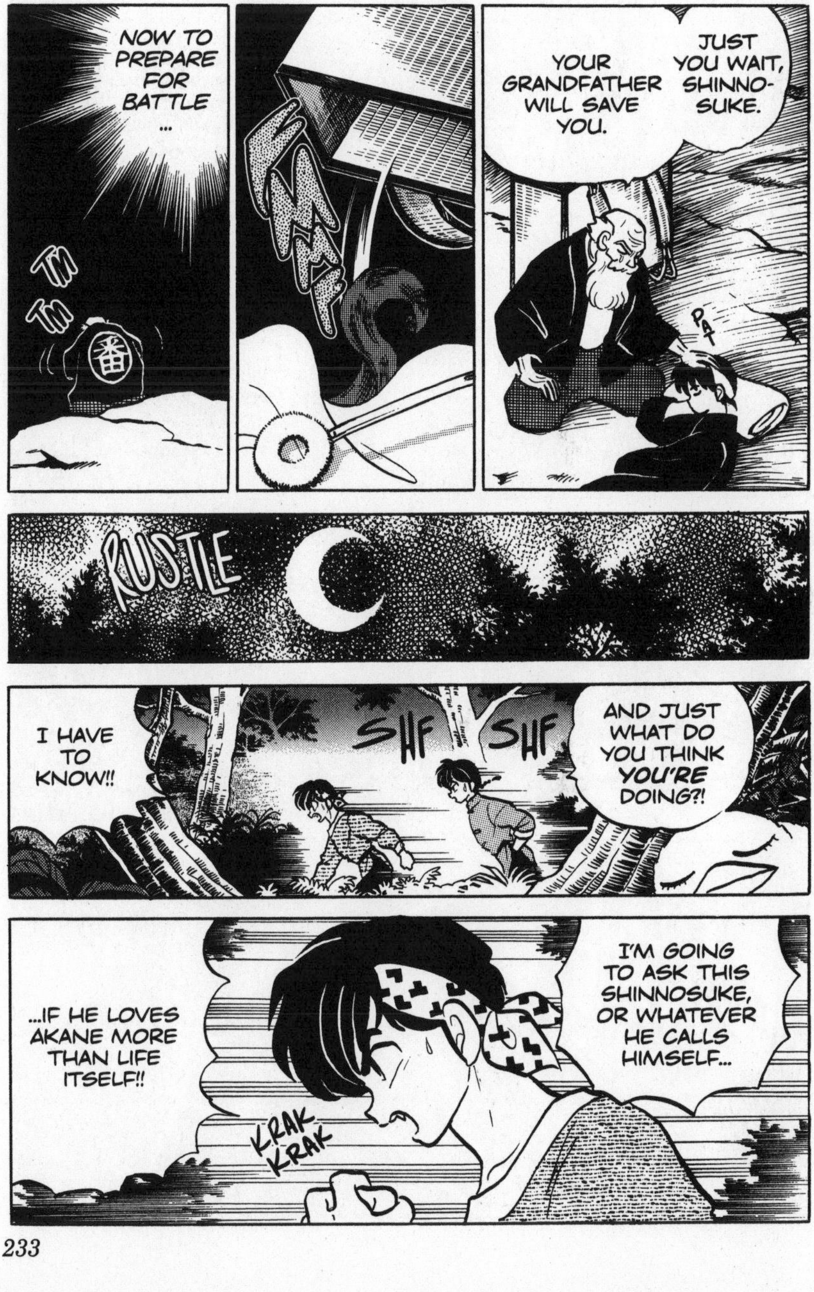
JUST YOU WAIT, SHINNOSUKE.
YOUR GRANDFATHER WILL SAVE YOU.
PAT
NOW TO PREPARE FOR BATTLE ...
TM TM
番
RUSTLE
AND JUST WHAT DO YOU THINK YOU'RE DOING?!
SHF SHF
I HAVE TO KNOW!!
I'M GOING TO ASK THIS SHINNOSUKE, OR WHATEVER HE CALLS HIMSELF...
KRAK KRAK
...IF HE LOVES AKANE MORE THAN LIFE ITSELF!!

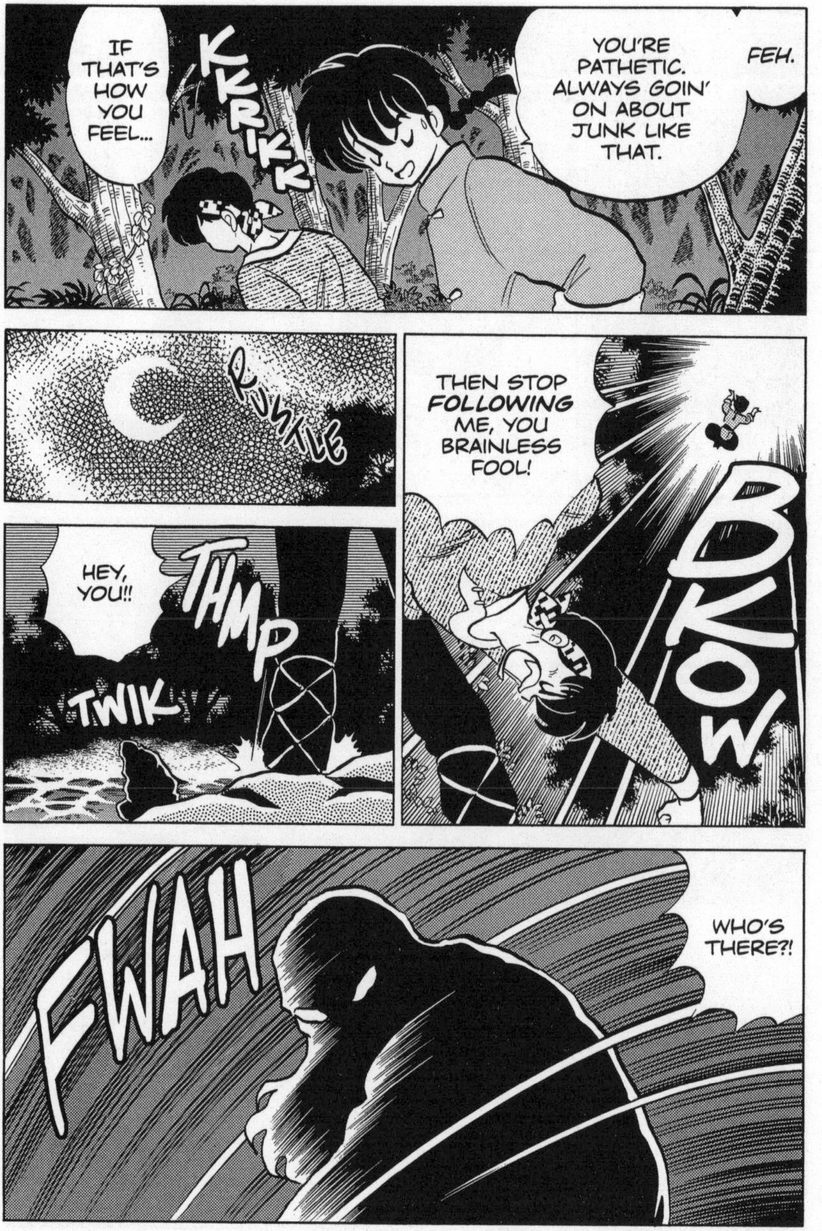
FEH.
YOU'RE PATHETIC. ALWAYS GOIN' ON ABOUT JUNK LIKE THAT.
KKRIKK
IF THAT'S HOW YOU FEEL...
THEN STOP **FOLLOWING** ME, YOU BRAINLESS FOOL!
BKOW
RUSTLE
HEY, YOU!!
THMP
TWIK
WHO'S THERE?!
FWAH

!!

GADONG
SHAAAAN

FWOB

HUH?!

!

BRR
BRR

P-CHAN
...

BLINK
BLINK

HHSSS

GRAND-
FATHER
...

GRAND-
FATHER
...?

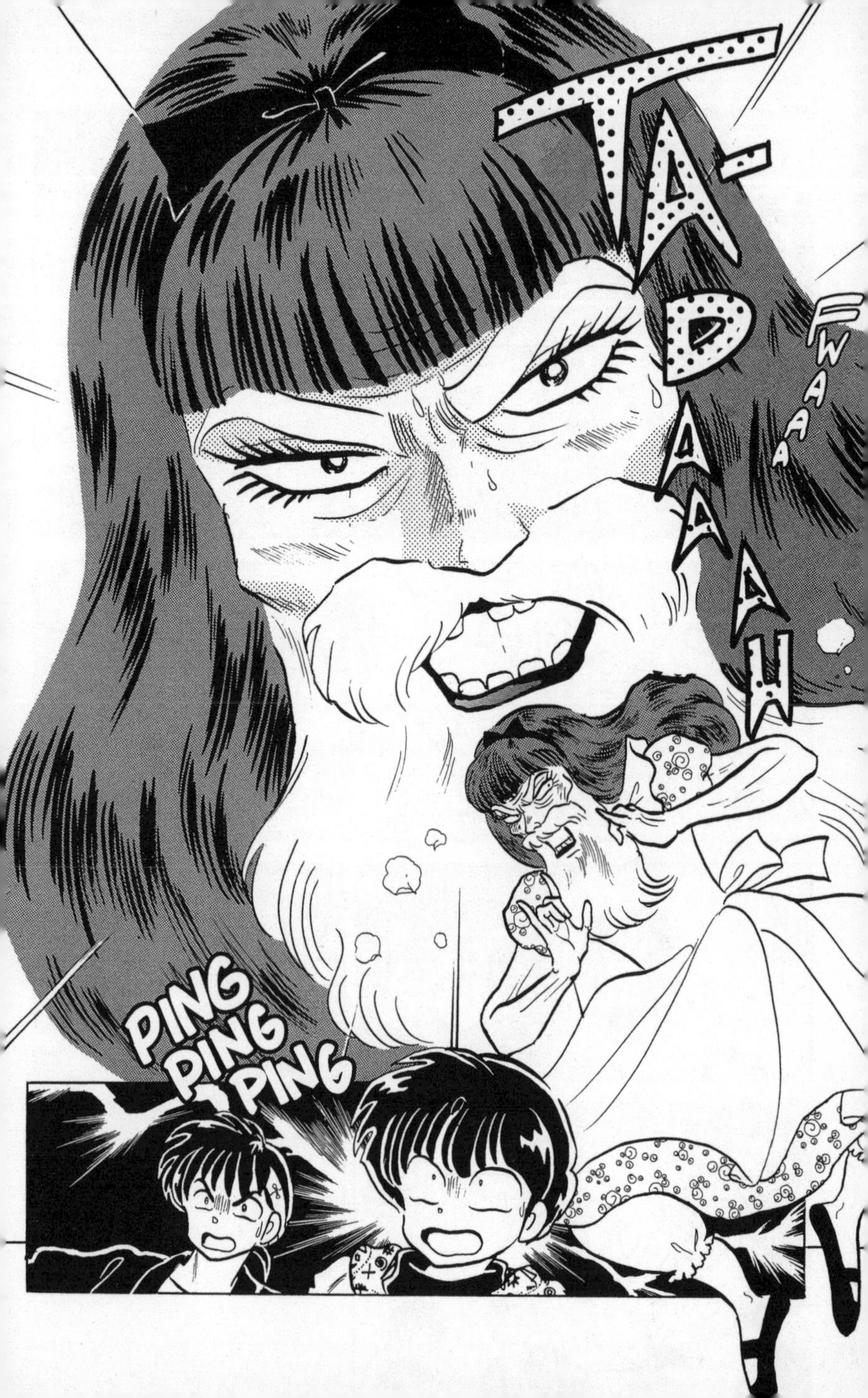
TA-DAAAAAAH
FWAAAA
PING PING PING

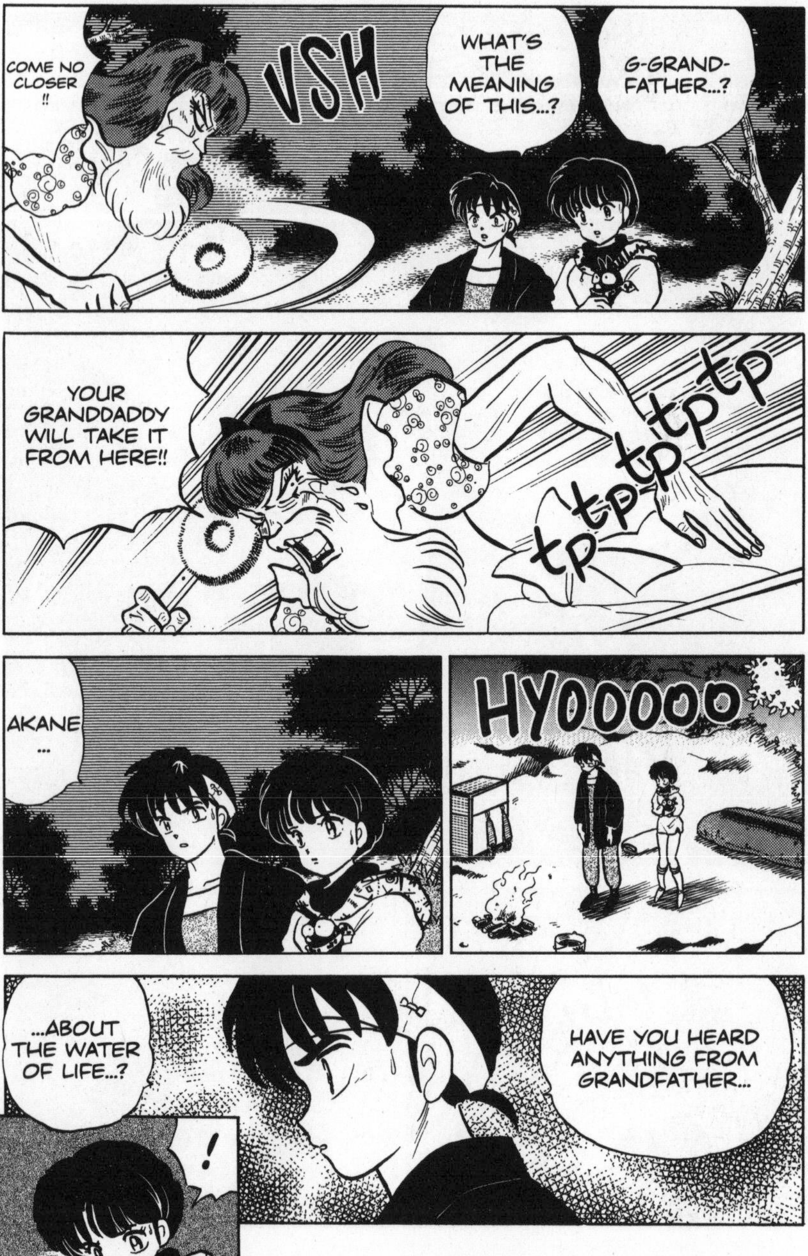
G-GRAND-FATHER...?
WHAT'S THE MEANING OF THIS...?
VSH
COME NO CLOSER !!
tp tp tp tp tp
YOUR GRANDDADDY WILL TAKE IT FROM HERE!!
HYOOOOO
AKANE ...
HAVE YOU HEARD ANYTHING FROM GRANDFATHER...
...ABOUT THE WATER OF LIFE...?
!

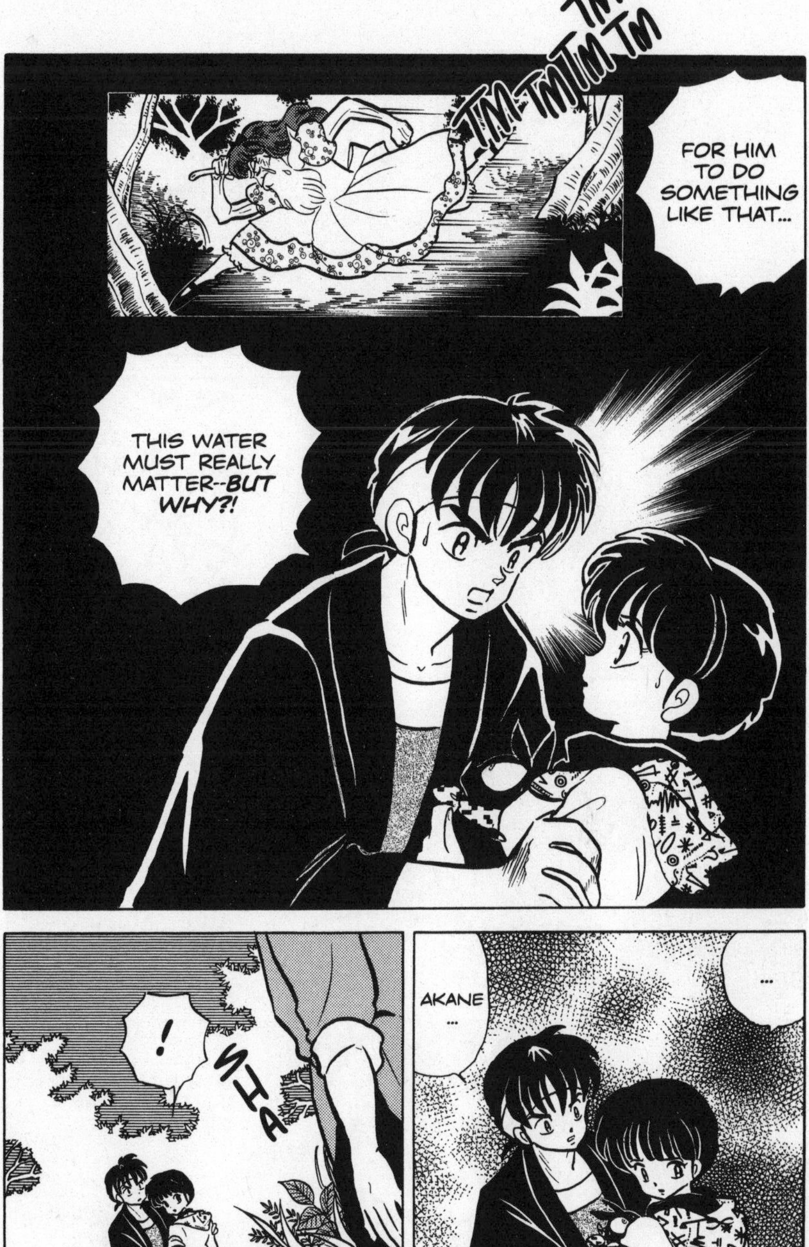
FOR HIM TO DO SOMETHING LIKE THAT...
TM TM TM TM TM TM
THIS WATER MUST REALLY MATTER--BUT WHY?!
...
AKANE ...
!
SHA

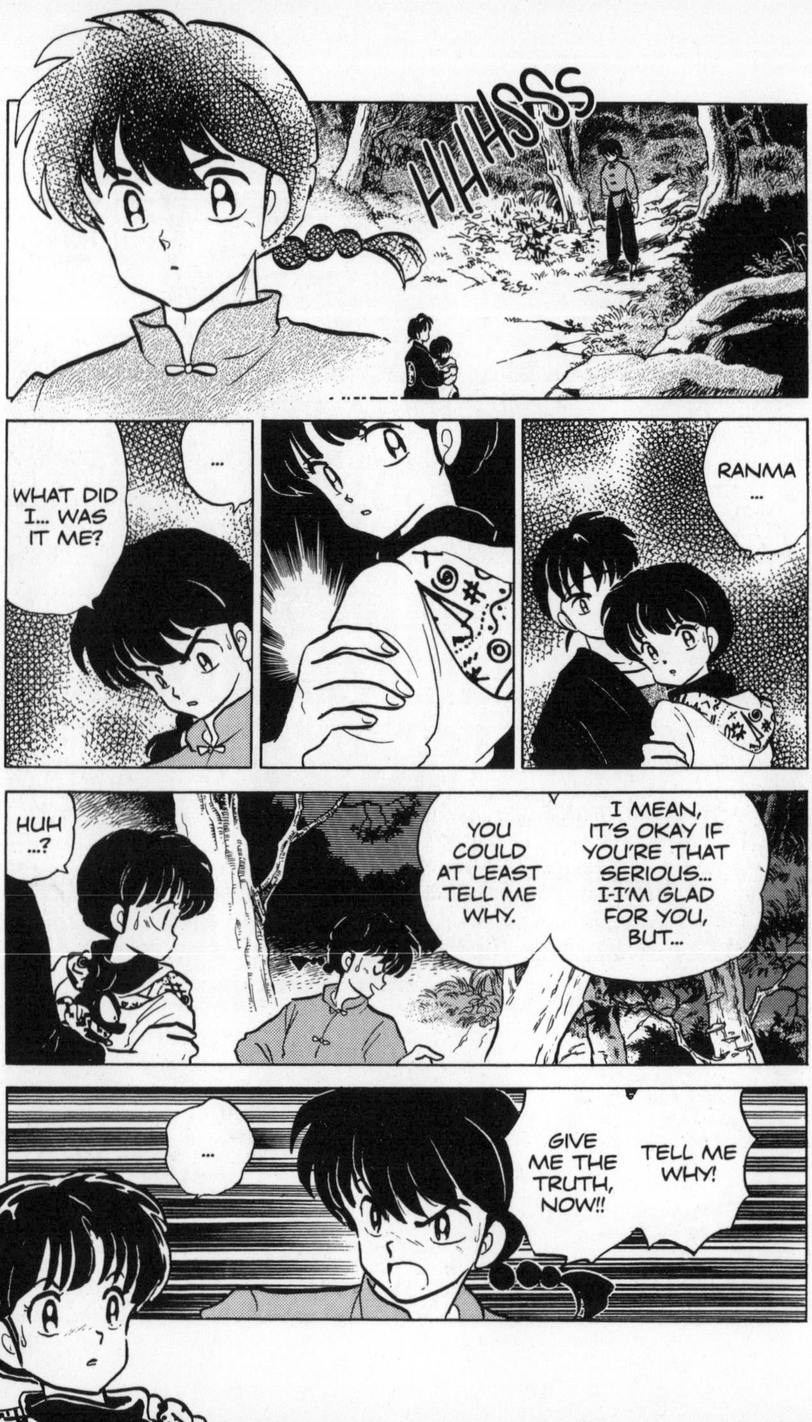
HHHSSS
RANMA ...
...
WHAT DID I... WAS IT ME?
I MEAN, IT'S OKAY IF YOU'RE THAT SERIOUS... I-I'M GLAD FOR YOU, BUT...
YOU COULD AT LEAST TELL ME WHY.
HUH ...?
TELL ME WHY!
GIVE ME THE TRUTH, NOW!!
...

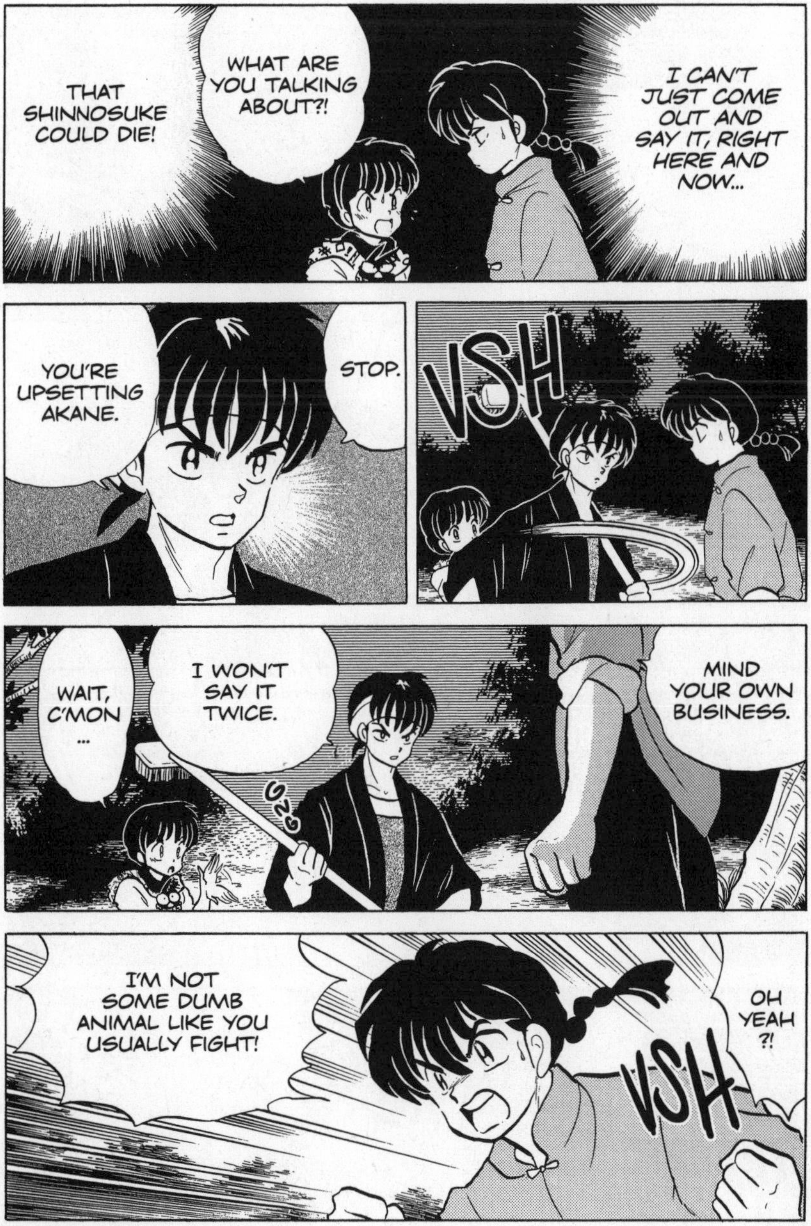

I CAN'T JUST COME OUT AND SAY IT, RIGHT HERE AND NOW...
WHAT ARE YOU TALKING ABOUT?!
THAT SHINNOSUKE COULD DIE!
VSH
STOP.
YOU'RE UPSETTING AKANE.
MIND YOUR OWN BUSINESS.
I WON'T SAY IT TWICE.
GNG
WAIT, C'MON ...
OH YEAH ?!
VSH
I'M NOT SOME DUMB ANIMAL LIKE YOU USUALLY FIGHT!

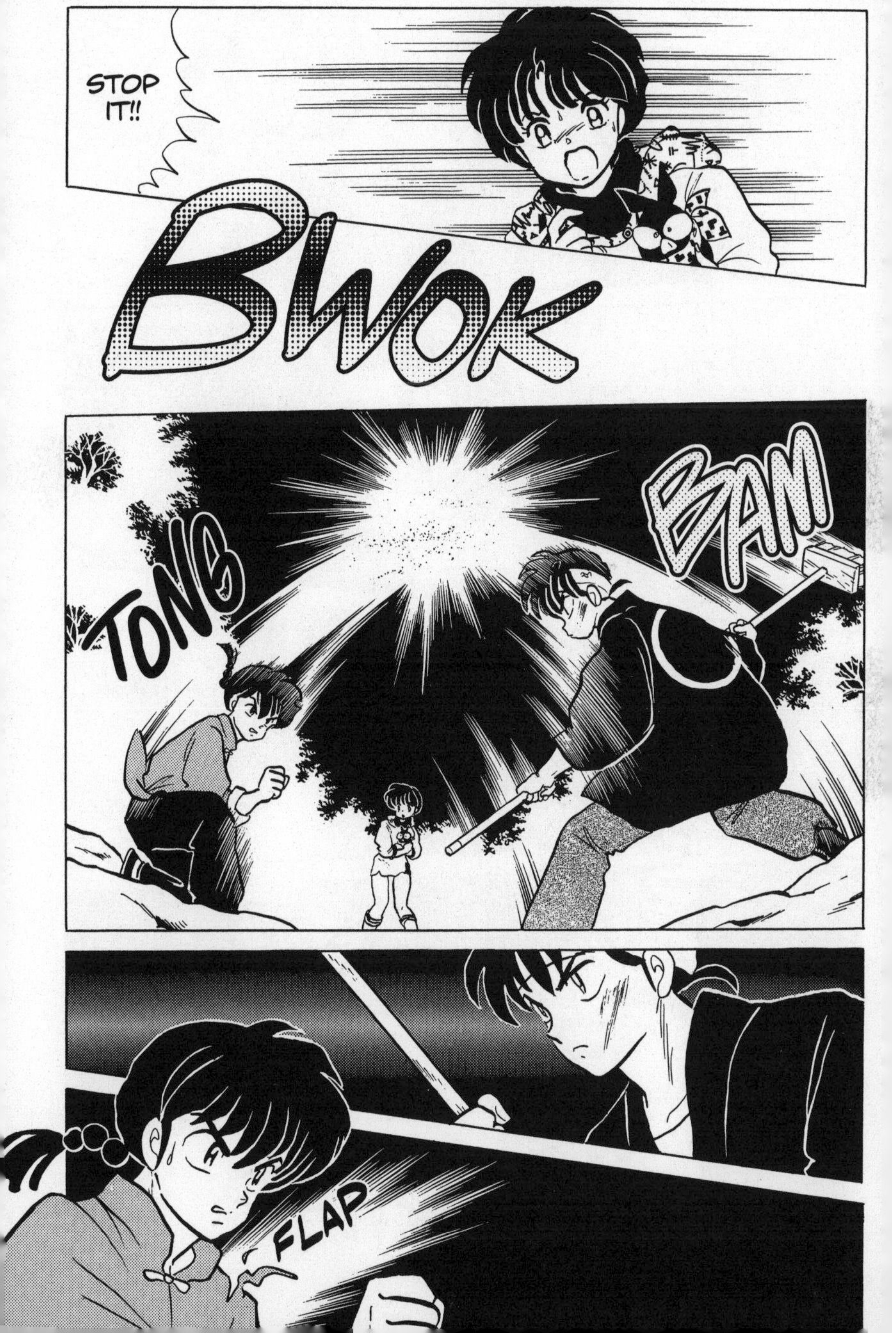
STOP IT!!
BWOK
BAM
TONG
FLAP

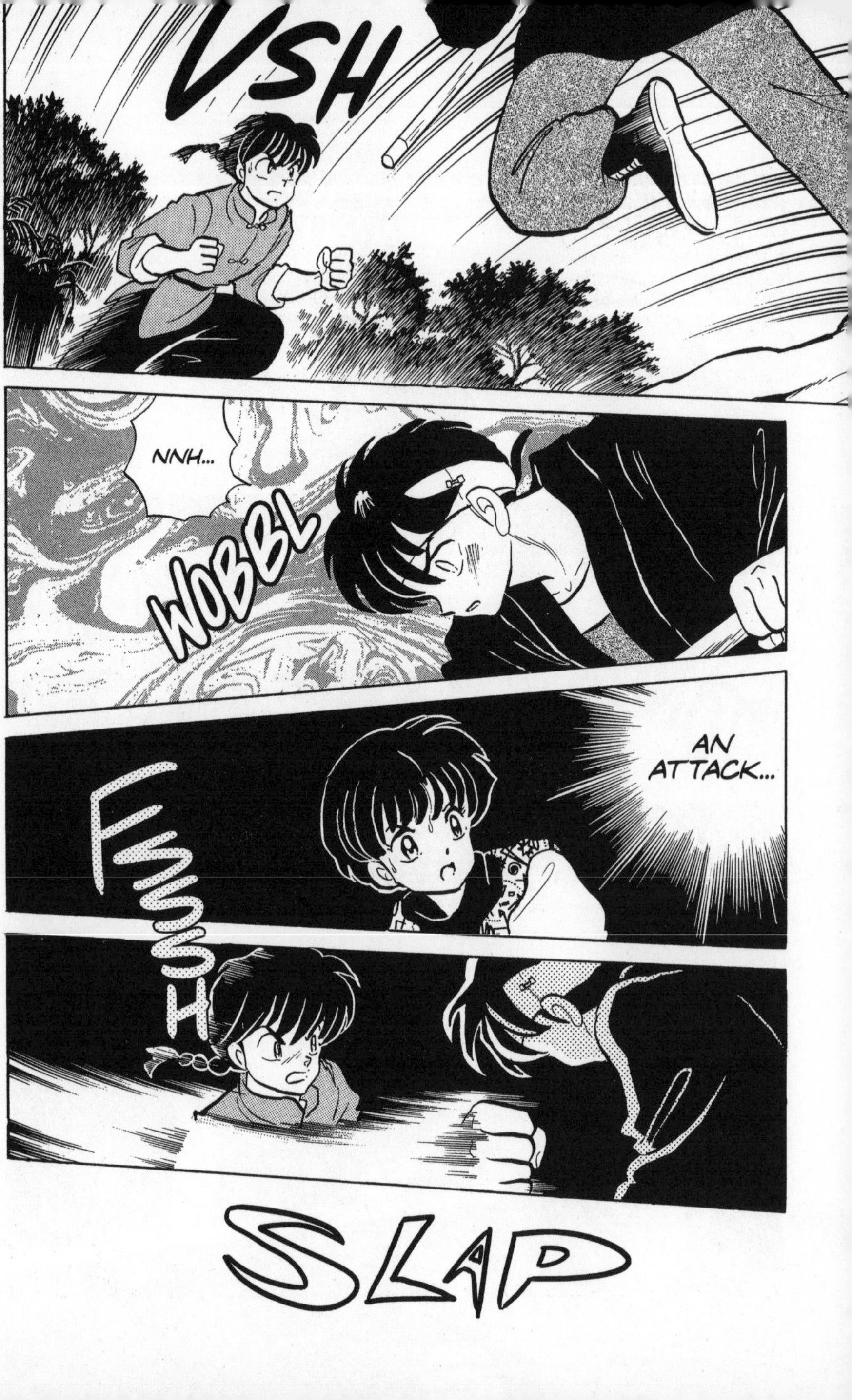
VSH
NNH...
WOBBL
AN ATTACK...
FWOSH
SLAP

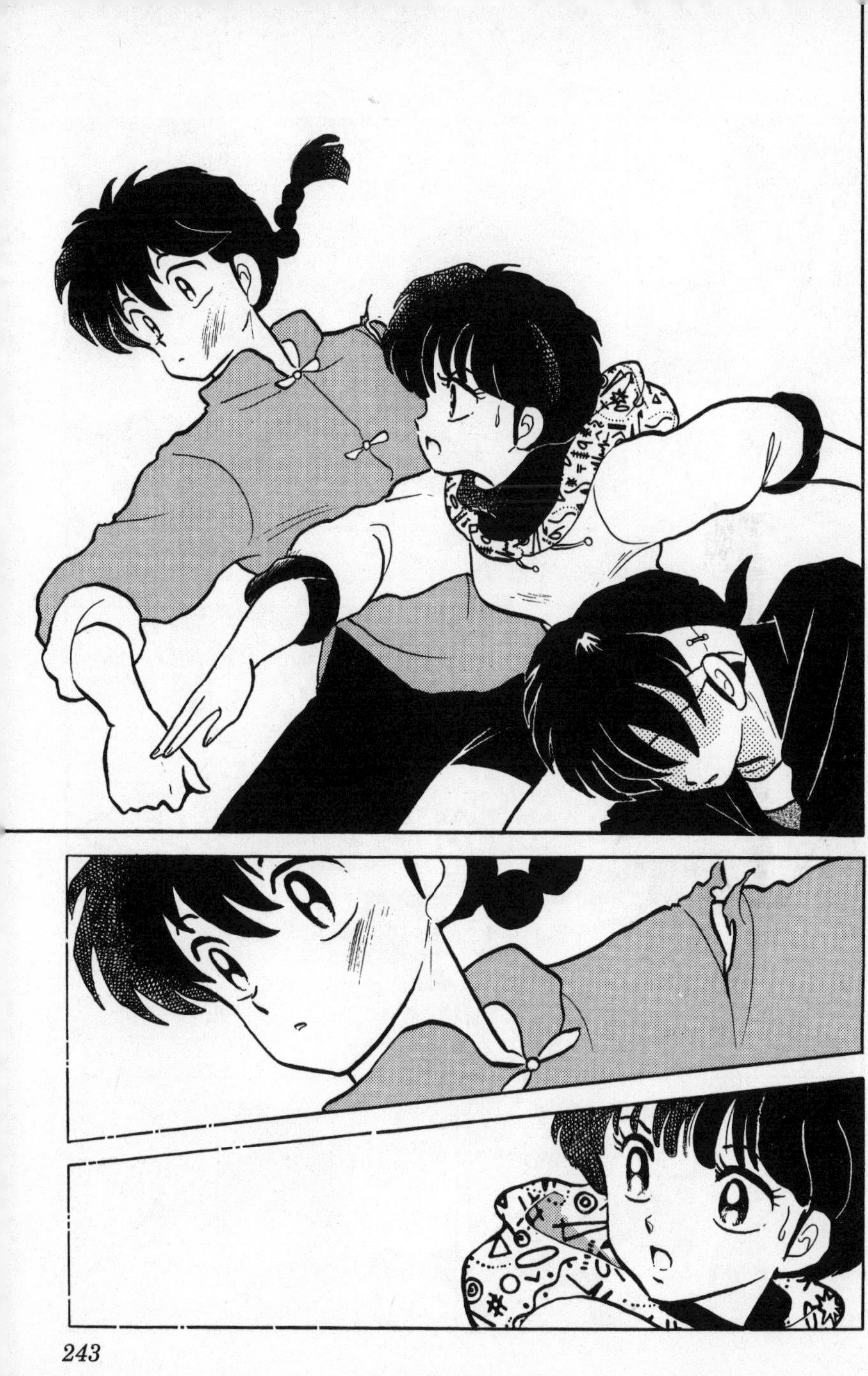

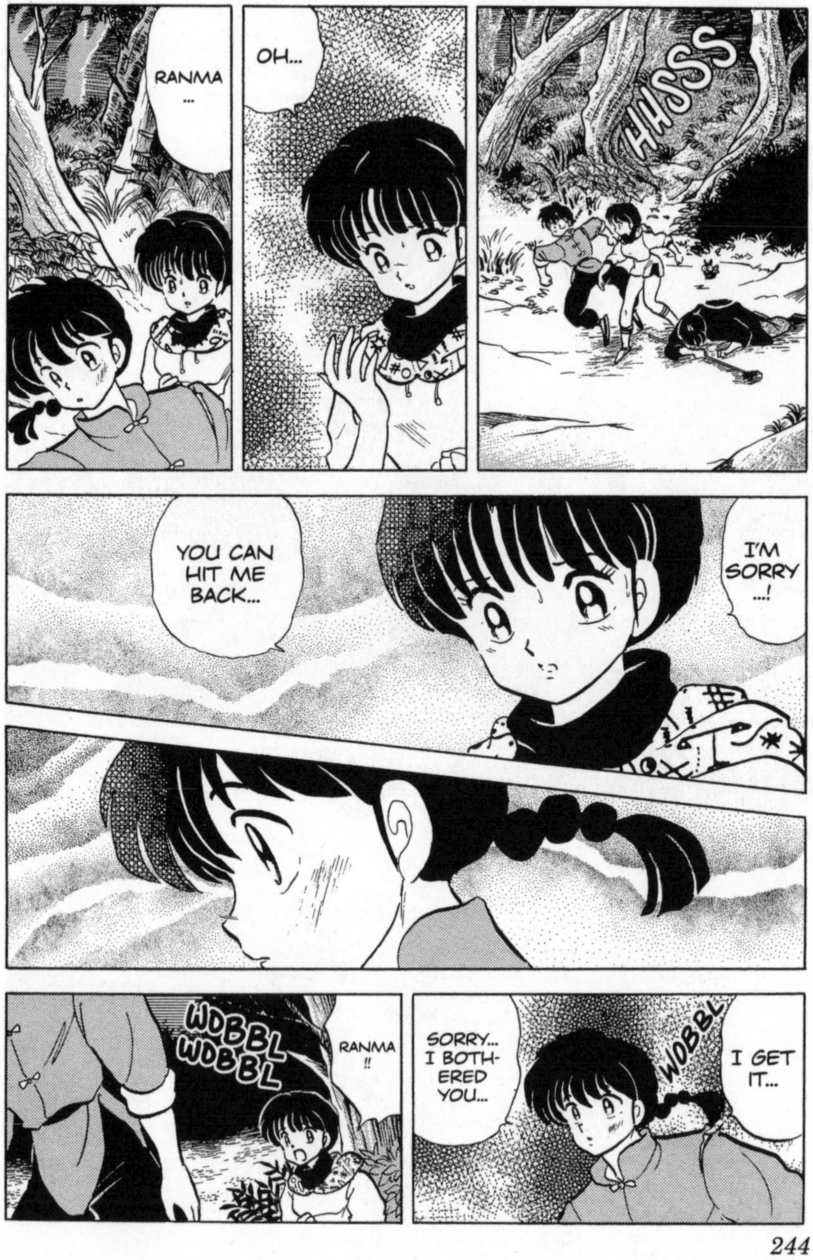
HHSSS
OH...
RANMA ...
I'M SORRY ...!
YOU CAN HIT ME BACK...
I GET IT...
WOBBL
SORRY... I BOTH-ERED YOU...
RANMA !!
WOBBL WOBBL

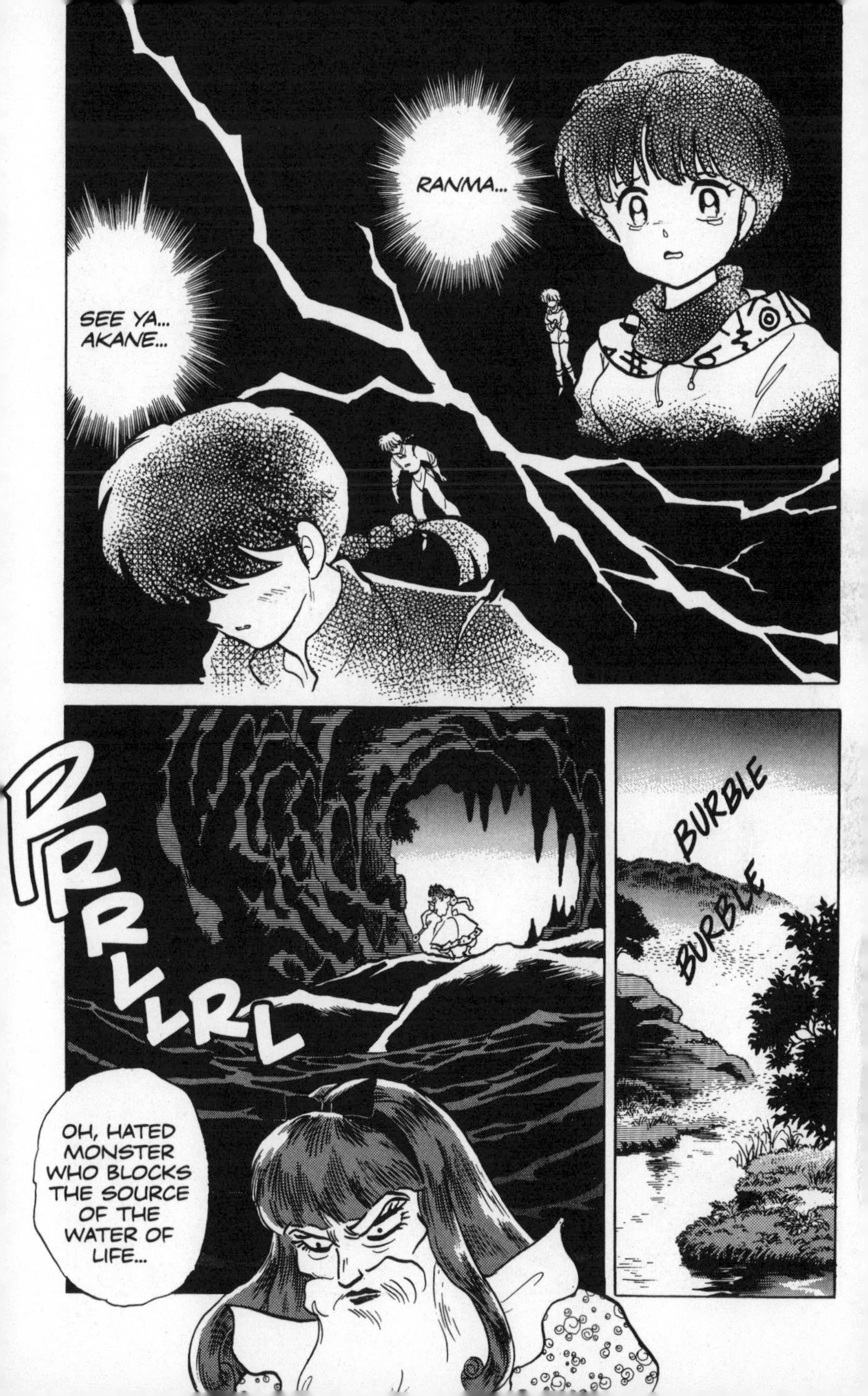
RANMA...
SEE YA... AKANE...
BURBLE
BURBLE
PRRLLRL
OH, HATED MONSTER WHO BLOCKS THE SOURCE OF THE WATER OF LIFE...

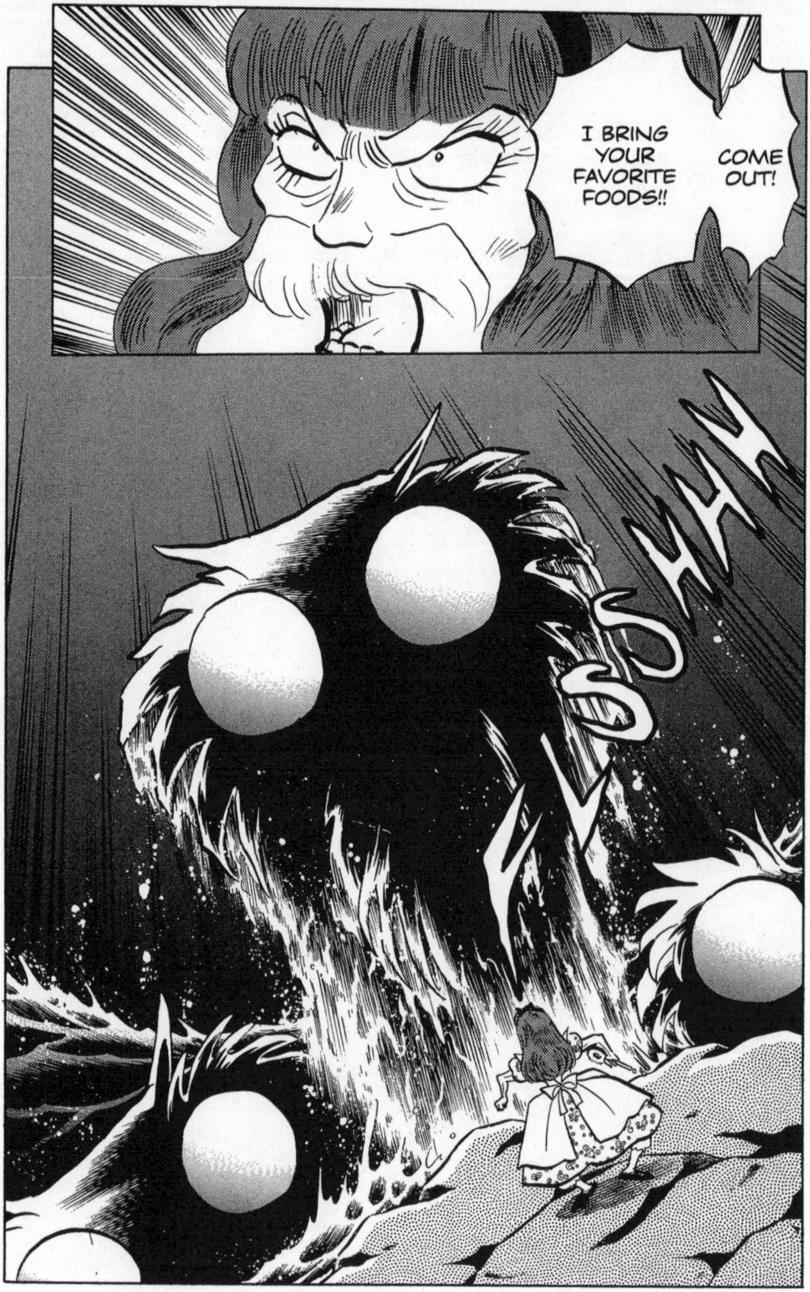
COME OUT!
I BRING YOUR FAVORITE FOODS!!
SSHHH

PART 16

THE KING OF BEASTS EMERGES!

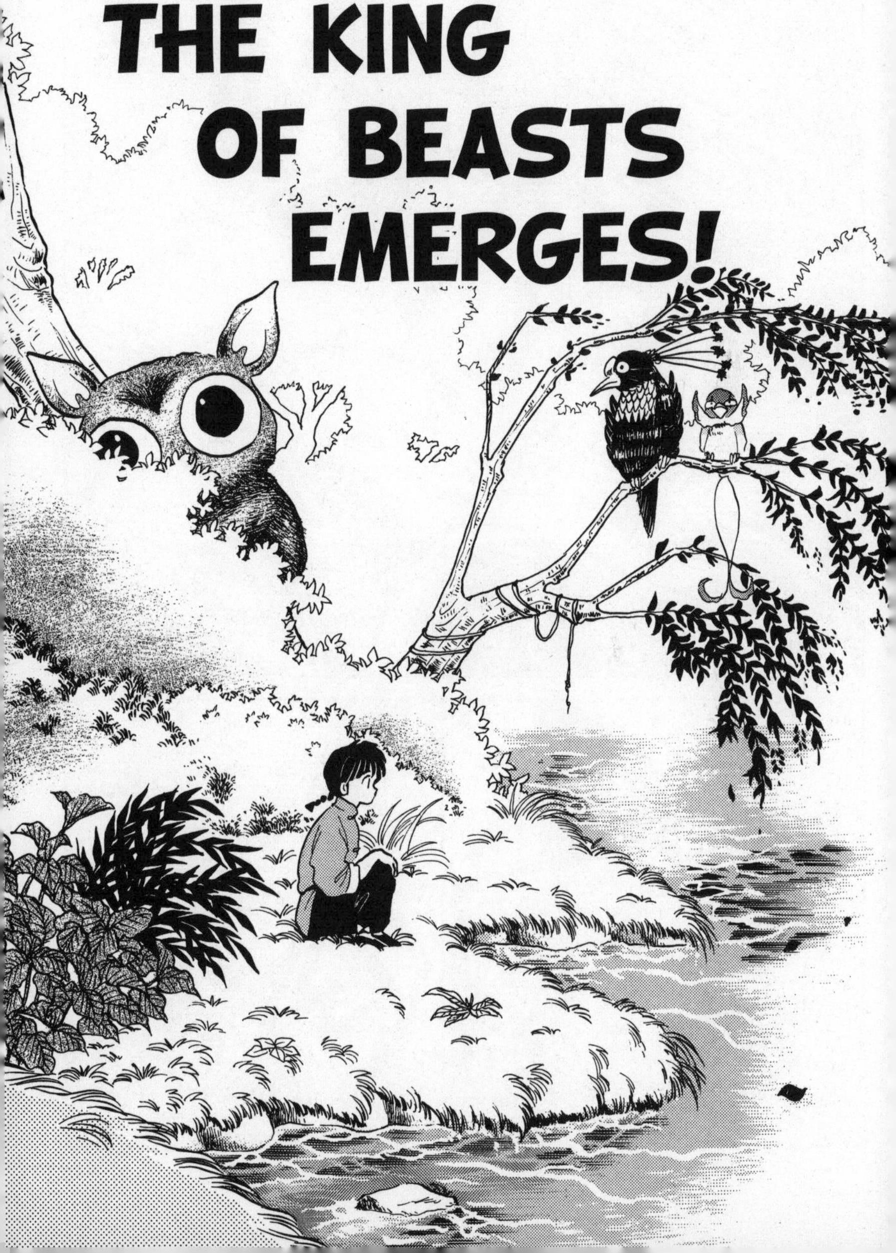

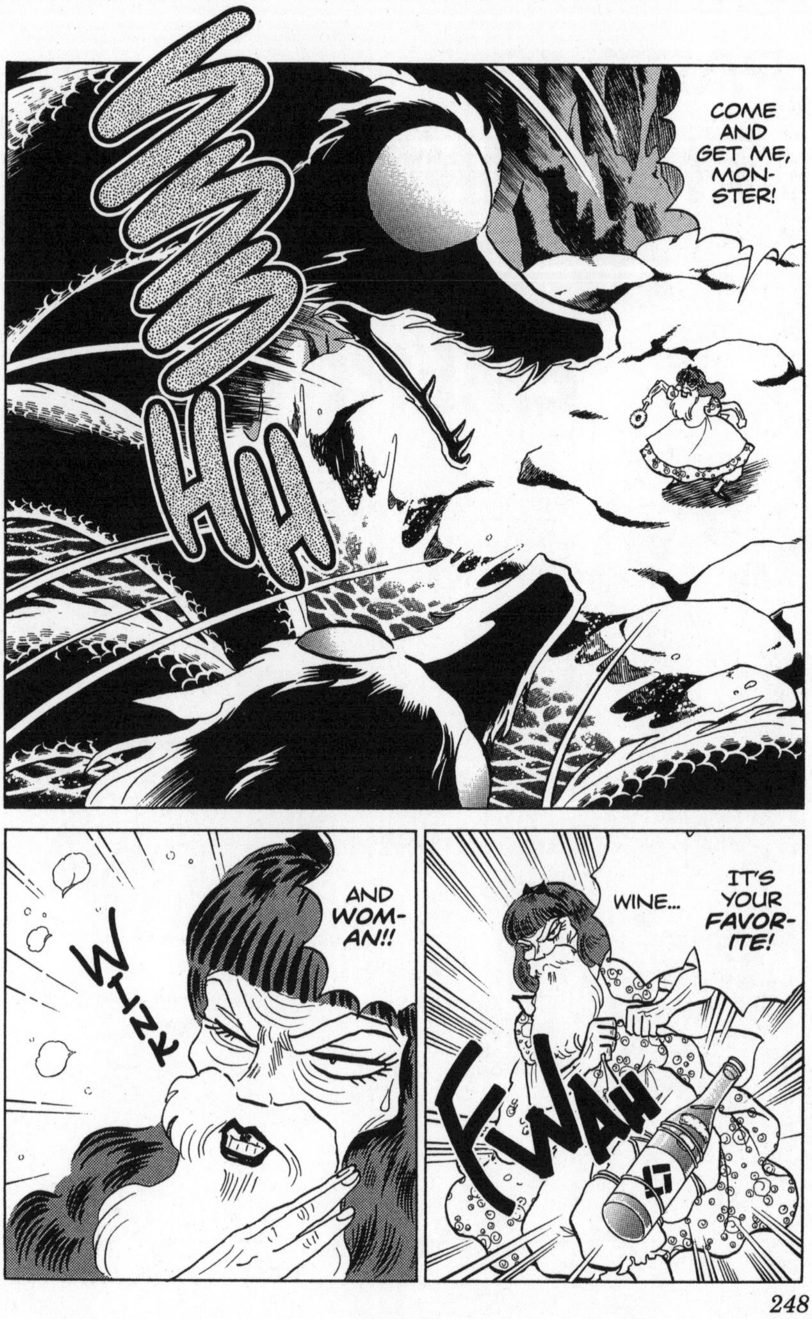
COME AND GET ME, MON-STER!
IT'S YOUR FAVOR-ITE!
WINE...
FWAH
AND WOM-AN!!
WINK

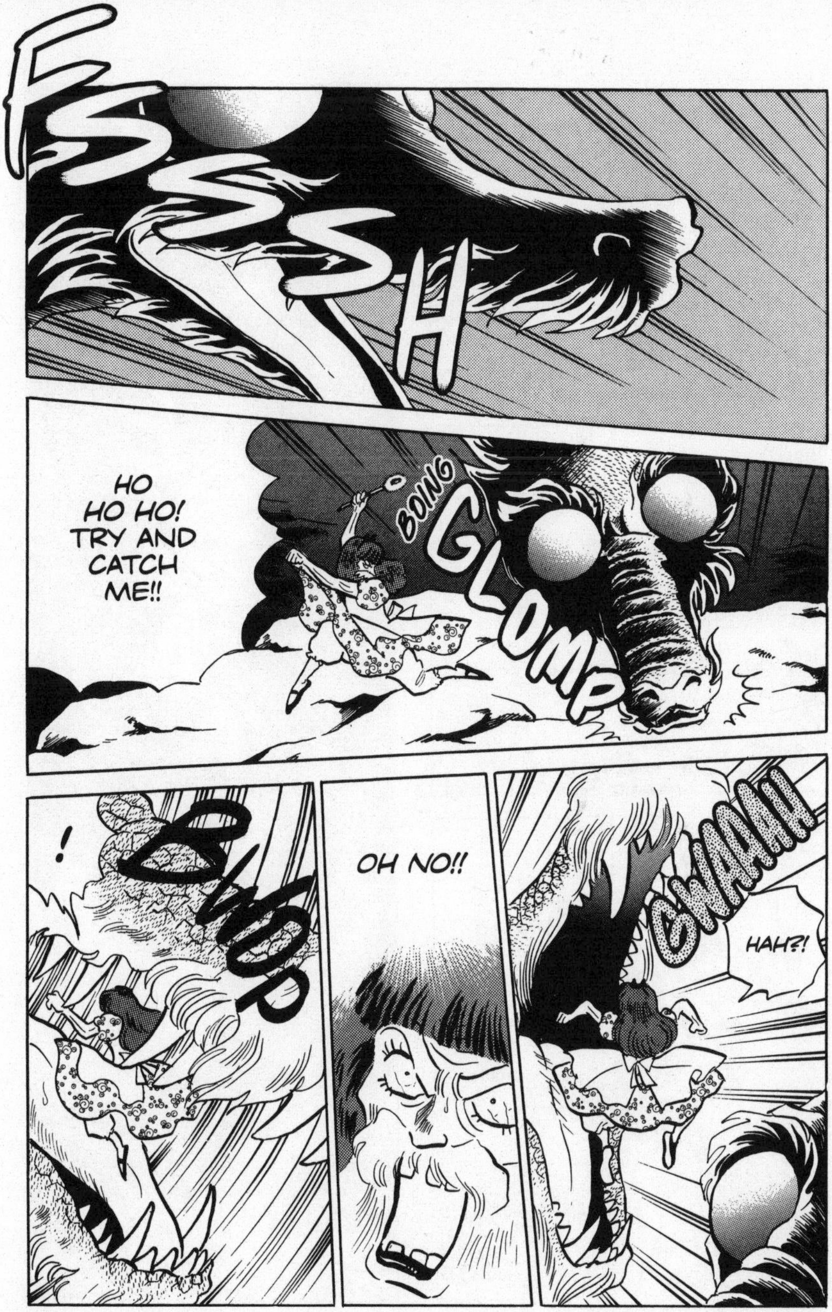
FSSSH
BOING
GLOMP
HO HO HO! TRY AND CATCH ME!!
GWAAAH
HAH?!
OH NO!!
!
BMOP

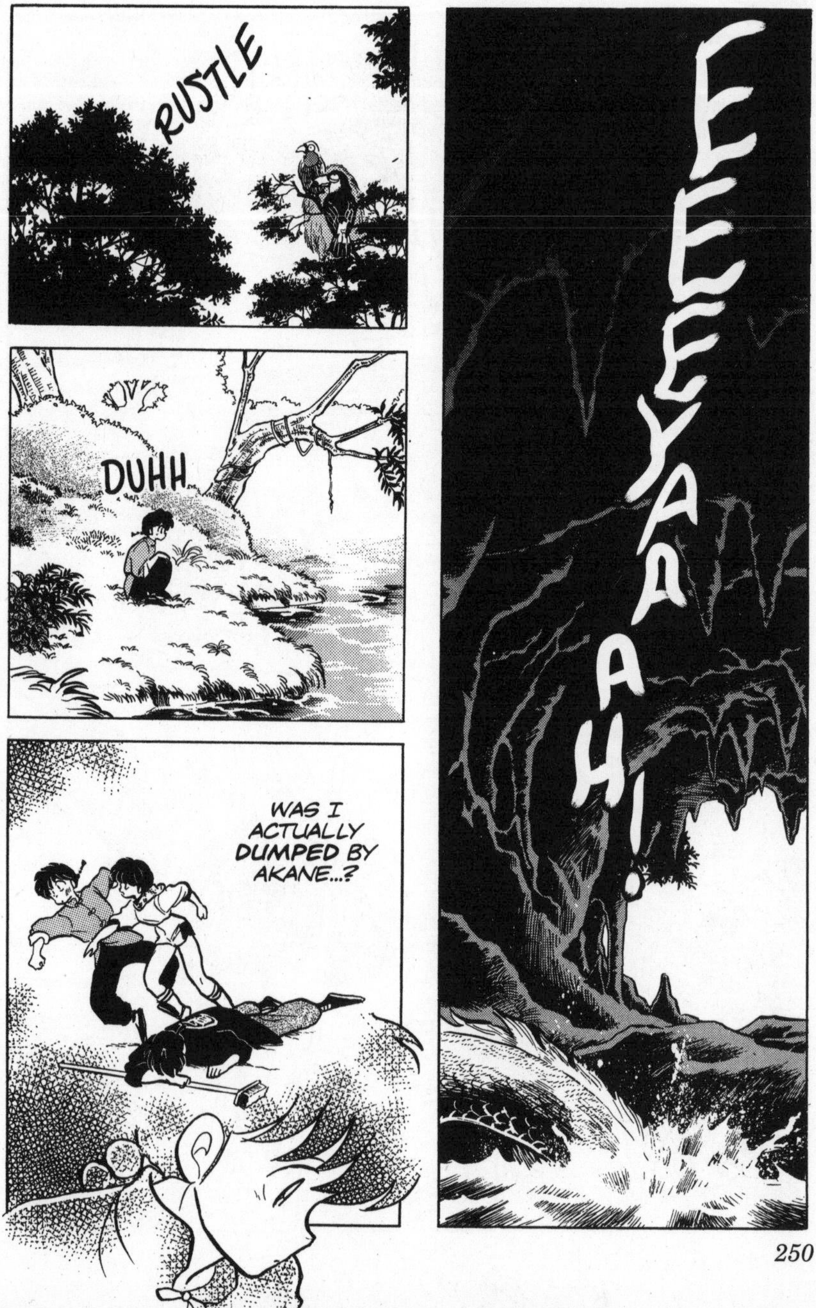
EEEEEYAAAH!
RUSTLE
DUHH
WAS I ACTUALLY DUMPED BY AKANE...?

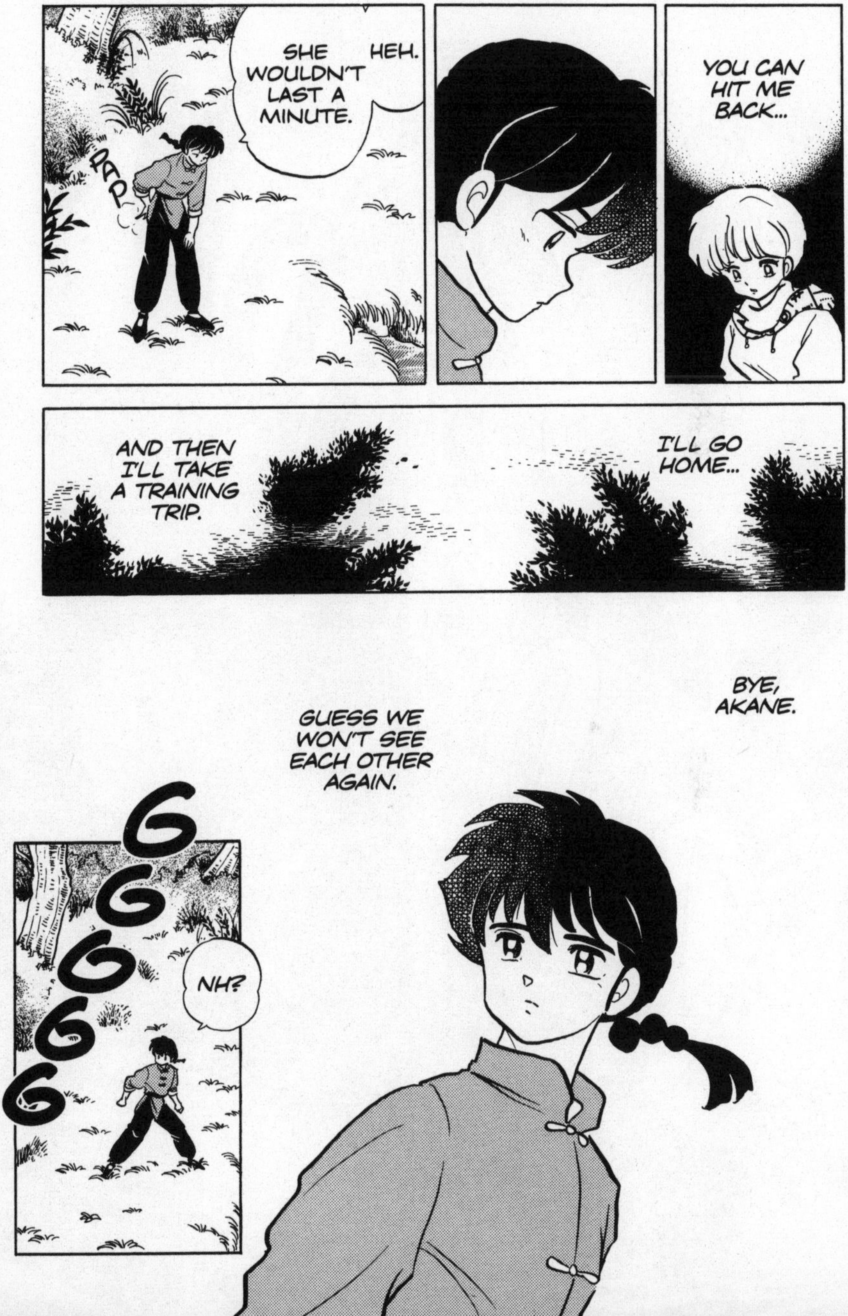
YOU CAN HIT ME BACK...
HEH. SHE WOULDN'T LAST A MINUTE.
PAP
I'LL GO HOME...
AND THEN I'LL TAKE A TRAINING TRIP.
BYE, AKANE.
GUESS WE WON'T SEE EACH OTHER AGAIN.
NH?
GGGGG

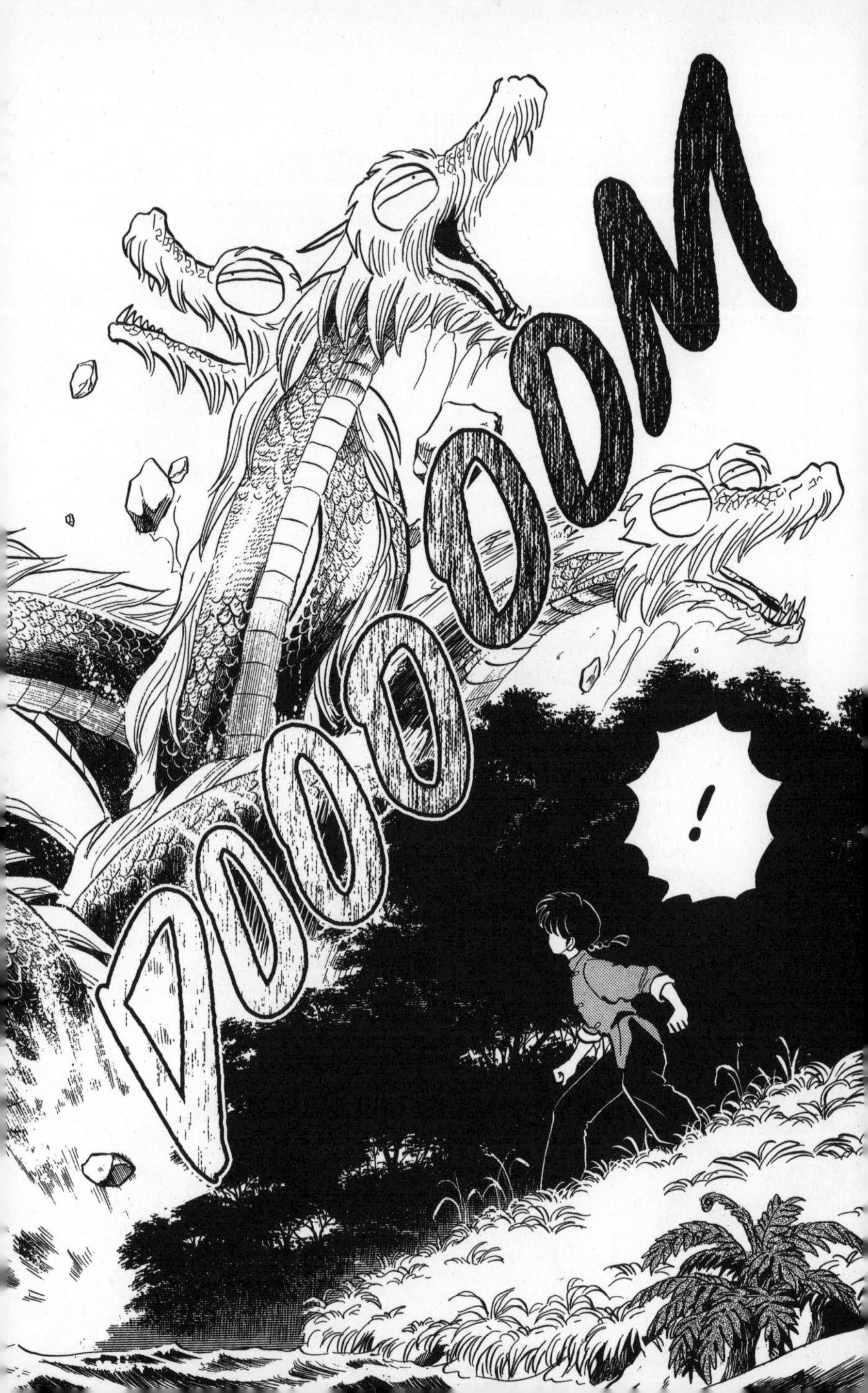
ZOOOOOOOM
!

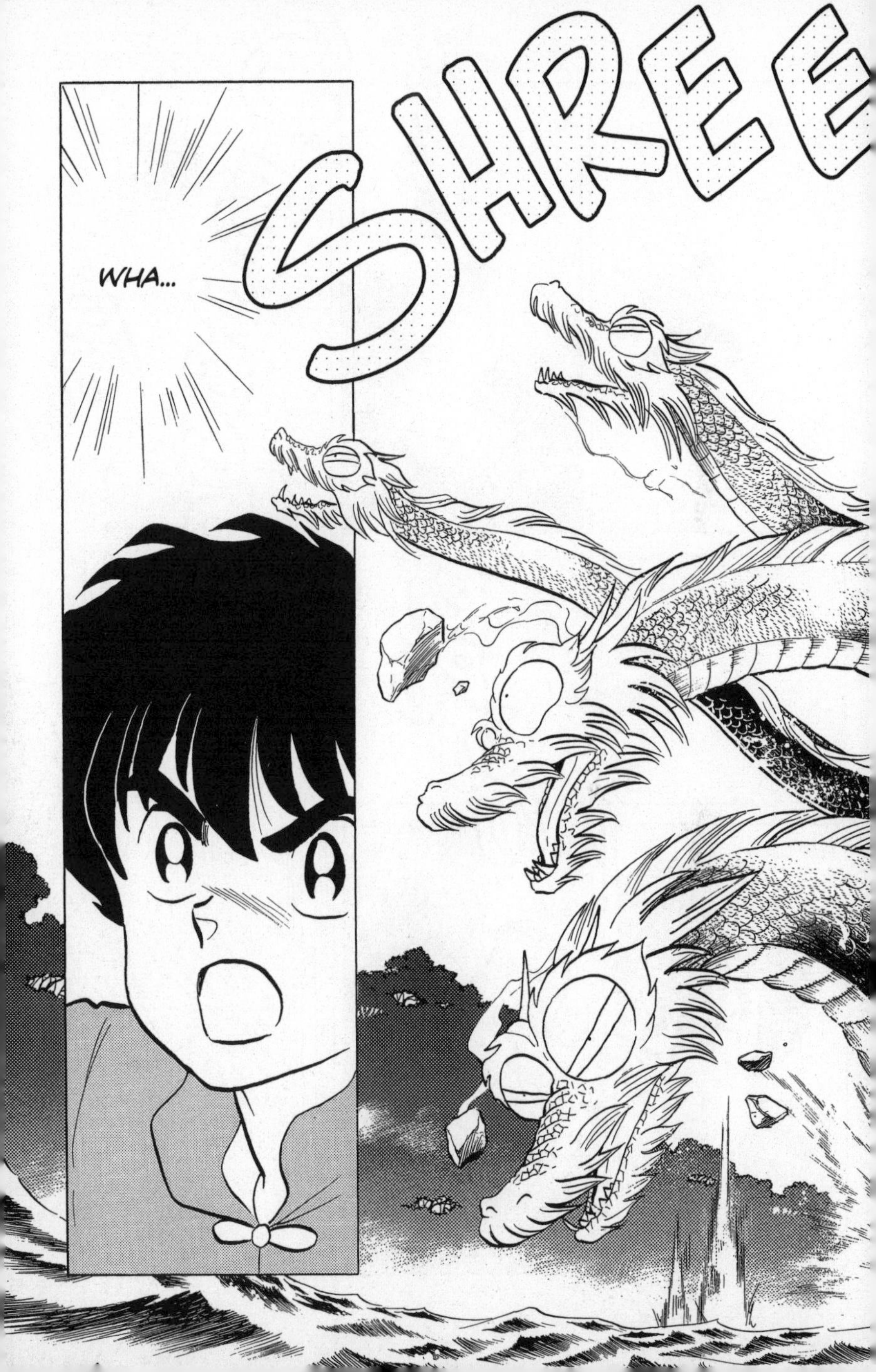
SHREE
WHA...

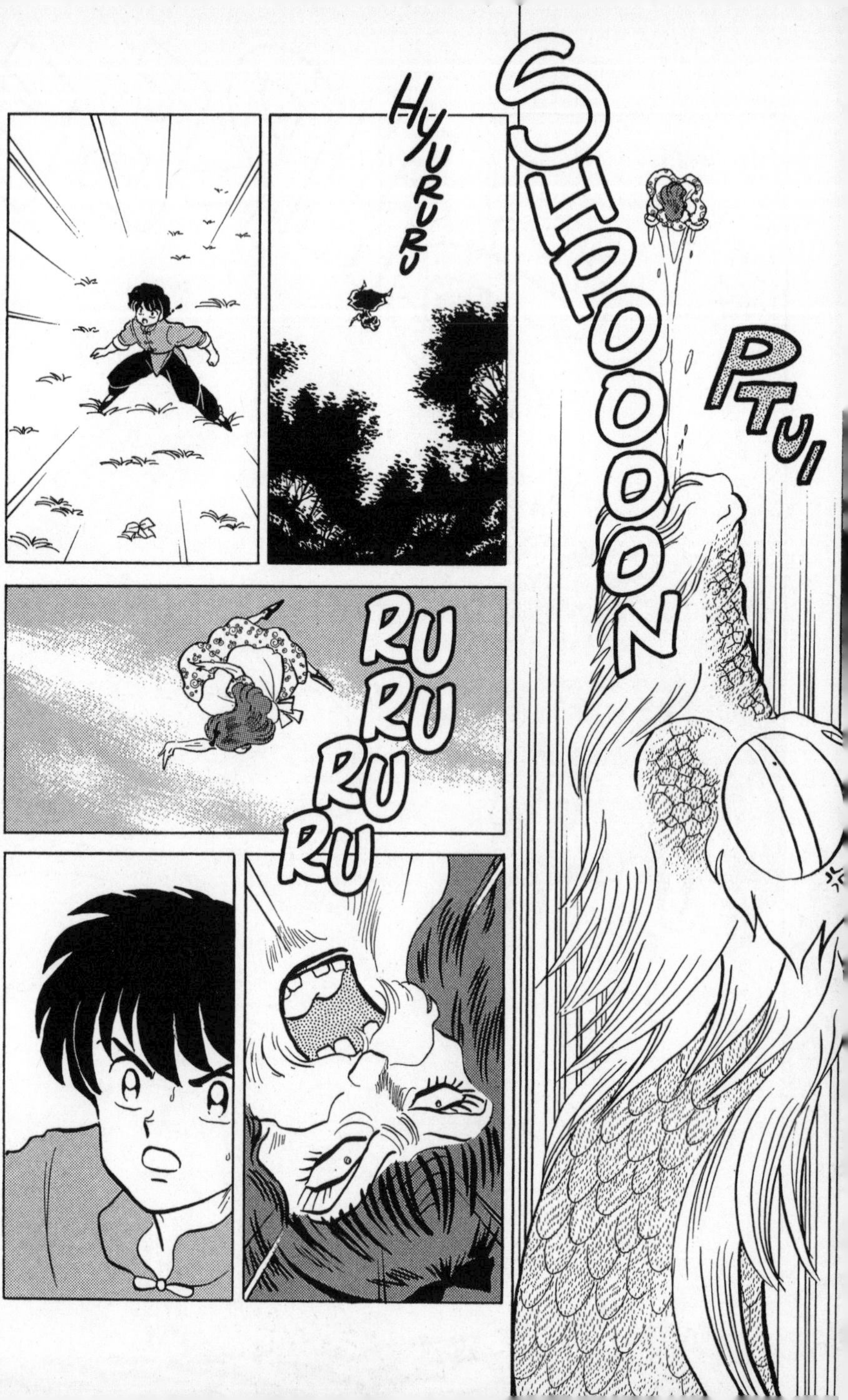
SHOOOOON
PTUI
HYURURURU
RU RU RU RU

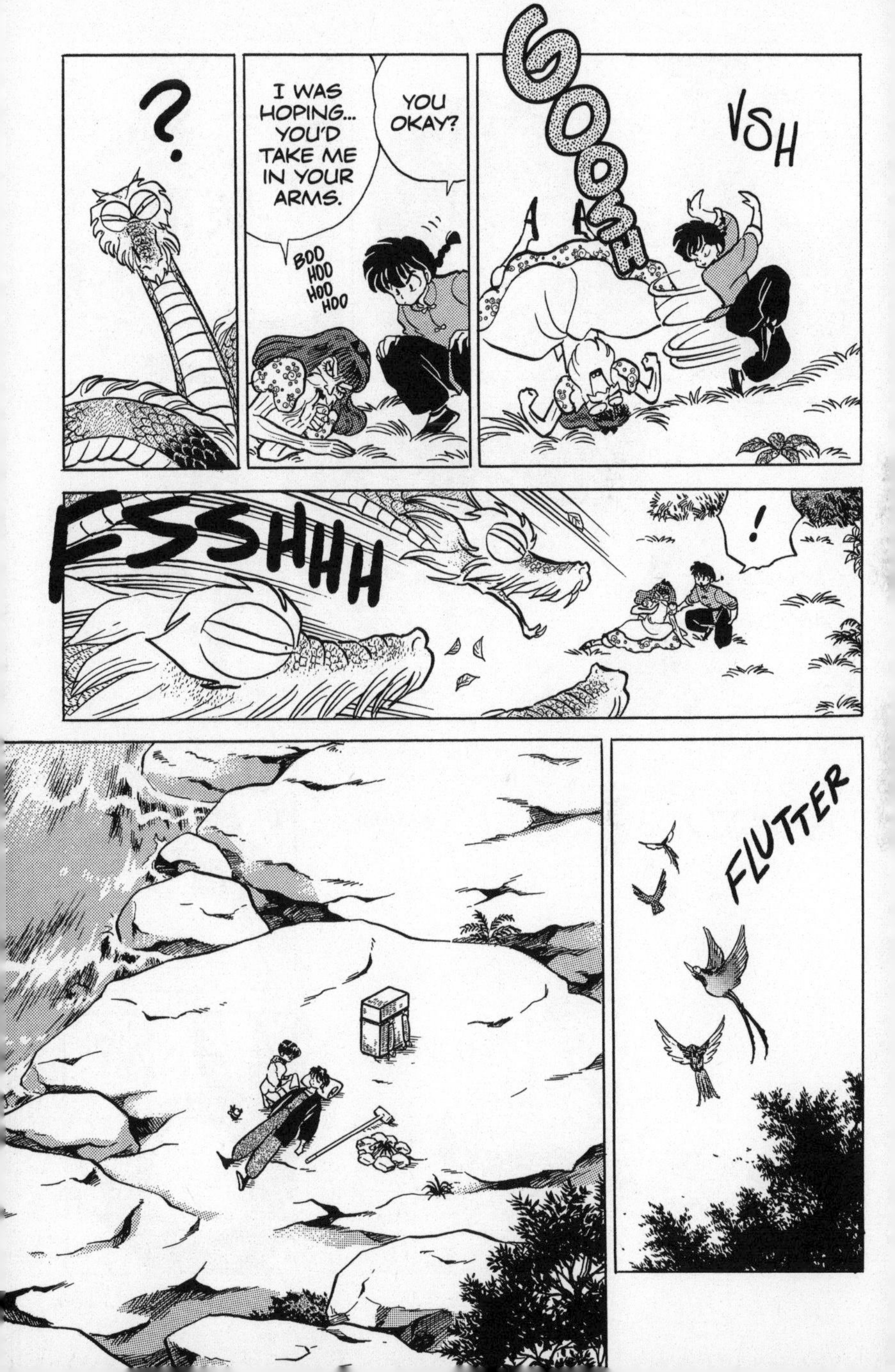
GOOMH
VSH
A A
YOU OKAY?
I WAS HOPING... YOU'D TAKE ME IN YOUR ARMS.
BOO HOO HOO HOO
?
!
FSSHHH
FLUTTER

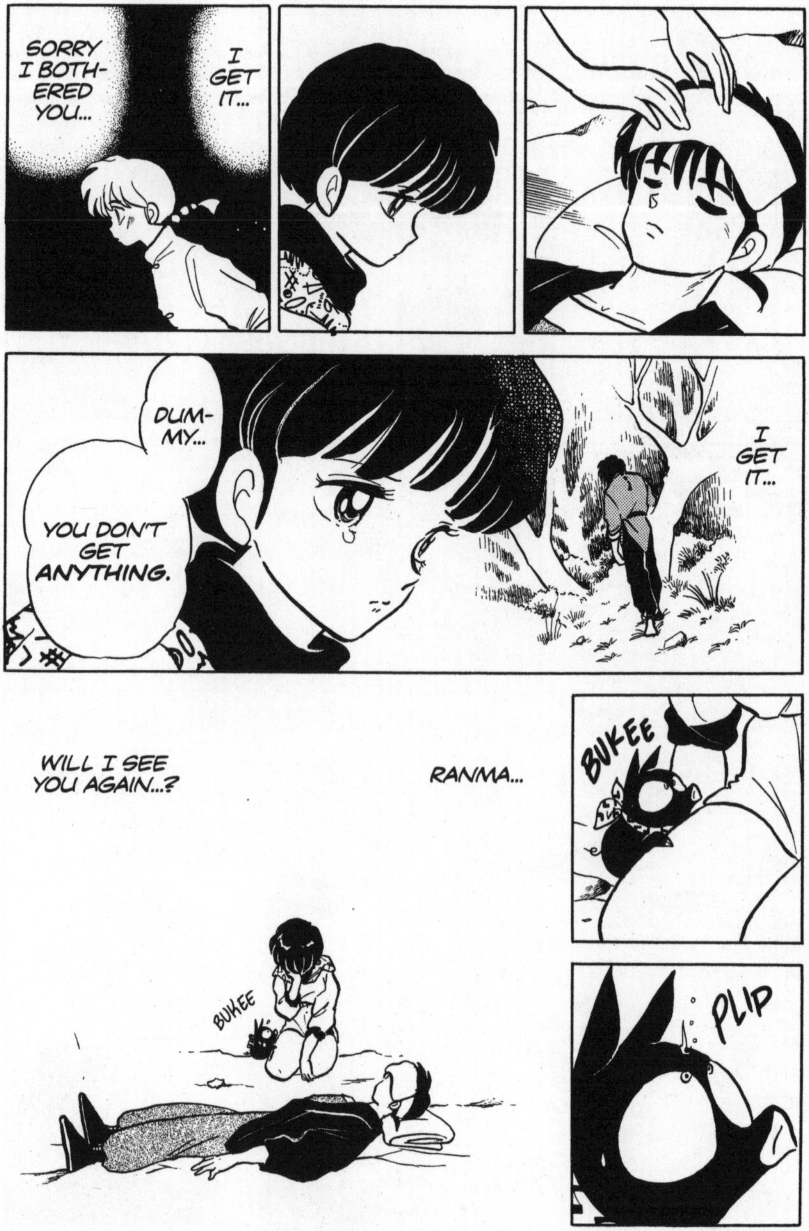
I GET IT...
SORRY I BOTHERED YOU...
I GET IT...
DUMMY...
YOU DON'T GET ANYTHING.
BUKEE
PLIP
RANMA...
WILL I SEE YOU AGAIN...?
BUKEE

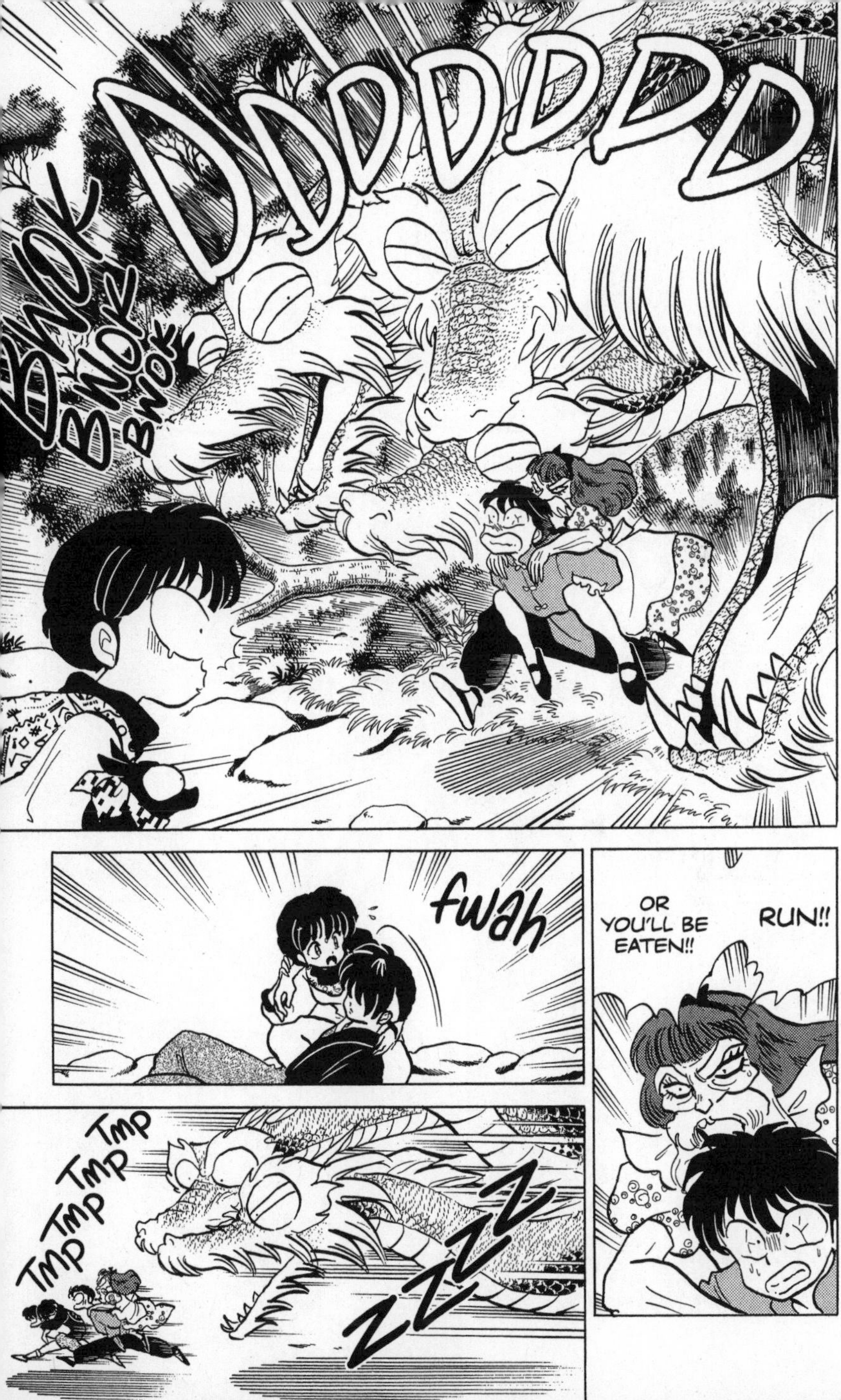
DDDDDDD
BWOK BWOK BWOK
RUN!!
OR YOU'LL BE EATEN!!
fwah
Tmp Tmp Tmp Tmp
ZZZZZ

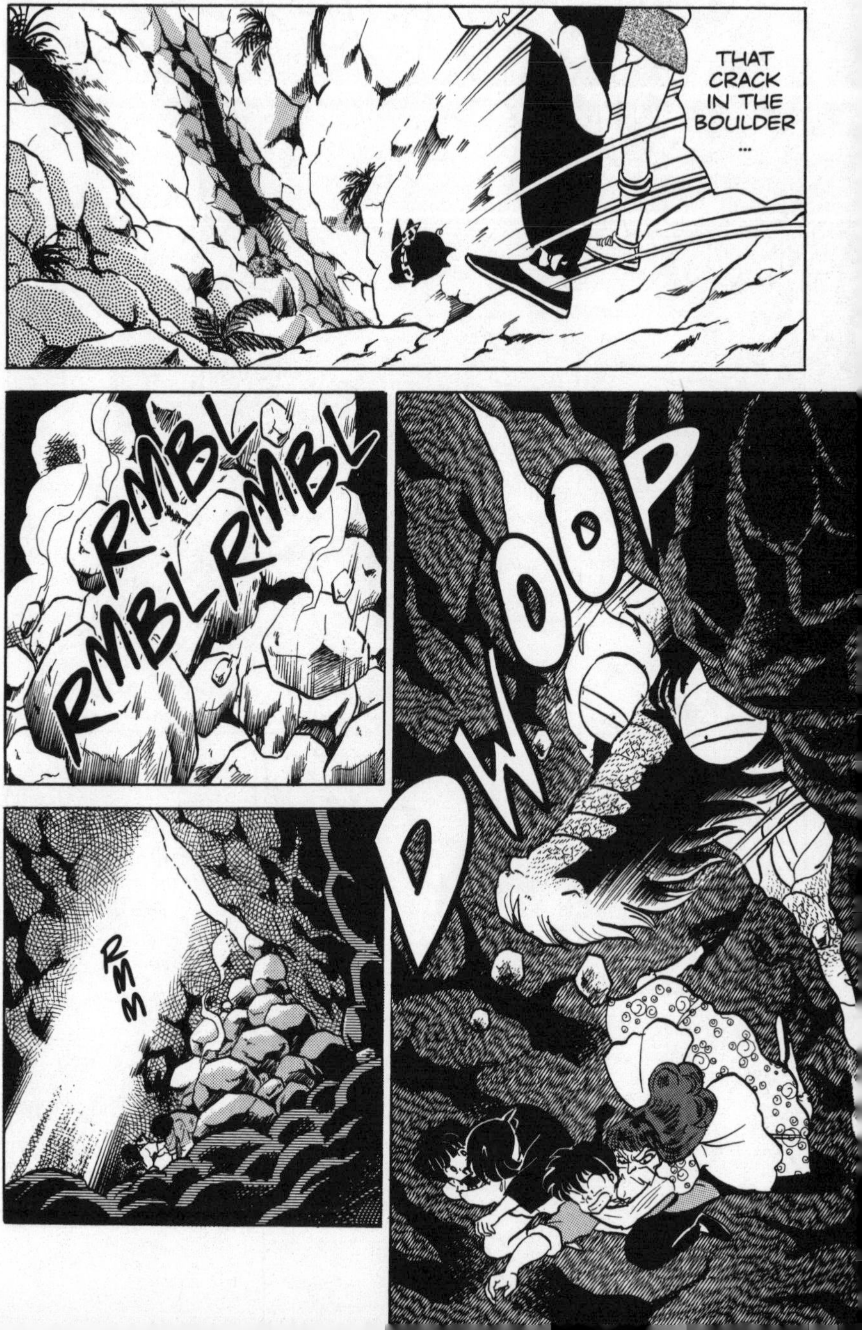
THAT CRACK IN THE BOULDER ...
DWOOP
RMBL RMBL
RMBL RMBL
RMM

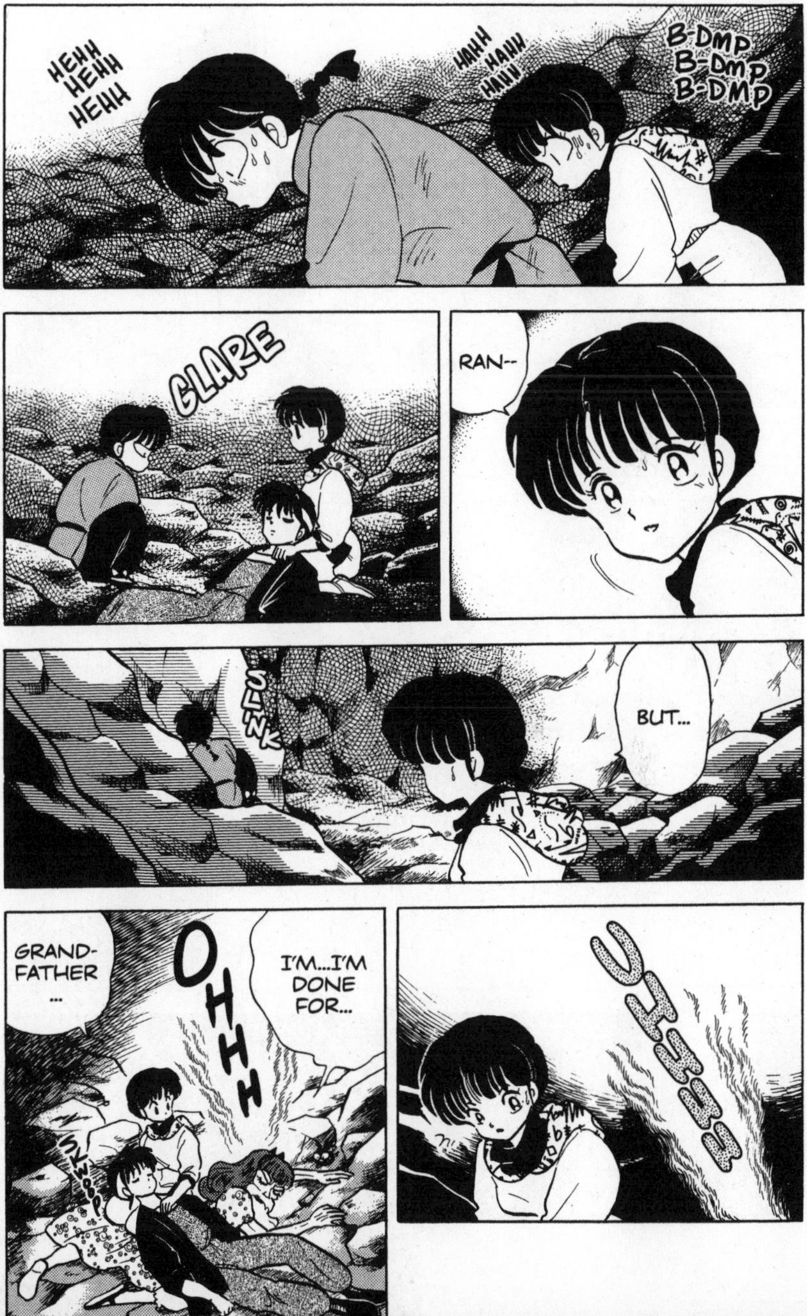
B-DMP B-DMP B-DMP
HAHH HAHH HAHH
HEHH HEHH HEHH
RAN--
GLARE
BUT...
SLINK
I'M...I'M DONE FOR...
OHHHH
GRAND-FATHER ...
SKWOOP

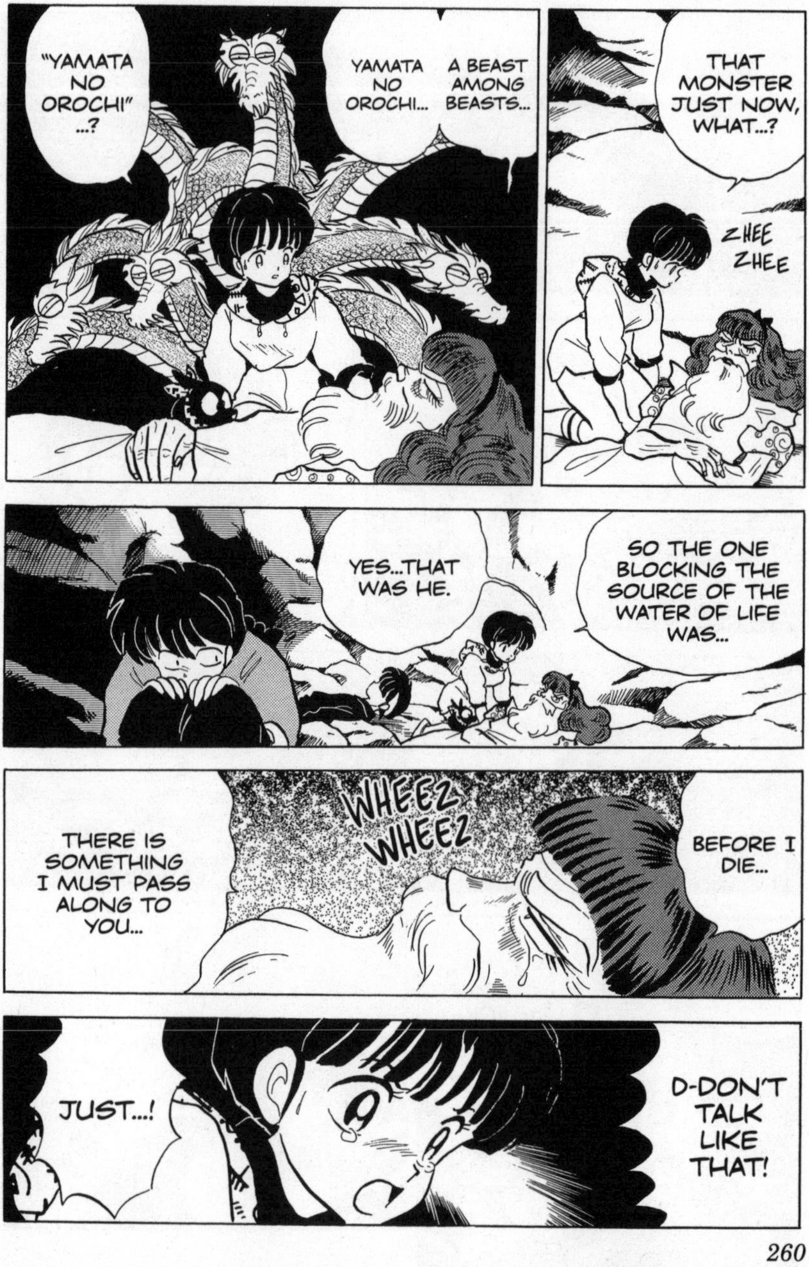
THAT MONSTER JUST NOW, WHAT...?
ZHEE ZHEE
YAMATA NO OROCHI... A BEAST AMONG BEASTS...
"YAMATA NO OROCHI" ...?
SO THE ONE BLOCKING THE SOURCE OF THE WATER OF LIFE WAS...
YES...THAT WAS HE.
BEFORE I DIE...
WHEEZ WHEEZ
THERE IS SOMETHING I MUST PASS ALONG TO YOU...
D-DON'T TALK LIKE THAT!
JUST...!

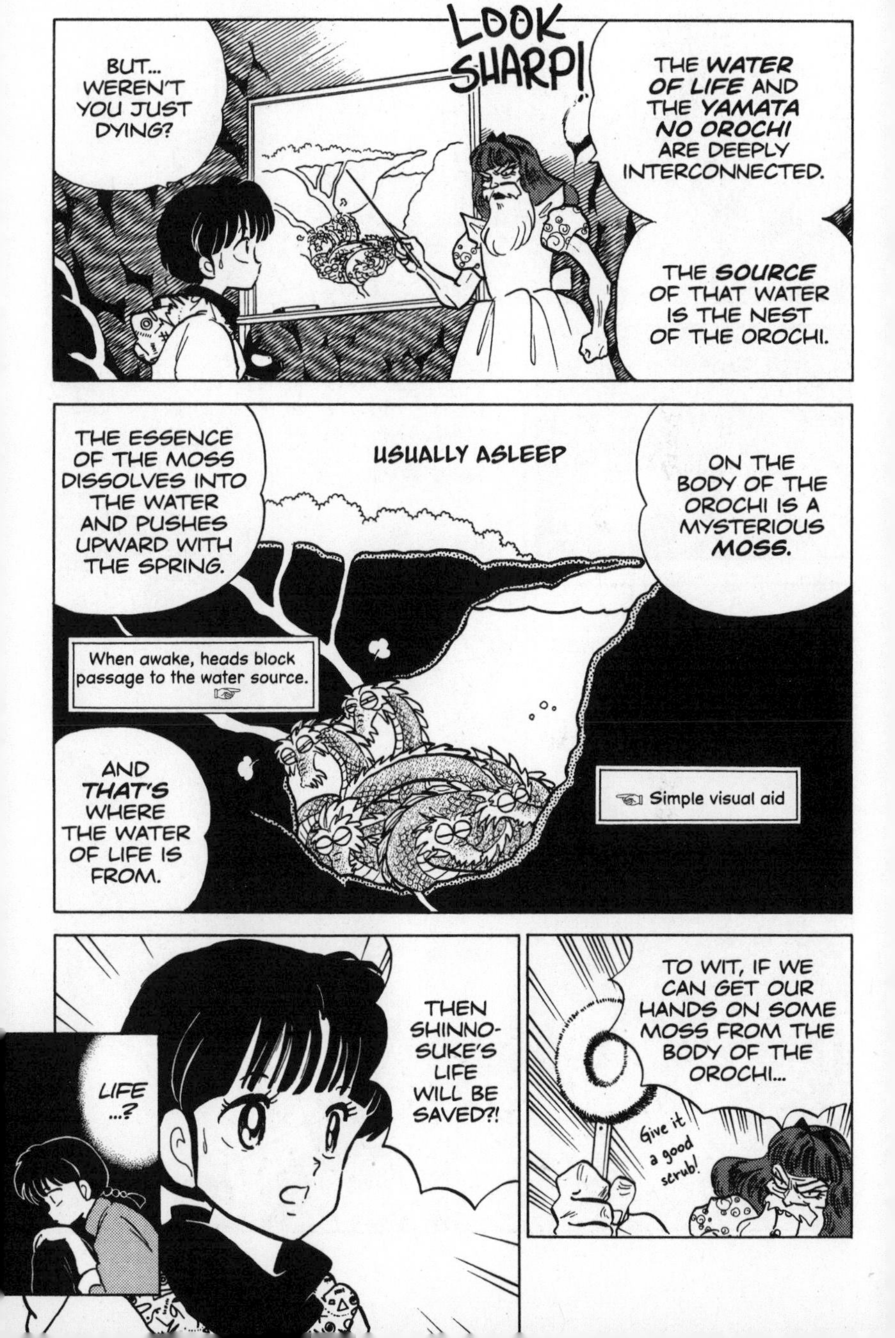
LOOK SHARP!
THE WATER OF LIFE AND THE YAMATA NO OROCHI ARE DEEPLY INTERCONNECTED.
BUT... WEREN'T YOU JUST DYING?
THE SOURCE OF THAT WATER IS THE NEST OF THE OROCHI.
ON THE BODY OF THE OROCHI IS A MYSTERIOUS MOSS.
USUALLY ASLEEP
THE ESSENCE OF THE MOSS DISSOLVES INTO THE WATER AND PUSHES UPWARD WITH THE SPRING.
When awake, heads block passage to the water source. ☞
☜ Simple visual aid
AND THAT'S WHERE THE WATER OF LIFE IS FROM.
TO WIT, IF WE CAN GET OUR HANDS ON SOME MOSS FROM THE BODY OF THE OROCHI...
Give it a good scrub!
THEN SHINNOSUKE'S LIFE WILL BE SAVED?!
LIFE ...?

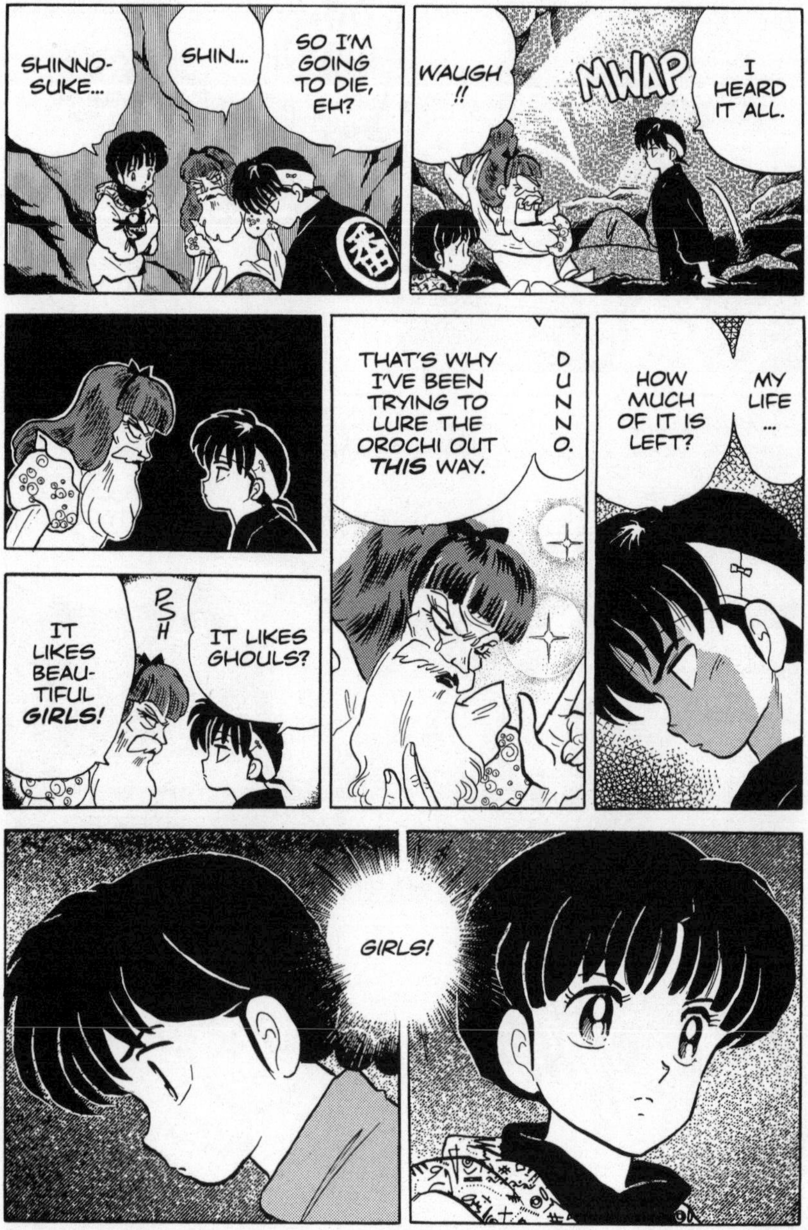
I HEARD IT ALL.
MWAP
WAUGH!!
SO I'M GOING TO DIE, EH?
SHIN...
SHINNO-SUKE...
MY LIFE...
HOW MUCH OF IT IS LEFT?
DUNNO.
THAT'S WHY I'VE BEEN TRYING TO LURE THE OROCHI OUT THIS WAY.
IT LIKES GHOULS?
PSH
IT LIKES BEAUTIFUL GIRLS!
GIRLS!

PART 17

THE FURY OF THE OROCHI!

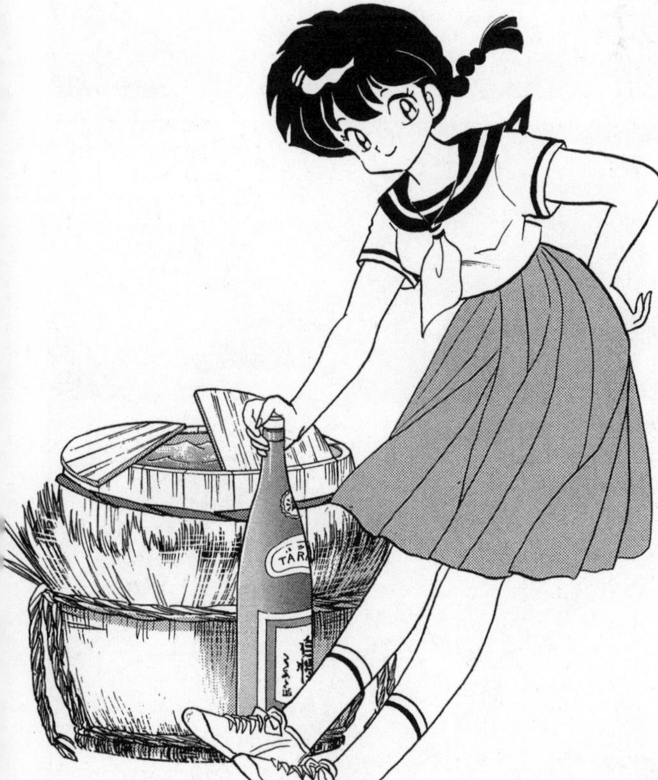
TARA

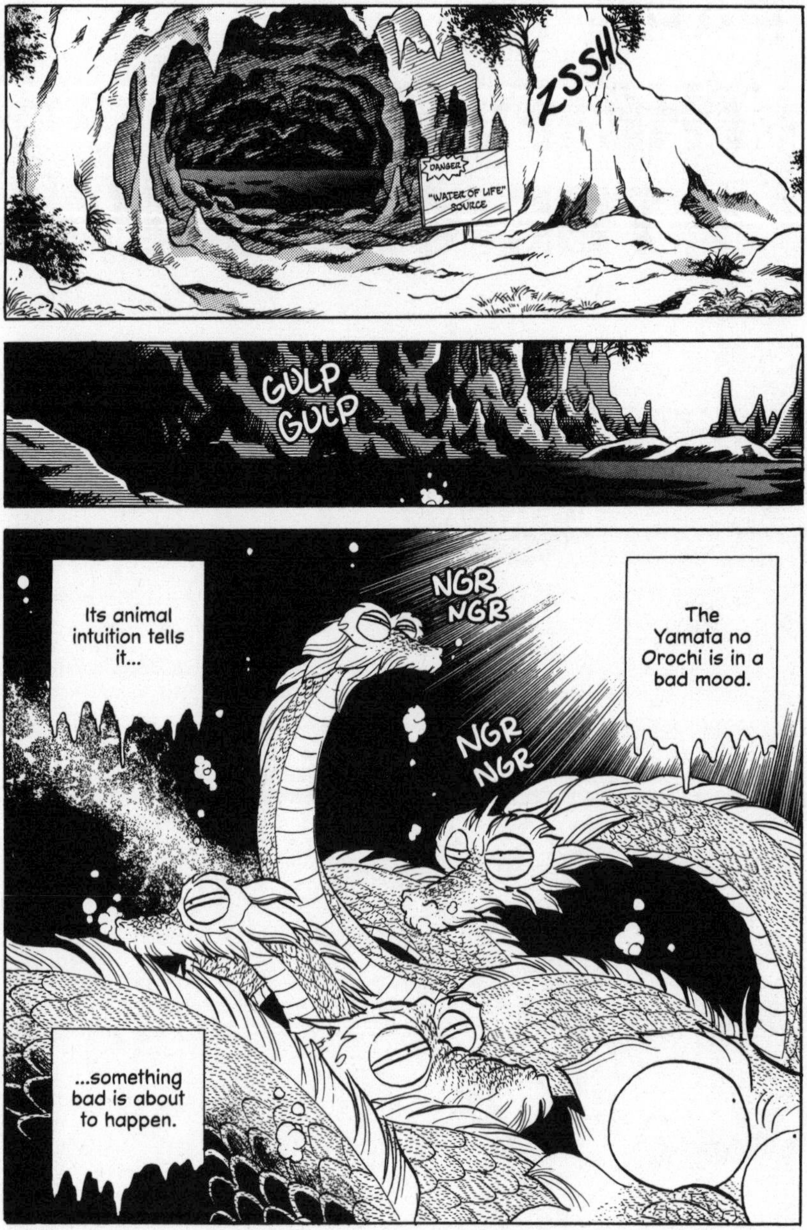
ZSSH
DANGER
"WATER OF LIFE" SOURCE
GULP GULP
The Yamata no Orochi is in a bad mood.
NGR NGR
NGR NGR
Its animal intuition tells it...
...something bad is about to happen.

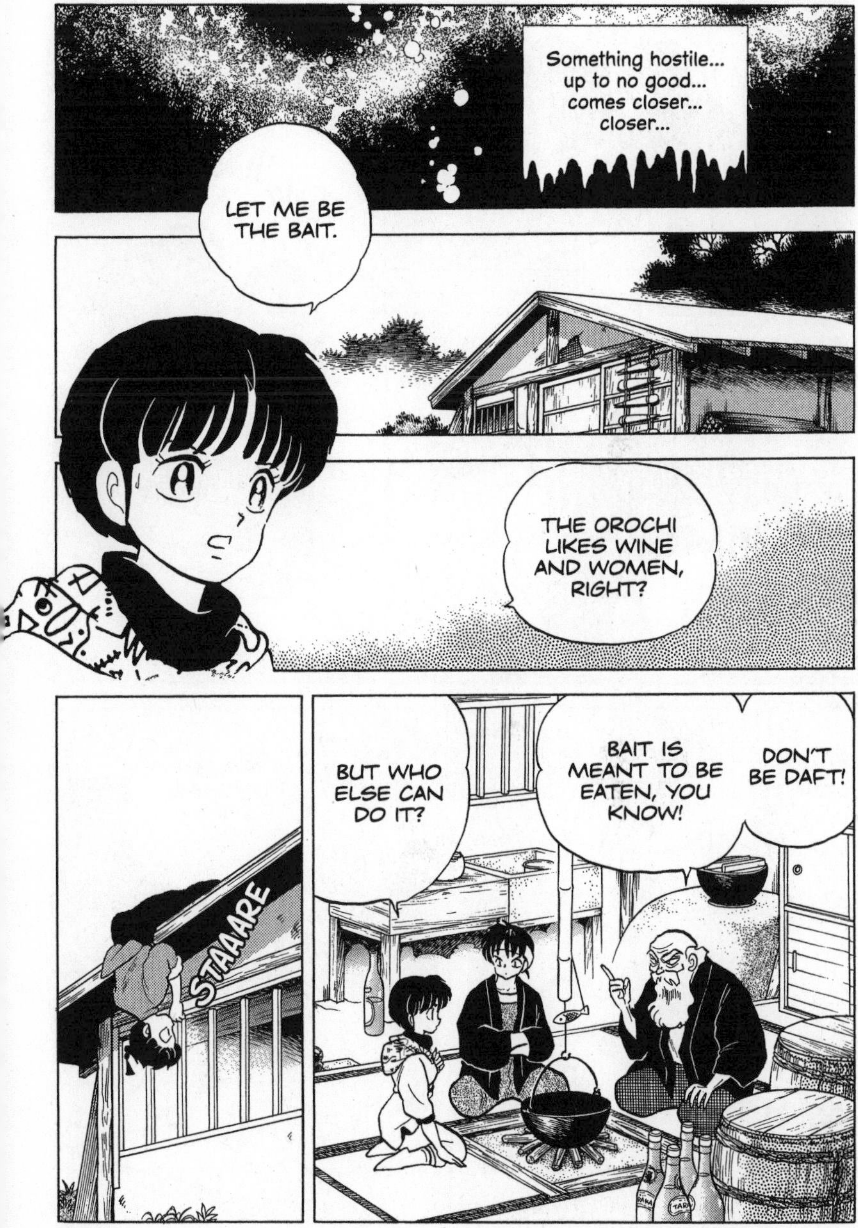
Something hostile... up to no good... comes closer... closer...
LET ME BE THE BAIT.
THE OROCHI LIKES WINE AND WOMEN, RIGHT?
DON'T BE DAFT!
BAIT IS MEANT TO BE EATEN, YOU KNOW!
BUT WHO ELSE CAN DO IT?
STAAARE

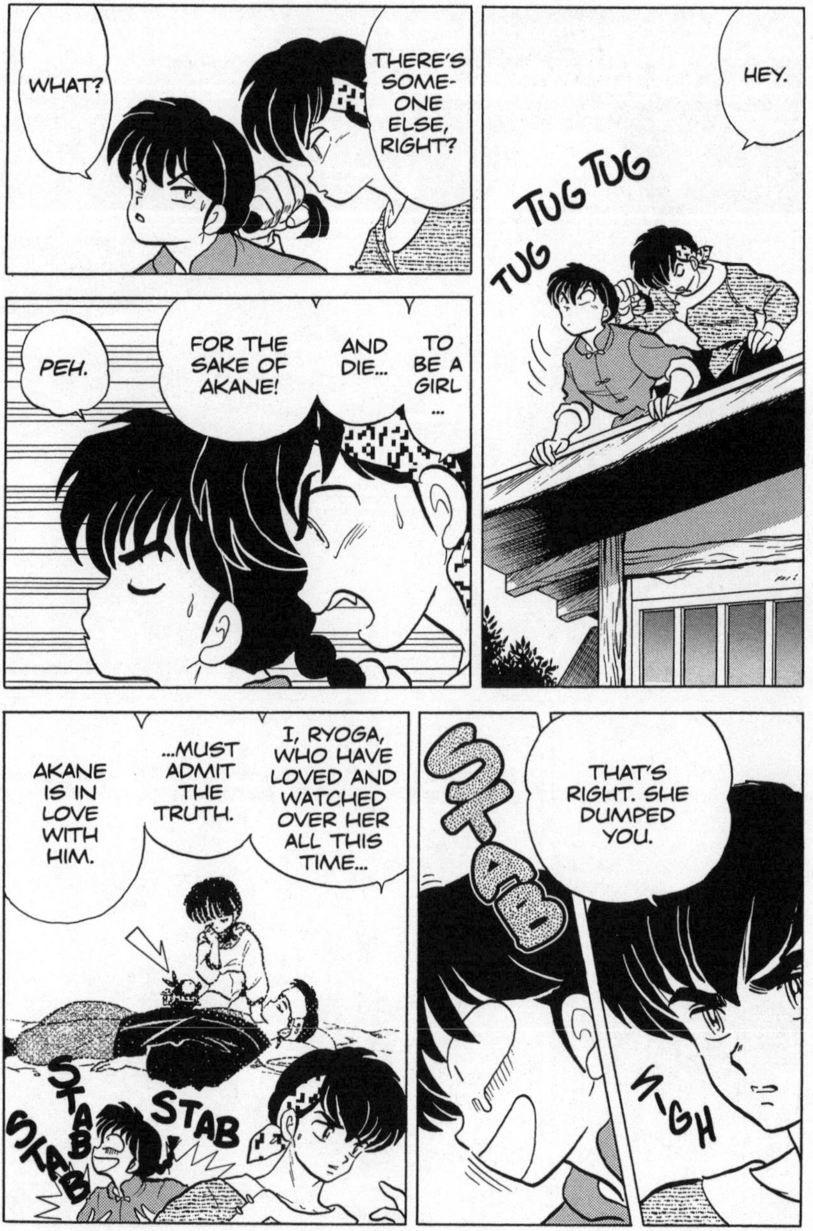
HEY.
TUG TUG TUG
THERE'S SOME-ONE ELSE, RIGHT?
WHAT?
TO BE A GIRL ...
AND DIE...
FOR THE SAKE OF AKANE!
PEH.
STAB
THAT'S RIGHT. SHE DUMPED YOU.
SIGH
I, RYOGA, WHO HAVE LOVED AND WATCHED OVER HER ALL THIS TIME...
...MUST ADMIT THE TRUTH.
AKANE IS IN LOVE WITH HIM.
STAB
STAB
STAB

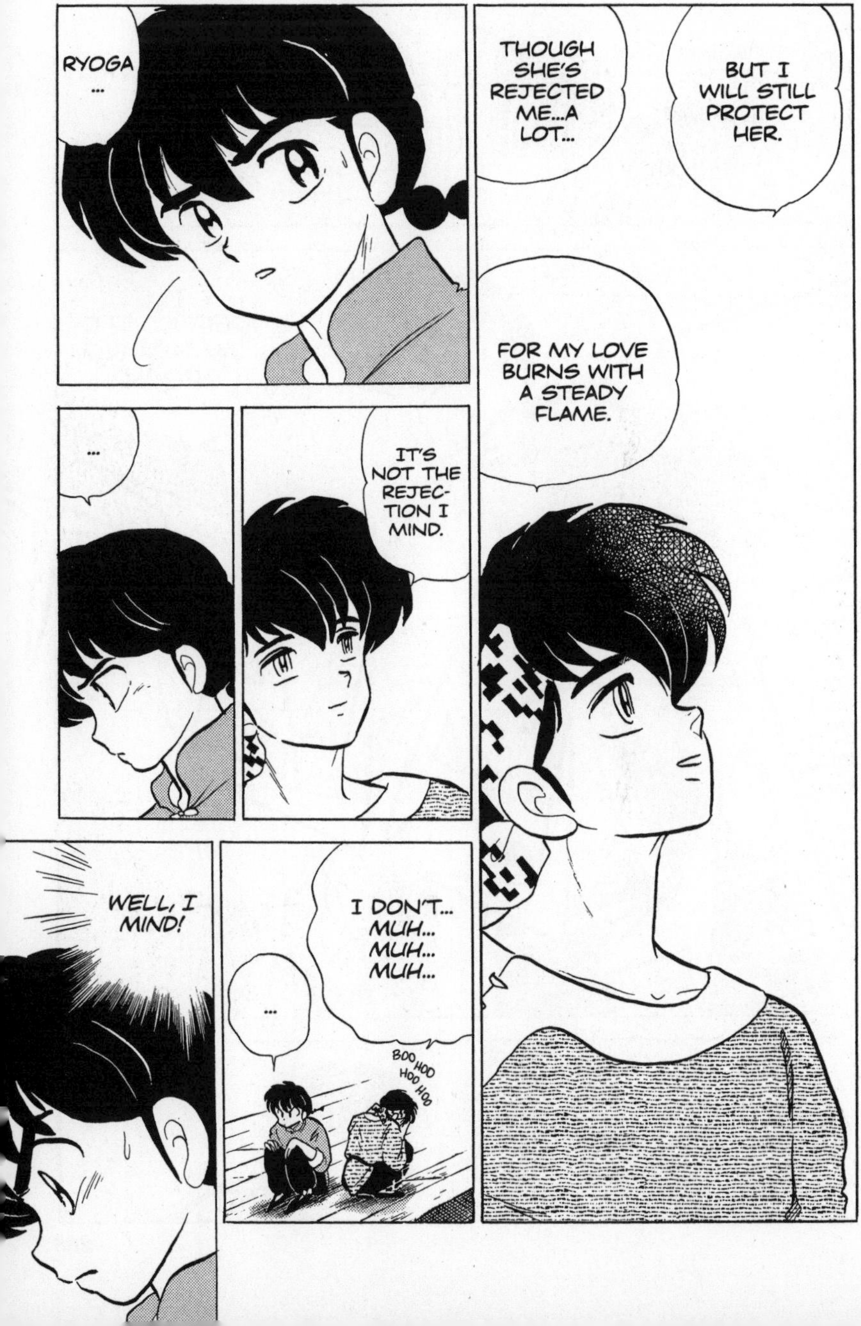
THOUGH SHE'S REJECTED ME...A LOT...
BUT I WILL STILL PROTECT HER.
FOR MY LOVE BURNS WITH A STEADY FLAME.
RYOGA ...
IT'S NOT THE REJECTION I MIND.
...
I DON'T... MUH... MUH... MUH...
...
BOO HOO HOO HOO
WELL, I MIND!

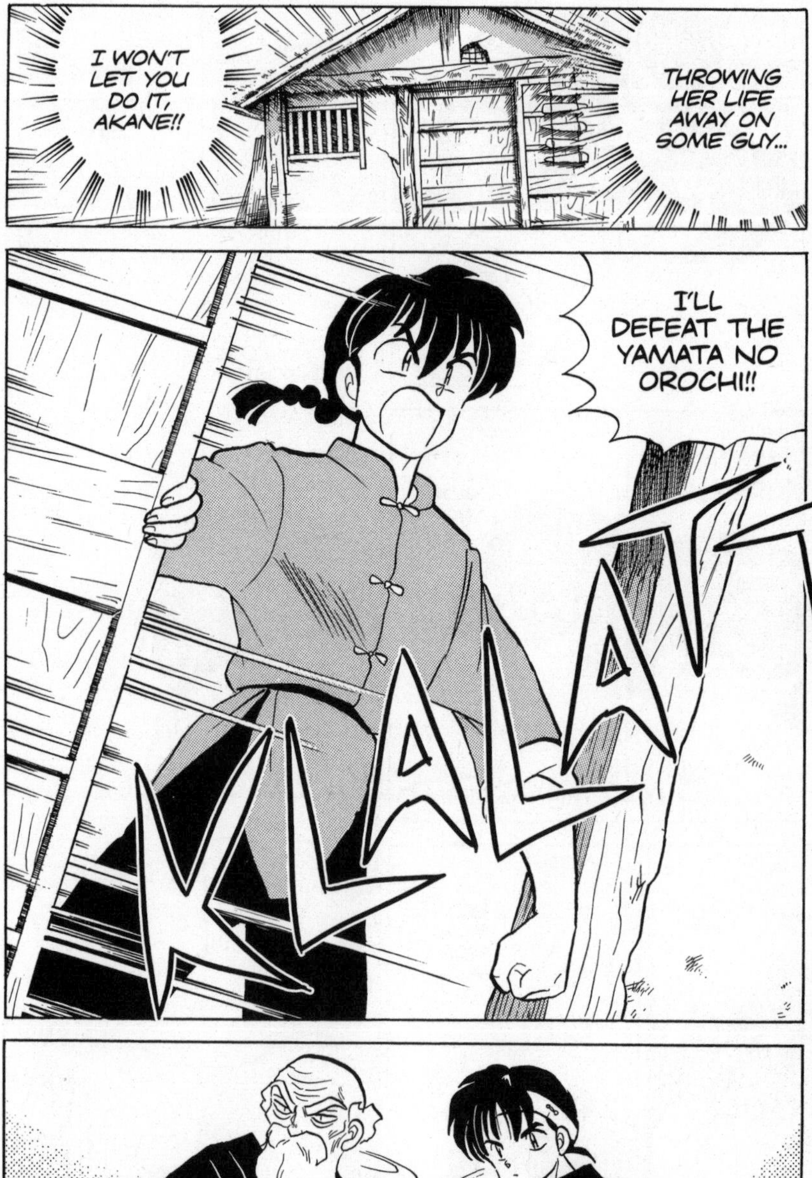
THROWING HER LIFE AWAY ON SOME GUY...
I WON'T LET YOU DO IT, AKANE!!
I'LL DEFEAT THE YAMATA NO OROCHI!!
KLALATT

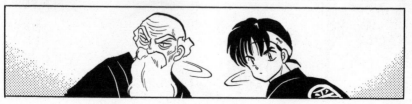

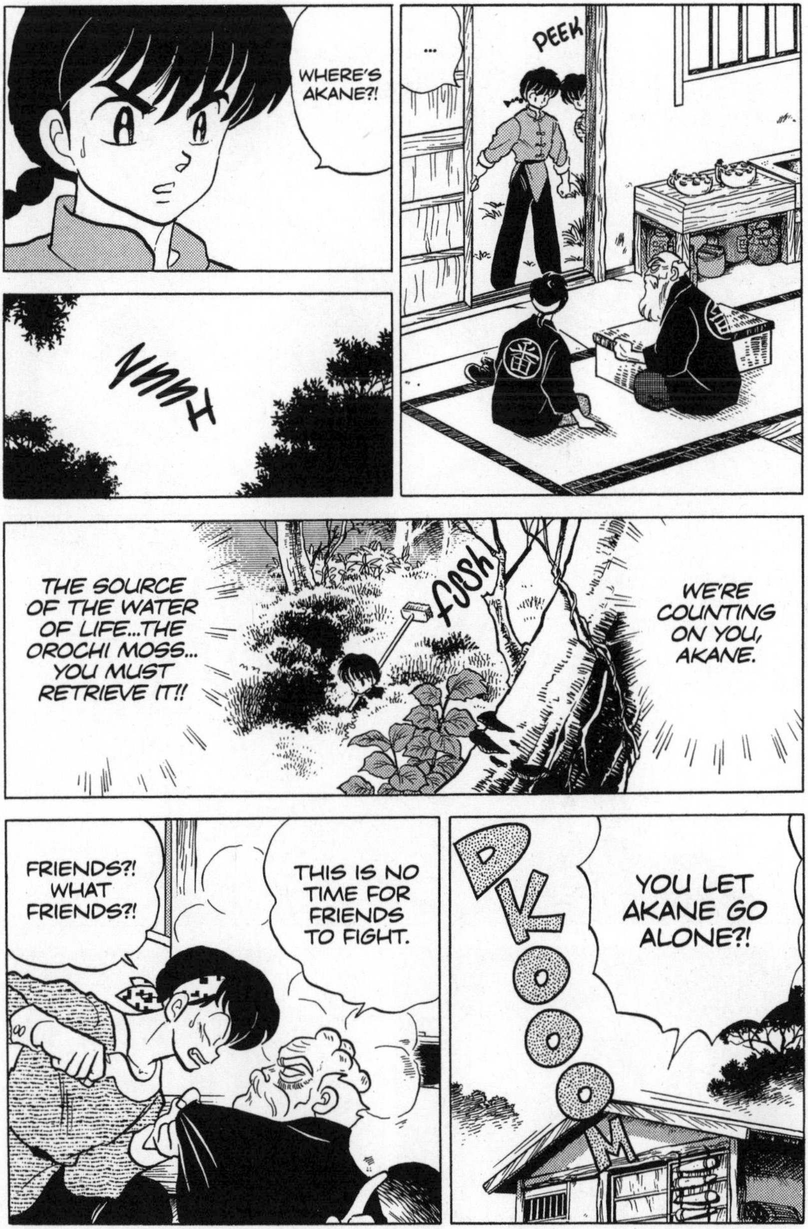
PEEK
...
WHERE'S AKANE?!
WE'RE COUNTING ON YOU, AKANE.
FSSH
THE SOURCE OF THE WATER OF LIFE...THE OROCHI MOSS... YOU MUST RETRIEVE IT!!
DKOOOOM
YOU LET AKANE GO ALONE?!
THIS IS NO TIME FOR FRIENDS TO FIGHT.
FRIENDS?! WHAT FRIENDS?!

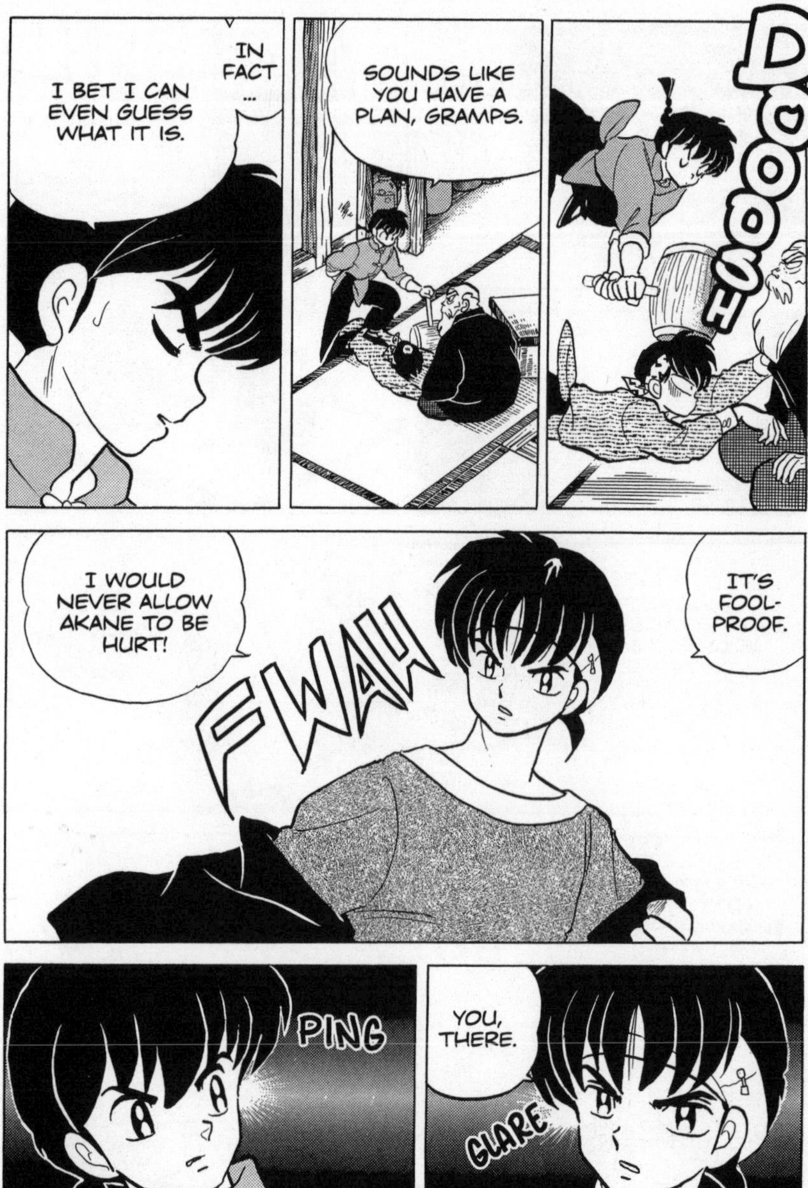
DOOOOSH
SOUNDS LIKE YOU HAVE A PLAN, GRAMPS.
IN FACT ...
I BET I CAN EVEN GUESS WHAT IT IS.
IT'S FOOL-PROOF.
FWAH
I WOULD NEVER ALLOW AKANE TO BE HURT!
YOU, THERE.
GLARE
PING

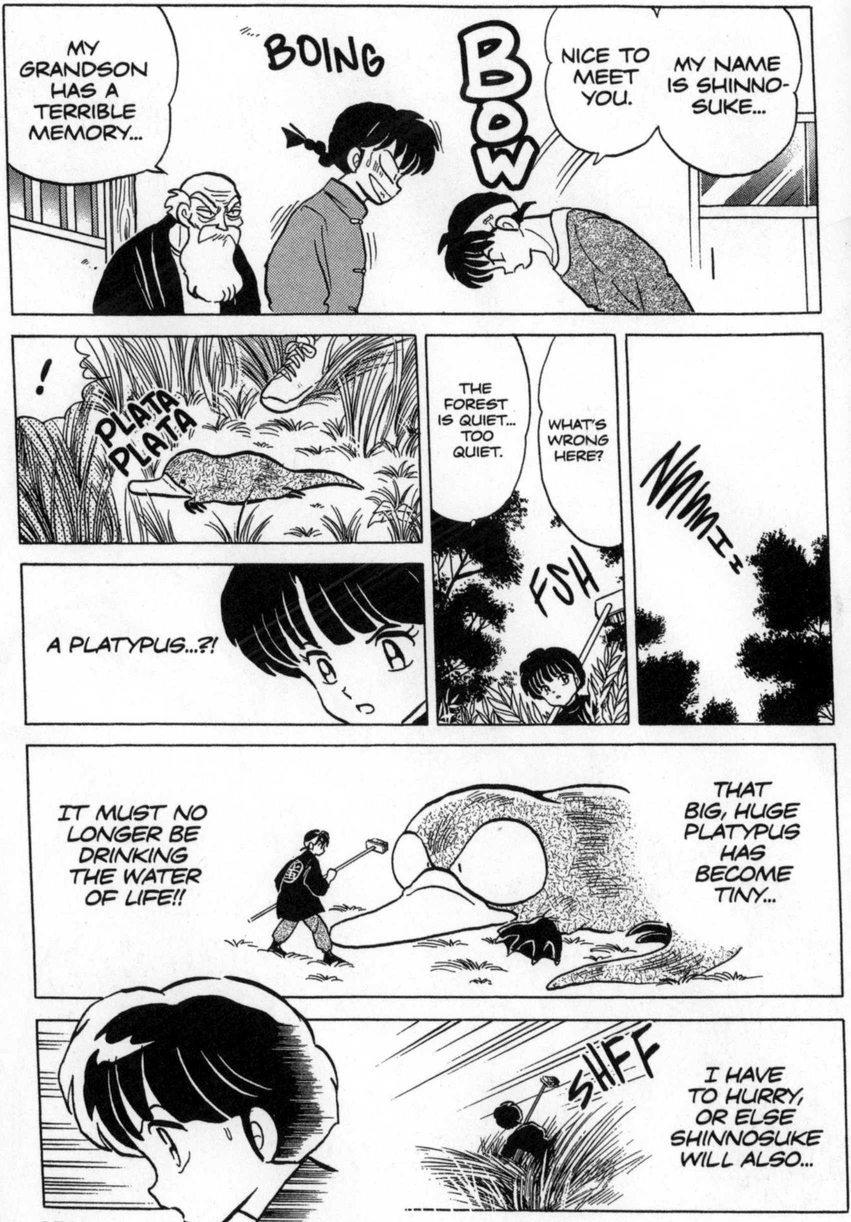
MY NAME IS SHINNO-SUKE...
NICE TO MEET YOU.
BOW
BOING
MY GRANDSON HAS A TERRIBLE MEMORY...
WHAT'S WRONG HERE?
THE FOREST IS QUIET... TOO QUIET.
FSH
!
PLATA PLATA
A PLATYPUS...?!
THAT BIG, HUGE PLATYPUS HAS BECOME TINY...
IT MUST NO LONGER BE DRINKING THE WATER OF LIFE!!
I HAVE TO HURRY, OR ELSE SHINNOSUKE WILL ALSO...
SHFF

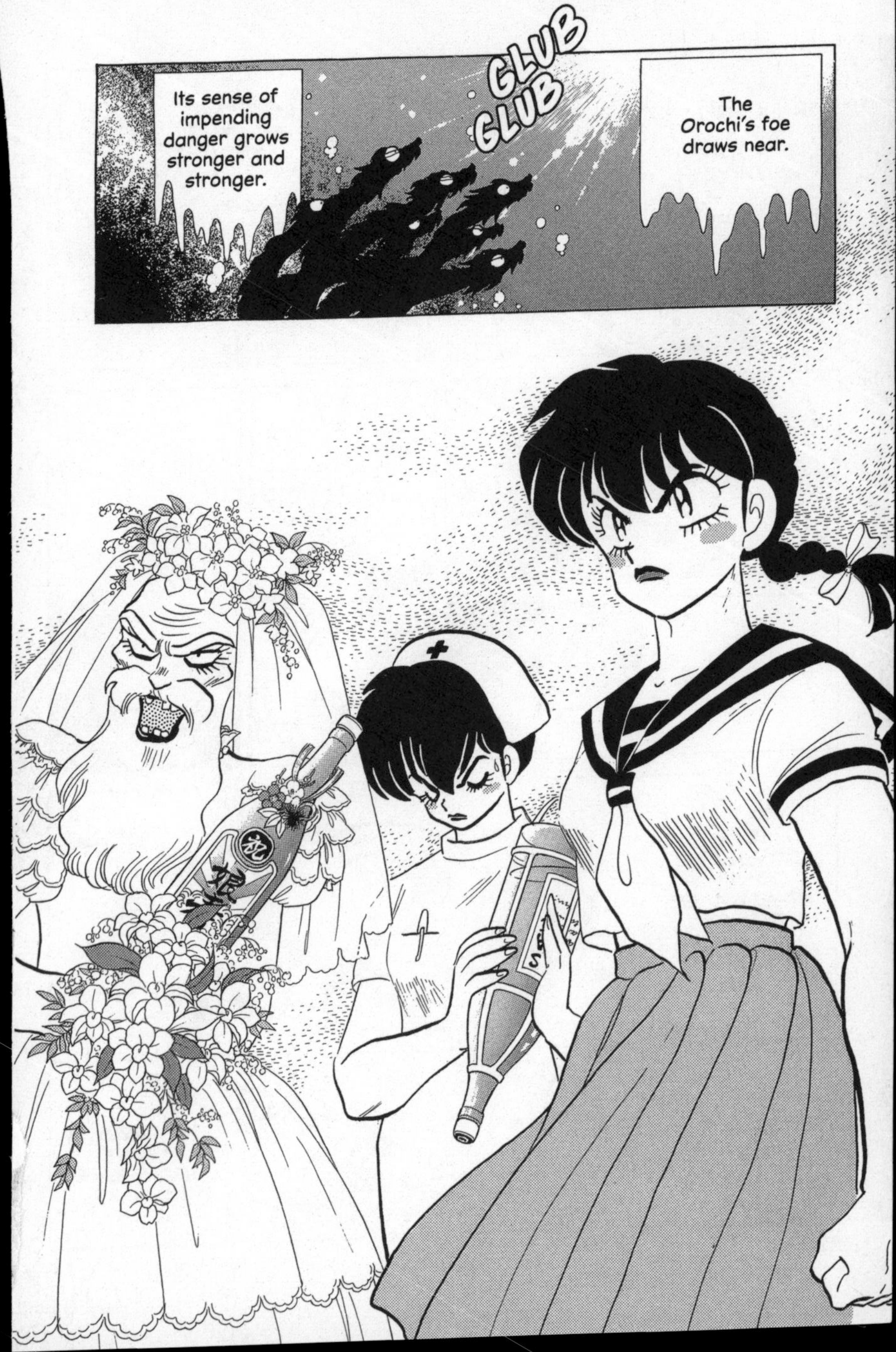
The Orochi's foe draws near.
GLUB GLUB
Its sense of impending danger grows stronger and stronger.

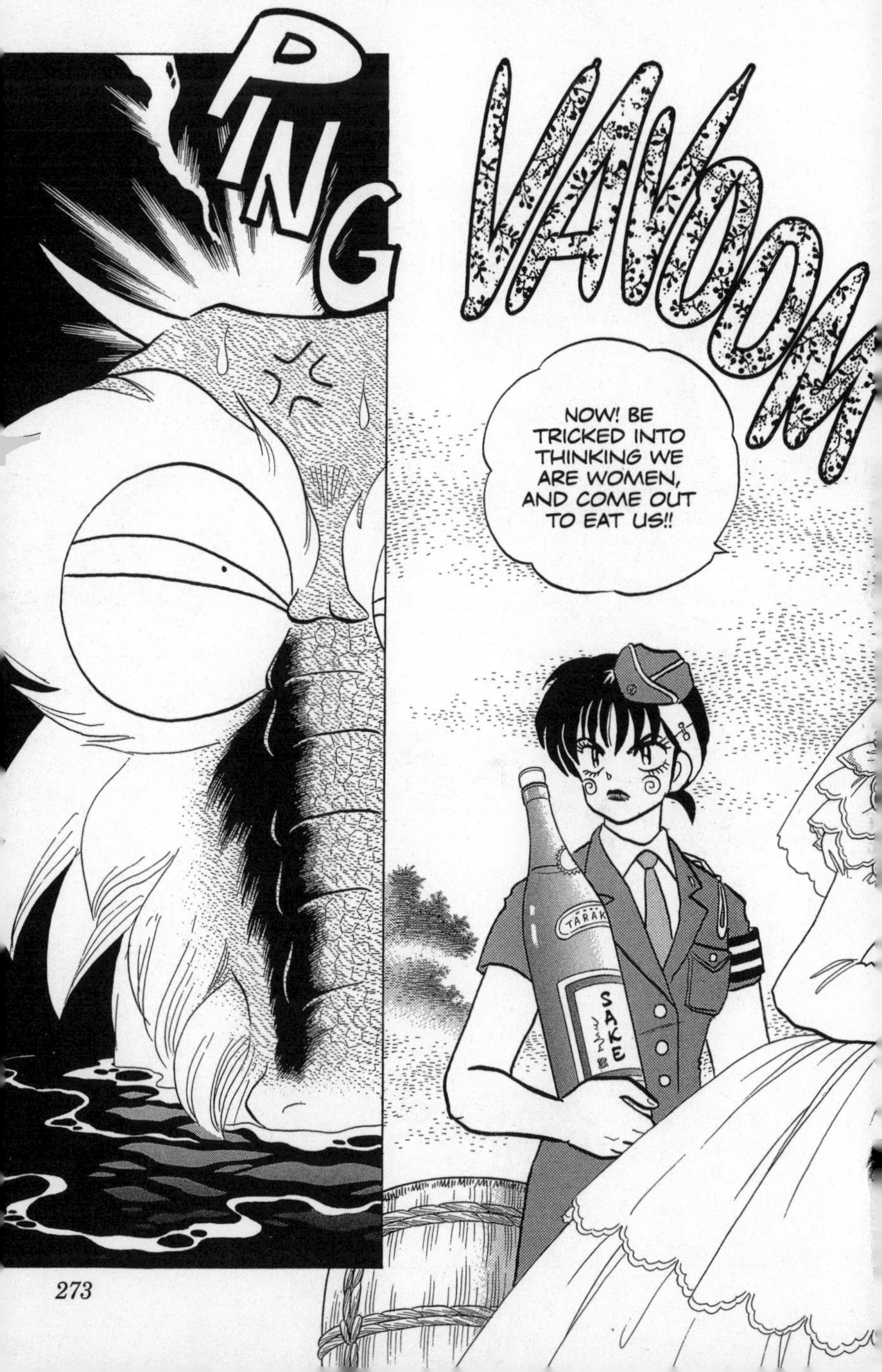
VAVOOM
NOW! BE TRICKED INTO THINKING WE ARE WOMEN, AND COME OUT TO EAT US!!
TARAK
SAKE
PING

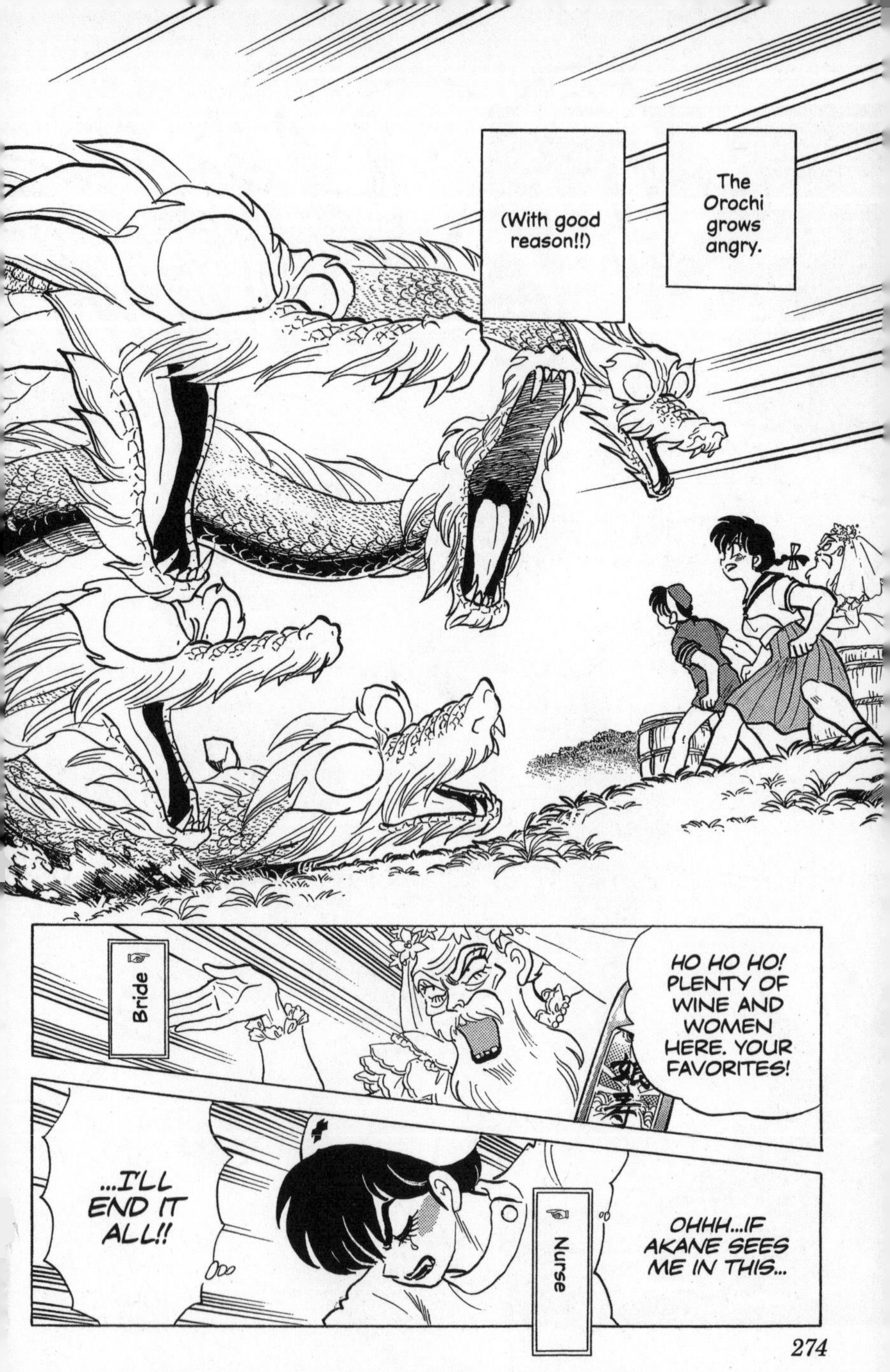
The Orochi grows angry.
(With good reason!!)
Bride
HO HO HO! PLENTY OF WINE AND WOMEN HERE. YOUR FAVORITES!
OHHH...IF AKANE SEES ME IN THIS...
Nurse
...I'LL END IT ALL!!

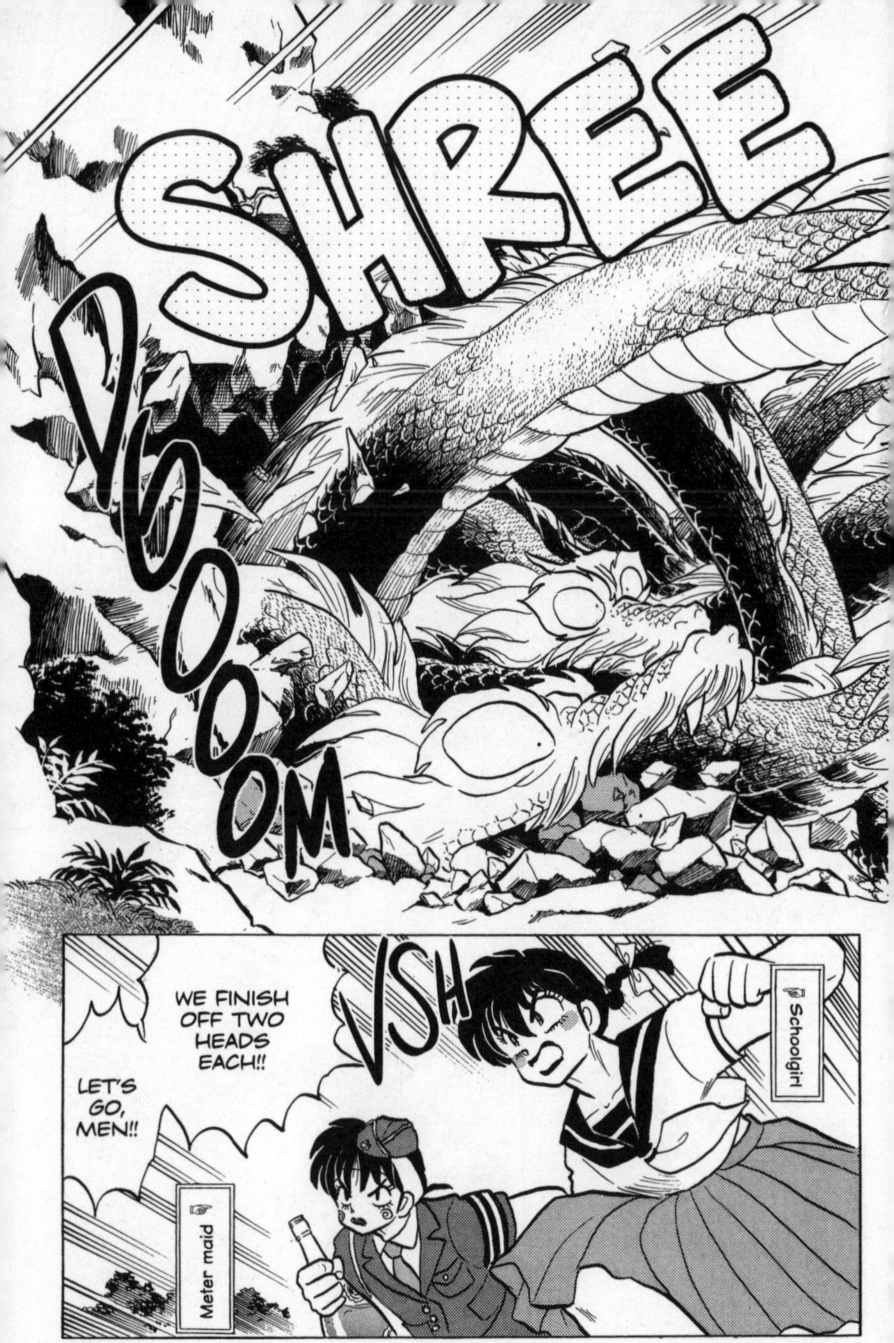
SHREE
DGOOOM
☞ Schoolgirl
VSH
WE FINISH OFF TWO HEADS EACH!!
LET'S GO, MEN!!
☞ Meter maid

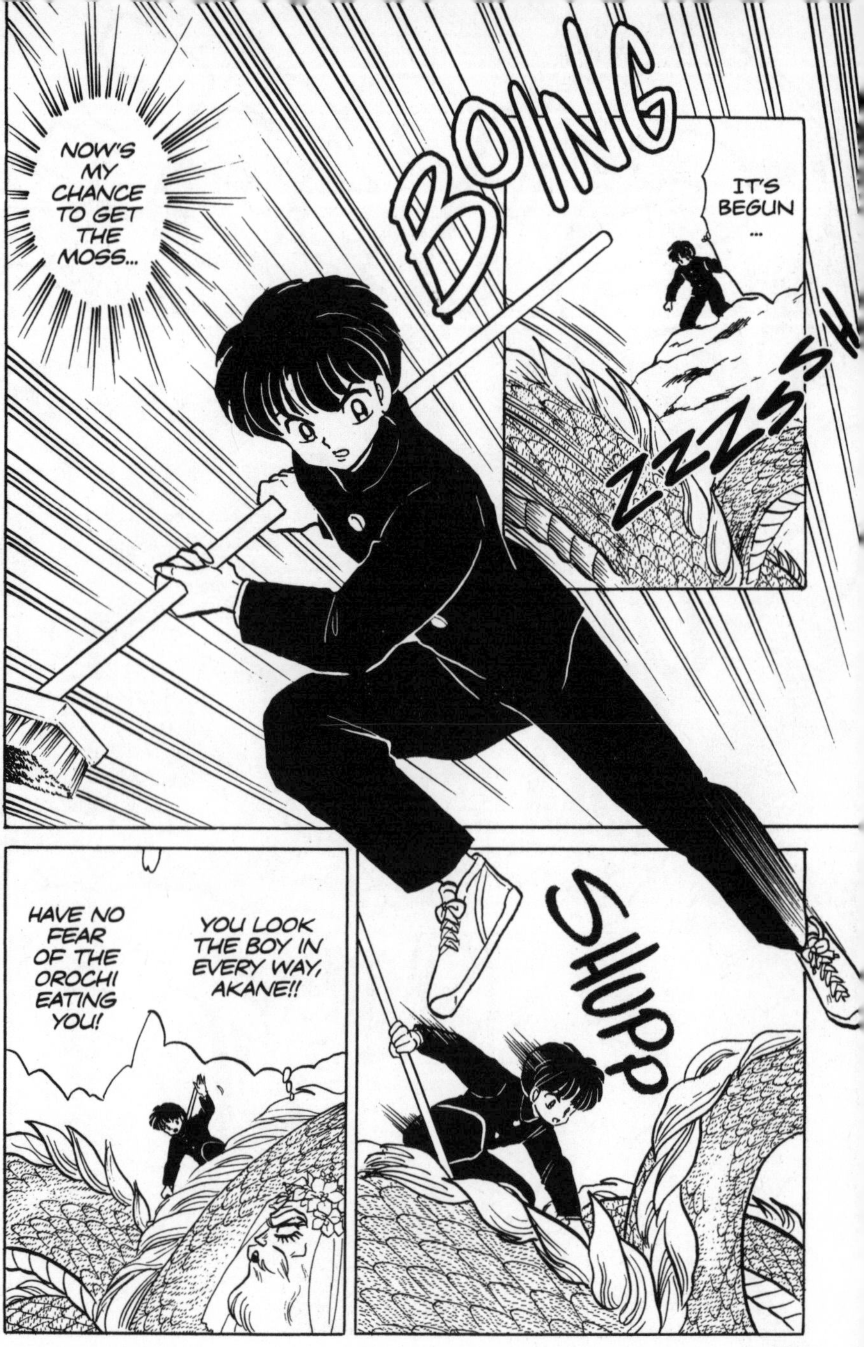
IT'S BEGUN ...
ZZZZSSSH
NOW'S MY CHANCE TO GET THE MOSS...
BOING
SHUPP
YOU LOOK THE BOY IN EVERY WAY, AKANE!!
HAVE NO FEAR OF THE OROCHI EATING YOU!

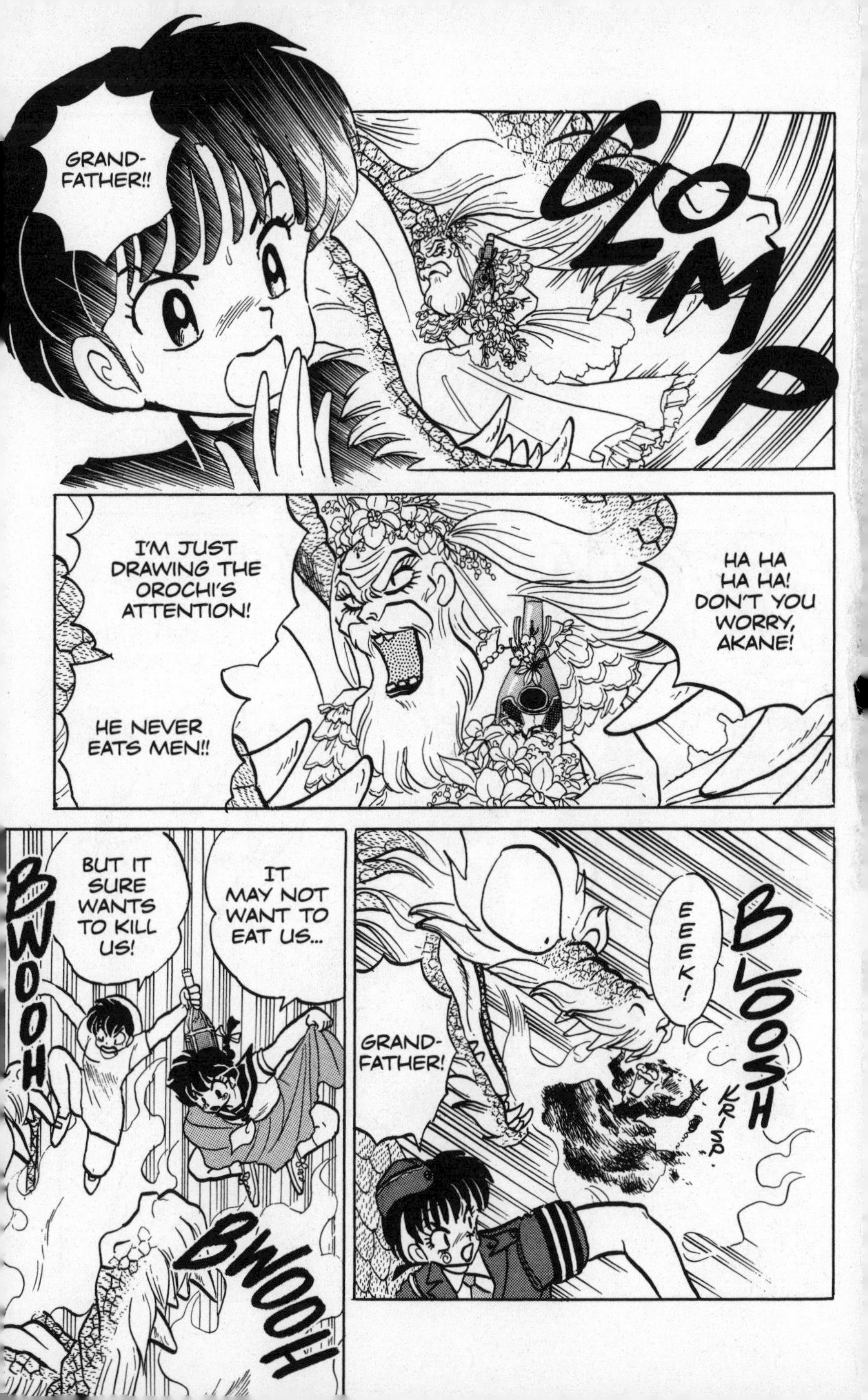
GLOMP
GRAND-FATHER!!
HA HA HA HA! DON'T YOU WORRY, AKANE!
I'M JUST DRAWING THE OROCHI'S ATTENTION!
HE NEVER EATS MEN!!
BLOOSH
EEEK!
GRAND-FATHER!
KRISP
IT MAY NOT WANT TO EAT US...
BUT IT SURE WANTS TO KILL US!
BWOOOH
BWOOOH

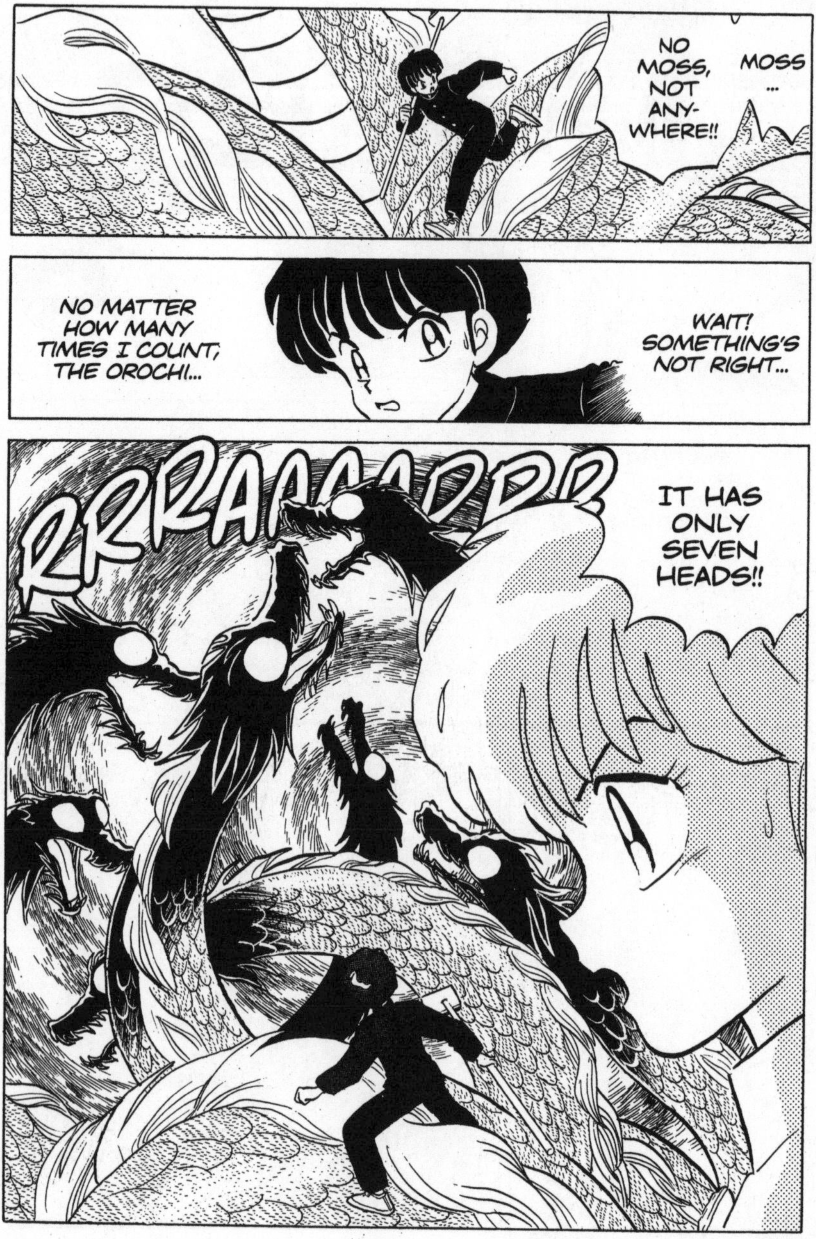
MOSS ...
NO MOSS, NOT ANY-WHERE!!
WAIT! SOMETHING'S NOT RIGHT...
NO MATTER HOW MANY TIMES I COUNT, THE OROCHI...
IT HAS ONLY SEVEN HEADS!!
RRRAAAARRR

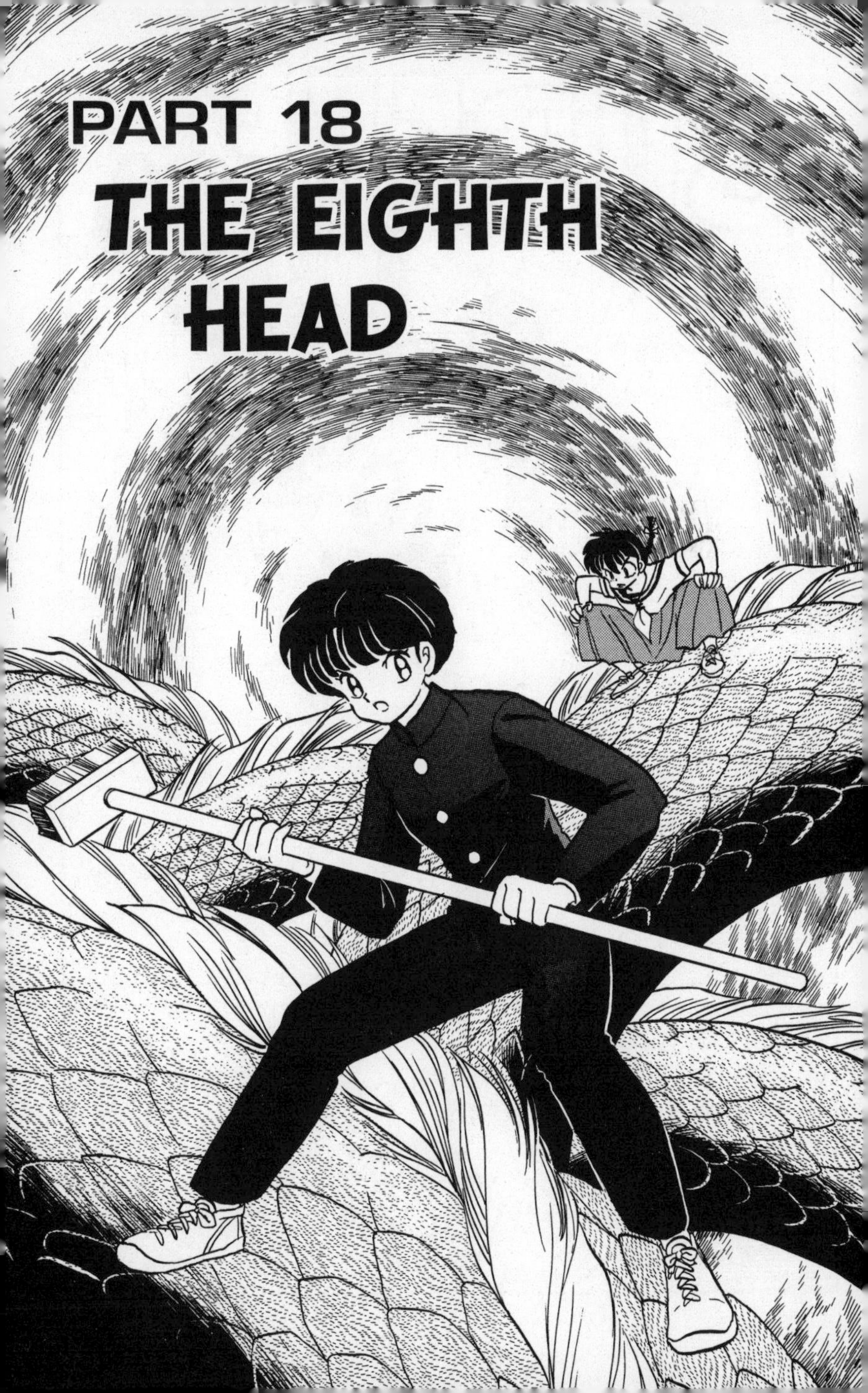
PART 18
THE EIGHTH HEAD

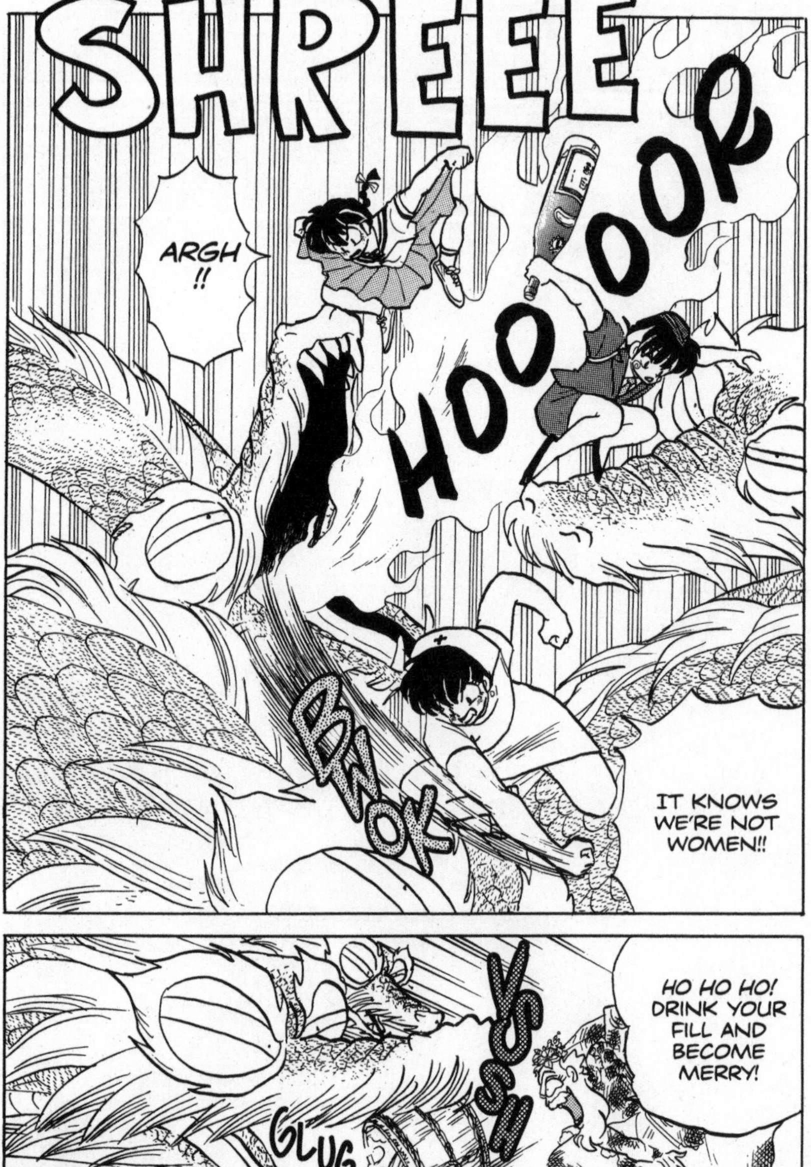
SHREEE
HOOOOP
ARGH!!
IT KNOWS WE'RE NOT WOMEN!!
BWOK
HO HO HO! DRINK YOUR FILL AND BECOME MERRY!
GLUG

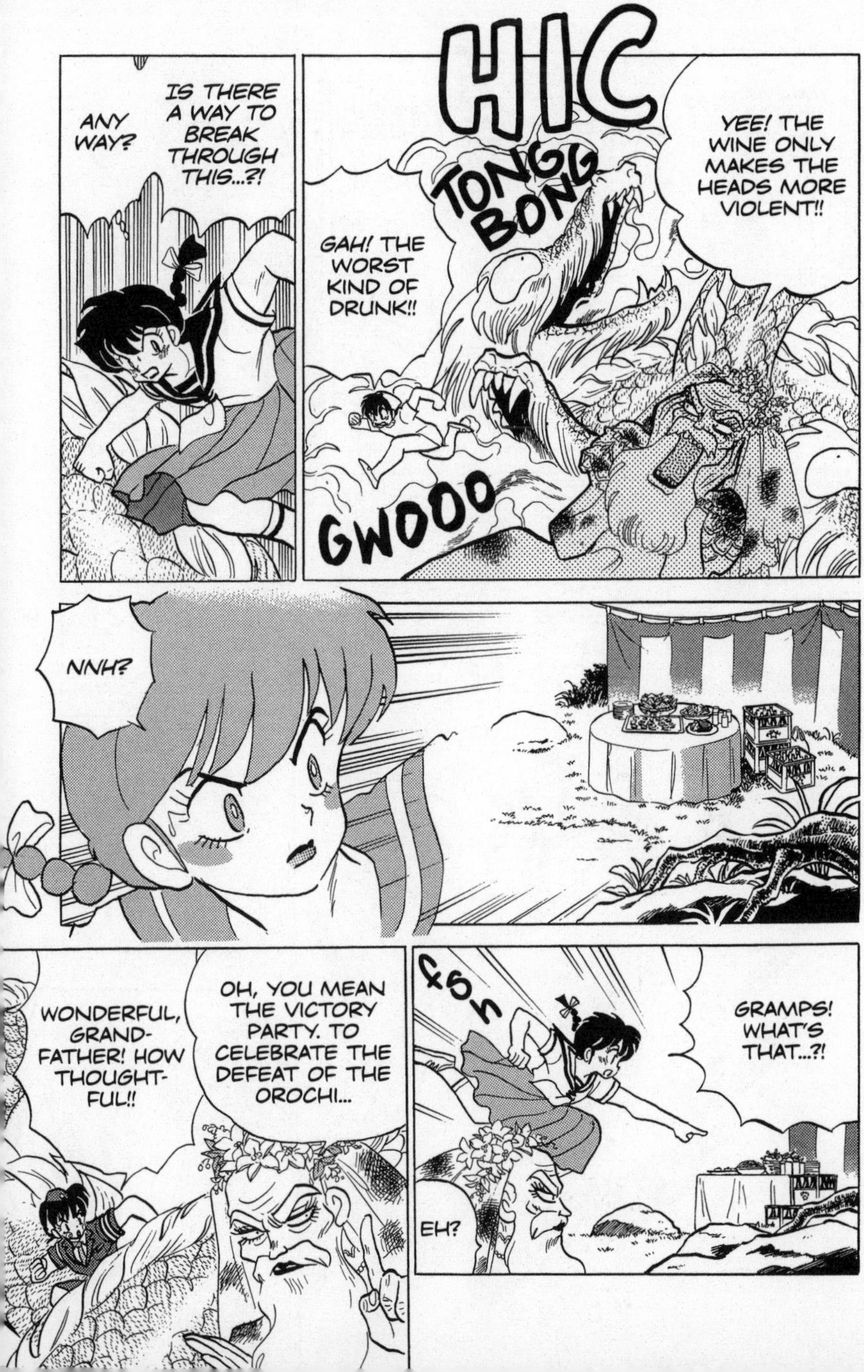
HIC
YEE! THE WINE ONLY MAKES THE HEADS MORE VIOLENT!!
TONG BONG
GAH! THE WORST KIND OF DRUNK!!
GWOOO
IS THERE A WAY TO BREAK THROUGH THIS...?!
ANY WAY?
NNH?
GRAMPS! WHAT'S THAT...?!
EH?
OH, YOU MEAN THE VICTORY PARTY. TO CELEBRATE THE DEFEAT OF THE OROCHI...
WONDERFUL, GRAND-FATHER! HOW THOUGHT-FUL!!

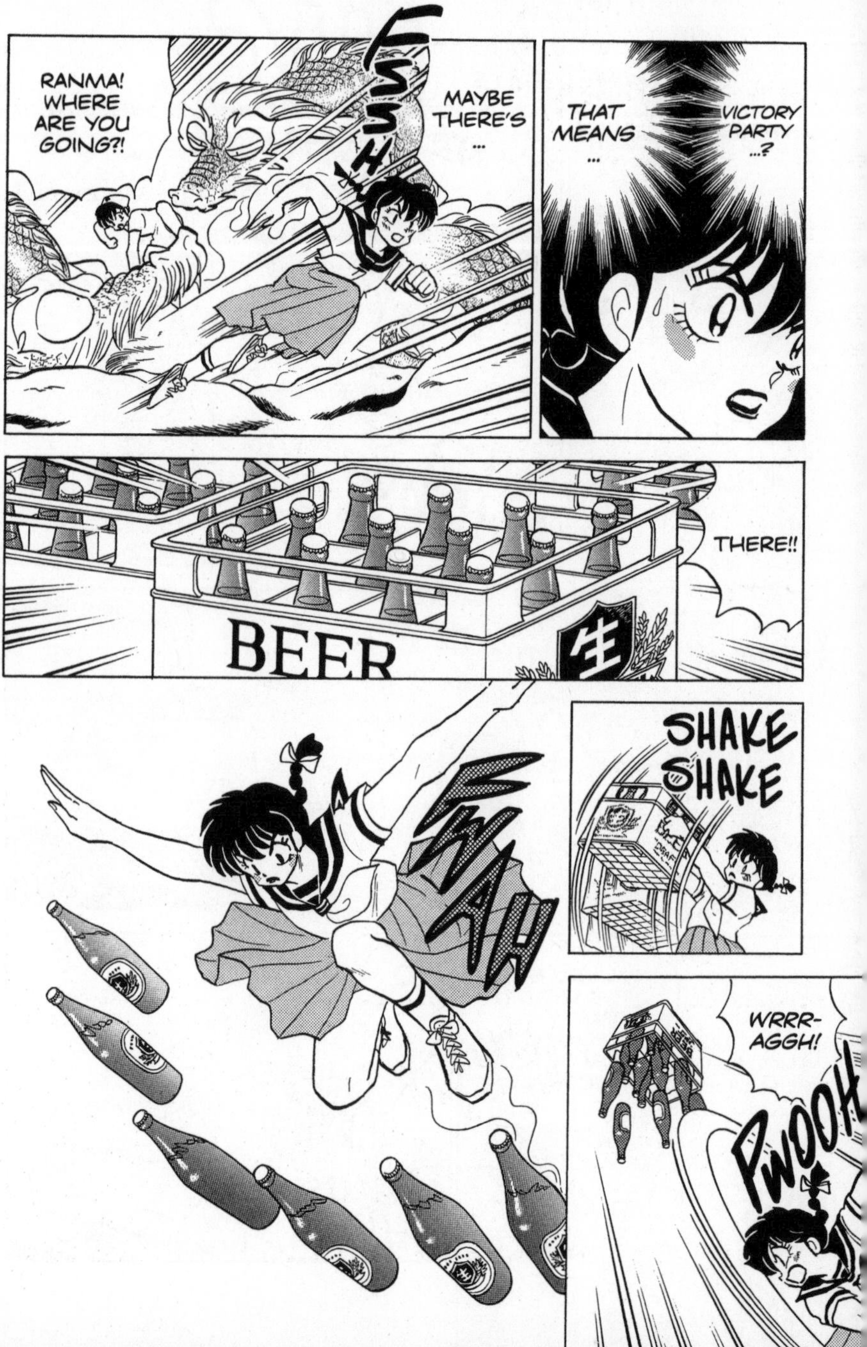
VICTORY PARTY ...?
THAT MEANS ...
MAYBE THERE'S ...
FSSH
RANMA! WHERE ARE YOU GOING?!
THERE!!
BEER
生
SHAKE SHAKE
WRRR-AGGH!
PWOOH
FWAH

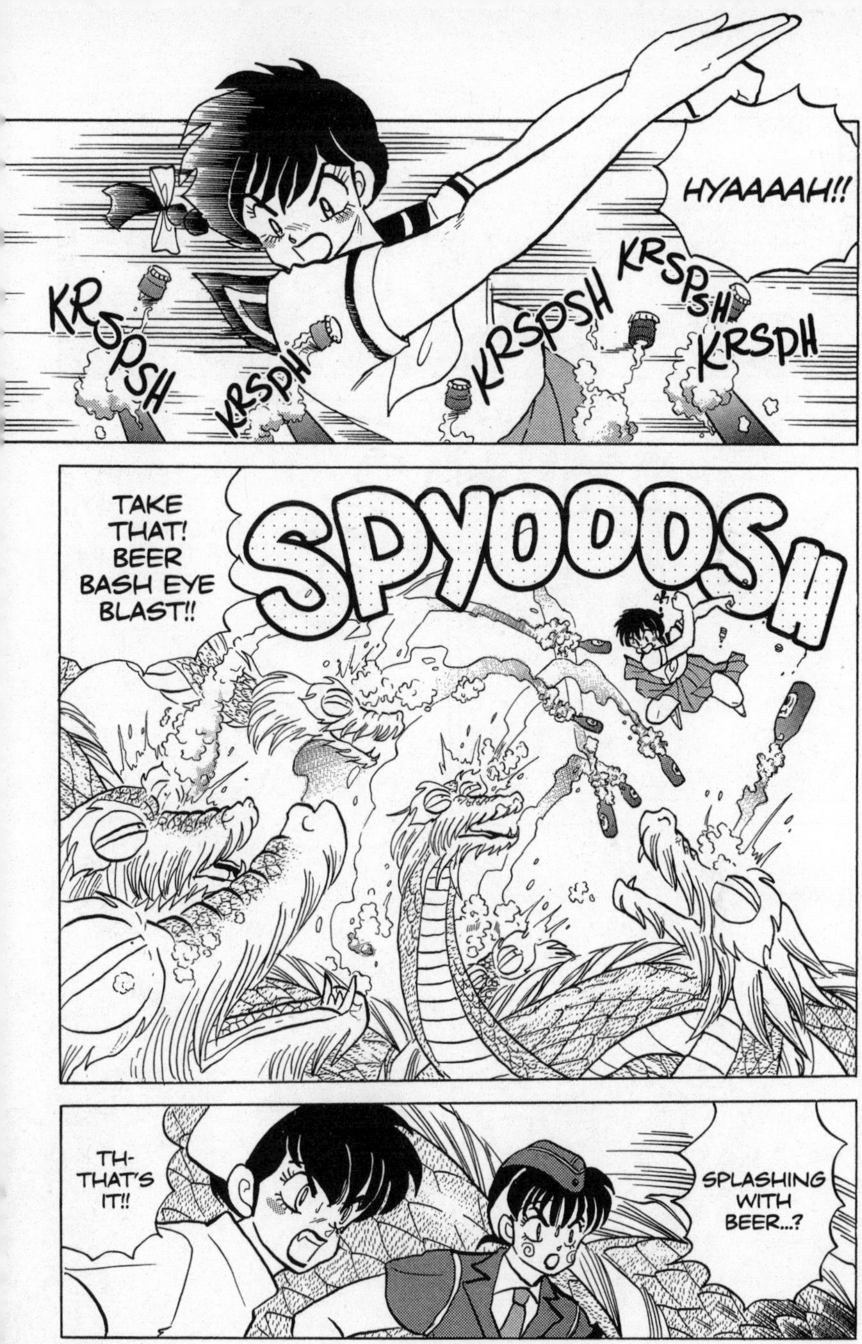
HYAAAAH!!
KRSPH
KRSPSH
KRSPSH
KRSPH
KRSPSH
SPYOOOSH
TAKE THAT! BEER BASH EYE BLAST!!
SPLASHING WITH BEER...?
TH- THAT'S IT!!

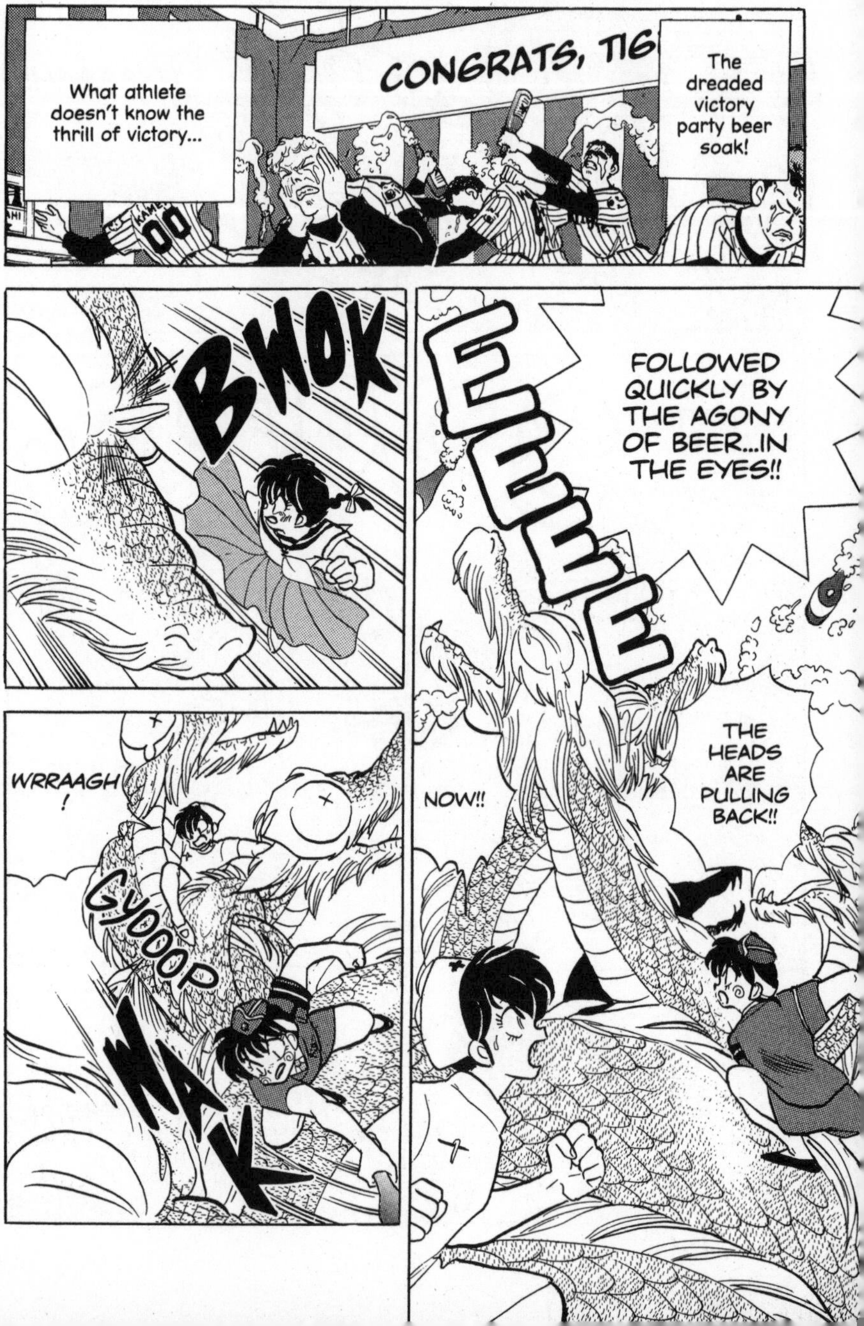
The dreaded victory party beer soak!
CONGRATS, TIG
What athlete doesn't know the thrill of victory...
FOLLOWED QUICKLY BY THE AGONY OF BEER...IN THE EYES!!
EEEEE
THE HEADS ARE PULLING BACK!!
NOW!!
BWOK
WRRAAGH!
GYOOOP
WAK

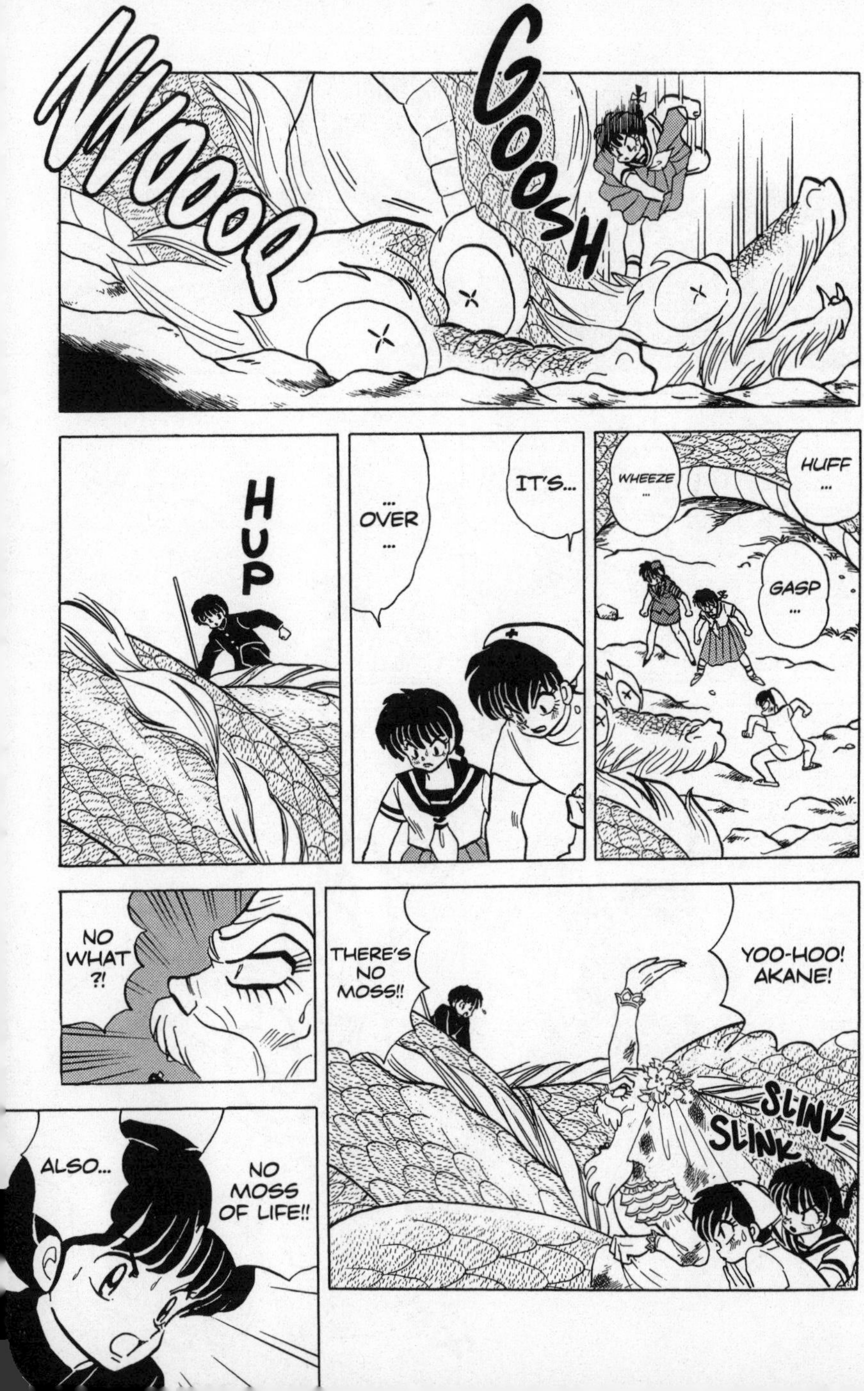
GOOSH
WHOOOP
HUFF ...
WHEEZE ...
GASP ...
IT'S...
... OVER ...
HUP
YOO-HOO! AKANE!
THERE'S NO MOSS!!
SLINK SLINK
NO WHAT ?!
NO MOSS OF LIFE!!
ALSO...

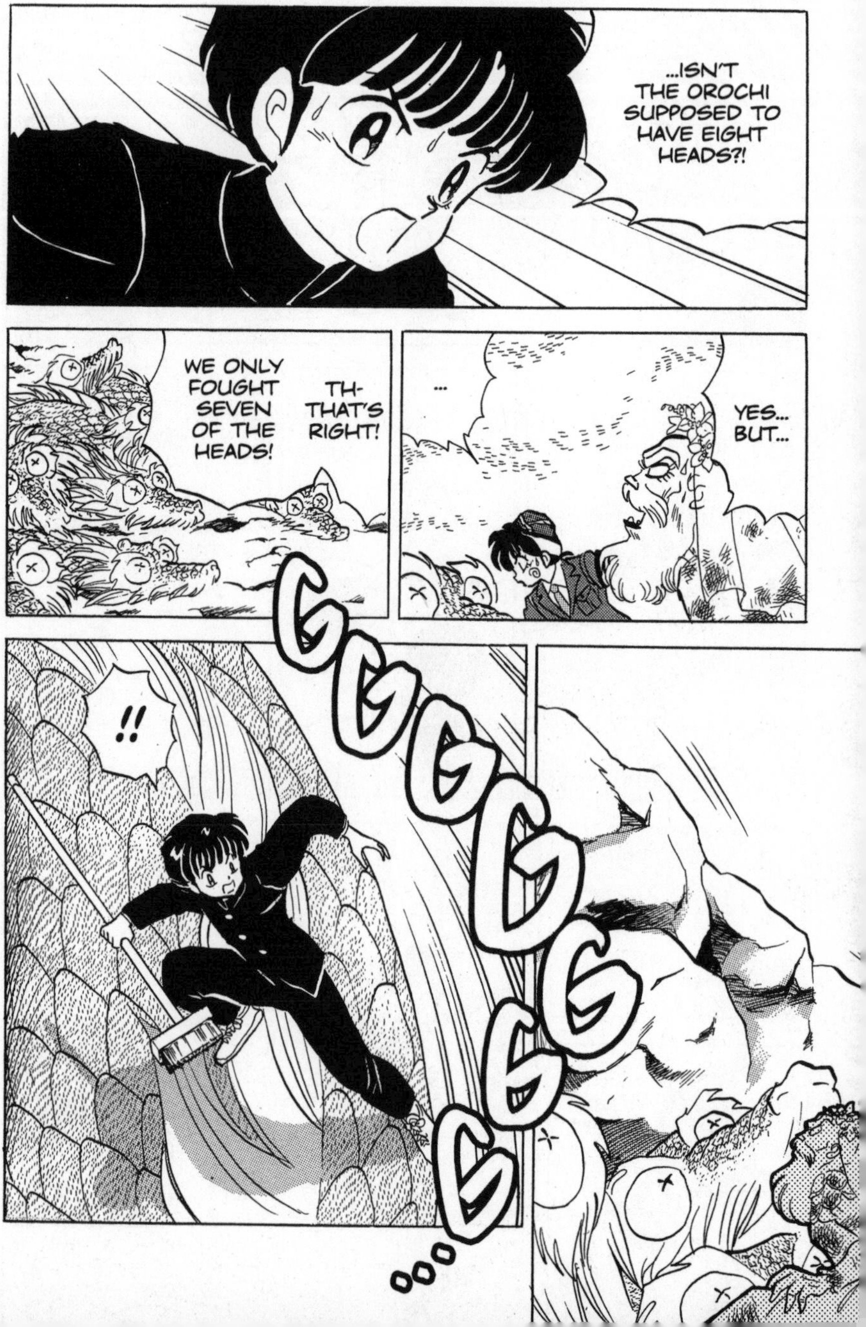
...ISN'T THE OROCHI SUPPOSED TO HAVE EIGHT HEADS?!
YES... BUT...
...
TH- THAT'S RIGHT!
WE ONLY FOUGHT SEVEN OF THE HEADS!
GGGGGGG...
!!

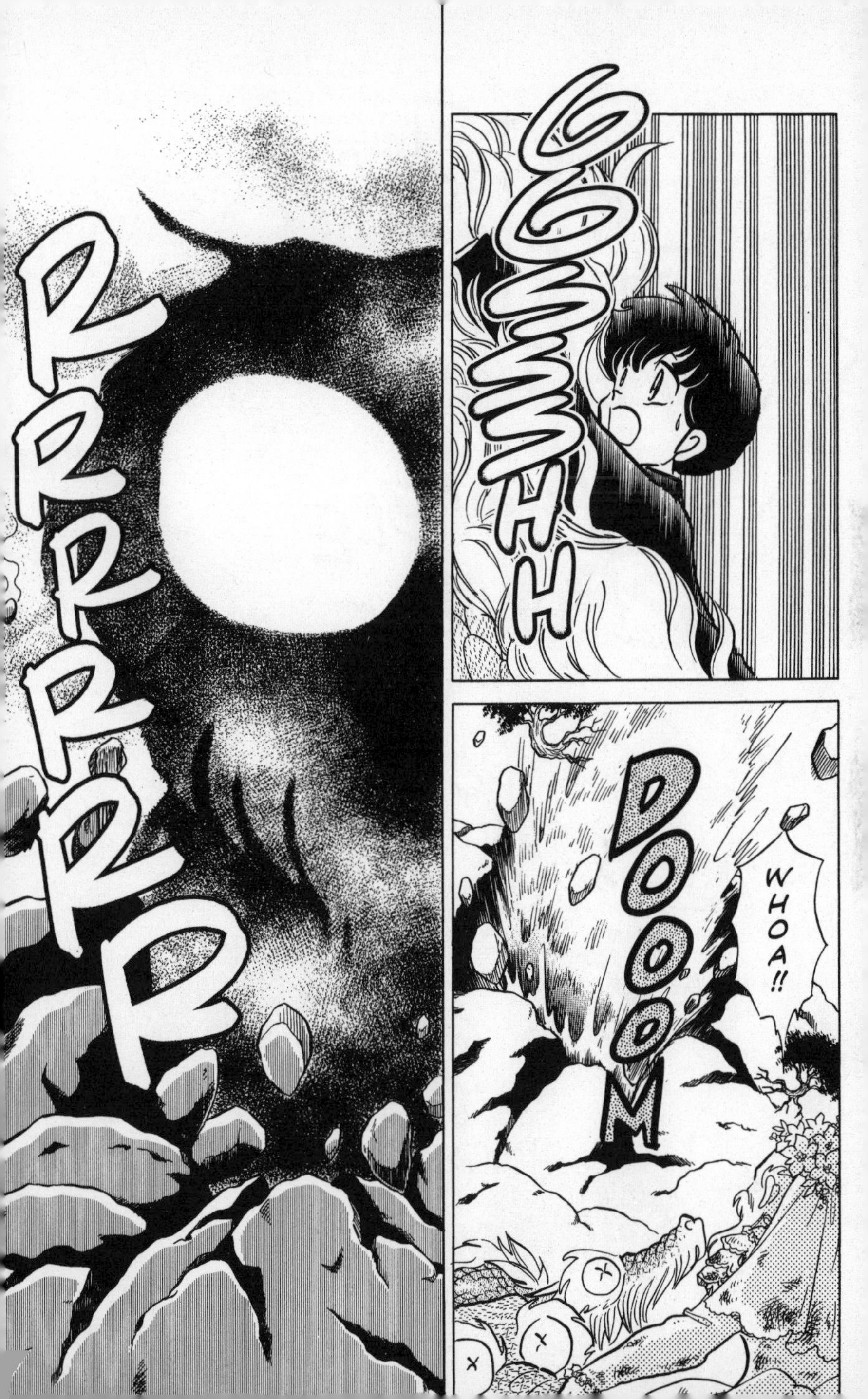
GGSSHH
DOOOOOM
WHOA!!
RRRRRR

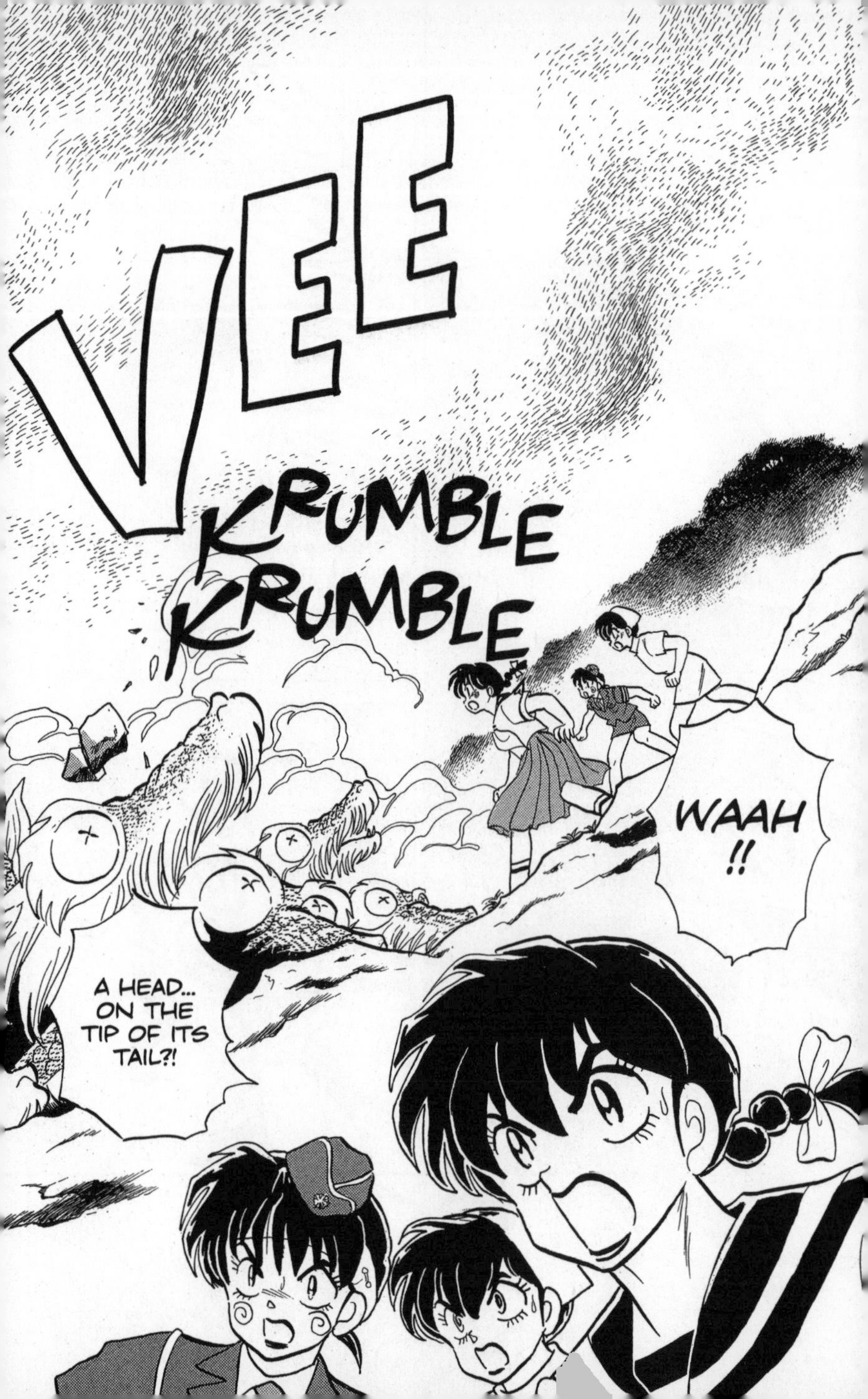
VEEE
KRUMBLE KRUMBLE
WAAH!!
A HEAD... ON THE TIP OF ITS TAIL?!

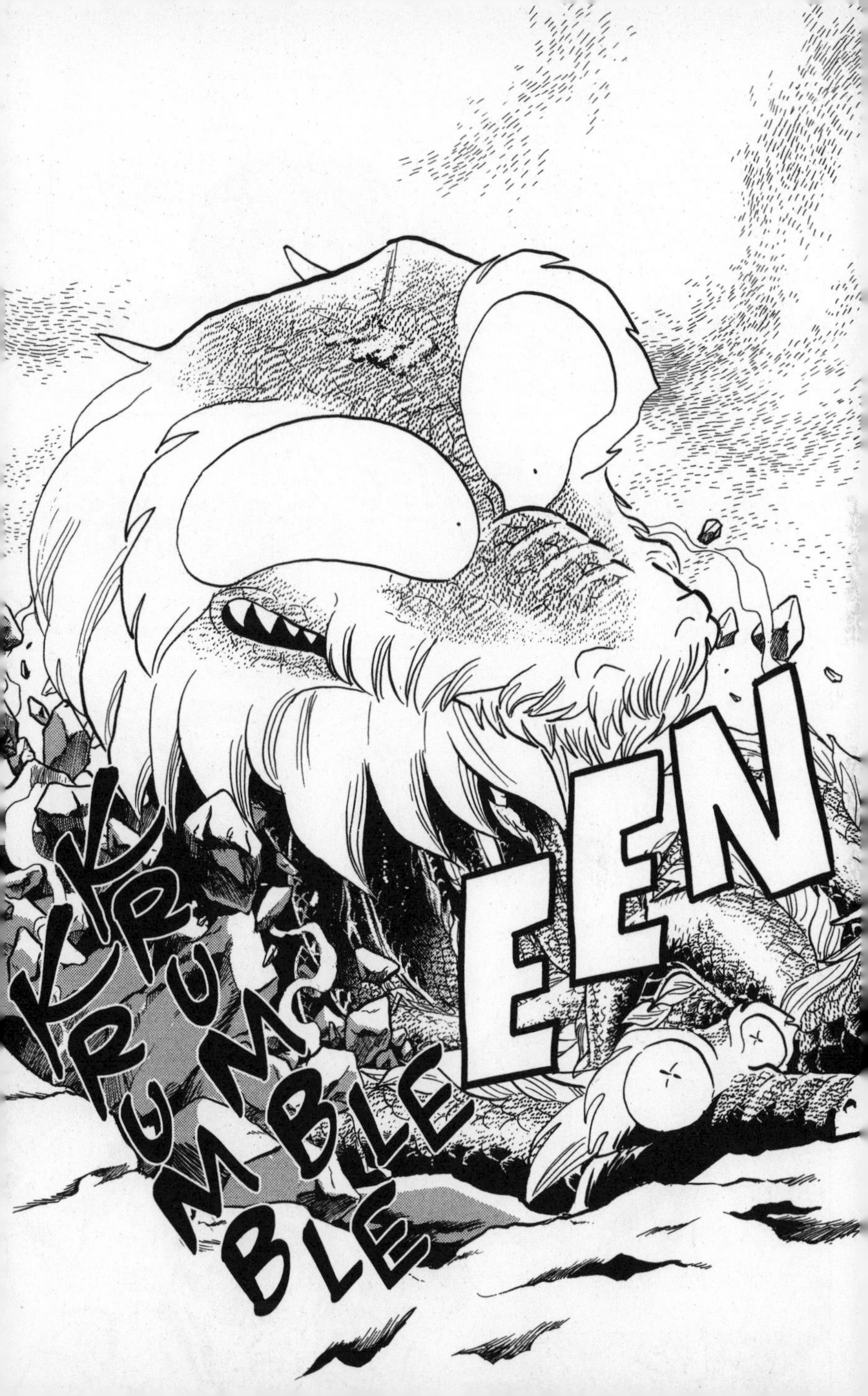
EEN
KRRUMBLE
KRUMBLE

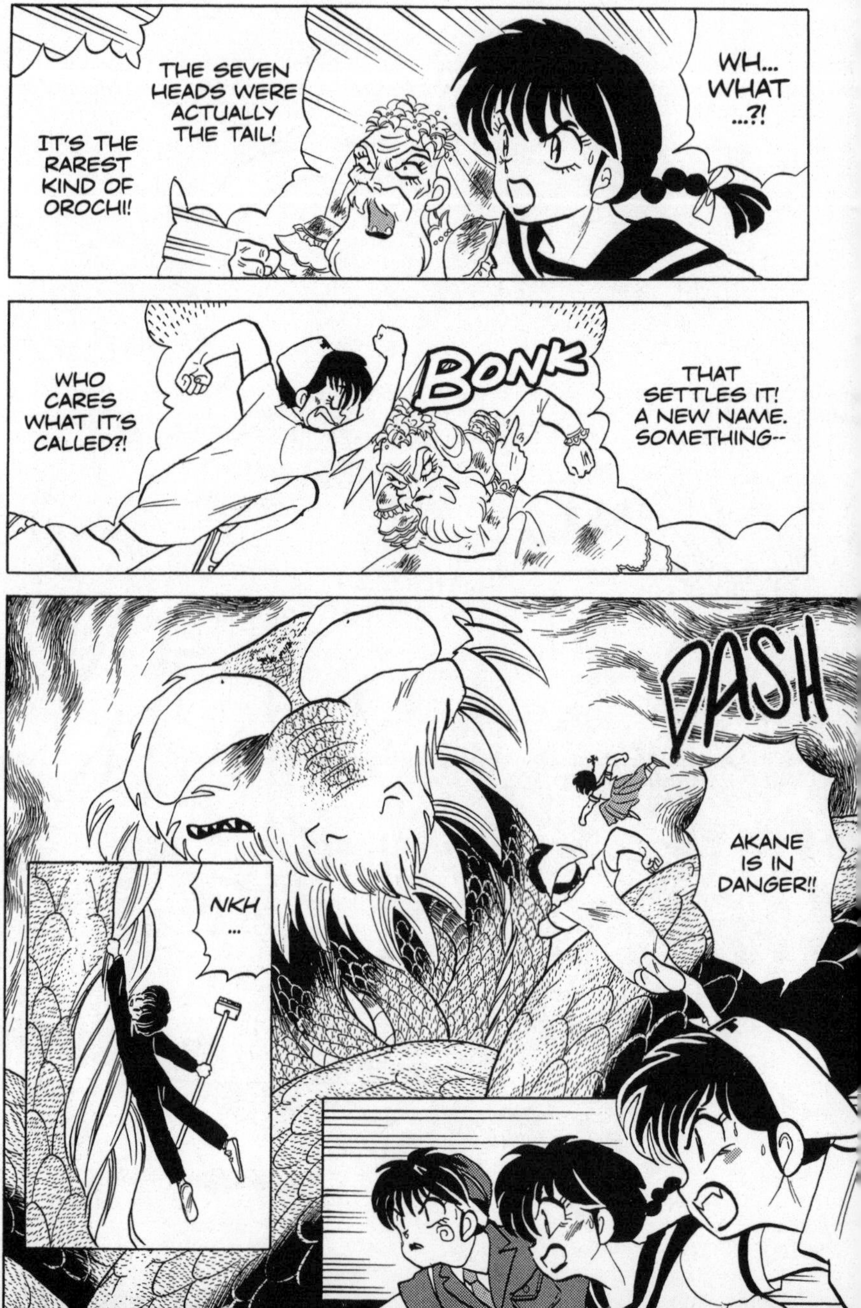
WH... WHAT ...?!
THE SEVEN HEADS WERE ACTUALLY THE TAIL!
IT'S THE RAREST KIND OF OROCHI!
THAT SETTLES IT! A NEW NAME. SOMETHING--
BONK
WHO CARES WHAT IT'S CALLED?!
DASH
AKANE IS IN DANGER!!
NKH ...

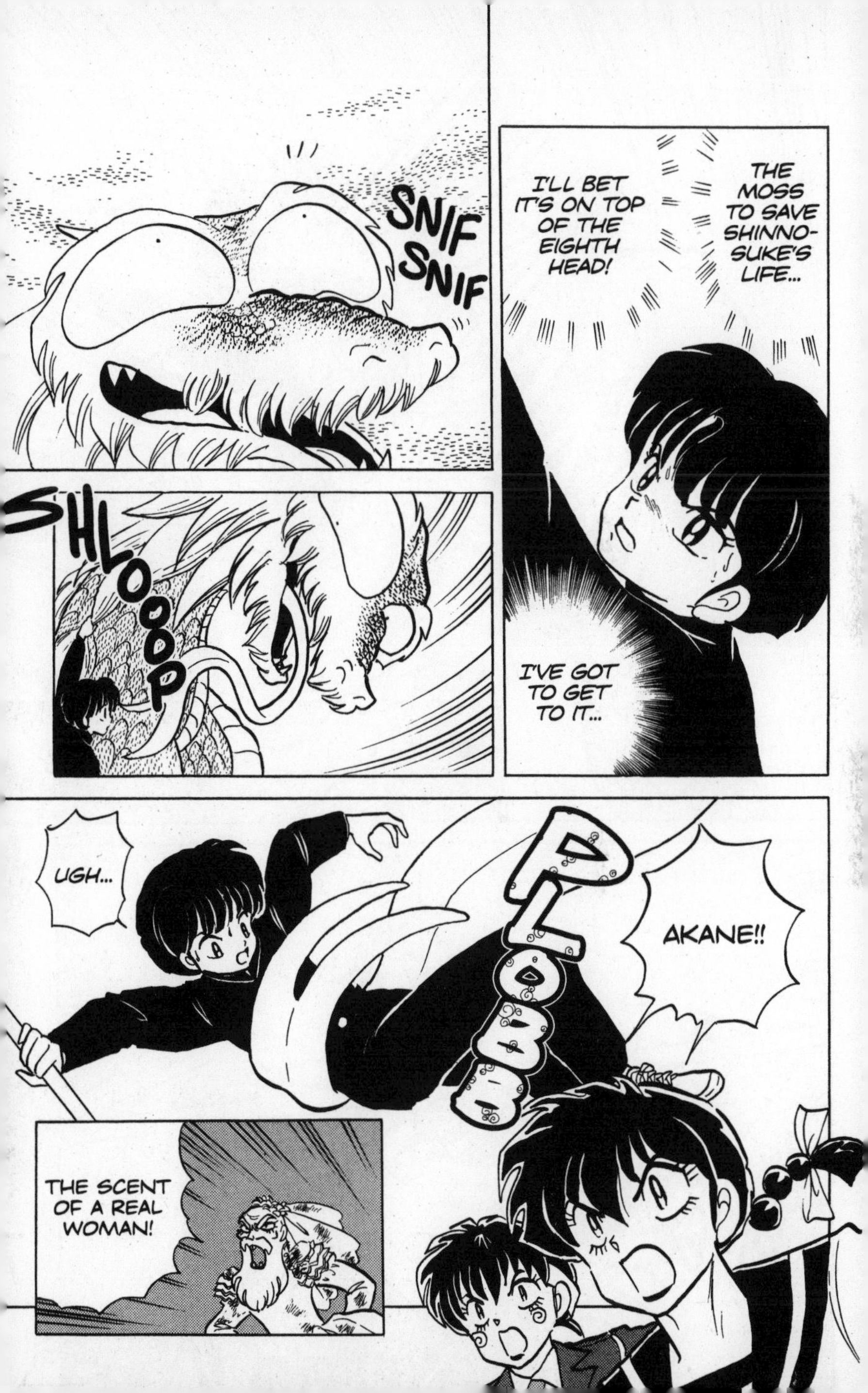
THE MOSS TO SAVE SHINNO-SUKE'S LIFE...
I'LL BET IT'S ON TOP OF THE EIGHTH HEAD!
I'VE GOT TO GET TO IT...
SNIF SNIF
SHLOOOP
AKANE!!
PLOMB
UGH...
THE SCENT OF A REAL WOMAN!

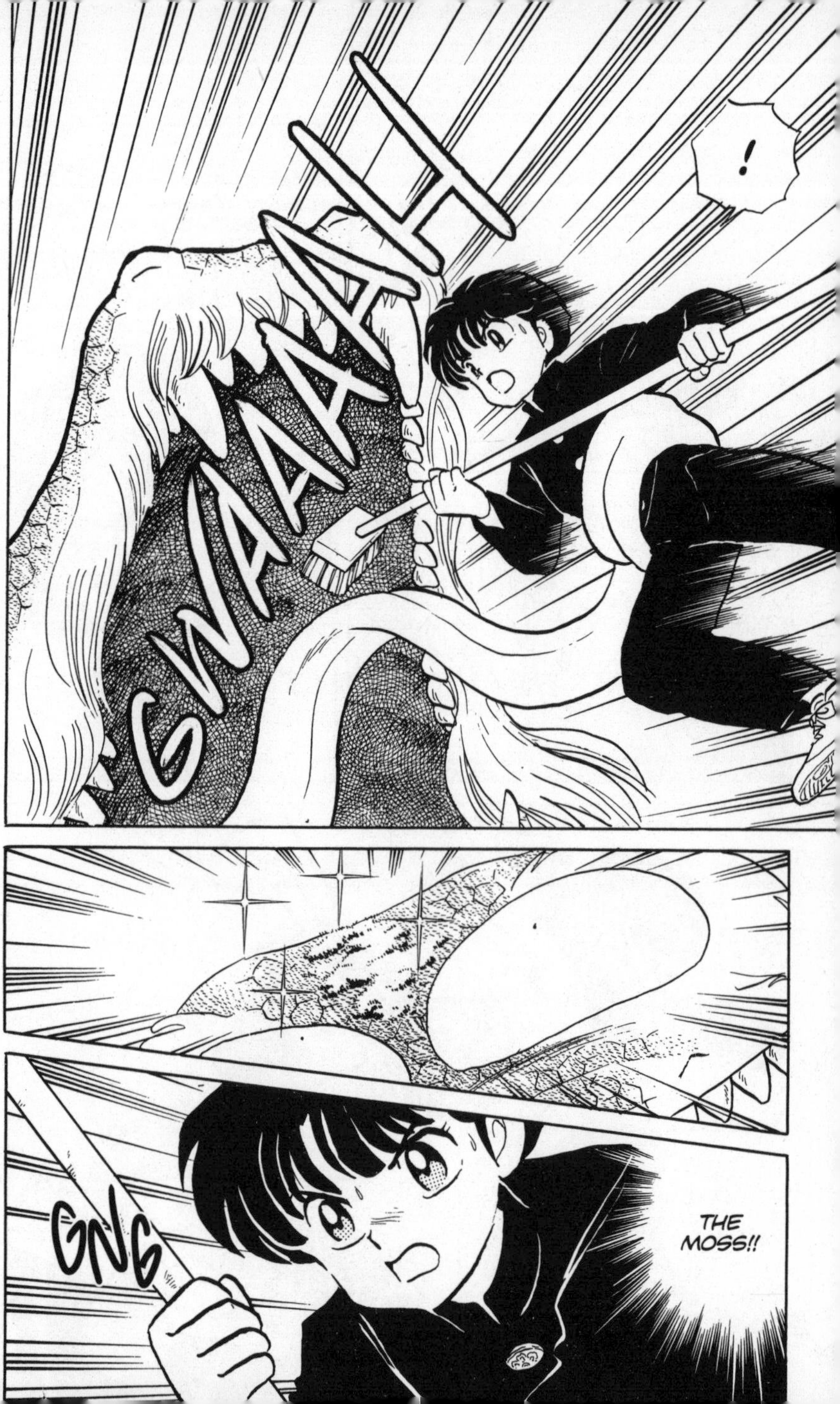
!
GWAAAH
THE MOSS!!
GNG

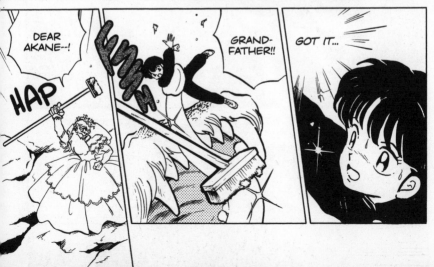

DEAR AKANE--!

HAP

GRAND-FATHER!!

GOT IT...

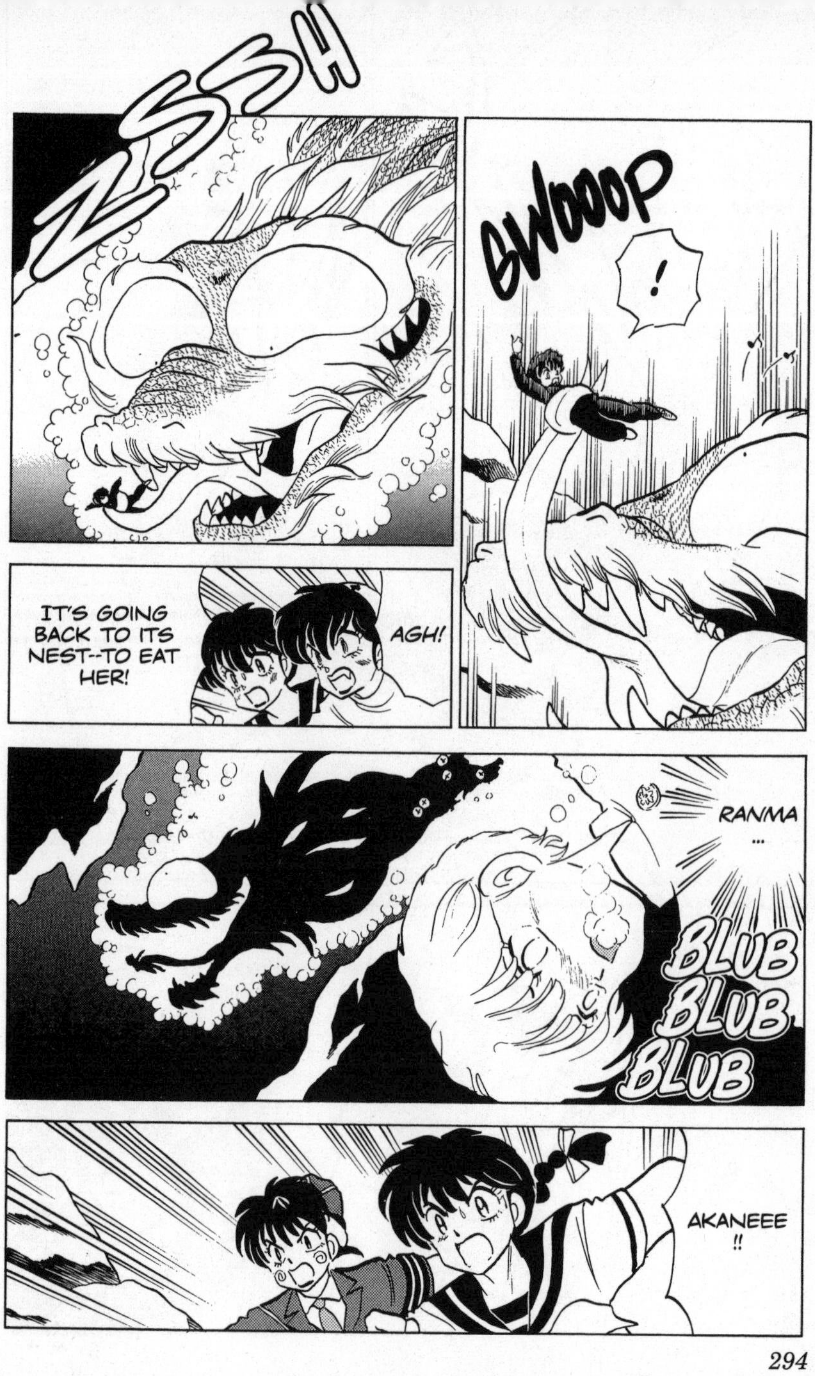
BWOOOP
!
ZSSH
AGH!
IT'S GOING BACK TO ITS NEST--TO EAT HER!
RANMA ...
BLUB BLUB BLUB
AKANEEE !!

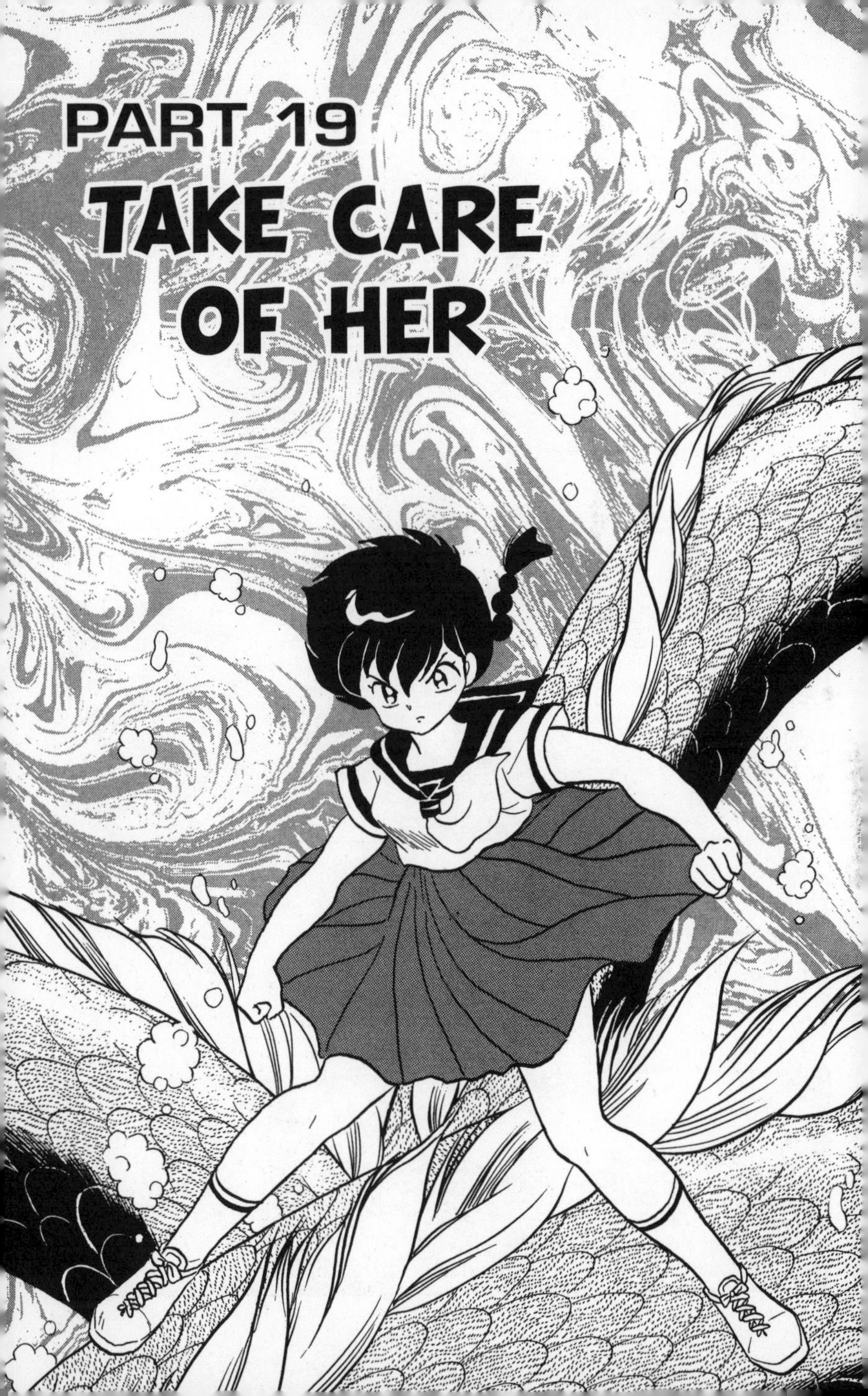
PART 19
TAKE CARE OF HER

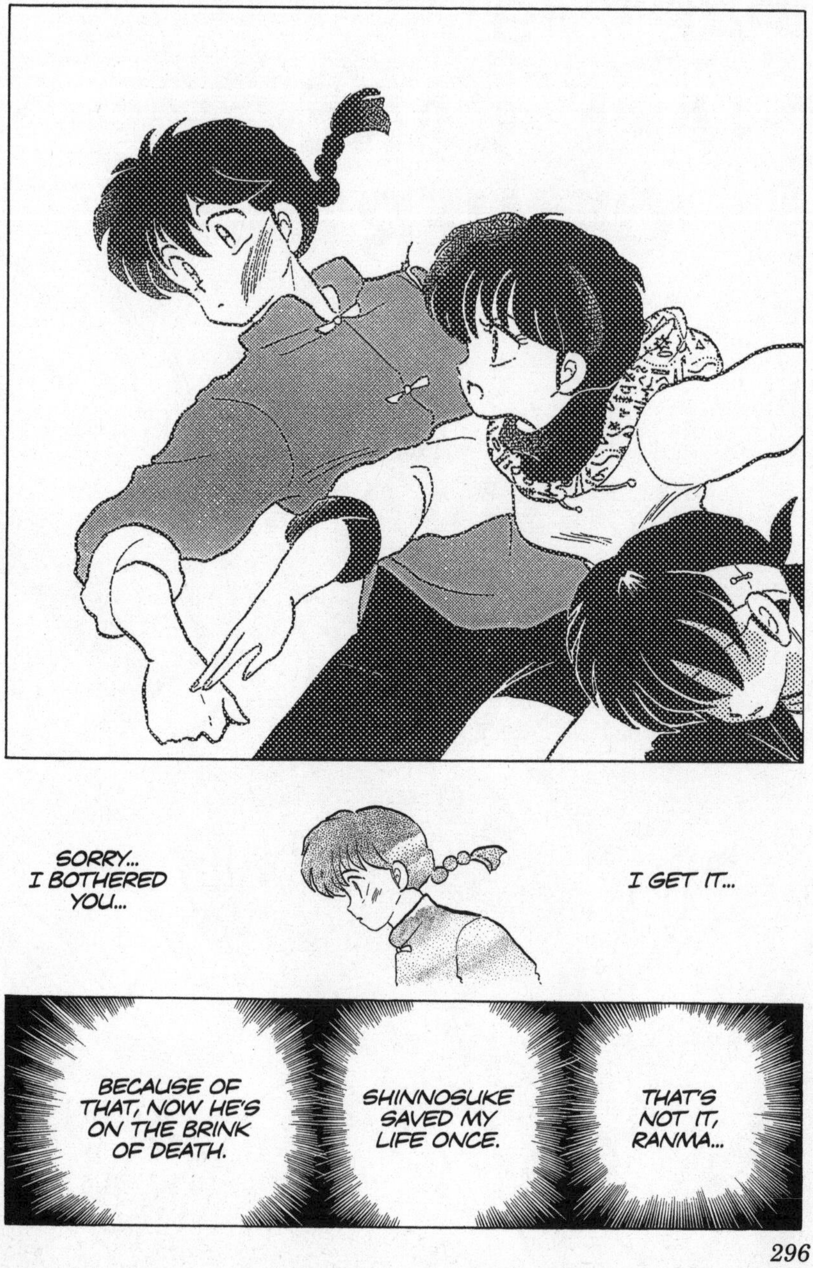
I GET IT...
SORRY... I BOTHERED YOU...
THAT'S NOT IT, RANMA...
SHINNOSUKE SAVED MY LIFE ONCE.
BECAUSE OF THAT, NOW HE'S ON THE BRINK OF DEATH.

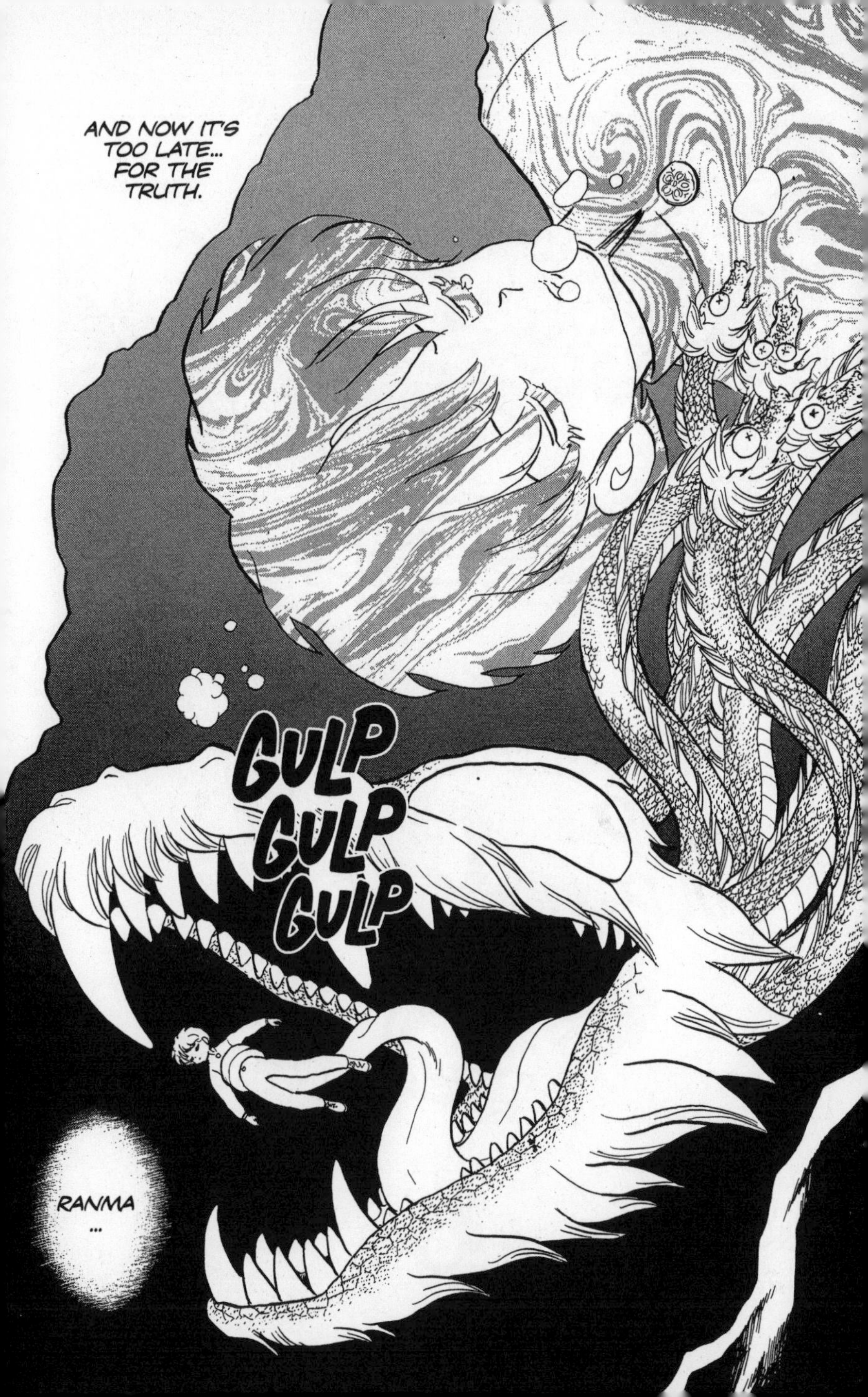
AND NOW IT'S TOO LATE... FOR THE TRUTH.
GULP GULP GULP
RANMA
...

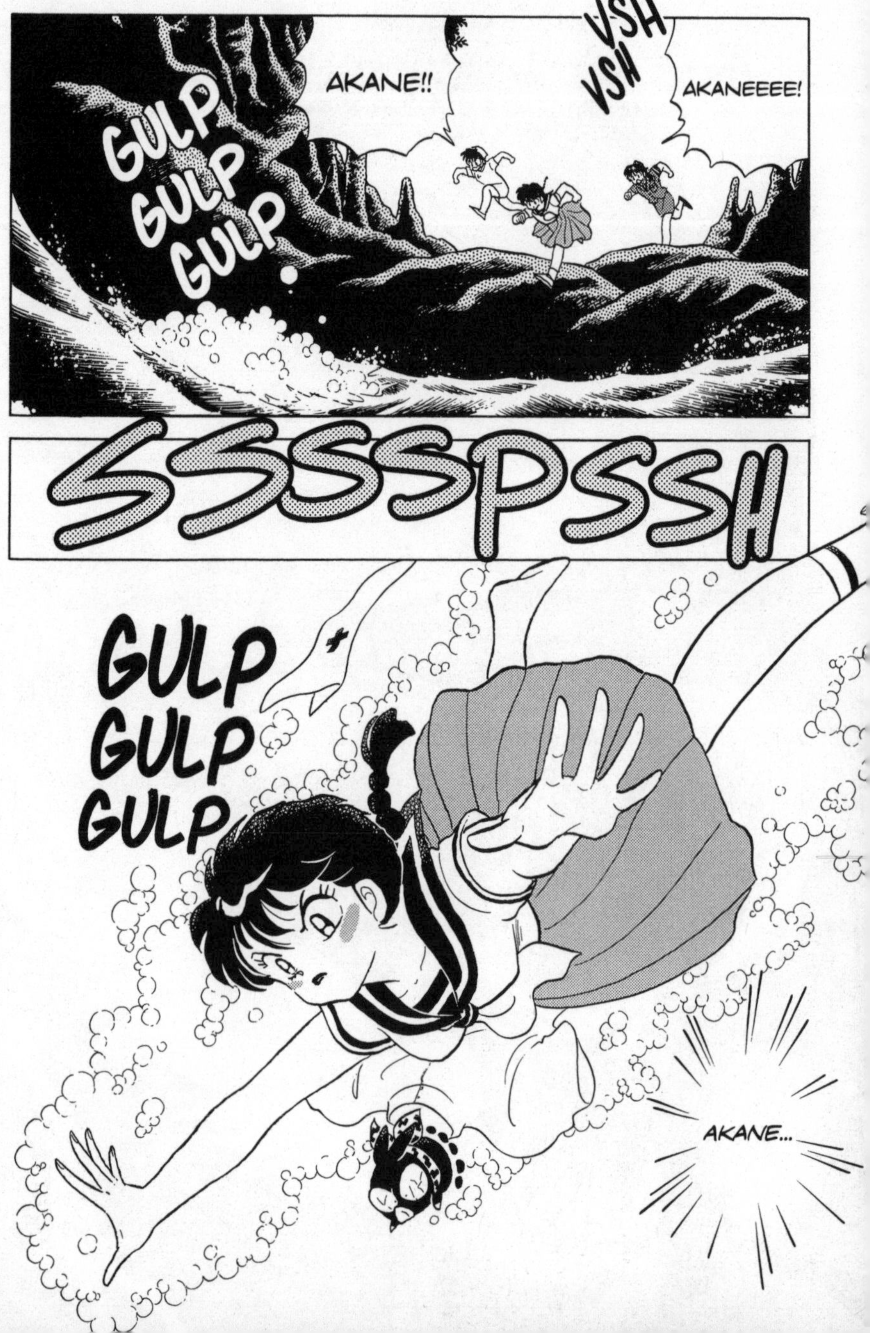
VSH VSH
AKANEEEE!
AKANE!!
GULP GULP GULP
SSSSPSSH
GULP GULP GULP
AKANE...

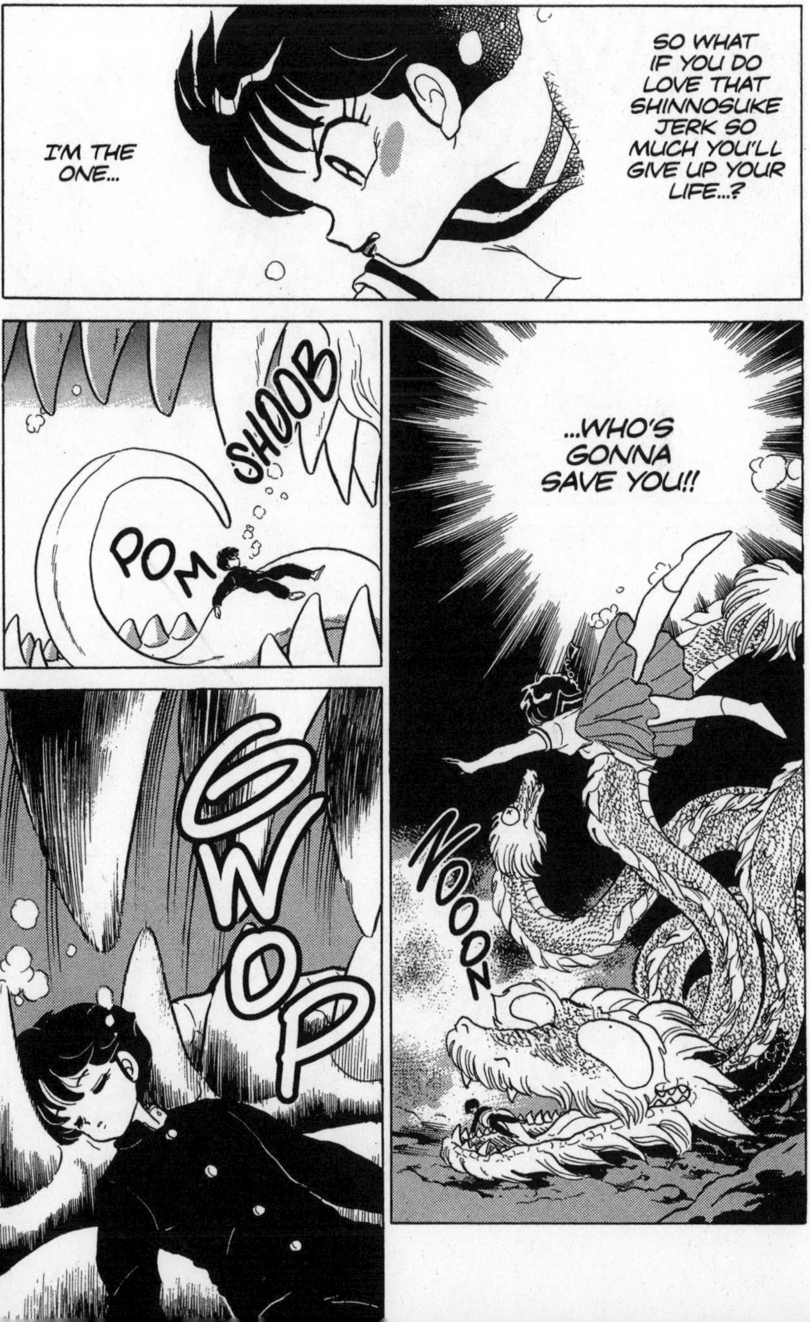
SO WHAT IF YOU DO LOVE THAT SHINNOSUKE JERK SO MUCH YOU'LL GIVE UP YOUR LIFE...?
I'M THE ONE...
...WHO'S GONNA SAVE YOU!!
NOOOON
SHOOB
POM
SWOOP

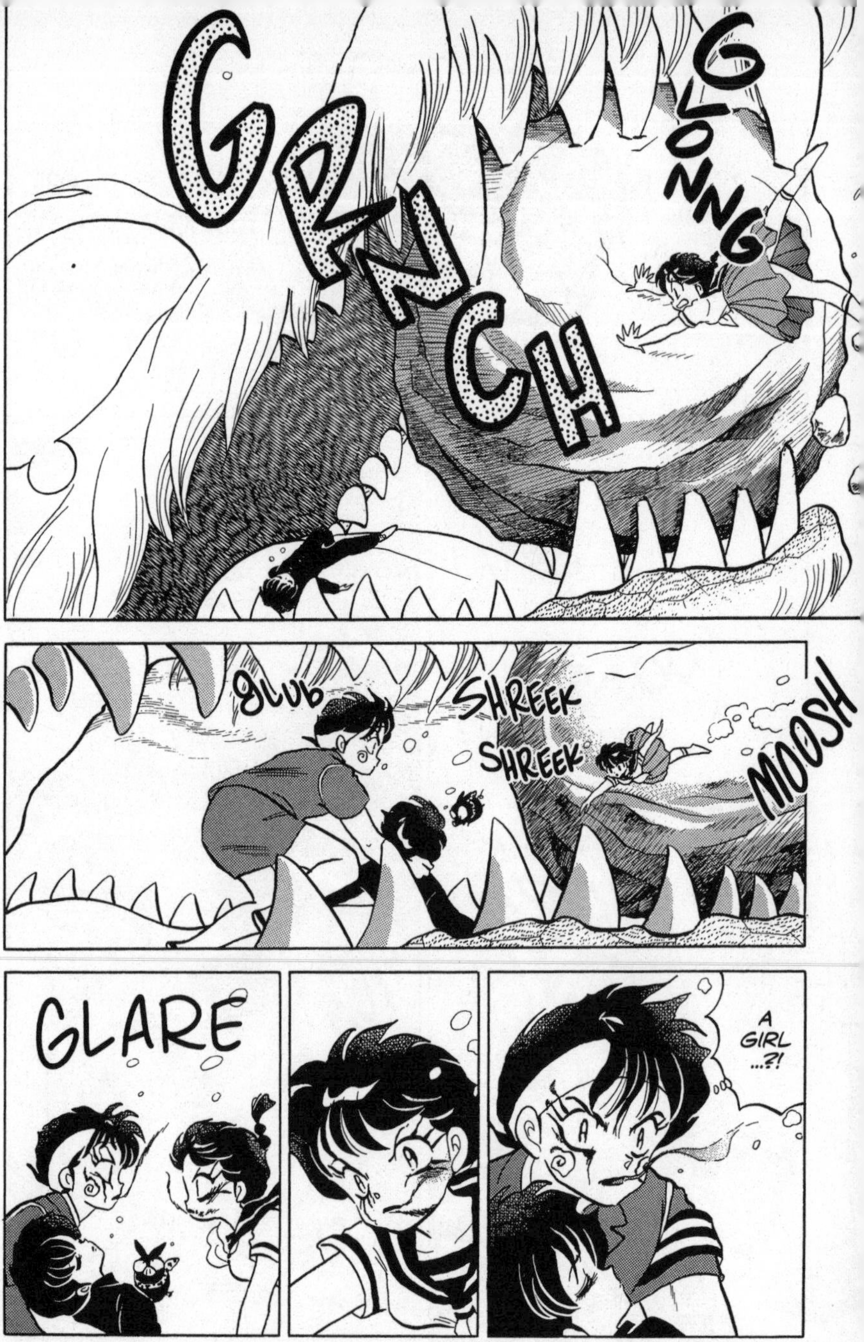
GLONNG
GRNCH
MOOSH
SHREEK
SHREEK
GLUB
A GIRL ...?!
GLARE

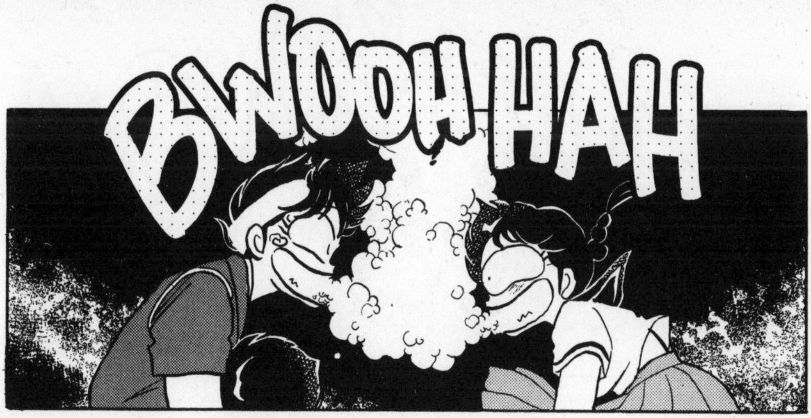
BWOOH HAH

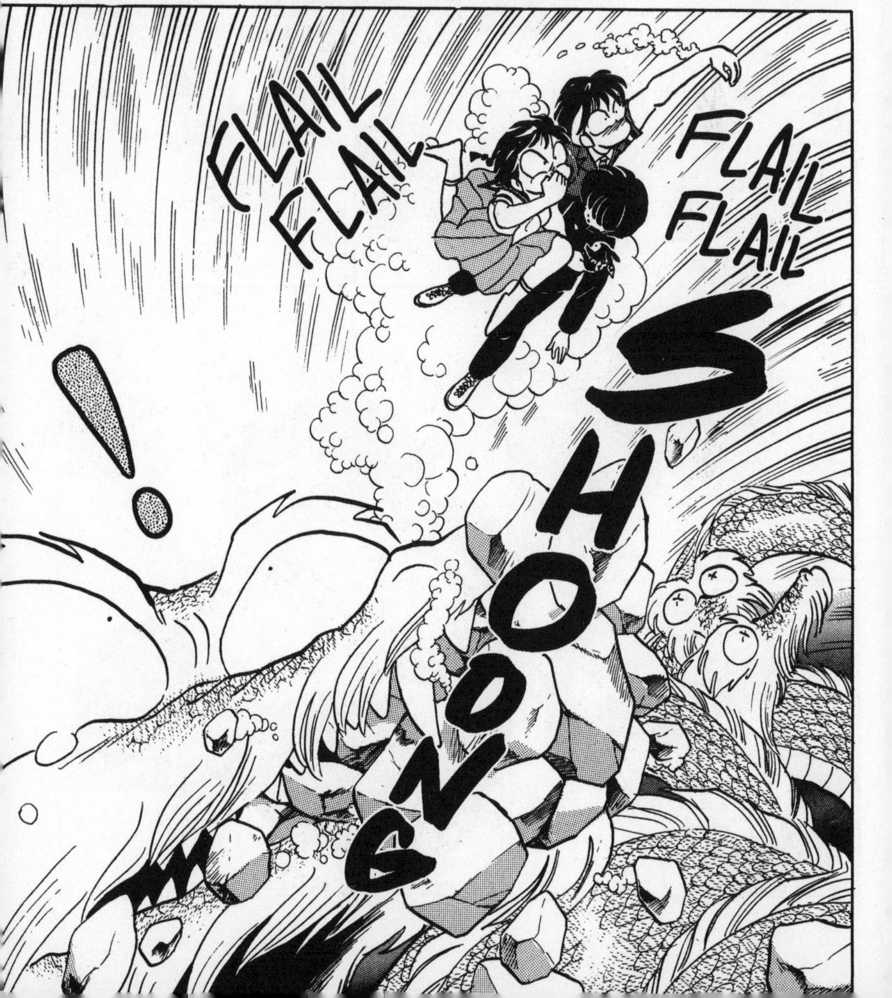
FLAIL FLAIL
SHOONG
FLAIL FLAIL
!

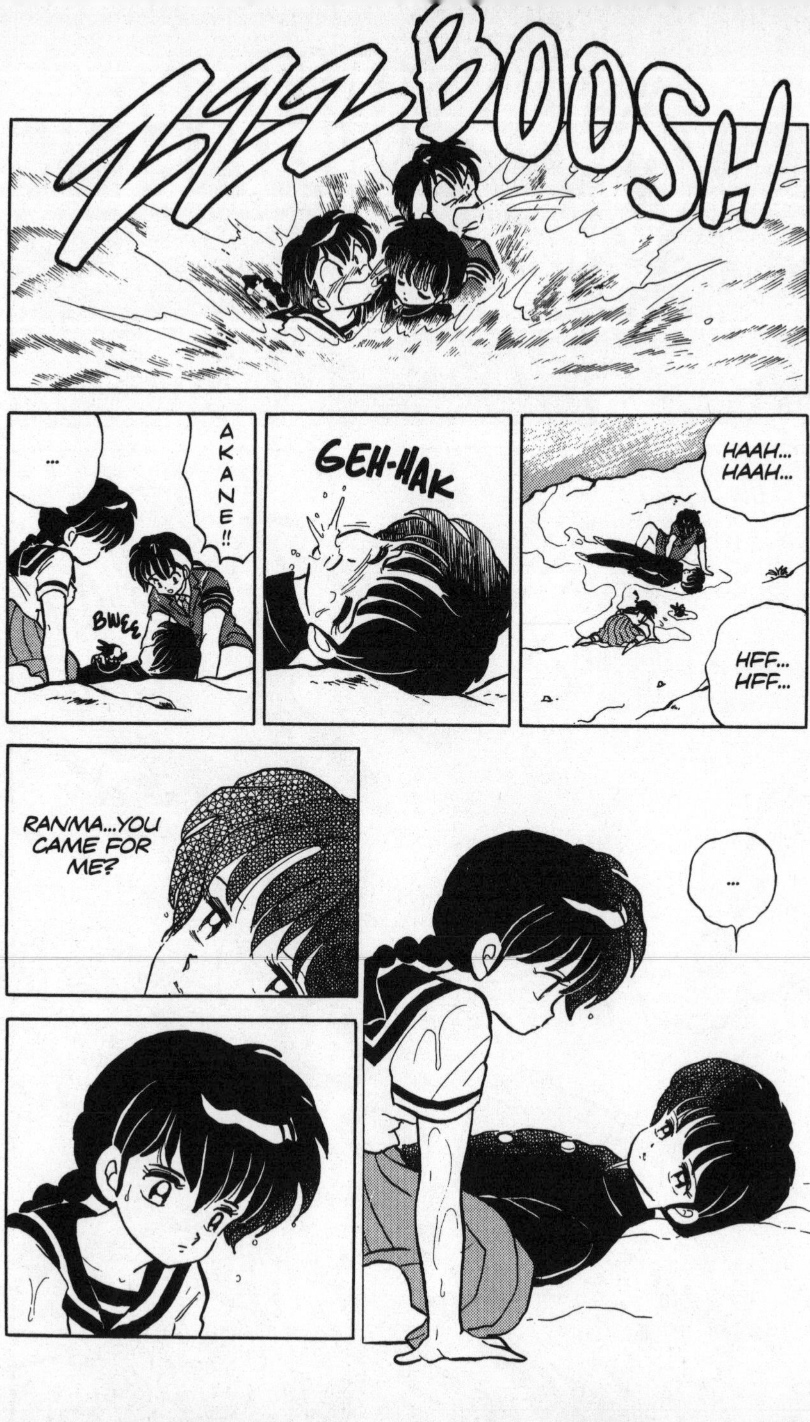
ZZZBOOSH
HAAH... HAAH...
HFF... HFF...
GEH-HAK
AKANE!!
...
BWEE
...
RANMA...YOU CAME FOR ME?

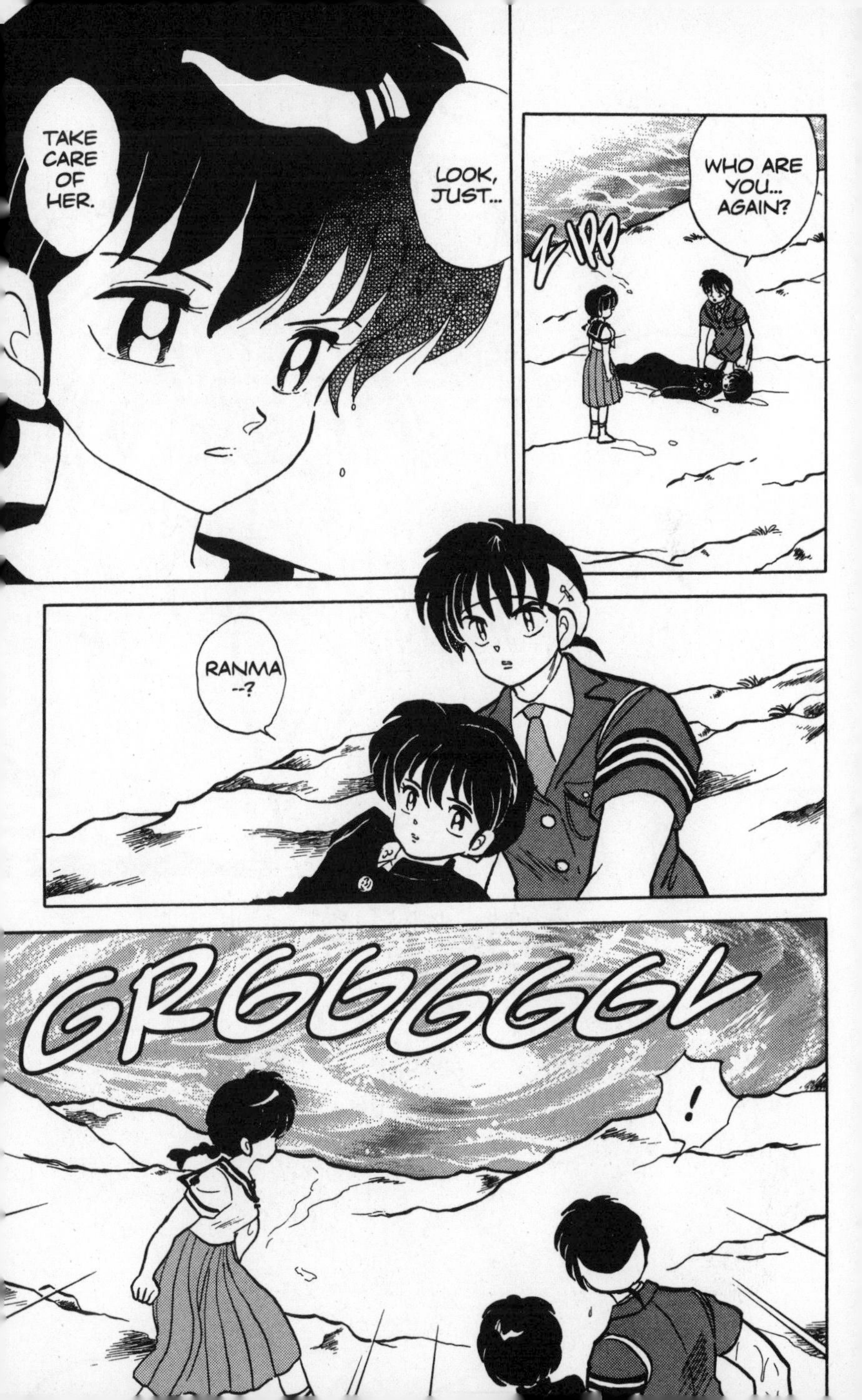
WHO ARE YOU... AGAIN?
ZIPP
LOOK, JUST...
TAKE CARE OF HER.
RANMA --?
GRGGGGGL
!

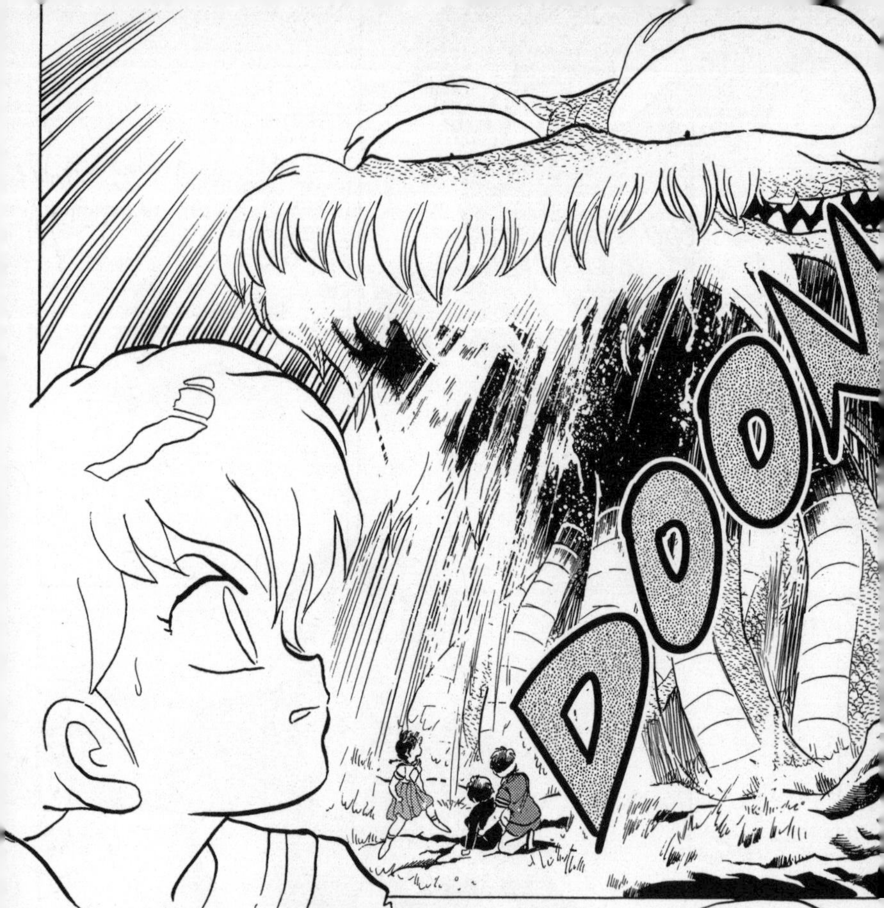
DOOO

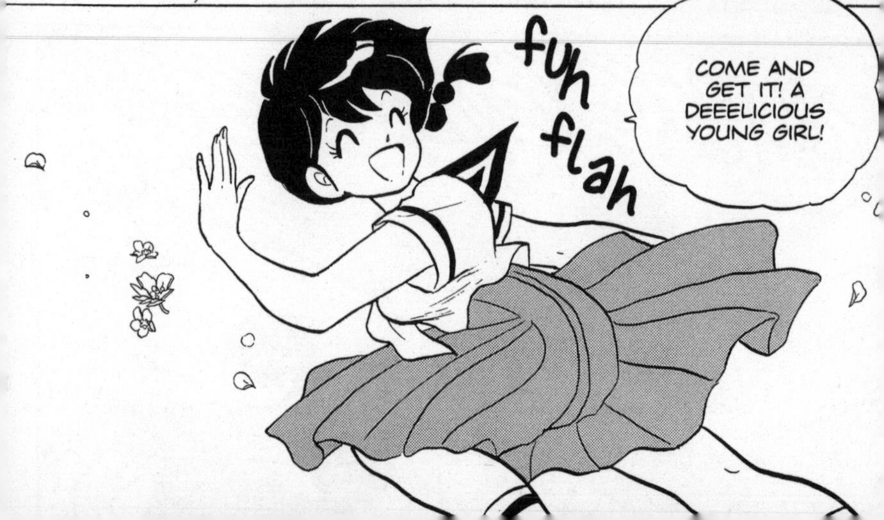
COME AND GET IT! A DEEELICIOUS YOUNG GIRL!
fuh flan

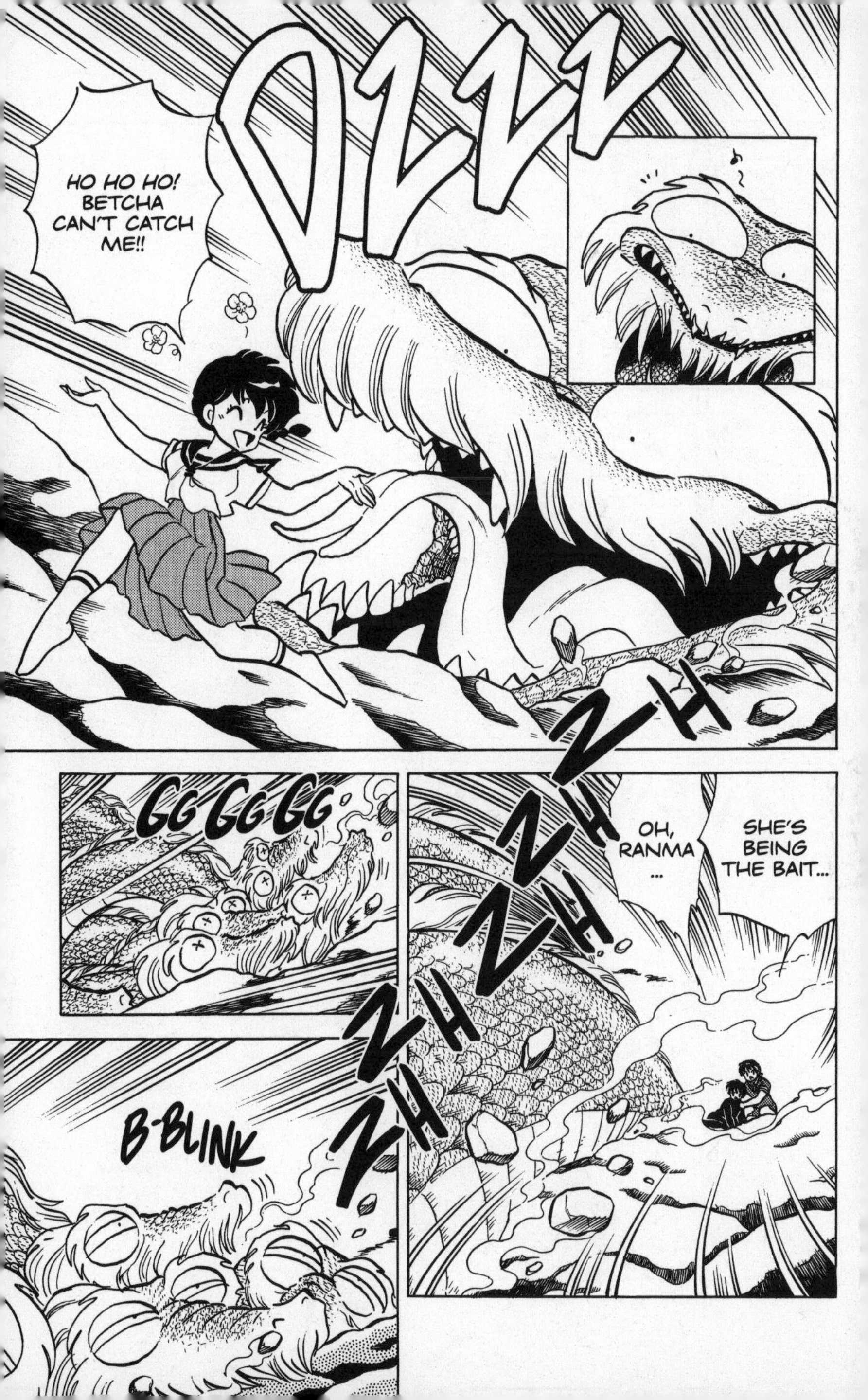
OZZZ
HO HO HO! BETCHA CAN'T CATCH ME!!
SHE'S BEING THE BAIT...
OH, RANMA ...
GG GG GG
B-BLINK

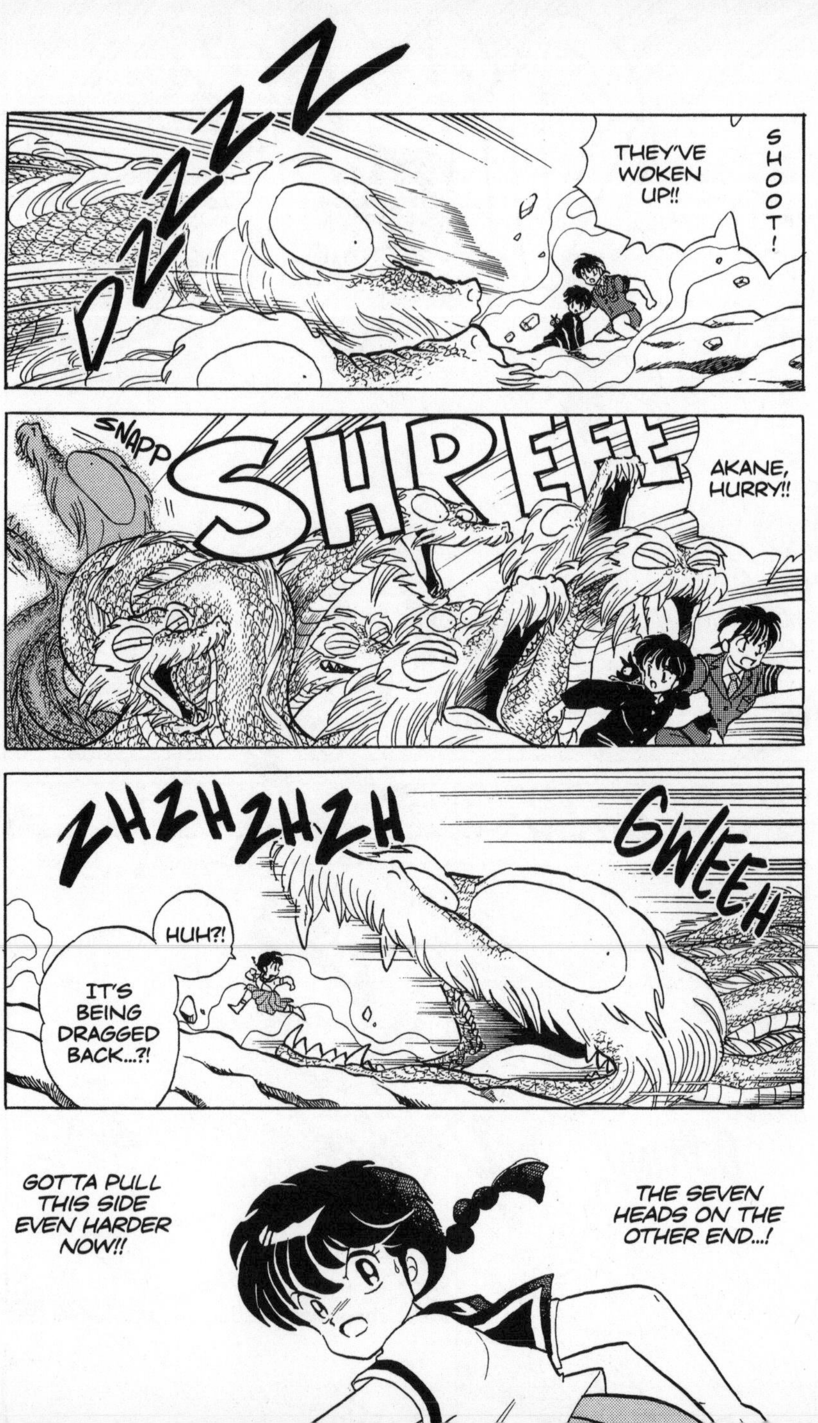

SHOOT!
THEY'VE WOKEN UP!!
DZZZZZ
AKANE, HURRY!!
SHREEE
SNAPP
GWEEH
ZHZHZHZHZH
HUH?!
IT'S BEING DRAGGED BACK...?!
THE SEVEN HEADS ON THE OTHER END...!
GOTTA PULL THIS SIDE EVEN HARDER NOW!!

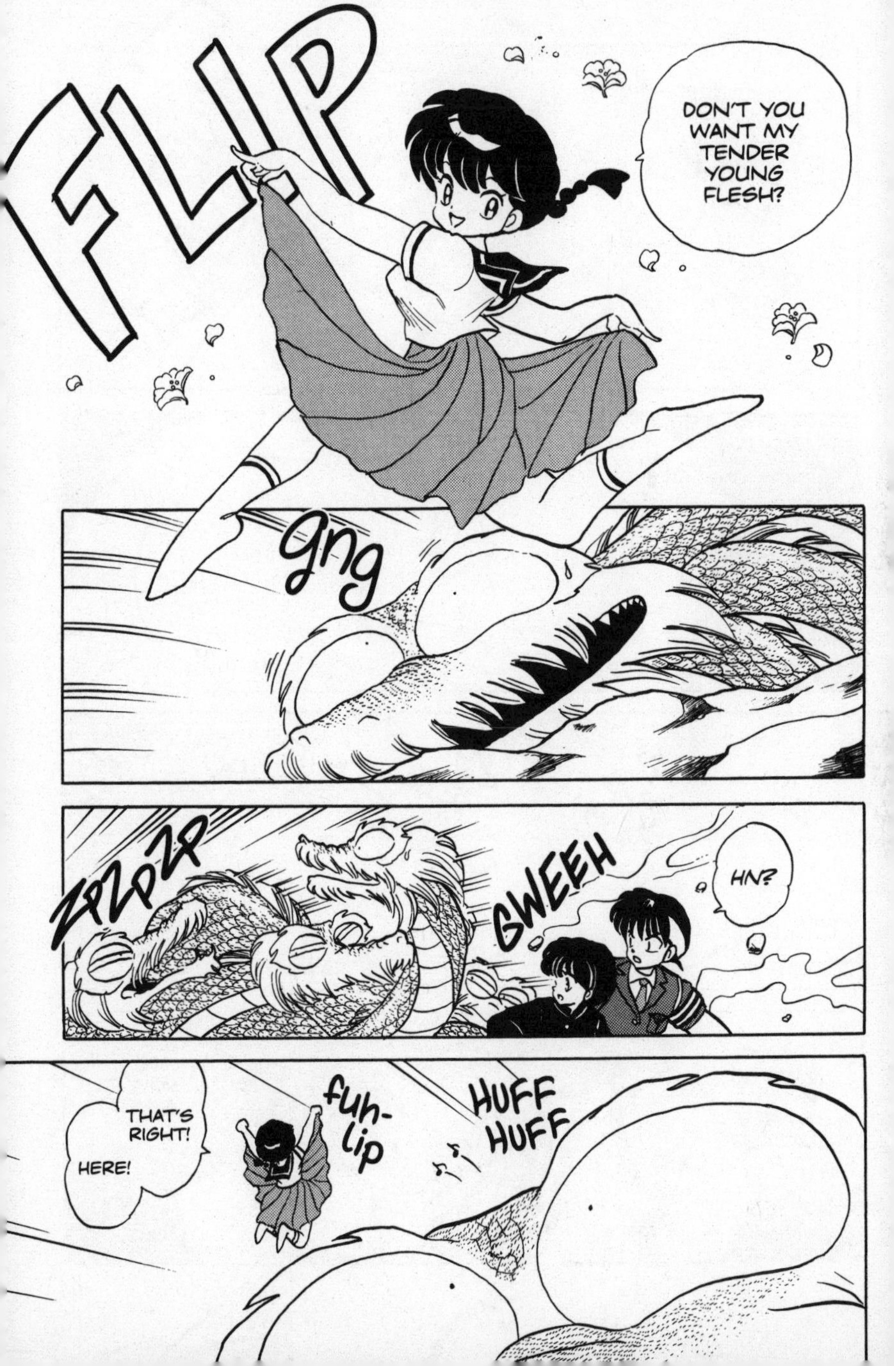
DON'T YOU WANT MY TENDER YOUNG FLESH?
FLIP
gng
HN?
GWEEH
ZPZPZP
HUFF HUFF
fuh-lip
THAT'S RIGHT!
HERE!

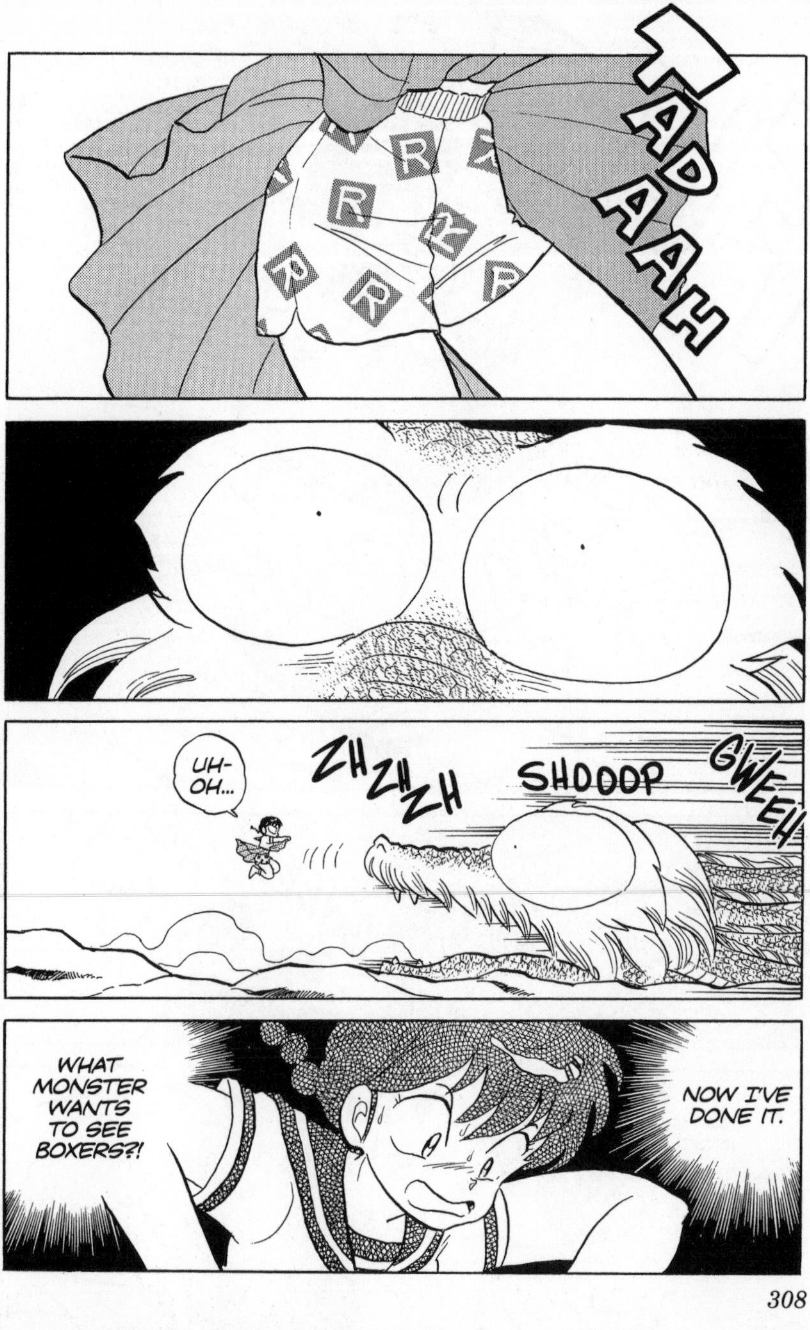
TADAAAH
GWEEH
SHOOOP
ZHZHZH
UH-OH...
NOW I'VE DONE IT.
WHAT MONSTER WANTS TO SEE BOXERS?!

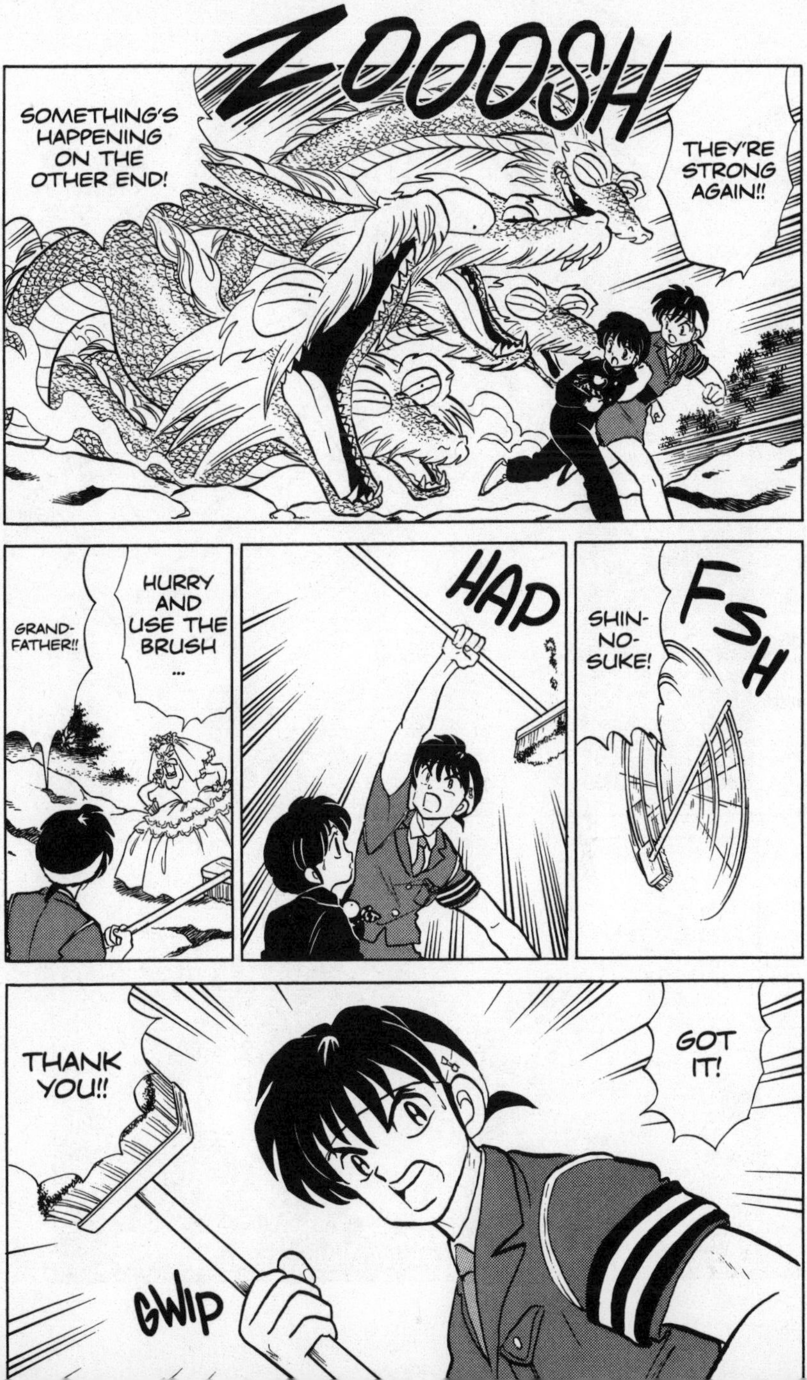
ZOOOSH
THEY'RE STRONG AGAIN!!
SOMETHING'S HAPPENING ON THE OTHER END!
FSH
SHIN-NO-SUKE!
HAP
HURRY AND USE THE BRUSH ...
GRAND-FATHER!!
GOT IT!
THANK YOU!!
GWIP

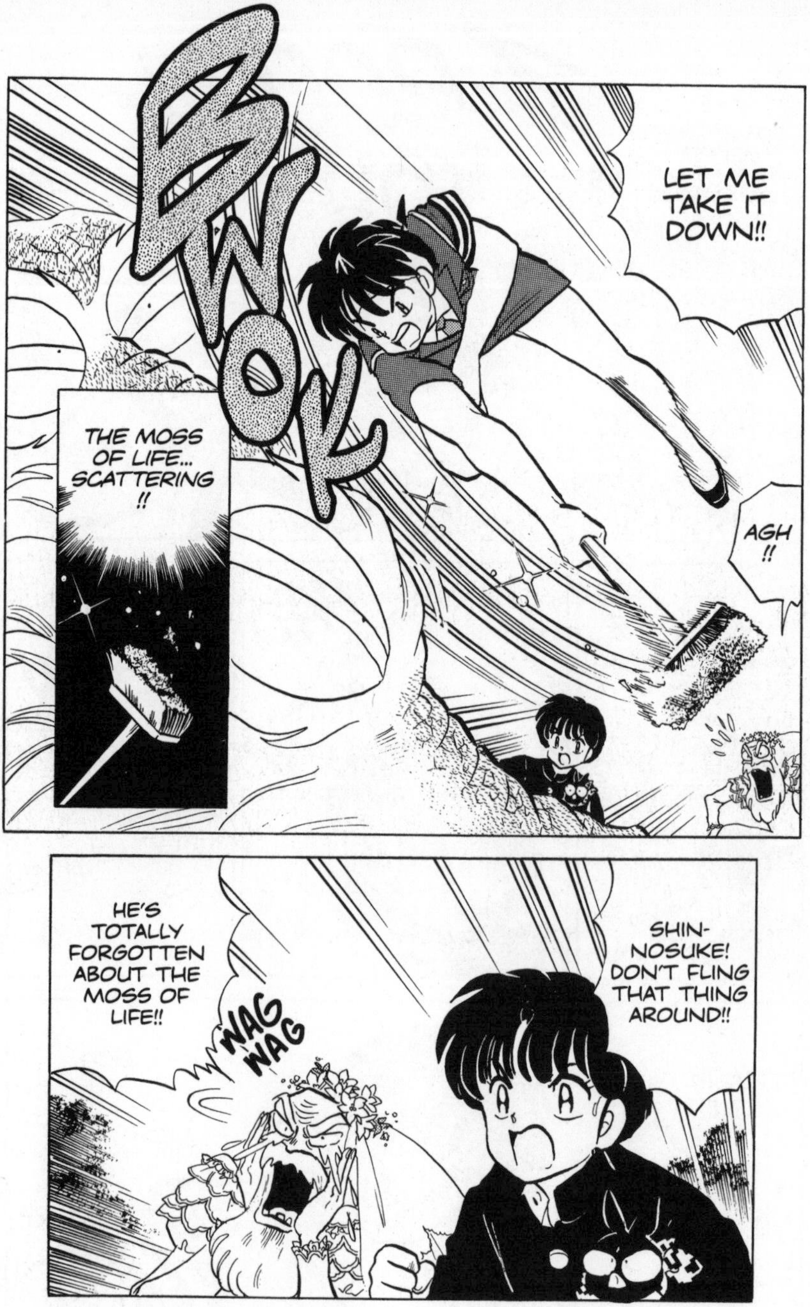
LET ME TAKE IT DOWN!!
BWOK
AGH !!
THE MOSS OF LIFE... SCATTERING !!
SHIN-NOSUKE! DON'T FLING THAT THING AROUND!!
HE'S TOTALLY FORGOTTEN ABOUT THE MOSS OF LIFE!!
WAG WAG

PART 20
BLOW YOUR HORN!

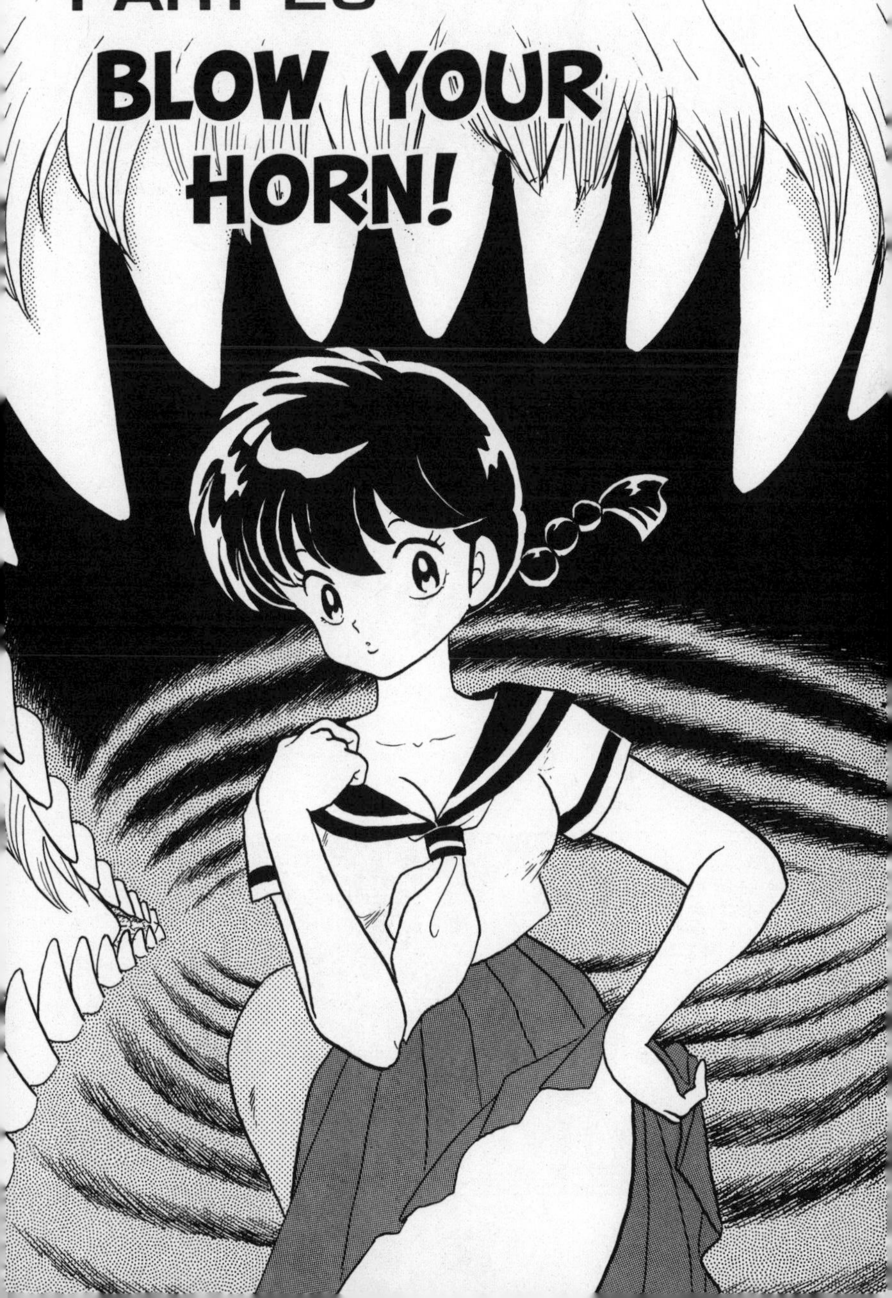

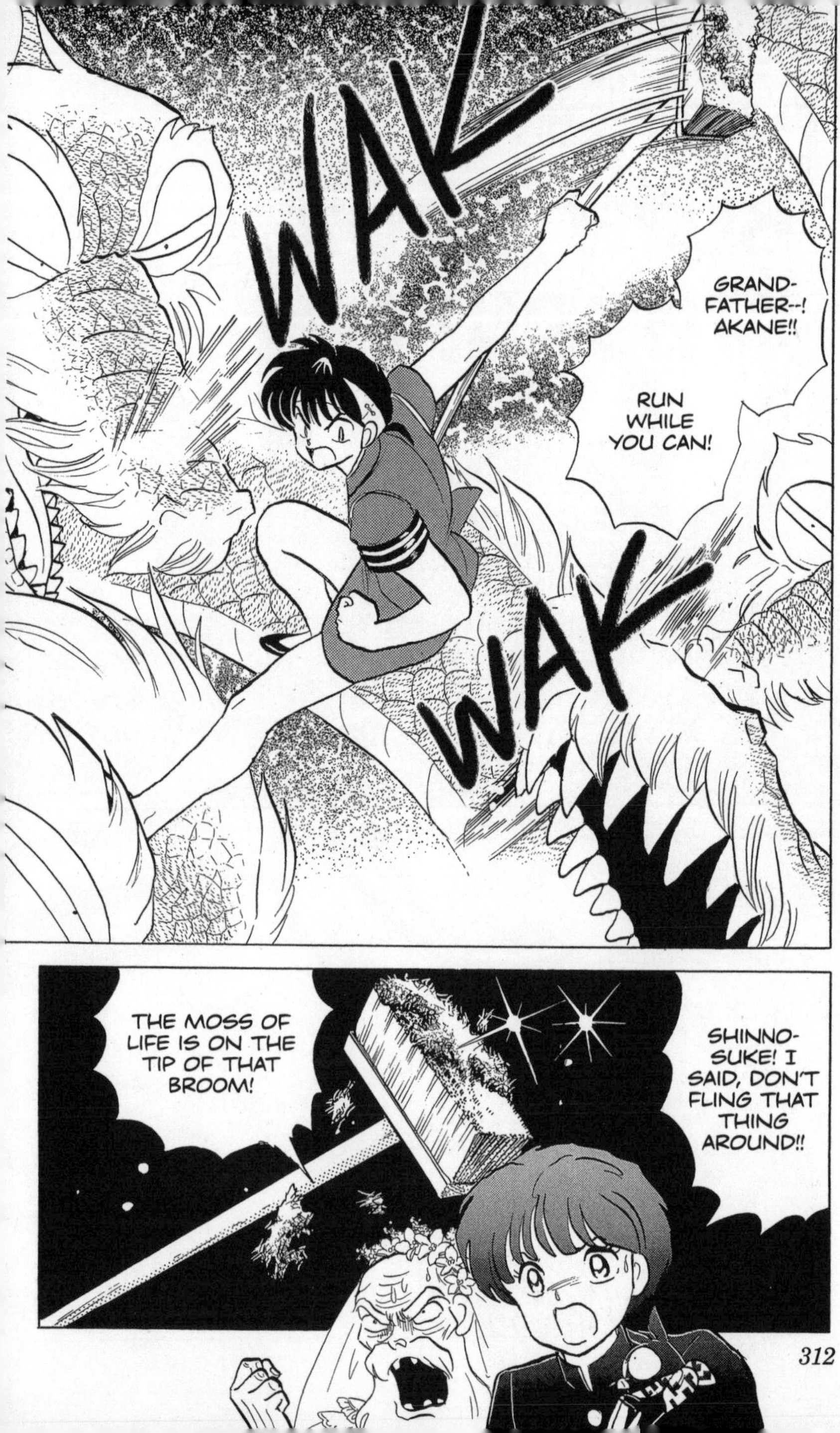
WAK
GRAND-FATHER--! AKANE!!
RUN WHILE YOU CAN!
WAK
SHINNO-SUKE! I SAID, DON'T FLING THAT THING AROUND!!
THE MOSS OF LIFE IS ON THE TIP OF THAT BROOM!

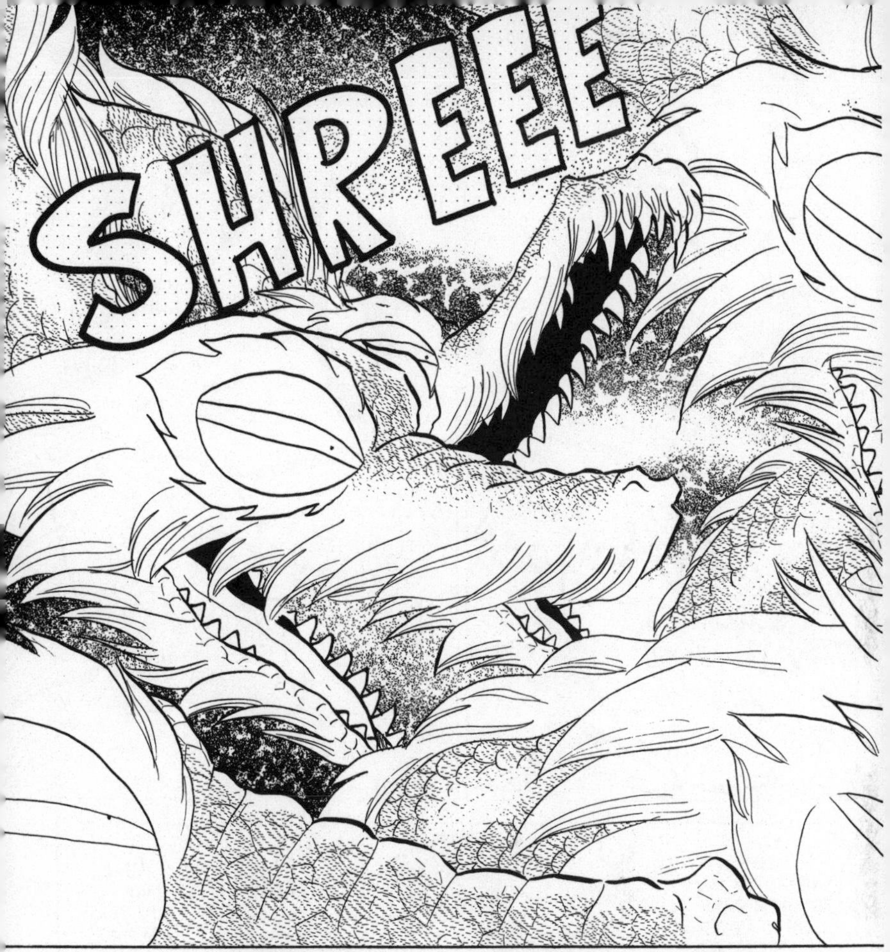
SHREEE

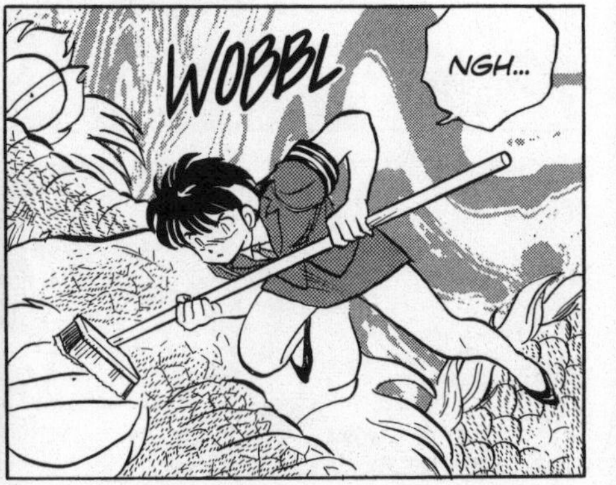
WOBBL
NGH...

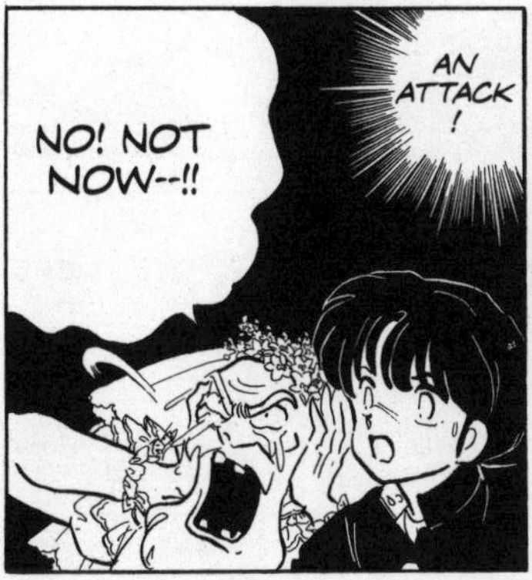
AN ATTACK!
NO! NOT NOW--!!

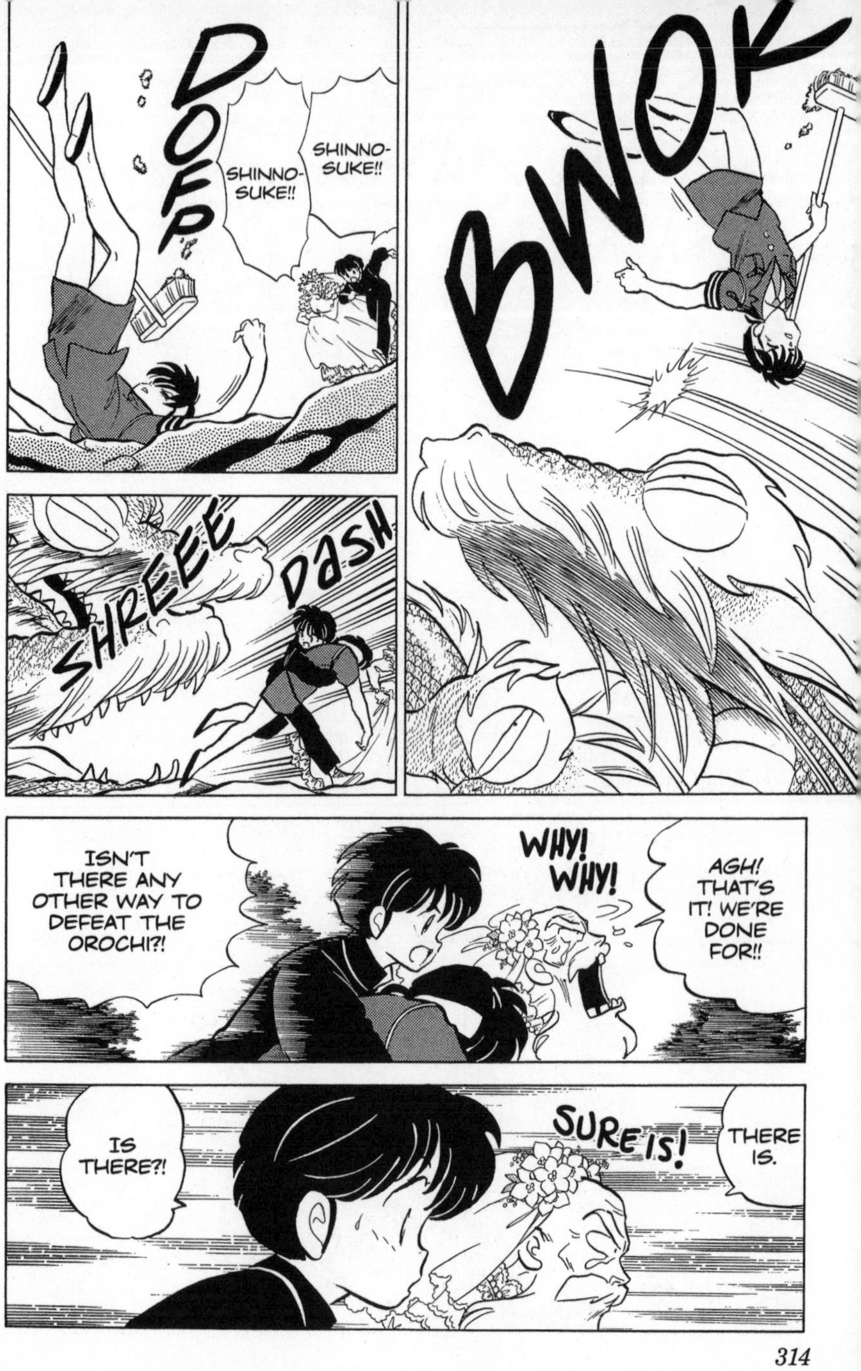
BWOK
SHINNO-SUKE!!
SHINNO-SUKE!!
DOFP
DASH
SHREEE
AGH! THAT'S IT! WE'RE DONE FOR!!
WHY! WHY!
ISN'T THERE ANY OTHER WAY TO DEFEAT THE OROCHI?!
THERE IS.
SURE IS!
IS THERE?!

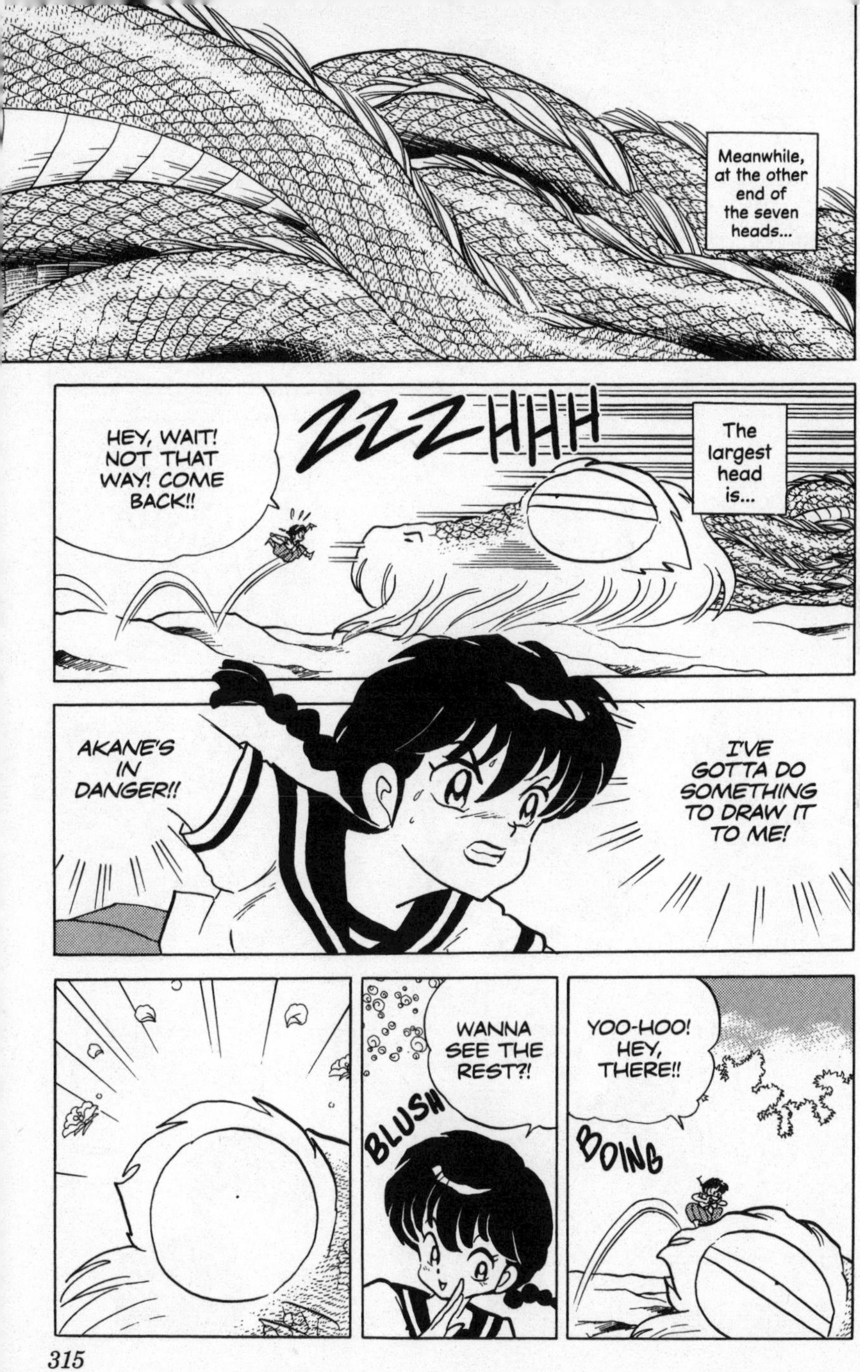
Meanwhile, at the other end of the seven heads...
The largest head is...
ZZZHHH
HEY, WAIT! NOT THAT WAY! COME BACK!!
I'VE GOTTA DO SOMETHING TO DRAW IT TO ME!
AKANE'S IN DANGER!!
YOO-HOO! HEY, THERE!!
BOING
WANNA SEE THE REST?!
BLUSH

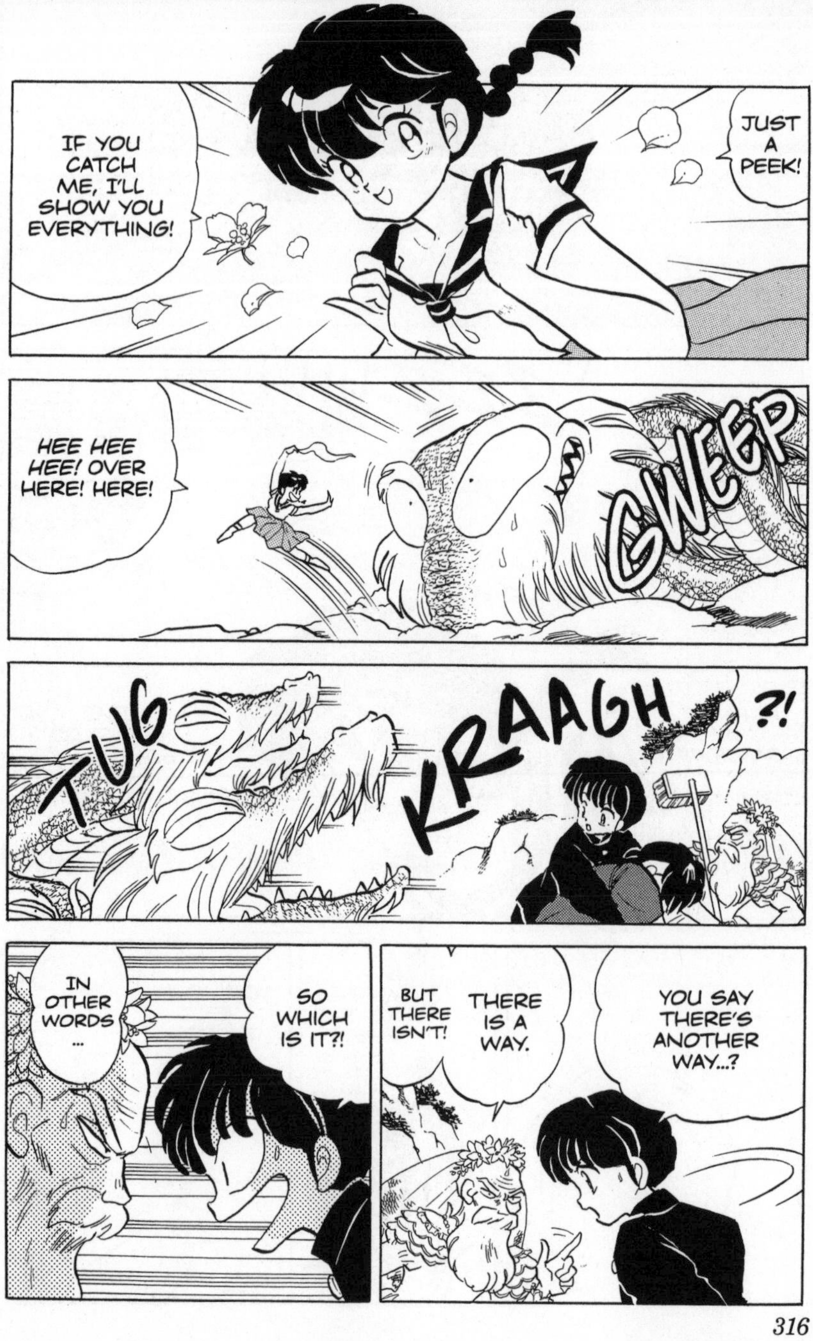
IF YOU CATCH ME, I'LL SHOW YOU EVERYTHING!
JUST A PEEK!
GWEEP
HEE HEE HEE! OVER HERE! HERE!
?!
KRAAGH
TUG
YOU SAY THERE'S ANOTHER WAY...?
THERE IS A WAY.
BUT THERE ISN'T!
SO WHICH IS IT?!
IN OTHER WORDS ...

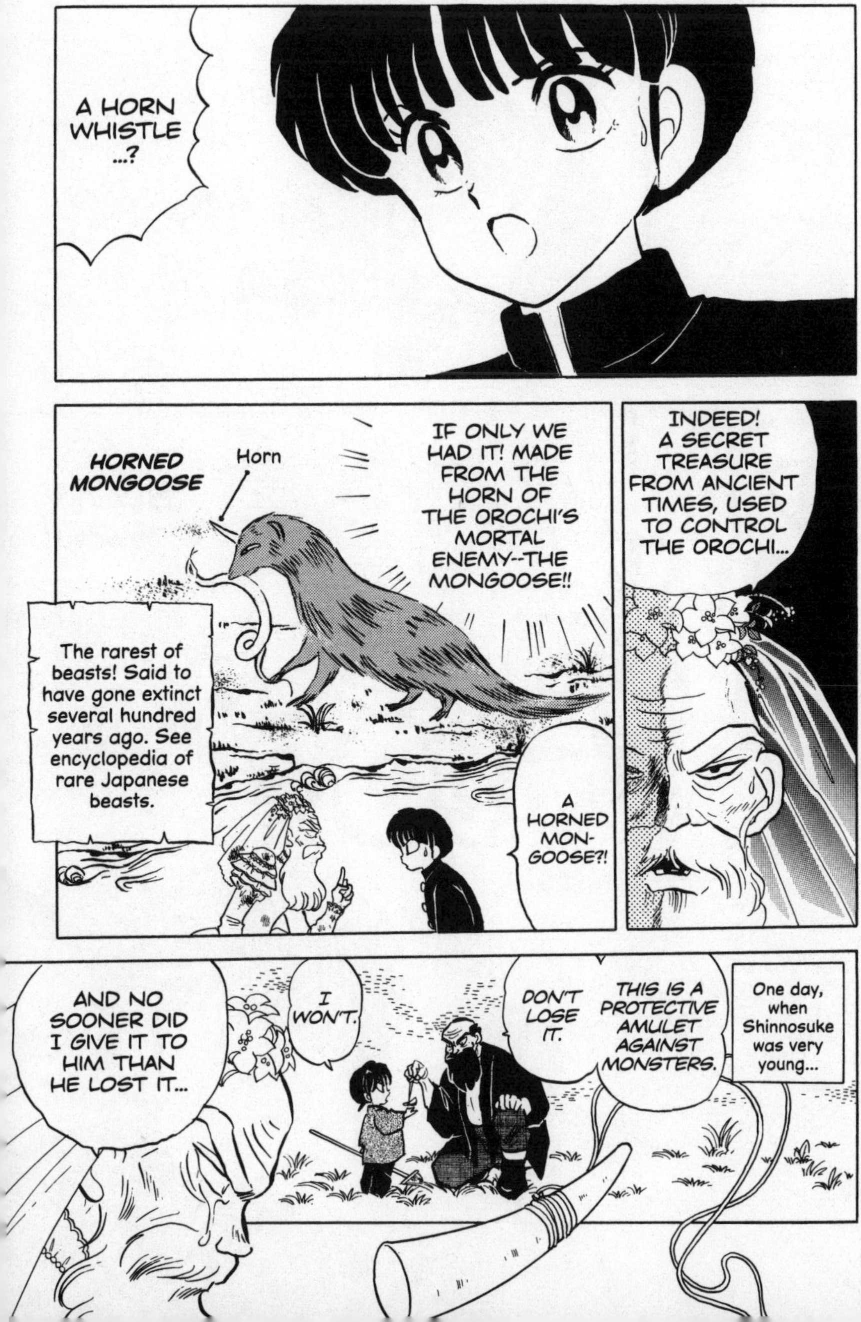
A HORN WHISTLE ...?
INDEED! A SECRET TREASURE FROM ANCIENT TIMES, USED TO CONTROL THE OROCHI...
IF ONLY WE HAD IT! MADE FROM THE HORN OF THE OROCHI'S MORTAL ENEMY--THE MONGOOSE!!
HORNED MONGOOSE
Horn
The rarest of beasts! Said to have gone extinct several hundred years ago. See encyclopedia of rare Japanese beasts.
A HORNED MON-GOOSE?!
One day, when Shinnosuke was very young...
THIS IS A PROTECTIVE AMULET AGAINST MONSTERS.
DON'T LOSE IT.
I WON'T.
AND NO SOONER DID I GIVE IT TO HIM THAN HE LOST IT...

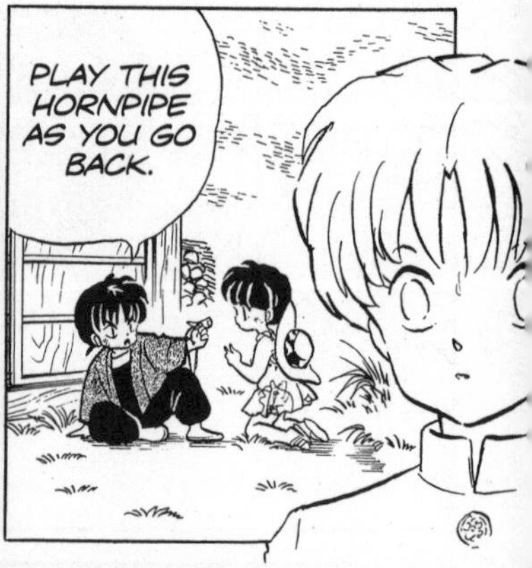
PLAY THIS HORNPIPE AS YOU GO BACK.
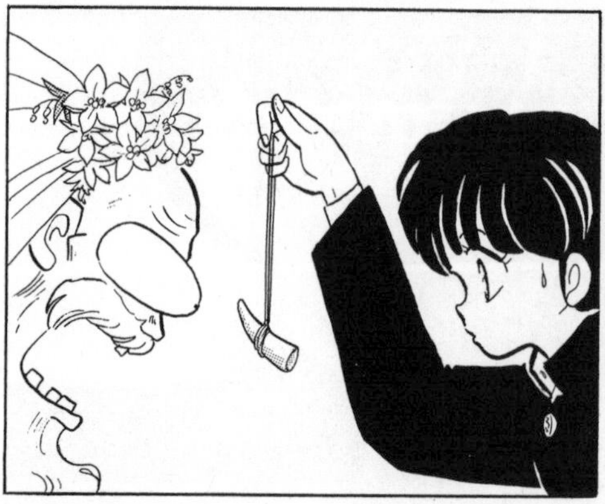
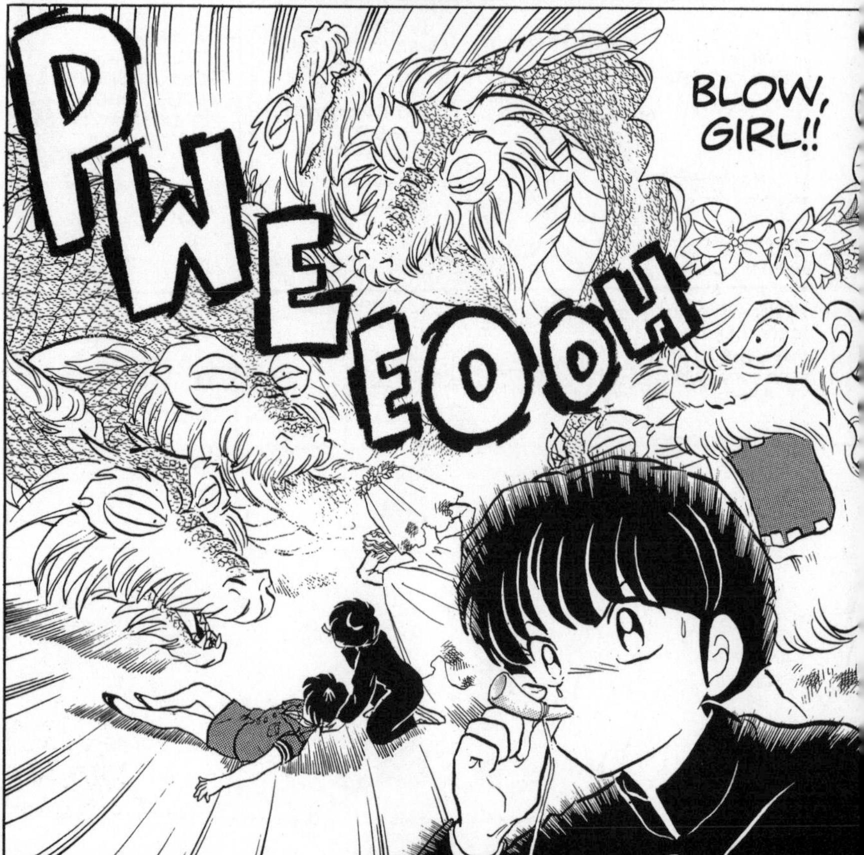
BLOW, GIRL!!
PWEEOOH

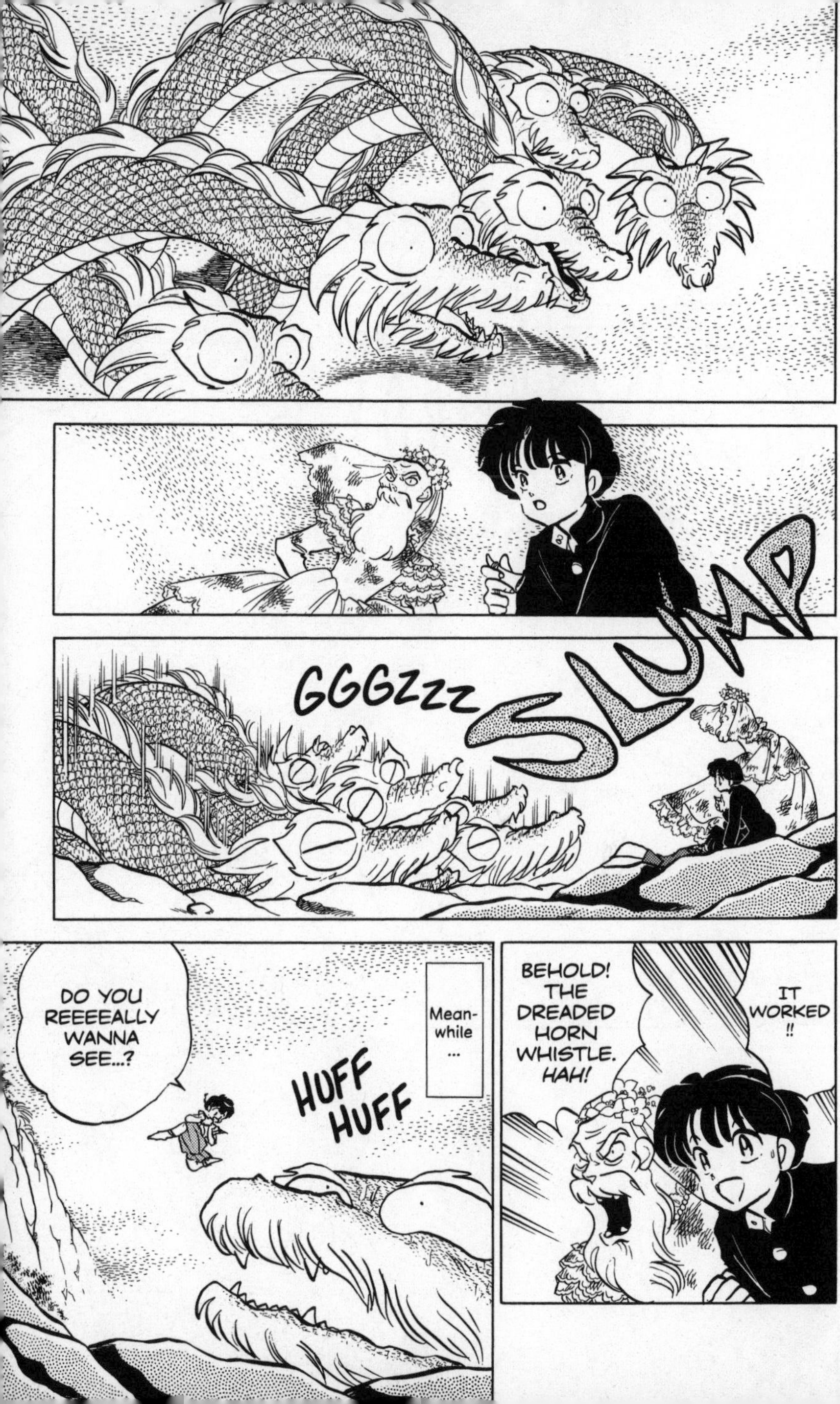
SLUMP
GGGZzz
IT WORKED!!
BEHOLD! THE DREADED HORN WHISTLE. HAH!
Mean-while...
DO YOU REEEEALLY WANNA SEE...?
HUFF HUFF

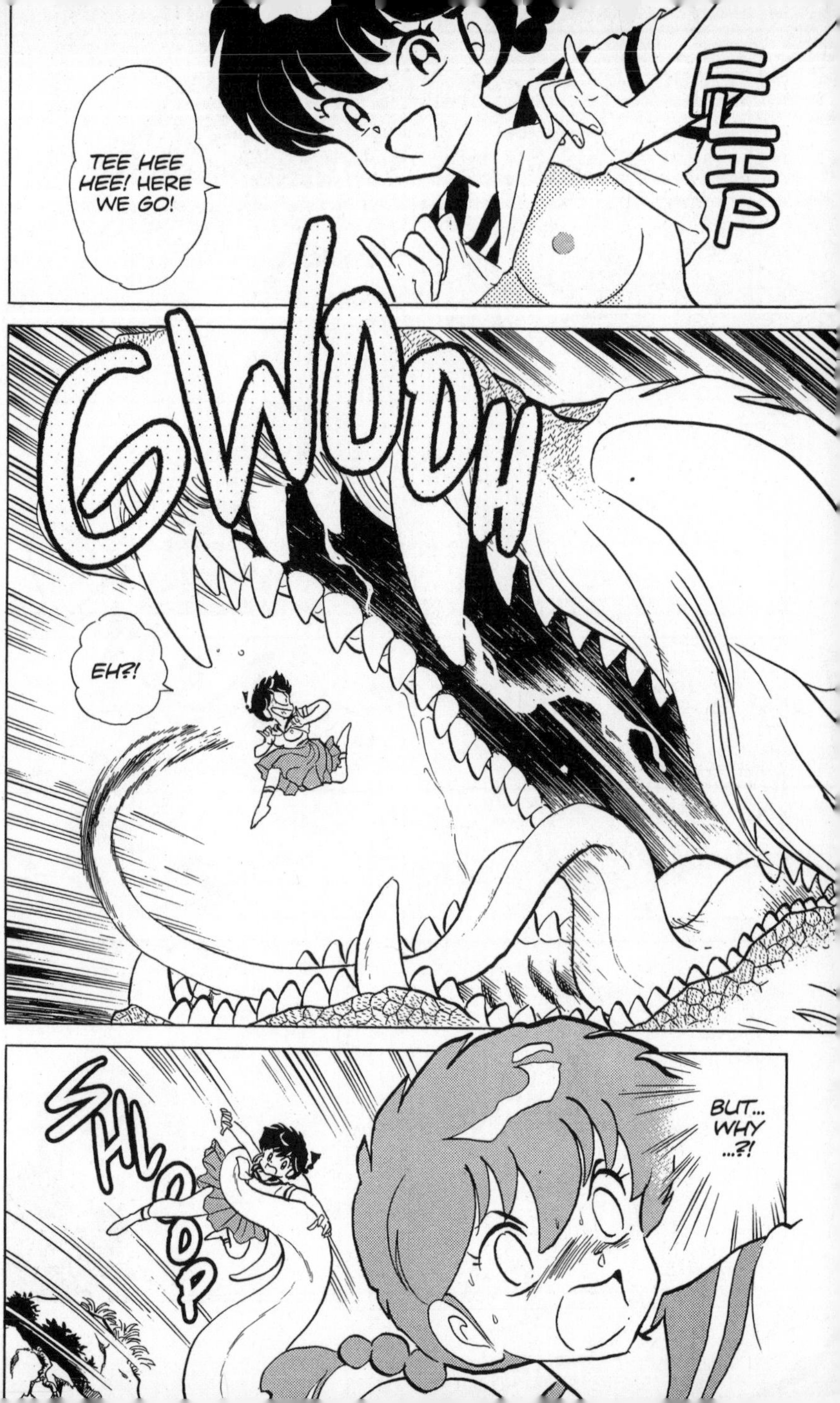
FLIP
TEE HEE HEE! HERE WE GO!
GWOOH
EH?!
BUT... WHY ...?!
SHLOOP

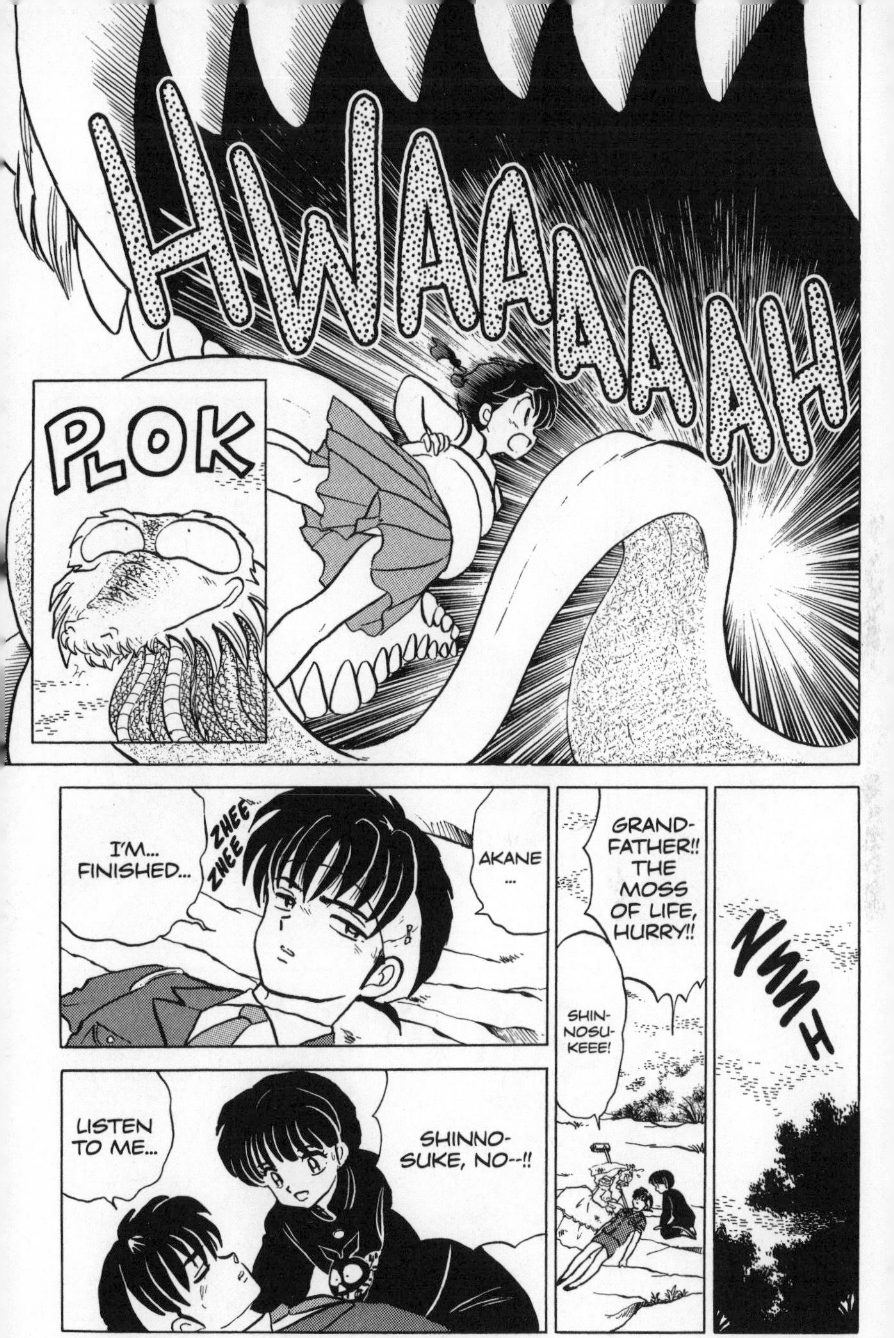
HWAAAAAH
PLOK
NWSH
GRAND-FATHER!! THE MOSS OF LIFE, HURRY!!
SHIN-NOSU-KEEE!
AKANE ...
ZHEE ZHEE
I'M... FINISHED...
SHINNO-SUKE, NO--!!
LISTEN TO ME...

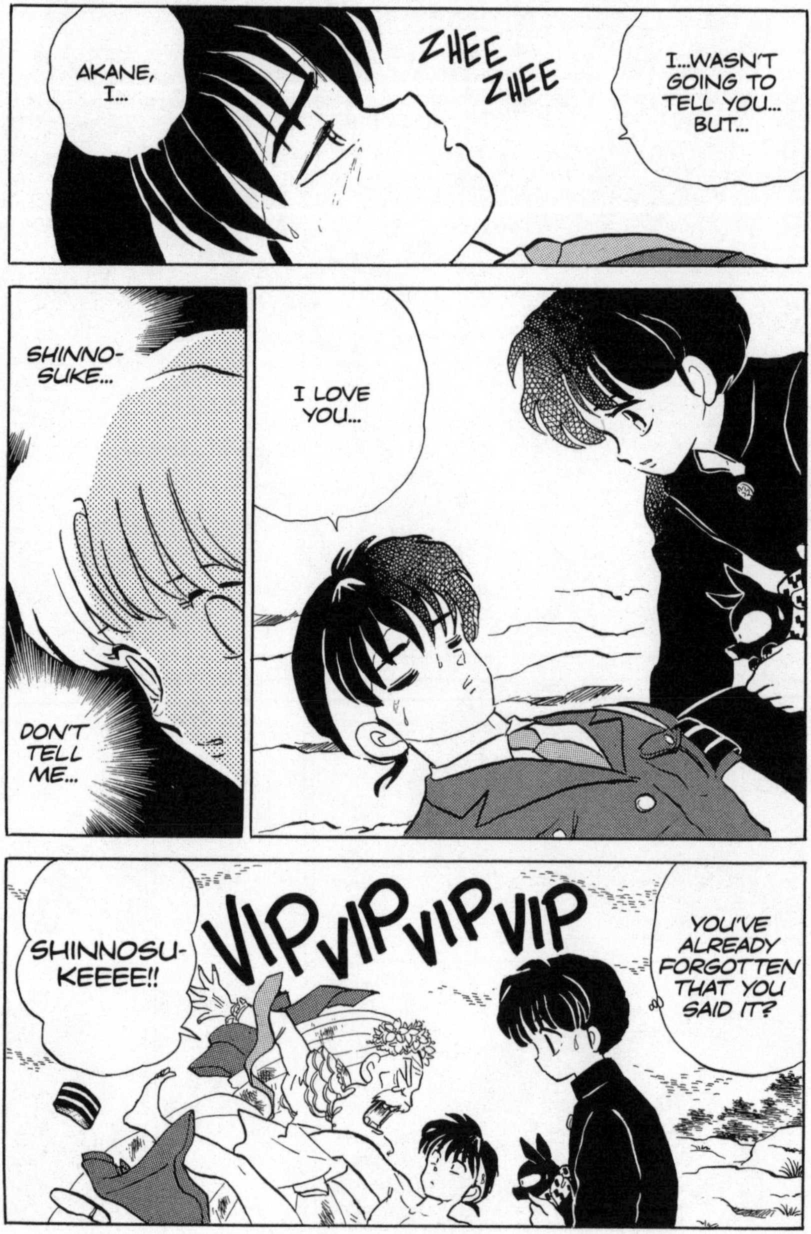
I...WASN'T GOING TO TELL YOU... BUT...
ZHEE ZHEE
AKANE, I...
I LOVE YOU...
SHINNO-SUKE...
DON'T TELL ME...
YOU'VE ALREADY FORGOTTEN THAT YOU SAID IT?
VIP VIP VIP VIP
SHINNOSU-KEEEE!!

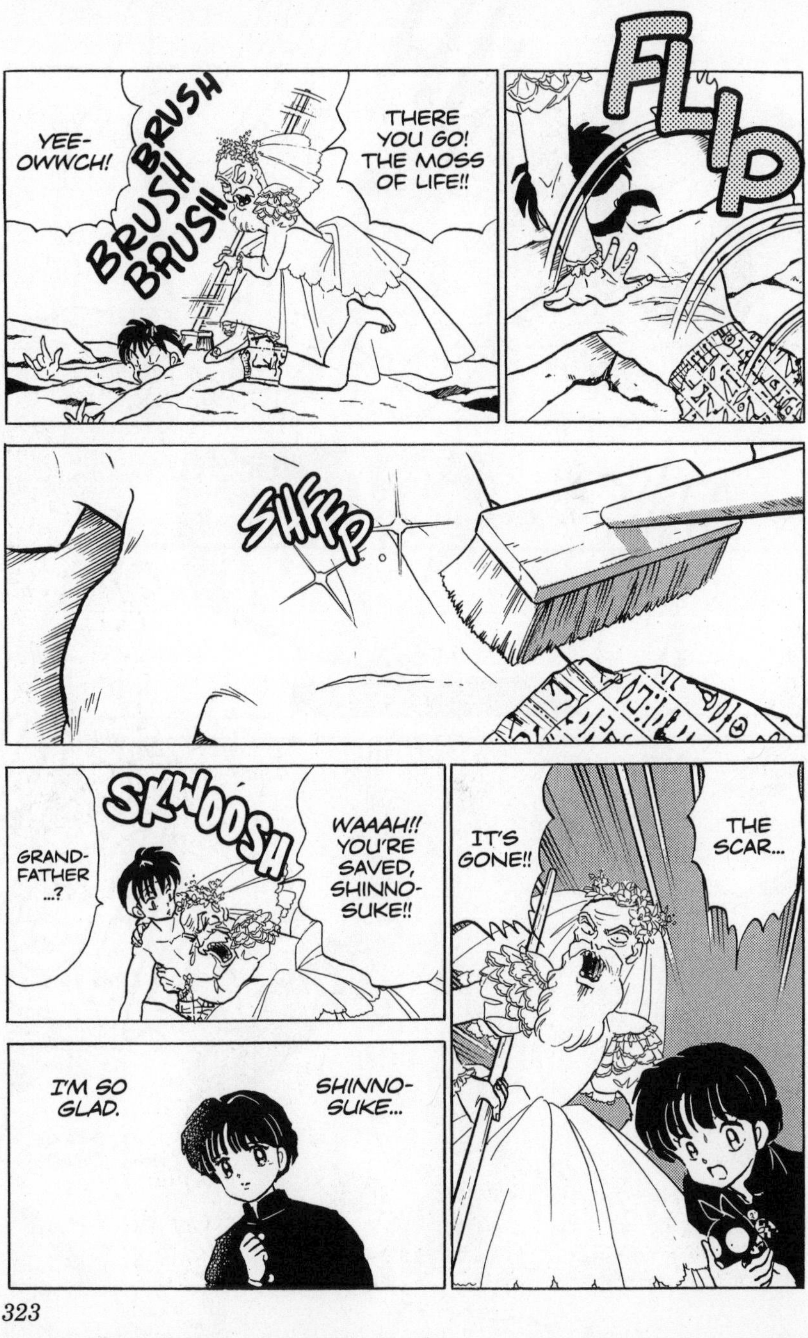
FLIP
THERE YOU GO! THE MOSS OF LIFE!!
BRUSH BRUSH BRUSH BRUSH
YEE-OWWCH!
SHFF
WAAAH!! YOU'RE SAVED, SHINNOSUKE!!
SKWOOSH
GRANDFATHER ...?
THE SCAR...
IT'S GONE!!
SHINNOSUKE...
I'M SO GLAD.

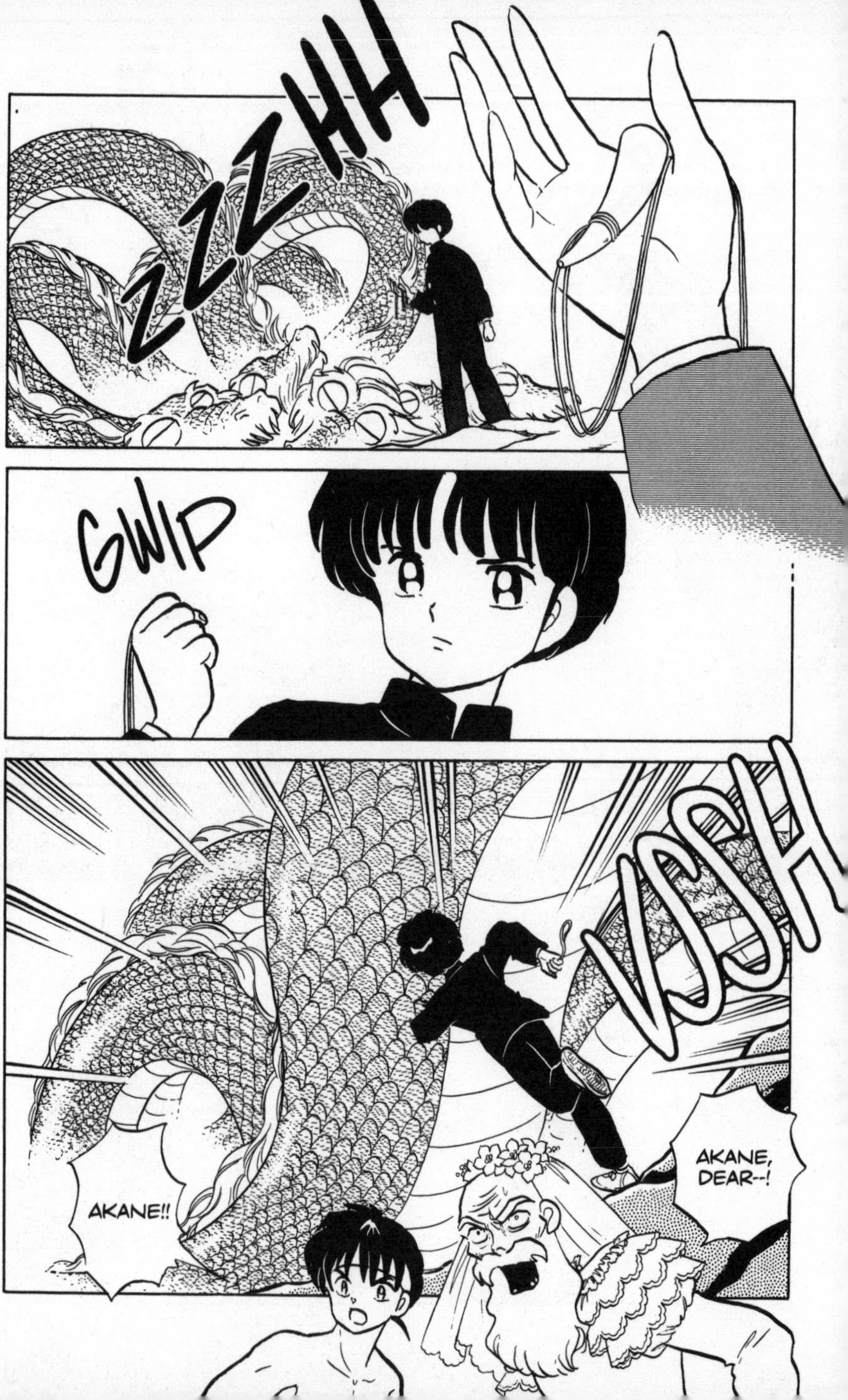
ZZZHH
GWIP
VOSH
AKANE, DEAR--!
AKANE!!

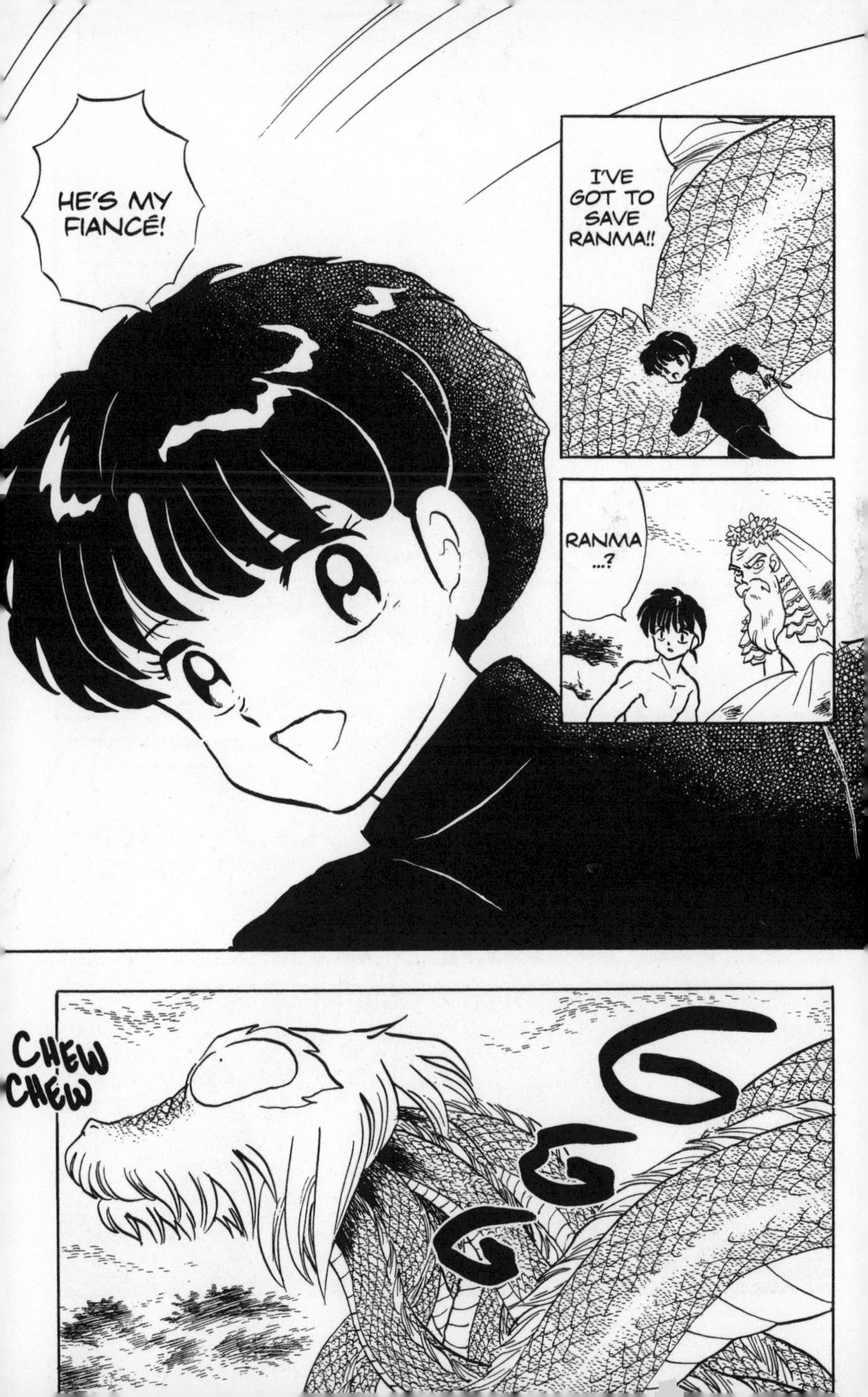
I'VE GOT TO SAVE RANMA!!
RANMA ...?
HE'S MY FIANCÉ!
CHEW CHEW
GGG

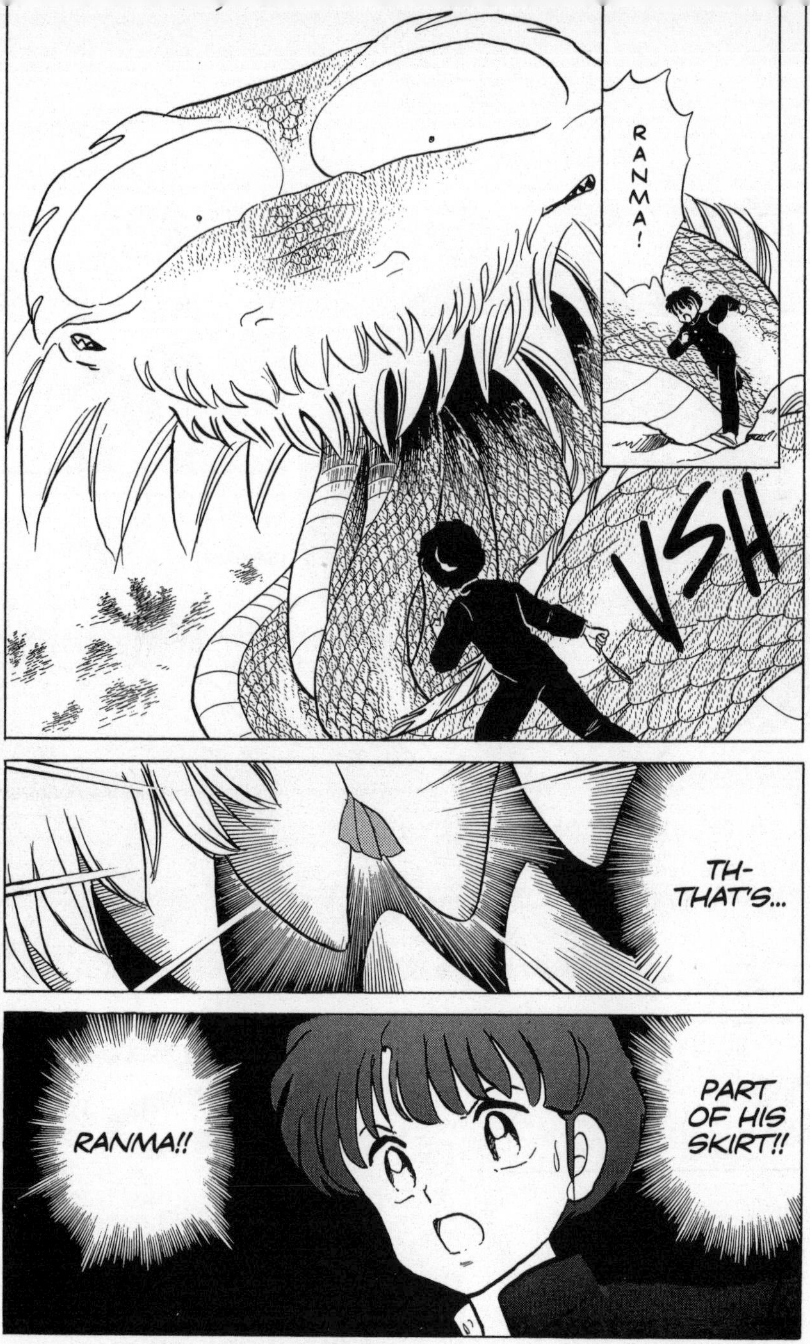
RANMA!
VSH
TH-THAT'S...
PART OF HIS SKIRT!!
RANMA!!

PART 21
LET'S GO HOME

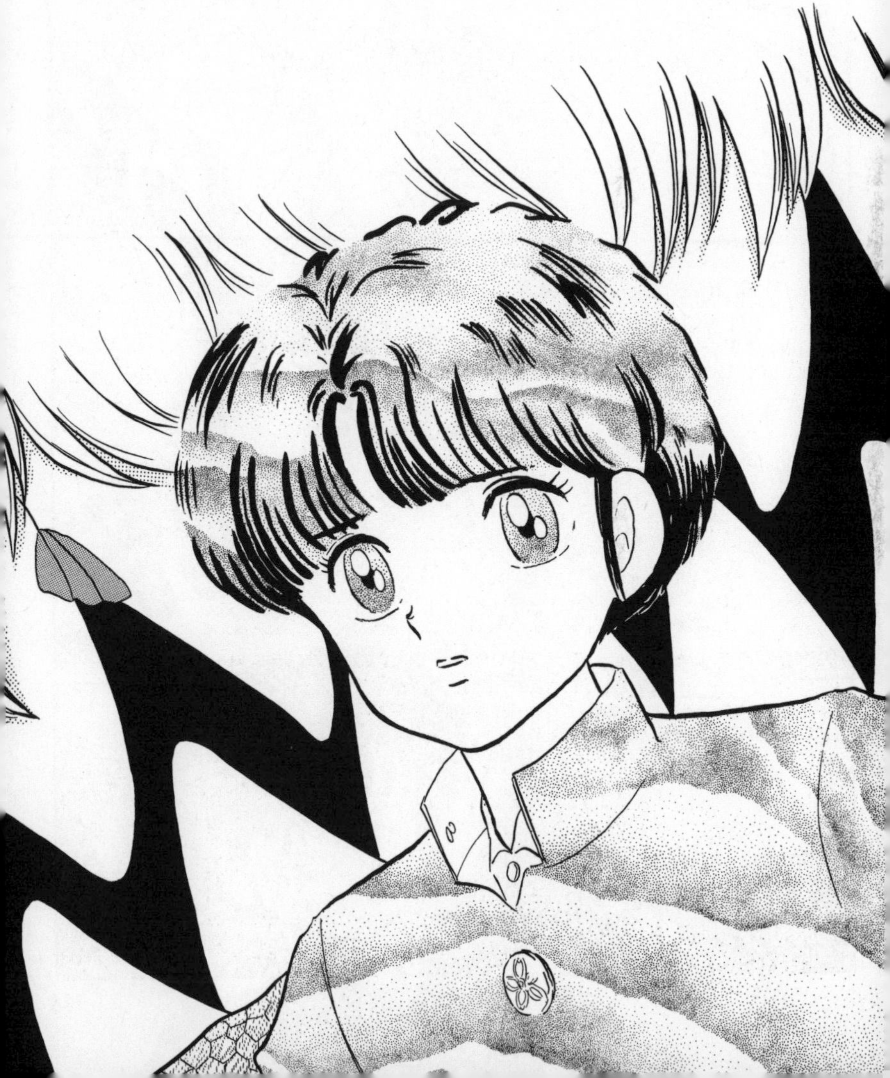

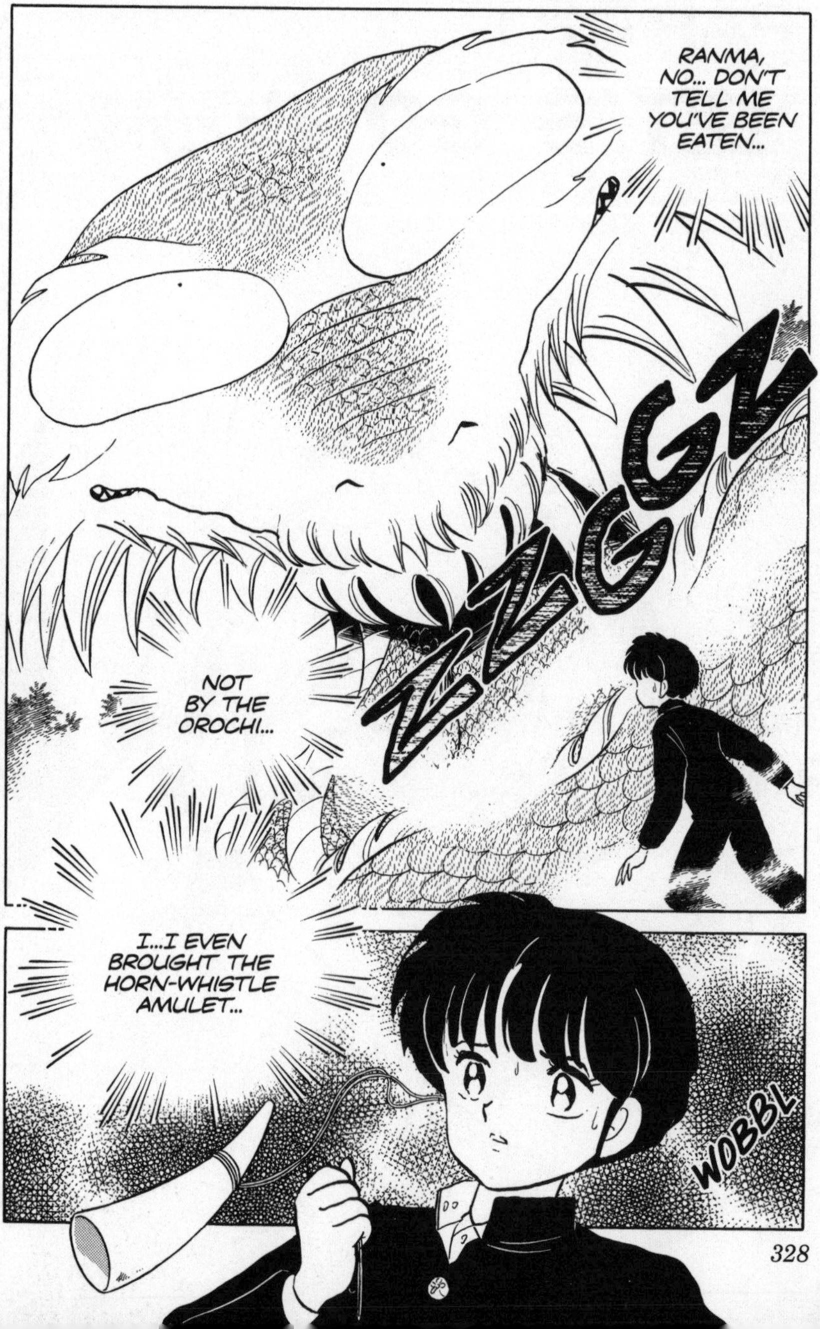
RANMA, NO... DON'T TELL ME YOU'VE BEEN EATEN...
ZZGGZ
NOT BY THE OROCHI...
I...I EVEN BROUGHT THE HORN-WHISTLE AMULET...
WOBBL

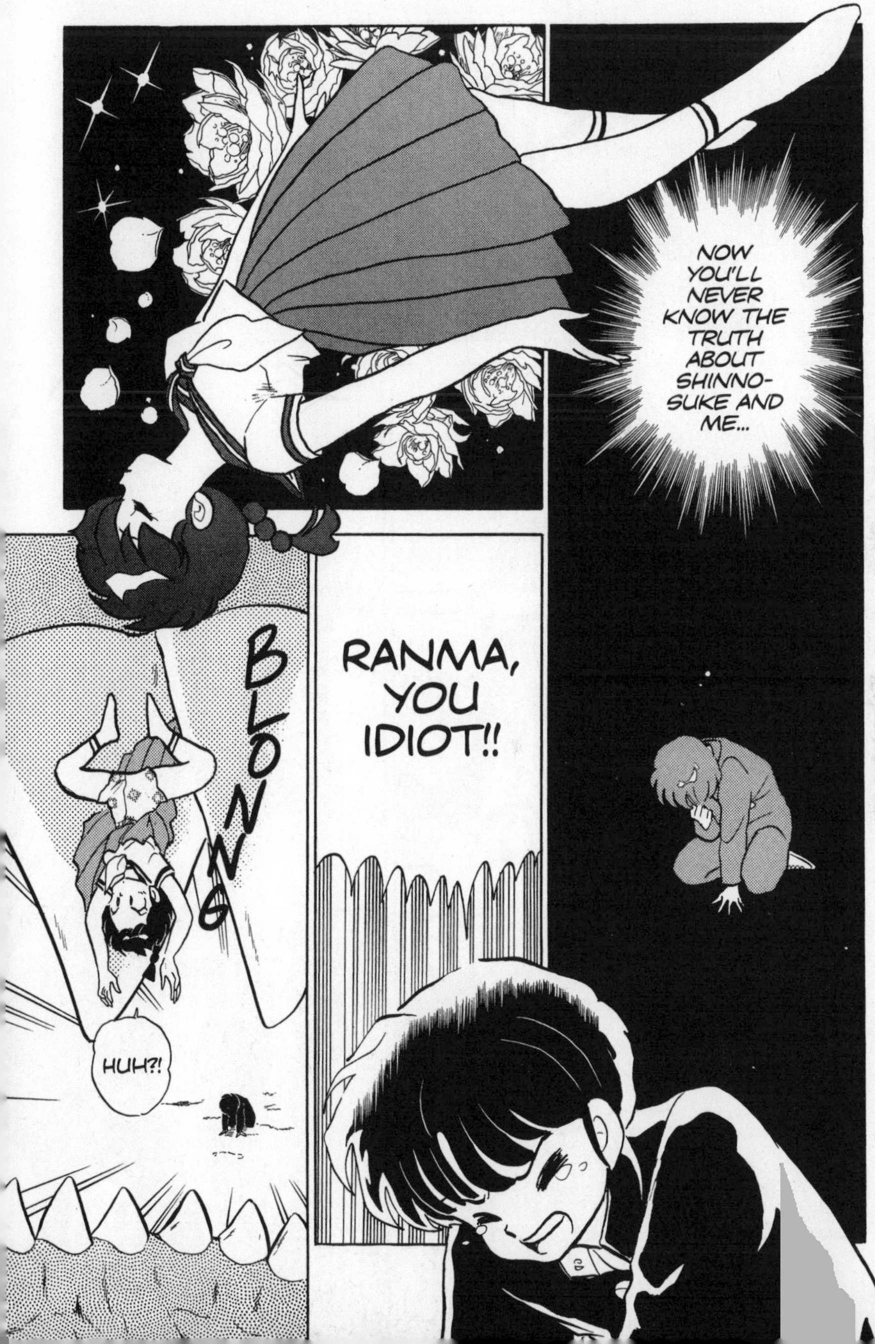
NOW YOU'LL NEVER KNOW THE TRUTH ABOUT SHINNO-SUKE AND ME...
RANMA, YOU IDIOT!!
BLONNG
HUH?!

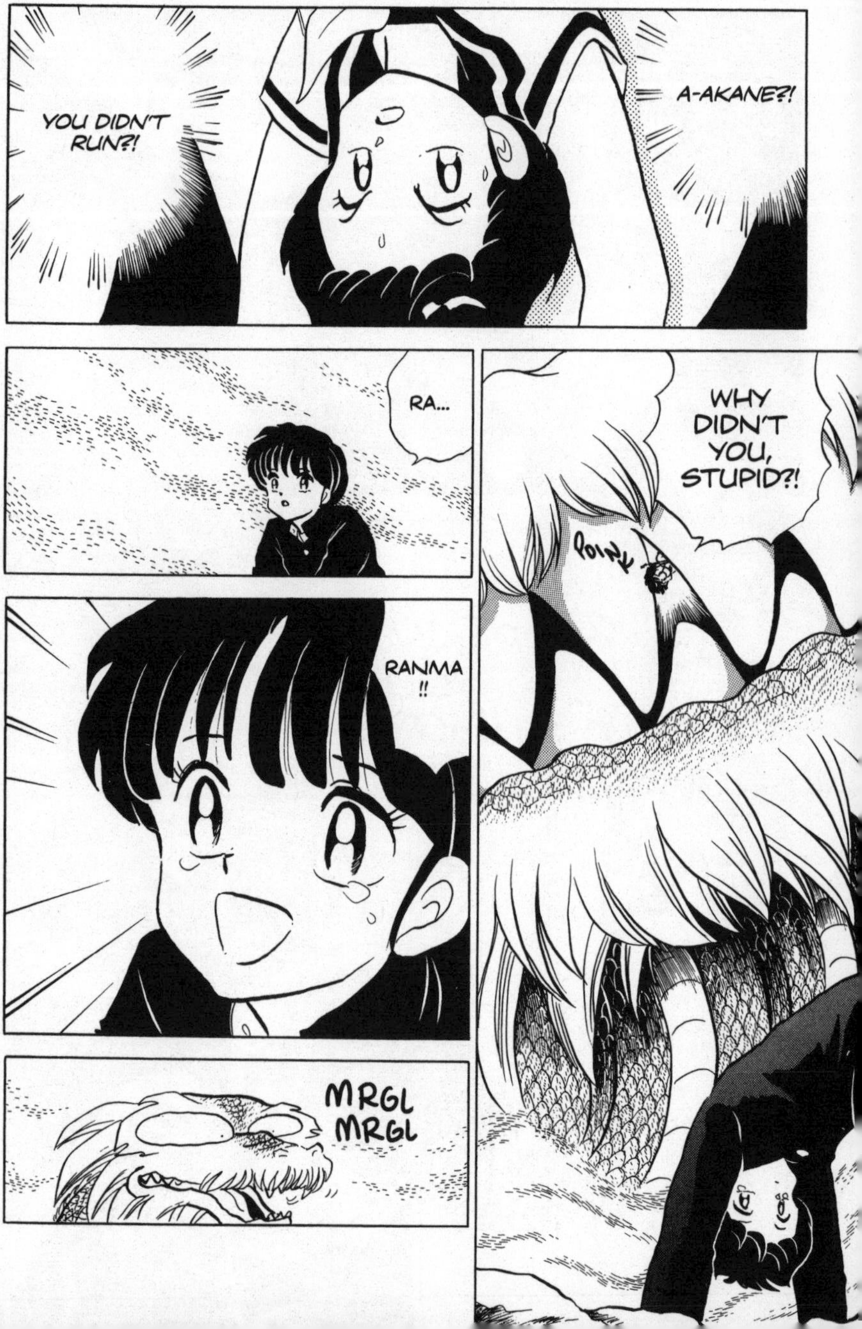
A-AKANE?!
YOU DIDN'T RUN?!
WHY DIDN'T YOU, STUPID?!
POINK
RA...
RANMA !!
MRGL MRGL

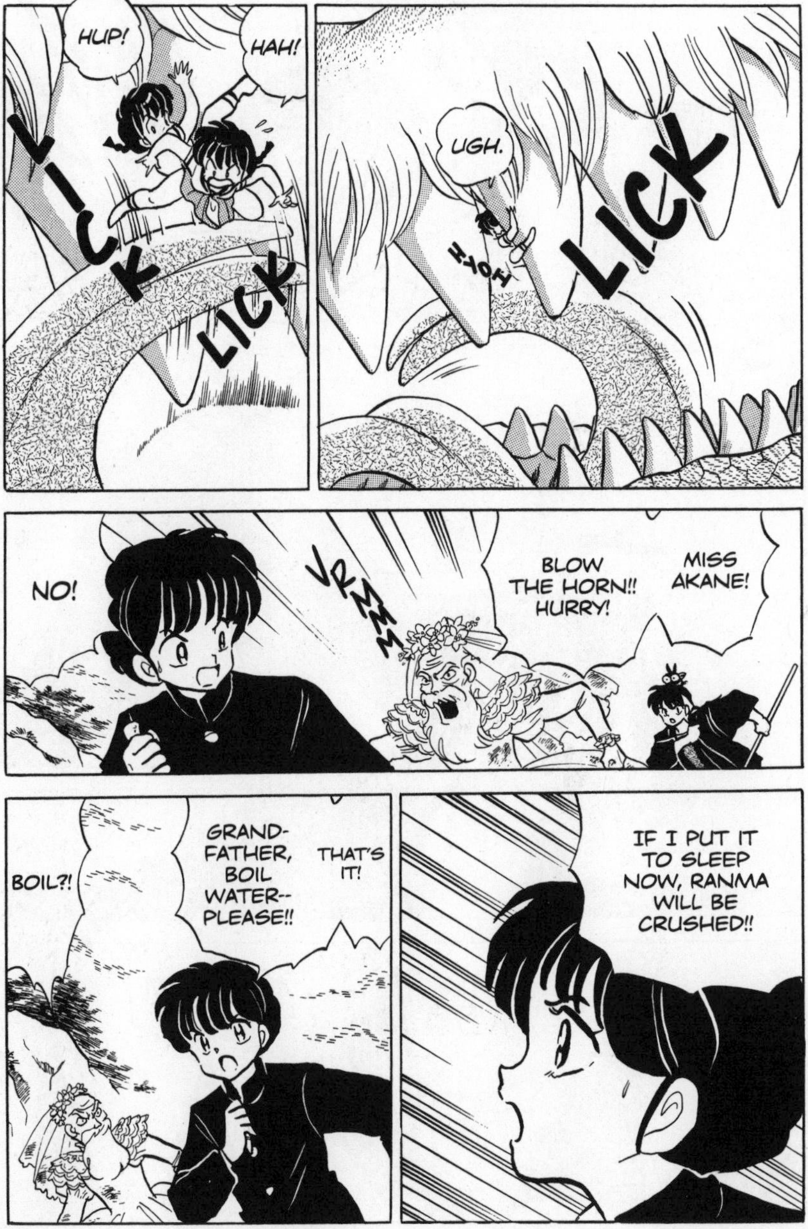
UGH.
LICK
HAH!
HUP!
LICK
LICK
MISS AKANE!
BLOW THE HORN!! HURRY!
NO!
IF I PUT IT TO SLEEP NOW, RANMA WILL BE CRUSHED!!
THAT'S IT!
GRAND-FATHER, BOIL WATER-- PLEASE!!
BOIL?!

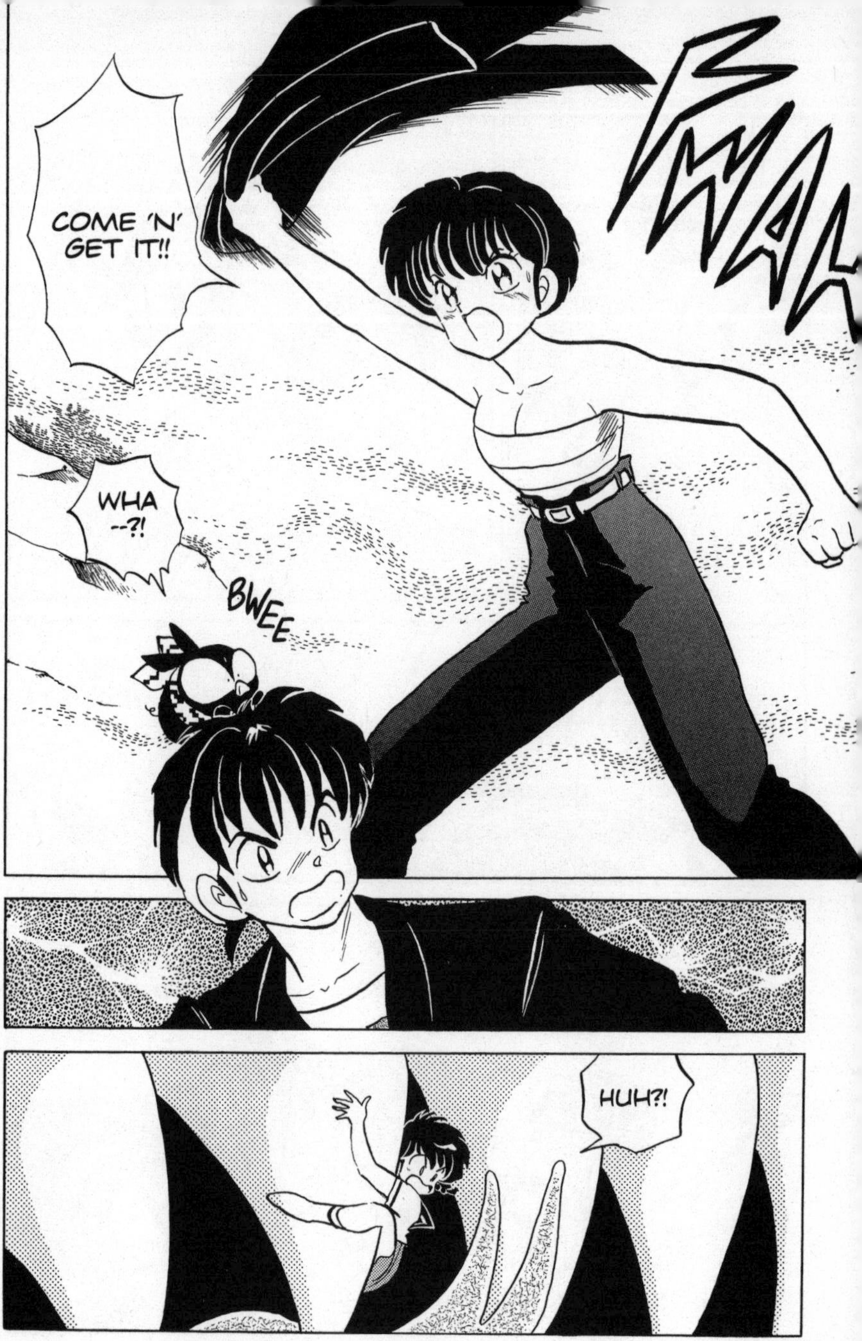
COME 'N' GET IT!!
WHA --?!
BWEE
HUH?!

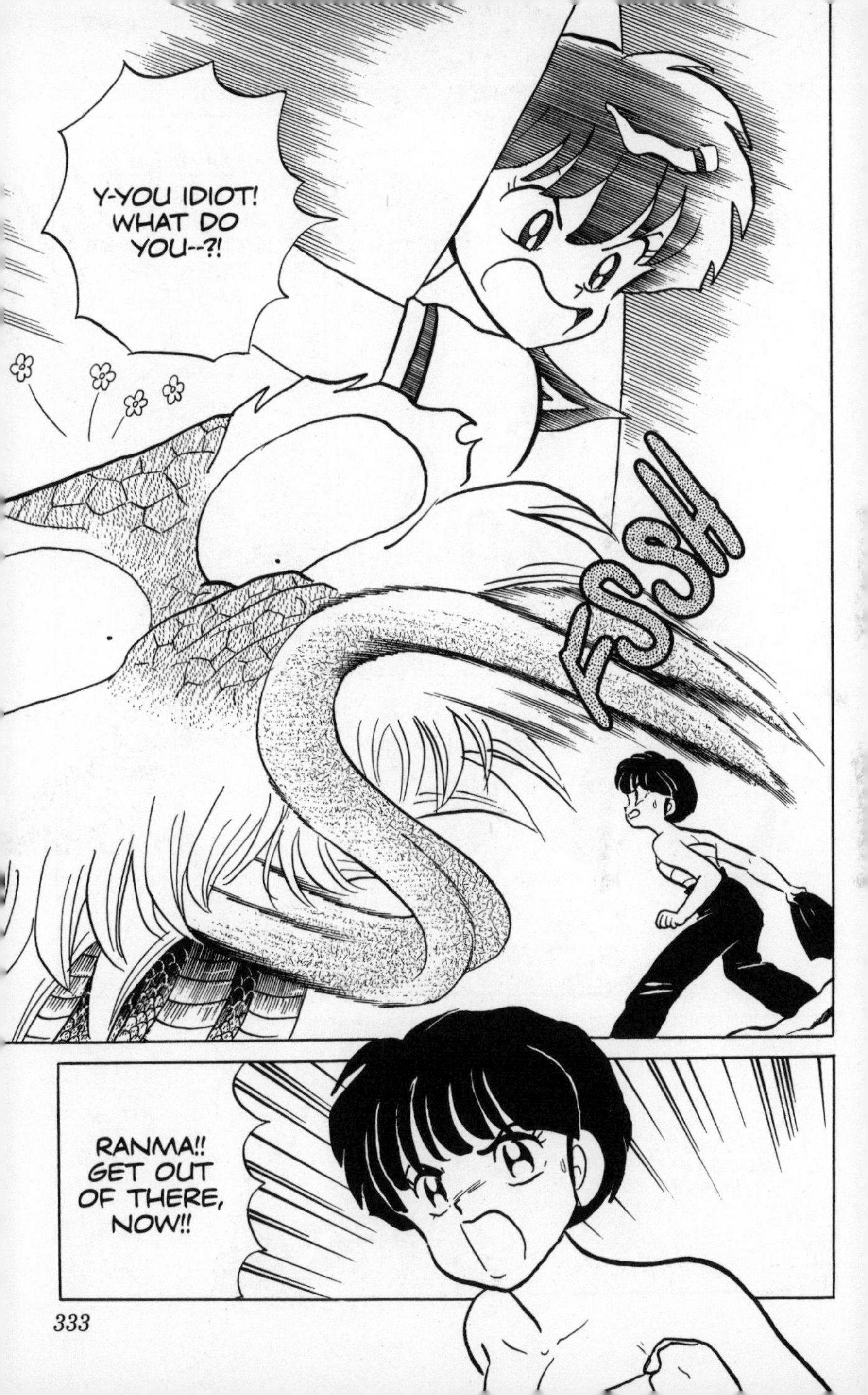
Y-YOU IDIOT! WHAT DO YOU--?!
FSSSH
RANMA!! GET OUT OF THERE, NOW!!

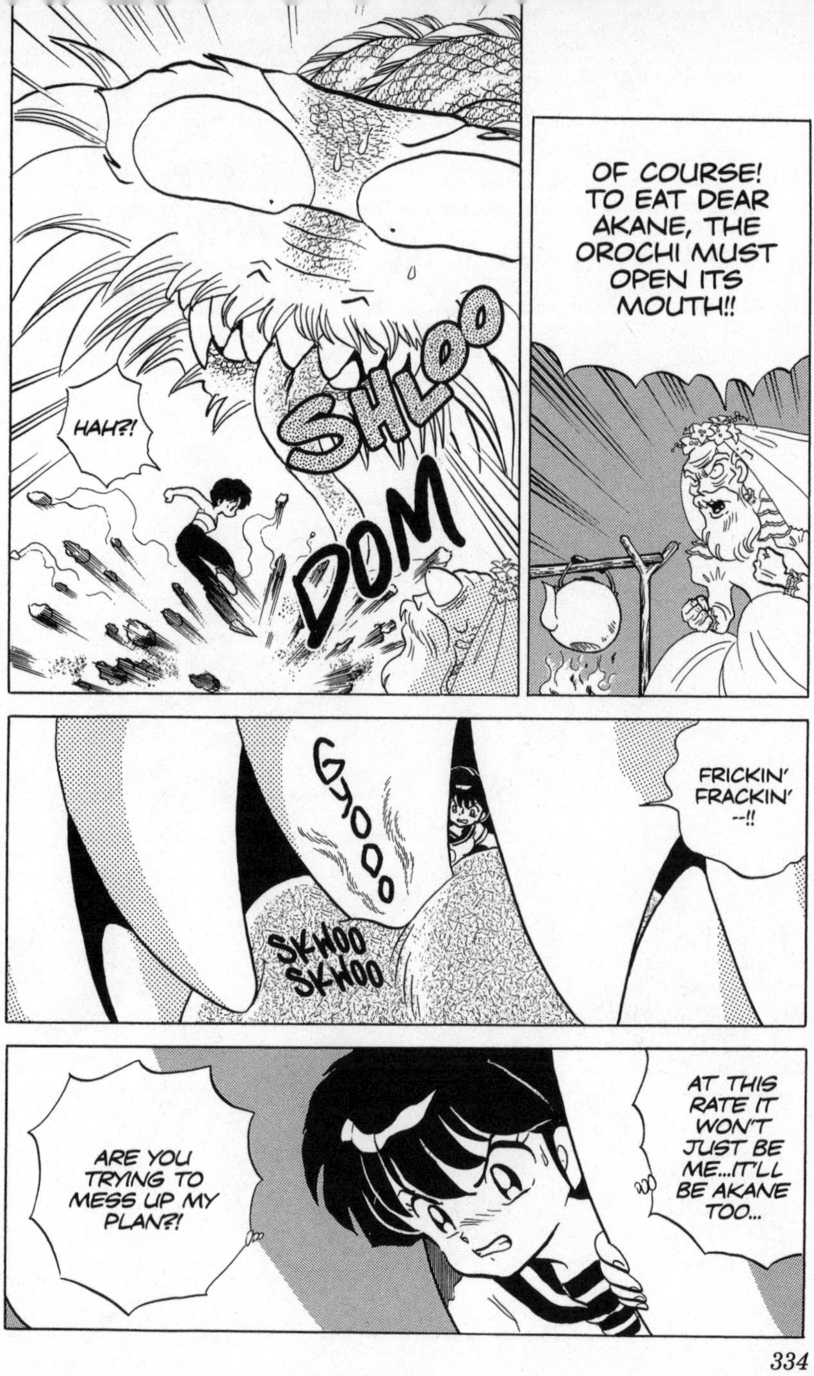
OF COURSE! TO EAT DEAR AKANE, THE OROCHI MUST OPEN ITS MOUTH!!
HAH?!
SHLOO
DOM
FRICKIN' FRACKIN' --!!
GYOOOO
SKWOO SKWOO
AT THIS RATE IT WON'T JUST BE ME...IT'LL BE AKANE TOO...
ARE YOU TRYING TO MESS UP MY PLAN?!

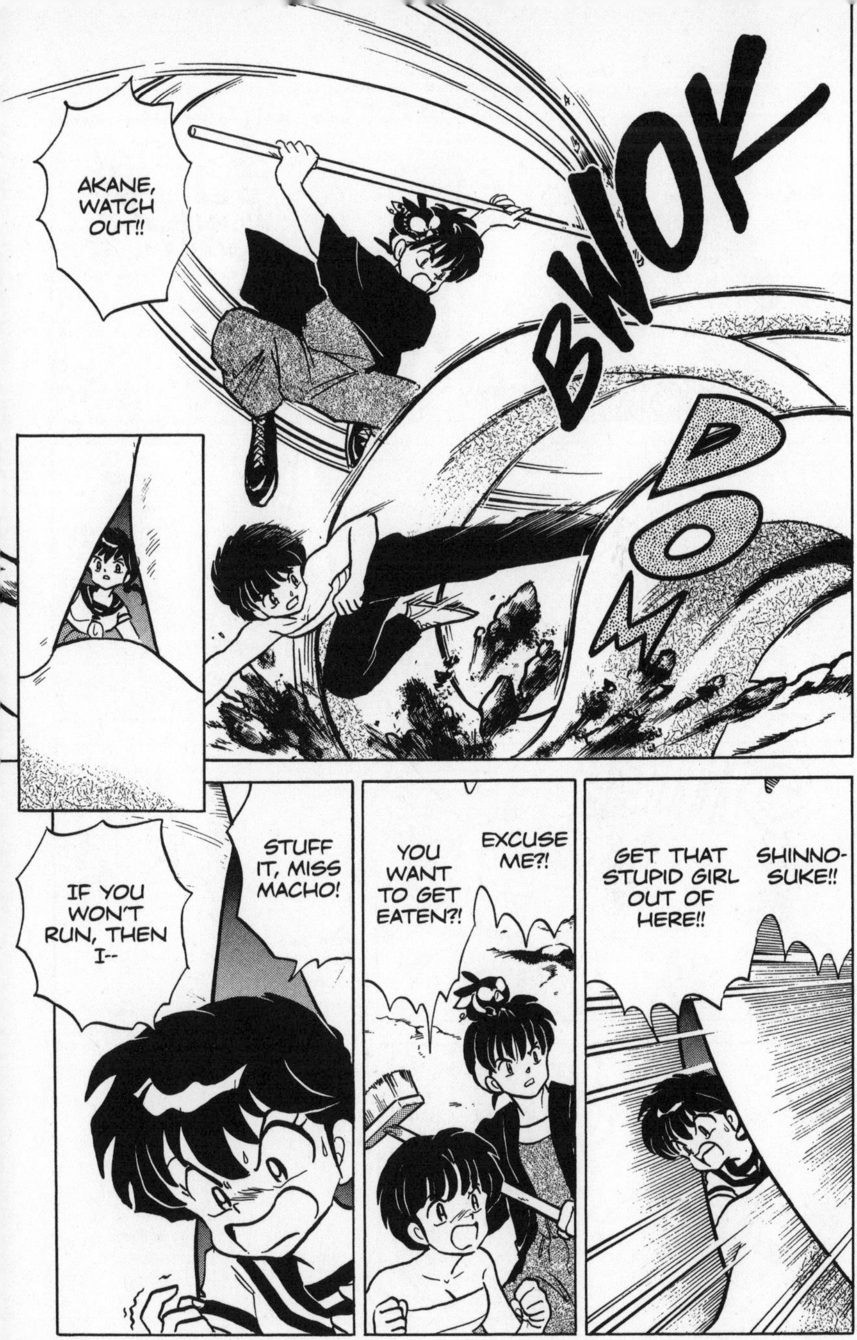
BWOK
AKANE, WATCH OUT!!
DOM
SHINNO-SUKE!!
GET THAT STUPID GIRL OUT OF HERE!!
EXCUSE ME?!
YOU WANT TO GET EATEN?!
STUFF IT, MISS MACHO!
IF YOU WON'T RUN, THEN I--

RANMA
...?!

HE DUCKED BACK?!

VIP

RUBBA...
RUBBA...
RUBBA...
RUBBA...

SIIIIGH

!

SHLOO

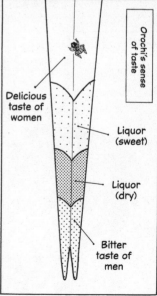

Orochi's sense of taste

Delicious taste of women

Liquor (sweet)

Liquor (dry)

Bitter taste of men

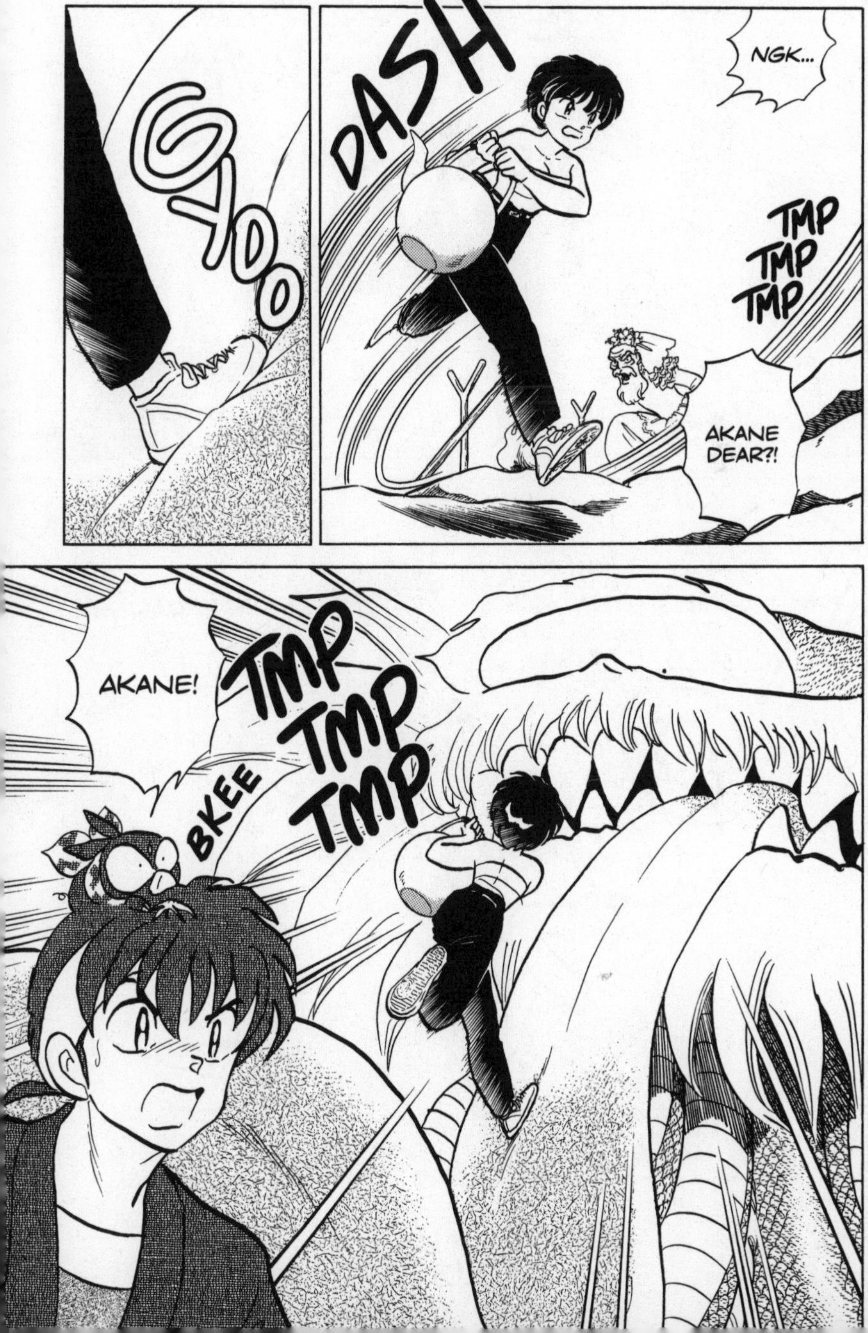
DASH
NGK...
TMP TMP TMP
AKANE DEAR?!
GYDOO
AKANE!
TMP TMP TMP
BKEE

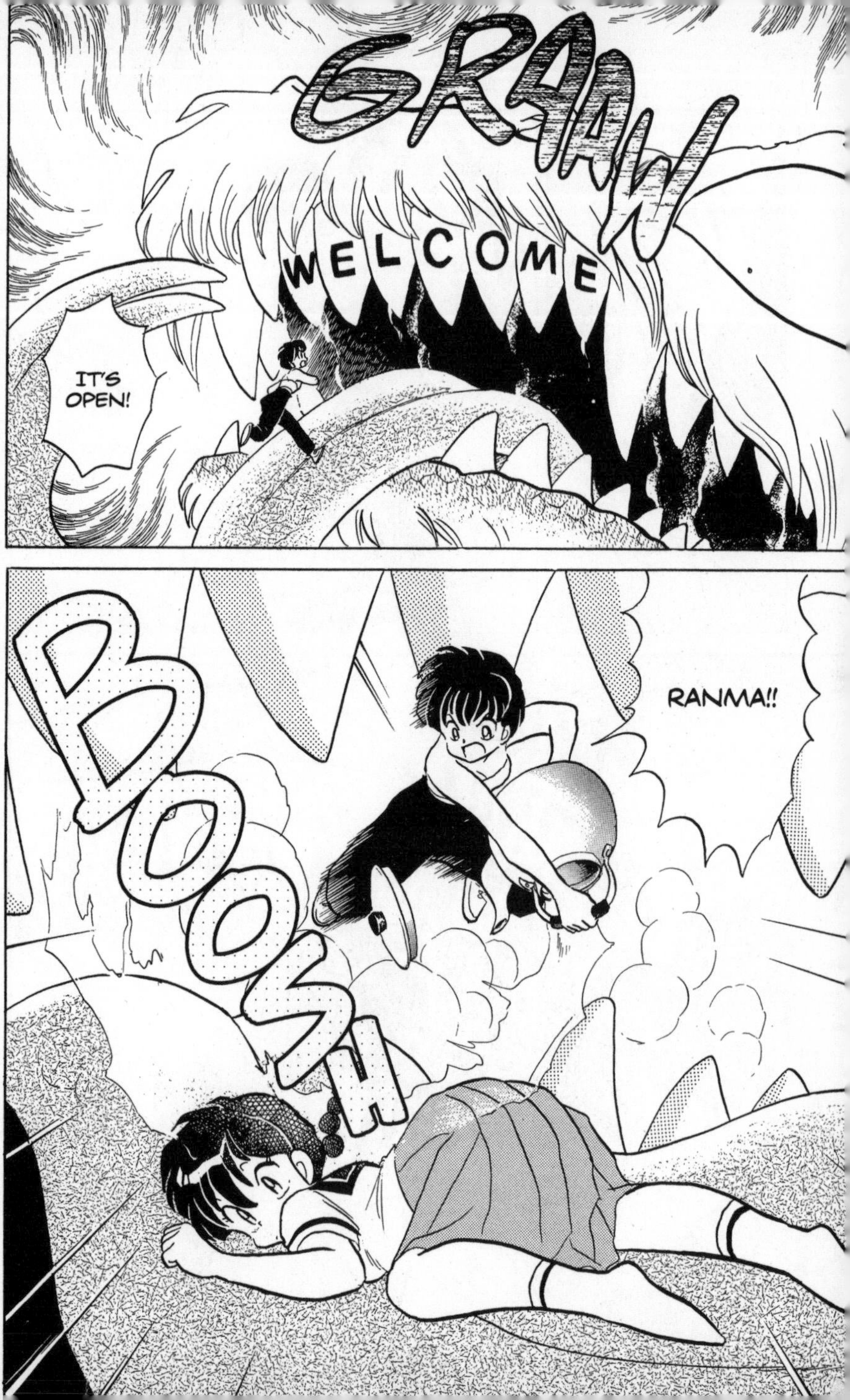
GRAAW
WELCOME
IT'S OPEN!
RANMA!!
BOOOSH

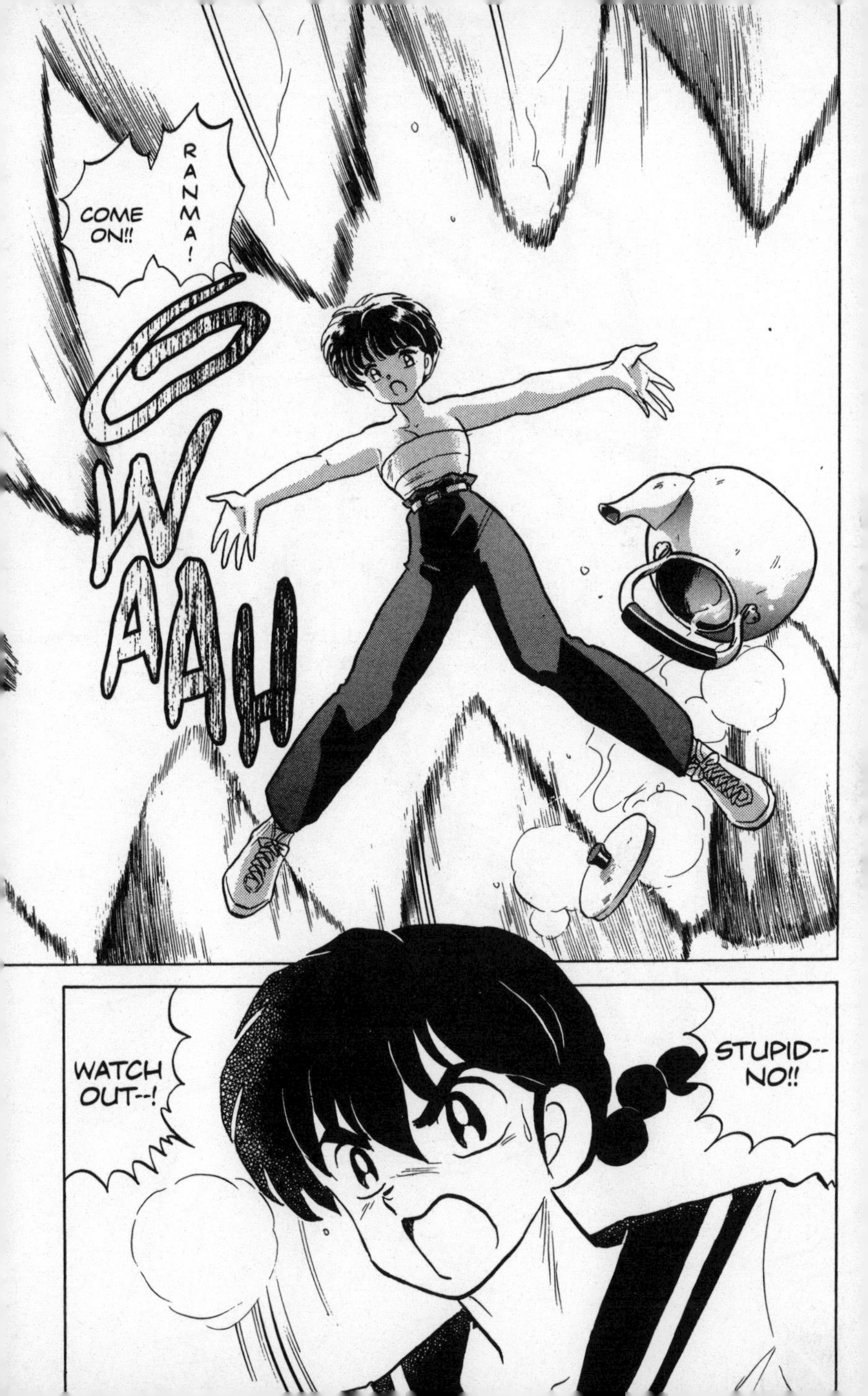
RANMA!
COME ON!!
OWAAH
STUPID-- NO!!
WATCH OUT--!

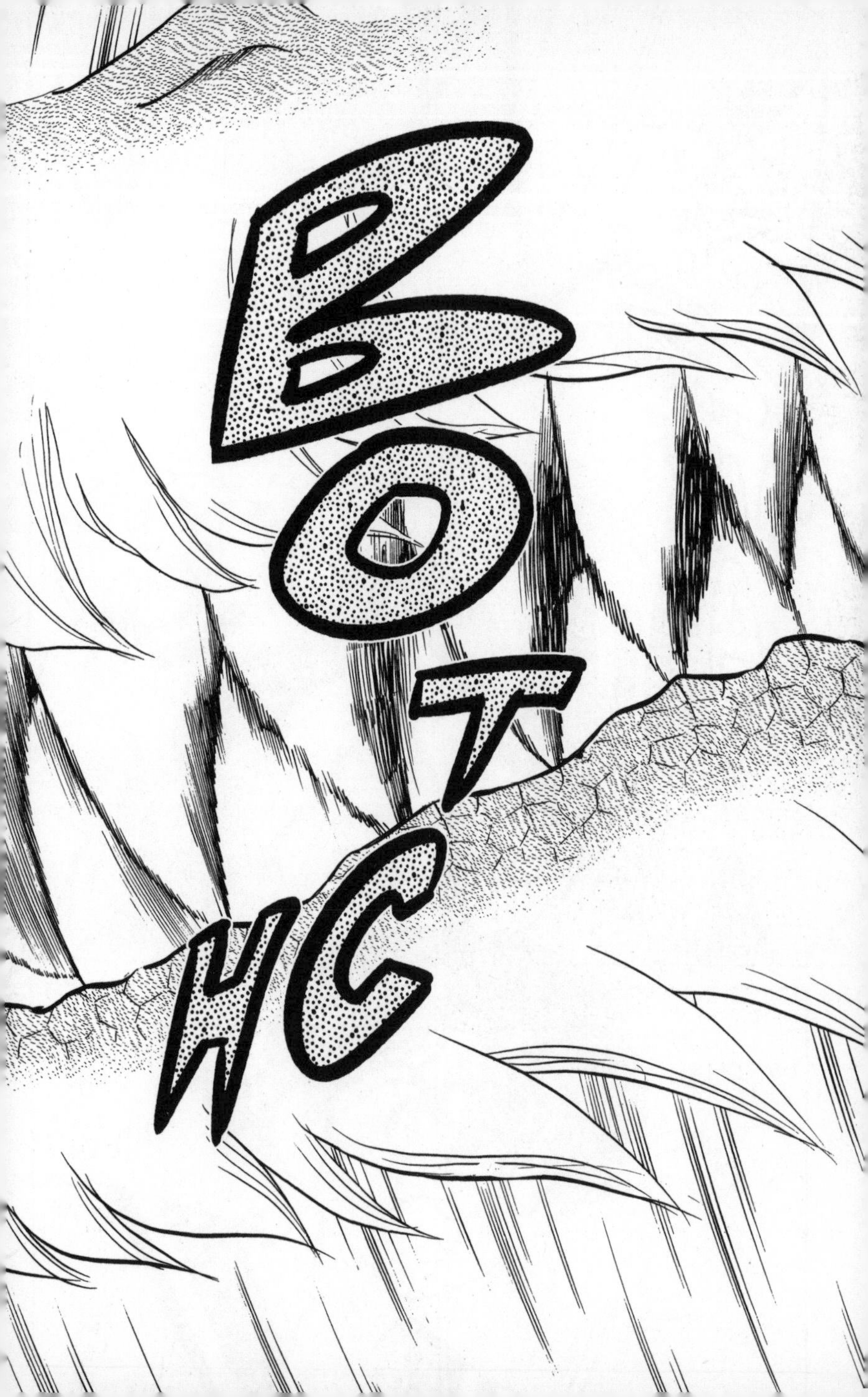
BOTCH

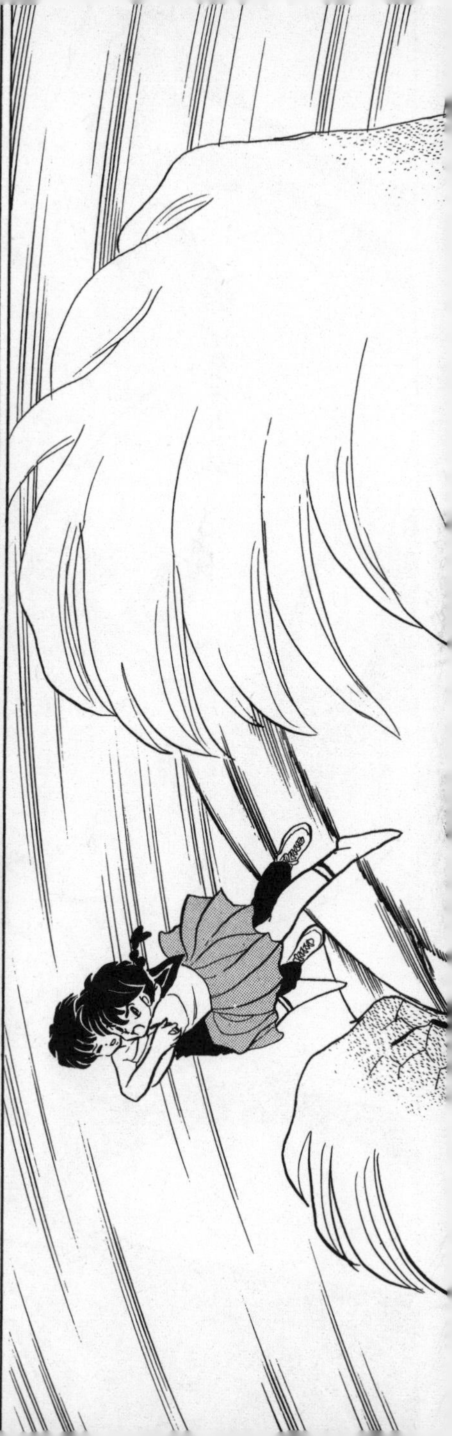

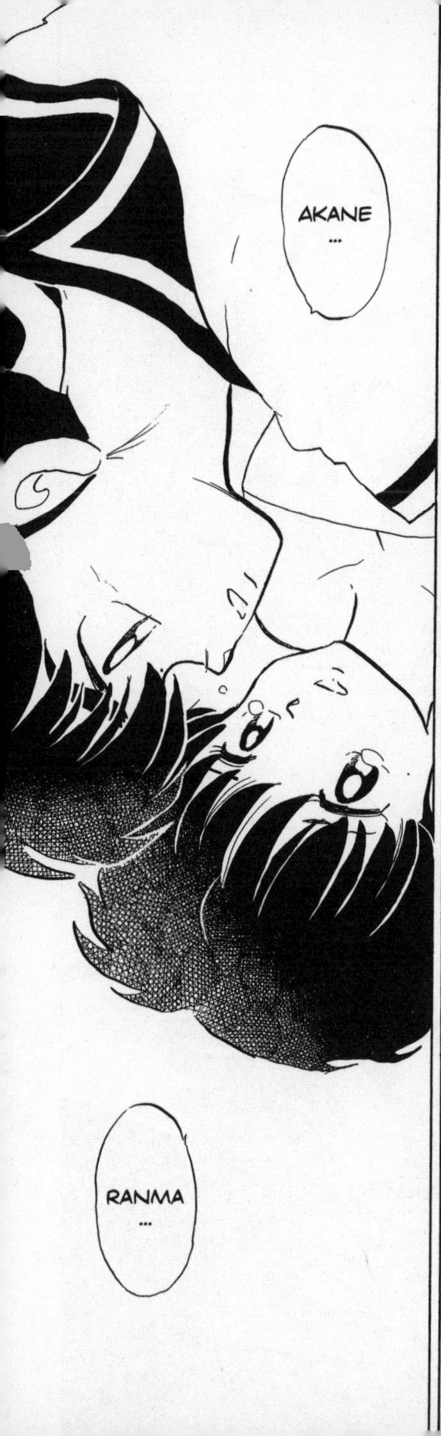
AKANE ...
RANMA ...

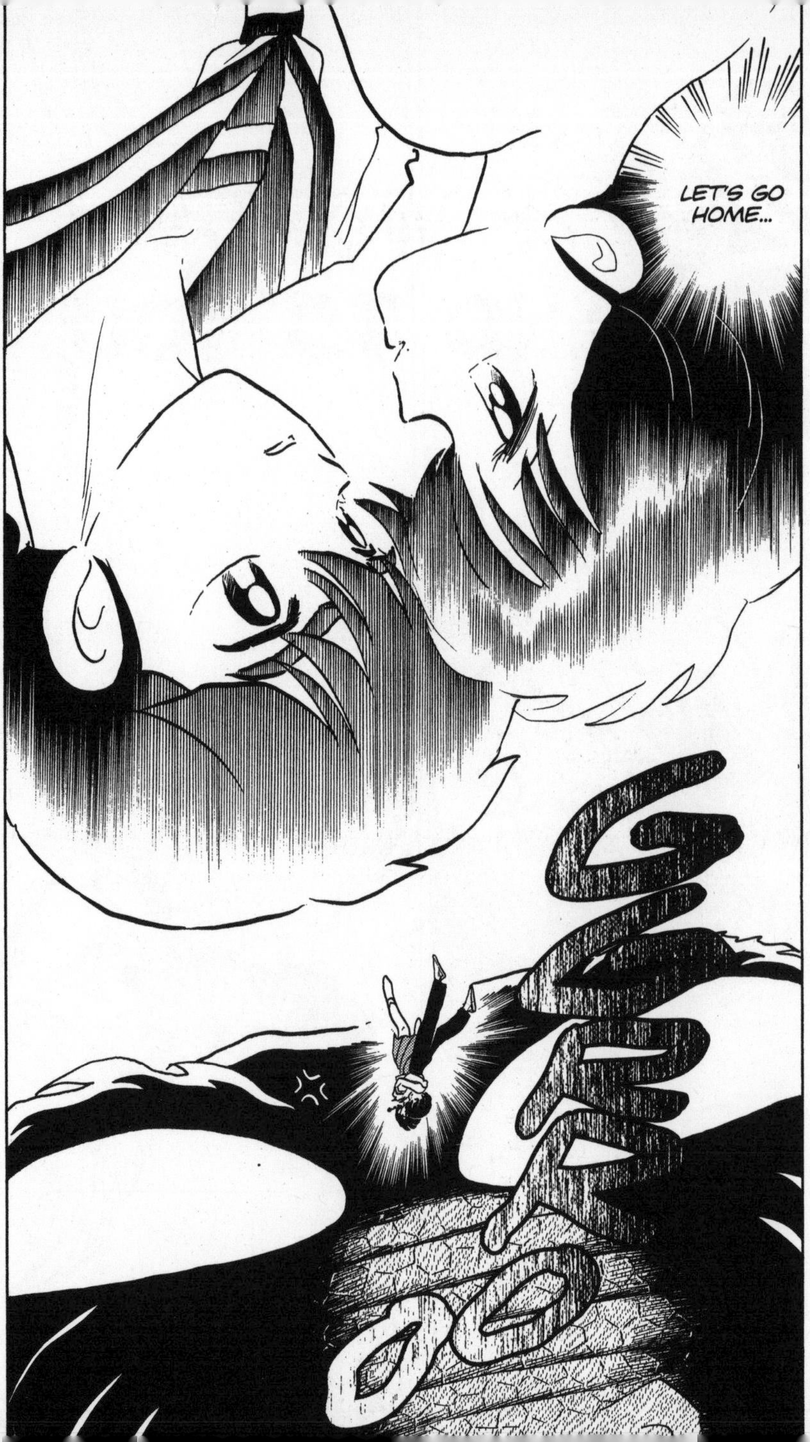
LET'S GO HOME...

PART 22
THESE WORDS I SEND TO YOU

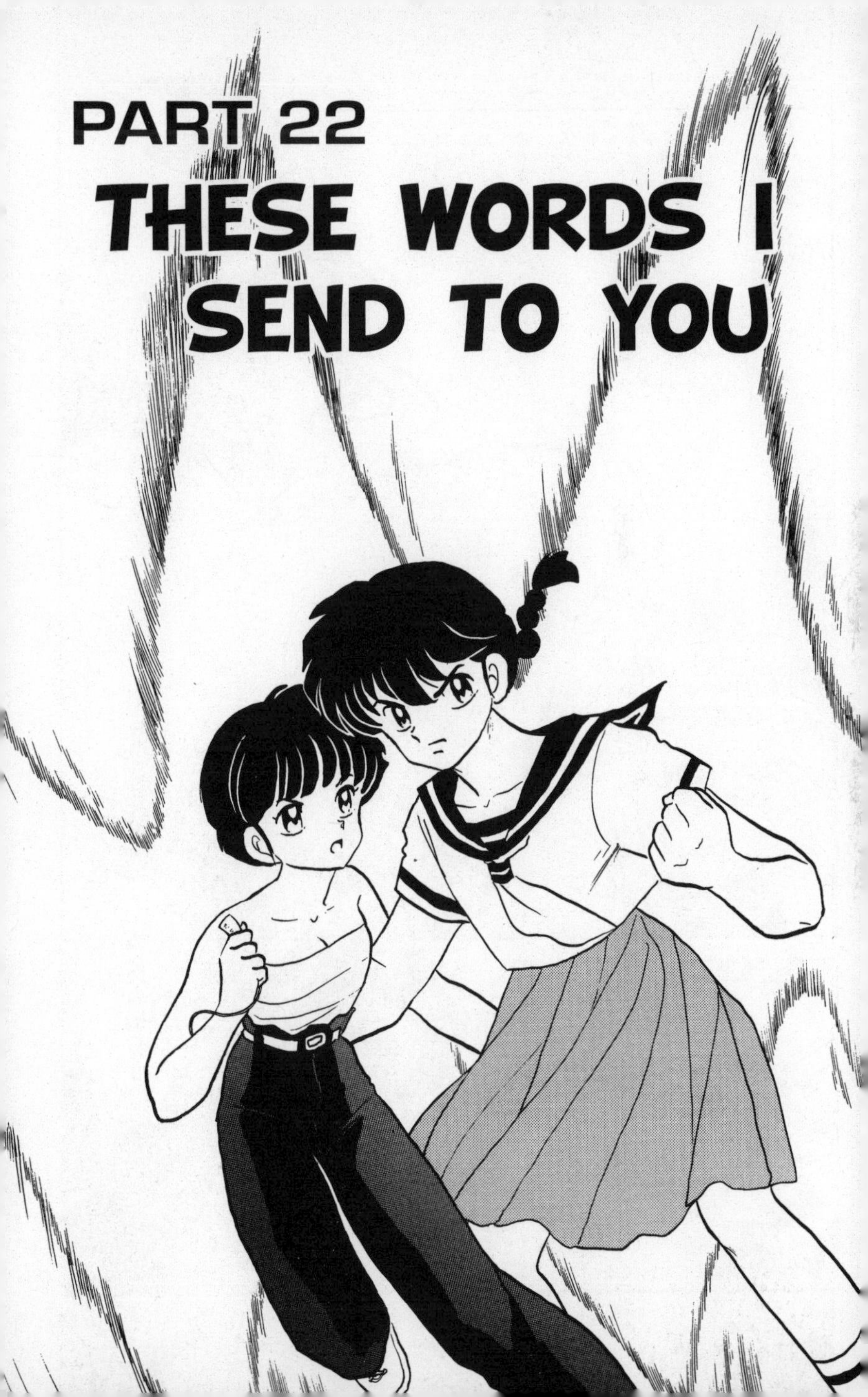

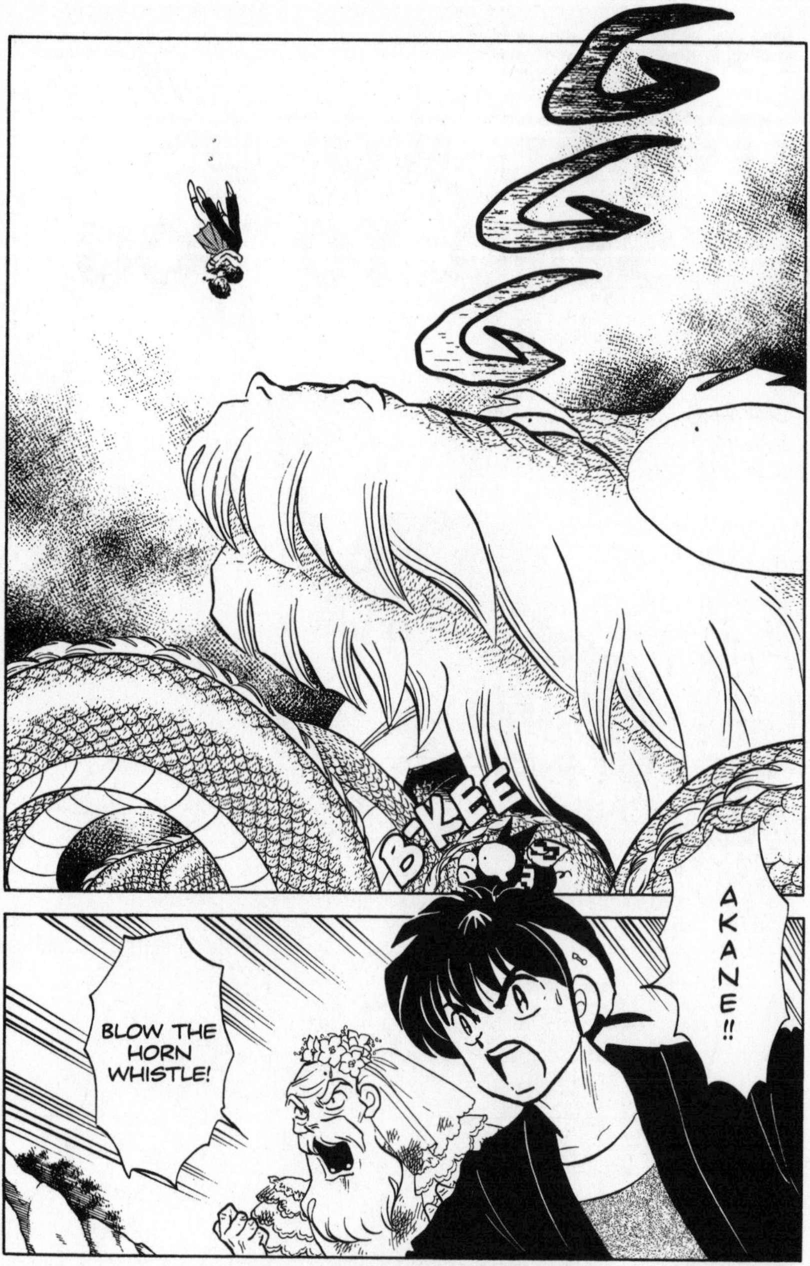
B-KEE
AKANE!!
BLOW THE HORN WHISTLE!

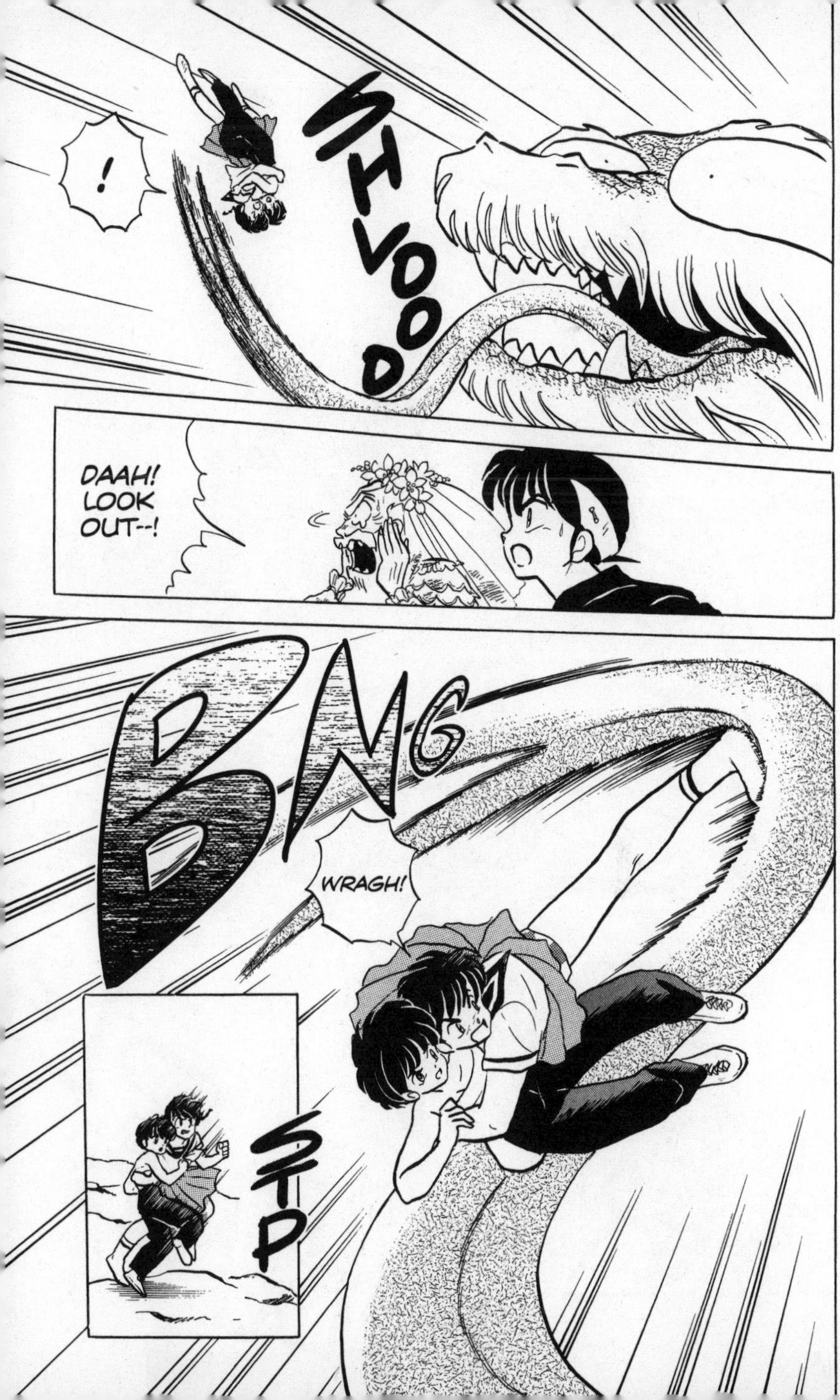

SHLOOD
!
DAAH! LOOK OUT--!
BANG
WRAGH!
STP

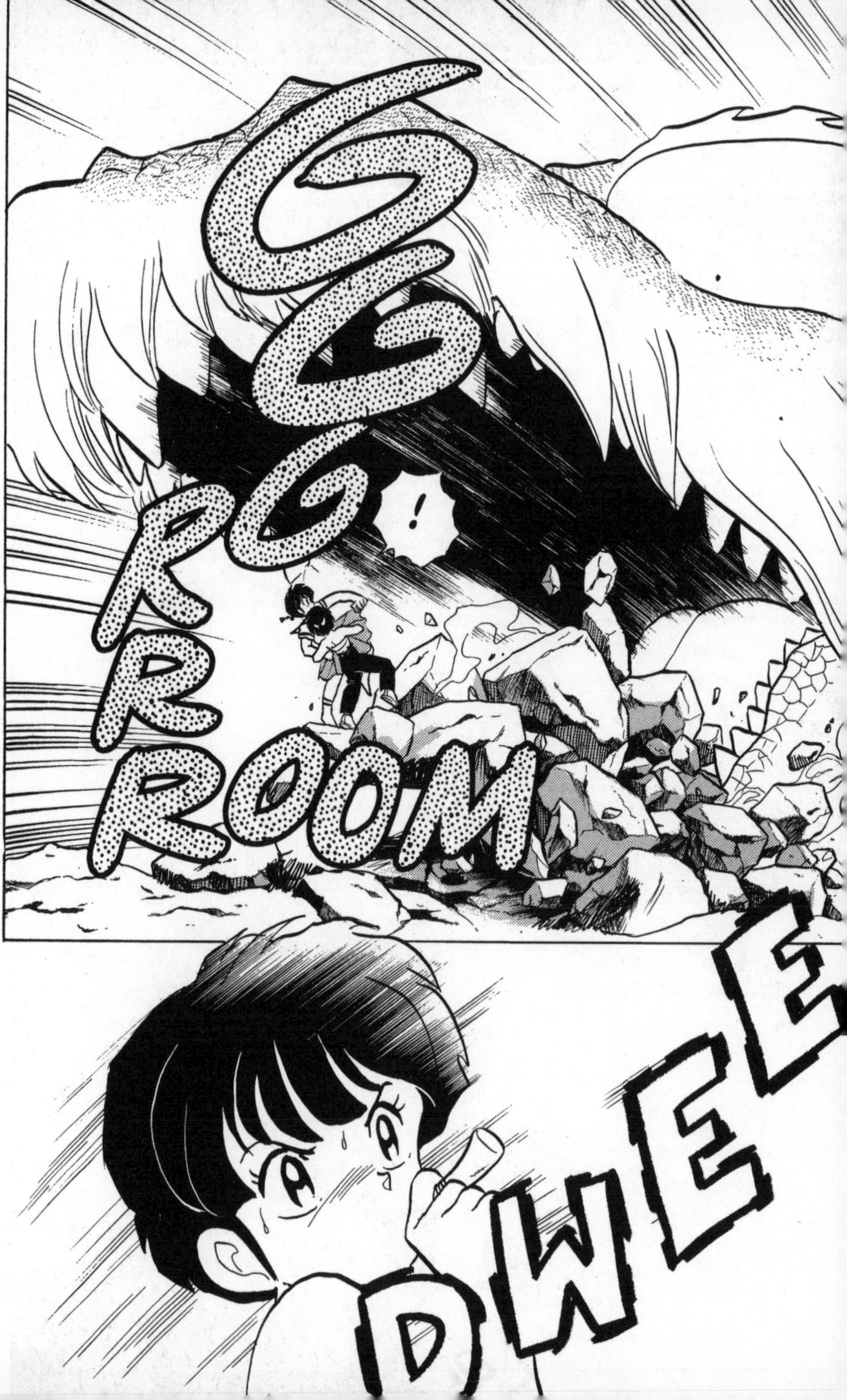
!
ROOM
DWEE

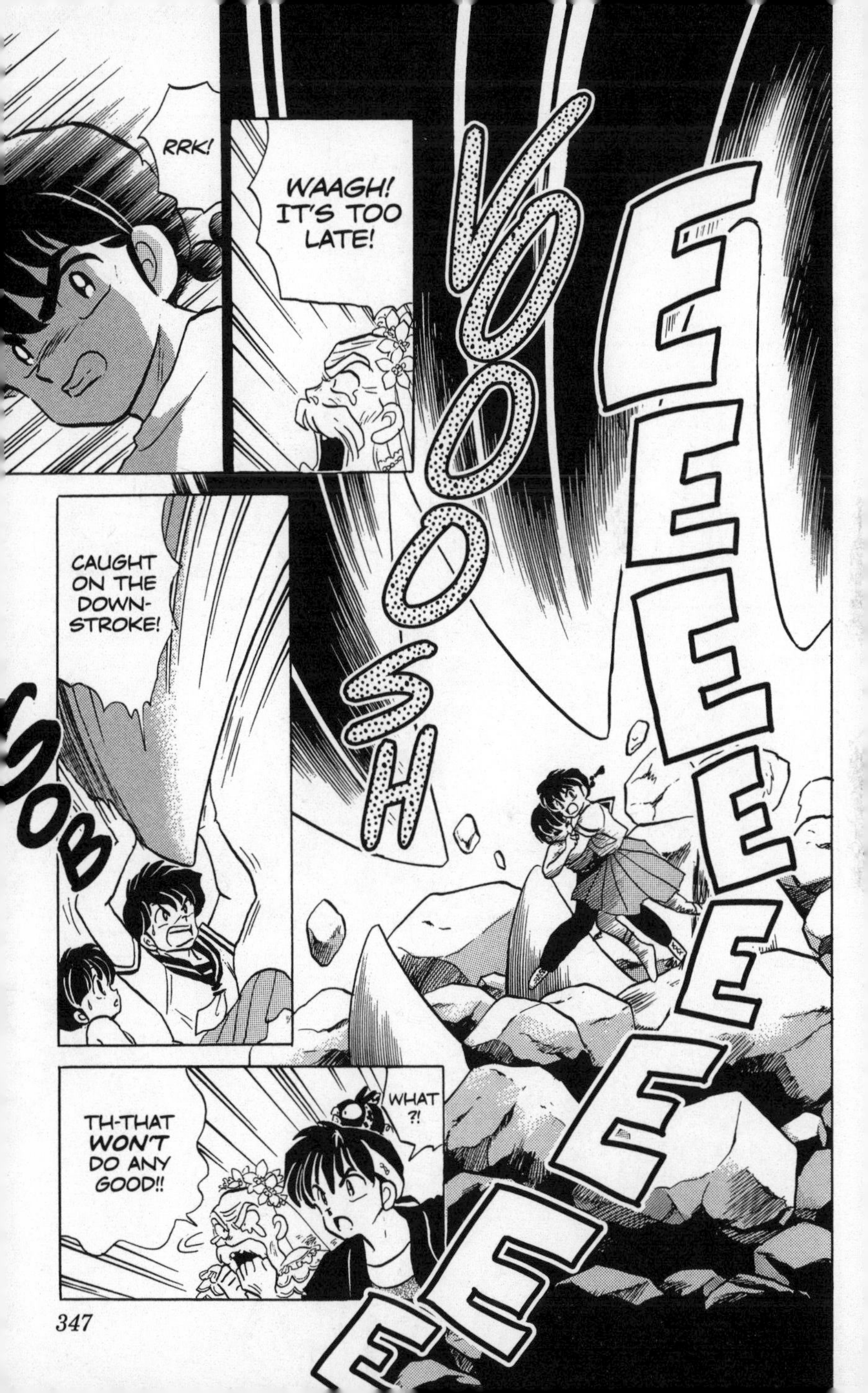
VOOOOSH
EEEEEEEEEEE
WAAGH! IT'S TOO LATE!
RRK!
CAUGHT ON THE DOWN-STROKE!
WHAT?!
TH-THAT WON'T DO ANY GOOD!!

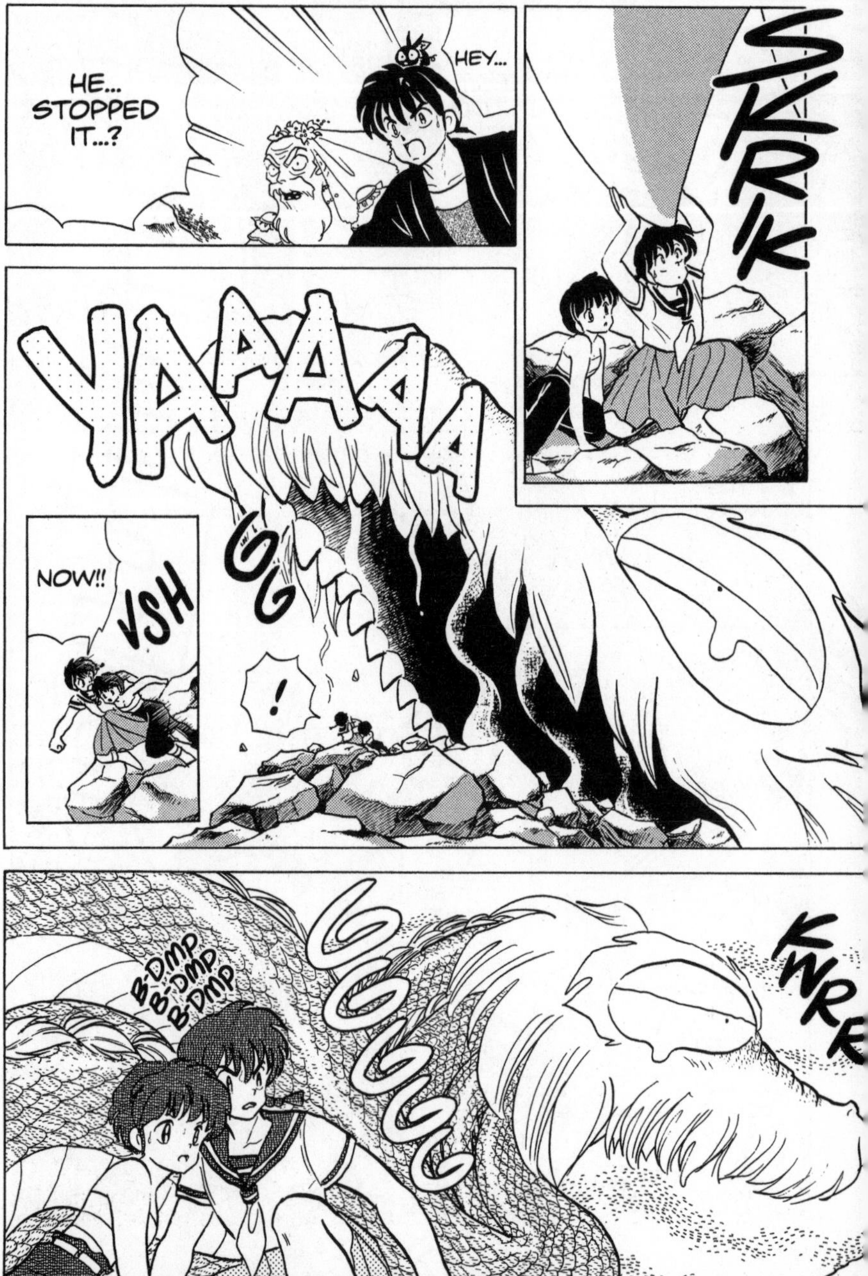
SKRIK
HEY...
HE... STOPPED IT...?
YAAAAAA
SG
!
NOW!!
VSH
KWRR
SGGGG
B-DMP B-DMP B-DMP

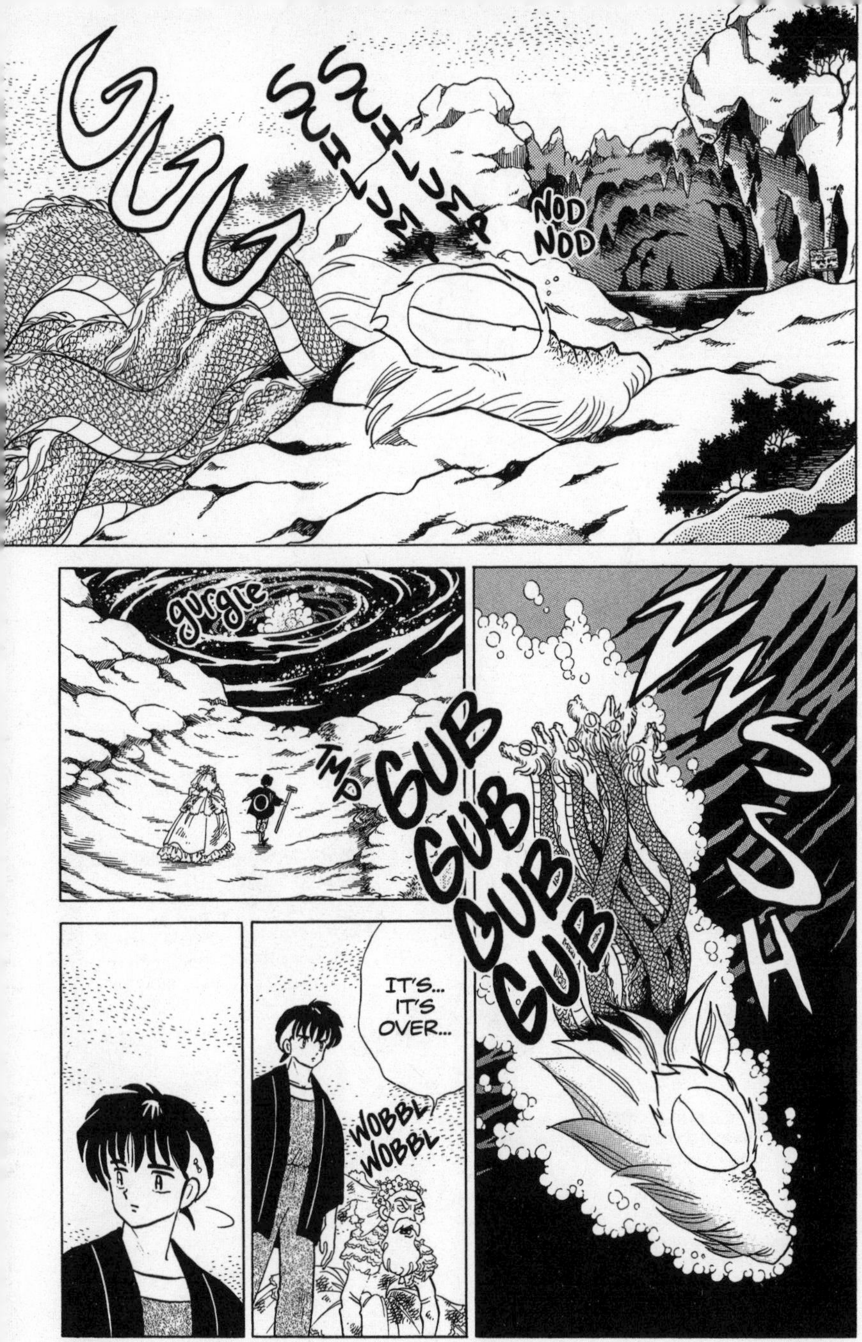
NOD NOD
SCHLUMP
SCHLUMP
ZZSSH
gurgle
TMP
GUB GUB GUB GUB
IT'S... IT'S OVER...
WOBBL WOBBL

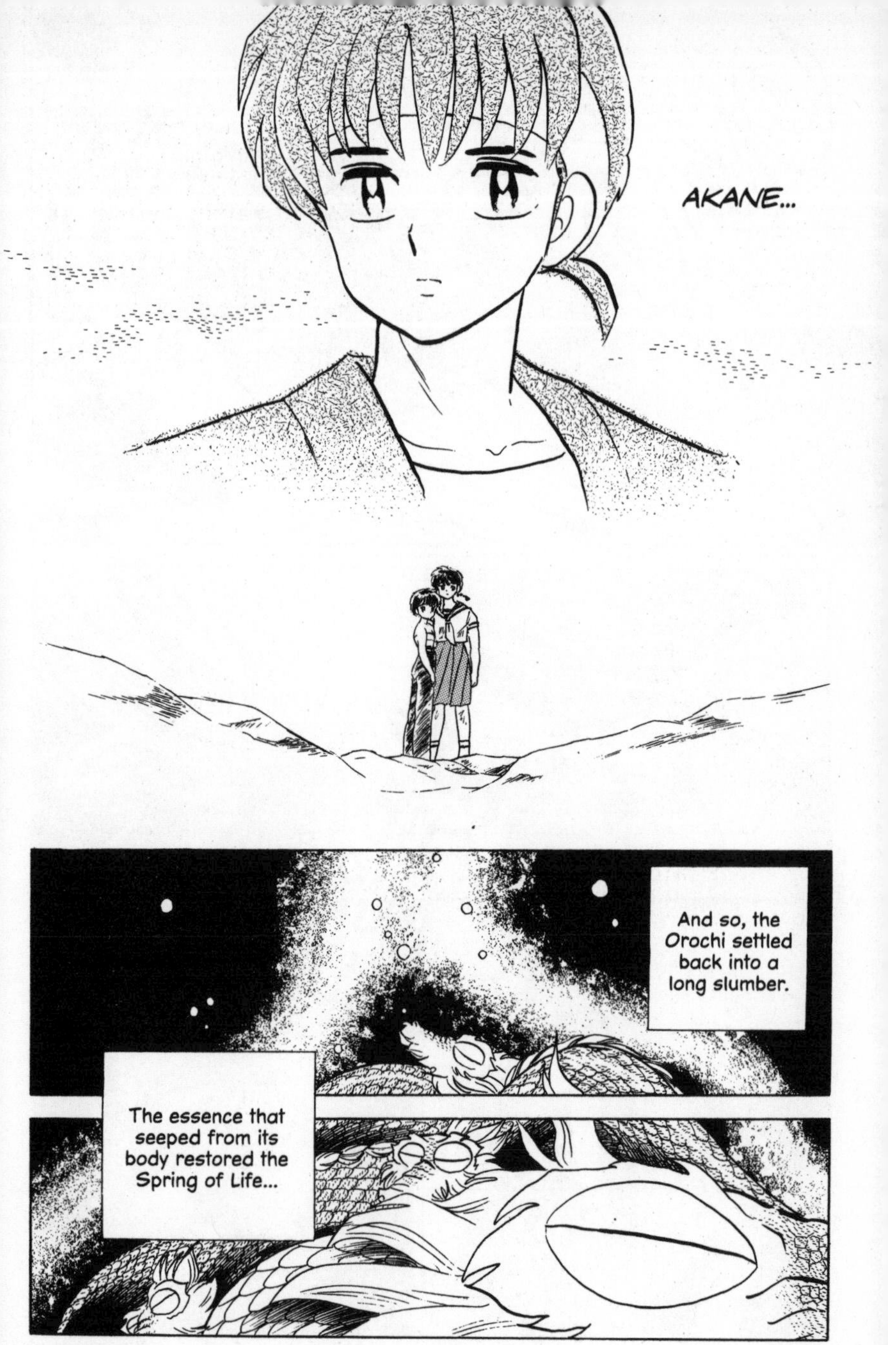
AKANE...
And so, the Orochi settled back into a long slumber.
The essence that seeped from its body restored the Spring of Life...

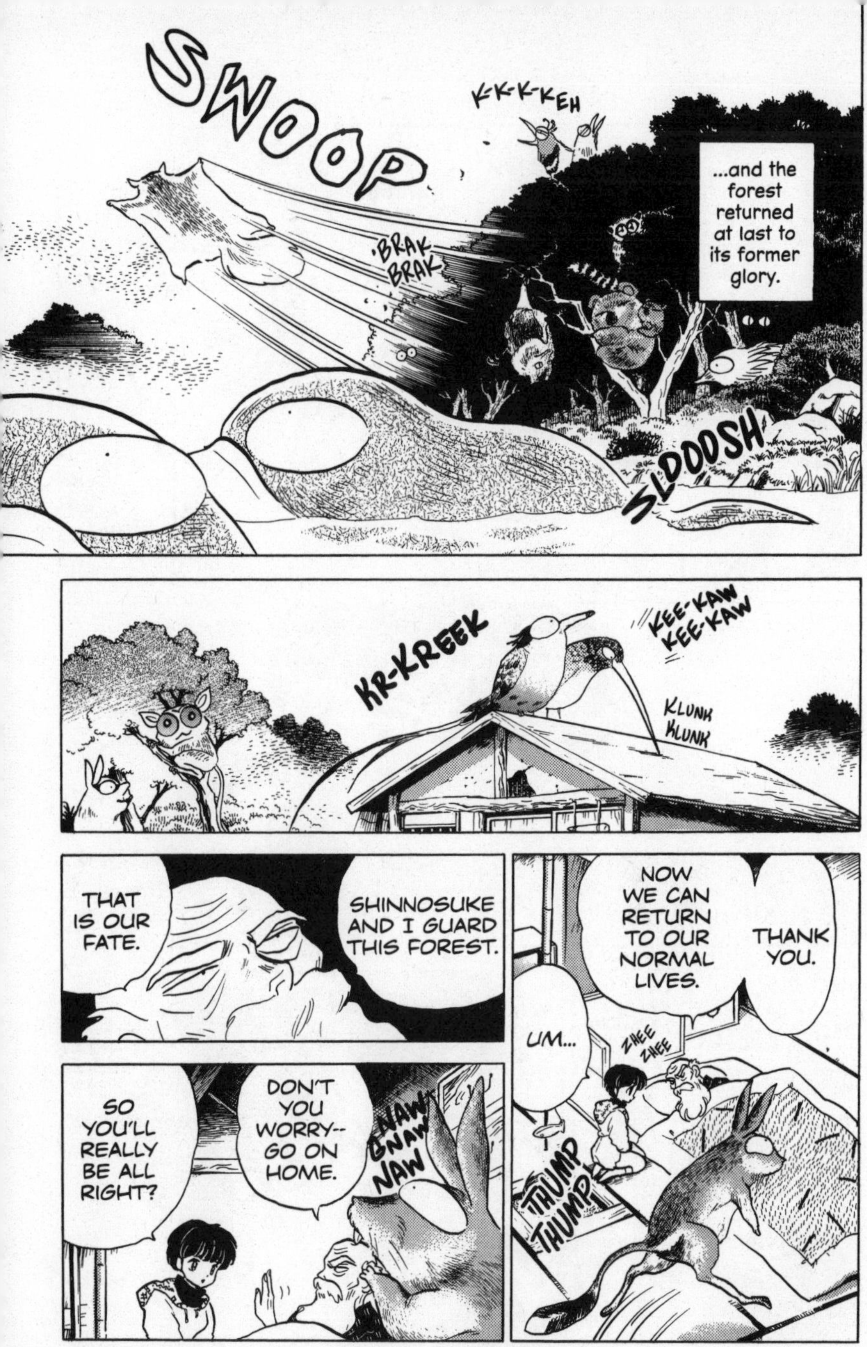
K-K-K-KEH
...and the forest returned at last to its former glory.
SWOOP
BRAK BRAK
SLDOOSH
KEE-KAW KEE-KAW
KLUNK KLUNK
KR-KREEK
THANK YOU.
NOW WE CAN RETURN TO OUR NORMAL LIVES.
UM...
ZHEE ZHEE
THUMP THUMP
SHINNOSUKE AND I GUARD THIS FOREST.
THAT IS OUR FATE.
GNAW GNAW NAW
DON'T YOU WORRY-- GO ON HOME.
SO YOU'LL REALLY BE ALL RIGHT?

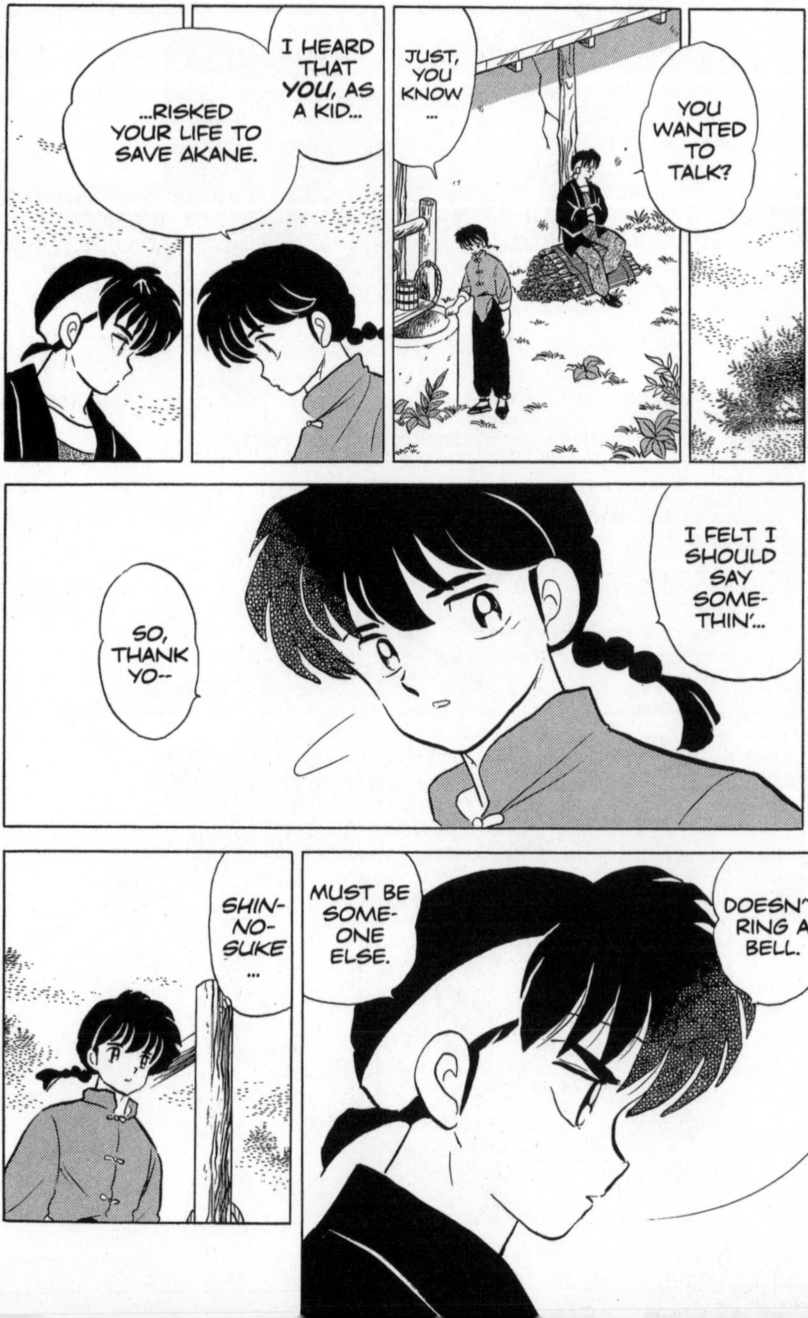
YOU WANTED TO TALK?
JUST, YOU KNOW ...
I HEARD THAT YOU, AS A KID...
...RISKED YOUR LIFE TO SAVE AKANE.
I FELT I SHOULD SAY SOME-THIN'...
SO, THANK YO--
DOESN'T RING A BELL.
MUST BE SOME-ONE ELSE.
SHIN-NO-SUKE ...

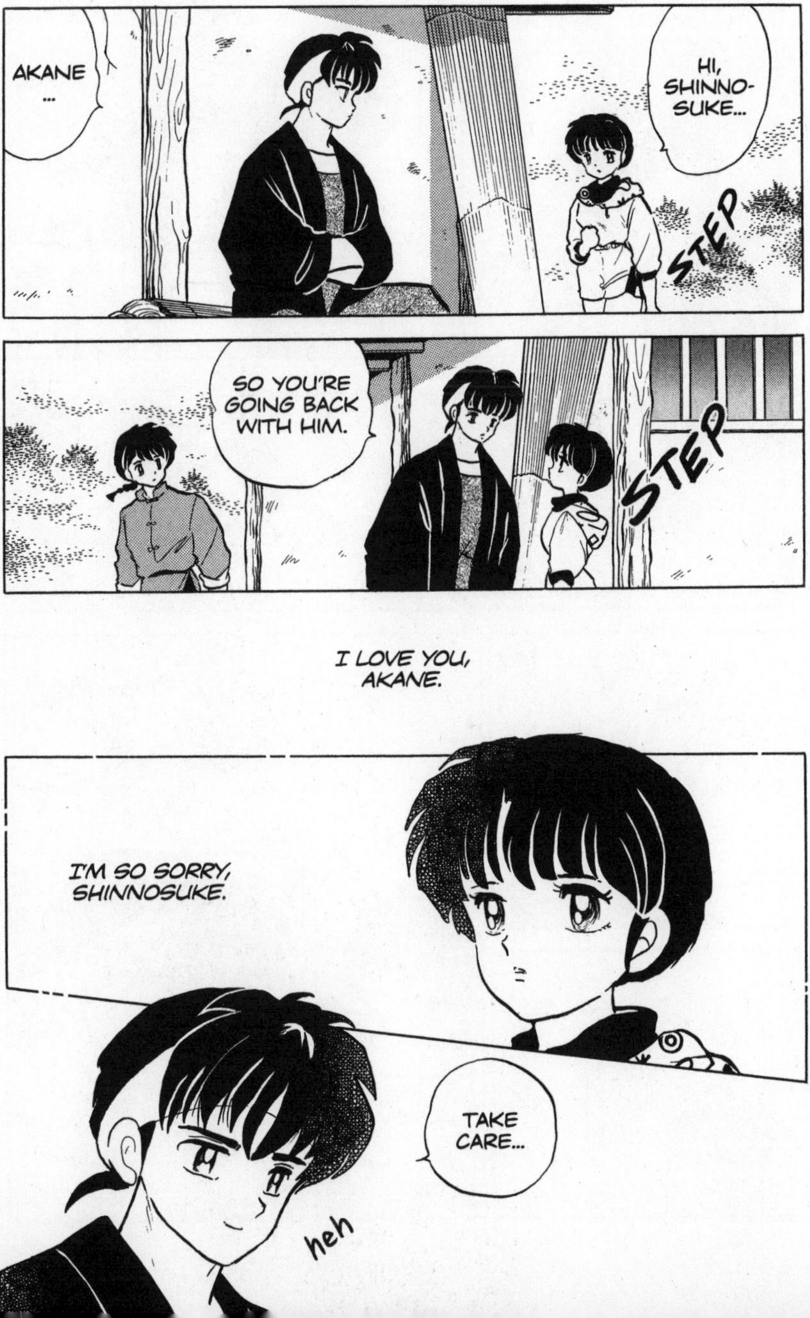
HI, SHINNO-SUKE...
STEP
AKANE ...
SO YOU'RE GOING BACK WITH HIM.
STEP
I LOVE YOU, AKANE.
I'M SO SORRY, SHINNOSUKE.
TAKE CARE...
heh

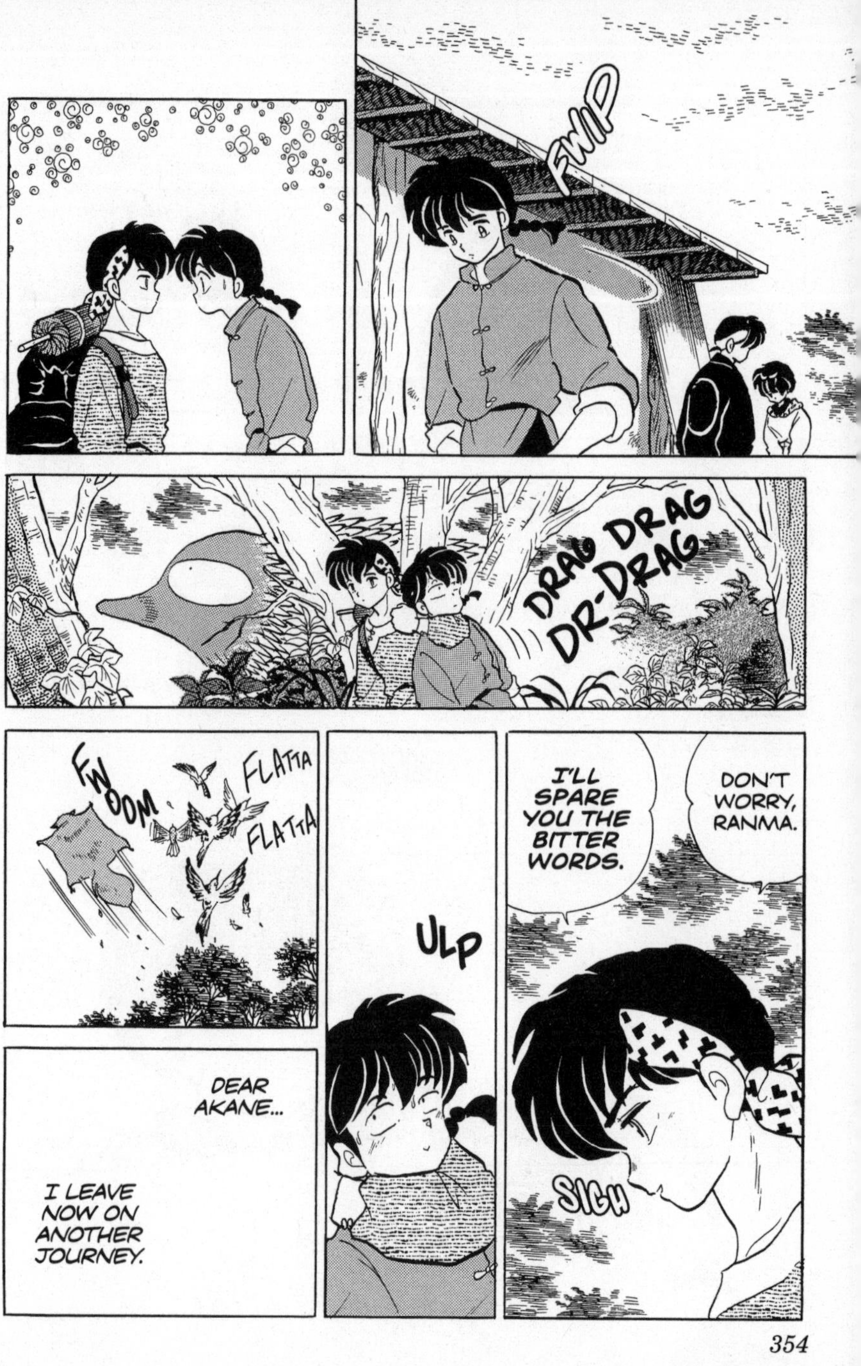
FWIP
DRAG DRAG
DR-DRAG
DON'T WORRY, RANMA.
I'LL SPARE YOU THE BITTER WORDS.
SIGH
ULP
FWOOM
FLATTA
FLATTA
DEAR AKANE...
I LEAVE NOW ON ANOTHER JOURNEY.

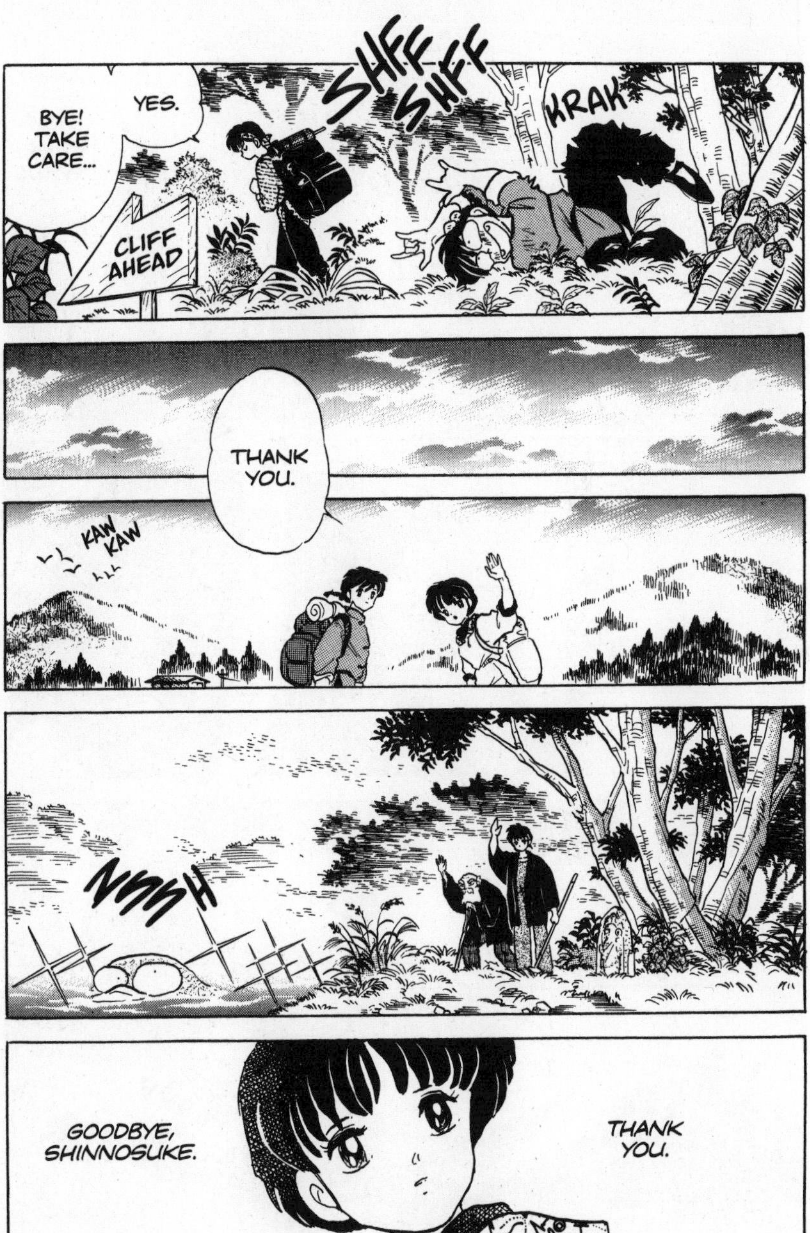
KRAK
SHFF SHFF
YES.
BYE! TAKE CARE...
CLIFF AHEAD
THANK YOU.
KAW KAW
NSSH
THANK YOU.
GOODBYE, SHINNOSUKE.

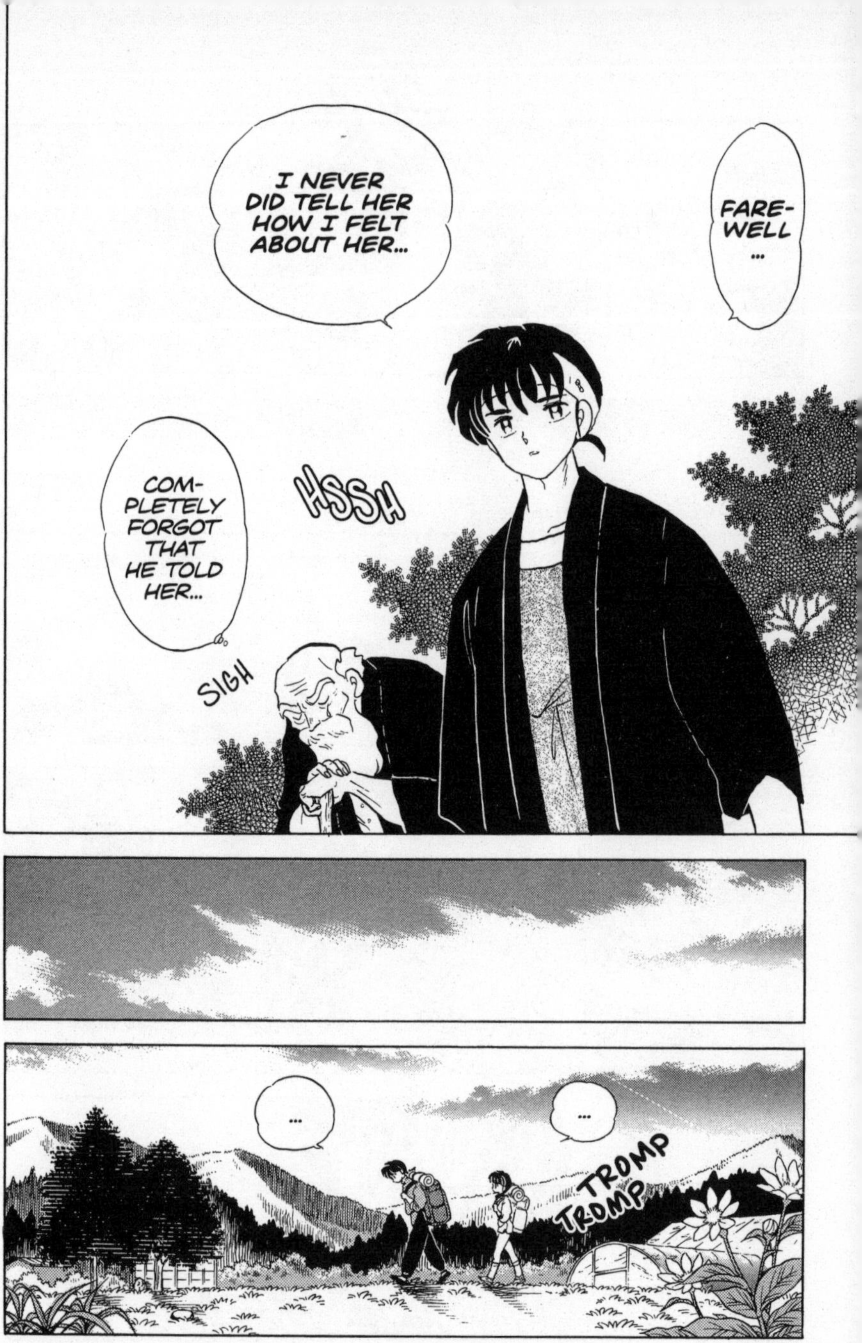
FARE-WELL ...
I NEVER DID TELL HER HOW I FELT ABOUT HER...
HSSH
COM-PLETELY FORGOT THAT HE TOLD HER...
SIGH
...
TROMP TROMP
...

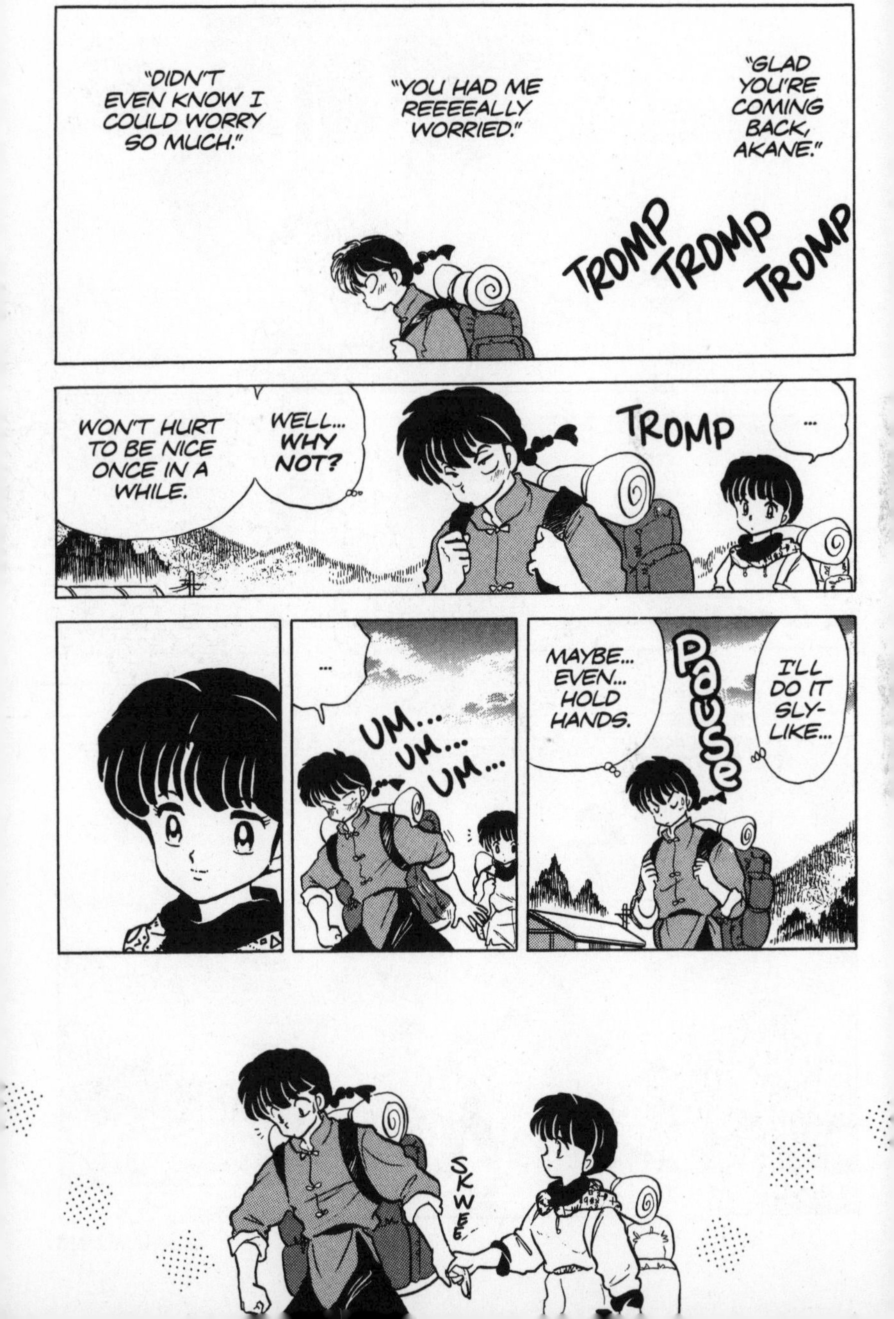
"GLAD YOU'RE COMING BACK, AKANE."
"YOU HAD ME REEEEALLY WORRIED."
"DIDN'T EVEN KNOW I COULD WORRY SO MUCH."
TROMP TROMP TROMP
...
TROMP
WELL... WHY NOT?
WON'T HURT TO BE NICE ONCE IN A WHILE.
I'LL DO IT SLY-LIKE...
Pause
MAYBE... EVEN... HOLD HANDS.
...
UM... UM... UM...
SKWEE

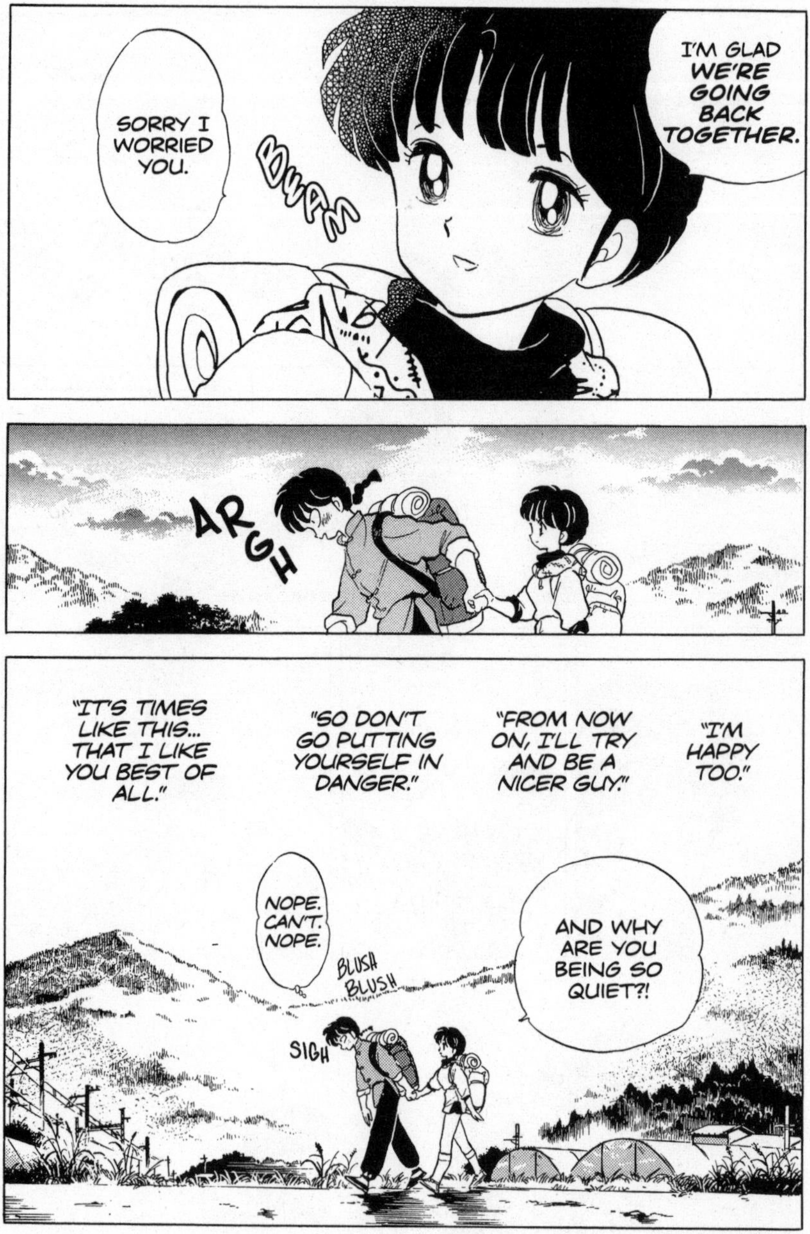
I'M GLAD WE'RE GOING BACK TOGETHER.
BWAM
SORRY I WORRIED YOU.
ARGH
"I'M HAPPY TOO."
"FROM NOW ON, I'LL TRY AND BE A NICER GUY."
"SO DON'T GO PUTTING YOURSELF IN DANGER."
"IT'S TIMES LIKE THIS... THAT I LIKE YOU BEST OF ALL."
AND WHY ARE YOU BEING SO QUIET?!
NOPE. CAN'T. NOPE.
BLUSH BLUSH
SIGH

To Be Continued

Rumiko Takahashi

The spotlight on Rumiko Takahashi's career began in 1978 when she won an honorable mention in Shogakukan's annual New Comic Artist Contest for *Those Selfish Aliens*. Later that same year, her boy-meets-alien comedy series, *Urusei Yatsura*, was serialized in *Weekly Shonen Sunday*. This phenomenally successful manga series was adapted into anime format and spawned a TV series and half a dozen theatrical-release movies, all incredibly popular in their own right. Takahashi followed up the success of her debut series with one blockbuster hit after another—*Maison Ikkoku* ran from 1980 to 1987, *Ranma ½* from 1987 to 1996, and *Inuyasha* from 1996 to 2008. Other notable works include *Mermaid Saga*, *Rumic Theater*, and *One-Pound Gospel*.

Takahashi won the prestigious Shogakukan Manga Award twice in her career, once for *Urusei Yatsura* in 1981 and the second time for *Inuyasha* in 2002. A majority of the Takahashi canon has been adapted into other media such as anime, live-action TV series, and film. Takahashi's manga, as well as the other formats her work has been adapted into, have continued to delight generations of fans around the world. Distinguished by her wonderfully endearing characters, Takahashi's work adeptly incorporates a wide variety of elements such as comedy, romance, fantasy, and martial arts. While her series are difficult to pin down into one simple genre, the signature style she has created has come to be known as the "Rumic World." Rumiko Takahashi is an artist who truly represents the very best from the world of manga.

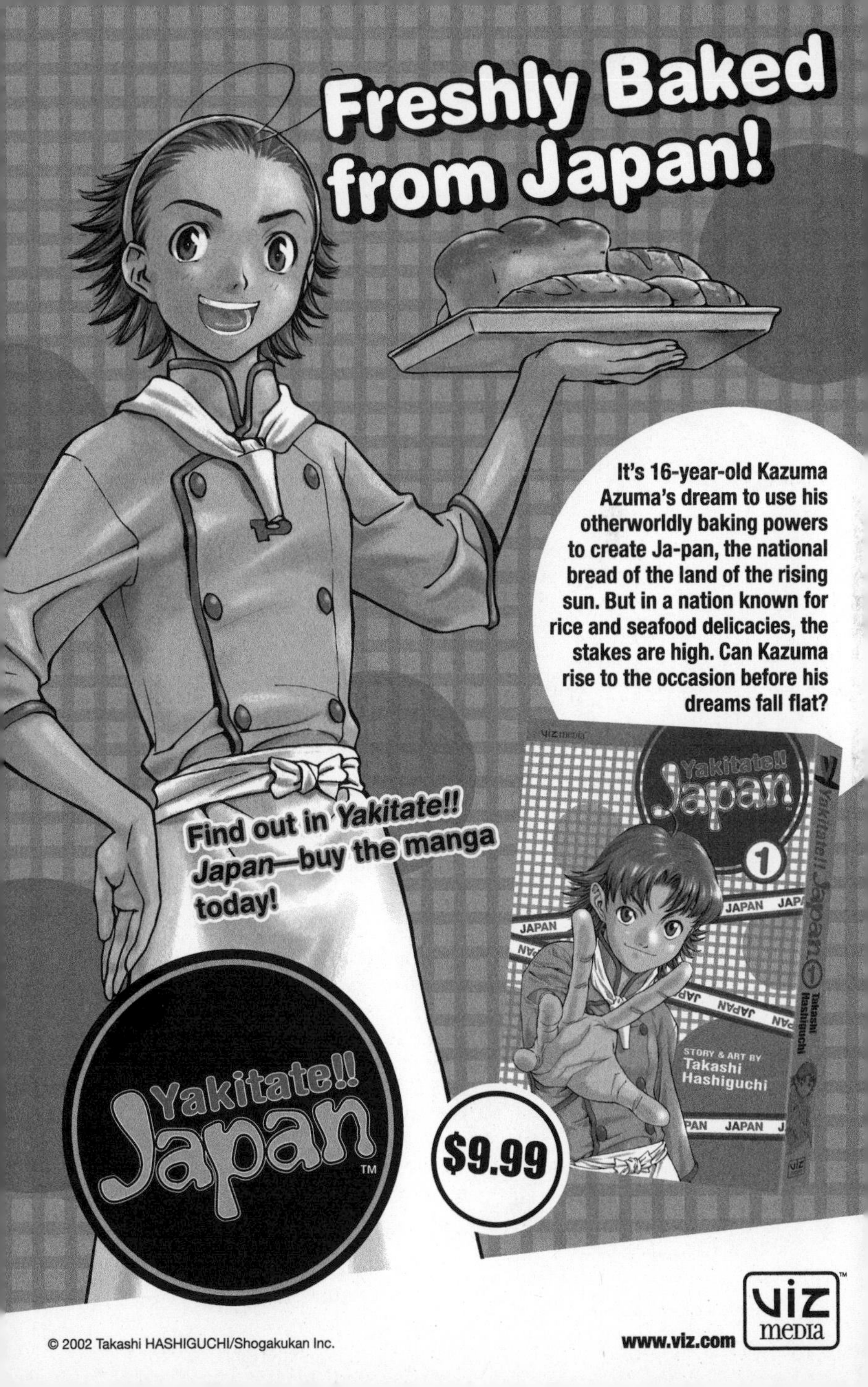
Freshly Baked from Japan!
It's 16-year-old Kazuma Azuma's dream to use his otherworldly baking powers to create Ja-pan, the national bread of the land of the rising sun. But in a nation known for rice and seafood delicacies, the stakes are high. Can Kazuma rise to the occasion before his dreams fall flat?
Find out in Yakitate!! Japan—buy the manga today!
Yakitate!! Japan™
Yakitate!! Japan 1
STORY & ART BY Takashi Hashiguchi
$9.99
VIZ MEDIA™
www.viz.com
© 2002 Takashi HASHIGUCHI/Shogakukan Inc.

A DETECTIVE IN NEED OF A CLUE

CASE CLOSED ™

With an innate talent for observation and intuition, Jimmy can solve mysteries that leave the most seasoned law enforcement officials baffled. But when a strange chemical transforms him from a high school teenager to a grade schooler who no one takes seriously, will this be one mystery this sleuth can't solve?

ONLY $9.99!

Start your graphic novel collection today!

www.viz.com
store.viz.com

VIZ MEDIA

©1994 Gosho AOYAMA/Shogakukan Inc.

CASE CLOSED™
One Truth Prevails™

CASE CLOSED IS A STEAL
THE PROOF IS IN THE PRICE

— CATCH THE CAPERS ON DVD FOR UNDER $30 A SEASON!

You should be watching funimation.com/case-closed

Based on the original graphic novel "Meitantei Conan" by Gosho Aoyama published by Shogakukan Inc.
© Gosho Aoyama / Shogakukan • YTV • TMS. Produced by TMS Entertainment Co., Ltd. Under License to FUNimation® Productions, Ltd. All Rights Reserved.

FUNIMATION

OWN THE FINAL CHAPTER OF RUMIKO TAKAHASHI'S FEUDAL FAIRYTALE

INUYASHA

The Final Act

The Complete Series

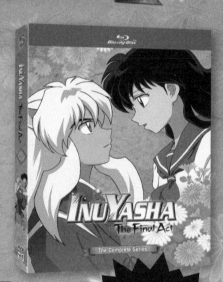

In their quest to restore the shattered Shikon Jewel, Inuyasha and Kagome face their ultimate enemy, the demon mastermind Naraku.

Own the complete 26 episode set today!

Now available at anime retailers everywhere.

BLU-RAY EXCLUSIVE SPECIAL FEATURES

- Production Art
- Storyboard Art
- 3 Original Japanese Trailers

As seen on Toonami!

Approx. 630 mins.   © Rumiko Takahashi / Shogakukan, Yomiuri TV, Sunrise 2009

www.viz.com

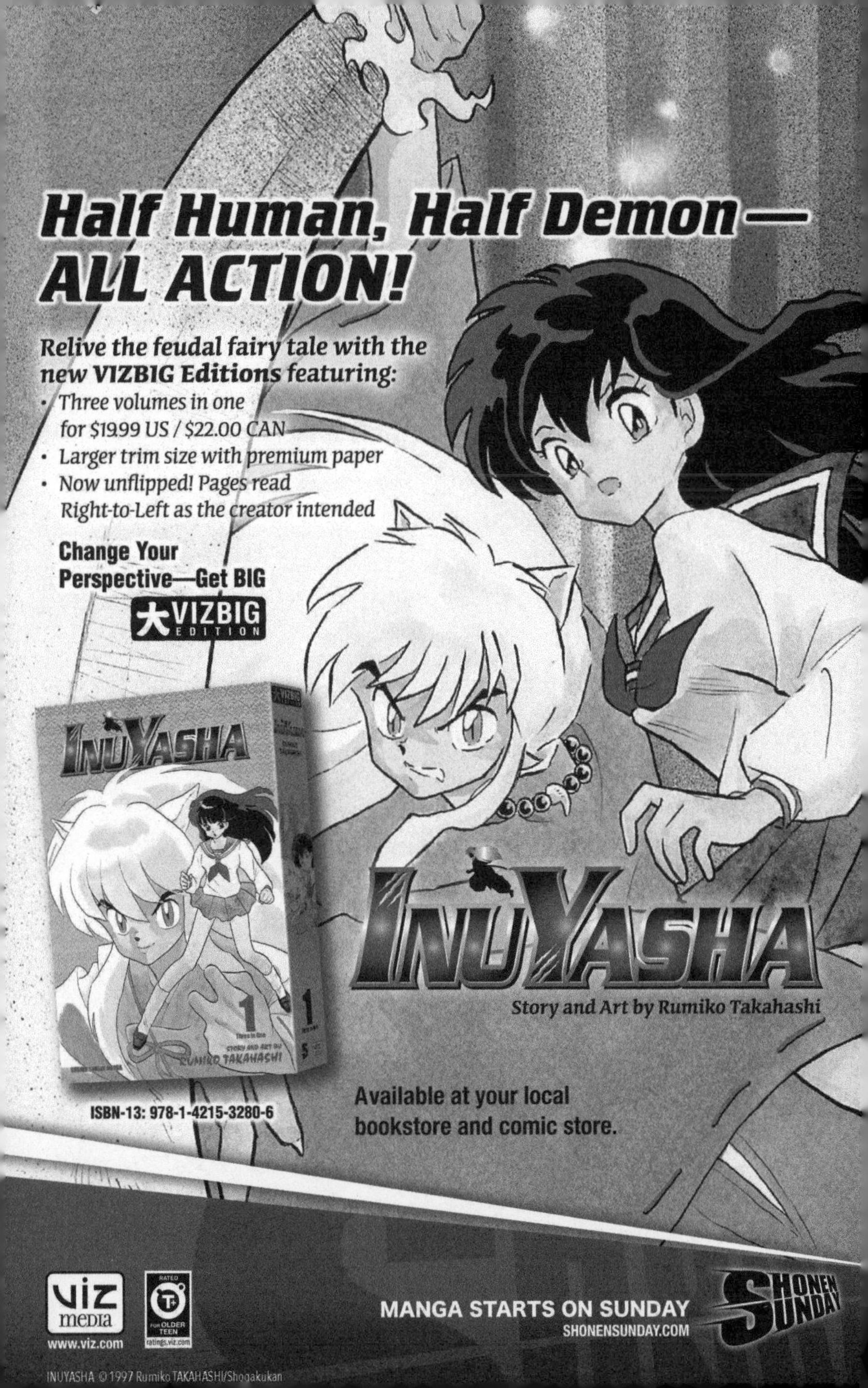
Half Human, Half Demon—
ALL ACTION!
Relive the feudal fairy tale with the new VIZBIG Editions featuring:
• Three volumes in one for $19.99 US / $22.00 CAN
• Larger trim size with premium paper
• Now unflipped! Pages read Right-to-Left as the creator intended
Change Your Perspective—Get BIG
大VIZBIG EDITION
INUYASHA
1
RUMIKO TAKAHASHI
ISBN-13: 978-1-4215-3280-6
INUYASHA
Story and Art by Rumiko Takahashi
Available at your local bookstore and comic store.
viz media
www.viz.com
RATED T+ FOR OLDER TEEN
ratings.viz.com
MANGA STARTS ON SUNDAY
SHONENSUNDAY.COM
SHONEN SUNDAY
INUYASHA © 1997 Rumiko TAKAHASHI/Shogakukan

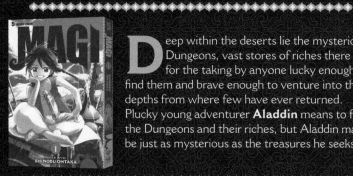

MAGI
The labyrinth of magic

Story & Art by
SHINOBU OHTAKA

A **fantasy adventure** inspired by
One Thousand and One Nights

Deep within the deserts lie the mysterious Dungeons, vast stores of riches there for the taking by anyone lucky enough to find them and brave enough to venture into the depths from where few have ever returned. Plucky young adventurer **Aladdin** means to find the Dungeons and their riches, but Aladdin may be just as mysterious as the treasures he seeks.

MANGA STARTS ON SUNDAY!

www.shonensunday.com

Available NOW!

RATED
T
FOR
TEEN
ratings.viz.com

VIZ
MEDIA
www.viz.com

MAGI © 2009 Shinobu OHTAKA/SHOGAKUKAN

STUDENTS BY DAY, DEMON-FIGHTERS BY NIGHT!

KEKKAISHI
【けっかいし】

Teenagers Yoshimori and Tokine are "kekkaishi"—demon-fighters that battle bad beings side-by-side almost every night. They also quarrel with each other, but their biggest fight is the one between their families. Can Yoshimori and Tokine fight together long enough to end their families' ancient rivalry and save the world?

Join this modern-day Romeo and Juliet adventure—graphic novels now available at *store.viz.com*!

ONLY $9.99!

VIZ media™

www.viz.com
store.viz.com

© 2004 Yellow Tanabe/Shogakukan, Inc.

Hey! You're Reading in the Wrong Direction!

This is the end of this graphic novel!

To properly enjoy this VIZ graphic novel, please turn it around and begin reading from right to left. Unlike English, Japanese is read right to left, so Japanese comics are read in reverse order from the way English comics are typically read.

This book has been printed in the original Japanese format in order to preserve the orientation of the original artwork. Have fun with it!

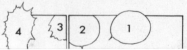

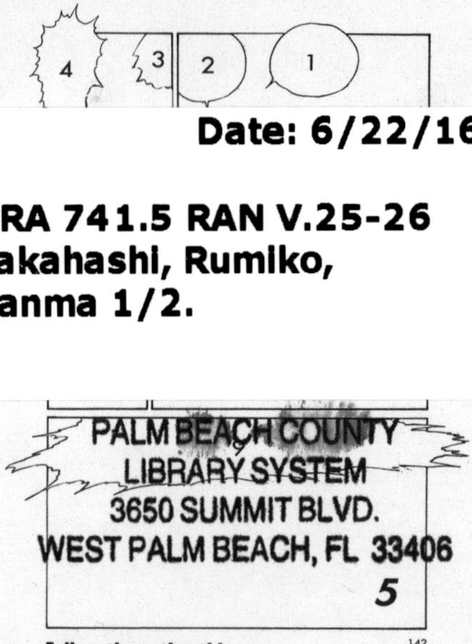

Date: 6/22/16

GRA 741.5 RAN V.25-26
Takahashi, Rumiko,
Ranma 1/2.

PALM BEACH COUNTY
LIBRARY SYSTEM
3650 SUMMIT BLVD.
WEST PALM BEACH, FL 33406

5

Follow the action this way